TALKING SHOP

TALKING SHOP

OVER 5,000 BUSINESS QUOTATIONS TO HELP
YOU THROUGH YOUR WORKING DAY

BLOOMSBURY

A BLOOMSBURY REFERENCE BOOK
Created from the Bloomsbury Business Database
www.ultimatebusinessresource.com

© Bloomsbury Publishing Plc 2003

First published in 2003 by
Bloomsbury Publishing Plc
38 Soho Square
London W1D 3HB

British Library Cataloguing in Publication Data
A CIP record for this book is available from the British Library.

ISBN 0-7475-6240-7

Design by Fiona Pike, Pike Design, Winchester
Typeset by RefineCatch Limited, Bungay, Suffolk
Printed in Great Britain by Clays Ltd, St Ives plc

All papers used by Bloomsbury Publishing are natural, recyclable products
made from wood grown in sustainable, well-managed forests. The
manufacturing processes conform to the environmental regulations of the
country of origin.

Contents

A NOTE TO THE USER

Talking Shop offers you one of the most extensive and up-to-date lists of business quotations available, and provides an accessible, practical source of thoughts and advice for presentations, reports, and speeches.

There are over 5,000 quotations in this collection from well over 1,500 authors and on more than 150 subjects, including *Corruption and Scandal, Leadership, Power,* and *Success*. As well as being thematically ordered, the quotations also offer comprehensive author and source details. All quotations retain the spelling used in the source from which they were drawn.

To help with the navigation through these quotations, we have included two indexes: a **keyword** index (p. 255) and an **author** index (p. 303). These are both simple to use, are arranged alphabetically, and have references to the number of the quotation and the theme under which the respective quotation will be found. The keyword index helps you to find a half-remembered quotation or a quotation that uses a specific word, while the author index allows you to find all the quotations by a particular author under different themes.

For more information about **BUSINESS: The Ultimate Resource**™ and other related titles, please visit:

www.ultimatebusinessresource.com

To register for free electronic upgrades, please go to **www.ultimatebusinessresource.com/register**, type in your e-mail address, and key in the password: **Welch**

The Quotations

ABILITY

1 Jill of all trades.

Anonymous. A permutation on the traditional saying 'Jack of all trades', used to describe a man with many skills. Quoted in *Liberation Management* (Tom Peters; 1992)

2 Behind an able man there are always other able men.

Anonymous. Chinese proverb.

3 When competencies are not developed at all levels, companies often get into trouble.

Ron Ashkenas (b. 1950) US writer. *The Boundaryless Organization* (co-written with Dave Ulrich, Todd Jick, and Steve Kerr; 1995)

4 The leader...is rarely the brightest person in the group. Rather, they have extraordinary taste, which makes them more curators than creators. They are appreciators of talent and nurturers of talent and they have the ability to recognize valuable ideas.

Warren Bennis (b. 1925) US educator and writer. Interview, *Strategy + Business* (July–September 1997)

5 The superior man is distressed by his want of ability.

Confucius (551–479 BC) Chinese philosopher, administrator, and writer. *Analects* (?500 BC)

6 Ability and achievement are *bona fides* no one dares question, no matter how unconventional the man who presents them.

J. Paul Getty (1892–1976) US entrepreneur, oil industry executive, and financier. *How to Be Rich* (1965)

7 Great ability develops and reveals itself increasingly with every new assignment.

Baltasar Gracián (1601–58) Spanish writer and priest. *The Oracle* (1647)

8 I found that there were these incredibly great people at doing certain things, and you couldn't replace one of these people with 50 average people. They could just do stuff that no number of average people could do.

Steve Jobs (b. 1955) US entrepreneur, co-founder and CEO of Apple Computer Company, and CEO of Pixar. Quoted in 'Steve's Two Jobs', *Time* (Michael Krantz; 18 October 1999)

9 You must make use of people according to their abilities and realise that absolutely no one is perfect.

Françoise d'Aubigné Maintenon (1635–1719) French wife of King Louis XIV. Letter to the Count d'Aubigné (25 September 1679)

10 From each according to his ability, to each according to his needs.

Karl Marx (1818–83) German political and economic philosopher. *Critique of the Gotha Programme* (1875)

11 Competence, like truth, beauty, and contact lenses, is in the eye of the beholder.

Laurence J. Peter (1919–90) Canadian academic and writer. *The Peter Principle: Why Things Always Go Wrong* (co-written with Raymond Hull; 1969)

ACCOMPLISHMENTS

1 It's not where you've reached that matters, it's how far you've had to travel to get there.

Anonymous. *Guardian* (27 July 2000)

2 Most people live and die with their music still unplayed. They never dare to try.

Mary Kay Ash (1915–2001) US entrepreneur, business executive, and founder of Mary Kay Cosmetics. *New York Times* (1985)

3 If you can run one business well, you can run any business well.

Richard Branson (b. 1950) British entrepreneur, business executive, and founder of the Virgin Group. *New York Times* (2000)

4 Sweat is the cologne of accomplishment.

Heywood Hale Broun (1918–2001) US broadcast journalist, actor, and author. CBS television interview (21 July 1973)

5 The best judgment we can make about managerial competence does not depend on what people say, but simply what the record says.

Warren Buffett (b. 1930) US entrepreneur and financier. Quoted in *Treasury of Investment Wisdom* (Bernice Cohen; 1999)

6 If you cannot communicate your many worthwhile achievements, no one will ever know what you have done.

Jac Fitz-Enz (b. 1948) US writer. *How to Measure Human Resources Management* (1995)

7 One worthwhile task carried to a successful conclusion is better than 50 half-finished tasks.

Bertie Charles Forbes (1880–1954) US publisher and writer. Quoted in *Reader's Digest* (1993)

8 No person can hope to be an all-rounder, let alone omni-competent, but he should know the essentials.

Indira Gandhi (1917–84) Indian prime minister. Speech (23 March 1968)

9 Later Marx was to recall his mother's words, 'If only Karl had made capital, instead of writing about it'.

Edna Healey (b. 1917) British author. Quoted in *Treasury of Investment Wisdom* (Bernice Cohen; 1999)

10 There is no end to what you can accomplish if you don't care who gets the credit.

Florence Luscomb (1887–1985) US campaigner for women's suffrage, architect, and pacifist. Quoted in *Moving the Mountain* (E. Cantorow; 1980)

11 The world is divided into people who do things and people who get the credit. Try, if you can, to belong to the first class. There's far less competition.

Dwight Morrow (1873–1931) US lawyer, banker, and diplomat. Written in a letter to his son. Quoted in *Dwight Morrow* (Harold Nicolson; 1935)

12 I wouldn't be human if I didn't feel pride and something that transcends pride...humility.

J.C. Penney (1875–1971) US founder of J.C. Penney stores. Said at the dedication of his company's Manhattan headquarters on 30 May 1965. *New York Herald Tribune* (1965)

13 It ain't bragging if you can do it.
Babe Ruth (1895–1948) US baseball player. Quoted in *Woodbury Reports Archives* (December 1994)

14 Man grows beyond his work, walks up the stairs of his concepts, emerges ahead of his accomplishment.
John Steinbeck (1902–68) US novelist. *The Grapes of Wrath* (1939)

15 It is better to deserve honors and not have them than to have them and not deserve them.
Mark Twain (1835–1910) US writer. Quoted in *Woodbury Reports Archives* (August 1995)

16 I am a woman who came from the cotton fields of the South. From there I was promoted to the washtub. From there I was promoted to the cook kitchen. And from there I promoted myself into the business of manufacturing hair goods and preparations…I have built my own factory on my own ground.
C.J. Walker (1867–1919) US business executive. Said in a speech to the National Negro Business League Convention, 1912. Quoted in *New York Times* (2000)

17 There is no royal flower-strewn path to success. And if there is, I have not found it for if I have accomplished anything in life it is because I have been willing to work hard.
C.J. Walker (1867–1919) US business executive. Quoted in *On Her Own Ground: The Life and Times of Madam C. J. Walker* (A'Lelia Bundles; 2000)

18 A few yes men may be born, but mostly they are made. Fear is a great breeder of them.
William Wrigley (1861–1932) US businessman and founder of Wrigley Company. *American Magazine* (March 1920)

ACCURACY

1 Facts, when combined with ideas, constitute the greatest force in the world. They are greater than armaments, greater than finance, greater than science, business, and law because they are the common denominator of them all.
Carl William Ackerman (1890–1970) US editor and writer. Address (26 September 1931)

2 ACCURACY, n. A certain uninteresting quality carefully excluded from human statements.
Ambrose Bierce (1842–?1914) US journalist and writer. *The Devil's Dictionary* (1911)

3 The attitude of disrespect that many executives have today for accurate reporting is a business disgrace. And auditors…have done little on the positive side. Though auditors should regard the investing public as their client, they tend to kowtow instead to the managers who choose them and dole out their pay.
Warren Buffett (b. 1930) US entrepreneur and financier. Chairman's Letter to Shareholders, *Berkshire Hathaway 1998 Annual Report* (1 March 1999)

4 It is the nature of greatness not to be exact.
Edmund Burke (1729–97) British philosopher and politician. Speech on American Taxation (1774)

5 I do not mind lying, but I hate inaccuracy.
Samuel Butler (1835–1902) British writer. 'Truth and Convenience', *Notebooks* (H. Festing-Jones, ed.; 1912)

6 If you don't get it right, what's the point?
Michael Cimino (b. 1943) US film director. Kodak advertisement. Quoted in *Variety* (23 July 1980)

7 For a successful technology, reality must take precedence over public relations, for nature cannot be fooled.
Richard Feynman (1918–88) US physicist. Speech (1986)

8 Measure what is measurable and make measurable what is not.
Galileo Galilei (1564–1642) Italian mathematician and scientist. Quoted in *Armchair Science Reader* (I. Gordon and S. Sortin, eds; 1959)

9 Nothing is more central to an organization's effectiveness than its ability to transmit accurate, relevant, understandable information among its members.
Saul W. Gellerman (b. 1929) US psychologist and writer. *The Management of Human Resources* (1976)

10 Accuracy is not an essential goal of reading.
Ken Goodman (b. 1927) US linguistics educator. *Daily Report Card* (18 November 1994)

11 Insanity is often the logic of an accurate mind overtasked.
Oliver Wendell Holmes (1809–94) US surgeon, teacher, and writer. *The Autocrat of the Breakfast-Table* (1858)

12 In all pointed sentences, some degree of accuracy must be sacrificed to conciseness.
Samuel Johnson (1709–84) British poet, lexicographer, essayist, and critic. 'The Bravery of the English Common Soldier', *The British Magazine* (1760)

13 A little inaccuracy sometimes saves tons of explanation.
H.H. Munro (Saki) (1870–1916) British short-story writer. 'Clovis on the Alleged Romance of Business', *The Square Egg* (1924)

14 Accuracy is to a newspaper what virtue is to a lady, but a newspaper can always print a retraction.
Adlai E. Stevenson (1900–65) US statesman and author. Quoted in *The Stevenson Wit* (Bill Adler; 1966)

15 The First Duty of a newspaper is to be Accurate. If it is Accurate, it follows that it is Fair.
Herbert Bayard Swope (1882–1958) US newspaper editor. Letter, *New York Herald Tribune* (16 March 1958)

16 The difference between the *almost* right word and the *right* word is really a large matter—it's the difference between the lightning bug and the lightning.
Mark Twain (1835–1910) US writer. Letter to George Bainton (15 October 1888)

ACHIEVING

1 The man who views the world at fifty the same as he did at twenty has wasted thirty years of his life.
Muhammad Ali (b. 1942) US boxer. *Playboy* (1975)

2 It took me fifteen years to discover that I had no talent for writing, but I couldn't give it up because by that time I was too famous.
Robert Benchley (1889–1945) US humorist. Quoted in *Robert Benchley* (Nathaniel Benchley; 1955)

3 Office is something that builds up a man only if he is somebody in his own right.
Tony Benn (b. 1925) British politician. Diary (April 1976)

4 Enthusiasm and hard work are indispensable ingredients of achievement. So is stick-to-it-iveness.
Clarence Birdseye (1886–1956) US businessman and founder of Birdseye. *American Magazine* (February 1951)

5 There is only one step from the sublime to the ridiculous.
Napoleon Bonaparte (1769–1821) French emperor. Referring to the retreat from Moscow. Comment (1812)

6 Do not think a man has done his full duty when he has performed the work assigned him. A man will never rise if he does only this. Promotion comes from exceptional work.
Andrew Carnegie (1835–1919) US industrialist and philanthropist. The fourth of his rules of business success. 'From Oakland: How to Succeed in Life', *The Pittsburgh Bulletin* (19 December 1903)

7 Cunning is the dark sanctuary of incapacity.
Lord Chesterfield (1694–1773) English statesman, orator, and letter writer. Letter (1783)

8 If anything terrifies me, I must try to conquer it.
Francis Charles Chichester (1901–72) British yachtsman and aviator. *Life* (June 1967)

9 By different methods different men excel: But where is he who can do all things well?
Charles Churchill (1731–64) British curate and satirist. *An Epistle to William Hogarth* (1763)

10 One of the things I learned long ago about auctions was that it's not about ego or talent. It's simply about raising your hand for the next bid. They won. We lost. Next.
Barry Diller (b. 1942) US media mogul. *BusinessWeek* (1994)

11 Owning the intellectual property is like owning land: You need to keep investing in it again and again to get a payoff; you can't simply sit back and collect rent.
Esther Dyson (b. 1951) US knowledge entrepreneur and government adviser. *Release 1.0* (1994)

12 Responsibility is the great developer of men.
Mary Parker Follett (1868–1933) US management thinker and author. *Dynamic Administration* (1941)

13 How you start is important, but it is how you finish that counts. In the race for success, speed is less important than stamina. The sticker outlasts the sprinter.
Bertie Charles Forbes (1880–1954) US publisher and writer. Quoted in *Reader's Digest* (1993)

14 The man who has the largest capacity for work and thought is the man who is bound to succeed.
Henry Ford (1863–1947) US industrialist, car manufacturer, and founder of Ford Motor Company. *My Life and Work* (co-written with Samuel Crowther; 1922)

15 Dreams seldom materialise on their own.
Dian Fossey (1932–85) US conservationist. *Gorillas in the Mist* (1983)

16 Effort only fully releases its reward after a person refuses to quit.
Napoleon Hill (1883–1970) US motivational author. *Think and Grow Rich* (1937)

17 Well, we knocked the bastard off.
Edmund Hillary (b. 1919) New Zealand explorer and mountaineer. Referring to his ascent of Everest. Press comment (1953)

18 The medal is not for yourself. We are educated in the principles of modesty, not individual honours.
Alberto Juantorena (b. 1950) Cuban athlete and businessman. 1976. Referring to gold medal achievement at Montreal Olympics. Quoted in *Running with the Legends* (Michael Sandrock; 1996)

19 If you can fill the unforgiving minute with sixty seconds worth of distance run.
Rudyard Kipling (1865–1936) British novelist, poet, and short-story writer. 'If' (1910)

20 Real power is creating stuff.
Geraldine Laybourne (b. 1947) US chairman of Oxygen Media. 'The 50 Most Powerful Women in American Business', *Fortune* (Patricia Sellers and Cora Daniels; October 1999)

21 They have not any difficulties on the way up because they fly, but they have many when they reach the summit.
Niccolò Machiavelli (1469–1527) Italian historian, statesman, and political philosopher. *The Prince* (1513)

22 Self-actualisation.
Abraham Maslow (1908–70) US behavioural psychologist. Referring to the theory that individuals should achieve their own personal potential. *Motivation and Personality* (1954)

23 I've taken less than the 150 years they thought it would take to achieve.
Robert Maxwell (1923–91) British publisher, business executive, and politician. Referring to Pergamon Press and its publication of scientific journals. Television interview (August 1972)

24 What the mind can believe, you can achieve.
Lorraine Moller (b. 1955) New Zealand athlete. Quoted in *Running with the Legends* (Michael Sandrock; 1996)

25 The worst fault of the working classes is telling their children they're not going to succeed, saying: 'There is life, but it's not for you'.
John Mortimer (b. 1923) British lawyer, dramatist, and writer. *Daily Mail* (May 1988)

26 I avoided the company because I wanted the opportunity to have a track record of starting a business where you are not the boss's son.
James Murdoch (b. 1973) Australian chief executive and chairman of Star TV. Referring to his father, Rupert Murdoch. *Forbes* (July 1998)

27 There are still worlds out there to conquer.
Rupert Murdoch (b. 1931) US CEO of News Corporation. *Forbes* (June 1998)

28 It is better to underpromise and overdeliver than vice versa. For this one need not break the law of the land. One has to only think global. Otherwise success will disappear like the dew in the morning sun.
Narayana Murthy (b. 1946) Indian founder and CEO of Infosys. 'Employee Satisfaction Crucial to Success', *Hindu Business Line* (2000)

29 I was actually too exhausted to realize at the moment that my life's purpose had been achieved.
Robert Edwin Peary (1856–1920) US Arctic explorer. Referring to reaching the North Pole. *The North Pole* (1910)

30 Knowledge is fine, but the ability to get things done is the most important thing in my book.
Jack Petchey (b. 1925) British investor. *Sunday Times* (September 2000)

31 I didn't come to NASA to make history.
Sally Kristen Ride (b. 1951) US astronaut. Referring to being the first US woman in space. *Newsweek* (June 1983)

32 Happiness...lies in the joy of achievement, in the thrill of creative effort. The joy and moral stimulation of work no longer must be forgotten in the mad chase of evanescent profits.
Franklin D. Roosevelt (1882–1945) US president. Presidential inaugural address (4 March 1933)

33 I wish to preach not the doctrine of ignoble ease, but the doctrine of the strenuous life.
Theodore Roosevelt (1858–1919) US president. Speech (1899)

34 A simple third-generation shopkeeper.
Marcus Sieff (1913–2001) British president of Marks & Spencer. Quoted in *A Passion for Excellence* (Tom Peters and Mary Austin; 1985)

35 If you do it right 51 percent of the time you will end up a hero.
Alfred P. Sloan (1875–1966) US president of General Motors. Quoted in *Corporate Cultures* (Deal and Kennedy; 1982)

36 To reach this chair from which the Nobel lecture is delivered...I have mounted not three or four temporary steps, but hundreds or even thousands.
Aleksander Solzhenitsyn (b. 1918) Russian author and winner of the 1970 Nobel Prize in Literature. Nobel Prize acceptance speech (1970)

37 A self-made man is one who believes in luck and sends his son to Oxford.
Christina Stead (1902–83) Australian writer. *House of all Nations* (1938)

38 If you join a big corporation, you have to aspire to getting as far as you can.
Tony Trahar (b. 1950) South African CEO of Anglo American. *Sunday Times* (May 2000)

39 But what those critics don't know is that these same assets that excite me in the chase often, once they are acquired, leave me bored.
Donald J. Trump (b. 1946) US property developer. *Trump: Surviving at the Top* (co-written with Charles Leerhsen; 1990)

40 Deals are my art form.
Donald J. Trump (b. 1946) US property developer. *Trump: The Art of the Deal* (co-written with Tony Schwartz; 1987)

41 To me, it's very simple; if you're going to be thinking anyway, you might as well think big.
Donald J. Trump (b. 1946) US property developer. *Trump: The Art of the Deal* (co-written with Tony Schwartz; 1987)

42 I can do more in communications than any conqueror could have done.
Ted Turner (b. 1938) US founder of Turner Broadcasting Systems. *Newsweek* (16 June 1980)

43 I'm in history and I like myself. I would not want to be anyone else.
Ted Turner (b. 1938) US founder of Turner Broadcasting Systems. *Saturday Evening Post* (March 1984)

44 To achieve great things we must live as though we were never going to die.
Luc de Clapiers Vauvenargues (1715–47) French soldier and writer. *Reflections and Maxims* (1746)

45 Character is a by-product; it is produced in the great manufacture of daily duty.
Woodrow Wilson (1856–1924) US president. Address (May 1915)

46 I believe in my own possibilities, and I feel I can do it all.
Oprah Winfrey (b. 1954) US talk show host, actor, and business executive. Quoted in *Oprah Winfrey: The Real Story* (George Mair; 1994)

ACTION

1 Never let an opportunity pass by, but always think twice before acting.
Anonymous. Japanese proverb.

2 Action without a name, without a 'who' attached to it, is meaningless.
Hannah Arendt (1906–75) US political philosopher. *The Human Condition* (1958)

3 Doubt is a necessary precondition to meaningful action. Fear is the great mover in the end.
Donald Barthelme (1931–89) US novelist and short-story writer. 'The Rise of Capitalism', *Sadness* (1972)

4 Freedom from activity is never achieved by abstaining from action.
Bhagavad Gita, Indian religious text. (?1st century BC), 3:4

5 Enough of talking—it is time now to do.

Tony Blair (b. 1953) British prime minister. Press conference (May 1997)

6 The world can only be grasped by action, not by contemplation. The hand is the cutting edge of man.

Jacob Bronowski (1908–74) Polish mathematician and philosopher. *The Ascent of Man* (1973)

7 One's objective should be to get it right, get it quick, get it out, and get it over...your problem won't improve with age.

Warren Buffett (b. 1930) US entrepreneur and financier. 'Interview with Warren Buffett', *Harvard Business Review* (Norman Augustine; November/December 1995)

8 We do not need, and indeed never will have, all the answers before we act...It is often through taking action that we can discover some of them.

Charlotte Bunch (b. 1944) US feminist theorist and writer. 'Not by Degrees', *Passionate Politics* (1987)

9 When I saw something that needed doing, I did it.

Nellie Cashman (1851–1925) Irish writer and explorer. Interview, *Daily British Colonist* (1898)

10 Give us the tools and we will finish the job.

Winston Churchill (1874–1965) British prime minister. Referring to the era before the US formally entered the second world war. Radio broadcast (February 1941)

11 If you're proactive, you don't have to wait for circumstances or other people to create perspective expanding experiences. You can consciously create your own.

Stephen Covey (b. 1932) US writer and psychologist. *The 7 Habits of Highly Effective People* (1989)

12 Whenever anything is being accomplished, it is being done, I have learned, by a monomaniac with a mission.

Peter F. Drucker (b. 1909) US management consultant and academic. *Adventures of a Bystander* (1979)

13 It is an immutable law in business that words are words, explanations are explanations, promises are promises—but only performance is reality.

Harold S. Geneen (1910–97) US telecommunications entrepreneur and CEO of ITT. *Managing* (co-written with Alvin Moscow; 1984)

14 I acted, and my action made me wise.

Thom Gunn (b. 1929) British poet. 'Incident on a Journey', *Fighting Terms* (1954)

15 Never confuse movement with action.

Ernest Hemingway (1899–1961) US author. Quoted in *Papa Hemingway* (A.E. Hotchner; 1966)

16 Action is at bottom a swinging and flailing of the arms to regain one's balance and keep afloat.

Eric Hoffer (1902–83) US philosopher. *The Passionate State of Mind* (1955)

17 Do that which consists in taking no action, and order will prevail.

Laozi (?570—?490 BC) Chinese philosopher, reputed founder of Daoism. *Daode Jing*, III

18 When action grows unprofitable, gather information; when information grows unprofitable, sleep.

Ursula K. Le Guin (b. 1929) US author. *The Left Hand of Darkness* (1969)

19 I don't believe there's a contradiction between contemplation and action. Action should be founded on contemplation, and those of us who act don't put enough time, don't give enough emphasis, to contemplation.

Robert S. McNamara (b. 1916) US politician and president of the World Bank. Interview, Conversations with History series, Institute of International Studies, University of California, Berkeley. 'A Life in Public Service' (16 April 1996)

20 Action to be effective must be directed to clearly conceived ends.

Jawaharlal Nehru (1889–1964) Indian prime minister. Quoted in *Glorious Thoughts of Nehru* (N.B. Sen; 1964)

21 'Tis the motive that exalts the action; 'Tis the doing, and not the deed.

Margaret Preston (1820–97) US poet and writer. 'The First Proclamation of Miles Standish' (?1875)

22 In politics if you want anything said, ask a man. If you want anything done, ask a woman.

Margaret Thatcher (b. 1925) British former prime minister. Quoted in *People* (15 September 1975)

23 It is ruinous to do what should not be done
And ruinous to leave undone what should be done.

Tiruvalluvar (*fl.* 1st century) Indian poet. *The Kural*, 466

24 Think and act; to act and then to think
Is folly.

Tiruvalluvar (*fl.* 1st century) Indian poet. *The Kural*, 467

ADVERSITY

1 Not only is there no God, but try getting a plumber on weekends.

Woody Allen (b. 1935) US actor, humorist, producer, and director. *Getting Even* (1971)

2 Prosperity doth best discover vice; but adversity doth best discover virtue.

Francis Bacon (1561–1626) English philosopher and statesman. 'Of Adversity', *Essays* (1597–1625)

3 Prosperity is not without many fears and distastes; and Adversity is not without comfort and hope.

Francis Bacon (1561–1626) English philosopher and statesman. 'Of Adversity', *Essays* (1597–1625)

4 Economic distress will teach men, if anything can, that realities are less dangerous than fancies, that fact-finding is more effective than fault-finding.

Carl Becker (1873–1945) US historian. *Progress and Power* (1935)

5 Whom prosperity maketh our friend, adversity will make our enemy.

Boethius (?480–524) Roman philosopher and statesman. *De Consolatione Philosophiae* (524), bk 3, ch. 4

6 Whenever our neighbour's house is on fire, it cannot be amiss for the engine to play a little on our own.

Edmund Burke (1729–97) British philosopher and politician. *Reflections on the Revolution in France* (1790)

7 Adversity is the first path to truth.

Lord Byron (1788–1824) British poet. *Don Juan* (1823), can. 12, st. 50

8 Adversity is sometimes hard upon a man; but for one man who can stand prosperity, there are a hundred that will stand adversity.

Thomas Carlyle (1795–1881) British historian and essayist. 'The Hero as Man of Letters', *On Heroes, Hero-Worship, and the Heroic in History* (1841)

9 If you have bright plumage, people will take pot shots at you.

Alan Clark (1928–99) British politician and diarist. *Independent* (25 June 1994)

10 Without humanity a man cannot long endure adversity, nor can he long enjoy prosperity.

Confucius (551–479 BC) Chinese philosopher, administrator, and writer. *Analects* (?500 BC)

11 There is no education like adversity.

Benjamin Disraeli (1804–81) British prime minister and novelist. *Endymion* (1880), ch. 61

12 After calamities, more caution.

Desiderius Erasmus (?1466–1536) Dutch writer, scholar, and humanist. *Adagia* (1523), chiliadis 4, centuria 3, no. 59

13 If afflictions refine some, they consume others.

Thomas Fuller (1654–1734) English physician and writer. *Gnomologia* (1732)

14 I think large organizations have a real tendency to block bad news from moving around the organization. People don't know how to deal with it...having it just be a matter of course that you get the bad news out there, and everybody is...talking about it on an open basis, I think is really fundamental.

Bill Gates (b. 1955) US entrepreneur, chairman and CEO of Microsoft. Speech, Microsoft's Second Annual CEO Summit, Seattle, Washington (28 May 1998)

15 Prosperity is a great teacher; adversity is a greater.

William Hazlitt (1778–1830) British essayist and journalist. 'On the Conversation of Cards', *Essays* (1819)

16 Adversity is wont to reveal genius, prosperity to hide it.

Horace (65–8 BC) Roman poet and satirist. *Satires* (30 BC), bk 2, Satire 8

17 He knows not his own strength who has not met adversity.

Ben Jonson (1572–1637) English playwright and poet. 'Explorata', *Timber, or Discoveries* (1640)

18 Life is truly known only to those who suffer, lose, endure adversity, and stumble from defeat to defeat.

Ryszard Kapuściński (b. 1932) Polish journalist and author. 'A Warsaw Diary', *Granta* (1985)

19 It is a common fault of men not to reckon on storms in fair weather.

Niccolò Machiavelli (1469–1527) Italian historian, statesman, and political philosopher. *The Prince* (1513), ch. 24

20 In adversity a man is saved by hope.

Menander (?342—?292 BC) Athenian dramatist. *Fragments* (?300 BC)

21 Feelings of anger or dismay, a sense of injustice—these are the responses to downward mobility shared by most of its victims.

Katherine S. Newman (b. 1953) US anthropologist. *Falling from Grace* (1988)

22 Prosperity proves the fortunate, adversity the great.

Pliny the Younger (62–113) Roman government official. *Panegyric on Trajan* (AD 100), sect. 31

23 The highest form of success...comes, not to the man who desires mere easy peace, but to the man who does not shrink from danger, from hardship, or from bitter toil, and who out of these wins the splendid ultimate triumph.

Theodore Roosevelt (1858–1919) US president. 10 April 1899. 'The Strenuous Life', *The Strenuous Life: Essays and Addresses* (1900)

24 Sweet are the uses of adversity, Which like the toad, ugly and venomous, Wears yet a precious jewel in his head.

William Shakespeare (1564–1616) English poet and playwright. *As You Like It* (1599), Act 2, Scene 1, ll. 12–13

25 If you can't stand the heat, get out of the kitchen.

Harry S. Truman (1884–1972) US president. *Mr. Citizen* (1960)

ADVERTISING

1 Time spent in the advertising business seems to create a permanent deformity like the Chinese habit of foot-binding.

Dean Acheson (1893–1971) US statesman. Quoted in *Among Friends* (David S. McLellan and David C. Acheson; 1980)

2 Good advertising can make people buy your product even if it sucks...A dollar spent on brainwashing is more cost-effective than a dollar spent on product improvement.

Scott Adams (b. 1957) US cartoonist and humorist. *The Dilbert Principle* (1996)

3 An advertising agency is 85 percent confusion and 15 percent commission.

Fred Allen (1894–1956) US comedian and satirist. *Treadmill to Oblivion* (1954)

4 Whatever happens, you get your pet back.

Anonymous. Slogan of a Manhattan firm founded by two brothers, one a vet, the other a taxidermist. Quoted in *Architect's Journal* (13 July 2000)

5 Tell me quick and tell me true, what your product's going to do, or else, my love, to hell with you.

Anonymous. Quoted in *Marketing* (July 2000)

6 Advertising challenges don't come much bigger than this.

Anonymous. Referring to the task of transforming the brand image of the Czech car maker Skoda. *Sunday Telegraph* (August 2000)

7 Advertising is the very essence of democracy.

Bruce Barton (1886–1967) US advertising executive and author. *Reader's Digest* (1955)

8 We read advertisements...to discover and enlarge our desires.

Daniel J. Boorstin (b. 1914) US Pulitzer-prize-winning historian. *The Image* (1961)

9 Advertising is the ability to sense, interpret...to put the very heart throbs of a business into type, paper, and ink.

Leo Burnett (1891–1971) US advertising executive and author. Quoted in *Leo Burnett: Star Reacher* (Joan Kufrin; 1995)

10 Don't act too guilty. Running apologetic ads would only call unnecessary attention to the glitch.

Clive Chajet (b. 1937) US management consultant. Speaking about America Online's loss of service for one day. 'AOL Takes Right Approach Offering Mea Culpa, Rebate', *USA Today* (1999)

11 It is pretty obvious that the debasement of the human mind caused by a constant flow of fraudulent advertising is not a trivial thing. There is more than one way to conquer a country.

Raymond Chandler (1888–1959) US writer. Quoted in *Raymond Chandler Speaking* (Dorothy Gardiner and Katherine S. Walker, eds; 1962)

12 Advertising nourishes the consuming power of men.

Winston Churchill (1874–1965) British prime minister. Quoted in *Confessions of an Advertising Man* (David Ogilvy; 1963)

13 Each day of our lives, twelve billion display ads, two and a half million radio commercials, and over three hundred thousand television commercials are dumped into the collective conscience.

Ronald Collins, US journalist. *Columbia Journalism Review* (November/December 1991)

14 A desirable advertisement will be reasonable, but never dull...original, but never self-conscious...imaginative, but never misleading.

Fairfax Cone (1903–77) US advertising executive. *Christian Science Monitor* (1963)

15 Advertising is the business of telling someone something that should be important to him. It is a substitute for talking to him.

Fairfax Cone (1903–77) US advertising executive. *Christian Science Monitor* (1963)

16 Advertising is what you do when you can't go see somebody. That's all it is.

Fairfax Cone (1903–77) US advertising executive. *Christian Science Monitor* (1963)

17 There have been many disputes by advertisers and their agencies about articles published in magazines to which they took exception, and scheduled advertising has been cancelled. But I can see no difference between this and the action of an irate individual who cancels his subscription because of an article or story that he doesn't like.

Fairfax Cone (1903–77) US advertising executive. Quoted in *Fables of Abundance: A Cultural History of Advertising in America* (Jackson Lears; 1994)

18 From Those Wonderful Folks Who Gave You Pearl Harbor

Jerry Della Femina (b. 1936) US advertising executive. Book title, originally suggested as an advertising slogan for Panasonic Corporation. *From Those Wonderful Folks Who Gave You Pearl Harbor* (1970)

19 A good ad should be like a good sermon: It must not only comfort the afflicted—it must *afflict the comfortable*!

Bernice Fitz-Gibbon (?1895–1982) US advertising executive. *Macy's, Gimbels and Me* (1967)

20 Of course advertising creates wants. Of course it makes people discontented, dissatisfied. Satisfaction with things as they are would defeat the American Dream.

Bernice Fitz-Gibbon (?1895–1982) US advertising executive. *Macy's, Gimbels and Me* (1967)

21 The things we have to sell won't take the place of the Ten Commandments...Copy can be casually optimistic, but no more.

Bernice Fitz-Gibbon (?1895–1982) US advertising executive. 'Suppressed News: FTC Brands Million-dollar Advertising Press & Air Campaigns False', *New York Times* (1947)

22 It is not necessary to advertise food to hungry people, fuel to cold people, or houses to the homeless.

J.K. Galbraith (b. 1908) US economist and diplomat. *American Capitalism* (1956)

23 The modern corporation must manufacture not only goods but the desire for the goods it manufactures.

J.K. Galbraith (b. 1908) US economist and diplomat. *The Affluent Society* (1958), ch. 20

24 To write down, frame, and publish your corporate values is all about self-deceit and ego. It is almost certainly bullshit.

Barry J. Gibbons (b. 1946) US chairman and CEO of Burger King, co-founder of Y Arriba Y Arriba, and author. Quoted in *How to Manage* (Ray Wild; 1995)

25 Advertising as a marketing and communications tool will never command the respect it deserves until the correlation between share of voice and profitable growth is firmly established.

DeWitt Frederick Helm Jr (b. 1933) US consultant. Speech (1993)

26 Give them quality. That's the best kind of advertising.

Milton Snavely Hershey (1857–1945) US industrialist. Quoted in *Low Cost Marketing* (Ros Jay; 1994)

27 It is far easier to write ten passably effective sonnets, good enough to take in the not too enquiring critic, than one effective advertisement that will take in a few thousand of the uncritical buying public.

Aldous Huxley (1894–1963) British novelist and essayist. *On the Margin* (1923)

28 Promise, large promise is the soul of an advertisement.

Samuel Johnson (1709–84) British poet, lexicographer, essayist, and critic. *The Idler* (1759), no. 40

29 I liked the shaver so much I bought the company.

Victor Kiam (1926–2001) US CEO of Remington Corporation. An advertising slogan for Remington electric razors. Kiam appeared in his company's advertisements. Quoted in *Collins Dictionary of Slogans* (Nigel Rees; 1997)

30 The list of sins committed by advertising is limited only by the creativity of its critics.

Jerry Kirkpatrick, US author. Quoted in *Journal of Advertising, vol. 15* (1986)

31 What is self-image? Who started talking about one? I rather fancy it was Madison Avenue.

Madeleine L'Engle (b. 1918) US novelist. *A Circle of Quiet* (1972)

32 Society drives people crazy with lust and calls it advertising.

John Lahr (b. 1941) US writer and critic. *Guardian* (August 1989)

33 Imagine if advertisers used their creative skills to make watching learning-oriented shows a first choice for kids.

Geraldine Laybourne (b. 1947) US chairman of Oxygen Media. 'It Takes Three to Tango', *www.childrennow.org/media* (2000)

34 Advertising may be described as the science of arresting human intelligence long enough to get money from it.

Stephen Leacock (1869–1944) Canadian humorist, essayist, economist, and historian. *The Perfect Salesman* (1924)

35 The way a lot of advertising works is negative, in an 'if you have this you'll be younger, better, perfect' sort of way. That's not my message.

Jeanine Lobell (b. 1964) US entrepreneur, founder and CEO of Stila cosmetics. 'Jeanine Lobell, A Fresh Face', *www.womenswire.com* (Evelyn Sheinkopf; 2000)

36 Advertising is the greatest art form of the twentieth century.

Marshall McLuhan (1911–80) Canadian sociologist and author. Attrib.

37 Our brand awareness went from 65 percent to 81 percent in one year. We weren't advertising so we know exactly what to blame.

Chris Moore (b. 1960) British marketing director of Domino's Pizza. *Marketing* (June 2000)

38 Beneath this slab
John Brown is stowed
He watched the ads
And not the road.

Ogden Nash (1902–71) US humorist and writer. 'Lather as You Go' (1942)

39 I think that I shall never see
A billboard lovely as a tree.
Indeed, unless the billboards fall
I'll never see a tree at all.

Ogden Nash (1902–71) US humorist and writer. 'Song of the Open Road', *Happy Days* (1933)

40 Political commercials encourage the deceptive, the destructive, and the degrading.

John O'Toole (1929–95) US advertising executive. Quoted in *The Want Makers: Inside the World of Advertising* (Eric Clark; 1988)

41 Advertising is only evil when it advertises evil things.

David Ogilvy (1911–99) British advertising executive, founder and chairman of Ogilvy & Mather. *Confessions of an Advertising Man* (1963)

42 Every advertisement should be thought of as a contribution to the complex symbol which is the brand image.

David Ogilvy (1911–99) British advertising executive, founder and chairman of Ogilvy & Mather. *Confessions of an Advertising Man* (1963)

43 I do not regard advertising as entertainment or an art form, but as a medium of entertainment.

David Ogilvy (1911–99) British advertising executive, founder and chairman of Ogilvy & Mather. *Confessions of an Advertising Man* (1963)

44 If you pretest your product with consumers and pretest your advertising, you will do well in the marketplace.

David Ogilvy (1911–99) British advertising executive, founder and chairman of Ogilvy & Mather. *Confessions of an Advertising Man* (1963)

45 I have never admired the belles lettres school of advertising. I have always thought them absurd; they did not give the reader a single fact.

David Ogilvy (1911–99) British advertising executive, founder and chairman of Ogilvy & Mather. *Confessions of an Advertising Man* (1963)

46 Never stop testing, and your advertising will never stop improving.

David Ogilvy (1911–99) British advertising executive, founder and chairman of Ogilvy & Mather. *Confessions of an Advertising Man* (1963)

47 Ninety per cent of advertising doesn't sell much of anything.

David Ogilvy (1911–99) British advertising executive, founder and chairman of Ogilvy & Mather. *Confessions of an Advertising Man* (1963)

48 The most important word in the vocabulary of advertising is TEST.

David Ogilvy (1911–99) British advertising executive, founder and chairman of Ogilvy & Mather. *Confessions of an Advertising Man* (1963)

49 Unless your campaign has a big idea, it will pass like a ship in the night.

David Ogilvy (1911–99) British advertising executive, founder and chairman of Ogilvy & Mather. *Confessions of an Advertising Man* (1963)

50 What you say in advertising is more important than how you say it.

David Ogilvy (1911–99) British advertising executive, founder and chairman of Ogilvy & Mather. *Confessions of an Advertising Man* (1963)

51 There is one category of advertising which is totally uncontrolled and flagrantly dishonest: the television commercials for candidates in Presidential elections.

David Ogilvy (1911–99) British advertising executive, founder and chairman of Ogilvy & Mather. *Ogilvy on Advertising* (1983)

52 When you have nothing to say, sing it.

David Ogilvy (1911–99) British advertising executive, founder and chairman of Ogilvy & Mather. *Ogilvy on Advertising* (1983)

53 All these bromides are interchangeable—any company could use any of them.

David Ogilvy (1911–99) British advertising executive, founder and chairman of Ogilvy & Mather. Referring to the blandness of corporate advertising slogans. *Ogilvy on Advertising* (1983)

54 Get rid of sad dogs that spell doom.

David Ogilvy (1911–99) British advertising executive, founder and chairman of Ogilvy & Mather. *Principles of Management* (1968)

55 Good copy can't be written with tongue in cheek, written just for a living. You've got to believe in the product.

David Ogilvy (1911–99) British advertising executive, founder and chairman of Ogilvy & Mather. Quoted in *The Quotable Executive* (J. Woods; 2000)

56 If it doesn't sell, it isn't creative.

David Ogilvy (1911–99) British advertising executive, founder and chairman of Ogilvy & Mather. Quoted in *The Quotable Executive* (J. Woods; 2000)

57 The more informative your advertising, the more persuasive it will be.

David Ogilvy (1911–99) British advertising executive, founder and chairman of Ogilvy & Mather. Quoted in *The Quotable Executive* (J. Woods; 2000)

58 Political advertising ought to be stopped. It's the only really dishonest kind of advertising that's left. It's totally dishonest.

David Ogilvy (1911–99) British advertising executive, founder and chairman of Ogilvy & Mather. Quoted in *The Want Makers: Inside the World of Advertising* (Eric Clark; 1988)

59 Modernity desacralized the human body, and advertising has used it as a marketing tool.

Octavio Paz (1914–98) Mexican writer. *The Double Flame* (1995)

60 The reality remains that the power to persuade has to be demonstrated in old-fashioned conventional terms.

Michael Perry (b. 1934) British business executive. *Marketing* (March 2000)

61 The enemies of advertising are the enemies of freedom.

Enoch Powell (1912–98) British politician. Attrib.

62 It is a bloodless extrapolation of a satisfying life. You dine off the advertiser's 'sizzle' and not the meat of the steak.

J.B. Priestley (1894–1984) British author. *New Statesman* (December 1975)

63 What do you want from me? Fine writing? Or would you like to see the goddam sales curve stop going down and start going up?

Rosser Reeves (1910–84) US advertising executive. Interview (1965)

64 Advertising began as an art...and too many advertising people want it to remain that way—a never-never land where they can say this is right because we feel it is right.

Rosser Reeves (1910–84) US advertising executive. *Reality in Advertising* (1961)

65 Advertising is merely a substitute for a personal sales force—an extension, if you will, of the merchant who cried about his wares.

Rosser Reeves (1910–84) US advertising executive. *Reality in Advertising* (1961)

66 A hard sell advertisement, like a diesel motor, must be judged on whether it performs what it was designed to do.

Rosser Reeves (1910–84) US advertising executive. Quoted in *The Mirror Makers* (Stephen Fox; 1984)

67 Creative people are like a wet towel. You wring them out and pick up another one.

Charles Revson (1906–75) US entrepreneur, business executive, and founder of Revlon, Inc. Attrib.

68 The cosmetics industry should be promoting health and well-being; instead it hypes an outdated notion of glamour and sells false hopes and fantasies.

Anita Roddick (b. 1942) British entrepreneur and founder of The Body Shop. *Body and Soul* (co-written with Russell Miller; 1991)

69 Those who prefer their English sloppy have only themselves to thank if the advertisement writer uses his mastery of vocabulary and syntax to mislead their weak minds.

Dorothy L. Sayers (1893–1957) British author. 'The Psychology of Advertising', *Spectator* (November 1937)

70 We do things much the same way we did 50, 60 or even 70 years ago. The answers may not be wrong, but we haven't experimented to see whether they are or not.

Martin Sorrell (b. 1945) British advertising executive. Referring to advertising. *Financial Times* (March 1997)

71 Until the rise of American advertising, it never occurred to anyone anywhere in the world that the teenager was a captive in a hostile world of adults.

Gore Vidal (b. 1925) US novelist and critic. *Rocking the Boat* (1962)

72 I know half the money I spend on advertising is wasted, but I can never find out which half.

John Wanamaker (1838–1922) US businessman. Quoted in 'How to Acquire Customers on the Web', *Harvard Business Review* (Donna L. Hoffman and Thomas P. Novak; 2000)

73 Any seeming deception in a statement is costly, not only in the expense of the advertising but in the detrimental effect produced upon the customer, who believes she has been misled.

John Wanamaker (1838–1922) US businessman. Quoted in *Whatever Happened to Madison Avenue?* (Martin Mayer; 1991)

74 In writing advertising it must always be kept in mind that the customer often knows more about the goods than the advertising writers because they have had experience in buying them.

John Wanamaker (1838–1922) US businessman. Quoted in *Whatever Happened to Madison Avenue?* (Martin Mayer; 1991)

75 I never felt anyone bought anything from a teacher.

Dan G. Wieden (b. 1945) US advertising executive. Referring to the need for advertising to sell. *New York Times* (October 1995)

76 Advertising is our printed salesman. It may not be pretty, but it has to be true.

William Wrigley (1861–1932) US businessman and founder of Wrigley Company. 'The Lowdown on Salesmanship', *American Magazine* (Neil M. Clark; October 1929)

77 Dull times are the very times when you need advertising most.

William Wrigley (1861–1932) US businessman and founder of Wrigley Company. 'Make a Fair Product for a Fair Price, then Tell the World', *Illustrated World* (S.J. Duncan-Clark; March 1922)

78 Make a Fair Product for a Fair Price, then Tell the World

William Wrigley (1861–1932) US businessman and founder of Wrigley Company. 'Make a Fair Product for a Fair Price, then Tell the World', *Illustrated World* (S.J. Duncan-Clark; March 1922)

ADVICE

1 Wall Street is the only place people ride to in a Rolls Royce to get advice from people who take the subway.

Warren Buffett (b. 1930) US entrepreneur and financier. *Newsday* (August 1991)

2 The field of consultancy and gurus and so on is very much like alchemy; no concepts, no rigorous definition, and just waffle and fiddling around.

Elliot Jacques (b. 1917) Canadian psychologist and sociologist. Radio broadcast (August 1997)

3 Advice almost never functions as a social lubricant; eight or nine times out of ten it makes people lose face, crushes their will, and creates a grudge.

Yukio Mishima (1925–70) Japanese novelist. 'Hagakure and its Author', *Mishima on Hagakure* (1977)

4 Get the advice of everybody whose advice is worth having—they are very few—and then do what you think best yourself.

Charles Stewart Parnell (1846–91) Irish politician. Quoted in *Parnell* (Conor Cruise O'Brien; 1957)

5 What a difficult thing it is to ask someone's advice on a matter without colouring his judgment by the way in which we present our problem.

Blaise Pascal (1623–62) French philosopher and mathematician. *Pensées* (1670)

6 You need to listen back. And you have to accept the fact that you will not always prevail. No matter how intelligent you think you are or how powerful your arguments are, you will lose. And you have to say, 'I fought the fight, I gave my advice, and I was overruled'.

Laura D'Andrea Tyson (b. 1947) US economist, academic, and chair of the Council of Economic Advisors and National Economic Council (1993–96). Interview, Conversations with History series, Institute of International Studies, University of California, Berkeley. Referring to giving advice. 'An Economist Goes to Washington' (14 January 1998)

7 I always pass on good advice. It is the only thing to do with it. It is never of any use to oneself.

Oscar Wilde (1854–1900) Irish writer and wit. Said by Lord Goring. *An Ideal Husband* (1895), Act 1

AMBITION

1 He wishes not to seem, but to be, the best.

Aeschylus (525–456 BC) Greek dramatist. *Seven Against Thebes* (?467 BC)

2 Position, in an intelligent man, is a sign of ambition.

W.H. Auden (1907–73) US poet. *The Life of That There Poet* (1958)

3 One of the reasons I started this business was I wanted to go to my class reunion in a limo. In school, I knew I was smart...but I was the kid least likely to succeed.

Terri Bowersock (b. 1956) US furniture company entrepreneur. Quoted in 'Terri Bowersock: Furniture Franchiser', *Women to Watch, womenswire.com* (Teresa O'Neil; 1996)

4 Managerial intellect wilted in competition with managerial adrenaline. The thrill of the chase blinded pursuers to the consequences of the chase.

Warren Buffett (b. 1930) US entrepreneur and financier. 'Acquisitions: The Process Can Be a Problem', *Harvard Business Review* (David B. Jemison and Sim B. Sitkin; 1986)

5 Well is it known that ambition can creep as well as soar.

Edmund Burke (1729–97) British philosopher and politician. *Letters on the Proposals for Peace with the Regicide Directory of France* (1797), no. 3

6 When you reach for the stars, you may not quite get one, but you won't come up with a handful of mud either.

Leo Burnett (1891–1971) US advertising executive and author. Quoted in *Reader's Digest* (January 1985)

7 My aspirations take a higher flight. Mine be it to have contributed to the enlightenment and the joys of the mind, to the things of the spirit, to all that tends to bring into the lives of the toilers of Pittsburgh sweetness and light. I hold this the noblest possible use of wealth.

Andrew Carnegie (1835–1919) US industrialist and philanthropist. Address at the presentation of the Carnegie Library, Pittsburgh, Pennsylvania (5 November 1895)

8 At the age of six I wanted to be a cook. At seven I wanted to be Napoleon. And my ambition has been growing steadily ever since.

Salvador Dali (1904–89) Spanish artist. *The Secret Life of Salvador Dali* (1948)

9 It goes back to all of us wanting to be in Hollywood. We're all dying to win an Oscar.

Jerry Della Femina (b. 1936) US advertising executive. *Wall Street Journal* (1987)

10 I don't think that ambition is a bad word if you work hard yourself.

Lynn Forrester (b. 1955) US business executive. *Sunday Times* (June 2000)

11 Nothing humbler than ambition, when it is about to climb.

Benjamin Franklin (1706–90) US politician, inventor, and journalist. The *Poor Richard's Almanack* series (1732–58) was originally published under the pseudonym Richard Saunders. *Poor Richard's Almanack* (1753)

12 A guy like Ted Turner has all the money that he can possibly use...he wants people to think of him in a certain way, that he's the man that founded CNN, that created an entirely new media business.

Francis Fukuyama (b. 1952) US economist and writer. Referring to the importance of the desire for recognition as a key motivating force for great entrepreneurs. Interview, *Booknotes, www.C-Span.org* (17 January 1992)

13 People want to be head of General Motors, or General Electric...they want those jobs certainly for the income that is returned. But the income is itself a measure of the prestige and power, authority, that goes with achieving those positions.

J.K. Galbraith (b. 1908) US economist and diplomat. Interview, Conversations with History series, Institute of International Studies, University of California, Berkeley. 'Intellectual Journey: Challenging the Conventional Wisdom' (27 March 1986)

14 Man's restlessness makes him strive.

Johann Wolfgang von Goethe (1749–1832) German poet, playwright, novelist, and scientist. *Faust* (1832), Part 2

15 Nothing arouses ambition so much in the hearer as the trumpet clang of another's fame.

Baltasar Gracián (1601–58) Spanish writer and priest. *The Art of Worldly Wisdom* (1647)

16 To him that will, ways are not wanting.

George Herbert (1593–1633) English poet. *Jacula Prudentum* (1651)

17 Man is the only creature that strives to surpass himself, and yearns for the impossible.

Eric Hoffer (1902–83) US philosopher. *New York Times* (21 July 1969)

18 Do you want to spend the rest of your life selling sugared water or do you want the chance to change the world?

Steve Jobs (b. 1955) US entrepreneur, co-founder and CEO of Apple Computer Company, and CEO of Pixar. Said to John Sculley, then president of PepsiCo, when inviting him to join Apple. *Fortune* (14 September 1987)

19 I grew up with a lot of brothers and sisters. I did all I could do to really stand out and that nurtured a lot of confidence and drive and ambition.

Madonna (b. 1958) US singer and actor. 1985. Quoted in *Rolling Stone* (9 May 1985)

20 Men do not desire to be *rich* but to be richer than other men.

John Stuart Mill (1806–73) British economist and philosopher. Posthumous Essay on Social Freedom, *Oxford and Cambridge Review* (January 1907)

21 A man always has two reasons for what he does—a good one and the real one.

J.P. Morgan (1837–1913) US financier. Quoted in *Roosevelt: The Story of a Friendship* (Owen Wister; 1930)

22 If ambition doesn't hurt you, you haven't got it.

Kathleen Norris (1880–1966) US novelist. *Hands Full of Living* (1931)

23 Don't waste your effort on a thing which ends in a petty triumph unless you are satisfied with a life of petty issues.

John D. Rockefeller (1839–1937) US industrialist, philanthropist, and founder of Standard Oil. *Random Reminiscenses of Men and Events* (1909)

24 The man who starts out simply with the idea of getting rich won't succeed, you must have a larger ambition.

John D. Rockefeller (1839–1937) US industrialist, philanthropist, and founder of Standard Oil. *Random Reminiscenses of Men and Events* (1909)

25 Ambition should be made of sterner stuff.

William Shakespeare (1564–1616) English poet and playwright. *Julius Caesar* (1599), Act 3, Scene 2, l. 94

26 The world continues to offer glittering prizes to those who have stout hearts and sharp swords.

Frederick E. Smith (1872–1930) British politician. Rectorial address (7 November 1923)

27 Ambition if it feeds at all, does so on the ambition of others.
Susan Sontag (b. 1933) US novelist and essayist. *The Benefactor* (1963), ch. 1

28 Ambition often puts men upon doing the meanest offices; so climbing is performed in the same posture with creeping.
Jonathan Swift (1667–1745) Irish writer and satirist. *Thoughts on Various Subjects* (1711)

29 What a man thinks of himself, that it is which determines, or rather indicates, his fate.
Henry David Thoreau (1817–62) US writer. *Walden, or Life in the Woods* (1854)

30 I wasn't satisfied just to earn a good living. I was looking to make a statement.
Donald J. Trump (b. 1946) US property developer. *Trump: The Art of the Deal* (co-written with Tony Schwartz; 1987)

31 What's the subject of life—to get rich? All of those fellows out there getting rich could be dancing around the real subject of life.
Paul A. Volcker (b. 1927) US economist and banker. *Newsweek* (24 February 1986)

32 My initial plan was to conquer the world, but in reality, the world is not an easy place to conquer. I learned through the years that I had to build step by step, solidly.
Lise Watier (b. 1942) Canadian proprietor of a cosmetics chain. Quoted in *Looking Good* (Rosa Harris-Adler; 1997)

33 The impulse to acquisition, pursuit of gain, of money, of the greatest possible amount of money, has in itself nothing to do with capitalism...One may say that it has been common to all sorts and conditions of men at all times and in all cultures of the earth, wherever the objective possibility of it is or has been given.
Max Weber (1864–1920) German economist and sociologist. *The Protestant Ethic and the Spirit of Capitalism* (1904–05)

34 Ambition, madam, is a great man's madness.
John Webster (?1580—?1625) English dramatist. *The Duchess of Malfi* (?1613), Act 1, Scene 1

35 I decided to be the best and the smartest.
Oprah Winfrey (b. 1954) US talk show host, actor, and business executive. Quoted in *Oprah Winfrey Speaks* (Janet Lowe; 1998)

36 I was like a hit album waiting to be released. I knew my day would come.
Oprah Winfrey (b. 1954) US talk show host, actor, and business executive. Quoted in *Oprah Winfrey Speaks* (Janet Lowe; 1998)

37 The idea was to prove...that you were one of the elected and anointed ones who had *the right stuff* and could move higher and higher and...join the special few at the very top.
Tom Wolfe (b. 1931) US novelist and journalist. *The Right Stuff* (1979), ch. 2

ATTITUDE

1 A thick skin is a gift from God.
Konrad J. Adenauer (1876–1967) German chancellor. *New York Times* (30 December 1959)

2 A professional is a man who can do his job when he doesn't feel like it. An amateur is a man who can't do his work when he does feel like it.
James Agate (1877–1947) British critic and essayist. Diary (19 July 1945)

3 What is of first importance is not the religious or non-religious character of the work done, but the inner attitude in which it is done.
Sri Aurobindo (1872–1950) Indian philosopher, mystic, and nationalist. Quoted in *Ethics in Management: Vedantic Perspectives* (S.K. Chakraborty; 1995)

4 If you look at life one way there is always cause for alarm.
Elizabeth Bowen (1899–1973) Irish writer. *The Death of the Heart* (1938)

5 If a gentleman is frivolous, he will lose the respect of his inferiors.
Confucius (551–479 BC) Chinese philosopher, administrator, and writer. *Analects* (?500 BC)

6 Your attitude determines your altitude.
Stephen Covey (b. 1932) US writer and psychologist. Quoted in *Woodbury Reports Archives* (October 1995)

7 Always trust a positive response, question any negative ones.
Jack Daniels (b. 1933) US athletics coach. *Daniels' Running Formula* (1998)

8 Take the place and attitude to which you see your unquestionable right, and all men acquiesce.
Ralph Waldo Emerson (1803–82) US essayist, lecturer, and poet. *Journals* (1836)

9 You can increase your brain power three to fivefold simply by laughing and having fun before working on a problem.
Doug Hall (b. 1959) US business writer. *Jump Start Your Brain* (1996)

10 Change is an attitude of mind and the place to start is within ourselves.
John Harvey-Jones (b. 1924) British management adviser, author, and former chairman of ICI. *Managing to Survive* (1993)

11 Without the right attitude, a business with everything going for it will fail.
Robert Heller (b. 1932) British management writer. Referring to research into company growth carried out by consultancy Binder Hamlyn. *Goldfinger* (1998)

12 Have faith and pursue the unknown end.
Oliver Wendell Holmes Jr (1841–1935) US jurist. Letter to John C.H. Wu (1924)

13 It depends on how we look at things, and not on how they are in themselves.
Carl Gustav Jung (1875–1961) Swiss psychiatrist. *Modern Man in Search of a Soul* (1933)

14 Think small and act small, and we'll get bigger. Think big and act big, and we'll get smaller.

Herb Kelleher (b. 1931) US businessman and founder of Southwest Airlines. *Sales and Marketing Management* (October 1996)

15 Two men look out through the same bars: One sees the mud, and one the stars.

Frederick Langbridge (1849–1923) British clergyman and writer. *A Cluster of Quiet Thoughts* (1896)

16 It is the disposition of the thought that altereth the nature of the thing.

John Lyly (?1554–1606) English writer and dramatist. *Euphues: The Anatomy of Wit* (1578)

17 Attitudes are more important than facts.

Karl Augustus Menninger (1893–1990) US psychiatrist. Attrib.

18 Drop the idea that you are Atlas carrying the world on your shoulders. The world would go on even without you. Don't take yourself so seriously.

Norman Vincent Peale (1898–1993) US religious leader. *Positive Thinking Every Day* (1995)

19 All seems infected that the infected spy, As all looks yellow to the jaundiced eye.

Alexander Pope (1688–1744) English poet. *An Essay on Criticism* (1711)

20 If I had to name a driving force in my life, I'd name passion every time.

Anita Roddick (b. 1942) British entrepreneur and founder of The Body Shop. *Body and Soul* (co-written with Russell Miller; 1991)

21 If you can't change your fate change your attitude.

Amy Tan (b. 1952) US writer. *The Joy Luck Club* (1989)

BANKING

1 The most hated sort, and with the greatest reason, is usury... For money was intended to be used in exchange, but not to increase at interest.

Aristotle (384–322 BC) Greek philosopher and scientist. 'Sort' refers to 'sort of money-making'. *Politics* (4th century BC), bk 1

2 Adventure is the life of commerce but caution, I had almost said timidity, is the life of banking.

Walter Bagehot (1826–77) British economist and journalist. *Lombard Street* (1873)

3 Every banker knows that if he has to *prove* that he is worthy of credit, however good may be his arguments, in fact his credit is gone.

Walter Bagehot (1826–77) British economist and journalist. *Lombard Street* (1873)

4 Thus English capital runs as surely and instantly where it is most wanted and where there is the most to be made of it, as water runs to find its own level.

Walter Bagehot (1826–77) British economist and journalist. On the role of the London banks and financial markets. *Lombard Street* (1873)

5 They're just cold-blooded fish sitting at the top of some bloody great building looking at stats—and they've got handbooks.

Peter de Savary (b. 1944) British entrepreneur. Referring to investment bankers. Quoted in *The Adventure Capitalists* (Jeff Grout and Lynne Curry; 1998)

6 Our joint objective is that bankers should become uniformly acceptable as wise counsellors and friends of the community as a whole and not merely as associates of particular sections of society.

Indira Gandhi (1917–84) Indian prime minister. Speech (30 September 1969)

7 Ensuring that our nation's financial system works for all Americans also means promoting access to high quality financial services for all Americans. Despite the strong national economy, 10 million American families still do not have a bank account.

Gary Gensler (b. 1957) US economist and politician. Speech, American Bankers Association Government Relations Council (19 September 2000)

8 There may be no greater challenges and no greater opportunities for the banking industry than those presented by rapidly changing technology. No industry is more suited to garnering the benefits of e-commerce.

Gary Gensler (b. 1957) US economist and politician. Speech, American Bankers Association Government Relations Council (19 September 2000)

9 A bank is a place that will lend you money if you can prove that you don't need it.

Bob Hope (b. 1903) US comedian and film actor. Quoted in 'The Tyranny of Forms', *Life in the Crystal Palace* (Alan Harrington; 1959)

10 Through the fat years, the bankers were always right there by our side. But in bad times they backed off in a hurry.

Lee Iacocca (b. 1924) US president of Ford Motor Company, chairman and CEO of Chrysler Corporation. The banks failed to support Chrysler when it was on the verge of bankruptcy; the company was eventually saved by a government loan. *Iacocca: An Autobiography* (1984)

11 Banking establishments are more dangerous than standing armies.

Thomas Jefferson (1743–1826) US president. Letter to Elbridge Gerry (26 January 1799)

12 I've come to the belief that banks are not in the business of banking. They're in the business of collecting fees.

Patrick C. Kelly (b. 1947) US sales executive. *Inc.* (October 1995)

13 Financial institutions such as insurance and banking were a powerful presence in the American economy at the turn of the century, and women...became office workers in record numbers between 1870 and 1930.

Angel Kwolek-Folland, US author. *Engendering Business* (1994)

14 Except for the con men borrowing money they shouldn't get and the widows who have to visit with the handsome young men in the trust department, no sane person ever enjoyed visiting a bank.
Martin Mayer (b. 1928) US author and journalist. *The Money Bazaars* (1984)

15 Quite a few banks have cleaned up their act rather than risk public exposure. In the process, they have discovered that there is profit to be made in lending to residents in underserved neighborhoods.
Ralph Nader (b. 1934) US lawyer and consumer-rights campaigner. 'Digital Democracy in Action', *Forbes* (12 February 1996)

16 To the chagrin of banks and other financial corporations, public interest groups...are using the new technology to plow through mountains of data to detect who gets mortgage loans and who gets shut out.
Ralph Nader (b. 1934) US lawyer and consumer-rights campaigner. 'Digital Democracy in Action', *Forbes* (12 February 1996)

17 Bankers are like everybody else, except richer.
Ogden Nash (1902–71) US humorist and writer. 'Bankers are like everybody else, except richer', *The Pocket Book of Ogden Nash* (1962)

18 I want to be a banker
Like the banker at Banker's Trust.
...I want to play at Banker's Trust like a hippety-hoppety bunny,
And best of all, oh best of all,
With really truly money.
Ogden Nash (1902–71) US humorist and writer. 'If He Were Alive Today, Mayhap Mr. Morgan Would Sit on the Midget's Lap', *There's Always Another Windmill* (1968)

19 I doubt if there is any occupation which is more consistently and unfairly demeaned, degraded, denounced, and deplored than banking.
William Proxmire (b. 1915) US politician. Quoted in *Fortune* (31 October 1983)

20 The distinctive function of the banker begins as soon as he uses the money of others.
David Ricardo (1772–1823) British economist. *Principles of Political Economy and Taxation* (1817)

21 Under the banner of deregulation and total faith in the marketplace we're impairing our greatest assets: the credibility of our capital markets and the faith in our financial institutions...The growing feeling today is that the capital markets have become the property of insiders and speculators.
Felix Rohatyn (b. 1928) US investment company executive. *Wall Street Journal* (March 1985)

22 A banker is a man who lends another man the money of a third man.
Guy de Rothschild (b. 1909) French banker. Interview, *Sunday Citizen* (21 March 1965)

23 Behind all its global responsibilities and impersonal style banking is still a 'people business'...it may be the most personal business of all for it always depends on the original concept of credit, meaning trust.
Anthony Sampson (b. 1926) British author and journalist. *The Moneylenders: Bankers in a Dangerous World* (1981), ch. 1

24 It has been the bankers' destiny...to find themselves on the dangerous edge of the world, pointing up the contradictions and cross-purposes. They are not often loved for it.
Anthony Sampson (b. 1926) British author and journalist. *The Moneylenders: Bankers in a Dangerous World* (1981), ch. 22

25 Before October, 1929, no one objected to short sellers except their own families. The families objected to going bankrupt.
Fred Schwed (1901–66) US author. *Where Are The Customers' Yachts?* (1940)

26 Bankers need a political sense, a second vision, just as sailors need a meteorological sense.
Fritz Stern (b. 1926) US historian and academic. *Gold and Iron* (1977)

27 I learned then what a bunch of gangsters the banks are. They *really* are gangsters.
Alan Sugar (b. 1947) British entrepreneur, founder and chairman of Amstrad electronics company. Referring to his experience during takeover negotiations. Quoted in *The Amstrad Story* (David Thomas; 1990)

28 It's one of life's ironies that the more you can prove that you don't need a loan, the better your chances usually are of getting one. This is especially true for start-up businesses.
Lillian Vernon (b. 1927) US entrepreneur and CEO of Lillian Vernon Corporation. Speech. 'The Entrepreneur and the Professional Manager: Getting the Best of Both Worlds' (1998)

29 All these financiers, all the little gnomes of Zürich and the other financial centres, about whom we keep on hearing.
Harold Wilson (1916–95) British prime minister. Speech, House of Commons (12 November 1956)

30 Whether we like it or not mankind now has a completely integrated international financial and informational marketplace capable of moving money and ideas to any place on this planet in minutes.
Walter Wriston (b. 1919) US banker. Speech, International Monetary Conference, London (11 June 1979)

31 Our banking system grew by accident; and whenever something happens by accident, it becomes a religion.
Walter Wriston (b. 1919) US banker. *BusinessWeek* (20 January 1975)

32 Information about money has become almost as important as money itself. The competitive advantage of the banks used to be that they knew more about their customers than anyone else. Now...that knowledge can be had at the push of a button. The guy with the competitive advantage is the one with the best technology.

Walter Wriston (b. 1919) US banker. November 1985.
Quoted in *The Financial Revolution: The Big Bang
Worldwide* (Adrian Hamilton; 1986), ch. 2

33 In its simplest terms, this scientific advance in
the art of communication has created...an
entirely new system of world finance based on
the incredibly rapid flow of information....I
would argue that the information standard has
replaced the gold standard as the basis of
world finance.
Walter Wriston (b. 1919) US banker. Quoted in *The
Financial Revolution: The Big Bang Worldwide* (Adrian
Hamilton; 1986), ch. 2

BLAME

1 To accuse is so easy that it is infamous to do so
where proof is impossible.
Zoë Akins (1886–1958) US poet and playwright. *Déclassée*
(1919)

2 Judge not, that ye be not judged.
Bible. Matthew, 7:1

3 By blaming others, we fail to find the real
solutions to our problems and we do not carry
out our own responsibilities.
Jeb Bush (b. 1953) US politician. *Foundation for Florida's
Future* (1996)

4 The pursuit of alibis for poor industry
performance is one of the great Australian art
forms.
John Button (b. 1933) Australian politician. Quoted in
'Sayings of the Week', *Sydney Morning Herald* (5 July 1986)

5 Everyone threw the blame on me...they
nearly always do. I suppose...they think I shall
be able to bear it best.
Winston Churchill (1874–1965) British prime minister. *My
Early Life* (1947), ch. 17

6 Things that are done, it is needless to speak
about...things that are past, it is needless to
blame.
Confucius (551–479 BC) Chinese philosopher, administrator,
and writer. *Analects* (?500 BC)

7 One must first learn to live oneself before one
blames others.
Fyodor Dostoevsky (1821–81) Russian novelist. *Notes from
the Underground* (1864)

8 Good men prefer to be accountable.
Michael Owen Edwardes (b. 1930) British company
executive. Quoted in *How to Manage* (Ray Wild; 1982)

9 Blameless people are always the most
exasperating.
George Eliot (1819–80) British novelist. *Middlemarch*
(1871–72)

10 Keep alive the light of justice, and much that
men say in blame will pass you by.
Euripides (?484–?406 BC) Greek playwright. *The Suppliant
Women* (?421 BC)

11 An expert is someone called in at the last
minute to share the blame.
Sam Ewing (1920–2001) US author. Quoted in *Reader's
Digest* (December 1992)

12 Even doubtful accusations leave a stain
behind them.
Thomas Fuller (1654–1734) English physician and writer.
Gnomologia (1732)

13 He who findeth fault meaneth to buy.
Thomas Fuller (1654–1734) English physician and writer.
Gnomologia (1732)

14 Those see nothing but faults that seek for
nothing else.
Thomas Fuller (1654–1734) English physician and writer.
Gnomologia (1732)

15 Success is never blamed.
Thomas Fuller (1654–1734) English physician and writer.
Gnomologia (1732), no. 4273

16 He that blames would buy.
George Herbert (1593–1633) English poet. *Jacula
Prudentum* (1651)

17 The offender never pardons.
George Herbert (1593–1633) English poet. *Jacula
Prudentum* (1651)

18 The man who acts the least upbraids the most.
Homer (*fl.* 800 BC) Greek poet. *Iliad* (Alexander Pope; tr.
1715–20)

19 I find that pain of a little censure, even when it
is unfounded, is more acute than the pleasure
of much praise.
Thomas Jefferson (1743–1826) US president. Letter to
F. Hopkinson (13 March 1789)

20 It is the fate of those who toil at the lower
employments of life...to be exposed to
censure, without hope of praise.
Samuel Johnson (1709–84) British poet, lexicographer,
essayist, and critic. *A Dictionary of the English Language*
(1755), Preface

21 He has great tranquillity of heart who cares
neither for the praises nor the fault-finding of
men.
Thomas à Kempis (?1380–1471) German mystic, monk, and
writer. *De Imitatione Christi* (1426)

22 The devil is always blaming someone.
Bricks of blame pave the floor of hell.
Brendan Kennelly (b. 1936) Irish poet and academic. 'Blame',
A Time for Voices (1990)

23 If we had no faults of our own, we should not
take so much pleasure in noticing those of
others.
François La Rochefoucauld (1613–80) French epigrammatist.
Reflections: or, Sentences and Moral Maxims, 5th edition
(1678)

24 If there is no intention, there is no blame.
Livy (59 BC–AD 17) Roman historian. *History of Rome*
(26 BC–AD 15)

25 I wonder how anyone can have the face to condemn others when he reflects upon his own thoughts.
W. Somerset Maugham (1874–1965) British novelist, short-story writer, and dramatist. *The Summing Up* (1938)

26 Rash and incessant scolding runs into custom and renders itself despised.
Michel Eyquem de Montaigne (1533–92) French essayist and moralist. 'Of Anger', *Essays* (1580–88)

27 They have a right to censure that have a heart to help.
William Penn (1644–1718) English colony builder. *Some Fruits of Solitude* (1693)

28 Some praise at morning what they blame at night;
But always think the last opinion right.
Alexander Pope (1688–1744) English poet. *An Essay on Criticism* (1711)

29 I accept the responsibility but not the blame.
Robert Semple (1873–1955) New Zealand politician. 1944. Quoted in *Dominion* (Richard Long; 1984)

30 Take each man's censure, but reserve thy judgement.
William Shakespeare (1564–1616) English poet and playwright. *Hamlet* (1601), Act 1, Scene 2

31 Underneath runs the main current of preoccupation, which is keeping one's nose clean at all times. This means that when things go wrong you have to pass the blame along the line, like pass-the-parcel, till the music stops.
Tom Stoppard (b. 1937) British playwright and screenwriter. *Neutral Ground* (1983)

32 Our culture peculiarly honors the act of blaming, which it takes as the sign of virtue and intellect.
Lionel Trilling (1905–75) US academic, writer, and literary critic. *The Liberal Imagination* (1950)

BOASTING

1 I'm not just the greatest, I'm the double greatest.
Muhammad Ali (b. 1942) US boxer. Press conference (1963)

2 Anything you can do I can do better,
I can do anything better than you.
Irving Berlin (1888–1989) US composer and songwriter. 'Anything You Can Do', *Annie Get Your Gun* (1946)

3 I'm a single, straight billionaire in Manhattan. What do you think? It's a wet dream.
Michael Bloomberg (b. 1942) US entrepreneur, business executive, and Mayor of New York. 'Terminal Velocity', *Wired* (David S. Bennahum; February 1999)

4 Thank you for making me nouveau riche.
Jerry Della Femina (b. 1936) US advertising executive. Engraving on a silver box presented to Mort Janklow after the successful sale of Della Femina's advertising agency. *New York* (1987)

5 If you wish in this world to advance
Your merits you're bound to enhance;
You must stir it and stump it,
And blow your own trumpet,
Or trust me, you haven't a chance.
W.S. Gilbert (1836–1911) British librettist and playwright. *Ruddigore* (1887), Act 1

6 I have helped to change society in a way that is beyond presidents and is going to make the world a better and happier place.
Hugh Hefner (b. 1926) US entrepreneur and publisher. *Mail and Femail* (18 December 1989)

7 I gotta tell ya, with our $2.4 billion in profits last year, they gave me a great big bonus. Really, it's almost obscene.
Lee Iacocca (b. 1924) US president of Ford Motor Company, chairman and CEO of Chrysler Corporation. 1985. Said in a speech to market analysts in Detroit. Quoted in *Time* (1 April 1985)

8 Boast not of what thou would'st have done, but do
Then what thou would'st.
John Milton (1608–74) English poet. *Samson Agonistes* (1671)

9 If I needed a banker, I would go to me. No one really does what I do.
Nancy Peretsman (b. 1955) US investment banker. Answering the question: 'Nancy, what makes you so special?' 'Smarter than Herbert's Dog', *Forbes Global* (Dyan Machan; 1999)

10 Deep down, we're all Texans at heart. We love big and bigger, and positively adore biggest.
Tom Peters (b. 1942) US management consultant and author. *Liberation Management* (1992)

11 Beware the manager who proclaims to the world he is a long-termer, beginning today.
Gifford Pinchot (b. 1942) US author and software CEO. *Harvard Business Review* (May–June 1986)

12 I don't meet competition. I crush it.
Charles Revson (1906–75) US entrepreneur, business executive, and founder of Revlon, Inc. *Time* (16 June 1958)

13 When I describe Semco to other business people, they laugh. 'What do you do?' they ask, 'make beads?' And I say no, among other things we make rocket-fuel-propellant mixers for satellites.
Ricardo Semler (b. 1959) Brazilian business executive and president of Semco. 'The Mavericks', *Fortune* (June 1995)

14 If I only had a little humility, I'd be perfect.
Ted Turner (b. 1938) US founder of Turner Broadcasting Systems. *New York Times* (1980)

15 It is very vulgar to talk about one's business. Only people like stockbrokers do that, and then merely at dinner parties.
Oscar Wilde (1854–1900) Irish writer and wit. Said by Algernon. *The Importance of Being Earnest* (1895), Act 2

BOLDNESS

1 Boldness is an ill keeper of promise.
Francis Bacon (1561–1626) English philosopher and statesman. 'Of Boldness', *Essays* (1597–1625)

2 In civil business: what first? Boldness; what second, and third? Boldness.
Francis Bacon (1561–1626) English philosopher and statesman. 'Of Boldness', *Essays* (1597–1625)

3 People love to recognize, not venture. The former is so much more comfortable and self-flattering.
Jean Cocteau (1889–1963) French poet, novelist, dramatist, and film director. Quoted in *Writers at Work* (George Plimpton, ed.; 1977)

4 Boldness, again boldness, and always boldness!
Georges Jacques Danton (1759–94) French lawyer and revolutionary leader. Speech to the Legislative Committee of General Defence (2 September 1792)

5 The difference between talents and character is adroitness to keep the old and trodden round, and power and courage to make a new road to new and better goals.
Ralph Waldo Emerson (1803–82) US essayist, lecturer, and poet. 'Circles', *Essays: First Series* (1841)

6 We must dare to think 'unthinkable' thoughts. We must learn to explore all the options and possibilities that confront us in a complex and rapidly changing world. We must learn to welcome and not fear the voices of dissent.
J. William Fulbright (1905–95) US educator and politician. Speech, US Senate (27 March 1964)

7 Boldness in business is the first, second, and third thing.
Thomas Fuller (1654–1734) English physician and writer. *Gnomologia* (1732)

8 I buy when other people are selling.
J. Paul Getty (1892–1976) US entrepreneur, oil industry executive, and financier. 1961. Quoted in *The Great Getty* (Robert Lenzner; 1985)

9 Challenging the status quo has to be the starting point for anything that goes under the label of strategy.
Gary Hamel (b. 1954) US academic, business writer, and consultant. Interview, *Strategy + Business* (October–December 1997)

10 Be bold; everywhere be bold; but be not bowled over.
O. Henry (1862–1910) US short-story writer. 'The Tale of a Tainted Tenner' (1907)

11 Don't study the idea to death with experts and committees. Get on with it and see if it works.
Kenneth Iverson (1925–2002) US industrialist, chairman and CEO of Nucor Corporation. Speech (5 February 1996)

12 All classes of society are trades unionists at heart, and differ chiefly in the boldness, ability, and secrecy with which they pursue their respective interests.
William Stanley Jevons (1835–82) British economist and mathematician. *The State in Relation to Labour* (1882)

13 Nothing will ever be attempted, if all possible objections must first be overcome.
Samuel Johnson (1709–84) British poet, lexicographer, essayist, and critic. *Rasselas, Prince of Abyssinia* (1759)

14 If the creator had a purpose in equipping us with a neck, he surely meant us to stick it out.
Arthur Koestler (1905–83) British writer and journalist. *The Sleepwalkers* (1959)

15 It is better to be impetuous than circumspect. Experience shows that (fortune) is more often subdued by men who do this than by those who act coldly.
Niccolò Machiavelli (1469–1527) Italian historian, statesman, and political philosopher. *The Prince* (1513)

16 Every week, an astonishing number of Internet start-ups get established, without objection from initial venture capital...They think everything is up for grabs...all the rules are to be changed.
William (Walid) Mougayar, US consultant and management theorist. *Opening Digital Markets* (1997), Preface to 2nd edition

17 Leaders...grasp nettles.
David Ogilvy (1911–99) British advertising executive, founder and chairman of Ogilvy & Mather. Speech, American Marketing Association (10 May 1972)

18 To a few rashness brings luck, to most misfortune.
Phaedrus (?15 BC–AD ?50) Roman writer. Fable 4, *Fables* (AD ?25), bk 5

19 Corporate risk takers are very much like entrepreneurs. They take personal risks to make new ideas happen.
Gifford Pinchot (b. 1942) US author and software CEO. *Intrapreneuring* (1985)

20 In great affairs there is no little step.
Cardinal de Retz (1613–79) French prelate and politician. *Mémoires du Cardinal de Retz* (1660–79)

21 There is a tide in the affairs of men
Which, taken at the flood, leads on to fortune;
Omitted, all the voyage of their life
Is bound in shallows and in miseries.
William Shakespeare (1564–1616) English poet and playwright. *Julius Caesar* (1599), Act 4, Scene 3

22 What is more mortifying than to feel that you have missed the plum for want of courage to shake the tree.
Logan Pearsall Smith (1865–1946) British essayist and critic. *Afterthoughts* (1931)

23 Be bold, be bold, and everywhere, Be bold.
Edmund Spenser (1552–99) English poet. *The Faerie Queen* (1590), bk 3, can. 11, st. 54

24 At some point a good leader with inadequate data will say, 'Ready, fire, aim—and if it doesn't work we'll correct it, but at least the timing is right to start with what we have.'
Robert Townsend (b. 1920) US business executive and author. 'Townsend's Third Degree in Leadership', *The Conference Board Challenge to Business: Industry Leaders Speak Their Minds* (Peter Krass and Richard E. Cavanagh, eds; 2000)

25 If you're going to be thinking only one thing, you might as well be thinking big.

Donald Trump (b. 1946) US property developer. Referring to the grand scale of his property deals. *Trump: The Art of the Deal* (1987)

26 Look with favour upon a bold beginning.

Virgil (70–19 BC) Roman poet. *Georgics* (36–29 BC), bk 1, l. 30

BOOM AND BUST

1 Steel prices cause inflation like wet sidewalks cause rain.

Roger Blough (1904–85) US business executive, chairman of US Steel Corporation. *Forbes* (1967)

2 The problem established firms seem unable to confront successfully is that of downward vision and mobility, in terms of the trajectory map.

Clayton M. Christensen (b. 1952) US writer. *The Innovator's Dilemma* (1997)

3 In the next economic downturn there will be an outbreak of bitterness and contempt for the supercorporate chieftains who pay themselves millions. In every major economic downturn in US history the 'villains' have been the 'heroes' during the preceding boom.

Peter F. Drucker (b. 1909) US management consultant and academic. Quoted in 'Seeing Things as They Really Are', *Forbes* (Robert Lenzner and Stephen S. Johnson; 1987)

4 Once again, Chairman Greenspan and the Federal Reserve have mugged America.

Henry Gonzalez (1916–2000) US politician. Referring to an interest-rate increase. *BusinessWeek* (1994)

5 Regrettably, history is strewn with the visions of such 'new eras' that, in the end, have proven to be a mirage. In short, history counsels caution.

Alan Greenspan (b. 1926) US economist and chairman of US Federal Reserve Board. 9 September 1997. Said in testimony before Congress on 9 September 1997. *Financial Times* (1997)

6 A depression is either a 12 percent unemployment rate for nine months or more, or a 15 percent unemployment rate for three to nine months.

Alan Greenspan (b. 1926) US economist and chairman of US Federal Reserve Board. 1982. *New York Times Magazine* (William Safire; 1997)

7 There is no evidence that the business cycle has been repealed.

Alan Greenspan (b. 1926) US economist and chairman of US Federal Reserve Board. *Wall Street Journal* (1997)

8 Gentlemen, you have come sixty days too late. The depression is over.

Herbert Hoover (1874–1964) US president. June 1930. Reply to a delegation calling for a public-works programme to alleviate some of the impact of the Great Crash of October 1929. The worst effects of the Great Depression were still to come. Quoted in *The Crisis of the Old Order* (Arthur M. Schlesinger Jr; 1957)

9 I see nothing in the present situation that is either menacing or warrants pessimism...I have every confidence that there will be a revival of activity in the spring, and that during this coming year 1930 the country will make steady progress.

Andrew William Mellon (1855–1937) US financier, industrialist, and public servant. 1929. Quoted in *American Chronicle* (Lois and Alan Gordon; 1987)

10 Liquidate labor, liquidate stocks, liquidate farmers.

Andrew William Mellon (1855–1937) US financier, industrialist, and public servant. Said to Herbert Hoover when Mellon was Treasury Secretary. Quoted in *Wall Street Journal* (1974)

11 Inflation is as violent as a mugger, as frightening as an armed robber, and as deadly as a hit man.

Ronald Reagan (b. 1911) US president and actor. *Los Angeles Times* (1978)

12 A depression is a situation of self-fulfilling pessimism.

Joan Robinson (1903–83) British economist. 'The Short Period', *Economic Heresies* (1970)

13 Wall Street Lays An Egg

Sime Silverman (1873–1933) US founder, publisher, and editor of *Variety*. Headline following the Wall Street crash. *Variety* (October 1929)

14 In certain circumstances, financial markets can affect the so-called fundamentals which they are supposed to reflect. When that happens, markets enter into a state of dynamic disequilibrium and behave quite differently from what would be considered normal by the theory of efficient markets. Such boom/bust sequences do not arise very often, but when they do, they can be very disruptive, exactly because they affect the fundamentals of the economy.

George Soros (b. 1930) US financier, entrepreneur, and philanthropist. Speech to the MIT Department of Economics, World Economy Laboratory Conference, Washington, D.C. 'The Theory of Reflexivity' (26 April 1994)

15 What we used to say was bring on the recession. Recession drove people to church, and they realised they were missing their Bible.

Hargis Thomas (b. 1950) US publisher. Speaking as director of Bible sales and marketing at Oxford University Press. *The Economist* (1996)

BRANDS

1 When you are marketing a drinks brand, it can take over your life.

Andrew Allan (b. 1964) British e-commerce executive. *Marketing* (September 2000)

2 Brand stewardship.

Charlotte Beers (b. 1935) US advertising executive and

former undersecretary of state for public diplomacy and public affairs in the US government. Annual report (1996)

3 It...involves a marketing dilemma: how can we establish a mainstream brand identity while maintaining our strength in the Indian restaurant market.

Karan Bilimoria (b. 1962) Indian entrepreneur and founder of Cobra. Referring to Cobra beer. *Sunday Times* (October 2000)

4 Hiccups in the international business scene are not new to us. Wedgwood china has survived upheavals before—the Napoleonic Wars, the Franco-Prussian War, the world wars. We do have a sense of continuity.

Arthur Bryan (b. 1923) British chairman of Josiah Wedgwood & Sons Ltd. *New York Times* (30 March 1980)

5 If I'm Philip Morris or R.J. Reynolds I'd go celebrate, because I know whatever brands I have now will never be seriously challenged by a new product.

Clive Chajet (b. 1937) US management consultant. 'Deal Won't Extinguish Tobacco Advertising', *USA Today* (1997)

6 What's being created is a very large group of consumers who are loyal to coupons not brands.

Len Dayham, US author. Referring to the tendency of sales promotions to weaken loyalty to individual brands. *Advertising Age* (August 1983)

7 What we're really selling here is the name Walt Disney.

Walt Disney (1901–66) US entertainment entrepreneur and founder of the Walt Disney Company. Internal memo (1939)

8 We know that for many people it is because of perceptions of the past. Debenhams is still a well-kept secret.

Belinda Earl (b. 1961) British retail executive. Referring to Debenhams's lack of strong brand image. *Sunday Times* (September 2000)

9 The name Disney is one of the world's most powerful brands.

Michael Eisner (b. 1942) US chairman and CEO of the Disney Corporation. Speech (April 1996)

10 Does the consumer really know who you are, or are they buying the brand that is being promoted this week?

Robert Evans, US chairman of Promotion Marketing Association of America. *Advertising Age* (1983)

11 As the retail trade consolidates, it will look more and more at big fresh brands that are constantly innovating.

Niall Fitzgerald (b. 1945) British CEO of Unilever and president of the Advertising Association. *Marketing* (July 2000)

12 This is a violation of the brand and we're not doing it.

Lou Gerstner (b. 1942) US chairman and CEO of IBM. *Fortune* (April 1997)

13 A lot of our communications have celebrated what we were not.

Rawdon Glover (b. 1968) British marketing executive. *Marketing* (June 2000)

14 The world is first a Coke world, then an orange world, then a lemon-lime world.

Roberto Goizueta (1931–97) US CEO of Coca-Cola. *Wall Street Journal* (February 1997)

15 Familiarity is the culmination of successful brand building.

Robert Heller (b. 1932) British management writer. Referring to research on brands carried out by the advertising agency Young & Rubicam. *Goldfinger* (1998)

16 Shoot my children if you ever see Howies in Marks & Spencer.

Dave Hieatt (b. 1965) British founder of anti-corporate marketing agency. Referring to the anti-corporate sports brand Howies. *Marketing* (October 2000)

17 Brands were never really dead. Brands have always been about the relationship between product and user...A brand signals a set of expectations and a core understanding that drives everything.

Shelly Lazarus (b. 1949) US chairperson of Ogilvy & Mather Worldwide. *Marketing News* (2000)

18 With the strongest brands, the CEO owns the brand. It must be owned by someone, the higher in the company the better.

Shelly Lazarus (b. 1949) US chairperson of Ogilvy & Mather Worldwide. *Marketing News* (2000)

19 You can get fame quickly but we're building a brand with depth and flavour.

Carl Lyons (b. 1970) British marketing director of lastminute.com. *Marketing* (August 2000)

20 I think it's quite clear that in the information age, the brand is what you compete on.

Andrew Neil (b. 1949) British publisher and broadcaster. *Marketing* (October 2000)

21 Truly great brands are far more than just labels for products; they are symbols that encapsulate the desires of consumers; they are standards that are held aloft under which the masses congregate.

Tony O'Reilly (b. 1936) Irish executive chairman of Independent News & Media and former CEO of Heinz Corporation. 1990. Speech, British Council of Shopping Centres. Quoted in *Granta* (Spring 1996)

22 Anybody who said that brands were irrelevant in the 1980s will be singing the blues in the next millennium.

Michael Ovitz (b. 1946) US film agent and head of Disney. *Fortune* (1997)

23 Brands are all about trust. You buy the brand because you consider it a friend.

Michael Perry (b. 1934) British business executive. *Marketing* (March 2000)

24 The white collar job as now configured is doomed. Soon. ('Downsizing' in the nineties will look like small change.) So what's the trick? There's only one: DISTINCTION. Or as we call it...turning yourself into a brand...Brand You.

Tom Peters (b. 1942) US management consultant and author. 'Work Matters!' movement manifesto, *www.tompeters.com* (September 1999)

25 You, me, all of us, must turn ourselves into distinctive one-person Brands.

Tom Peters (b. 1942) US management consultant and author. 'Work Matters!' movement manifesto, *www.tompeters.com* (September 1999)

26 For lots of big companies, their brand is worth so much to them that they can't endanger their reputation for being a quality company without really endangering their business performance.

Clare Short (b. 1946) British politician. *Management Today* (November 1999)

27 When you build a brand it is often tempting to force-fit success—you want it to jump and you want it to jump fast.

Ric Simcock (b. 1965) British advertising executive. *Marketing* (September 2000)

28 If we had launched Orange in the US, which is considered the home of branding, it would never have worked.

Hans Snook (b. 1948) German chairman of Carphone Warhouse and former CEO of Orange. *Sunday Times* (June 2000)

29 Running a media brand is about harnessing the value of people...journalists, DJs, editors— all of them are the brand.

Vijay Solanki (b. 1969) Kenyan marketing executive. *Marketing* (August 2000)

30 I'm a brand.

Martha Stewart (b. 1942) US chairperson of Martha Stewart Living Omnimedia. *People magazine* (1995)

BUDGETING

1 The budget is God.

Anonymous. Slogan at Japanese optical company Topcom. Quoted in *The Economist* (13 January 1996)

2 Watch the costs and the profits will take care of themselves.

Andrew Carnegie (1835–1919) US industrialist and philanthropist. Quoted in *The Entrepreneurs—An American Adventure* (R. Sobel and D.B. Silicia; 1986)

3 We didn't actually overspend our budget. The Health Commission allocation simply fell short of our expenditure.

Keith Davis (b. 1926) Australian administrator and physician. Quoted in *Sydney Morning Herald* (14 November 1981)

4 Balance sheets are meaningless. Our accounting system is still based on the assumption that 80 per cent of costs are manual labour.

Peter F. Drucker (b. 1909) US management consultant and academic. Interview, *Hot Wired* (July/August 1993)

5 My father would look at my books and pull his hair, I just never got involved with the whole cash-flow thing. My attitude was, creativity will see me through.

Adrienne Landau (b. 1950) US fashion designer. 'An Artisan Discovers Cash Flow', *Forbes Global* (Richard C. Morais; October 1999)

6 Whenever I think about the budgetary problems, I think about the problems of Errol Flynn...reconciling net income with gross habits.

Malcolm Rifkind (b. 1946) British politician. Quoted in *Film Yearbook* (1986)

BUREAUCRACY

1 A memorandum is written not to inform the reader but to protect the writer.

Dean Acheson (1893–1971) US statesman. Quoted in *Wall Street Journal* (8 September 1977)

2 The giant power wielded by pygmies.

Honoré de Balzac (1799–1850) French writer. Referring to bureaucracies. *Les Employés* (1836)

3 The problem is that lots of people in organizations may have vision, but there's absolutely zero meaning...They've...forgotten why they are there, which is why bureaucracies become stodgy and obsolete and filled with inertia.

Warren Bennis (b. 1925) US educator and writer. Interview, *Strategy + Business* (July–September 1997)

4 Bureaucracy emerged out of the organization's need for order and precision and the workers' demands for impartial treatment. It was an organization ideally suited to the values and demands of the Victorian age.

Warren Bennis (b. 1925) US educator and writer. 'The Coming Death of Bureaucracy', *Think* (1966)

5 Poor fellow, he suffers from files.

Aneurin Bevan (1897–1960) British politician. Referring to the administrator Sir Walter Citrine. Quoted in *Aneurin Bevan* (Michael Foot; 1962), vol. 1

6 Guidelines for bureaucrats: (1) When in charge, ponder. (2) When in trouble, delegate. (3) When in doubt, mumble.

James H. Boren (b. 1925) US lecturer and satirist. *New York Times* (9 November 1970)

7 A committee is a cul-de-sac down which ideas are lured and then quietly strangled.

Barnett Cocks (b. 1907) British author. Quoted in *New Scientist* (1973)

8 'Corpocracy' is large-scale corporate America's tendency to be like the government bureaucracy.

Richard G. Darman (b. 1943) US investment banker, academic, and presidential adviser. *New York Times* (9 November 1986)

9 It seems to me that there must be an ecological limit to the number of paper pushers the earth can sustain.

Barbara Ehrenreich (b. 1941) US writer, sociologist, and feminist. 1986. 'Premature Pragmatism', *The Worst Years of Our Lives* (1991)

10 We try to substitute discussion for thought by organizing committees.

Harvey Firestone (1868–1938) US founder of Firestone Tire and Rubber. *Men and Rubber* (co-written with Samuel Crowther; 1926)

11 Gradually I contracted the chart fever.

Harvey Firestone (1868–1938) US founder of Firestone Tire and Rubber. Referring to the creation of department and organisation charts. *Men and Rubber* (co-written with Samuel Crowther; 1926)

12 Administrative purpose usually outruns the facts. Indeed the administrative official's ardor for facts usually begins when he wants to change the facts!

Mary Parker Follett (1868–1933) US management thinker and author. *Creative Experience* (1924)

13 The real problem for any government coming to power is to control the civil servants. They will all explain why it is quite impossible to do things other than the way they are currently done.

Milton Friedman (b. 1912) US economist and winner of the 1976 Nobel Prize in Economics. *Evening Standard* (26 February 1980)

14 In an information society, neither governments nor corporations will rely exclusively on formal, bureaucratic rules...Instead, they will have to decentralize and...rely on the people over whom they have nominal authority to be self-organizing.

Francis Fukuyama (b. 1952) US economist and writer. *The Great Disruption: Human Nature and the Reconstruction of Social Order* (1999), ch. 1

15 Large, rigid bureaucracies, which sought to control everything...have been undermined by the shift toward a knowledge-based economy, which serves to 'empower' individuals by giving them access to information.

Francis Fukuyama (b. 1952) US economist and writer. *The Great Disruption: Human Nature and the Reconstruction of Social Order* (1999), ch. 1

16 The modern business mania is to build greater and ever greater paper-shuffling empires.

J. Paul Getty (1892–1976) US entrepreneur, oil industry executive, and financier. *How to Be Rich* (1965)

17 I don't believe there's any difference under the microscope between the bureaucracy of General Motors, the Pentagon, the Kremlin, the Vatican or any of these major bureaucracies.

James Goldsmith (1933–97) British entrepreneur, financier, and politician. Quoted in *Company Man: The Rise and Fall of Corporate Life* (Anthony Sampson; 1995)

18 Few great men could pass Personnel.

Paul Goodman (1911–72) US educator, psychoanalyst, and writer. *Growing Up Absurd* (1960)

19 Bureaucracy is ever desirous of spreading its influence and power.

Herbert Hoover (1874–1964) US president. Presidential campaign speech, New York (22 October 1928)

20 The most important thing American industry needs to do is reduce the number of management layers.

Kenneth Iverson (1925–2002) US industrialist, chairman and CEO of Nucor Corporation. Quoted in *Thriving on Chaos* (Tom Peters; 1987)

21 Bureaucracy...carries much of the function in modern industrialized society that was carried by the extended family, the village and the surrounding community before the industrial revolution.

Elliot Jacques (b. 1917) Canadian psychologist and sociologist. *A General Theory of Bureaucracy* (1976)

22 Bureaucracy is...a potentially powerful force in the direction of freedom and justice in industrial society, by acting to ensure openness and social mobility.

Elliot Jacques (b. 1917) Canadian psychologist and sociologist. *A General Theory of Bureaucracy* (1976)

23 The manifest picture of bureaucratic organisation is a confusing one.

Elliot Jacques (b. 1917) Canadian psychologist and sociologist. *A General Theory of Bureaucracy* (1976)

24 We have a very simple, clear organization. It's very easy to know who has authority for what, who has responsibility for what. There's no politics about it, they're virtually politics-free organizations.

Steve Jobs (b. 1955) US entrepreneur, co-founder and CEO of Apple Computer Company, and CEO of Pixar. Quoted in 'Steve's Two Jobs', *Time* (Michael Krantz; 18 October 1999)

25 Officials are highly educated but one-sided; in his own department an official can grasp whole trains of thought from a single word, but let him have something from another department explained to him...he won't understand a word of it.

Franz Kafka (1883–1924) Czech novelist. *The Castle* (1926)

26 Bureaucratic and risk-averse environments are career killers because of their impact on learning.

John P. Kotter (b. 1947) US writer. *The New Rules* (1995)

27 A committee is an animal with four back legs.

John Le Carré (b. 1931) British novelist. *Tinker, Tailor, Soldier, Spy* (1974)

28 The bureaucracies of the Industrial Age will appear to the new inter-corporate, transcontinental networks like old Royal typewriters do to PC owners.

Jessica Lipnack (b. 1947) US journalist. *St. Louis Post-Dispatch* (December 1991)

29 It is a characteristic of committee discussions and decisions that every member has a vivid recollection of them and that every member's recollection differs violently from every other member's recollection.

Jonathan Lynn (b. 1943) British writer and film director. *Yes Prime Minister* (co-written with Antony Jay; 1987)

30 The only thing that saves us from the bureaucracy is inefficiency. An efficient bureaucracy is the greatest threat to liberty.

Eugene McCarthy (b. 1916) US politician and writer. *Time* (12 February 1979)

31 Bureaucracy, the rule of no-one, has become the modern form of despotism.

Mary McCarthy (1912–89) US author and critic. 'The Vita Activa', *New Yorker* (18 October 1958)

32 An administrator in a bureaucratic world is a man who can feel big by merging his non-entity with an abstraction. A real person in touch with real things inspires terror in him.
Marshall McLuhan (1911–80) Canadian sociologist and author. Letter to Ezra Pound (1951)

33 Bureaucracies indicate a lack of trust and mutual regard and respect.
Shiv Nadar (b. 1946) Indian business executive and software developer. Quoted in *Giant Killers* (Geoffrey James; 1996)

34 Generally, large companies are so inwardly directed that staff memorandums about growing bureaucracy get more attention than the dwindling competitive advantage of being big in the first place. David, who has a life, needn't use a slingshot. Goliath, who doesn't, is too busy reading office memos.
Nicholas Negroponte (b. 1943) US academic, co-founder and director of MIT Media Laboratory. 'Get a Life?', *Wired Magazine* (3 September 1995)

35 Bureaucratic time...slower than geologic time but more expensive than time spent with Madame Claude's girls in Paris.
P.J. O'Rourke (b. 1947) US humorist and journalist. *Parliament of Whores* (1991)

36 Government proposes, bureaucracy disposes. And the bureaucracy must dispose of government proposals by dumping them on us.
P.J. O'Rourke (b. 1947) US humorist and journalist. *Parliament of Whores* (1991)

37 Too many diversified companies strangle individual businesses with red tape in the form of financial and bureaucratic guidelines.
Kenichi Ohmae (b. 1943) Japanese management consultant and theorist. *The Mind of the Strategist* (1982), ch. 13

38 It's all papers and forms, the entire Civil Service is like a fortress made of papers, forms, and red tape.
Aleksandr Nikolayevich Ostrovsky (1823–86) Russian playwright. Attrib.

39 I despise bureaucrats. I despise administrators...There has been an overgrowth of an arrogant master class of administrators...who regard themselves as being in charge and everyone else as being their *lackeys*.
Camille Paglia (b. 1947) US academic, educator, and writer. Interview, *Reason Magazine* (August–September 1995)

40 Time spent on any item of the agenda will be in inverse proportion to the sum involved.
C. Northcote Parkinson (1909–93) British political scientist and author. *Parkinson's Law: The Pursuit of Progress* (1958)

41 In a hierarchy every employee tends to rise to his level of incompetence.
Laurence J. Peter (1919–90) Canadian academic and writer. *The Peter Principle: Why Things Always Go Wrong* (co-written with Raymond Hull; 1969)

42 Muddle is the extra unknown personality in any committee.
Anthony Sampson (b. 1926) British author and journalist. *Anatomy of Britain Today* (1965)

43 The bureaucratic method of building an integrated Europe has exhausted its potential.
George Soros (b. 1930) US financier, entrepreneur, and philanthropist. 'Can Europe Work?', *Foreign Affairs* (1996)

44 So many signatures for such a small heart.
Mother Teresa (1910–97) Albanian missionary. Referring to filling in forms in a Californian hospital. Quoted in *Evening Standard* (3 January 1992)

45 Bureaucracy, safely repeating today what it did yesterday, rolls on as ineluctably as some vast computer, which, once penetrated by error, duplicates it forever.
Barbara W. Tuchman (1912–89) US historian. *The March of Folly* (1984)

46 The heroic role of the captain of industry is that of a deliverer from an excess of business management. It is a casting out of businessmen by the chief of businessmen.
Thorstein Veblen (1857–1929) US economist and social scientist. *The Theory of Business Enterprise* (1904)

47 There is something about a bureaucrat that does not like a poem.
Gore Vidal (b. 1925) US novelist and critic. *Sex, Death, and Money* (1968), Preface

48 Confucius...emphasized that benevolence should be regarded as the highest ideal of morality and as the basis of administrative power.
Zhong-Ming Wang, Chinese academic and business author. 'Management in China', *Management in Asia Pacific* (Malcolm Warner, ed.; 2000)

49 However many people complain about the 'red tape', it would be sheer illusion to think for a moment that continuous administrative work can be carried out except by means of officials working in offices...The choice is only that between bureaucracy and dilettantism in the field of administration.
Max Weber (1864–1920) German economist and sociologist. Quoted in *Economy and Society* (Guenther Roth and Claus Wittich, eds; 1968)

50 Bureaucratic administration means fundamentally the exercise of control on the basis of knowledge.
Max Weber (1864–1920) German economist and sociologist. 1924. *The Theory of Social and Economic Organization* (A.M. Henderson and T. Parsons, eds and trs; 1947)

51 Capitalism...strongly tends to foster the development of bureaucracy...Conversely, capitalism is the most rational economic basis for bureaucratic administration and enables it to develop in the most rational form.
Max Weber (1864–1920) German economist and sociologist. *The Theory of Social and Economic Organization* (A.M. Henderson and T. Parsons, eds and trs; 1947)

52 The development of the modern form of the organization of corporate groups in all fields is nothing less than identical with the development and continual spread of bureaucratic administration.
Max Weber (1864–1920) German economist and sociologist. *The Theory of Social and Economic Organization* (A.M. Henderson and T. Parsons, eds and trs; 1947)

53 The purely bureaucratic type of administrative organization...is superior to any other form in precision, in stability, in the stringency of its discipline, and in its reliability.
Max Weber (1864–1920) German economist and sociologist. *The Theory of Social and Economic Organization* (A.M. Henderson and T. Parsons, eds and trs; 1947)

54 The speed with which bureaucracy has invaded almost every branch of human activity is something astounding once one thinks about it.
Simone Weil (1909–43) French philosopher and activist. 1933. *Oppression and Liberty* (1955)

55 The Treasury could not, with any marked success, run a fish and chip shop.
Harold Wilson (1916–95) British prime minister. Quoted in 'Sayings of the Week', *Observer* (18 March 1984)

BUSINESS ETHICS

1 A nation of shopkeepers are very seldom so disinterested.
Samuel Adams (1722–1803) US revolutionary leader. Referring to Britain. Speech (August 1776)

2 A company's ethical conduct is something like a big flywheel. It might have a lot of momentum, but it will eventually slow down and stop unless you add energy.
William Adams (b. 1934) US financial consultant. Quoted in *Managing Corporate Ethics* (Francis J. Aguilar; 1994)

3 If you allow men to use you for your own purposes, they will use you for theirs.
Aesop (?620–?560 BC) Greek writer. 'The Horse, Hunter, and Stag' (6th century BC)

4 In all industries, including the media, a few names are as common as muck. This isn't talent telling, it's unashamed favouritism.
Anonymous. Referring to nepotism. *Guardian* (27 July 2000)

5 The presumption that because you share a surname with someone who is good at their job, you'll be good at it too, is patently nonsense. Yet nothing seems to help you more in life than your signature.
Anonymous. Referring to nepotism. *Guardian* (27 July 2000)

6 If you run in the forest, plant a tree.
Arturo Barrios (b. 1962) US athlete. Quoted in *Running with the Legends* (Michael Sandrock; 1996)

7 I ran the wrong kind of business, but I did it with integrity.
Sydney Biddle Barrows (b. 1952) US brothel owner. 'Mayflower Madam Tells All', *Boston Globe* (1986)

8 The nature of business is swindling.
August Bebel (1840–1913) German politician. Speech (1892)

9 Copying other organizations' activities sounds like industrial espionage to some people, but the truth is that benchmarking is perfectly legal and ethical.
Warren Bennis (b. 1925) US educator and writer. *The 21st Century Organization* (co-written with Michael Mische; 1995)

10 If all corporations were run like Fininvest, there would be no problems of public morality in Italy.
Silvio Berlusconi (b. 1936) Italian media entrepreneur and prime minister. August 1994. Spoken before investigations into corruption in his Fininvest consortium. Quoted in *Guardian* (December 31 1994)

11 COMMERCE, n. A kind of transaction in which A plunders from B the goods of C, and for compensation B picks the pocket of D of money belonging to E.
Ambrose Bierce (1842–?1914) US journalist and writer. *The Devil's Dictionary* (1911)

12 Businessmen and businesswomen are mute not only when they fail to speak up about flagrant abuse they become aware of...but also when they fail to speak up for causes or projects that they judge to be morally valuable.
Frederick Bruce Bird (b. 1938) US writer. *The Muted Conscience* (1996)

13 In the culture I grew up in, you did your work and you did not put your arm around it to stop other people from looking. You took the earliest possible opportunity to make knowledge available.
James Black (b. 1924) British pharmacologist and winner of the 1988 Nobel Prize in Medicine. *Daily Telegraph* (December 1995)

14 We can be richer by being greener.
Tony Blair (b. 1953) British prime minister. Press conference (October 2000)

15 Heavy-handed state intervention, the battle between capitalism and socialism...is dead and buried. But the idea of values, of collective purpose, and therefore of collective action is not. It is being renewed.
Tony Blair (b. 1953) British prime minister. January 2000. Speech, World Economic Forum, Davos, Switzerland. Quoted in *World Link* (March–April 2000)

16 A well-run business must have high and consistent standards of ethics.
Richard Branson (b. 1950) British entrepreneur, business executive, and founder of the Virgin Group. Speech to the Institute of Directors, London. 'Growing Bigger While Still Staying Small' (May 1993)

17 What is robbing a bank compared with founding a bank?
Bertolt Brecht (1898–1956) German playwright and poet. *The Threepenny Opera* (1928)

18 Occasionally, a man must rise above principles.
Warren Buffett (b. 1930) US entrepreneur and financier. Annual report (1991)

19 We will only do with your money what we would do with our own.
Warren Buffett (b. 1930) US entrepreneur and financier. Annual report (1989)

20 The face of evil is always the face of total need.
William S. Burroughs (1914–97) US novelist. *The Naked Lunch* (1959)

21 It isn't etiquette to cut anyone you've been introduced to.
Lewis Carroll (1832–98) British writer and mathematician. Said by the Red Queen. *Through the Looking Glass* (1872)

22 'Organizational values' always derive from 'individual values'—especially those of the founding fathers and of the very top executives.
S.K. Chakraborty (b. 1957) Indian academic. *Management by Values: Towards Cultural Congruence* (1991)

23 Values serve the process of 'becoming', in the sense of transformation of the level of consciousness to purer, higher levels.
S.K. Chakraborty (b. 1957) Indian academic. *Management by Values: Towards Cultural Congruence* (1991)

24 What is a value in IBM could be the reverse in an Indian firm.
S.K. Chakraborty (b. 1957) Indian academic. *Management by Values: Towards Cultural Congruence* (1991)

25 There are two parties involved in every corrupt transaction, typically a government official and a business person. Yet those who pay bribes are often depicted as innocent victims...The reality is that both parties conspire to defraud the public.
Lynda Chalker (b. 1942) British politician. 'Public Sector Corruption from an International Perspective'. Speech, University of Glasgow, Scotland (19 February 1999)

26 Such is the brutalization of commercial ethics in this country no one can feel anything more delicate than the velvet touch of a soft buck.
Raymond Chandler (1888–1959) US writer. Letter to his publisher. *Raymond Chandler Speaking* (Dorothy Gardiner and Katherine S. Walker, eds; 1962)

27 Thieves respect property. They merely wish the property to become their property that they may more perfectly respect it.
G.K. Chesterton (1874–1936) British novelist, poet, and critic. *The Man Who Was Thursday* (1908)

28 Just to the windward of the law.
Charles Churchill (1731–64) British curate and satirist. *The Ghost* (1762)

29 The good of the people is the chief law.
Cicero (106–43 BC) Roman orator and statesman. Attrib.

30 In every era, society must strike the right balance between the freedom businesses need to compete for a market share and to make profits and the preservation of family and community values.
Hillary Clinton (b. 1947) US lawyer, politician, and former first lady. *It Takes a Village* (1996)

31 Thou shalt not cheat; an empty feat when it's so lucrative to cheat.
Arthur Hugh Clough (1819–61) British poet. 'The Latest Decalogue' (1862)

32 At the risk of a horrible mixed metaphor, we can say that the Celtic Tiger needs a human face and a human heart.
Cahal Daly (b. 1917) Irish Roman Catholic archbishop and cardinal. Referring to the economic boom in Ireland. *Irish Times* (10 January 1998)

33 These mobsters had enjoyed power for many years. They weren't going to roll over and play dead.
Miguel Angel Davila (b. 1966) Mexican entrepreneur. Referring to labour problems in Mexico. *Forbes* (May 1998)

34 No longer can a manufacturer afford to treat a supplier like a vendor from whom every last ounce of cost-saving must be wrung. Nor can a customer be treated simply like a market for products and services at the best possible price.
Michael Dell (b. 1965) US chairman and CEO of Dell Computer Corporation. Speech to the 1998 World Congress on Information Technology, Vienna, Virginia. 'Collaborating in a Connected Economy: The Power of Virtual Integration' (24 June 1998)

35 We are human beings, not businessmen trying to shaft the consumer at home.
James Dyson (b. 1947) British entrepreneur. *Management Today* (July 1999)

36 People should be given the opportunity to vote with their wallets.
Noel Edmonds (b. 1948) British broadcaster and media executive. 1991. Referring to ethical products. Quoted in *Noel Edmonds* (Alison Bowyer; 1999)

37 All we did was to try to take information that was hidden and bring it into the light.
Larry D. Ellison (b. 1945) US CEO of Oracle Corporation. Referring to corporate intelligence. *Sunday Times* (July 2000)

38 We will ship them our garbage. We believe in full disclosure.
Larry D. Ellison (b. 1945) US CEO of Oracle Corporation. Referring to corporate spying during Microsoft hearings. *Sunday Times* (July 2000)

39 We know the good but we do not practise it.
Euripides (?484–?406 BC) Greek playwright. Attrib.

40 The camera cannot lie but it can be an accessory to untruth.
Harold Evans (b. 1928) British newspaper editor and publisher. *Good Times, Bad Times* (1983)

41 It was the first takeover I had experienced. It wasn't merely insensitive and unjust: it was rebellious in its consequences for the company.

Harold Evans (b. 1928) British newspaper editor and publisher. Referring to Rupert Murdoch's acquisition of *The Times* and the *Sunday Times*. *Good Times, Bad Times* (1983)

42 He has made a profession out of a business and an art out of a profession.

Clifton Fadiman (1904–99) US editor and author. Referring to Alfred A. Knopf, recalled on Knopf's death on 11 August 1984. *New York Times* (1984)

43 Customers must trust an organisation and its people.

Tom Farmer (b. 1940) British chairman and CEO of Kwik-Fit. *Management Today* (July 1999)

44 Scientific knowledge is an enabling power to do either good or bad. But it does not carry instructions on how to use it.

Richard Feynman (1918–88) US physicist. Address (1957)

45 I believe in the market and the power of the market to generate wealth. But you have to deal with wealth in a responsible way and ensure everyone in your society has an even chance to participate.

Niall Fitzgerald (b. 1945) British CEO of Unilever and president of the Advertising Association. *Marketing* (July 2000)

46 If you don't drive your business, you will be driven out of business.

Bertie Charles Forbes (1880–1954) US publisher and writer. Quoted in *Forbes* (1974)

47 A business that makes nothing but money is a poor kind of business.

Henry Ford (1863–1947) US industrialist, car manufacturer, and founder of Ford Motor Company. Quoted in *The Arizona Republic* (1999)

48 We must find ways to live together, cooperate, understand our differences, respect them, but also work for all the things that build our friendship, our common interests, our mutual responsibilities.

Carlos Fuentes (b. 1928) Mexican writer. Referring to relations between Mexico and the United States. *A New Time for Mexico* (1994)

49 If networks are to be more efficient...this will come about only on the basis of a high level of trust and the existence of shared norms of ethical behavior between network members.

Francis Fukuyama (b. 1952) US economist and writer. *Trust: The Social Virtues and the Creation of Prosperity* (1995)

50 Now there is one outstandingly important fact regarding Spaceship Earth, and that is that no instruction book came with it.

R. Buckminster Fuller (1895–1983) US inventor, architect, and philosopher. *Operating Manual for Planet Earth* (1969)

51 The greater the wealth, the thicker will be the dirt.

J.K. Galbraith (b. 1908) US economist and diplomat. *The Affluent Society* (1958)

52 It is difficult but not impossible to conduct strictly honest business. What is true is that honesty is incompatible with the amassing of a large fortune.

Mahatma Gandhi (1869–1948) Indian nationalist leader and philosopher. *Non-Violence in Peace and War* (1948)

53 Business now shares in much of the responsibility for our global quality of life.

Roberto Goizueta (1931–97) US CEO of Coca-Cola. Speech (October 1992)

54 Ethical conduct is not a matter of conformity to some preset plan. It is more concerned with acceptable and desirable parameters of conduct.

Damian Grace (b. 1950) Australian academic. *Australian Problems and Cases* (1995)

55 If there is no conception that a decision entails ethical considerations, and if there is no adequate conceptual vocabulary to make sense of ethical requirements, then reasonable ethical standards in business become a matter of luck.

Damian Grace (b. 1950) Australian academic. *Australian Problems and Cases* (1995)

56 Unless managers are aware of ethical issues...they will fail to institutionalise ethics in corporate life. Ignorance can be as pernicious as malice.

Damian Grace (b. 1950) Australian academic. *Australian Problems and Cases* (1995)

57 If there's no money in poetry, neither is there poetry in money.

Robert Graves (1895–1985) British poet, novelist, and classical scholar. Speech (December 1963)

58 Our track record is good. We've been investigated by the government before, and we got a clean bill of health. We've been sued in about half a dozen private antitrust suits, and they all got dismissed. I don't think it's an accident. We...try to impose the legality and the ethics of competing fairly on all elements of our business. That's what we worry about.

Andrew S. Grove (b. 1936) US entrepreneur, author, and chairman of Intel Corporation. On the Antitrust Division of the Department of Justice's investigation into the practices of dominant industry players such as Intel and Microsoft. Interview, *Upside Magazine* (12 October 1997)

59 No plagiarist can excuse the wrong by showing how much of his work he did not pirate.

Learned Hand (1872–1961) US judge. Trial speech (1936)

60 The Spirit of Liberty is the spirit which is not too sure that it is right.

Learned Hand (1872–1961) US judge. *The Spirit of Liberty* (1952)

61 We have corporate CEOs who raise their pay 20 percent or more in years when they lay off thousands of people. It's obscene.

Charles Handy (b. 1932) British business executive and author. Quoted in *Business Week* (25 April 1994)

62 Our Shari'ah legal code does not permit our participating in interest bearing instruments. That means that owning a savings account or

a certificate of deposit is a mortal sin for
Muslims.
Hasnita Dato Hashim (b. 1962) Malaysian investment banker.
Forbes (June 2000)

63 To take a simple example, a construction
company is, on the face of it, a perfectly
appropriate investment. But if a great deal of
its activity involves the building of casinos,
then it is not for an Islamic investor.
Hasnita Dato Hashim (b. 1962) Malaysian investment banker.
Forbes (June 2000)

64 When participation is suggested in terms of
control over overall goals, it is usually a sham.
Frederick Herzberg (1923–2000) US psychologist. *The
Motivation to Work* (1959)

65 Oh God, that bread should be so dear
And flesh and blood so cheap.
Thomas Hood (1799–1845) British poet. 'The Song of the
Shirt' (1843)

66 That action is best, which provides the
greatest happiness for the greatest numbers.
Francis Hutcheson (1694–1746) Irish philosopher. *An
Inquiry into the Origin of our Ideas of Beauty and Virtue*
(1725)

67 Inequality is not only about income, where
real poverty has grown, it is about self-esteem.
Will Hutton (b. 1950) British author and newspaper editor.
The State We're In (1995)

68 We at Chrysler borrow money the
old-fashioned way. We pay it back.
Lee Iacocca (b. 1924) US president of Ford Motor Company,
chairman and CEO of Chrysler Corporation. *New York
Times* (1983)

69 Ministers and merchants love nobody.
Thomas Jefferson (1743–1826) US president. Letter to John
Langdon (11 September 1785)

70 There's nothing wrong with big companies. A
lot of people think big business in America is a
bad thing. I think it's a really good thing. Most
people in business are ethical, hard-working,
good people. And it's a meritocracy.
Steve Jobs (b. 1955) US entrepreneur, co-founder and CEO
of Apple Computer Company, and CEO of Pixar. Interview,
'The Next Insanely Great Thing', *Wired Magazine* (February
1996)

71 Too seldom does the world pause to consider
how much kinder and more humane business
has become since women invaded the
market-place.
Edith Johnson (1891–1954) US writer and educator. *To
Women of the Business World* (1923)

72 I think we are in danger of a populous
backlash. I think it will be against big
institutions of all kind, government and big
business.
Rosabeth Moss Kanter (b. 1943) US management theorist,
academic, and writer. Interview, *www.pbs.org/newshour*
(1995)

73 Two half truths do not make a truth.
Arthur Koestler (1905–83) British writer and journalist. *The
Ghost in the Machine* (1967)

74 Ethical traps are more common now than a
generation ago…In a volatile world, it is easy
to step over moral boundaries.
John P. Kotter (b. 1947) US writer. *The New Rules* (1995)

75 Original research tends to be a novel concept.
Ashok Kumar (b. 1964) Indian investment analyst. *Forbes*
(September 2000)

76 Not property is wrong, not profits are wrong,
nor money or gain, but the swollen
disproportionate gain that can turn a monied
group to be the bosses of their fellow men.
Stephen Leacock (1869–1944) Canadian humorist, essayist,
economist, and historian. *While There Is Time* (1945)

77 These capitalists generally act harmoniously
and in concert to fleece the people.
Abraham Lincoln (1809–65) US president. Speech (January
1837)

78 Civilized men think as they trade, not in kind,
but by means of a circulating medium.
Thomas Babington Macaulay (1800–59) British politician and
historian. Attrib.

79 The leader should know how to enter into evil
when necessity commands.
Niccolò Machiavelli (1469–1527) Italian historian, statesman,
and political philosopher. *The Prince* (1513)

80 The mission of a manufacturer should be to
overcome poverty, to relieve society as a
whole from misery and bring it wealth.
Konosuke Matsushita (1894–1989) Japanese electronics
executive, entrepreneur, and inventor. *Quest for Prosperity*
(1988)

81 We take society's capital, we take their people,
we take their materials, yet without a good
profit we are using precious resources that
could be used better elsewhere.
Konosuke Matsushita (1894–1989) Japanese electronics
executive, entrepreneur, and inventor. *Quest for Prosperity*
(1988)

82 I would have been a success in anything. But I
have chosen an activity that was socially
useful and that aspect gives me extra
satisfaction.
Robert Maxwell (1923–91) British publisher, business
executive, and politician. Interview (July 1967)

83 So long as commerce specializes in business
methods which take no account of human
nature and social motives, so long may we
expect strikes and sabotage to be the ordinary
accompaniment of industry.
Elton Mayo (1880–1949) US psychologist. *The Human
Problems of an Industrial Civilization* (1933)

84 These issues are not simply about PR and
reputation, but about the fundamental nature
of business and ensuring our long-term
success. Business can no longer operate in a
vacuum, insulated from the demands and
concerns of the outside world, even if it
wanted to.
Mark Moody-Stuart (b. 1940) British chairman of Anglo
American, and former chairman of Committee of Managing
Directors Royal Dutch/Shell Group. Speech to the World

Congress of the International Society of Business, Economics and Ethics, São Paolo, Brazil. Referring to ethical issues. 'Putting Principles into Practice: The Ethical Challenge to Global Business' (19 July 2000)

85 The sceptics should consider the business reputation impact of this emerging agenda. In recent years, public concern over the environment, human rights, and ethical issues has directly affected a wide range of household name companies, including Shell, BP Amoco, Disney, Monsanto, Nike and Nestlé. Consumer boycotts, NGO campaigns and political pressure are all facts of business life.

Mark Moody-Stuart (b. 1940) British chairman of Anglo American, and former chairman of Committee of Managing Directors Royal Dutch/Shell Group. Speech to the World Congress of the International Society of Business, Economics and Ethics, São Paolo, Brazil. Referring to the growing importance of business ethics and corporate responsibility. 'Putting Principles into Practice: The Ethical Challenge to Global Business' (19 July 2000)

86 I think one of the more interesting conclusions emerging from this ever more complicated business environment, is that values do matter. Sustainable business will have to be responsible and sensitive to the needs of everyone involved.

Mark Moody-Stuart (b. 1940) British chairman of Anglo American, and former chairman of Committee of Managing Directors Royal Dutch/Shell Group. Speech, St Paul's Cathedral, London. 'The Values of Sustainable Business in the Next Century' (12 July 1999)

87 The final task of industry, therefore, is to organise participation in these activities, even in the most backward communities and countries.

James Mooney (1884–1957) US business executive. *Onward Industry* (co-written with Alan Reiley; 1931)

88 The highest development of the techniques both of production and distribution will be futile to supply the material wants of those who, because of poverty, are unable to acquire through purchase.

James Mooney (1884–1957) US business executive. *Onward Industry* (co-written with Alan Reiley; 1931)

89 We would never do violence such as you see in a Nintendo game.

Rupert Murdoch (b. 1931) US CEO of News Corporation. In response to the question, 'What won't you do?' 'What Won't You Do?', *The New Yorker* (Ken Auletta; 1993)

90 It's possible to live in this country and create wealth legally and ethically.

Narayana Murthy (b. 1946) Indian founder and CEO of Infosys. Referring to India. *Forbes* (October 2000)

91 Should we really let our people starve so we can pay our debts.

Julius Nyerere (1922–99) Tanzanian president. *Guardian* (March 1985)

92 Negotiating with them reminded me of haggling over a fake Rolex on the streets of Bangkok.

Sandy Oh (b. 1971) Malaysian investment banker. *BusinessWeek* (September 2000)

93 I am I plus my surroundings, and, if I do not preserve the latter, I do not preserve myself.

Jose Ortega y Gasset (1883–1955) Spanish author and philosopher. *Meditaciones del Quijote* (1914)

94 There are only two kinds of men: those righteous who believe themselves sinners; the other sinners who believe themselves righteous.

Blaise Pascal (1623–62) French philosopher and mathematician. *Pensées* (1670), no. 562

95 An activist—the guy who clears the river, not the guy who concludes it's dirty.

H. Ross Perot (b. 1930) US entrepreneur, venture capitalist, and politician. Quoted in *Ross Perot* (Ken Gross; 1992)

96 He's a businessman...I'll make him an offer he can't refuse.

Mario Puzo (1920–99) US novelist. The offer referred to is a death threat. *The Godfather* (1969), bk 1, ch. 1

97 Businesses which forego profits to build communities, or keep production local...risk losing business to cheaper competitors without such commitments, and being targeted for take-over by...corporate raiders. Reinforced by the weight of the WTO.

Anita Roddick (b. 1942) British entrepreneur and founder of The Body Shop. Speech to the International Forum on Globalisation Teach-In, Seattle, Washington. 'Trading with Principles' (27 November 1999)

98 To run this business...you need...optimism, humanism, enthusiasm, intuition, curiosity, love, humour, magic and fun and that secret ingredient—euphoria.

Anita Roddick (b. 1942) British entrepreneur and founder of The Body Shop. *Body and Soul* (co-written with Russell Miller; 1991)

99 Which of us...is to do the hard and dirty work for the rest—and for what pay? who is to do the pleasant and clean work, and for what pay?

John Ruskin (1819–1900) British art critic and writer. *Sesame and Lillies* (1865)

100 Machines are worshipped because they are beautiful, and valued because they confer power; they are hated because they are hideous, and loathed because they impose slavery.

Bertrand Russell (1872–1970) British philosopher and writer. *Sceptical Essays* (1928)

101 Fashion is something barbarous for it produces innovation without reason and imitation without benefit.

George Santayana (1863–1952) US philosopher, novelist, and poet. *The Life of Reason* (1905)

102 We continue to struggle with the old question...of whether to obey a superior even when the order is unjust.

John Ralston Saul (b. 1947) Canadian writer. *The Unconscious Civilization* (1995)

103 I think that the best companies are companies that have a real purpose.

Marjorie Scardino (b. 1947) US CEO of Pearson. *Fortune* (October 2000)

104 One can't say that figures lie. But figures, as used in financial arguments, seem to have the bad habit of expressing a small part of the truth forcibly, and neglecting the other part, as do some people we know.

Fred Schwed (1901–66) US author. *Where Are The Customers' Yachts?* (1940)

105 Companies have to be socially responsible or the shareholders pay eventually.

Warren Shaw (b. 1950) US former CEO of Chancellor LGT Asset Management. 'The Players', *Fortune* (Eileen Gunn; April 1997)

106 The first line of defence is to vote with my feet.

Warren Shaw (b. 1950) US former CEO of Chancellor LGT Asset Management. Referring to the achievements of African Americans in business. 'The Players', *Fortune* (Eileen Gunn; April 1997)

107 Biopiracy is the Columbian 'discovery' 500 years after Columbus.

Vandana Shiva (b. 1944) Indian academic. *Globalisation: Gandhi and Swadeshi* (2000)

108 Patents on life...the enclosure of the intellectual and biological commons.

Vandana Shiva (b. 1944) Indian academic. *Globalisation: Gandhi and Swadeshi* (2000)

109 I strongly believe that core business interests are advanced by socially responsible policies that help promote development in poorer countries.

Clare Short (b. 1946) British politician. *Management Today* (November 1999)

110 The latter-day robber barons are discovering that better conditions and rewards for workers pay off in a world where consumers increasingly demand ethical standards.

Clare Short (b. 1946) British politician. *Management Today* (November 1999)

111 Smaller businesses often say the words, but can't get in on the act.

Clare Short (b. 1946) British politician. Referring to the difficulties of maintaining ethical standards in the face of severe competition. *Management Today* (November 1999)

112 Whenever we have compromised on our principles, we and our customers have been the losers.

Marcus Sieff (1913–2001) British president of Marks & Spencer. *Don't Ask the Price, George* (1987)

113 Markets reduce everything, including human beings and nature, to commodities.

George Soros (b. 1930) US financier, entrepreneur, and philanthropist. *Atlantic Monthly* (January 1998)

114 As an anonymous participant in financial markets, I never had to weigh the social consequences of my actions...I felt justified in ignoring them on the grounds that I was playing by the rules.

George Soros (b. 1930) US financier, entrepreneur, and philanthropist. *The Crisis of Global Capitalism* (1998)

115 Our whole economy is based on planned obsolescence.

Brooks Stevens (1911–95) US industrial designer. Quoted in *The Waste Makers* (Vance Packard; 1960)

116 When I build something for somebody...My guys come in, they say it's going to cost $75 million. I say it's going to cost $125 million, and I build it for $100 million. Basically, I did a lousy job. But they think I did a great job.

Donald J. Trump (b. 1946) US property developer. 1984. Said to a meeting of US Football League owners. Quoted in *New York Times* (1 July 1986)

117 Always do right. This will gratify some people, and astonish the rest.

Mark Twain (1835–1910) US writer. Speech to the Young People's Society, Greenpoint Baptist Church, Brooklyn, New York (1901)

118 One of the most striking differences between a cat and a lie is that the cat has only nine lives.

Mark Twain (1835–1910) US writer. *Pudd'nhead Wilson* (1894)

119 Commercialism is doing well that which should not be done at all.

Gore Vidal (b. 1925) US novelist and critic. *Listener* (August 1975)

120 A solid business must build on justice, fairness, and transparency.

Gaston Vizcarra (b. 1952) Peruvian ecological entrepreneur and president of Candela Peru. *Forbes* (April 2000)

121 Conservation is business too.

Gaston Vizcarra (b. 1952) Peruvian ecological entrepreneur and president of Candela Peru. *Forbes* (April 2000)

122 An artist is someone who produces things that people don't need to have but that he—for some reason—thinks it would be a good idea to give them.

Andy Warhol (1928–87) US artist and film maker. *The Philosophy of Andy Warhol (from A to B and Back Again)* (1975)

123 Control and learning are deeply embedded in the specific cultural and institutional ethos of an organization.

Yanni Yan (b. 1958) Chinese business author and academic. 'Managerial and Organization—Learning in Chinese Firms', *China's Managerial Revolution* (Malcolm Warner, ed.; 1999)

124 Nothing is illegal if 100 businessmen decide to do it.

Andrew Jackson Young Jr (b. 1932) US diplomat and civil rights advocate. Press conference (1976)

CAPITALISM

1 The trouble with a free market economy is that it requires so many policemen to make it work.

Dean Acheson (1893–1971) US statesman. Quoted in *Observer* (26 May 1985)

2 Capital must be propelled by self-interest; it cannot be enticed by benevolence.
Walter Bagehot (1826–77) British economist and journalist. *Economic Studies* (1880)

3 Capitalism without bankruptcy is like Christianity without hell.
Frank Borman (b. 1928) US astronaut and business executive. Remark (21 April 1986)

4 The dynamics of capitalism is postponement of enjoyment to the constantly postponed future.
Norman O. Brown (1913–2002) US cultural critic. *Love's Body* (1966)

5 We accept and welcome, therefore, as conditions to which we must accommodate ourselves, great inequality of environment, the concentration of business, industrial and commercial, in the hands of a few, and the law of competition between these, as being not only beneficial, but essential for the future progress of the race.
Andrew Carnegie (1835–1919) US industrialist and philanthropist. 'Wealth', *North American Review* (June 1889)

6 The pursuit of modern life is economic and the fundamental principle of economic production is individual independence.
Chen Duxiu (1879–1942) Chinese scholar and reformer. *The New Youth* (December 1916)

7 Capitalism still possesses quite substantial and far from exhausted resources.
Konstantin Ustinovich Chernenko (1911–85) Soviet president. Quoted in 'Sayings of the Week', *Observer* (23 June 1984)

8 Predatory capitalism created a complex industrial system and an advanced technology; it permitted a considerable extension of democratic practice and fostered certain liberal values, but within limits that are now being pressed and must be overcome.
Noam Chomsky (b. 1928) US linguist and political activist. *For Reasons of State* (1973)

9 The chief business of the American people is business.
Calvin Coolidge (1872–1933) US president. 1925. *New York Times* (2000)

10 One of the things about the free enterprise capitalism system is that life is brutal.
Bernard Cornfeld (1927–95) US business executive. Interview, *Daily Mail* (17 January 1970)

11 If there is a man on this earth who is entitled to all the comforts and luxuries of this life...it is the man whose labor produces them...Does he get them in the present system?
Eugene V. Debs (1855–1926) US politician and trade union leader. Speech at Girard, Kansas. 'The Issue' (23 May 1908)

12 Capitalism is truly miraculous. What other system enables us to cooperate with millions of other people...in an incredible, complex web of commercial transactions?
Steve Forbes (b. 1947) US publishing executive. 'Three Cheers for Capitalism', *Imprimis* (September 1993)

13 Capitalism works better than any of us can conceive. It is also the only truly moral system of exchange. It encourages individuals to devote their energies...to the satisfaction of others' wants and needs.
Steve Forbes (b. 1947) US publishing executive. 'Three Cheers for Capitalism', *Imprimis* (September 1993)

14 One of the dynamics of capitalism is that because it's in constant change, there are always people who feel they're going to be hurt by change and are going to resist it.
Steve Forbes (b. 1947) US publishing executive. February 1991. Interview, *Reason Magazine* (May 1991)

15 It is in the very design of democratic capitalist countries like the United States that the most talented and ambitious natures should tend to go into business rather than into politics, the military, universities, or the church.
Francis Fukuyama (b. 1952) US economist and writer. *The End of History and the Last Man* (1991)

16 Capital as such is not evil; it is its wrong use that is evil. Capital in some form or other will always be needed.
Mahatma Gandhi (1869–1948) Indian nationalist leader and philosopher. *Harijan* (1940)

17 This is called capitalism. We create a product called Windows. Who decides what's in Windows. It's the customers who buy Windows.
Bill Gates (b. 1955) US entrepreneur, chairman and CEO of Microsoft. *Wall Street Journal* (October 1997)

18 In the capitalist urban milieu...the routinisation of day-to-day activities is stripped away from tradition...they become matters of habit or of 'dull economic compulsion'.
Anthony Giddens (b. 1938) British sociologist and author. *A Contemporary Critique of Historical Materialism* (1985)

19 The prevailing theory of capitalism suffers from one central and disabling flaw, a profound distrust and incomprehension of capitalism.
George Gilder (b. 1939) US economist. *The Spirit of Enterprise* (1984)

20 Much of what we took for granted in our free-market system was not nature at all, but culture. The dismantling of the central planning function did not, as some had supposed, automatically establish market capitalism.
Alan Greenspan (b. 1926) US economist and chairman of US Federal Reserve Board. Quoted in 'Genuflecting at the Altar of Market Economics', *International Herald Tribune* (14 July 1997)

21 I have said to the people we mean to have less of Government in business as well as more business in Government.

Warren Harding (1865–1923) US president. Speech to Congress on 12 April 1921. *East Valley Tribune* (2000)

22 Capitalism, as practiced, is a financially profitable, non-sustainable aberration in human development.

Paul Hawken (b. ?1946) US entrepreneur and business author. *Natural Capitalism* (co-written with Amory B. Lovins and L. Hunter Lovins; 1999)

23 The system of private property is the most important guarantee of freedom, not only for those who own property, but scarcely less for those who do not.

Friedrich August von Hayek (1899–1992) British economist. *The Road to Serfdom* (1944), ch. 8

24 It does not, it destroys some things and distorts others: it makes new separations, based on privilege and buying power, differences which increase social divisions.

Richard Hoggart (b. 1918) British academic, cultural critic, and author. Discussing the argument that the 'market solves, decides, and justifies all'. *The Way We Live Now* (1995), pt 1, ch. 1

25 It is just as important that business keep out of government as that government keep out of business.

Herbert Hoover (1874–1964) US president. October 22, 1928. Quoted in *East Valley Tribune* (2000)

26 Co-operative capitalism does not spontaneously emerge from free markets—it needs to be designed.

Will Hutton (b. 1950) British author and newspaper editor. *The State We're In* (1995)

27 Successful capitalism demands a fusion of co-operation and competition and a means of grafting such a hybrid into the soil of the economic, political and social system.

Will Hutton (b. 1950) British author and newspaper editor. *The State We're In* (1995)

28 The great challenge of the twentieth century...is to create a new financial architecture in which private decisions produce a less degenerate capitalism.

Will Hutton (b. 1950) British author and newspaper editor. *The State We're In* (1995)

29 Armaments, universal debt, and planned obsolescence—these are the three pillars of Western prosperity.

Aldous Huxley (1894–1963) British novelist and essayist. *Island* (1962), ch. 9

30 Capitalism, wisely managed, can probably be made more efficient for attaining economic ends than any alternative system yet in sight.

John Maynard Keynes (1883–1946) British economist. *The End of Laissez-Faire* (1926)

31 Market competition is the only form of organization which can afford a large measure of freedom to the individual.

Frank H. Knight (1885–1972) US economist. *Freedom and Reform* (1947), ch. 13

32 The wealth of societies in which the capitalist mode of production prevails appears as an 'immense collection of commodities'; the individual commodity appears as its elementary form.

Karl Marx (1818–83) German political and economic philosopher. Opening line. *Das Kapital* (1867), vol. 1

33 We have an underdeveloped democracy and overdeveloped plutocracy.

Ralph Nader (b. 1934) US lawyer and consumer-rights campaigner. *The Economist* (1996)

34 I do believe that capitalism is inherently Darwinian and that a totally free market is ultimately inhumane, because you'll have what happened in the 19th century—a kind of piling up of profits at the very top...there should be some kind of safety net, we should not tolerate, in an affluent society, extreme levels of poverty or deprivation.

Camille Paglia (b. 1947) US academic, educator, and writer. Interview, *Reason Magazine* (August–September 1995)

35 Capitalism is an art form, an Apollonian fabrication to rival nature...Everyone born into capitalism has incurred a debt to it. Give Caesar his due.

Camille Paglia (b. 1947) US academic, educator, and writer. *Sexual Personae: Art and Decadence from Nefertiti to Emily Dickinson* (1990)

36 Our democratic capitalist society has converted Eros into an employee of Mammon.

Octavio Paz (1914–98) Mexican writer. Attrib.

37 Capitalism with near-full employment was an impressive sight.

Joan Robinson (1903–83) British economist. 'The Second Crisis of Economic Theory', *The Second Crisis of Economic Theory* (Rendigs Fels, ed.; 1972)

38 Capitalism is a hotel. Its penthouse suites are always filled, but not necessarily with the same people.

Paul Samuelson (b. 1915) US economist and winner of the 1970 Nobel Prize in Economics. *US News & World Report* (July 1986)

39 Few ideas are as capitalist as profit-sharing, which rewards with part of a company's earnings the people who help generate this blessed surplus.

Ricardo Semler (b. 1959) Brazilian business executive and president of Semco. *Maverick!* (1993)

40 Social opportunities of education and health care, which may require public action, complement individual opportunities of economic and political participation and also help to foster our own initiatives in overcoming our respective deprivations.

Amartya Sen (b. 1933) Indian economist and winner of the 1998 Nobel Prize in Economics. *Development as Freedom* (1999)

41 The twentieth century has established democratic and participatory governance as the preeminent model of political

organization. Concepts of human rights and political liberty are now...part of the prevailing rhetoric.
Amartya Sen (b. 1933) Indian economist and winner of the 1998 Nobel Prize in Economics. *Development as Freedom* (1999)

42 While there are successes of market economies, there are also needs for supplementation in other fields in terms of public intervention, in terms of political participation, and so forth.
Amartya Sen (b. 1933) Indian economist and winner of the 1998 Nobel Prize in Economics. Interview, *NewsHour, Online Focus* (PBS; 15 October 1998)

43 The ideology of capitalism makes us all connoisseurs of liberty—of the indefinite expansion of possibility.
Susan Sontag (b. 1933) US novelist and essayist. *Aids and its Metaphors* (1989), ch. 7

44 My critique of the global capitalist system has three major themes. First, the system favors financial capital but financial markets are inherently unstable and global markets even more so. Second, the excessive reliance on market values and their penetration into areas where they do not properly belong has undermined the stability of our society. Third, we cannot have a global economy without a global society.
George Soros (b. 1930) US financier, entrepreneur, and philanthropist. Speech to the Council on Foreign Relations, New York City. 'The Crisis of Global Capitalism: Open Society Endangered' (10 December 1998)

45 War is capitalism with the gloves off.
Tom Stoppard (b. 1937) British playwright and screenwriter. *Travesties* (1974), Act 1

46 The spread of capitalism needs to be tempered by public purpose: by policies...institutions and agreements that give businesses and people a clear framework in which to operate... the same must be true at the global level.
Lawrence H. Summers (b. 1954) US president of Harvard University, economist, and politician. Speech, School for Advanced International Studies, Washington, D.C. 'Rising to the Challenge of Global Economic Integration' (20 September 2000)

47 Private property is a necessary institution, at least in a fallen world; men work more and dispute less when goods are private than when they are in common.
Richard Tawney (1880–1962) British economic historian and social critic. *Religion and the Rise of Capitalism* (1926), ch. 1, sect. 1

48 Running other companies out of business and gaining market share is what capitalistic competition is all about. Efficiency and lower prices flow from that all-out economic life-and-death struggle.
Lester Thurow (b. 1938) US economist, management theorist, and writer. 'Microsoft Case is about a Good Capitalist Practice: Running Your Competitor out of Business', *www.lthurow.com* (3 November 1999)

49 Economic acquisition is no longer subordinated to man as the means for the satisfaction of his material needs. This...is evidently as definitely a leading principle of capitalism as it is foreign to all peoples not under capitalist influence.
Max Weber (1864–1920) German economist and sociologist. *The Protestant Ethic and the Spirit of Capitalism* (1904–05)

50 Man is dominated by the making of money, by acquisition as the ultimate purpose of his life.
Max Weber (1864–1920) German economist and sociologist. Referring to the impact of capitalism. *The Protestant Ethic and the Spirit of Capitalism* (1904–05)

51 What breaks capitalism, all that will ever break capitalism is capitalists.
Raymond Williams (1921–88) British academic, critic, and novelist. *Loyalties* (1985)

52 Sometimes it's tough for African Americans to embrace capitalism.
Deborah Wright (b. 1958) US CEO of Carver Federal Savings and former president of Upper Manhattan Empowerment Zone. 'The Players', *Fortune* (Eileen Gunn; April 1997)

CAPITALISM VERSUS SOCIALISM

1 You can talk about capitalism and communism...but the important thing is the struggle everybody is engaged in to get better living conditions, and they are not interested too much in government.
Bernard Baruch (1870–1965) US financier and economist. *The Times* (20 August 1964)

2 The twentieth-century struggle between capitalism and socialism is, at an ideological level, a fight about the content of progress.
John Berger (b. 1926) British novelist, essayist, and art critic. *Pig Earth* (1991), Introduction

3 To speak of limits to growth under a capitalistic market economy is as meaningless as to speak of limits of warfare under a warrior society.
Murray Bookchin (b. 1921) US writer and environmentalist. *Remaking Society* (1990)

4 Capitalism is using its money; we socialists throw it away.
Fidel Castro (b. 1927) Cuban president. Quoted in *Observer* (8 November 1964)

5 The worker is the slave of the capitalist society, the female worker is the slave of that slave.
James Connolly (1868–1916) Irish political activist. *The Re-conquest of Ireland* (1915)

6 Liberal democracy is really all there is now. We've seen that in the Soviet Union and eastern Europe. Communism was...undermined by the fact that people did not believe it was a viable form of government.

Francis Fukuyama (b. 1952) US economist and writer. Interview, *Booknotes, www.C-Span.org* (17 January 1992)

7 You cannot go to sleep with one form of economic system and wake up the next morning with another.
Mikhail Gorbachev (b. 1931) Russian former president. *Guardian* (7 December 1990)

8 Economic modernization...spawns indigenous types of capitalism that owe little to any western model.
John Gray (b. 1948) British academic and writer. *False Dawn* (1998)

9 Global democratic capitalism is as unrealizable a condition as worldwide communism.
John Gray (b. 1948) British academic and writer. *False Dawn* (1998)

10 The natural counterpart of a free market economy is a politics of insecurity.
John Gray (b. 1948) British academic and writer. *False Dawn* (1998)

11 Stalin was not a man you could do business with. Stalin didn't understand the importance of business.
Armand Hammer (1898–1990) US industrialist, philanthropist, founder and CEO of Occidental Petroleum. Interview, *Sunday Times Magazine* (24 June 1984)

12 Less than seventy-five years after it officially began, the contest between capitalism and socialism is over: capitalism has won.
Robert L. Heilbroner (b. 1919) US economist. 'Reflections: The Triumph of Capitalism', *New Yorker* (23 January 1989)

13 Capitalism is at its liberating best in a noncapitalist environment. The crypto-businessman is the true revolutionary in a Communist country.
Eric Hoffer (1902–83) US philosopher. *Reflections on the Human Condition* (1973)

14 Communism has failed, but capitalism has not succeeded.
William Keegan (b. 1938) British author and journalist. *The Spectre of Capitalism* (1992)

15 Totalitarianism is not so good at industrial innovation and adaptation to consumer demand.
William Keegan (b. 1938) British author and journalist. *The Spectre of Capitalism* (1992)

16 Marxian Socialism must always remain a portent to the historians of Opinion—how a doctrine so illogical and so dull can have exercised so powerful and enduring an influence over the minds of men...
John Maynard Keynes (1883–1946) British economist. *The End of Laissez-Faire* (1926)

17 The twentieth century marks the turning-point from the old capitalism to the new, from the domination of capital in general to the domination of financial capital.
Vladimir Ilich Lenin (1870–1924) Russian revolutionary

leader and political theorist. *Imperialism, the Higher Stages of Capitalism* (1917)

18 There are not only trade unions in England, but also alliances between workers and capitalists in a particular industry for the purpose of raising prices and robbing everybody else.
Vladimir Ilich Lenin (1870–1924) Russian revolutionary leader and political theorist. *Selected Works*, vol. 7

19 It is Capitalism that is being tried. We told you...that the time would come when finance would be more powerful than industry. That day has come.
Ramsay MacDonald (1866–1937) British prime minister. Speech, Llandudno, Wales (7 October 1930)

20 You show me a capitalist, I'll show you a bloodsucker.
Malcolm X (1925–65) US black consciousness leader. *Malcolm X Speaks* (1965)

21 Between the capitalist and communist systems of society lies the period of the revolutionary transformation of the one into the other...the revolutionary dictatorship of the proletariat.
Karl Marx (1818–83) German political and economic philosopher. *Critique of the Gotha Programme* (1875)

22 During its rule of scarce one hundred years, capitalism has created more massive and more colossal productive forces than have all preceding generations together.
Karl Marx (1818–83) German political and economic philosopher. *The Communist Manifesto* (co-written with Friedrich Engels; 1848)

23 The old Communists who run Vietnam actually believe they defeated decadent Western capitalism. So where did the little girl in Hoan Kiem Park, in the middle of downtown Hanoi, get a hula hoop?
P.J. O'Rourke (b. 1947) US humorist and journalist. *All the Trouble in the World* (1994)

24 In the end we beat them with Levi 501 jeans. Seventy-two years of Communist indoctrination and propaganda was drowned out by a three-ounce Sony Walkman.
P.J. O'Rourke (b. 1947) US humorist and journalist. 'The Death of Communism', *Rolling Stone* (November 1989)

25 I just made a smart deal for myself. This is America. This isn't the Soviet Union. It's the supply-and-demand of the marketplace.
Michael Ovitz (b. 1946) US film agent and head of Disney. Quoted in *Ovitz: The Inside Story of Hollywood's Most Controversial Power Broker* (Robert Slates; 1997)

26 I feel that capitalism has a very bad press with the pseudo-leftists who clog our best college campuses and that...modern capitalism has allowed the birth of the independent woman who is no longer economically dependent on her husband.
Camille Paglia (b. 1947) US academic, educator, and writer. Interview, *Reason Magazine* (August–September 1995)

27 Remember this, Griffin. The revolution eats its own. Capitalism re-creates itself.
Mordecai Richler (1931–2001) Canadian novelist. *Cocksure* (1968)

28 The contradiction in the system which produced conflict, movement and change...is the increasingly social, cooperative nature of production...and the individual ownership of the means of production.
Eric Roll (b. 1907) British economist. Discussing the causes of capitalist change. *A History of Economic Thought* (1942)

29 Man is born perfect. It is the capitalist system which corrupts him.
Arthur Scargill (b. 1938) British former trade union leader. Speech, Wakefield, England (20 November 1981)

30 As a matter of practical necessity, socialist democracy may eventually turn out to be more of a sham than capitalist democracy ever was.
Joseph Alois Schumpeter (1883–1950) US economist and social theorist. *Capitalism, Socialism and Democracy* (1942), ch. 1

31 Capitalism inevitably and by virtue of the very logic of its civilization creates, educates and subsidizes a vested interest in social unrest.
Joseph Alois Schumpeter (1883–1950) US economist and social theorist. *Capitalism, Socialism and Democracy* (1942), ch. 13

32 I personally believe that capitalism, as it is now, won't survive unless it becomes more socially responsible.
Jim Slater (b. 1929) British business executive and author. *Financial Times* (11 January 1973)

33 Let us look at the capitalist roots of the racial miseries in our country, South Africa. The real question is not whether a system works but for whom it works.
Joe Slovo (1926–95) South African politician and lawyer. Quoted in obituary, *Guardian* (7 January 1995)

34 Globalization will not go away...The questions are whether global capitalism finds acceptance or if the backlash against the present hardships and inequities is going to bring forth a quite different economic paradigm.
Theo Sommer (b. 1930) German newspaper publisher, journalist, and author. Speech, 5th Workshop on Inventing the Organisation of the 21st Century, Munich, Germany. 'Shareholder Values or Shared Values? The Politics and Ethics of the Global Economy in the Post-Cold War World' (February 1999)

35 The opening up of economies must be combined with social integration. Without it the institutions of the market would quickly lose their political legitimization...Revolution is not in the offing, but it still is in the political armory.
Theo Sommer (b. 1930) German newspaper publisher, journalist, and author. Speech, 5th Workshop on Inventing the Organisation of the 21st Century, Munich, Germany. 'Shareholder Values or Shared Values? The Politics and Ethics of the Global Economy in the Post-Cold War World' (February 1999)

36 The fact that global capitalism is flawed does not mean that we should turn to communism or withdraw into national isolation, just as the failure of communism does not mean that markets are perfect.
George Soros (b. 1930) US financier, entrepreneur, and philanthropist. Speech to the Council on Foreign Relations, New York City. 'The Crisis of Global Capitalism: Open Society Endangered' (10 December 1998)

37 Market fundamentalism undermines the democratic political process and the inefficiency of the political process is a powerful argument in favor of market fundamentalism.
George Soros (b. 1930) US financier, entrepreneur, and philanthropist. *The Crisis of Global Capitalism* (1998)

38 Communism may have been defeated, but the Communists often have not been.
Margaret Thatcher (b. 1925) British former prime minister. Quoted in *Fortune* (18 October 1993)

39 The Western Colonial system shook all the societies in the world loose from their old moorings. But it seems indifferent whether or not they reach safe harbour in the end.
Barbara Ward (1914–81) British economist, journalist, and educator. *The Rich Nations and the Poor Nations* (1962)

40 Mr Heath talks about the unacceptable face of capitalism, but intrinsically it doesn't have an unacceptable face.
Arnold Weinstock (1924–2002) British managing director of General Electric Company. Referring to prime minister Edward Heath's description of Lonrho as 'the unacceptable face of capitalism'. Quoted in *Daily Telegraph* (17 June 1974)

41 My biggest challenge in transforming the company was fear. Under socialism, people learned to be afraid to express their opinions.
Peter Zwack (b. 1928) Hungarian business executive. *Forbes* (April 2000)

CAREERS

1 The emerging work paradox is that in a post-job world, the only viable long-term career is to be a temp.
Anonymous. Quoted in *Management Today* (February 1995)

2 No man likes to acknowledge that he has made a mistake in the choice of his profession.
Charlotte Brontë (1816–55) British novelist and poet. *The Professor* (1857), ch. 4

3 People don't choose their careers; they are engulfed by them.
John Dos Passos (1896–1970) US novelist. *New York Times* (25 October 1959)

4 A young person entering the work force in 2000...has almost no chance of working for the same company even a decade hence. In this world people must take responsibility for their own futures. They cannot simply count on ascending a career ladder.

Peter F. Drucker (b. 1909) US management consultant and academic. 'Putting More Now into the Internet', *www.Forbes.com* (15 March 2000)

5 The best augury of a man's success in his profession is that he thinks it the finest in the world.

George Eliot (1819–80) British novelist. *Daniel Deronda* (1876)

6 Total commitment to family and total commitment to career is possible, but fatiguing.

Muriel Fox (b. 1928) US business executive. Quoted in 'Wait Late to Marry', *New Woman* (Barbara Jordan Moore; October 1971)

7 Unlike a straight academic career, you end up fully recognizing that hypotheses matter, that actions matter, and the ideas that you come up with matter.

Alan Greenspan (b. 1926) US economist and chairman of US Federal Reserve Board. Referring to his experience as Federal Reserve chairman. Speech accepting appointment to fourth term as US Federal Reserve chairman, Washington, D.C. (4 January 2000)

8 Portfolio working.

Charles Handy (b. 1932) British business executive and author. Referring to changing career patterns. *The Age of Unreason* (1989)

9 Tomorrow's typical career will be neither linear nor continuous, nor will it always be upwards. Instead, one's life work will take more of a zig-zag course.

Tom Horton (b. 1926) US chairman of American Management Association. *Management Review* (1990)

10 I'm just a guy who probably should have been a semi-talented poet on the Left Bank. I got sort of side-tracked here.

Steve Jobs (b. 1955) US entrepreneur, co-founder and CEO of Apple Computer Company, and CEO of Pixar. *Fortune* (1 October 1984)

11 The power of the position is giving way to the power of the person. A formal title and its placement on an organization chart have less to do with career prospects and success...than the skills and ideas a person brings to that work.

Rosabeth Moss Kanter (b. 1943) US management theorist, academic, and writer. *When Giants Learn to Dance: Mastering the Challenges of Strategy, Management and Careers in the 1990s* (1992), ch. 11

12 The traditional corporate career may soon share the fate of the dad-at-work-mom-at home-two-kids nuclear family: an oft-invoked ideal that applies to fewer and fewer people.

Rosabeth Moss Kanter (b. 1943) US management theorist, academic, and writer. *When Giants Learn to Dance: Mastering the Challenges of Strategy, Management and Careers in the 1990s* (1992), ch. 11

13 In many corporations managers now work with one eye on their résumé. Assignments that used to be seen in terms of their political value in the promotion game are now assessed for their résumé value.

Rosabeth Moss Kanter (b. 1943) US management theorist,

academic, and writer. *When Giants Learn to Dance: Mastering the Challenges of Strategy, Management and Careers in the 1990s* (1992), ch. 12

14 I suppose in my case shouting about all that stinking, rotten business going on in Washington simply takes the place of shouting at the devil.

Vivien Kellems (1896–1975) US industrialist, feminist, and lecturer. Explaining why she didn't succeed her father as a Disciples of Christ minister. *Toil, Taxes, and Trouble* (1952)

15 Your career is literally your business.

Theodore Levitt (b. 1925) US management theorist, writer, and editor. *Only the Paranoid Survive* (1996)

16 Copywriters don't usually run the company. But the great thing about this business is it isn't really traditional.

Judy McGrath (b. 1952) US president of MTV. 'MTV Honcho Judy McGrath', *www.womenswire.com* (Jonathan Sapers; 2000)

17 I learned I was a better copywriter than writer-writer.

Judy McGrath (b. 1952) US president of MTV. Referring to why she left journalism. 'MTV Honcho Judy McGrath', *www.womenswire.com* (Jonathan Sapers; 2000)

18 The life-fate of the modern individual depends not only upon the family into which he was born or which he enters by marriage, but increasingly upon the corporation in which he spends the most alert hours of his best years.

L. Wright Mills (1916–62) US sociologist. *The Power Elite* (1956), ch. 1

19 I've got her tits but I didn't want her career.

Tara Newley (b. 1965) British actor. Referring to her mother, actor Joan Collins. *Style* (August 2000)

20 The world's best poker players don't hanker for jobs in casino management.

Tom Peters (b. 1942) US management consultant and author. *Liberation Management* (1992)

21 Soon the emphasis will be on getting a life instead of a career, and work will be viewed as a series of gigs or projects.

Jonas Ridderstråle, Swedish academic and author. *Funky Business* (co-written with Kjell Nordström; 2000)

22 I have yet to hear a man ask for advice on how to combine marriage and a career.

Gloria Steinem (b. 1934) US entrepreneur, editor, and writer. Radio interview, LBC (2 April 1984)

23 Project management is the furnace in which successful careers are made.

Thomas A. Stewart (b. 1948) US journalist and author. *Intellectual Capital* (1997)

24 I should have worked just long enough to discover that I didn't like it.

Paul Theroux (b. 1941) US travel writer. *Observer Magazine* (1979)

25 Whether it's choosing a career or deciding what charity to get involved with, the choice should come from your heart. Ultimately, you are the one who has to get up every morning and enjoy what you are doing, so make sure it matters to you.

Dave Thomas (1932–2002) US founder of Wendy's. 'Dave Thomas Serves up Advice for Graduates of All Ages', *USA Today* (2000)

26 I got my start by giving myself a start.

C.J. Walker (1867–1919) US business executive. Quoted in *On Her Own Ground: The Life and Times of Madam C. J. Walker* (A'Lelia Bundles; 2000)

27 Never burn bridges. Today's junior prick, tomorrow's senior partner.

Sigourney Weaver (b. 1949) US actor. Said as executive Katharine Parker, from the screenplay by Kevin Wade. *Working Girl* (1988)

28 Companies that have been around for 50 years are another world to me. I entered the technology arena the same year that Microsoft was started. And the arena has always felt like a meritocracy, though there were never many women.

Ann Winblad (b. 1953) US venture capitalist. 'Women in the New Workplace', *BusinessWeek* (Mica Schneider; 2000)

29 When you retire...you go from who's who to who's that, like stepping off the pier (or) achieving statutory senility.

Walter Wriston (b. 1919) US banker. On retiring as chairman of Citibank Corp. *New York Times* (1985)

CHALLENGE

1 We specialize in the wholly impossible.

Nannie Burroughs (1883–1961) US educationlist and journalist. Motto of the National Training School for Girls in Washington. Quoted in *Black Women in White America* (1972)

2 It is so tempting to try the most difficult thing possible.

Jennie Churchill (1854–1921) US socialite and writer. Quoted in *Daily Chronicle* (8 July 1909)

3 In a stable world, knowledge of standard situations and the routine ways of dealing with them is sufficient. Not so in a changing world...judgments from the past may be inadequate, misleading, and dangerous.

Edward de Bono (b. 1933) British creative-thinking theorist, educator, and writer. 'Away with the Gang of Three', *Guardian* (25 January 1997)

4 You may not realize it when it happens, but a kick in the teeth may be the best thing in the world for you.

Walt Disney (1901–66) US entertainment entrepreneur and founder of the Walt Disney Company. Attrib.

5 Never talk defeat. Use words like hope, belief, faith, victory.

Brendan Kennelly (b. 1936) Irish poet and academic. *The Power of Positive Thinking* (1952)

6 If we see light at the end of the tunnel, it's the light of the oncoming train.

Robert Lowell (1917–77) US poet. *Day by Day* (1977)

7 In every difficult situation is potential value. Believe this, then begin looking for it.

Norman Vincent Peale (1898–1993) US religious leader. *Positive Thinking Every Day* (1995)

8 You must do the thing you think you cannot do.

Eleanor Roosevelt (1884–1962) US reformer, author, and first lady. *You Learn by Living* (1960)

9 When the sea was calm, all boats alike
Show'd mastership in floating.

William Shakespeare (1564–1616) English poet and playwright. *Coriolanus* (1623), Act 4, Scene 1

10 I relished the challenge of working on the lowest circulations in Fleet Street in one of the most competitive markets in the world.

Trish Wadley (b. 1962) Australian marketing director. 'Independently Minded', *Independent* (Poppy Brech; 2000)

CHANGE

1 Faced with change, employees have one question: 'What's going to happen to me?' A successful change management communication program will avoid that question.

Scott Adams (b. 1957) US cartoonist and humorist. *The Dilbert Principle* (1996)

2 Change means movement. Movement means friction.

Saul Alinsky (1909–72) US activist. *Rules for Radicals* (1971)

3 Paradigm Shift: A euphemism companies use when they realize the rest of their industry has expanded into Guangdong while they were investing in Orange County.

Anonymous. *Fortune* (15 February 1995)

4 When the wind of change blows, some build walls, others build windmills.

Anonymous

5 To change and to improve are two different things.

Anonymous. German proverb.

6 Structure will become a dynamic enabler of both change and unchange, the ultimate model of organizational chaos.

Igor Ansoff (1918–2002) US author and academic. *Corporate Structure Present and Future* (February 1974)

7 It is change...that is the dominant factor in society today. No sensible decision can be made without taking into account not only the world as it is, but the world as it will be.

Isaac Asimov (1920–92) US novelist, critic, and scientist. 1978. 'My Own View', *Asimov on Science Fiction* (1981)

8 Better never means better for everyone...It always means worse, for some.

Margaret Atwood (b. 1939) Canadian poet and novelist. *The Handmaid's Tale* (1985)

9 Most of us are about as eager to be changed as we were to be born, and go through our changes in a similar state of shock.

James Baldwin (1924–87) US writer. 'Every Good-Bye Ain't Gone', *New York* (19 December 1977)

10 When you are through changing, you are through.

Percy Barnevik (b. 1941) Swedish former CEO of ABB. Quoted in *Financial Times Handbook of Management* (Stuart Crainer, ed.; 1995)

11 You can't permit a honeymoon of small changes over a year or two. A long series of small changes just prolongs the pain.

Percy Barnevik (b. 1941) Swedish former CEO of ABB. *Harvard Business Review* (March/April 1991)

12 You cannot renew a company without revitalising its people.

Christopher Bartlett (b. 1945) Australian business writer. *The Individualised Corporation* (co-written with Sumantra Ghoshal; 1997)

13 If I were to give off-the-cuff advice to anyone trying to institute change, I would say, 'How clear is the metaphor?'

Warren Bennis (b. 1925) US educator and writer. 'Why Leaders Can't Lead', *Amacom* (1976)

14 It's time to make things ship-shape, to get rid of the debt, to get a bit of a cash box to work from, to enjoy life a bit more.

Conrad Black (b. 1944) Canadian newspaper proprietor and business executive. Referring to disposals from his media group. *New York Times* (April 2000)

15 I am not the one who transforms the company...The marketplace is what is changing France Télécom; the customers and the competition are its alpha and its omega. A company requires a leader, but individually no one can pretend to be the driving force.

Michel Bon (b. 1943) French former CEO of France Télécom. Interview, *Strategy + Business* (April–June 1999)

16 We don't want to do it for a quick pop in share price.

Peter Bonfield (b. 1944) British former CEO of British Telecom. Said at a British Telecom annual general meeting. Referring to possible restructuring of BT. Remark (July 2000)

17 No one has ever accused us of lagging behind. In fact, I am willing to turn an entire company upside down if it's time to do that. We're in perpetual evolution.

Richard Branson (b. 1950) British entrepreneur, business executive, and founder of the Virgin Group. Interview, *ASAP* (27 February 1997)

18 Recognize that transition has a characteristic shape.

William Bridges (b. 1933) US transition management thinker. *Transitions: Making Sense of Life's Changes* (1980)

19 Thinking about change is a redundancy. All thinking is about change.

Edgar Bronfman Jr (b. 1955) Canadian CEO of the Seagram Corporation. Quoted in *How to Manage* (Ray Wild; 1995)

20 A state without the means of some change is without the means of its conservation.

Edmund Burke (1729–97) British philosopher and politician. *Reflections on the Revolution in France* (1790)

21 It is idle to speak of organizational transformation without individuals being transformed, especially the leader.

S.K. Chakraborty (b. 1957) Indian academic. *Ethics in Management: Vedantic Perspectives* (1995)

22 People are no longer content to talk merely of 'organizational change'...the new aspiration is for 'organizational transformation'.

S.K. Chakraborty (b. 1957) Indian academic. *Ethics in Management: Vedantic Perspectives* (1995)

23 Outworn policies may remain in force simply because of sheer inertia or lack of perception amongst policy makers.

S.K. Chakraborty (b. 1957) Indian academic. *Management by Objectives: An Integrated Approach* (1976)

24 Even when the universe made it quite clear to me that I was mistaken in my certainties...I did not break. The shattering of my sureties did not shatter me.

Lucille Clifton (b. 1936) US poet and author. Quoted in *The Black Woman's Gumbo Ya-Ya* (Terri L. Jewell; 1993)

25 It is only the very wisest and the very stupidest who cannot change.

Confucius (551–479 BC) Chinese philosopher, administrator, and writer. *Analects* (?500 BC)

26 Passion for change drives great business people. It moves them restlessly from industry to industry.

Paul Corrigan (b. 1948) British author. *Shakespeare on Management* (1999)

27 Management, a science? Of course not, it's just a wastepaper basket full of recipes which provided the dish of the day during a few years of plenty and economic growth. Now the recipes are inappropriate and the companies which persist in following them will disappear.

Léon Courville (b. 1945) Canadian banker. Quoted in *The Unconscious Civilization* (John Ralston Saul; 1995)

28 The first step toward change is acceptance. Once you accept yourself, you open the door to change.

Stephen Covey (b. 1932) US writer and psychologist. *First Things First: To Live, To Love, To Learn, To Leave a Legacy* (1994)

29 As times change, you want to really revere your heredity, but you don't want to be a shrine—to light candles and kneel.

Kitty d'Alessio, US business executive. Referring to conflicts after she succeeded company founder Coco Chanel to become president of Chanel Inc. *New York Times* (28 July 1985)

30 Open the windows, let in the year we're living in.

Kitty d'Alessio, US business executive. Referring to the conflict between tradition and modernity after she succeeded company founder Coco Chanel to become president of Chanel Inc. *New York Times* (1985)

31 This is an age that calls for cunning, speed, and enterprise.

Richard D'Aveni (b. 1950) US strategist. 'The Mavericks', *Fortune* (June 1995)

32 I would constructively rebel by changing the rules but, once agreed, I would observe them.
Howard Davies (b. 1951) British chairman of the Financial Services Authority. *Sunday Times* (July 2000)

33 We're fast approaching the point at which there is really no distinction between the .com companies and traditional businesses. The only distinction will be between the winners and losers, and of course, the pace of change at which companies become winners or losers.
Michael Dell (b. 1965) US chairman and CEO of Dell Computer Corporation. Speech to the DirectConnect Customer Conference, Austin, Texas. 'DirectConnect' (25 August 1999)

34 Unlike other industries, our pace of change is so fast that I don't think it's right to expect the same type of concentration as in the auto industry.
Michael Dell (b. 1965) US chairman and CEO of Dell Computer Corporation. *Wall Street Journal* (February 1997)

35 Only management can change the system.
W. Edwards Deming (1900–93) US consultant and author. Quoted in *In Search of European Excellence* (Robert Heller; 1997)

36 Change is inevitable in a progressive country. Change is constant.
Benjamin Disraeli (1804–81) British prime minister and novelist. 29 October 1867. Speech, Edinburgh, Scotland. Quoted in *The Times* (30 October 1867)

37 All great change in business has come from outside the firm, not from inside.
Peter F. Drucker (b. 1909) US management consultant and academic. Quoted in 'Seeing Things as They Really Are', *Forbes* (Robert Lenzner and Stephen S. Johnson; 1987)

38 Corporations once built to last like pyramids are now more like tents. Tomorrow they're gone or in turmoil.
Peter F. Drucker (b. 1909) US management consultant and academic. Quoted in *How to Manage* (Ray Wild; 1995)

39 The stepladder is gone, and there's not even the implied structure of an industry's rope ladder. It's more like vines, and you bring your own machete.
Peter F. Drucker (b. 1909) US management consultant and academic. Referring to to the impact of rapid organisational change. Quoted in *How to Manage* (Ray Wild; 1995)

40 Organizations that are change leaders are designed for change. But people need continuity...they do not function well if the environment is not predictable, not understandable, not known.
Peter F. Drucker (b. 1909) US management consultant and academic. *Management Challenges for the 21st Century* (1999)

41 Every organization of today has to build into its very structure the management of change.
Peter F. Drucker (b. 1909) US management consultant and academic. *Post-capitalist Society* (1993)

42 To make knowledge productive...requires the systematic exploitation of opportunities for change.
Peter F. Drucker (b. 1909) US management consultant and academic. *Post-capitalist Society* (1993)

43 The Age of Discontinuity
Peter F. Drucker (b. 1909) US management consultant and academic. Book title. *The Age of Discontinuity* (1969)

44 The Times They Are A-Changin'
Bob Dylan (b. 1941) US singer. Song title. 'The Times They Are A-Changin'' (1964)

45 I never think of the future. It comes soon enough.
Albert Einstein (1879–1955) US physicist. Interview (December 1930)

46 The fertility of happy invention denied its full fruit by the grimy rules of union demarcation.
Harold Evans (b. 1928) British newspaper editor and publisher. Referring to union opposition to new technology in the newspaper industry. *Good Times, Bad Times* (1983)

47 Consolidation is going to take place and it's better to lead than to follow. If you lead you have the best opportunity to gain the best partners.
Niall Fitzgerald (b. 1945) British CEO of Unilever and president of the Advertising Association. *Marketing* (July 2000)

48 I realised that if you want to change something, nine times out of ten you can change it more effectively from within.
Niall Fitzgerald (b. 1945) British CEO of Unilever and president of the Advertising Association. *Marketing* (July 2000)

49 Change is inevitable, but it is in us to control its content and directions.
Indira Gandhi (1917–84) Indian prime minister. Speech (8 January 1967)

50 If the 1980s were about quality and the 1990s were about reengineering, then the 2000s will be about velocity.
Bill Gates (b. 1955) US entrepreneur, chairman and CEO of Microsoft. *Business@the Speed of Thought* (co-written with Collins Hemingway; 1999)

51 One of the lessons from the Darwinian world is that the excellence of an organism's nervous system helps determine its ability to sense change and quickly respond, thereby surviving or even thriving.
Bill Gates (b. 1955) US entrepreneur, chairman and CEO of Microsoft. 'Leaders Must Be Candid, Consistent', *New York Times* (21 May 1997)

52 The information highway will transform our culture as dramatically as Gutenberg's press did the Middle Ages.
Bill Gates (b. 1955) US entrepreneur, chairman and CEO of Microsoft. *The Road Ahead* (co-written with Nathan Myhrvold and Peter N. Rinearson; 1995)

53 You can't fight against the future. Time is on our side.
William Ewart Gladstone (1809–98) British prime minister. Speech (1866)

54 Don't wrap the flag of Coca-Cola around you to prevent change taking place.

Roberto Goizueta (1931–97) US CEO of Coca-Cola. Speech. Quoted in *Fortune* (December 1995)

55 It is extremely important that you show some insensitivity to your past in order to show the proper respect for the future.

Roberto Goizueta (1931–97) US CEO of Coca-Cola. Speech. Quoted in *Fortune* (December 1995)

56 From now on, change will be the constant. The individuals best prepared to succeed are those who can learn, modify, and grow, regardless of age, experience, or ego.

Danny Goodman (b. 1950) US writer. *Living at Light Speed: Your Survival Guide to Life on the Information Superhighway* (1994)

57 Let chaos reign, then rein in chaos.

Andrew S. Grove (b. 1936) US entrepreneur, author, and chairman of Intel Corporation. Attrib.

58 The new environment dictates two rules; first everything happens faster; second, anything that can be done will be done, if not by you, then by someone else, somewhere.

Andrew S. Grove (b. 1936) US entrepreneur, author, and chairman of Intel Corporation. Attrib.

59 There are two options: adapt or die.

Andrew S. Grove (b. 1936) US entrepreneur, author, and chairman of Intel Corporation. Attrib.

60 The possible use of automated equipment in the over-the-counter marketplace has become an increasingly important subject.

Robert W. Haack (1917–92) US president of New York Stock Exchange. *The Wall Street Journal* (1967)

61 Perseverance may be just as important as speed in the battle for the future.

Gary Hamel (b. 1954) US academic, business writer, and consultant. *Competing for the Future* (co-written with C.K. Prahalad; 1994)

62 This extraordinary arrogance that change must start at the top is a way of guaranteeing that change will not happen in most companies.

Gary Hamel (b. 1954) US academic, business writer, and consultant. Interview, *Strategy + Business* (October–December 1997)

63 Complex processes are the work of the devil.

Michael Hammer (b. 1948) US author and academic. *BusinessWeek* (August 1996)

64 To succeed at re-engineering, you have to be a missionary, a motivator, and a leg breaker.

Michael Hammer (b. 1948) US author and academic. *Fortune* (August 1993)

65 America's business problem is that it is entering the twenty-first century with companies designed during the nineteenth century to work well in the twentieth.

Michael Hammer (b. 1948) US author and academic. *Re-engineering the Corporation* (co-written with James Champy; 1993)

66 Business re-engineering isn't about fixing anything—it's about starting again, about re-inventing our corporation from top to bottom.

Michael Hammer (b. 1948) US author and academic. *Re-engineering the Corporation* (co-written with James Champy; 1993)

67 Unless companies change these rules, any superficial re-organizations they perform will be no more effective than dusting the furniture in Pompeii.

Michael Hammer (b. 1948) US author and academic. *Re-engineering the Corporation* (co-written with James Champy; 1993)

68 What I really do is I'm reversing the Industrial Revolution.

Michael Hammer (b. 1948) US author and academic. *Re-engineering the Corporation* (co-written with James Champy; 1993)

69 Change means avoiding the predictable and known ways of doing things which we learn to adjust to.

John Harvey-Jones (b. 1924) British management adviser, author, and former chairman of ICI. *Managing to Survive* (1993)

70 Business leaders must not cling to old ways of doing business, or allow inertia or complacency to prevent them from making the decisions that they will eventually be forced to make.

Patricia Hewitt (b. 1948) British government minister. *Digital Britain* (January 2000)

71 Others appear frozen in the headlights—aware of the likely impact, yet paralysed by the fear of major transformations.

Patricia Hewitt (b. 1948) British government minister. *Digital Britain* (January 2000)

72 A business cannot stand still. It has to be dynamic. The world around us changes all the time and there can be no holy cows.

Nicola Horlick (b. 1960) British fund manager. *Can You Have It All?* (1997)

73 Only man is not content to leave things as they are but must always be changing them, and when he has done so, is seldom satisfied at the result.

Elspeth Huxley (1907–97) British author. *The Mottled Lizard* (1962)

74 In order for an ideal to become a reality, there must be a person, a personality to translate it.

Jesse Jackson (b. 1941) US churchman, civil rights activist, and presidential candidate. Eulogy (October 1972)

75 If one is going to change things, one has to make a fuss and catch the eye of the world.

Elizabeth Janeway (b. 1913) US feminist and writer. *Open Secrets* (1972)

76 I am captivated more by dreams of the future than by history of the past.

Thomas Jefferson (1743–1826) US president. Attrib.

77 I want to put a ding in the universe.

Steve Jobs (b. 1955) US entrepreneur, co-founder and CEO of Apple Computer Company, and CEO of Pixar. Quoted in *Made in the USA* (Phil Patton; 1992)

78 Large companies not paying attention to change will get hurt. The Web will be one more area of significant change and those who don't pay attention will get hurt, while those who see it early enough will get rewarded. The Web is just going to be one more of those major change factors that businesses face every decade.
Steve Jobs (b. 1955) US entrepreneur, co-founder and CEO of Apple Computer Company, and CEO of Pixar. Interview, 'The Next Insanely Great Thing', *Wired Magazine* (February 1996)

79 Companies that stay ahead of change are ones in which their people see change as something they themselves accomplish and not something that is imposed on them. They see lots of opportunities to take initiative.
Rosabeth Moss Kanter (b. 1943) US management theorist, academic, and writer. Interview, *Strategy + Business* (July–September 1999)

80 The more things change, the more they are the same.
Alphonse Karr (1808–90) French author. *Les Guêpes* (1849)

81 Bankers regard research as most dangerous and a thing that makes banking hazardous due to the rapid changes it brings about in industry.
Charles Franklin Kettering (1876–1958) US businessman and engineer. Address (1927)

82 Corporate insiders...can seldom transform an organisation beset by inertia.
John P. Kotter (b. 1947) US writer. Quoted in *In Search of European Excellence* (Robert Heller; 1997)

83 Anyone in a large organization who thinks major change is impossible should probably get out.
John P. Kotter (b. 1947) US writer. *The New Rules* (1995)

84 If we want everything to remain as it is, it will be necessary for everything to change.
Giuseppe di Lampedusa (1896–1957) Italian writer. *The Leopard* (1955), ch. 1

85 Our future must depend on the kind of future we deserve to have.
Stephen Leacock (1869–1944) Canadian humorist, essayist, economist, and historian. *While There Is Time* (1945)

86 If you want truly to understand something, try to change it.
Kurt Lewin (1890–1947) US author. Attrib.

87 The reformer has enemies in all who profit by the old order, and only lukewarm defenders in all those who would profit by the new order.
Niccolò Machiavelli (1469–1527) Italian historian, statesman, and political philosopher. *The Prince* (1513)

88 There is nothing more difficult to take in hand, more perilous to conduct, or more uncertain in its success, than to take the lead in the introduction of a new order of things.
Niccolò Machiavelli (1469–1527) Italian historian, statesman, and political philosopher. *The Prince* (1513)

89 When business conditions got tough in recent years, we did not take meat cleavers to our product.
Colin Marshall (b. 1933) British CEO of British Airways. *Harvard Business Review* (November–December 1995)

90 Social relations are closely bound up with productive forces. In acquiring new productive forces men change their mode of production; and in changing their mode of production, in changing the way of earning their living, they change all their social relations.
Karl Marx (1818–83) German political and economic philosopher. *The Poverty of Philosophy* (1847)

91 The mode of production of material life conditions the general process of social, political and spiritual life...changes in the economic foundation lead sooner or later to the transformation of the whole immense superstructure.
Karl Marx (1818–83) German political and economic philosopher. *Towards a Critique of Political Economy* (1859)

92 Power is the ability to influence individuals and institutions in ways that change ideas.
Carl McCall (b. 1935) US former Comptroller of New York State. Referring to the achievements of African Americans in business. 'The Players', *Fortune* (Eileen Gunn; April 1997)

93 You can't change anything if you don't bring people with you.
Carolyn McCall (b. 1962) British managing director of Guardian Newspapers. *Marketing* (April 2000)

94 There can be no major change in a complex organization unless there are both sufficient resources and substantial readiness.
Robert H. Miles (b. 1944) US writer. *Leading Corporate Transformation* (1997)

95 Transformational change requires enormous energy.
Robert H. Miles (b. 1944) US writer. *Leading Corporate Transformation* (1997)

96 Remember when railway companies were the reigning industrial forces? Then, airlines companies came along...How many railway companies became airline companies? None! How many industrial companies will become information companies? Not too many!
William (Walid) Mougayar, US consultant and management theorist. Interview, *EMarketer* (10 August 1998)

97 I'm not going to claim that we fought the battle of Wapping because we wanted to bring a silver age to British journalism.
Rupert Murdoch (b. 1931) US CEO of News Corporation. Speech (1989)

98 Discontinuous change, because it shatters the framework of the existing organization and scrambles the internal patterns of informal relationships, presents its own very special set of issues for leaders of change.
David A. Nadler (b. 1948) US author and organisational behaviour specialist. *Champions of Change* (1998)

99 There are two broad ways to categorize large-scale change. The first is on the basis of scope, or the breadth of change. The second is on the basis of the timing of the industry change cycles.

David A. Nadler (b. 1948) US author and organisational behaviour specialist. *Champions of Change* (1998)

100 Economies of scale are giving way to economies of scope, finding the right size for synergy, market flexibility and, above all, speed.

John Naisbitt (b. ?1929) US business executive and author. *Megatrends* (1982)

101 The most reliable way to anticipate the future is by understanding the past.

John Naisbitt (b. ?1929) US business executive and author. *Megatrends* (1982)

102 It is as absurd to argue men, as to torture them into believing.

John Henry Newman (1801–90) British theologian. Sermon (December 1831)

103 I missed the buzz. I was like a barbecued chicken roasting in Portugal with nothing to do.

Denis O'Brien (b. 1958) Irish telecommunications entrepreneur. Referring to a period between jobs. *Sunday Times* (October 2000)

104 We set sail within a vast sphere, ever drifting in uncertainty, driven from end to end.

Blaise Pascal (1623–62) French philosopher and mathematician. *Pensées* (1670)

105 If it ain't broke, break it.

Richard Pascale (b. 1938) US academic and author. *Managing on the Edge* (1990)

106 Incremental change is not enough. The whole command and control tradition is being turned on its head.

Richard Pascale (b. 1938) US academic and author. *Managing on the Edge* (1990)

107 The incremental approach to change is effective when what you want is more of what you've already got.

Richard Pascale (b. 1938) US academic and author. *Managing on the Edge* (1990)

108 Wisdom lies neither in fixity nor in change, but in the dialectic between the two.

Octavio Paz (1914–98) Mexican writer. *The Times* (8 June 1989)

109 Revitalising General Motors is like teaching an elephant to tap dance. You find the sensitive spot and start poking.

H. Ross Perot (b. 1930) US entrepreneur, venture capitalist, and politician. *International Management* (February 1987)

110 The nanosecond nineties.

Tom Peters (b. 1942) US management consultant and author. Referring to pace of change during the 1990s. *Liberation Management* (1992)

111 We haven't touched—or really even bothered with white collar productivity. Until now...The White Collar Revolution is finally on...I believe that 90+ percent of White Collar Jobs will disappear or be reconfigured beyond recognition. Within 10 to 15 years.

Tom Peters (b. 1942) US management consultant and author. 'Work Matters!' movement manifesto, *www.tompeters.com* (September 1999)

112 Each age has its own techniques.

Jackson Pollock (1912–56) US painter. Radio interview (1950)

113 Changing the direction of a large company is like trying to turn an aircraft carrier. It takes a mile before anything happens. And if it was a wrong turn, getting back on course takes even longer.

Al Ries (b. 1926) US advertising executive and chairman of Trout & Ries Advertising, Inc. *Positioning: The Battle for Your Mind* (co-written with Jack Trout; 1980)

114 In today's mercurial, unpredictable economy, businesses that fail to grow and change will stagnate and die. Taking care of business means having your feet firmly on the ground.

Heather Robertson (b. 1942) Canadian author. *Taking Care of Business* (1997)

115 Change is scientific, progress is ethical; change is indubitable, whereas progress is a matter of controversy.

Bertrand Russell (1872–1970) British philosopher and writer. *Unpopular Essays* (1950)

116 Technology changes. Economics does not.

Carl Shapiro (b. 1955) US academic and author. *Information Rules* (co-written with Hal L. Varian; 1999)

117 If we don't change, we don't grow. If we don't grow, we aren't really living.

Gail Sheehy (b. 1937) US journalist and author. *Passages* (1976)

118 With the only certainty in our daily existence being change, and a rate of change growing always faster in a kind of technological leapfrog game, speed helps people think they are keeping up.

Gail Sheehy (b. 1937) US journalist and author. *Speed is of the Essence* (1971)

119 The rapidity of technological change makes the search for facts a permanently necessary feature.

Alfred P. Sloan (1875–1966) US president of General Motors. *My Years with General Motors* (1964)

120 If the shoe doesn't fit, must we change the foot?

Gloria Steinem (b. 1934) US entrepreneur, editor, and writer. *Outrageous Acts and Everyday Rebellions* (1983)

121 A company with no sense of crisis and no appetite for reform will eventually lose the battle against time and disappear.

Kunio Takeda, Japanese business executive. Quoted in *Fortune* (March 2003)

122 Economics are the method. The object is to change the soul.

Margaret Thatcher (b. 1925) British former prime minister. *Sunday Times* (April 1975)

123 When you sell 30 percent of a business, it is like taking two limbs off a body—it's not surprising there is a negative effect on the rest of the business.
Clive Thompson (b. 1943) British chairman of the Confederation of British Industry and former CEO of Rentokil. *Sunday Times* (October 2000)

124 Change is not merely necessary to life, it is life.
Alvin Toffler (b. 1928) US social commentator. *Future Shock* (1970)

125 Future shock is the disorientation that affects an individual, a corporation, or a country when he or it is overwhelmed by change and the prospect of change...we are in collision with tomorrow.
Alvin Toffler (b. 1928) US social commentator. *Observer* (1972)

126 Inside the world of business, as in the larger world outside, force, wealth and knowledge...remain the primary roots of power. Failure to understand how they are changing is a ticket to economic oblivion.
Alvin Toffler (b. 1928) US social commentator. *Powershift* (1990), pt 2, ch. 3

127 The coming world quake means more than just new machines. It promises to restructure all the human relationships and roles in the office as well.
Alvin Toffler (b. 1928) US social commentator. *The Third Wave* (1980)

128 We need a readiness to enter a room in the dark and stumble over unfamiliar furniture until the pain in our shins reminds us of where things are.
Fons Trompenaars (b. 1952) Dutch author and management consultant. *Financial Times* (July 1996)

129 Management that wants to change an institution must first show that it loves that institution.
John Tusa (b. 1936) British broadcaster and managing director of the Barbican. *Observer* (February 1994)

130 But change and the willingness to change, to try anything, try anyone's idea, it might not work. But it won't break the company when it doesn't.
Sam M. Walton (1918–92) US entrepreneur and founder of Wal-Mart, Inc. 'CEO of the Decade, Sam M. Walton', *Financial World* (Sharron Reier; April 1989)

131 Look, you can take anything away from IBM...but leave our people and this business will re-create itself overnight.
Thomas J. Watson Jr (1914–93) US CEO of IBM. *Father, Son & Co.: My Life at IBM and Beyond* (co-written with Peter Petre; 1990)

132 The inevitability of gradualness.
Sidney Webb (1859–1947) British economist, historian, and social reformer. Speech, Labour Party Conference (1920)

133 It isn't the changes that do you in, it's the transition.
Daniel Webster (1782–1852) US statesman, orator, and lawyer. *Managing Transitions* (1991)

134 Men are going to have to learn to be managers in a world where the organization will come close to consisting of all chiefs and one Indian. The Indian, of course, is the computer.
Thomas L. Whisler, US academic. *Christian Science Monitor* (21 April 1964)

CHARACTER

1 There may be said to be two classes of people in the world: Those who constantly divide the people of the world into two classes and those who do not.
Robert Benchley (1889–1945) US humorist. Quoted in *Washingtonian* (November 1978)

2 My trouble is I lack what the English call character. By which they mean the power to refrain.
Alan Bennett (b. 1934) British playwright. 'An Englishman Abroad', *Single Spies* (1989)

3 The rough broad difference between the American and the European business man is that the latter is anxious to leave his work, while the former is anxious to get to it.
Arnold Bennett (1867–1931) British novelist, playwright, and essayist. *Those United States* (1926)

4 Courtesy is the ornament of a noble man.
Bhartrihari (*fl.* ?570—?651) Indian poet and philosopher. *Niti Sataka* (7th century)

5 A man is known by the company he organizes.
Ambrose Bierce (1842—?1914) US journalist and writer. Quoted in *The Whiz Kids* (J.A. Byrne; 1993)

6 Be polite. Write diplomatically. Even in a declaration of war one observes the rules of politeness.
Otto Edward Leopold von Bismarck (1815–98) Prussian chancellor. Attrib.

7 You know what charm is: a way of getting the answer yes without having asked any clear question.
Albert Camus (1913–60) French novelist and essayist. *The Fall* (1956)

8 Do not make riches, but usefulness, your first aim; and let your chief pride be that your daily occupation is in the line of progress and development; that your work, in whatever capacity it may be, is useful work, honestly conducted, and as such ennobling to your life.
Andrew Carnegie (1835–1919) US industrialist and philanthropist. 'From Oakland: How to Succeed in Life', *The Pittsburgh Bulletin* (19 December 1903)

9 Be more concerned with your character than with your reputation. Your character is what you really are, while your reputation is what others think you are.
Dale Carnegie (1888–1955) US consultant and author. *How to Win Friends and Influence People* (1936)

10 Every man is as Heaven made him, and sometimes a great deal worse.
Miguel de Cervantes (1547–1616) Spanish novelist and playwright. *Don Quixote* (1615), pt 2, ch. 4

11 Chief executives seem no more able to resist their biological urge to merge, than dogs can resist chasing rabbits.

Philip Coggan (b. 1959) British journalist. Quoted in *Treasury of Investment Wisdom* (Bernice Cohen; 1999)

12 Men's natures are alike; it is their habits that carry them apart.

Confucius (551–479 BC) Chinese philosopher, administrator, and writer. *Analects* (?500 BC)

13 Though meaning to let a man have something, to be grudging about bringing it out from within, that is called behaving like a petty functionary.

Confucius (551–479 BC) Chinese philosopher, administrator, and writer. *Analects* (?500 BC)

14 Though intelligence is powerless to modify character, it is a dab hand at finding euphemisms for its weaknesses.

Quentin Crisp (1908–99) British writer. *The Naked Civil Servant* (1968)

15 Humour is by far the most significant activity of the human brain.

Edward de Bono (b. 1933) British creative-thinking theorist, educator, and writer. *Daily Mail* (29 January 1990)

16 Nurture your mind with great thoughts. To believe in the heroic makes heroes.

Benjamin Disraeli (1804–81) British prime minister and novelist. Quoted in *Light From Many Lamps* (Lillian Eichler Watson; 1988)

17 A man who lies to himself, and believes his own lies, becomes unable to recognize the truth, either in himself or in anyone else, and he ends up losing respect for himself as well as for others.

Fyodor Dostoevsky (1821–81) Russian novelist. *The Brothers Karamazov* (1879–80)

18 What e'r he did was done with so much ease, In him alone, 'twas Natural to please.

John Dryden (1631–1700) English poet and playwright. *Absalom and Achitophel* (1680), pt 1

19 We cannot judge either of the feelings or of the character of men with perfect accuracy, from their actions or their appearance in public; it is from their careless conversation...that we may hope...to discover their real character.

Maria Edgeworth (1767–1849) British writer. *Castle Rackrent* (1800)

20 Desire for approval and recognition is a healthy motive but the desire to be acknowledged as better, stronger, or more intelligent than a fellow being or fellow scholar easily leads to an excessively egoistic psychological adjustment.

Albert Einstein (1879–1955) US physicist. *Ideas and Opinions* (1954)

21 A character is like an acrostic or Alexandrian stanza; read it forward, backward, or across, it still spells the same thing.

Ralph Waldo Emerson (1803–82) US essayist, lecturer, and poet. 'Self-Reliance', *Essays: First Series* (1841)

22 Women are definitely more intuitive. They interact with people differently; people can be much more open with a woman.

Grace Fey, US vice-president and director of Frontier Capital Management. Quoted in *Women of the Street* (Sue Herera; 1997)

23 There are people whose external reality is generous because it is transparent, because you can read everything, accept everything, understand everything about them: people who carry their own sun with them.

Carlos Fuentes (b. 1928) Mexican writer. *The Old Gringo* (1985)

24 Many would be cowards if they had courage enough.

Thomas Fuller (1654–1734) English physician and writer. *Gnomologia* (1732), no. 3366

25 Deep down, I'm pretty superficial.

Ava Gardner (1922–90) US actor. Quoted in *Ava* (Roland Flamini; 1983), ch. 8

26 If my parents hadn't forced me time after time, there would have been no driving sustained effort to top the field.

Amadeo Giannini (1870–1949) US banker and founder of Bank of America. 'The Story of an Unusual Career', *Forbes* (November 1923)

27 Talent is formed in quiet, character in the stream of human life.

Johann Wolfgang von Goethe (1749–1832) German poet, playwright, novelist, and scientist. *Torquato Tasso* (1790), Act 1, Scene 2

28 The ability to control impulse is the basis of will and character.

Daniel Goleman (b. 1946) US behavioural scientist, journalist, and author. *Emotional Intelligence* (1995)

29 Bury your ego. Don't be the star. Be the star maker!

Bud Hadfield (b. 1923) US entrepreneur and founder of Kwik Kopy. *Wealth within Reach: Winning Strategies for Success from the Unconventional Wisdom of Bud Hadfield* (1995)

30 A bad reference is as hard to find as a good employee.

Robert Half (b. 1918) US consultant. *Half on Hiring* (1985), ch. 9

31 To keep your character you cannot stoop to filthy acts. It makes it easier to stoop the next time.

Katharine Hepburn (1907–2003) US actor. Quoted in *Los Angeles Times* (November 1974)

32 I think that, as life is action and passion, it is required of a man that he should share the passion and action of his time at peril of being judged not to have lived.

Oliver Wendell Holmes Jr (1841–1935) US jurist. Memorial Day Address (1884)

33 Having a character that consists mainly of defects, I try to correct them one by one, but there are limits to the altitude that can be attained by hauling on one's own boot-straps.

Clive James (b. 1939) Australian writer and broadcaster. *Unreliable Memoirs* (1980), ch. 3

34 What is character but the determination of incident? What is incident but the illustration of character?

Henry James (1843–1916) US novelist. 'The Art of Fiction', *Partial Portraits* (1888)

35 And so, my fellow Americans: ask not what your country can do for you. Ask what you can do for your country.

John F. Kennedy (1917–63) US president. Presidential inaugural speech (20 January 1961)

36 I can't do anything without first putting on lipstick.

Geraldine Laybourne (b. 1947) US chairman of Oxygen Media. Quoted in '10 to Watch: Geraldine Laybourne', *The Standard* (Kenneth Li; 2000)

37 Between ourselves and our real natures we interpose that wax figure of idealizations and selections which we call our character.

Walter Lippmann (1889–1974) US political commentator, editor, and writer. *A Preface to Politics* (1914), ch. 6

38 Women are less likely to have their egos tied up in their decisions, and therefore are more able to reverse direction if necessary

Elizabeth MacKay, US investment strategist and managing director of Bear Stearns. Quoted in *Women of the Street* (Sue Herera; 1997)

39 For every five well-adjusted and smoothly functioning Americans, there are two who never had the chance to discover themselves. It may well be because they have never been alone with themselves.

Marya Mannes (1904–90) US essayist and journalist. 'To Save the Life of "I"', *Vogue* (1964)

40 One of the best strengtheners of character and developers of stamina...is to assume the part you wish to play; to assert stoutly the possession of whatever you lack.

Orison Swett Marden (1848–1924) US author. *The Young Man Entering Business* (1903)

41 We don't love qualities, we love persons; sometimes by reason of their defects as well as of their qualities.

Jacques Maritain (1882–1973) French philosopher. *Reflections on America* (1958), ch. 3

42 I recognize that I am made up of several persons and that the person that at the moment has the upper hand will inevitably give place to another. But which is the real one? All of them or none?

W. Somerset Maugham (1874–1965) British novelist, short-story writer, and dramatist. *Of Human Bondage* (1915)

43 A little Consideration, a little Thought for Others, makes all the difference.

A.A. Milne (1882–1956) British children's author. Said by Eeyore after Pooh sat on a thistle. *Winnie-the-Pooh* (1926)

44 Too many lives are needed to make just one.

Eugenio Montale (1896–1981) Italian poet. 'Summer', *Le Occasioni* (1939)

45 The first thing is character...before money or anything else. Money cannot buy it...because a man I do not trust could not get money from me on all the bonds in Christendom.

J.P. Morgan (1837–1913) US financier. Statement to US Congressional banking committee (1912)

46 You've got to learn to survive a defeat. That's when you develop character.

Richard Milhous Nixon (1913–94) US president. *Dallas Times-Herald* (10 December 1978)

47 It is with narrow-souled people as with narrow-necked bottles: the less they have in them, the more noise they make in pouring it out.

Alexander Pope (1688–1744) English poet. *Thoughts on Various Subjects* (1741)

48 While animals survive by adjusting themselves to their background, man survives by adjusting his background to himself.

Ayn Rand (1905–82) US writer. *For the New Intellectual* (1961)

49 A woman is like a tea bag—only in hot water do you realize how strong she is.

Nancy Reagan (b. 1921) US actor and former first lady. *Observer* (March 1981)

50 You can tell a lot about a fellow's character by his way of eating jelly beans.

Ronald Reagan (b. 1911) US former president and actor. Quoted in *New York Times* (15 January 1981)

51 A radical is a man with both feet firmly planted in the air.

Franklin D. Roosevelt (1882–1945) US president. Radio broadcast (26 October 1939)

52 How is a legend different from a brand? An alternative spelling of 'legend' is g-u-t-s.

Harriet Rubin (b. 1952) US author. 'We Won't See Great Leaders Until We See Great Women Leaders. As Role Models, Men Are Going Flat', *Fast Company* (2000)

53 Children with Hyacinth's temperament don't know better as they grow older; they merely know more.

H.H. Munro (Saki) (1870–1916) British short-story writer. 'Hyacinth', *The Toys of Peace* (1919)

54 He looked like the kind of a guy that wouldn't talk to you much unless he wanted something off you. He had a lousy personality.

J.D. Salinger (b. 1919) US novelist. *The Catcher in the Rye* (1951), ch. 11

55 Character is the basis of happiness and happiness the sanction of character.

George Santayana (1863–1952) US philosopher, novelist, and poet. 'Reason in Common Sense', *The Life of Reason* (1906), ch. 9

56 A certain person may have, as you say, a wonderful presence: I do not know. What I do know is that he has a perfectly delightful absence.

Idries Shah (1924–96) British writer. 'Presence and Absence', *Reflections* (1968)

57 Give me that man
That is not passion's slave, and I will wear him
In my heart's core, ay, in my heart of heart,
As I do thee.
William Shakespeare (1564–1616) English poet and
playwright. *Hamlet* (1601), Act 3, Scene 2, l. 76–79

58 The analysis of character is the highest human
entertainment.
Isaac Bashevis Singer (1904–91) US novelist and short-story
writer. *New York Times* (26 November 1978)

59 Never cheat, but do not be soft. It is a hard
world. Be harder. But, and this is the test, at
the same time, obviously, a good fellow.
Gerald Sparrow (1903–88) British business executive and
writer. *How to Become a Millionaire* (1960)

60 A man with so-called character is often a
simple piece of mechanism; he has often only
one point of view for the extremely
complicated relationships of life.
J. August Strindberg (1849–1912) Swedish playwright and
novelist. 1886. *The Son of a Servant* (Claud Field, tr.; 1913)

61 If a man's character is to be abused, say what
you will, there's nobody like a relation to do
the business.
William Makepeace Thackeray (1811–63) British novelist.
Vanity Fair (1847), ch. 19

62 I'm not hard—I'm frightfully soft. But I will not
be hounded.
Margaret Thatcher (b. 1925) British former prime minister.
Daily Mail (1972)

63 Don't be afraid to be unique or speak your
mind because that's what makes you different
from everyone else.
Dave Thomas (1932–2002) US founder of Wendy's. 'Dave
Thomas Serves Up Advice for Graduates of All Ages', *USA
Today* (2000)

64 The depths and strength of a human character
are defined by its moral reserves. People
reveal themselves completely only when they
are thrown out of the customary conditions of
their life, for only then do they have to fall
back on their reserves.
Leon Trotsky (1879–1940) Russian revolutionary leader and
Marxist theorist. 5 April 1935. *Diary in Exile* (1959)

65 I've got a virtually limitless supply of bullshit.
Ted Turner (b. 1938) US founder of Turner Broadcasting
Systems. Interview, *Playboy* (1978)

66 To arrive at a just estimate of a renowned
man's character one must judge it by the
standards of his time, not ours.
Mark Twain (1835–1910) US writer. *Joan of Arc* (1896),
Preface

67 He is a man of brick. As if he was born as a
baby literally of clay and decades of exposure
have baked him to the color and hardness of
brick.
John Updike (b. 1932) US novelist and critic. *Rabbit, Run*
(1960)

68 The best index to a person's character is (a)
how he treats people who can't do him any
good, and (b) how he treats people who can't
fight back.
Abigail Van Buren (b. 1918) US advice consultant. 'Dear
Abby', syndicated newspaper column (16 May 1974)

69 I think the atmosphere of imminent doom in
which we lived during my formative years led
to a lifelong sense of panic and anxiety.
Lillian Vernon (b. 1927) US entrepreneur and CEO of Lillian
Vernon Corporation. *An Eye For Winners* (1996)

70 I'm very neat. I like to know where things are.
I think people have a tendency to want to be
neat.
Lillian Vernon (b. 1927) US entrepreneur and CEO of Lillian
Vernon Corporation. 'For Lillian Vernon, a Career Made to
Order', *Washington Post* (Megan Rosenfeld; 2000)

71 I don't think I'll ever run out of anything.
Lillian Vernon (b. 1927) US entrepreneur and CEO of Lillian
Vernon Corporation. 'For Lillian Vernon, a Career Made to
Order', *Washington Post* (Megan Rosenfeld; 2000)

72 Have you no sense of decency, sir? At long
last, have you left no sense of decency?
Joseph N. Welch (1890–1960) US lawyer. 1954. Said to
Senator Joseph McCarthy at the Army-McCarthy hearings in
1954. Quoted in *Mesa Tribune* (1999)

73 It is only the superficial qualities that last.
Man's deeper nature is soon found out.
Oscar Wilde (1854–1900) Irish writer and wit. Said by Cecily.
The Importance of Being Earnest (1895), Act 3

74 If you will think about what you ought to do
for other people, your character will take care
of itself. Character is a by-product, and any
man who devotes himself to its cultivation in
his own case will become a selfish prig.
Woodrow Wilson (1856–1924) US president. Speech,
Pittsburgh, Pennsylvania (24 October 1914)

75 As a rule, from what I've observed, the
American captain of industry doesn't do
anything out of business hours. When he has
put the cat out and locked up the office for the
night, he just relapses into a state of coma
from which he emerges only to start being a
captain of industry again.
P.G. Wodehouse (1881–1975) US writer and humorist.
'Leave it to Jeeves', *My Man Jeeves* (1919)

CHOICE

1 Once the *what* is decided the *how* always
follows. We must not make the *how* an excuse
for not facing and accepting the *what*.
Pearl S. Buck (1892–1973) US writer. *To My Daughters with
Love* (1967)

2 It is your own conviction which compels you;
that is, choice compels choice.
Epictetus (?55—?135) Greek philosopher. Attrib.

3 Any color you like as long as it's black.
Henry Ford (1863–1947) US industrialist, car manufacturer,
and founder of Ford Motor Company. Slogan advertising the

mass-produced Model-T Ford. Attrib. *Ford* (Allan Nevins; 1954), vol. 2, ch. 15

4 No choice among stinking fish.

Thomas Fuller (1654–1734) English physician and writer. *Gnomologia* (1732)

5 Business is often about killing your favourite children to allow others to succeed.

John Harvey-Jones (b. 1924) British management adviser, author, and former chairman of ICI. 'Troubleshooter', BBC TV series (1990)

6 From a narrow either/or society with a limited range of personal choices, we are exploding into a free-wheeling multiple option society.

John Naisbitt (b. ?1929) US business executive and author. *Megatrends* (1982)

7 Commerce is the agency by which the power of choice is obtained.

John Ruskin (1819–1900) British art critic and writer. *Munera Pulveris* (1872)

8 Even children learn in growing up that 'both' is not an admissible answer to a choice of 'which one'?

Paul Samuelson (b. 1915) US economist and winner of the 1970 Nobel Prize in Economics. Attrib.

9 Things are in their essence what we choose to make them.

Oscar Wilde (1854–1900) Irish writer and wit. *De Profundis* (1905)

CIVILISATION

1 The market, whether stock, bond or super, is a barometer of civilization.

Jason Alexander (b. 1959) US actor and director. *Philosophy for Investors* (1979)

2 If civilization has risen from the Stone Age, it can rise again from the Wastepaper Age.

Jacques Barzun (b. 1907) US educator, historian, and writer. *The House of Intellect* (1959)

3 Wealth may not produce civilization, but civilization produces money.

Henry Ward Beecher (1813–87) US clergyman and reformer. *Proverbs from Plymouth Pulpit* (1887)

4 Upon the sacredness of property civilization itself depends—the right of the laborer to his hundred dollars in the savings bank, and equally the legal right of the millionaire to his millions.

Andrew Carnegie (1835–1919) US industrialist and philanthropist. 'Wealth', *North American Review* (June 1889)

5 A good civilisation spreads over us freely like a tree, varying and yielding because it is alive. A bad civilisation stands up and sticks out above us like an umbrella—artificial, mathematical in shape; not merely universal, but uniform.

G.K. Chesterton (1874–1936) British novelist, poet, and critic. 'Cheese', *Alarms and Discursions* (1910)

6 What will be more important in the 21st century—our differences or our common humanity?

Bill Clinton (b. 1946) US former president. Referring to problems of global terrorism after 11 September 2001. Speech (December 2001)

7 Another existence swallowed up in the fearful rush of what is called civilization, but is very like chaos.

Marceline-Félicité-Josèphe Desbordes-Valmore (1786–1859) French actor and poet. 26 March 1854. Letter to her niece, Camille. *Memoirs of Madame Debordes-Valmore* (1872)

8 Increased means and increased leisure are the two civilizers of man.

Benjamin Disraeli (1804–81) British prime minister and novelist. Speech to the Conservatives of Manchester (3 April 1872)

9 Everything's so repressive now—it's the No generation.

Michael Douglas (b. 1944) US actor. Quoted in *Independent on Sunday* (5 April 1992)

10 Mechanics, not microbes, are the menace to civilization.

Norman Douglas (1868–1952) British novelist and essayist. *The Norman Douglas Limerick Book* (1965), Introduction

11 The true test of civilization is...the kind of men the country turns out.

Ralph Waldo Emerson (1803–82) US essayist, lecturer, and poet. *Society and Solitude* (1870)

12 Bare-faced covetousness was the moving spirit of civilization from its first dawn to the present day; wealth, and again wealth, and for the third time wealth; wealth, not of society, but of the puny individual, was its only and final aim.

Friedrich Engels (1820–95) German social philosopher and political economist. *The Origin of the Family* (1885)

13 The civilized man is a larger mind but a more imperfect nature than the savage.

Margaret Fuller (1810–50) US writer and social reformer. *Summer on the Lakes* (1844)

14 I think it would be an excellent idea.

Mahatma Gandhi (1869–1948) Indian nationalist leader and philosopher. Said when asked what he thought of Western civilisation. Attrib.

15 The meek shall inherit the earth but not the mineral rights.

J. Paul Getty (1892–1976) US entrepreneur, oil industry executive, and financier. Quoted in *BusinessWeek* (1986)

16 In a state of nature, the weakest go to the wall; in a state of over-refinement, both the weak and the strong go to the gutter.

Elbert Hubbard (1856–1915) US humorist. *The Philistine* (1895–1915)

17 A nation advances in civilisation by increasing in wealth and population, and by multiplying the accessories and paraphernalia of life.

William Ralph Inge (1860–1954) British prelate and writer. 'Our Present Discontents', *Outspoken Essays: First Series* (1919)

18 Labor is the foundation of all, and those that labor are the Caryatides that support the structure and glittering dome of civilization and progress.
Robert Green Ingersoll (1833–99) US lawyer and writer. *How to Reform Mankind* (1896)

19 The true civilization is where every man gives to every other every right that he claims for himself.
Robert Green Ingersoll (1833–99) US lawyer and writer. Interview, *Washington Post* (14 November 1880)

20 Commerce is the great civilizer. We exchange ideas when we exchange fabrics.
Robert Green Ingersoll (1833–99) US lawyer and writer. Said to Indianapolis clergy. Attrib.

21 Superdevelopment, which consists in an excessive availability of every kind of material goods for the benefit of certain social groups, easily makes people slaves of 'possession' and of immediate gratification.
John Paul II (b. 1920) Polish pontiff. *Solicitudo rei socialis* (1988)

22 A decent provision for the poor is the true test of civilization.
Samuel Johnson (1709–84) British poet, lexicographer, essayist, and critic. 1770. Quoted in *The Life of Samuel Johnson* (James Boswell; 1791)

23 In civilised society, personal merit will not serve you so much as money will. Sir, you may make the experiment. Go into the street, and give one man a lecture on morality, and another a shilling, and see which will respect you the most.
Samuel Johnson (1709–84) British poet, lexicographer, essayist, and critic. 20 July 1763. Quoted in *The Life of Samuel Johnson* (James Boswell; 1791)

24 Ours is not so much an age of vulgarity as of vulgarization; everything is tampered with or touched up, or adulterated or watered down, in an effort to make it palatable, in an effort to make it pay.
Louis Kronenberger (1904–80) US writer. 'The Spirit of the Age', *Company Manners* (1954)

25 Avarice and luxury, those evils which have been the ruin of every great state.
Livy (59 BC–AD 17) Roman historian. *History of Rome* (26 BC–AD 15)

26 Private property being individualism, and its abolition being socialism, the two are correlative and must yield to each other just as rapidly as experience and necessity dictate. Civilization is a growth both ways—an intensification of private property in certain ways, an abolition of it in others.
Henry Demarest Lloyd (1847–1903) US journalist and reformer. *Man the Social Creator* (1906)

27 The earth we abuse and the living things we kill will, in the end, take their revenge; for in exploiting their presence we are diminishing our future.
Marya Mannes (1904–90) US essayist and journalist. *More in Anger* (1958)

28 We have in fact passed beyond that stage of human organization in which effective communication and collaboration were secured by established routines of relationship.
Elton Mayo (1880–1949) US psychologist. *The Social Problems of an Industrial Civilization* (1945)

29 Civilization has developed executive powers far beyond its understanding.
Maude Meagher (1895–1977) US writer. *Fantastic Traveler* (1931)

30 Civilization is the progress towards a society of privacy...the process of setting man free from men.
Ayn Rand (1905–82) US writer. *The Fountainhead* (1943)

31 Out of this modern civilization economic royalists have carved new dynasties.
Franklin D. Roosevelt (1882–1945) US president. Speech accepting re-nomination for a second presidential term, Philadelphia (27 June 1936)

32 To be able to fill leisure intelligently is the last product of civilization.
Bertrand Russell (1872–1970) British philosopher and writer. *The Conquest of Happiness* (1930)

33 Money, as a physical medium of exchange, has made a diversified civilisation possible.
Josiah Stamp (1880–1941) British economist. *The Money Illusion* (Irving Fisher; 1928), Foreword

34 Civilization advances by extending the number of important operations which we can perform without thinking about them.
A.N. Whitehead (1861–1947) British philosopher and mathematician. *An Introduction to Mathematics* (1911)

35 Business underlies everything in our national life, including our spiritual life. Witness the fact that in the Lord's Prayer the first petition is for daily bread. No one can worship God or his neighbor on an empty stomach.
Woodrow Wilson (1856–1924) US president. 1912. Quoted in *Phoenix Home and Garden* (1999)

36 A few suits of clothes, some money in the bank, and a new kind of fear constitute the main differences between the average American today and the hairy men with clubs who accompanied Attila to the city of Rome.
Philip Gordon Wylie (1902–71) US writer. *Generation of Vipers* (1942)

37 A great invention of human civilisation.
Xu Jiatun (b. 1916) Chinese politician who defected to the United States after the Tiananmen Square massacre. 1988. Referring to capitalism. Quoted in *Wen Wei Po* (Hong Kong) (22 March 1988)

COMMON SENSE

1 Common sense is part of the home-made ideology of those...deprived of learning, of those...kept ignorant...common sense can never teach itself, can never advance beyond its own limits.

John Berger (b. 1926) British novelist, essayist, and art critic. *A Fortunate Man* (1967)

2 Common sense (which, in truth, is very uncommon) is the best sense I know of.
Lord Chesterfield (1694–1773) English statesman, orator, and letter writer. Letter (27 September 1748)

3 Common sense is the best distributed commodity in the world, for every man is convinced that he is well supplied with it.
René Descartes (1596–1650) French philosopher and mathemetician. *Le Discours de la méthode* (1637), pt 1

4 Common sense is the collection of prejudices acquired by age eighteen.
Albert Einstein (1879–1955) US physicist. Quoted in *Scientific American* (February 1976)

5 Nothing astonishes men so much as common sense and plain dealing.
Ralph Waldo Emerson (1803–82) US essayist, lecturer, and poet. 'Art', *Essays: First Series* (1841)

6 Common sense is a very tricky instrument; it is as deceptive as it is indispensable.
Susanne K. Langer (1895–1985) US philosopher. *Philosophical Studies* (1962)

7 Common-sense knowledge is prompt, categorical, and inexact.
Susanne K. Langer (1895–1985) US philosopher. *Philosophy in a New Key* (1942)

8 We seldom attribute common sense except to those who agree with us.
François La Rochefoucauld (1613–80) French epigrammatist. *Reflections: or, Sentences and Moral Maxims* (1665)

9 Success is more a function of consistent common sense than it is of genius.
An Wang (1920–90) US entrepreneur, business executive, electrical engineer, and founder of Wang Laboratories. *Boston Magazine* (December 1986)

COMMUNICATION

1 To ask the hard question is simple.
W.H. Auden (1907–73) US poet. 'Poem' (1933)

2 One of the indispensable functions of informal organizations...is that of communication.
Chester Barnard (1886–1961) US business executive and management theorist. *Organization and Management* (1948)

3 If we could get them moving in roughly the same direction, we would be unstoppable.
Percy Barnevik (b. 1941) Swedish former CEO of ABB. Referring to the problem of communicating with large numbers of employees. *Harvard Business Review* (March/April 1991)

4 A quotation is what a speaker wants to say, unlike a soundbite which is all that an interviewer allows you to say.
Tony Benn (b. 1925) British politician. Letter (1996)

5 Reflective back talk increases a leader's ability to make good decisions.
Warren Bennis (b. 1925) US educator and writer. *On Becoming a Leader* (1989)

6 Communication is best achieved through simple planning and control...Most conversations...drift along; in business, this is wasteful; as a manager...seek communication rather than chatter.
Gerald M. Blair (b. 1959) US writer. *Conversation as Communication* (2000)

7 My principal inspiration comes from the employees...I try to go to the field on a weekly basis...I come back with fresh ideas and a clearer understanding of our needs...These people...set the pace of what we can do by clearly understanding the strategy and overall goals of the company.
Michel Bon (b. 1943) French former CEO of France Télécom. Interview, *Strategy + Business* (April–June 1999)

8 Society cannot share a common communication system so long as it is split into warring factions.
Bertolt Brecht (1898–1956) German playwright and poet. 'A Short Organum for the Theatre' (1949)

9 I say what I mean, you hear what I say. That is the end of it.
Barbara Cassani (b. 1960) US former CEO of Go. *Management Today* (August 1999)

10 Words are so futile, so feeble.
Charlie Chaplin (1889–1977) US actor and producer. Acadamy Awards speech (1972)

11 When you have nothing to say, say nothing.
Charles Caleb Colton (?1780–1832) British clergyman and writer. *Lacon* (1820–22), vol. 1

12 Let us write as if we were writing to a skeptical aunt. All the rest of the world can look over our aunt's shoulder.
Fairfax Cone (1903–77) US advertising executive. *Christian Science Monitor* (1963)

13 Avoid fight or flight, talk through differences.
Stephen Covey (b. 1932) US writer and psychologist. *Thirty Methods of Influence* (1991)

14 Just as 'location, location, location' defines value in real estate, in business today it's connectivity that equals competitiveness.
Mary J. Cronin (b. 1947) US business author. *Doing More Business on the Internet* (1995)

15 There is mathematics, there are computers, and there are pictures, but the bulk of our communicated thinking is done with language.
Edward de Bono (b. 1933) British creative-thinking theorist, educator, and writer. 'Message for Today', *www.edwdebono.com* (4 September 2000)

16 If it's important enough, it will be followed up with a more formal approach, but the starting point will always be looking into people's eyes and telling them the way it is.
Ron Dennis (b. 1949) British entrepreneur and Formula 1

motor racing team owner. Quoted in *The Adventure Capitalists* (Jeff Grout and Lynne Curry; 1998)

17 Electronic communication, as fast and efficient as it has become, does not automatically lead to better communication.
Dan Dimancescu (b. 1943) US consultant and writer. *World-class New Product Development* (co-written with Kemp Dwenger; 1996)

18 At office-managerial level...you do not read more than the first two sentences of any given report. You believe that anything which cannot be put into two sentences is not worth attending to.
Penelope Fitzgerald (1916–2000) British novelist and biographer. 'The Axe', *The Means of Escape* (2000)

19 Communication, whether it be in the dance, or whether it be in the spoken word, is now the great need of the world.
Martha Graham (1894–1991) US dancer and choreographer. *Notebooks of Martha Graham* (1973)

20 Even the frankest and bravest of subordinates do not talk with their boss the same way they talk with colleagues.
Robert Greenleaf (1904–90) US director of Management Research for AT&T and author. *Servant Leadership: A Journey into the Nature of Legitimate Power and Greatness* (1977)

21 Many attempts to communicate are nullified by saying too much.
Robert Greenleaf (1904–90) US director of Management Research for AT&T and author. *Servant Leadership: A Journey into the Nature of Legitimate Power and Greatness* (1977)

22 We have needed to define ourselves by reclaiming the words that define us. They have used language as weapons. When we open ourselves to what they say and how they say it, our narrow prejudices evaporate and we are nourished and armed.
Selma James (b. 1951) US activist and writer. *The Ladies and the Mammies: Jane Austen and Jean Rhys* (1983)

23 Through the picture I see reality; through the word I understand it.
Peter Kindersley (b. 1941) British publisher, co-founder of Dorling-Kindersley. 1975. Referring to the importance of both words and images in communication and publishing. Quoted in *Goldfinger* (Robert Heller; 1998)

24 The more you talk and listen to a bad character the more you lose your dislike for him.
Henry Lawson (1867–1922) Australian poet and short-story writer. *Joe Wilson and His Mates* (1902)

25 If figures of speech based on sports and fornication were suddenly banned, American corporate communication would be reduced to pure mathematics.
Jay McInerney (b. 1955) US author. *Brightness Falls* (1992)

26 It is ironic but true that in this era of electronic communications, personal interaction is becoming more important than ever.

Regis McKenna (b. 1939) US marketing entrepreneur and chairman of The McKenna Group. Quoted in *Thriving on Chaos* (Tom Peters; 1987)

27 The feedback loop, connecting company and customer, is central to the operating definition of a truly market-driven company.
Regis McKenna (b. 1939) US marketing entrepreneur and chairman of the McKenna Group. *Relationship Marketing* (1991)

28 Propaganda ends where dialogue begins.
Marshall McLuhan (1911–1980) Canadian sociologist and author. *Understanding Media* (1964)

29 Chief executives repeatedly fail to recognize that for communication to be effective, it must be two-way.
Robert N. McMurry US management and personnel specialist. 'Clear Communication for Chief Executives', *Harvard Business Review* (1965)

30 Just as a pit crew monitors a driver by computer, laptops keep us in constant touch with our representatives.
Doug Nelson (b. 1944) US regional vice-president of Altria Group Inc. (formerly Philip Morris). 'The Mavericks', *Fortune* (June 1995)

31 It used to be you needed lots of meetings between middle managers to exchange information that is now instantly available to all employees via an intranet.
Masahiro Noilia (b. 1939) Japanese business executive. *Wired Asia* (June 2000)

32 If an organization is to work effectively, the communication should be through the most effective channel regardless of the organization chart.
Tom Peters (b. 1942) US management consultant and author. *In Search of Excellence: Lessons from America's Best-Run Companies* (co-written with Robert H. Waterman Jr; 1988)

33 Today, communication itself is the problem. We have become the world's first overcommunicated society. Each year we send more and receive less.
Al Ries (b. 1926) US advertising executive and chairman of Trout & Ries Advertising, Inc. *Positioning: The Battle for Your Mind* (co-written with Jack Trout; 1980)

34 By creating conversation, we let our customers spread our message by word of mouth.
Anita Roddick (b. 1942) British entrepreneur and founder of The Body Shop. *Body and Soul* (co-written with Russell Miller; 1991)

35 In companies whose wealth is intellectual capital, networks, rather than hierarchies, are the right organizational design.
Thomas A. Stewart (b. 1948) US journalist and author. *Intellectual Capital* (1997)

36 Listen to everyone in your company and figure out ways to get them talking.
Sam M. Walton (1918–92) US entrepreneur and founder of Wal-Mart, Inc. *Made in America* (co-written with John Huey; 1992)

37 Real communication takes countless hours of eyeball to eyeball, back and forth...It is human beings coming to see and accept things through a constant interactive process aimed at consensus.
Jack Welch (b. 1935) US former chairman and CEO of General Electric. *Harvard Business Review* (September–October 1989)

38 There is a commodity in human experience. If it has happened to one person, it has happened to thousands of others.
Oprah Winfrey (b. 1954) US talk show host, actor, and business executive. *Time* (August 1988)

39 One man saying that everything is wrong can command coast-to-coast attention in living colour, a power not given to an absolute monarch a century ago.
Walter Wriston (b. 1919) US banker. *Risk and Other Four Letter Words* (1986)

COMMUNISM AND SOCIALISM

1 Socialism substitutes for individual energy the energy of the government...for human personality the blind, mechanical power of the State.
Benjamin Nathan Cardozo (1870–1938) US jurist and writer. Commencement oration, Columbia College, New York (1889)

2 The strike is the weapon of the oppressed, of men capable of appreciating justice and having the courage to resist wrong and contend for principle.
Eugene V. Debs (1855–1926) US politician and trade union leader. 1888. Speaking during the strike of engineers and firefighters on the Chicago, Burlington, and Quincy Rail Line. Quoted in *The Arizona Republic* (2000)

3 In moving towards the market we are moving not away from socialism, but towards a fuller realisation of society's capabilities.
Mikhail Gorbachev (b. 1931) Russian former president. Speech, 28th Congress of the Soviet Communist Party (3 July 1990)

4 The market came with the dawn of civilisation and is not the invention of capitalism. If the market leads to the improvement of people's daily lives, then there is no contradiction with socialism.
Mikhail Gorbachev (b. 1931) Russian former president. Responding to allegations by conservative critics that his perestroika policies were an attempt to restore capitalism in the Soviet Union. Speech, Moscow (June 1990)

5 It would be very superficial to think that the Soviet Union can be bought for dollars.
Mikhail Gorbachev (b. 1931) Russian former president. *Guardian* (14 September 1990)

6 A community in which power, wealth and opportunity are in the hands of the many not the few...in which the enterprise of the market and the rigour of competition are joined with the forces of partnership and co-operation.
Labour Party, British political party. This new version of the Labour Party Constitution's Clause Four compares with the 1918 (revised 1928) original: 'To secure for workers...the full fruits of their industry and the most equitable distribution thereof that may be possible upon the basis of common ownership of the means of production, distribution, and exchange'. Clause Four, *Labour Party Constitution* (29 April 1995)

7 Accounting and control—that is *mainly* what is needed for the 'smooth working', for the proper functioning, of the first phase of communist society.
Vladimir Ilich Lenin (1870–1924) Russian revolutionary leader and political theorist. *The State and Revolution* (1924), ch. 5

8 To the ordinary working man, the sort you would meet in any pub on Saturday night, Socialism does not mean much more than better wages and shorter hours, and nobody bossing you about.
George Orwell (1903–50) British novelist, critic, and essayist. *The Road to Wigan Pier* (1937)

9 The most remarkable thing about socialist competition is that it creates a basic change in people's view of labour, since it changes the labour from a shameful and heavy burden into a matter of honour..., valour, and heroism.
Joseph Stalin (1879–1953) Soviet secretary-general. Speech (27 June 1930)

10 Socialism proposes no adequate substitute for the motive of enlightened selfishness that to-day is at the basis of all human labor and effort, enterprise and new activity.
William Howard Taft (1857–1930) US president. *Popular Government* (1913)

11 Marxism is above all a method of analysis.
Leon Trotsky (1879–1940) Russian revolutionary leader and Marxist theorist. *Permanent Revolution* (1928)

COMPETITION

1 Under increasing returns, and under very specific mathematical conditions, markets become unstable. One product, one company, can take a great deal of the market...Think of America Online, think of Microsoft's dominance...think of Java.
W. Brian Arthur (b. 1945) US economist. Interview, *Strategy + Business* (April–June 1998)

2 The largest profits go to those businesses which most devotedly follow a policy of insisting on a competitive advantage, no matter how small, for every product or service they market.
R.H. Beeby (b. ?1932) US president of Pepsi-Cola International. Quoted in *Offensive Marketing* (Hugh Davidson; 1987)

3 Removing the non-productive cancer that has spread through engineering and manufacturing will hurt, but it is the only way to survive competitors.

C. Gordon Bell (b. 1934) US inventor and computer pioneer. *Spectrum* (February 1989)

4 In a world driven by rapid changes in technology, empirical evidence indicates that the firms that prosper are far more likely to be those that face fierce rivalry in their home markets than the sheltered monopolists...the fear of being left behind is more likely to spur innovation than the security bred of stable market power.

Anne K. Bingaman (b. 1943) US lawyer. Speech, University of Kansas Law School (19 September 1996)

5 IBM was a leader in mainframes in the 1950s. Then Digital became the leader of the minicomputer revolution in the 1960s. The PC era launched new names—Dell and Compaq, Microsoft. In each case the leader of one phase failed to dominate the next phase.

Michael Bloomberg (b. 1942) US entrepreneur, business executive, and Mayor of New York. 'Terminal Velocity', *Wired* (David S. Bennahum; February 1999)

6 I believe that if you're going to take someone on, you might as well take on the biggest brand in the world.

Richard Branson (b. 1950) British entrepreneur, business executive, and founder of the Virgin Group. 'The Mavericks', *Fortune* (June 1995)

7 Most people who have been around as long as Coke have become quite fat. I believe they've got very vulnerable skin.

Richard Branson (b. 1950) British entrepreneur, business executive, and founder of the Virgin Group. 'The Mavericks', *Fortune* (June 1995)

8 Nothing focuses the mind better than the constant sight of a competitor who wants to wipe you off the map.

Wayne Calloway (1935–98) US CEO of Pepsico. *Fortune* (11 March 1991)

9 The price which society pays for the law of competition, like the price it pays for cheap comforts and luxuries, is also great; but the advantages of this law are also greater still, for it is to this law that we owe our wonderful material development, which brings improved conditions in its train.

Andrew Carnegie (1835–1919) US industrialist and philanthropist. 'Wealth', *North American Review* (June 1889)

10 Whether the law be benign or not, we must say of it...It is here; we cannot evade it; no substitutes for it have been found; and while the law may be sometimes hard for the individual, it is best for the race, because it insures the survival of the fittest in every department.

Andrew Carnegie (1835–1919) US industrialist and philanthropist. On 'the law of competition'. 'Wealth', *North American Review* (June 1889)

11 There are two ways to compete—in stable conditions, you plan and you compete on scale. In unstable times, you live by your wits.

Dick Cavanagh (b. 1946) US business executive. *The Winning Performance* (1989)

12 Thou shalt not covet, but tradition Approves all forms of competition.

Arthur Hugh Clough (1819–61) British poet. 'The Latest Decalogue' (1862), ll. 19–20

13 The truth is if you don't say you can do a job, someone else in the world will, and you'll be left behind.

Richard D'Aveni (b. 1950) US strategist. 'The Mavericks', *Fortune* (June 1995)

14 This is not an age of castles, moats, and armour where people can sustain a competitive advantage for very long.

Richard D'Aveni (b. 1950) US strategist. 'The Mavericks', *Fortune* (June 1995)

15 Surpetition.

Edward de Bono (b. 1933) British creative-thinking theorist, educator, and writer. Referring to an extreme form of competition. Quoted in *In Search of European Excellence* (Robert Heller; 1997)

16 Again and again in business history, an unknown competitor comes from nowhere and in a few short years overtakes the established leaders without apparently even breathing hard.

Peter F. Drucker (b. 1909) US management consultant and academic. *Harvard Business Review* (January/February 1995)

17 The domestic appliance industry is dominated by the multinational companies which all know what their rivals are doing and which have no interest in upsetting the status quo.

James Dyson (b. 1947) British entrepreneur. *Financial Times* (January 1997)

18 You can't win without being completely different. When everyone else says we are crazy, I say, gee we really must be on to something.

Larry D. Ellison (b. 1945) US CEO of Oracle Corporation. *Forbes* (October 2000)

19 A zealous sense of mission is only possible where there is opposition to it.

D.W. Ewing (b. 1923) US writer and editor of *Harvard Business Review*. 'Tension Can Be an Asset', *Harvard Business Review* (September/October 1964)

20 To win against opponents, companies need strategies for three related tasks: outwitting, outmaneuvering, and outperforming competitors.

Liam Fahey (b. 1951) British writer and consultant. *Competitors* (1999)

21 Competition rarely puts anyone out of business—a man usually puts himself out of business either by not making a good article or by wrong methods in sales or finance.

Harvey Firestone (1868–1938) US founder of Firestone Tire and Rubber. *Men and Rubber* (co-written with Samuel Crowther; 1926)

22 The bigger they come the harder they fall.

Bob Fitzsimmons (?1862–1917) New Zealand boxer. Said before a fight. Remark (June 1899)

23 I found that competition was supposed to be a menace and that a good manager circumvented his competitors by getting a monopoly by artificial means.

Henry Ford (1863–1947) US industrialist, car manufacturer, and founder of Ford Motor Company. *My Life and Work* (co-written with Samuel Crowther; 1922)

24 Perfect competition is a theoretical concept like the Euclidean line, which has no width and no depth. Just as we've never seen that line there has never been truly free enterprise.

Milton Friedman (b. 1912) US economist and winner of the 1976 Nobel Prize in Economics. *There's No Such Thing as a Free Lunch* (1975), Introduction

25 Oil is like a wild animal. Whoever captures it has it.

J. Paul Getty (1892–1976) US entrepreneur, oil industry executive, and financier. Quoted in *The Great Getty* (Robert Lenzner; 1985)

26 It's the classic case of being at the party too early. Nobody was there yet and nobody had had a drink. By the time we got there, the party was raging.

Mark Getty (b. ?1978) US Internet entrepreneur. Referring to early attempts to market digital images. *Sunday Times* (October 2000)

27 Competition is warfare. Mostly it is played by prescribed rules—there is a sort of Geneva Convention for competition—but it's thorough and often brutal.

Andrew S. Grove (b. 1936) US entrepreneur, author, and chairman of Intel Corporation. *New Yorker* (October 1997)

28 In a garage somewhere, an entrepreneur is forging a bullet with your company's name on it.

Gary Hamel (b. 1954) US academic, business writer, and consultant. *Digital Britain* (January 2000)

29 Assessing the current tactical advantages of known competitors will not help you understand the resolution, stamina, and inventiveness of potential competitors.

Gary Hamel (b. 1954) US academic, business writer, and consultant. *Harvard Business Review* (1989)

30 Too many companies are expending enormous energy simply to reproduce the cost and quality advantages that global competitors already have.

Gary Hamel (b. 1954) US academic, business writer, and consultant. *Harvard Business Review* (1989)

31 We are ruined by Chinese cheap labour.

Bret Harte (1836–1902) US author. *Plain Language from Truthful James* (1870)

32 Business is becoming more and more akin to intellectual sumo wrestling.

John Harvey-Jones (b. 1924) British management adviser, author, and former chairman of ICI. *All Together Now* (1994)

33 The idea is to grind the opposition into the ground. That's on and off the table.

Barry Hearn (b. 1948) British sports promoter. Referring to his work as a snooker promoter. *Independent* (15 April 1989)

34 Leveraging America's diversity will give employers a competitive advantage. We speak every language. We know every culture. And capitalizing on our diversity and immigration trends will position us to compete and win everywhere.

Alexis M. Herman (b. 1947) US politician. Labor Day address, New York (3 September 1999)

35 Men often compete with one another until the day they die; comradeship consists of rubbing shoulders jocularly with a competitor.

Edward Hoagland (b. 1932) US novelist, essayist, and naturalist. 'Heaven and Nature', *Harper's Magazine* (March 1988)

36 So far as power is concerned, does anyone believe the premiums of insurance companies are all almost uniform by accident?

Jimmy Hoffa (1913–?1975) US trade union leader. Interview, *Playboy* (December 1975)

37 We need to re-establish the blue water between ourselves and the competition.

Roger Holmes (b. 1960) British business executive. *Sunday Times* (September 2000)

38 We are a nation which has no illusions about the nature of international economic competition. It is never a race against one's economic past but only ever a fierce contest with present day economic realities.

John Winston Howard (b. 1939) Australian prime minister. Speech, World Economic Forum, Melbourne, Victoria, Australia (11 September 2000)

39 The Japanese are masters at making you peel the onion. You get through one layer and you are looking at another one just like it.

Lee Iacocca (b. 1924) US president of Ford Motor Company, chairman and CEO of Chrysler Corporation. Speech (January 1992)

40 In any competition an important element of grand strategy is to understand the strengths of the competitor. The more that Western companies understand what are the ingredients of the Japanese revolution in quality the more effective will be the Western response.

Joseph M. Juran (b. 1904) US business thinker. Paper presented at the 25th conference of the European Organisation for Quality Control, Paris, June 1981. 'Product Quality—A Prescription for the West', *www.juran.com* (2000)

41 Cheap labor is not going to be the way we compete in the United States. It's going to be brain power.

Rosabeth Moss Kanter (b. 1943) US management theorist, academic, and writer. Interview (1995)

42 We've created a solid niche—our main competition is the automobile. We're taking people away from Toyota and Ford.

Herb Kelleher (b. 1931) US businessman and founder of Southwest Airlines. *Time* (January 1993)

43 I feel sorry for those who live without competition...fat, dumb, and unhappy in cradle-to-grave security.
Donald M. Kendall (b. 1921) US CEO of Pepsico, Inc. Quoted in *How to Manage* (Ray Wild; 1995)

44 Forgive your enemies, but never forget their names.
John F. Kennedy (1917–63) US president. Attrib.

45 It's ridiculous to call this an industry—it's not. This is rat eat rat, dog eat dog.
Ray Kroc (1902–84) US founder of McDonald's. Quoted in *Big Mac* (Max Boas and Steve Chain; 1976)

46 What do you do when your competitor's drowning? Get a live hose and stick it in his mouth.
Ray Kroc (1902–84) US founder of McDonald's. *Wall Street Journal* (October 1997)

47 Never wrestle with a pig. You get dirty and only the pig enjoys himself.
Mark McCormack (1930–2003) US entrepreneur, founder and CEO of the International Management Group. *What You'll Never Learn on the Internet* (2000)

48 If we had just continued the way we were going, we would end up being nibbled to death.
David Michels (b. 1946) British CEO of Hilton Hotels. Referring to competition from smaller companies on the Internet. *Sunday Times* (May 2000)

49 Sustainable business must be built on recognition of fundamental economic laws. That must include an acknowledgment of competition, of its positive benefits and the severe penalties it can exact.
Mark Moody-Stuart (b. 1940) British chairman of Anglo American, and former chairman of Committee of Managing Directors Royal Dutch/Shell Group. Speech, St Paul's Cathedral, London. 'The Values of Sustainable Business in the Next Century' (12 July 1999)

50 You can't measure the value of being first.
Chris Moore (b. 1960) British marketing director of Domino's Pizza. *Marketing* (June 2000)

51 Competition as most of us have routinely thought of it is dead.
James F. Moore (b. 1948) US writer and business consultant. *The Death of Competition* (1997)

52 Atom-based companies are finding themselves competing increasingly with bit-based companies that have an organizational structure advantage—a fact of the new economy.
William (Walid) Mougayar, US consultant and management theorist. 'What you can learn from the portals', *Computerworld* (31 August 1998)

53 On the Internet...competitive advantage has shrunk to a few months. If they don't keep innovating, they'll be overtaken. They have to keep adding digital value, adding services, building their brand.
William (Walid) Mougayar, US consultant and management theorist. Interview, *UpsideToday* (1998)

54 I want to be at the table as a player when they move the pieces around in America.
Rupert Murdoch (b. 1931) US CEO of News Corporation. Quoted in *Murdoch* (William Shawcross; 1992)

55 A prosperous competitor is often less dangerous than a desparate one.
Barry J. Nalebuff, US author. *Co-opetition* (co-written with Adam M. Brandenburger; 1997)

56 There is no gap in the market unless you have sharp elbows.
Andrew Neil (b. 1949) British publisher and broadcaster. *Sunday Times* (September 2000)

57 These people ought to realise that we are taking them to the cleaners.
Andrew Neil (b. 1949) British publisher and broadcaster. Referring to a newspaper circulation war. *Sunday Times* (September 2000)

58 When the competition is moving at 200 miles an hour, every second you're in the pits matters a lot.
Doug Nelson (b. 1944) US regional vice-president of Altria Group Inc. (formerly Philip Morris). 'The Mavericks', *Fortune* (June 1995)

59 Don't look back, something might be gaining on you.
Leroy Paige (1906–82) US baseball player. Personal saying (1952)

60 The sovereign right of every listener in America to snap the switch and shut off his radio or to shift his dial from one station to another has been the greatest single factor in broadcasting's onward march.
William S. Paley (1901–90) US founder of Columbia Broadcasting Corporation. *Theatre Arts* (November 1943)

61 And then, if you're IBM's Akers, you continue to wonder why 50,000 competitors, most of them microscopic, are eating your lunch.
Tom Peters (b. 1942) US management consultant and author. *Liberation Management* (1992)

62 Competitive battles are Niche Inc. v. Niche Inc., not Master Inc. v. Master Inc.
Tom Peters (b. 1942) US management consultant and author. *Liberation Management* (1992)

63 Overall size is largely irrelevant for competitive advantage.
Michael Porter (b. 1947) US strategist. *The Economist* (1990)

64 Some people think that Japan's success is due to cartels and collaboration. It is not. In the industries in which Japan is internationally successful, it has many fiercely competitive local rivals.
Michael Porter (b. 1947) US strategist. *The Economist* (9 June 1990)

65 Complete freedom of competition is the safest, the most exacting, and, from the point of view of the nation and the state, the most profitable method of control of domestic and external trade.
François Quesnay (1694–1774) French political economist.

General Rules for the Economic Government of an Agricultural Kingdom (1757)

66 As you seek to change every procedure and job description to aid responsiveness, remember the bygone days when we whipped big competitors by being faster and fleeter of foot.
Ronald Reagan (b. 1911) US former president and actor. Quoted in *Thriving on Chaos* (Tom Peters; 1987)

67 It's like saying McDonald's can't serve chips with its burgers and asking it to give its secret recipe to Burger King.
Oliver Roll (b. 1966) British marketing executive. Referring to proposals to break up Microsoft. *Marketing* (July 2000)

68 We're eyeball to eyeball and I think the other fellow just blinked.
Dean Rusk (1909–94) US politician. Speech (October 1962)

69 Competition policy is intended to ensure a fair fight, not to punish winners or protect losers.
Carl Shapiro (b. 1955) US academic and author. *Information Rules* (co-written with Hal L. Varian; 1999)

70 Competition is the final price determinant and competitive prices may result in profits which force you to accept a rate of return less than you hoped for.
Alfred P. Sloan (1875–1966) US president of General Motors. *My Years with General Motors* (1964)

71 The goal of competitors is to prevail, not to preserve competition in the markets.
George Soros (b. 1930) US financier, entrepreneur, and philanthropist. *Atlantic Monthly* (January 1998)

72 Mobile voice communications competition is basically over; there is no real differentiator among competitors.
Keiji Tachikawa (b. 1939) Japanese IT executive. *Forbes* (May 2000)

73 Copycats are on the prowl at all times in all industries.
Michael Treacy, US author. *Discipline of Market Leaders* (1995)

74 There is no such thing as a man being too proud to fight.
Woodrow Wilson (1856–1924) US president. Speech (May 1915)

75 Tough is passé. Today, you're dealing with a variety of head game. That's where the cruelty is.
Abraham Zaleznik (b. 1924) US psychologist. *Fortune* (October 1993)

COMPUTERS

1 The search button on the browser no longer provides an objective search, but a commercial one.
Tim Berners-Lee (b. 1955) British computer scientist and founder of the World Wide Web. Referring to the commercialisation of the Internet. *Weaving the Web* (1999)

2 Many view the Internet merely as a sales channel and treat it as an add-on without fundamentally questioning their current business system.
Alex Birch, British consultant and author. *The Age of E-Tailing* (co-written with Phillip Gerbert and Dirk Schneider; 2000)

3 The one thing computers have done is let us make bigger mistakes. We have to be careful not to depend on our machines.
Michael Bloomberg (b. 1942) US entrepreneur, business executive, and Mayor of New York. Quoted in 'Terminal Velocity', *Wired* (David S. Bennahum; February 1999)

4 A modern computer hovers between the obsolescent and the non-existent.
Sydney Brenner (b. 1927) British scientist and winner of the 2002 Nobel Prize in Medicine. *Society* (January 1990)

5 Take Wrigley's Chewing Gum. I don't think the Internet is going to change how people chew gum.
Warren Buffett (b. 1930) US entrepreneur and financier. Interview *Fortune* (July 1998)

6 The Weightless World
Diane Coyle, British economist and journalist. Book title. Referring to an economy in which information is more important than physical products. *The Weightless World* (1997)

7 You must accept that if the computer is a tool, it is the job of the tool user to know what to use it for.
Peter F. Drucker (b. 1909) US management consultant and academic. Quoted in *Techno Vision* (C.B. Wang; 1994)

8 Computers are like bikinis. They save people a lot of guesswork.
Sam Ewing (1920–2001) US author. Quoted in *Sun* (25 May 1999)

9 What if computing were nearly free?
Bill Gates (b. 1955) US entrepreneur, chairman and CEO of Microsoft. Referring to the falling price of computing components. *The Road Ahead* (co-written with Nathan Myhrvold and Peter N. Rinearson; 1995)

10 While new PCs outship new TVs on a worldwide basis, we still have a long way to go before we win this 'war for eyeballs'.
Andrew S. Grove (b. 1936) US entrepreneur, author, and chairman of Intel Corporation. Speech (November 1986)

11 The PC is the LSD of the 90s.
Timothy Leary (1920–96) US psychologist. *Guardian* (June 1996)

12 A sort of cognitive equivalent of a condom—it's a layer of contraceptive rubber between the direct experience and the cognitive system.
Jonathan Miller (b. 1934) British theatre director and writer. Referring to reading from a computer screen. *Independent on Sunday* (January 1996)

13 The value of e-commerce is not in the e, but in the commerce.
Octavio Paz (1914–98) Mexican writer. Quoted in *Management Today* (June 2000)

14 Computers are useless. They can only give us answers.
Pablo Picasso (1881–1973) Spanish artist and sculptor. Quoted in *.con* (Gerry Griffin; 1999)

15 As an environment that can sustain economic life, the Web has given birth to entirely new species of start-ups and enterprises that could not have existed previously.
Evan Schwartz, US author and journalist. *Digital Darwinism* (1999)

16 I would say that hardware is the bone of the head, the skull. The semiconductor is the brain within the head. The software is the wisdom and data is the knowledge.
Masayoshi Son (b. 1943) Taiwanese CEO of Softbank Corporation. *Harvard Business Review* (January/February 1992)

17 The advanced economy could not run for thirty seconds without computers.
Alvin Toffler (b. 1928) US social commentator. *Powershift* (1990)

18 Even a partial shift towards the electronic office will be enough to trigger an eruption of social, psychological, and economic consequences.
Alvin Toffler (b. 1928) US social commentator. *The Third Wave* (1980)

19 A computer can tell you down to the dime what you've sold, but it can never tell you how much you could have sold.
Sam M. Walton (1918–92) US entrepreneur and founder of Wal-Mart, Inc. *Made in America* (co-written with John Huey; 1992)

CONFIDENCE

1 Some men are just as firmly convinced of what they think as others are of what they know.
Aristotle (384–322 BC) Greek philosopher and scientist. *Nicomachean Ethics* (4th century BC)

2 I've learned the perimeter of my circle of confidence.
Warren Buffett (b. 1930) US entrepreneur and financier. Quoted in *Treasury of Investment Wisdom* (Bernice Cohen; 1999)

3 Trust comes back to the character, behaviour, and values of the company. You only achieve trust and retain it if you behave in a way which inspires trust.
Dominic Cadbury (b. 1940) British business executive. Quoted in *The Winning Streak Mark II* (Walter Goldsmith and David Clutterbuck; 1997)

4 Confidence is that feeling by which the mind embarks on great and honourable courses with a sure hope and trust in itself.
Cicero (106–43 BC) Roman orator and statesman. *Rhetorical Invention* (1st century BC), bk 1

5 Danger breeds best on too much confidence.
Pierre Corneille (1606–84) French playwright. *Le Cid* (1636)

6 I am very careful about bringing people into my confidence. I want to see the color of their eyes.
E. Gerald Corrigan (b. 1941) US investment banker and managing director of Goldman Sachs. Referring to

becoming president of the Federal Reserve Bank in Minneapolis. *New York Times* (30 December 1984)

7 Ignorance more frequently begets confidence than does knowledge: it is those who know little, and not those who know much, who so positively assert that this or that problem will never be solved by science.
Charles Darwin (1809–82) British scientist and evolutionary theorist. *The Descent of Man* (1871)

8 Confidence as an outgoing act is directness and courage in meeting the facts of life, trusting them to bring instruction and support to a developing self.
John Dewey (1859–1952) US philosopher and educational theorist. *Human Nature and Conduct* (1922)

9 I see before me the statue of a celebrated minister, who said that confidence was a plant of slow growth. But I believe, however gradual may be the growth of confidence, that of credit requires still more time to arrive at maturity.
Benjamin Disraeli (1804–81) British prime minister and novelist. Speech (9 November 1867)

10 I always went into an area that was in last place, with a philosophy, 'you can't fall off the floor'.
Michael Eisner (b. 1942) US chairman and CEO of the Disney Corporation. Speech (June 1994)

11 Self-trust is the essence of heroism.
Ralph Waldo Emerson (1803–82) US essayist, lecturer, and poet. 'Heroism', *Essays: First Series* (1841)

12 Speak what you think to-day in words as hard as cannon-balls and to-morrow speak what to-morrow thinks in hard words again, though it contradict every thing you said to-day
Ralph Waldo Emerson (1803–82) US essayist, lecturer, and poet. 'Self-Reliance', *Essays: First Series* (1841)

13 The greatest success is confidence.
Ralph Waldo Emerson (1803–82) US essayist, lecturer, and poet. 'Behavior', *The Conduct of Life* (1860)

14 We should do everything both cautiously and confidently at the same time.
Epictetus (?55—?135) Greek philosopher. *Discourses* (2nd century AD), bk 2

15 Whether you believe you can, or whether you believe you can't, you're absolutely right.
Henry Ford (1863–1947) US industrialist, car manufacturer, and founder of Ford Motor Company. Attrib.

16 We often take a minimal level of trust and honesty for granted and forget that they pervade everyday economic life and are crucial to its smooth functioning.
Francis Fukuyama (b. 1952) US economist and writer. *Trust: The Social Virtues and the Creation of Prosperity* (1995)

17 The superior confidence which people repose in the tall man is well merited. Being tall, he is more visible than other men and being more visible, he is much more closely watched.
J.K. Galbraith (b. 1908) US economist and diplomat. *The Scotch* (1964)

18 Attempt easy tasks as if they were difficult, and difficult as if they were easy: in the one case that confidence may not fall asleep, in the other that it may not be dismayed.

Baltasar Gracián (1601–58) Spanish writer and priest. *The Art of Worldly Wisdom* (1647)

19 Building up the confidence of an organisation can sometimes lead to feelings of arrogance and superiority towards those on whom you are actually dependent for making a living.

John Harvey-Jones (b. 1924) British management adviser, author, and former chairman of ICI. Warning against building up the company's confidence at the expense of customers and suppliers. *Managing to Survive* (1993)

20 As is our confidence, so is our capacity.

William Hazlitt (1778–1830) British essayist and journalist. *Characteristics* (1823)

21 If the public doesn't believe the message conveyed by your product and its promotion, the marketing game is lost.

Robert Heller (b. 1932) British management writer. *The Supermarketers* (1987)

22 A reasonable probability is the only certainty.

Ed Howe (1853–1937) US journalist and writer. *Country Town Sayings* (1911)

23 The better people think they are, the better they will be. Positive self-image creates success.

Liisa Joronen (b. 1944) Finnish CEO of SOL (formerly Lindström). Interview in *The Winning Streak Mark II* (Walter Goldsmith and David Clutterbuck; 1997)

24 The confidence which we have in ourselves gives birth to much of that which we have in others.

François La Rochefoucauld (1613–80) French epigrammatist. *Reflections: or, Sentences and Moral Maxims* (5th ed.) (1678)

25 In times of great prosperity it's easy to forget that investors commit capital because they have a basic confidence in the quality and integrity of America's markets. That faith does more than fuel markets—it makes markets possible.

Arthur Levitt Jr (b. 1931) US author and former chairman of the US Securities and Exchange Commission. Speech to the New York University Center for Law and Business, New York City. 'Renewing the Covenant with Investors' (10 May 2000)

26 If you once forfeit the confidence of your fellow citizens, you can never regain their respect and esteem. It is true that you may fool all the people some of the time; you can even fool some of the people all the time; but you can't fool all of the people all the time.

Abraham Lincoln (1809–65) US president. Quoted in *Lincoln's Yarns and Stories* (Alexander K. McClure; 1904)

27 The final test of a leader is that he leaves behind him in other men the conviction and the will to carry on.

Walter Lippmann (1889–1974) US political commentator, editor, and writer. 'Roosevelt Has Gone', *New York Herald Tribune* (14 April 1945)

28 Confidence placed in another often compels confidence in return.

Livy (59 BC–AD 17) Roman historian. *History of Rome* (26 BC–AD 15)

29 My parents...gave me the biggest gift a parent can give a child: Confidence.

Elizabeth MacKay, US investment strategist and managing director of Bear Stearns. Quoted in *Women of the Street* (Sue Herera; 1997)

30 I don't really see the hurdles. I sense them like a memory.

Edwin Moses (b. 1955) US athlete. Attrib.

31 No one can build or construct anything beautiful unless he has faith.

Jawaharlal Nehru (1889–1964) Indian prime minister. Quoted in *Glorious Thoughts of Nehru* (N.B. Sen; 1964)

32 Confidence is a mark of respect—and respect is appreciated by anyone of courage and honour.

Anne-Marie-Louise d' Orléans (1627–93) French noblewoman and author. *Mademoiselle's Portrait Gallery* (1657)

33 If you don't know where you are going, you will probably end up somewhere else.

Laurence J. Peter (1919–90) Canadian academic and writer. *The Peter Principle: Why Things Always Go Wrong* (co-written with Raymond Hull; 1969)

34 You are never dedicated to something you have complete confidence in. No one is fanatically shouting that the sun is going to rise tomorrow.

Robert M. Pirsig (b. 1928) US author. *Zen and the Art of Motorcycle Maintenance* (1974), pt 2, ch. 13

35 Confidence is a plant of slow growth in an aged bosom; youth is the season of credulity.

William Pitt (1708–78) British prime minister. Speech to the House of Commons (14 January 1766)

36 You gain strength, courage and confidence by every experience in which you really stop to look fear in the face.

Eleanor Roosevelt (1884–1962) US reformer, author, and first lady. *You Learn by Living* (1960)

37 Lack of confidence is not the result of difficulty; the difficulty comes from lack of confidence.

Seneca (?4 BC–AD 65) Roman politician, philosopher, and writer. *Letters to Lucilius* (1st century AD)

38 There's one blessing only, the source and cornerstone of beatitude—confidence in self.

Seneca (?4 BC–AD 65) Roman politician, philosopher, and writer. *Letters to Lucilius* (1st century AD)

39 One man that has a mind and knows it can always beat ten men who haven't and don't.

George Bernard Shaw (1856–1950) Irish writer and critic. *The Apple Cart* (1929), Act 1

40 When it comes to mergers, hope triumphs over experience.

Irwin Stelzer (b. 1932) US economist. Quoted in *Treasury of Investment Wisdom* (Bernice Cohen; 1999)

41 If one advances confidently in the direction of his dreams, and endeavors to live the life which he has imagined, he will meet with a success unexpected in common hours.
Henry David Thoreau (1817–62) US writer. *Walden, or Life in the Woods* (1854), Conclusion

42 All you need in this life is ignorance and confidence; then success is sure.
Mark Twain (1835–1910) US writer. Letter to Mrs Foote (2 December 1887)

43 They can do all because they think they can.
Virgil (70–19 BC) Roman poet. *Aeneid* (26–19 BC)

44 Confidence is a thing not to be produced by compulsion. Men cannot be forced to trust.
Daniel Webster (1782–1852) US statesman, orator, and lawyer. Speech in the Senate (1834)

45 Las Vegas has always represented the tremendous freedom to do nutty things.
Steve Wynn (b. 1942) US hotel entrepreneur. *The Economist* (1996)

CONSCIENCE

1 Management's total loyalty to the maximization of profit is the principal obstacle to achieving higher standards of ethical practice.
Kenneth R. Andrews (b. 1916) US business author. *Harvard Business Review* (September/October 1989)

2 Conscience gets a lot of credit that belongs to cold feet.
Anonymous. US proverb.

3 Conscience is an imitation within ourselves of the government without us.
Alexander Bain (1818–1903) British philosopher and psychologist. *The Emotions and the Will* (1859)

4 There cannot be a situation where a businessman says, 'I base all my business on moral considerations'. Equally, you can't say you can run a business without morality.
Timothy Bevan (b. 1927) British banker. Said as Chairman of Barclays Bank Ltd, when asked about Barclays' withdrawal from South Africa. *Observer* (30 November 1986)

5 The world has achieved brilliance without conscience. Ours is a world of nuclear giants and ethical infants.
Omar Nelson Bradley (1893–1981) US general. Armistice Address (1948)

6 A business must have a conscience as well as a counting house.
Montague Burton (1885–1952) British tailor and founder of the Burton Group. Attrib.

7 In many walks of life, a conscience is a more expensive encumbrance than a wife or a carriage.
Thomas De Quincey (1785–1859) British writer. 'Preliminary Confessions', *Confessions of an English Opium-Eater* (1821–56)

8 The task of the conscience activities is not to help the organization improve on its present activities. Its task is to hold the organization to its own standards, to remind the organization what it should be, but isn't, doing.
Peter F. Drucker (b. 1909) US management consultant and academic. Recommending support activities which 'set standards, create vision, and demand excellence in all key areas where a business needs to strive for excellence'. *Management* (1974)

9 There is one thing alone that stands the brunt of life throughout its course: a quiet conscience.
Euripides (?484–?406 BC) Greek playwright. *Hippolytus* (428 BC)

10 Freedom of conscience entails more dangers than authority and despotism.
Michel Foucault (1926–84) French philosopher. *Madness and Civilization* (1965)

11 The more productively one lives, the stronger one's conscience, and, in turn, the more it furthers one's productiveness.
Erich Fromm (1900–80) US psychoanalyst and social philosopher. *Man for Himself* (1947)

12 Debt is an evil conscience.
Thomas Fuller (1654–1734) English physician and writer. *Gnomologia* (1732)

13 It is always term-time in the court of conscience.
Thomas Fuller (1654–1734) English physician and writer. *Gnomologia* (1732)

14 Conscience is a coward, and those faults it has not strength to prevent, it seldom has justice enough to accuse.
Oliver Goldsmith (1730–74) British playwright, writer, and poet. *The Vicar of Wakefield* (1766)

15 The mind is fearless so long as there is no reproach of conscience. When that comes, come breakage and bondage and a host of terrors.
Louise Imogen Guiney (1861–1920) US poet and essayist. *Goose Quill Papers* (1885)

16 A society dedicated to the enrichment and enhancement of the self will only survive and certainly will only prosper if the dominant ethic is the support and encouragement of others.
Charles Handy (b. 1932) British business executive and author. *The Age of Unreason* (1991)

17 They feel neither shame, remorse, gratitude nor goodwill.
William Hazlitt (1778–1830) British essayist and journalist. Referring to corporations. *Table Talk* (1821–22), no. 27

18 The market has no morality.
Michael Heseltine (b. 1933) British politician and publisher. Interview, 'Panorama', BBC Television (June 1988)

19 Conscience is the name which the orthodox give to their prejudices.
John Oliver Hobbes (1867–1906) British novelist and dramatist. *A Bundle of Life* (1894)

20 If we cannot be powerful and happy and prey on others, we invent conscience and prey on ourselves.
Elbert Hubbard (1856–1915) US humorist. *The Philistine* (1895–1915)

21 The glory of good men is in their conscience and not in the mouths of men.
Thomas à Kempis (?1380–1471) German mystic, monk, and writer. *De Imitatione Christi* (1426)

22 Conscience: self-esteem with a halo.
Irving Layton (b. 1912) Canadian poet. *The Whole Bloody Bird* (1969)

23 A man's conscience begins life with him; if he does not keep friends with it, he is continually at warfare with this principle within.
Hannah Farnham Lee (1780–1865) US author. *Elinor Fulton* (1837)

24 Our conscience is not the vessel of eternal verities. It grows with our social life and a new social condition means a radical change in conscience.
Walter Lippmann (1889–1974) US political commentator, editor, and writer. 'Some Necessary Iconoclasm', *A Preface to Politics* (1914)

25 Sufficient conscience to bother him, but not sufficient to keep him straight.
David Lloyd-George (1863–1945) British prime minister. Referring to Ramsay MacDonald. Quoted in *Life with Lloyd George* (A.J. Sylvester; 1975)

26 It is neither safe nor prudent to do aught against conscience.
Martin Luther (1483–1546) German theologian. *Table Talk* (1569)

27 Conscience is the guardian in the individual of the rules which the community has evolved for its own preservation.
W. Somerset Maugham (1874–1965) British novelist, short-story writer, and dramatist. *The Moon and Sixpence* (1919)

28 Conscience is the inner voice that warns us somebody may be looking.
H.L. Mencken (1880–1956) US journalist, essayist, and critic. *A Mencken Chrestomathy* (1948)

29 The difference between a moral man and a man of honor is that the latter regrets a discreditable act, even when it has worked and he has not been caught.
H.L. Mencken (1880–1956) US journalist, essayist, and critic. *Prejudices, Fourth Series* (1924)

30 There is no witness so dreadful, no accuser so terrible as the conscience that dwells in the heart of every man.
Polybius (?200–?118 BC) Greek politician and historian. *History*, bk 18

31 Wisdom entereth not into a malicious mind, and science without conscience is but the ruin of the soul.
François Rabelais (?1483–1553) French writer, physician, and priest. *Gargantua and Pantagruel* (1534), bk 2

32 I believe it is my duty to make money and still more money and to use the money I make for the good of my fellow man according to the dictates of my conscience.
John D. Rockefeller (1839–1937) US industrialist, philanthropist, and founder of Standard Oil. Interview (1905)

33 Making money doesn't oblige people to forfeit their honour or their conscience.
Guy de Rothschild (b. 1909) French banker. *The Whims of Fortune* (1985)

34 Makes us rather bear those ills we have
Than fly to others we know not of?
Thus conscience does make cowards of us all.
William Shakespeare (1564–1616) English poet and playwright. *Hamlet* (1601), Act 3, Scene 1

35 A peace above all earthly dignities,
A still and quiet conscience.
William Shakespeare (1564–1616) English poet and playwright. *Henry VIII* (1613), Act 3, Scene 2

36 If there be not a conscience to be used in every trade we shall never prosper.
William Shakespeare (1564–1616) English poet and playwright. *Pericles* (1606–08), Act 4, Scene 2

37 Most people sell their souls and live with a good conscience on the proceeds.
Logan Pearsall Smith (1865–1946) British essayist and critic. 'Other People', *Afterthoughts* (1931)

38 Trust that man in nothing who has not a conscience in everything.
Laurence Sterne (1713–68) British novelist and humorist. *The Life and Opinions of Tristram Shandy, Gentleman* (1760), bk 2

39 I've got just as much conscience as any man in business can afford to keep—just a little, you know, to swear by as 't were.
Harriet Beecher Stowe (1811–96) US writer. *Uncle Tom's Cabin* (1852), ch. 1

40 A man cannot be comfortable without his own approval.
Mark Twain (1835–1910) US writer. 'What is Man' (1906)

41 In all the ages, three-fourths of the support of the great charities has been conscience money.
Mark Twain (1835–1910) US writer. *A Humane Word from Satan* (1905)

42 Conscience and cowardice are really the same things. Conscience is the trade-name of the firm.
Oscar Wilde (1854–1900) Irish writer and wit. *The Picture of Dorian Gray* (1891), ch. 1

CONSUMERS

1 Food comes first, then morals.
Bertolt Brecht (1898–1956) German playwright and poet. *The Threepenny Opera* (1928)

2 There is enough in the world for everyone's need, but not for everyone's greed.

Frank Buckman (1878–1961) US evangelist. *Remaking the World* (1947)

3 Make no mistake: Customers are in control today.

Anne Busquet (b. ?1951) US president of American Express Relationship Services. 'Next Stop—The 21st Century', *Fast Company* (Lucy McCauley; 1999)

4 Many people believe that we have entered the age of the Internet. Actually, it's more accurate to say that we're living in the age of the customer.

Anne Busquet (b. ?1951) US president of American Express Relationship Services. 'Next Stop—The 21st Century', *Fast Company* (Lucy McCauley; 1999)

5 Man wants but little here below but likes that little good—and not too long in coming.

Samuel Butler (1835–1902) British writer. *Further Extracts from the Notebooks* (A. Bartholomew, ed.; 1934)

6 Arguably the only goods people need these days are food and nappies.

Terence Conran (b. 1931) British business executive, retailer, and founder of Habitat. Quoted in *Observer* (21 February 1988)

7 The consumer is the most important part of the production line.

W. Edwards Deming (1900–93) US consultant and author. *Out of the Crisis* (1992)

8 The consumer dictates whether we're in business or not.

Niall Fitzgerald (b. 1945) British CEO of Unilever and president of the Advertising Association. *Marketing* (June 2000)

9 With every decision we make, the last question we ask is what does the consumer think of this.

Niall Fitzgerald (b. 1945) British CEO of Unilever and president of the Advertising Association. *Marketing* (June 2000)

10 You could not have got more knowledge about detergents anywhere in the world...I asked, could anyone who has washed their own clothes in the past three months put their hands up. Not one hand went up.

Niall Fitzgerald (b. 1945) British CEO of Unilever and president of the Advertising Association. Referring to Unilever's problems with a washing powder. *Marketing* (July 2000)

11 Teenagers travel in droves, packs, swarms. To the librarian, they're a gaggle of geese. To the cook, they're a scourge of locusts. To department stores they're a big beautiful exaltation of larks, all lovely and loose and jingly.

Bernice Fitz-Gibbon (?1895–1982) US advertising executive. *New York Times* (1960)

12 The individual serves the industrial system not by supplying it with savings and the resulting capital; he serves it by consuming its products.

J.K. Galbraith (b. 1908) US economist and diplomat. *The New Industrial State* (1967)

13 What I'm learning from customers is that there is an excess of technology out there.

Lou Gerstner (b. 1942) US chairman and CEO of IBM. *Fortune* (1993)

14 Business is about supplying the needs and desires of human society and is therefore about human goods and the best means to provide them.

Damian Grace (b. 1950) Australian academic. *Australian Problems and Cases* (1995)

15 Consumers resent it when a company presumes to judge the quality of its products on their behalf.

Andrew S. Grove (b. 1936) US entrepreneur, author, and chairman of Intel Corporation. *Fortune* (May 1995)

16 People want economy and they will pay any price to get it.

Lee Iacocca (b. 1924) US president of Ford Motor Company, chairman and CEO of Chrysler Corporation. *New York Times* (1974)

17 In a consumer society there are inevitably two kinds of slaves: the prisoners of addiction and the prisoners of envy.

Ivan Illich (1926–2002) US priest and educator. *Tools for Conviviality* (1973)

18 Customers do not care about industry boundaries; they want service and convenience.

Peter G.W. Keen (b. 1930) US information technology consultant. 'Basic Change', *The Process Edge* (1999)

19 New consumers are never-satisfied consumers.

Regis McKenna (b. 1939) US marketing entrepreneur and chairman of The McKenna Group. *Relationship Marketing* (1991)

20 Advertising is an environmental striptease for a world of abundance.

Marshall McLuhan (1911–80) Canadian sociologist and author. Quoted in *Subliminal Seduction: Ad Media's Manipulation of a Not So Innocent America* (Wilson Bryan Key; 1974)

21 The car, the furniture, the wife, the children—everything has to be disposable. Because you see, the main thing today is shopping.

Arthur Miller (b. 1915) US dramatist. *The Price* (1968)

22 Unsafe at Any Speed

Ralph Nader (b. 1934) US lawyer and consumer-rights campaigner. Book title, concerned with the automotive industry, and referring to the Chevy Corvair. *Unsafe at Any Speed* (1965)

23 Our gadget-filled paradise suspended in a hell of insecurity.

Reinhold Niebuhr (1892–1971) US theologian. *Pious and Secular America* (1957)

24 The consumer isn't a moron; she is your wife.

David Ogilvy (1911–99) British advertising executive, founder and chairman of Ogilvy & Mather. *Confessions of an Advertising Man* (1963)

25 Man is the only creature that consumes without producing.

George Orwell (1903–50) British novelist, critic, and essayist. *Animal Farm* (1945)

26 The most exciting thing happening in business is the rise of vigilante consumers.

Anita Roddick (b. 1942) British entrepreneur and founder of The Body Shop. Interview, *Marketing Week* (24 February 2000)

27 On the whole businesses do not listen to the consumer. Consumers have not been told effectively enough that they have huge power and that purchasing and shopping involve a moral choice.

Anita Roddick (b. 1942) British entrepreneur and founder of The Body Shop. Interview, *Share International* (April 1998)

28 No other man-made device since the shields and lances of ancient knights fulfills a man's ego like an automobile.

William Rootes (1894–1964) British car manufacturer. Speech (1958)

29 The consumer, so it is said, is the king…each is a voter who uses his money as votes to get the things done that he wants done.

Paul Samuelson (b. 1915) US economist and winner of the 1970 Nobel Prize in Economics. *Economics* (1970)

30 Trying to get consumers to re-evaluate their behaviour is what I enjoy most.

Ric Simcock (b. 1965) British advertising executive. *Marketing* (September 2000)

31 Consumption is the sole end and purpose of production; and the interest of the producer ought to be attended to only so far as it may be necessary for promoting that of the consumer.

Adam Smith (1723–90) British economist and philosopher. *An Inquiry into the Nature and Causes of the Wealth of Nations* (1776)

32 Prosumers.

Alvin Toffler (b. 1928) US social commentator. Meaning consumers who contribute directly to product development. *The Third Wave* (1980)

33 While Chinese youth may desire the same clothing and popular music as the West, the core values are very resistant to change.

Rosalie L. Tung (b. 1948) Canadian academic and business educator. *International Management in China: Cross-cultural Issues* (Jan Selmer, ed.; 1998)

34 America is a vast conspiracy to make you happy.

John Updike (b. 1932) US novelist and critic. *Problems* (1980)

35 In the kingdom of consumption the citizen is king…The dictatorship of consumer goods has finally destroyed the barriers of blood, lineage, and race.

Raoul Vaneigem (b. 1934) Belgian philosopher. *The Revolution of Everyday Life* (1967)

36 Work to survive, survive by consuming, survive to consume: the hellish cycle is complete.

Raoul Vaneigem (b. 1934) Belgian philosopher. *The Revolution of Everyday Life* (1967)

37 Conspicuous consumption of valuable goods is a measure of reputability to the gentlemen of leisure.

Thorstein Veblen (1857–1929) US economist and social scientist. *The Theory of the Leisure Class* (1899)

38 The superior gratification derived from the use and contemplation of costly and supposedly beautiful products is, commonly, in great measure a gratification of our sense of costliness masquerading under the name of beauty.

Thorstein Veblen (1857–1929) US economist and social scientist. *The Theory of the Leisure Class* (1899)

39 I probably spend some time once a month listening in on calls or talking to customers. I encourage my executives to do the same.

Lillian Vernon (b. 1927) US entrepreneur and CEO of Lillian Vernon Corporation. 'My Biggest Mistake', *Inc.* (1999)

40 There are so many flukes in the catalog industry that you have to constantly assess what your customers want and need.

Lillian Vernon (b. 1927) US entrepreneur and CEO of Lillian Vernon Corporation. 'My Biggest Mistake', *Inc.* (1999)

41 Buying is much more American than thinking and I'm as American as they come.

Andy Warhol (1928–87) US artist and film maker. *The Philosophy of Andy Warhol (from A to B and Back Again)* (1975)

42 What's great about this country is that America started the tradition where the richest consumers buy essentially the same things as the poorest.

Andy Warhol (1928–87) US artist and film maker. *The Philosophy of Andy Warhol (from A to B and Back Again)* (1975)

43 The Internet has certainly brought us face to face with the consumer. And the consumer has everything to gain here.

Ann Winblad (b. 1953) US venture capitalist. *www.womenswire.com* (Soledad O'Brien; 2000)

CONTRACTS

1 Make your bargain before beginning to plough.

Anonymous. Arab proverb.

2 You'll have the legal authority to use my skin for lampshades so far as I can see.

Robert Bolt (1924–95) British screenwriter and dramatist. Referring to a punitive contract. Letter (July 1963)

3 Contracts are agreements made up of big words and little type.

Sam Ewing (1920–2001) US author. Quoted in *Saturday Evening Post* (May 1993)

4 A verbal contract isn't worth the paper it's written on.

Samuel Goldwyn (1882–1974) US film producer. Quoted in *The Great Goldwyn* (Alva Johnson; 1937)

5 A contract is a mutual promise.
William Paley (1743–1805) British theologian and philosopher. *The Principles of Moral and Political Philosophy* (1784), bk 3, pt 1, ch. 6

6 Contract: an agreement that is binding on the weaker party.
Frederick Sawyer (b. 1947) US writer. Attrib.

7 Every law is a contract between the king and the people and therefore to be kept.
John Selden (1584–1654) English jurist, antiquary, and politician. *Table Talk* (1689)

8 Men keep their agreements when it is an advantage to both parties not to break them.
Solon (?638—?559 BC) Athenian statesman, legislator, and poet. Quoted in 'Solon', *Parallel Lives* (Plutarch; 1st century AD)

9 My style of dealmaking is quite simple and straightforward. I just keep pushing and pushing to get what I'm after.
Donald J. Trump (b. 1946) US property developer. *Time* (1989)

10 There is nothing more likely to start disagreement among people or countries than an agreement.
E.B. White (1899–1985) US writer. Attrib.

CO-OPERATION

1 Gung Ho!
Work Together!
Rewi Alley (1897–1987) New Zealand reformer and educator. Motto of the Chinese Industrial Co-operative Association. Quoted in *Rewi Alley of China* (Chapple; 1980)

2 Successful cooperation in or by formal organizations is the abnormal, not the normal, condition.
Chester Barnard (1886–1961) US business executive and management theorist. *Organization and Management* (1948)

3 Two are better than one; because they have a good reward for their labour.
For if they fall, the one will lift up his fellow: but woe to him that is alone when he falleth; for he hath not another to help him up.
Bible. Ecclesiastes, 4:9–10

4 *Coopetition* Cooperation between competitors...especially common in the computer industry, where consumers want to know in advance that a broad range of companies will support a given technology...companies will compete on actual products even as they cooperate on technical standards, sacrificing a degree of independence to increase the odds of success for the technology as a whole.
John Browning, US writer and consultant. *Encyclopedia of the New Economy* (co-written with Spencer Reiss; 2000)

5 Both suppliers and customers must be treated as partners and collaborators—jointly looking for ways to improve efficiency across the ENTIRE spectrum of the value chain...In this way, deeper, more enduring relationships can be created that result in SHARED efficiencies...and greatly enhanced long-term value for all.
Michael Dell (b. 1965) US chairman and CEO of Dell Computer Corporation. Speech to the 1998 World Congress on Information Technology, Vienna, Virginia. 'Collaborating in a Connected Economy: The Power of Virtual Integration' (24 June 1998)

6 The companies that fully capitalize on the promise of the Internet will be those that look at their businesses as more than building and selling products and services. In the virtual economy, collaboration is a new competitive imperative.
Michael Dell (b. 1965) US chairman and CEO of Dell Computer Corporation. Speech to the 1998 World Congress on Information Technology, Vienna, Virginia. 'Collaborating in a Connected Economy: The Power of Virtual Integration' (24 June 1998)

7 It used to be that you would do things yourself...you felt you had to have control and you could not necessarily get the other things from other partners. But now...it is much easier to connect suppliers and customers...we no longer have these closed business systems, we have more collaborative business systems
Michael Dell (b. 1965) US chairman and CEO of Dell Computer Corporation. Speech to the Canadian Club of Toronto, Canada. 'Leadership in the Internet Economy' (7 April 2000)

8 The speed of the Internet provides a fundamentally different perspective on how business relationships occur...The approach relies on collaboration, not on competition...on sharing information, and understanding what we as businesses do best.
Michael Dell (b. 1965) US chairman and CEO of Dell Computer Corporation. Speech to the Executives' Club of Chicago. 'NetSpeed: The Supercharged Effect of the Internet' (23 October 1998)

9 The key to using the Internet to extend and build relationships is to view ownership of information differently—you need to bring customers inside your business to create information partnerships...relationships become the differentiator, more than products or services. Businesses become intertwined.
Michael Dell (b. 1965) US chairman and CEO of Dell Computer Corporation. Speech (3 March 1999)

10 The CEO's role in raising a company's corporate IQ is to establish an atmosphere that promotes knowledge sharing and collaboration.
Bill Gates (b. 1955) US entrepreneur, chairman and CEO of Microsoft. *Business@the Speed of Thought* (co-written with Collins Hemingway; 1999)

11 The close relationships we form between researchers and product groups have already shown we can move the great ideas as they come along, without a schedule, into the products.
Bill Gates (b. 1955) US entrepreneur, chairman and CEO of Microsoft. *Net News* (10 August 1997)

12 As work becomes more complex and collaborative, companies where people work together best have a competitive edge.
Daniel Goleman (b. 1946) US behavioural scientist, journalist, and author. *Working with Emotional Intelligence* (1998)

13 These are two independent and aggressive companies serving their own purposes, but they are at the same time immensely pragmatic. We recognize that we have to work together, and at various times we recognize that we need to work independently. Some of those times we end up figuring out that we're better off working together after all, and we go back and forth.
Andrew S. Grove (b. 1936) US entrepreneur, author, and chairman of Intel Corporation. Referring to Intel's relationship with Microsoft Corporation. Interview, *Upside Magazine* (12 October 1997)

14 Talent wins games, but teamwork wins championships.
Michael Jordan (b. 1963) US basketball player. 1996. Attrib.

15 Working cooperatively is crucial because you can't count on the power of your position anymore; you have to count on the power of your ideas.
Rosabeth Moss Kanter (b. 1943) US management theorist, academic, and writer. Interview, *Strategy + Business* (July–September 1999)

16 In an e-business environment, leaders must manage not just teams, but large crowds...Because power lies in the network, all parts of it must adjust its actions in the light of what others are doing.
Rosabeth Moss Kanter (b. 1943) US management theorist, academic, and writer. 'How E-Smart Are You?', *World Link* (January–February 2000)

17 Within and outside of the enterprise, success in an Internet environment is more likely when there is seamless cooperation across product lines, functional areas, business units, and geographies.
Rosabeth Moss Kanter (b. 1943) US management theorist, academic, and writer. 'How E-Smart Are You?', *World Link* (January–February 2000)

18 Only recently have people begun to recognise that working with suppliers is just as important as listening to customers.
Barry J. Nalebuff, US author. *Co-opetition* (co-written with Adam M. Brandenburger; 1997)

19 Co-opetition
Barry J. Nalebuff, US author. Book title. *Co-opetition* (co-written with Adam M. Brandenburger; 1997)

20 The ultimate power of a successful general staff lies, not in the brilliance of its individual members, but in the cross-fertilisation of its collective abilities.
Reg Revans (1907–2003) British academic. *Action Learning* (1979)

21 Like a team of specialists in any field, our performance depended both on individual excellence and on how well we worked together...we all tried to figure out ways to make our combination more effective.
Bill Russell (b. 1934) US professional basketball player, coach, and sports commentator. *Second Wind: Memoirs of an Opinionated Man* (co-written with T. Branch; 1979)

22 Our win/loose mentality in hierarchical organizations...has taught us to look for others' weaknesses...True teaming is only possible if each of us gets good at discovering and building upon the capabilities of our colleagues.
Charles M. Savage, US management consultant and theorist. Speech, 4th Workshop on Inventing the organisation of the 21st Century, Munich, Germany. 'Leadership & Management in the Knowledge Era' (February 1998)

23 Building trust between partners in a joint venture can be seen as the first necessary step in developing a successful alliance.
Jan Selmer (b. 1942) Swedish academic and author. *International Management in China: Cross-cultural Issues* (Jan Selmer, ed.; 1998)

24 Shared vision is vital for the learning organization because it provides the focus and energy for learning.
Peter Senge (b. 1947) US academic and author. *The Fifth Discipline: The Art and Practice of the Learning Organization* (1990)

25 Men will find that they can...avoid far more easily the perils which beset them on all sides by united action.
Baruch Spinoza (1632–77) Dutch philosopher. *Ethics* (1677), pt 4, proposition 35, note

26 A sharing of control with local partners will lead to a greater contribution from them, which can assist in coping with circumstances that are unfamiliar to the foreign partner.
Yanni Yan (b. 1958) Chinese business author and academic. 'Managerial and Organization—Learning in Chinese Firms', *China's Managerial Revolution* (Malcolm Warner, ed.; 1999)

27 Where...one parent company has a special knowledge of technology, and the other a knowledge of the market, a shared management venture is the appropriate solution.
Yanni Yan (b. 1958) Chinese business author and academic. 'Managerial and Organization—Learning in Chinese Firms', *China's Managerial Revolution* (Malcolm Warner, ed.; 1999)

28 When you collaborate with other people, you tend to regard your own individual contribution as the most important.
Yang Jiang (b. 1911) Chinese playwright and writer. *A Cadre School Life* (1980)

CORPORATE CULTURE

1 Very often it's hard to distinguish between working and socialising because the whole industry is built around the social occasion.

Andrew Allan (b. 1964) British e-commerce executive. Referring to the drinks industry. *Marketing* (September 2000)

2 Some firms hardly dare change the wallpaper without consulting a guru.

Anonymous. Quoted in *Corporate Man to Corporate Skunk* (Stuart Crainer; 1997)

3 If you change the way you work, you will change the way you think.

Anonymous. Statement by the London-based St Lukes Advertising Agency. *Management Today* (April 1999)

4 The combined board creates a strong signal of unity inside and outside the company. It is an important symbolic and practical change.

Percy Barnevik (b. 1941) Swedish former CEO of ABB. Referring to the re-organisation of a multinational company. Quoted in *In Search of European Excellence* (Robert Heller; 1997)

5 Organisational psychology.

Christopher Bartlett (b. 1945) Australian business writer. The term created by the authors to describe the collection of corporate values and beliefs that can be managed. *Managing Across Borders* (co-written with Sumantra Ghoshal; 1989)

6 Constructive confrontation.

Christopher Bartlett (b. 1945) Australian business writer. *The Individualised Corporation* (co-written with Sumantra Ghoshal; 1997)

7 The oppressive atmosphere in most companies resembles downtown Calcutta in summer.

Christopher Bartlett (b. 1945) Australian business writer. *The Individualised Corporation* (co-written with Sumantra Ghoshal; 1997)

8 I believe in provocative disruption.

Charlotte Beers (b. 1935) US advertising executive and former under secretary of state for public diplomacy and public affairs in the US government. *Fortune* (August 1996)

9 One square foot less and it would be adulterous.

Robert Benchley (1889–1945) US humorist. Referring to the size of a shared office. Quoted in *New Yorker* (January 1946)

10 Trust is essential to all organizations.

Warren Bennis (b. 1925) US educator and writer. *Leaders: The Strategies for Taking Charge* (1985)

11 The single most important determinant of corporate culture is the behavior of the chief executive officer. He or she is the one clearly responsible for shaping the beliefs, motives, commitments, and predispositions of all.

Warren Bennis (b. 1925) US educator and writer. 'Leaders and Visions: Orchestrating the Corporate Culture', *The Conference Board Challenge to Business: Industry Leaders Speak Their Minds* (Peter Krass and Richard E. Cavanagh, eds; 2000)

12 There's No Business Like Show Business

Irving Berlin (1888–1989) US composer and songwriter. Song title. 'There's No Business Like Show Business' (1946)

13 A corporation does seem like a family. Not necessarily that one big happy family they

like to boast about…but just like every family, a hotbed of passion, rivalry, and dreams that build or destroy careers.

Paula Bernstein (b. 1933) US writer. *Family Ties, Corporate Bonds* (1985)

14 We're not a company that seeks out controversy, but we sure do find it.

Jeff Bezos (b. 1964) US founder and CEO of Amazon.com. *Sunday Telegraph* (July 2000)

15 Indians in general have tended to under-market themselves. That comes because it's part of our culture…you don't go and say I have created the world's greatest software.

Subeer Bhatia (b. 1967) Indian IT entrepreneur and founder of Hotmail. *BusinessWeek* (September 2000)

16 When you are sitting under the stern gaze of Lord Reith, you wouldn't dare say things you might in other circumstances.

Christopher Bland (b. 1938) British media executive and chairman of BT. Referring to his own outspoken comments earlier in his career. *Management Today* (July 1999)

17 The big danger in mega-mergers is that they are seen as a mating of dinosaurs.

Peter Bonfield (b. 1944) British former CEO of BT. *Sunday Times* (July 2000)

18 In all successful professional groups, regard for the individual is based not on title, but on competence, stature, and leadership.

Marvin Bower (1903–2003) US CEO of McKinsey & Company. *The Will to Manage* (1966)

19 The way to rebuild our corporate world is a blend of both male and female energy.

Terri Bowersock (b. 1956) US furniture company entrepreneur. 'She Could Have Gone To Jail, But Ended Up a Millionaire Instead', *Entrepreneur Illustrated* (1999)

20 Boxing is just show business with blood.

Frank Bruno (b. 1961) British boxer. *Guardian* (November 1991)

21 In the insurance business, there is no statute of limitation on stupidity.

Warren Buffett (b. 1930) US entrepreneur and financier. Annual report (1991)

22 Lethargy bordering on sloth remains the cornerstone of our investment style.

Warren Buffett (b. 1930) US entrepreneur and financier. *Newsweek* (May 1991)

23 IBM is like the Stepford Wives. It takes the best people from the best universities and colleges and then snips out some part of the brain so that they become mindless clones.

Bill Campbell (b. 1940) US CEO of Intuit Corporation. Quoted in *Giant Killers* (Geoffrey James; 1996)

24 Of course when you shut the door, other people look across and say, 'ooh, what's going on'.

Barbara Cassani (b. 1960) US former CEO of Go. *Management Today* (August 1999)

25 Indian management has to pursue processes which conform to the underlying grain of the Indian temper.

S.K. Chakraborty (b. 1957) Indian academic. *Management by Values: Towards Cultural Congruence* (1991)

26 Creative swiping provides energy to an organization.

Chuck Chambers, US CEO of SLD. Quoted in *Liberation Management* (Tom Peters; 1992)

27 A for-profit think tank.

Jim Clifton (b. 1951) US CEO of Gallup. Referring to Gallup. *Financial Times* (October 2000)

28 Nobody here cares which washroom you use.

Debi Coleman (b. 1953) US business executive and chief financial officer of Apple Computers. *US News & World Report* (September 1987)

29 Perfect freedom is reserved for the man who lives by his own work and, in that work, does what he wants to do.

R.G. Collingwood (1889–1943) British philosopher. *Speculum Mentis* (1924)

30 NCOs had evaluated themselves by the thickness of their carpets.

Bill Creech (b. 1958) US commanding general of US Air Force Tactical Air Command. Quoted in *A Passion for Excellence* (Tom Peters and Nancy Austin; 1985)

31 They tried to Wal-Martise me and it worked.

Carlos Criado-Perez (b. 1952) Argentinian business executive. *Sunday Times* (July 2000)

32 The key to effective leadership in corporations is reading and responding to cultural clues.

Terrence Deal, US author. *The New Corporate Cultures* (co-written with Allan Kennedy; 1999)

33 It's a vibrant special place, it really is like being in Italy during the Renaissance.

Donna Dubinsky (b. 1955) US IT executive. Referring to Silicon Valley. *Sunday Telegraph* (August 2000)

34 When I first started on Wall Street there was a lot of drinking...you would meet...people after work and have drinks, drinks, drinks. But that's all changed. It's mineral water now.

Gail Dudack (b. 1948) US managing director and chief investment strategist of UBS Securities Ltd. Quoted in *Women of the Street* (Sue Herera; 1997)

35 I could buy companies, tart up their products and put my name on them, but I don't want to do that. That's what our competitors do.

James Dyson (b. 1947) British entrepreneur. *Management Today* (July 1999)

36 My interest is in the practice of making and engineering things and doing it with a complete lack of marketing hype.

James Dyson (b. 1947) British entrepreneur. *Management Today* (July 1999)

37 The term synergy may be the object of ridicule throughout the world, but not here in Burbank, California.

Michael Eisner (b. 1942) US chairman and CEO of the Disney Corporation. Speech (April 1996)

38 I'm a child of the corporate struggle.

Michael Eisner (b. 1942) US chairman and CEO of the Disney Corporation. *Time* (April 1988)

39 A happy atmosphere is something that customers pick up on.

Tom Farmer (b. 1940) British chairman and CEO of Kwik-Fit. *Digital Britain* (January 2000)

40 Intense decentralization that gives managers the freedom usually reserved for entrepreneurs.

James W. Farnell, US CEO of Illinois Tool Works, Inc. *BusinessWeek* (1995)

41 Too many people are on boards because they want to have nice-looking visiting cards.

Utz Felcht (b. 1947) German chairman of Degussa. *Sunday Times* (October 2000)

42 Anytime you have a fiercely-competitive, change-oriented growth business where results count and merit matters, women will rise to the top.

Carly Fiorina (b. 1954) US president and CEO of Hewlett-Packard. 'The 50 Most Powerful Women in American Business', *Fortune* (Patricia Sellers and Cora Daniels; October 1999)

43 A company needs smart young men with the imagination and the guts to turn everything upside down if they can. It also needs old figures to keep them from turning upside down those things that ought to be rightside up.

Henry Ford (1919–87) US car manufacturer and CEO of Ford Motor Company. Speech (1966)

44 I really enjoyed going into the office...it was a party every day. I would be right in the middle of an econometric model and someone would pull a champagne cork because it was a birthday, or someone had adopted a baby.

Elaine Garzarelli (b. 1951) US CEO and president of Garzarelli Investment Management. Referring to working in Wall Street. Quoted in *Women of the Street* (Sue Herera; 1997)

45 Synergy, the most screwball buzzword of the past decade.

Harold S. Geneen (1910–97) US telecommunications entrepreneur and CEO of ITT. *The Synergy Myth* (co-written with Brent Bowers; 1997)

46 I'm almost not trying to understand IBM's culture.

Lou Gerstner (b. 1942) US chairman and CEO of IBM. *Fortune* (1993)

47 There is a misconception that small is always more beautiful than big.

Lou Gerstner (b. 1942) US chairman and CEO of IBM. *Fortune* (May 1993)

48 That state is a state of slavery in which a man does what he likes to do in his spare time and, in his working time, that which is required of him.

Eric Gill (1882–1940) British sculptor and engraver. *Art—Nonsense and Other Essays* (1929)

49 A company's culture is often buried so deeply inside rituals, assumptions, attitudes, and values that it becomes transparent to an organization's members only when, for some reason, it changes.

Rob Goffee (b. 1952) US writer, consultant, and professor at London Business School. *The Character of a Corporation* (co-written with Gareth Jones; 1998)

50 The character of a corporation can be illuminated by identifying its sociability and solidarity.

Rob Goffee (b. 1952) US writer, consultant, and professor at London Business School. *The Character of a Corporation* (co-written with Gareth Jones; 1998)

51 We don't manage people here. People manage themselves.

Wilbert Lee Gore (d. 1986) US founder of Goretex. Quoted in *A Passion for Excellence* (Tom Peters and Nancy Austin; 1985)

52 Discrimination is against the interests of business—yet business people too often practice it...they erect barriers to the free flow of capital and labor to their most profitable employment, and the distribution of output is distorted. In the end, costs are higher, less real output is produced, and national wealth accumulation is slowed.

Alan Greenspan (b. 1926) US economist and chairman of US Federal Reserve Board. Speech to the National Association of Urban Bankers, Urban Financial Services Coalition, San Francisco, California. 'Evolving Challenges for Bankers and Supervisors' (25 May 2000)

53 There is nothing more short term than a 60-year-old CEO holding a fistful of share options.

Gary Hamel (b. 1954) US academic, business writer, and consultant. *Competing for the Future* (co-written with C.K. Prahalad; 1994)

54 You might merge with another organisation, but two drunks don't make a sensible person.

Gary Hamel (b. 1954) US academic, business writer, and consultant. *Competing for the Future* (co-written with C.K. Prahalad; 1994)

55 Every company has its own language, its own version of its own history (its myths), and its own heroes and villains (its legends), both historical and contemporary.

Michael Hammer (b. 1948) US author and academic. *Beyond Re-engineering* (1996)

56 The people are not bad, but they have stopped questioning themselves.

Guy Hands (b. 1959) Zimbabwean CEO of Terra Firma Capital Partners. Referring to complacency of established companies. *Management Today* (October 1999)

57 People weren't allowed to put the whole puzzle together. Instead, they were given small parts because they feared what people would do if they knew and saw the whole puzzle.

Charles Handy (b. 1932) British business executive and author. Interview (February 1994)

58 The microdivision of labour has fostered a basic distrust of human beings.

Charles Handy (b. 1932) British business executive and author. Interview (February 1994)

59 To hold people to the corporation, there has to be some kind of continuity and some sense of belonging...With the way corporations are evolving...unless we develop a more sophisticated model of the organization, the corporation will become just a box of contracts with no commitment on anyone's part.

Charles Handy (b. 1932) British business executive and author. Interview, *Strategy + Business* (October–December 1995)

60 He draws the bonds of his new engagements closer and tighter about him. He loses sight, by degrees, of all common sense...in the petty squabbles, intrigues, feuds, and airs of affected importance to which he has made himself accessory.

William Hazlitt (1778–1830) British essayist and journalist. Describing the corporate employee. 'On Corporate Bodies', *Table Talk* (1821–22), Essay 27

61 Even though the leviathans have remained rich and powerful, mass has slowed them down and given openings to the new and nimble.

Robert Heller (b. 1932) British management writer. *In Search of European Excellence* (1997)

62 We know assistive technology...is making it easier for people with disabilities to join the labor force. But we also know that...about three out of four people with disabilities who want to work are not working.

Alexis M. Herman (b. 1947) US politician. Labor Day address, New York (3 September 1999)

63 In some of these family-owned companies, you can't tell the father to fire the son. We feel we need more control.

Ta-Lin Hsu (b. 1943) Chinese investor. *Forbes* (December 1998)

64 We are trying to apply Silicon Valley techniques to some of our Asian investments.

Ta-Lin Hsu (b. 1943) Chinese investor. *Forbes* (December 1998)

65 We were forced to become a fix-it company because we don't have money to buy $50 million stations.

Cathy Hughes (b. ?1947) US broadcasting executive. *Forbes* (September 1999)

66 If you're not scared, you're too stupid to work here.

Lee Iacocca (b. 1924) US president of Ford Motor Company, chairman and CEO of Chrysler Corporation. Speech (1990)

67 Corporations have been pre-occupied with the qualifications, experience and achievements of individuals.

Anthony Jay (b. 1930) British author and business consultant. Quoted in *Management Teams—Why They Succeed* (R. Meredith Belbin; 1984)

68 If you're not happy with yourself, how can you make the customer happy?

Liisa Joronen (b. 1944) Finnish CEO of SOL (formerly Lindstrom). *Fast Company* (1997)

69 It's just a very different way of thinking. My workers don't look at me as a boss, but as a friend, someone they can deal with in confidence.

Alberto Juantorena (b. 1950) Cuban athlete and businessman. Quoted in *Running with the Legends* (Michael Sandrock; 1996)

70 How the hell can I ask people who work for me to travel cheaply if I am travelling in luxury.

Ingvar Kamprad (b. 1926) Swedish business executive and founder of IKEA. *Forbes* (August 2000)

71 I don't want to feel responsible to outsiders with financial concerns that may differ from those of the welfare of IKEA.

Ingvar Kamprad (b. 1926) Swedish business executive and founder of IKEA. *Forbes* (August 2000)

72 My answer is to stay close to ordinary people because at heart I am one.

Ingvar Kamprad (b. 1926) Swedish business executive and founder of IKEA. *Forbes* (August 2000)

73 For us to get out of a business would involve firing people and that cannot be done easily in Japan.

Tsutomu Kanai (b. 1929) Japanese chairman of Hitachi. *Fortune* (May 1996)

74 When I work in this place, it's my rest.

Mehmet Kanbur (b. 1948) Turkish entrepreneur. *Forbes* (October 1999)

75 Corporate values are a genuine competitive advantage...an enduring factor amid so many changes in products and services.

Rosabeth Moss Kanter (b. 1943) US management theorist, academic, and writer. Speech (1991)

76 Unlike a more communal environment...those who run the bureaucratic corporation often rely on outward manifestation to determine 'the right sort of person'.

Rosabeth Moss Kanter (b. 1943) US management theorist, academic, and writer. *The Economist* (March 1992)

77 Ambivalence about family responsibilities has a long history in the corporate world.

Rosabeth Moss Kanter (b. 1943) US management theorist, academic, and writer. *When Giants Learn to Dance: Mastering the Challenges of Strategy, Management and Careers in the 1990s* (1992), ch. 10

78 The corporation's edict to its members could be phrased as: 'While you are here, you will act as though you have no other responsibilities, no other life'.

Rosabeth Moss Kanter (b. 1943) US management theorist, academic, and writer. *When Giants Learn to Dance: Mastering the Challenges of Strategy, Management and Careers in the 1990s* (1992), ch. 10

79 Companies...are likely to find hierarchies turned upside down. Juniors teach seniors, subordinates lead teams with their bosses on them...A decision-making hierarchy is replaced by an internal marketplace of ideas.

Rosabeth Moss Kanter (b. 1943) US management theorist, academic, and writer. 'How E-Smart Are You?', *World Link* (January–February 2000)

80 It's excitement, animation, a show. You're in show business 365 days a year.

Donna Karan (b. 1948) US fashion designer. Referring to fashion business. *Style* (August 2000)

81 The new economy favors intangible things— ideas, information, and relationships.

Kevin Kelly (b. 1958) US executive editor of *Wired* magazine. *New Rules for the New Economy: 10 Radical Strategies for a Connected World* (1998)

82 In an age of incessant searching for a grail of business and personal success that recedes as surely as Gatsby's green light into the distance, of the making of management gurus there is no foreseeable end.

Carol Kennedy (b. 1952) British business executive, editor, and author. *Guide to the Management Gurus* (1991)

83 Diversity raises the intelligence of groups.

Nancy Kline (b. 1946) US author, educator, and consultant. *Time to Think* (1999)

84 More and more CEOs have become conscious that they are the CEO of marketing. You're selling trust.

Philip Kotler (b. 1931) US marketing management thinker. Quoted in *BusinessWeek* (9 December 1996)

85 Anyone in an environment that is not preparing him or her for a tougher future should move out fast.

John P. Kotter (b. 1947) US writer. *The New Rules: How to Succeed in Today's Post-Corporate World* (1995)

86 I believe in God, family, and McDonald's and, in the office, that order is reversed.

Ray Kroc (1902–84) US founder of McDonald's. Quoted in *McDonald's—Behind the Arches* (John F. Love; 1986)

87 If I had a brick for every time I've repeated the phrase 'Quality, Service, Cleanliness and Value', I'd probably be able to bridge the Atlantic Ocean with them.

Ray Kroc (1902–84) US founder of McDonald's. *McDonald's Annual Report* (1980)

88 Modelers build intricate decision trees whose pretension to utility is exceeded only by the awe in which high-level managers hold the technocrats who constrain them.

Theodore Levitt (b. 1925) US management theorist, writer, and editor. 'A Heretical View of Management Science', *Fortune* (December 1978)

89 Not as priest or soldier or judge does youth seek honor today, but as a man of offices. The business subaltern, charming and gallant as the jungle-gallopers of Kipling, drills files, not of troops, but of correspondence.

Sinclair Lewis (1885–1951) US writer and social critic. *The Job* (1916)

90 Men are quite humorless about their own businesses.
Betty MacDonald (1908–58) US writer. *The Egg and I* (1945)

91 It's a dream of mine to make the Japanese market more democratic.
Oki Matsumoto (b. 1964) Japanese IT executive. *BusinessWeek* (September 2000)

92 We've got to change the way companies go public, or we'll never see Japanese capital markets develop.
Oki Matsumoto (b. 1964) Japanese IT executive. *BusinessWeek* (September 2000)

93 In a company of 2500 people, there are 2500 egos running around, each with his or her own view of reality.
Mark McCormack (1930–2003) US entrepreneur, founder and CEO of the International Management Group. *What They Don't Teach You at Harvard Business School* (1984)

94 Never pick up someone else's ringing phone.
Mark McCormack (1930–2003) US entrepreneur, founder and CEO of the International Management Group. *What You'll Never Learn on the Internet* (2000)

95 I need to be part of something that is constantly evolving, that's not established.
Judy McGrath (b. 1952) US president of MTV. 'The 50 Most Powerful Women in American Business', *Fortune* (Patricia Sellers and Cora Daniels; October 1999)

96 A corporate Woodstock.
Regis McKenna (b. 1939) US marketing entrepreneur and chairman of The McKenna Group. Referring to Apple Computers. Quoted in *Infinite Loop* (Michael S. Malone; 1999)

97 Tolerance is not acceptance, and indifference is not assimilation.
Carey McWilliams (1905–80) US lawyer, journalist, and writer. *Brothers under the Skin* (1945)

98 The missionary configuration would have its own prime co-ordinating mechanism— socialisation, or, if you like, the standardisation of norms—and a corresponding main design parameter— indoctrination.
Henry Mintzberg (b. 1939) Canadian academic and management theorist. *The Structuring of Organisations* (1979)

99 The organisation would have...an ideology. The perceptive reader visitor would sense it immediately.
Henry Mintzberg (b. 1939) Canadian academic and management theorist. *The Structuring of Organisations* (1979)

100 Clearly, there will be a first among equals, but my brothers and I really are joined at the hip. That may actually make it easier for us to do what our dad did.
Elisabeth Murdoch (b. 1968) Australian film and television executive. Referring to Rupert Murdoch's family. *Forbes* (July 1998)

101 I don't get involved in the details. I do get involved in the choice of editors.
Rupert Murdoch (b. 1931) US CEO of News Corporation. Referring to Murdoch's 'hands-on' style as a newspaper proprietor. *Forbes* (June 1998)

102 John D. Rockefeller wanted to dominate oil, but Microsoft wants it all, you name it: cable, media, banking, car dealerships.
Ralph Nader (b. 1934) US lawyer and consumer-rights campaigner. *Newsweek* (October 1997)

103 I want all our people to believe they are working for the best agency in the world. A sense of pride works wonders.
David Ogilvy (1911–99) British advertising executive, founder and chairman of Ogilvy & Mather. *Principles of Management* (1968)

104 It is more of an entrepreneurial approach where the people close to the market and product create the business.
Kenichi Ohmae (b. 1943) Japanese management consultant and theorist. Quoted in *Thriving on Chaos* (Tom Peters; 1987)

105 Success goes to those with a corporate culture that assures the ability to anticipate and meet customer demand.
Tadashi Okamura (b. 1938) Japanese president and CEO of Toshiba Group. Message, *www.toshiba.com* (1999)

106 It's good business for our people to have confidence that we will not lay them off just to help our profit short-term.
Ken Olsen (b. 1926) US computer designer and founder of Digital Equipment Corporation. Speech (1982)

107 One company, one strategy, one message.
Ken Olsen (b. 1926) US computer designer and founder of Digital Equipment Corporation. Quoted in *The Ultimate Entrepreneur* (Glenn Rifkin and George Harrar; 1988)

108 The open bins and store rooms were symbols of trust, a trust that is central to the way HP does business.
David Packard (1912–96) US entrepreneur and co-founder of Hewlett-Packard. *The HP Way* (1995)

109 I've often thought that after you get organized, you ought to throw away the organization chart.
David Packard (1912–96) US entrepreneur and co-founder of Hewlett-Packard. 'Lessons of Leadership', *The Nation's Business* (January 1974)

110 I come from an environment where, if you see a snake, you kill it. At General Motors, if you see a snake, the first thing you do is hire a consultant on snakes.
H. Ross Perot (b. 1930) US entrepreneur, venture capitalist, and politician. Speech (December 1991)

111 You need to have what could be called seduction skills—this is not a world of command and control.
Raoul Pinnell (b. 1951) British branding and marketing communications director of Shell International Petroleum. *Marketing* (June 2000)

112 The clichés of a culture sometimes tell the deepest truths.
Faith Popcorn (b. 1947) US trend expert and founder of BrainReserve. *The Popcorn Report* (1991)

113 We will be creating two swans out of ugly ducklings.

Peter Ratcliffe (b. 1948) British CEO of P&O leisure division. *Sunday Times* (October 2000)

114 When people look at you as an independent company, they are in a position to judge you and understand you better and they give you the value that you believe is there.

Peter Ratcliffe (b. 1948) British CEO of P&O leisure division. *Sunday Times* (October 2000)

115 The kind of brain-dead, gum chewing assistant you find in so many shops drives me wild. I want everyone who works for me to feel the same excitement that I feel.

Anita Roddick (b. 1942) British entrepreneur and founder of The Body Shop. *Body and Soul* (co-written with Russell Miller; 1991)

116 I'm forcing more men into my company to get more sexual tension into the business...I love the buzz and...sexuality of verbal foreplay.

Anita Roddick (b. 1942) British entrepreneur and founder of The Body Shop. *Marketing* (3 August 1989)

117 We have our values from the Church, the temple, the mosque. Do not rob, do not murder. But our behaviour changes the minute we go into the corporate place. Suddenly all of this is irrelevant.

Anita Roddick (b. 1942) British entrepreneur and founder of The Body Shop. Interview, *Marketing Week* (24 February 2000)

118 They trawl me out when the City comes down to see us, just to give them shock therapy.

Anita Roddick (b. 1942) British entrepreneur and founder of The Body Shop. Quoted in *The Adventure Capitalists* (Jeff Grout and Lynne Curry; 1998)

119 We don't so much have a marketing department, as anthropologists working for us.

Anita Roddick (b. 1942) British entrepreneur and founder of The Body Shop. Referring to the ethical attitudes of The Body Shop. Quoted in *The Adventure Capitalists* (Jeff Grout and Lynne Curry; 1998)

120 Green was the colour which is so strongly seen as the environmental colour. It was also the only colour which covered the damp patches.

Anita Roddick (b. 1942) British entrepreneur and founder of The Body Shop. Referring to the origins and attitudes of The Body Shop, an ethical retailer. Quoted in *The Adventure Capitalists* (Jeff Grout and Lynne Curry; 1998)

121 The origin of corporatism in the second half of the nineteenth century lay in two things—the rejection of citizen-based democracy and the desire to react in a stable way to the Industrial Revolution.

John Ralston Saul (b. 1947) Canadian writer. *The Unconscious Civilization* (1995)

122 Apple has to be more pragmatic and less religious. And the only one who can really do that is the person who created the religion in the first place.

John Sculley (b. 1939) US partner of Sculley Brothers, former president of Pepsi, and CEO of Apple Computers. *Newsweek* (1996)

123 A true democracy, a place run on trust and freedom, not fear.

Ricardo Semler (b. 1959) Brazilian business executive and president of Semco. 'The Mavericks', *Fortune* (June 1995)

124 This system sounds chaotic, can be frustrating and is, in some ways, uncontrollable. It has destroyed any semblance of corporate security. And...it has worked very well.

Ricardo Semler (b. 1959) Brazilian business executive and president of Semco. 'The Mavericks', *Fortune* (June 1995)

125 We use minimal hierarchies, ad hoc structures, self-control, and the discipline of our own community marketplace of jobs and responsibilities to achieve high quality, on-time performance.

Ricardo Semler (b. 1959) Brazilian business executive and president of Semco. Referring to the revolutionary business structure he introduced at Semco. 'Why My Former Employees Still Work For Me', *Harvard Business Review* (January/February 1994)

126 Inertia of deeply-entrenched mental models.

Peter Senge (b. 1947) US academic and author. Quoted in *In Search of European Excellence* (Robert Heller; 1992)

127 Dividing an elephant in half does not produce two elephants.

Peter Senge (b. 1947) US academic and author. *The Fifth Discipline: The Art and Practice of the Learning Organization* (1990)

128 Real commitment is rare in today's organisation...90 percent of the time what passes for commitment is compliance.

Peter Senge (b. 1947) US academic and author. *The Fifth Discipline: The Art and Practice of the Learning Organization* (1990)

129 Corporate totalitarianism...rules through dispensability rather than exploitation. It treats communities, people, countries, ecosystems, species as disposable and dispensable.

Vandana Shiva (b. 1944) Indian academic. *Globalisation: Gandhi and Swadeshi* (2000)

130 If the washroom isn't good enough for the people in charge, then it's not good enough for the people in the store.

Marcus Sieff (1913–2001) British president of Marks & Spencer. Quoted in *A Passion for Excellence* (Tom Peters and Mary Austin; 1985)

131 Sometimes I am forced to the conclusion that GM is so large and its inertia so great that it is impossible for us to be leaders.

Alfred P. Sloan (1875–1966) US president of General Motors. Quoted in *The Bigness Complex* (Walter Adams and James Brock; 1992)

132 Orange was never just another mobile phone company. It was a promise deliverer.

Hans Snook (b. 1948) German chairman of Carphone Warhouse and former CEO of Orange. *Sunday Times* (June 2000)

133 You know the saying, 'a horse always knows when the rider is afraid'? That is true for business as well.

Dennis Stevenson (b. 1946) British company director. *Management Today* (April 1999)

134 Any engineer that doesn't need to wash his hands at least three times a day is a failure.

Shoichiro Toyoda (b. 1925) Japanese chairman of Toyota Motor Corporation. Referring to the importance of manufacturing in Japanese industry. Quoted in *How to Manage* (Ray Wild; 1995)

135 We need to develop more black management throughout the group, particularly in South Africa. Equally you have to be careful not to disillusion the existing management. It's a difficult balancing act.

Tony Trahar (b. 1950) South African CEO of Anglo American. *Sunday Times* (May 2000)

136 So far I like it fine. Most entrepreneurs don't last very long in big companies. But I'm not normal.

Ted Turner (b. 1938) US founder of Turner Broadcasting Systems. *New York Times* (November 1996)

137 We need a can-do, vibrant, innovation-driven culture. Not wearing a tie is just a snippet of that.

Paul Walsh (b. 1955) British CEO of Diageo. *Sunday Times* (September 2000)

138 It certainly helped me with the socialisation aspect of business.

Paul Walsh (b. 1955) British CEO of Diageo. Referring to working in the United States. *Sunday Times* (September 2000)

139 If the associates treat the customers well, the customers will return again and again, and that's where the real profit in the retail business lies.

Sam M. Walton (1918–92) US entrepreneur and founder of Wal-Mart, Inc. *Made in America* (co-written with John Huey; 1992)

140 The way management treats their associates is exactly how the associates will then treat the customers.

Sam M. Walton (1918–92) US entrepreneur and founder of Wal-Mart, Inc. 'The Hot Ticket in Retailing', *New York Times* (Isadore Barmash; July 1984)

141 We believe that an organization should pursue all tasks with the idea that they can be accomplished in superior fashion.

Thomas J. Watson Jr (1914–93) US CEO of IBM. *A Business and Its Beliefs* (1963)

142 I looked for those sharp, scratchy, harsh, almost unpleasant guys who see and tell you about things as they really are.

Thomas J. Watson Jr (1914–93) US CEO of IBM. *Fortune* (August 1987)

143 Business is a game, the greatest game in the world if you know how to play it.

Thomas J. Watson Sr (1874–1956) US founder and president of IBM. Quoted in *Father, Son & Co.: My Life at IBM and Beyond* (Thomas J. Watson Jr and Peter Petre; 1990)

144 Clothes don't make the man—but they go a long way towards making a businessman.

Thomas J. Watson Sr (1874–1956) US founder and president of IBM. Quoted in *IBM: Colossus in Transition* (Robert Sobel; 1981)

145 You cannot be a success in any business without believing that it is the greatest business in the world.

Thomas J. Watson Sr (1874–1956) US founder and president of IBM. Quoted in *IBM: Colossus in Transition* (Robert Sobel; 1981)

146 You have to put your heart in the business and the business in your heart.

Thomas J. Watson Sr (1874–1956) US founder and president of IBM. Quoted in *IBM: Colossus in Transition* (Robert Sobel; 1981)

147 Wild ducks.

Thomas J. Watson Sr (1874–1956) US founder and president of IBM. Referring to a group of IBM Fellows, whose role is to shake up the organisation. Quoted in *In Search of Excellence* (Tom Peters and Robert Waterman; 1982)

148 Our dream for the 1990s is a boundaryless company...where we knock down the walls that separate us from each other on the inside and from our key constituencies on the outside.

Jack Welch (b. 1935) US former chairman and CEO of General Electric. *General Electric annual report* (1990)

149 Power is a very dangerous word.

Ann Winblad (b. 1953) US venture capitalist. 'The 50 Most Powerful Women in American Business', *Fortune* (Patricia Sellers and Cora Daniels; October 1999)

150 The software industry as a whole tends to be slightly managed chaos. It was a giant group grope in the 1970s, when this whole thing started...effectively there are no rules.

Ann Winblad (b. 1953) US venture capitalist. Quoted in *Giant Killers* (Geoffrey James; 1996)

151 If you look at the companies where the CEO stayed on till he's 80, those are the people who confuse themselves with the company.

Walter Wriston (b. 1919) US banker. *New York Times* (April 1993)

152 We're not in cultures which support learning; we're in cultures that give us the message consistently: 'Don't mess up, don't make mistakes, don't make the boss look bad, don't give us any surprises'. So we're asking for a kind of predictability, control, respect and compliance that has nothing to do with learning.

Walter Wriston (b. 1919) US banker. Interview with Scott London, *US National Public Radio* (November 1996)

CORPORATE RESPONSIBILITY

1 I would never make a decision which might be damaging to Turin's local administration. A Texan capitalist couldn't care less about local government, he couldn't care less about the federal government.

Giovanni Agnelli (1921–2003) Italian business executive and president of Fiat. Fiat's headquarters are based in Turin. Quoted in *Interview on Modern Capitalism* (Arrigo Levi; 1983)

2 In every half-case, people see compensation. Compensatitis must be the worst disease that we have in the country at the moment.
Bertie Ahern (b. 1951) Irish prime minister. 'This Week They Said', *Irish Times* (13 December 1997)

3 The distinguishing mark of the executive responsibility is that it requires not merely conformance to a complex code of morals but also the creation of moral codes for others.
Chester Barnard (1886–1961) US business executive and management theorist. *The Functions of the Executive* (1938)

4 Economic activity should not only be efficient in its use of resources but should also be socially just, and environmentally and ecologically sustainable.
Warren Bennis (b. 1925) US educator and writer. *Beyond Leadership: Balancing Economics, Ethics and Ecology* (co-written with Jagdish Parikh and Ronnie Lessem; 1994)

5 CORPORATION, n. An ingenious device for obtaining individual profit without individual responsibility.
Ambrose Bierce (1842—?1914) US journalist and writer. *The Devil's Dictionary* (1911)

6 Take care of those who work for you and you'll float to greatness on their achievements.
H.S.M. Burns (1900–71) British oil industry executive, geophysicist, and president of Shell Oil Company. Quoted in *Men at the Top* (Osborn Elliott; 1959)

7 Few trends could so thoroughly undermine the very foundations of our free society as the acceptance by corporate officials of a social responsibility other than to make as much money for their stockholders as possible.
Milton Friedman (b. 1912) US economist and winner of the 1976 Nobel Prize in Economics. *Capitalism and Freedom* (1962)

8 There is a price to be paid for success in a family business. Our approach has been that, first, everyone has a responsibility to create wealth in the company.
Terri L. Gardner (b. 1956) US CEO and president of Soft Sheen Products. Quoted in 'Terri Gardner: Making Permanent Waves', *www.womenswire.com* (Janet Kidd Stuart; 2000)

9 Corporate bodies are more corrupt and profligate than individuals because they have more power to do mischief and are less amenable to disgrace or punishment. They feel neither shame, remorse, gratitude, nor goodwill.
William Hazlitt (1778–1830) British essayist and journalist. 'On Corporate Bodies', *Table Talk* (1821–22), Essay 27

10 Only the little people pay taxes.
Leona Helmsley (b. 1920) US hotelier. *New York Times* (July 1989)

11 Tensions and conflict between work life and personal life will never be fully resolved...We must give people the support they need to pursue business opportunities fully without shortchanging the human relationships that are of equal importance.
Rosabeth Moss Kanter (b. 1943) US management theorist, academic, and writer. *When Giants Learn to Dance: Mastering the Challenges of Strategy, Management and Careers in the 1990s* (1992), ch. 10

12 To last, a company must strive to add long-term value rather than going for the quick buck...it must be guided by the desire for continued relations with its principal constituencies—employees, customers, suppliers, stockholders.
Charles G. Koch (b. 1935) US management theorist, author, chairman and CEO of Koch Industries. 'Market-based Management', *Imprimis* (August 1996)

13 I have come to view strong corporate governance as indispensable to resilient and vibrant capital markets. It is the blood that fills the veins of transparent corporate disclosure...the muscle that moves a viable and accessible financial reporting structure. And without financial reporting premised on sound, honest numbers, capital markets will collapse upon themselves, suffocate and die.
Arthur Levitt Jr (b. 1931) US author and former chairman of the US Securities and Exchange Commission. Speech to the Audit Committee Symposium, New York City. 'An Essential Next Step in the Evolution of Corporate Governance' (29 June 1999)

14 While it is clear that new opportunities summon new challenges and that new possibilities bring forth new risks, let us never forget that the fundamental credibility of our system remains the single most important obligation. Trust and professionalism should never be just catchwords in a company's or firm's brochure.
Arthur Levitt Jr (b. 1931) US author and former chairman of the US Securities and Exchange Commission. Speech to the Securities Industry Association Annual Meeting, Boca Raton, Florida. 'Meeting the Challenges of a 21st Century Marketplace' (6 November 1998)

15 Too many CEO's are being judged today not by how effectively they manage operations, but by how they manage the Street. Too many analysts are being judged not by how well they analyze a particular company, but by how well they assist in selling the latest deal.
Arthur Levitt Jr (b. 1931) US author and former chairman of the US Securities and Exchange Commission. Speech, New York University Center for Law and Business, New York City. 'Renewing the Covenant with Investors' (10 May 2000)

16 Increasingly, I have become concerned that the motivation to meet Wall Street earnings expectations may be overriding common sense business practices...Managing may be giving way to manipulation; Integrity may be losing out to illusion.
Arthur Levitt Jr (b. 1931) US author and former chairman of the US Securities and Exchange Commission. Speech to the

New York University Center for Law and Business, New York City. 'The Numbers Game' (28 September 1998)

17 The dynamic nature of today's capital markets creates issues that increasingly move beyond the bright line of right and wrong...financial market participants grapple with questions in a gray area where there are no easy answers. It is in this realm where judgment and integrity are indispensable for effective corporate governance

Arthur Levitt Jr (b. 1931) US author and former chairman of the US Securities and Exchange Commission. Speech, Directors' College, Stanford Law School, Stanford University, California (22 March 1999)

18 There are too many boards that overlook more than they oversee; too many boards that substitute CEO directive for board initiative; too many boards that are re-active instead of pro-active; and too many boards who never rejected an easy answer and never pursued a tough question.

Arthur Levitt Jr (b. 1931) US author and former chairman of the US Securities and Exchange Commission. Speech, Directors' College, Stanford Law School, Stanford University, California (22 March 1999)

19 Corporations can have no soul but they can love each other.

Henry Demarest Lloyd (1847–1903) US journalist and reformer. *Wealth Against Commonwealth* (1894)

20 In the future, the successful companies will be those who work hardest to make sure that they are in tune with the needs and aspirations of society...And as the Shell experience demonstrates, reporting and greater openness has real benefits for business. Not only does it promote improved environmental management, it can also improve business competitiveness.

Mark Moody-Stuart (b. 1940) British chairman of Anglo American and former chairman of Committee of Managing Directors Royal Dutch/Shell Group. Speech to the World Congress of the International Society of Business, Economics and Ethics, São Paolo, Brazil. 'Putting Principles into Practice: The Ethical Challenge to Global Business' (19 July 2000)

21 We can no longer draw a line around business and say that is not our problem. If it is a problem for society, it is our problem also. The question is not whether it is our problem, but what our capacity and legitimacy is as a business to contribute to a solution.

Mark Moody-Stuart (b. 1940) British chairman of Anglo American and former chairman of Committee of Managing Directors Royal Dutch/Shell Group. Speech, St Paul's Cathedral, London. 'The Values of Sustainable Business in the Next Century' (12 July 1999)

22 Without profitability nothing is possible. However mere profitability is unlikely to be sufficient in, and of, itself. Much more will be expected by our own people, our customers; the other businesses we deal with, and political institutions.

Mark Moody-Stuart (b. 1940) British chairman of Anglo American and former chairman of Committee of Managing Directors Royal Dutch/Shell Group. Speech, St Paul's Cathedral, London. 'The Values of Sustainable Business in the Next Century' (12 July 1999)

23 At all times the idea of doing not only first-class business...has been before our minds. We have never been satisfied with simply keeping within the law, but have constantly sought to...fully observe the professional code.

J.P. Morgan Jr (1867–1943) US banker and financier. Statement to Congress (1933)

24 Natural resources are morally neutral. As such they can be a source of great good...or dreadful ill. The key element is not the resource itself, but how it is exploited.

Nicky Oppenheimer (b. 1945) South African chairman of De Beers. Speech, Southern Africa Business Association, London (26 June 2000)

25 You can't look the troops in the eye and say, 'It's been a bad year, we can't do anything for you', but then say, 'By the way, we're going to pay ourselves a $1 million bonus'.

H. Ross Perot (b. 1930) US entrepreneur, venture capitalist, and politician. 1986. Referring to his resignation from the General Motors board following GM's decision to freeze profit-sharing payments to workers while going ahead with executive bonus payments. Quoted in *Thriving on Chaos* (Tom Peters; 1987)

26 The chief problem of big business today is to shape its policies so that each worker will feel...a vital part of his company with a personal responsibility for its success and a chance to share in that success.

William Cooper Procter (1862–1934) US president of Procter & Gamble. 1887. Speaking at the introduction of an innovatory employee profit-sharing scheme. Quoted in *Eyes on Tomorrow: The Evolution of Procter and Gamble* (Oscar Schisgall; 1981)

27 Business has to be a force for social change. It is not enough to avoid hideous evil—it must, we must, actively do good. If business stays parochial, without moral energy or codes of behaviour, claiming there are no such thing as values, then God help us all. If you think morality is a luxury business can't afford, try living in a world without it.

Anita Roddick (b. 1942) British entrepreneur and founder of The Body Shop. Speech to the International Forum on Globalisation Teach-In, Seattle, Washington. 'Trading with Principles' (27 November 1999)

28 Today's corporations have global responsibilities because their decisions affect world problems concerning economics, poverty, security and the environment.

Anita Roddick (b. 1942) British entrepreneur and founder of The Body Shop. *Body and Soul* (co-written with Russell Miller; 1991)

29 Being good is good business.

Anita Roddick (b. 1942) British entrepreneur and founder of The Body Shop. *Sunday Express* (2 November 1986)

30 Businesses should play to win, but they should also play by the rules. It is in our own interests that our social norms put common interests above the interests of the individual.

George Soros (b. 1930) US financier, entrepreneur, and philanthropist. January 2000. Speech, World Economic Forum, Davos, Switzerland. Quoted in *World Link* (March–April 2000)

31 Corporate courage is usually no greater than personal courage.

Edward Teller (b. 1908) US nuclear scientist. Interview, *Playboy* (August 1979)

32 The public be damned. I am working for my stockholders.

William Henry Vanderbilt (1821–85) US industrialist. Refusing to speak to a reporter. Quoted in Letter from A.W. Cole, *New York Times* (25 August 1918)

33 Today, wealth creation by major companies is taken for granted by the public, but economic performance and making profit are no longer enough. The real question is *how* do we make a profit, *how* do we define economic progress, and how sustainable is our business in the long-term?

Jeroen Van der Veer (b. 1947) Dutch Advisory Director of Unilever, vice-chairman of the Royal Dutch/Shell Group, and president of Royal Dutch Petroleum Company. Speech, 'Earning the Licence to Grow' (26 November 1999)

34 The drive and creativity of business is essential if society is to make progress towards sustainable development. Businesses can only contribute by being profitable and competitive. But equally, we will only continue to be profitable if we respond to people's concerns and meet their expectations.

Philip Watts (b. 1945) British managing director of Shell Petroleum Company and group managing director of Royal Dutch/Shell Group. Speech at Templeton College, Oxford, United Kingdom. 'Pursuing Sustainable Development—A Shell Journey' (15 May 2000)

CORRUPTION AND SCANDAL

1 Enron so engineered its reported financial position and results of operations that its financial statements bore little resemblance to its actual financial condition or performance.

Neal Balson, US government official. *Enron bankruptcy report* (March 2003)

2 Prepays were the quarter-to-quarter cashflow lifeblood of Enron.

Neal Balson, US government official. Referring to Enron's accounting practices. *Enron bankruptcy report* (March 2003)

3 I think as a profession we have taken a hit.

Joseph Berardino (b. 1951) US business executive. Referring to accounting scandals. Quoted in *BusinessWeek* (14 December 2001)

4 What was done was not in keeping with the values and heritage of this firm. It was wrong, there's no other word for it.

Joseph Berardino (b. 1951) US business executive. Referring to the part played by accountant's Arthur Andersen in the collapse of Enron. Quoted in *Guardian* (June 2002)

5 Greed is all right...Greed is healthy. You can be greedy and still feel good about yourself.

Ivan Boesky (b. 1937) US financier convicted of insider dealing in 1987. After success as a trader on Wall Street, in 1987 he was convicted of securities fraud, imprisoned for two years, and fined US$100 million. Commencement address, Berkeley, California (18 May 1986)

6 Get me inside any boardroom and I'll get any decision I want.

Alan Bond (b. 1938) Australian entrepreneur and founder of the Bond Corporation, convicted of corporate fraud in 1997. Bond was noted for his agressive business style. His company collapsed in 1990 causing widespread shock waves; in 1995 he was arrested and charged with misconduct relating to corporate deals in the 1980s. *Daily Telegraph* (27 June 1989)

7 When I'm older I'm going to buy and sell people like you.

Alan Bond (b. 1938) Australian entrepreneur and founder of the Bond Corporation, convicted of corporate fraud in 1997. As a boy, speaking to one of his teachers. Quoted in *Sunday Telegraph* (2 June 1989)

8 No office anywhere on earth is so puritanical, impeccable, elegant, sterile or incorruptible as not to contain the yeast for at least one affair...just let a yeast raiser into the place and first thing you know—bread!

Helen Gurley Brown (b. 1922) US writer and editor. *Sex and the Office* (1964)

9 The business pages of American newspapers should not read like a scandal sheet.

George W. Bush (b. 1946) US president. Referring to a series of high-profile accounting scandals. Speech (July 2002)

10 The misdeeds now being uncovered in some quarters of corporate America are threatening the financial well being of many workers and investors.

George W. Bush (b. 1946) US president. Referring to a series of high-profile accounting scandals. Speech (July 2002)

11 At this moment, America's greatest economic need is higher ethical standards—standards enforced by strict laws and upheld by responsible business leaders.

George W. Bush (b. 1946) US president. Said at a time when a number of high-profile accounting scandals were discovered. Speech (July 2002)

12 It is a capital mistake to theorise before one has data. Insensibly one begins to twist facts to suit theories, instead of theories to suit facts.

Arthur Conan Doyle (1859–1930) British writer and doctor. 'Scandal in Bohemia', *The Adventures of Sherlock Holmes* (1892)

13 I mean, we could have boards, literally, and management teams, tied up examining every process—is that the best use of a board and senior management time?

Carly Fiorina (b. 1954) US president and CEO of Hewlett-Packard. Referring to government plans to improve corporate responsibility after a series of accounting scandals. Interview, *Fortune* (November 2002)

14 The key to running an entrepreneurial business with feet on four continents lies in constant access to information.

Lycourgos Kyprianou (b. 1955) Greek Cypriot entrepreneur recently under investigation for fraud and insider dealing. *Forbes* (August 2000)

15 If there is anything material and we're not reporting it, we'll be breaking the law. We don't break the law.
Kenneth Lay (b. 1942) US business executive. Referring to Enron's accounting practices. Quoted in *Business Week* (24 August 2001)

16 There is so much wriggle room in the language of the notification that we may not be getting what we think we are getting.
Bill Leacock, US lawyer. Said at a time when a number of high-profile accounting scandals were discovered. Quoted in *Guardian* (16 August 2002)

CREATIVITY

1 Creativity is allowing oneself to make mistakes. Art is knowing which ones to keep.
William Adams (b. 1934) US financial consultant. *The Dilbert Principle* (1996)

2 Many people are inventive, sometimes cleverly so. But real creativity begins with the drive to work on and on and on.
Margueritte Bro (1894–1977) US writer. *Sarah* (1949)

3 An intellectual is someone whose mind watches itself.
Albert Camus (1913–60) French novelist and essayist. *Notebooks* (1963)

4 The decisive moment.
Henri Cartier-Bresson (b. 1908) French photographer. Essay (1952)

5 But my art, I thought, is perhaps a wild art, a blazing quicksilver, a blue soul flashing on my canvas.
Marc Chagall (1887–1985) French painter. *My Life* (1931)

6 If you want creative workers, give them enough time to play.
John Cleese (b. 1939) British comedian, actor, and writer. *East Valley Tribune* (1999)

7 Minds are like parachutes. They only function when they are open.
James Dewar (1842–1923) British physicist. Attrib.

8 Inventors and men of genius have almost always been regarded as fools at the beginning (and very often at the ends) of their careers.
Fyodor Dostoevsky (1821–81) Russian novelist. *The Idiot* (1868)

9 As a human being, one has been endowed with just enough intelligence to be able to see clearly how utterly inadequate that intelligence is when confronted with what exists.
Albert Einstein (1879–1955) US physicist. Letter (September 1932)

10 For people who live in the imagination, there is no lack of subjects. To seek for the exact moment at which inspiration comes is false. Imagination floods us with suggestions all the time, from all directions.
Federico Fellini (1920–93) Italian film director. *Autobiography* (1974)

11 Puzzle drive.
Richard Feynman (1918–88) US physicist. Address (1957)

12 Creativity often consists of merely turning up what is already there. Did you know that right and left shoes were thought up only a little over a century ago?
Bernice Fitz-Gibbon (?1895–1982) US advertising executive. Quoted in her obituary. *New York Times* (1982)

13 Curious people have an appetite for learning new things and they realise the necessity for change.
Brad Fregger, US CEO of 1st World Library. 'On Achieving Excellence' (July 1991)

14 In the middle of a hard project, I remind people to do something else. Sometimes people need to work on something completely different to get their best ideas.
Brad Fregger, US CEO of 1st World Library. 'On Achieving Excellence' (July 1991)

15 One doesn't discover new lands without consenting to lose sight of the shore for a very long time.
André Gide (1869–1951) French novelist and essayist. *The Counterfeiters* (1926)

16 All the great work comes from people's obsession and imagination, not from focus groups.
Michael Grade (b. 1943) British television executive. *Marketing* (June 2000)

17 I don't think I am creative. I think I recognise creativity.
Michael Grade (b. 1943) British television executive. *Marketing* (June 2000)

18 Shakespeare didn't walk up and down at the Globe and ask 'What do you fancy'...he just wrote what he felt like.
Michael Grade (b. 1943) British television executive. *Marketing* (June 2000)

19 Originality is deliberate and forced, and partakes of the nature of a protest.
Eric Hoffer (1902–83) US philosopher. *The Passionate State of Mind* (1955)

20 When you ask creative people how they did something, they feel a little guilty because they didn't really *do* it, they just *saw* something...That's because they were able to connect experiences they've had and synthesize new things.
Steve Jobs (b. 1955) US entrepreneur, co-founder and CEO of Apple Computer Company, and CEO of Pixar. Interview, 'The Next Insanely Great Thing', *Wired Magazine* (February 1996)

21 Firms that take a creative approach to looking for a process edge may discover or invent processes that open new avenues of opportunity without massive capital investment or abandoning currently successful ways of doing business.
Peter G.W. Keen (b. 1930) US information technology consultant. 'Basic Change', *The Process Edge* (1999)

22 True creativity often starts where language ends.
Arthur Koestler (1905–83) British writer and journalist. *The Act of Creation* (1964)

23 Every creative act is a sudden cessation of stupidity.
Edwin Land (1909–91) US inventor and founder of Polaroid Corporation. *Forbes* (June 1975)

24 Intense concentration for hour after hour can bring out resources in people that they didn't know they had.
Edwin Land (1909–91) US inventor and founder of Polaroid Corporation. *Forbes* (June 1975)

25 I think human beings in the mass are fun at square dances, exciting to be with in a theatre audience... At the same time, I think, whether outside science or within science, there is no such thing as group originality or group creativity.
Edwin Land (1909–91) US inventor and founder of Polaroid Corporation. 'Thinking Ahead', *Harvard Business Review* (September–October 1959)

26 We as technologists in industry do not use these minds at all. Instead of regarding them as minds, we substitute other criteria for usefulness.
Edwin Land (1909–91) US inventor and founder of Polaroid Corporation. *Selected Papers in Industry* (Polaroid Corporation; 1983)

27 We created an environment in which a man was expected to sit and think for two years.
Edwin Land (1909–91) US inventor and founder of Polaroid Corporation. *Selected Papers in Industry* (Polaroid Corporation; 1983)

28 Creativity is never enough.
Adrienne Landau (b. 1950) US fashion designer. 'An Artisan Discovers Cash Flow', *Forbes Global* (Richard C. Morais; October 1999)

29 All too often, people believe that creativity automatically leads to innovation. It doesn't.
Theodore Levitt (b. 1925) US management theorist, writer, and editor. 'Ideas Are Useless Unless Used', *Inc.* (February 1981)

30 Creative people tend to pass the responsibility for getting down to brass tacks to others.
Theodore Levitt (b. 1925) US management theorist, writer, and editor. 'Ideas Are Useless Unless Used', *Inc.* (February 1981)

31 Creativity is thinking new things. Innovation is doing new things.
Theodore Levitt (b. 1925) US management theorist, writer, and editor. 'Ideas Are Useless Unless Used', *Inc.* (February 1981)

32 Since business is a 'get things done' institution, creativity without action-oriented follow-through is a barren form of behavior.
Theodore Levitt (b. 1925) US management theorist, writer, and editor. 'Ideas Are Useless Unless Used', *Inc.* (February 1981)

33 If you are possessed by an idea, you find it expressed everywhere, you even smell it.
Thomas Mann (1875–1955) German writer. *Death in Venice* (1913)

34 I have no children but I have the heart of a child.
Mari Matsunaga (b. 1954) Japanese IT designer. *Fortune* (October 2000)

35 Less is more.
Ludwig Mies van der Rohe (1886–1969) German architect. Quoted in *Mies van der Rohe* (P. Johnson; 1947)

36 Planning, by its very nature, defines and preserves categories. Creativity, by its very nature, creates categories or re-arranges established ones.
Henry Mintzberg (b. 1939) Canadian academic and management theorist. *The Rise and Fall of Strategic Planning* (1994)

37 Strategic planning can neither provide creativity nor deal with it when it emerges by other means.
Henry Mintzberg (b. 1939) Canadian academic and management theorist. *The Rise and Fall of Strategic Planning* (1994)

38 Have nothing in your houses that you do not know to be useful, or believe to be beautiful.
William Morris (1834–96) British craftsman, artist, and writer. *Hopes and Fears for Art* (1882)

39 Organisations with decision-making speed and imagination will thrive as nobody can claim to have a monopoly over creativity.
Narayana Murthy (b. 1946) Indian founder and CEO of Infosys. 'The Future Is Inorganic', *www.rediff.com* (1998)

40 Could Henry Ford produce the Book of Kells? Certainly not. He would quarrel initially with the advisability of such a project and then prove it was impossible.
Flann O'Brien (1911–66) Irish writer. *Myles Away from Dublin* (1990)

41 The majority of businessmen are incapable of original thought because they are unable to escape from the tyranny of reason.
David Ogilvy (1911–99) British advertising executive, founder and chairman of Ogilvy & Mather. Quoted in *The Creative Organisation* (Gary A. Steiner, ed.; 1965)

42 That's an actor's life. Complete freedom and versatility.
Laurence Olivier (1907–89) British actor and director. Interview (1986)

43 Controlled accident.
Jackson Pollock (1912–56) US painter. Referring to his painting technique. Interview (1946)

44 The great creators—the thinkers, the artists, the scientists, the inventors—stood alone against the men of their time.
Ayn Rand (1905–82) US writer. *The Fountainhead* (1943)

45 As far as creativity is concerned, the power is in the unexpected.
Alan G. Robinson (b. 1958) US author. *Corporate Creativity* (co-written with Sam Stern; 1997)

46 The majority of creative acts are unplanned, and each begins with awareness of an unexpected opportunity.
Alan G. Robinson (b. 1958) US author. *Corporate Creativity* (co-written with Sam Stern; 1997)

47 The mind thinks, not with data, but with ideas whose creation and elaboration cannot be reduced to a set of predictable values.
Theodore Roszak (1933–81) US historian, writer, and editor. *The Cult of Information* (1994)

48 Creativity can be described as letting go of certainties.
Gail Sheehy (b. 1937) US journalist and author. *Speed is of the Essence* (1971)

49 Less is a bore.
Robert Venturi (b. 1925) US architect. Alluding to Mies van der Rohe's maxim 'Less is more'. *Complexity and Contradiction in Architecture* (1966)

50 Intelligence is quickness to apprehend as distinct from ability which is capacity to act wisely on the thing apprehended.
A.N. Whitehead (1861–1947) British philosopher and mathematician. *Dialogues* (1954)

51 Every human brain is born, not as a blank tablet waiting to be filled in by experience, but as an exposed negative waiting to be slipped into developer fluid.
Edward O. Wilson (b. 1929) US biologist. *Independent on Sunday* (February 1997)

CRITICISM

1 A negative judgement gives you more satisfaction than praise, providing it smacks of jealousy.
Jean Baudrillard (b. 1929) French philosopher. *Cool Memories* (1987)

2 No man can tell another his faults so as to benefit him, unless he loves him.
Henry Ward Beecher (1813–87) US clergyman and reformer. *Proverbs from Plymouth Pulpit* (1887)

3 Everything you reprove in another, you must carefully avoid in yourself.
Cicero (106–43 BC) Roman orator and statesman. *In Verrem* (1st century BC), no. 2

4 Why is it so necessary to sneer at people who are successful? I still take it all very personally. I often ask myself why do I go on.
Terence Conran (b. 1931) British business executive, retailer, and founder of Habitat. *Daily Express* (5 October 1981)

5 We are tough and brave in war. We are soft and compromising in business.
Michael Owen Edwardes (b. 1930) British company executive. Referring to British managers. Speech, Institute of Personnel Management Annual Conference (27 October 1984)

6 Praise should always be given in public, criticism should always be given in private.
J. Paul Getty (1892–1976) US entrepreneur, oil industry executive, and financier. *How to Be Rich* (1965)

7 Criticism is one of the most important tasks a manager has.
Daniel Goleman (b. 1946) US behavioural scientist, journalist, and author. *Emotional Intelligence* (1996)

8 Cheers hearten a man. But jeers are just as essential. They help maintain his sense of balance and proportion.
Jay E. House (1870–1936) US journalist and columnist. 'On Second Thoughts', *On Second Thoughts* (1936)

9 You may scold a carpenter who has made you a bad table, though you cannot make a table. It is not your trade to make tables.
Samuel Johnson (1709–84) British poet, lexicographer, essayist, and critic. 15 June 1763. Quoted in *The Life of Samuel Johnson* (James Boswell; 1791)

10 Critical remarks are only made by people who love you.
Federico Mayor (b. 1934) Spanish politician and former director-general of UNESCO. Quoted in *Guardian* (24 June 1988)

11 Next to the joy of the egotist is the joy of the detractor.
Agnes Repplier (1858–1950) US writer and historian. 'Writing an Autobiography', *Under Dispute* (1924)

12 No one can make you feel inferior without your consent.
Eleanor Roosevelt (1884–1962) US reformer, author, and first lady. *This is My Story* (1937)

13 Fashion is merely the lowest form of ideology.
John Ralston Saul (b. 1947) Canadian writer. *The Unconscious Civilization* (1995)

14 A free society is a society where it is safe to be unpopular.
Adlai E. Stevenson (1900–65) US statesman and author. Speech (October 1952)

15 I can't tell you the number of times that I meet with Internet entrepreneurs or executives, and how little theory they have, and how little cognitive behavior they seem to exhibit about what it is they're doing.
Jay S. Walker, US entrepreneur and founder of Priceline.com, CEO of Walker Digital Corporation. Interview, *Strategy + Business* (April/June 2000)

CUSTOMERS

1 The customer isn't king anymore. The customer is dictator.
Anonymous. Said by a retailer. *Fortune* (Autumn-Winter 1993)

2 Everything changes when there is a real customer yelling at you from the other end of the phone.
Percy Barnevik (b. 1941) Swedish former CEO of ABB. Quoted in *Liberation Management* (Tom Peters; 1992)

3 Above all, we wish to avoid having a dissatisfied customer. We consider our customers a part of our organization, and we want them to feel free to make any criticism they see fit in regard to our merchandise or service.

L.L. Bean (1872–1967) US outdoor clothing and equipment retailer. 1934. *L.L. Bean catalogue* (1999)

4 If someone thinks they are being mistreated by us, they won't tell 5 people, they'll tell 5000.

Jeff Bezos (b. 1964) US founder and CEO of Amazon.com. *Wall Street Journal* (May 1996)

5 It is difficult to make people happy but I know we should try harder.

Christopher Bland (b. 1938) British media executive and chairman of BT. Referring to the BBC's policy of achieving programme balance. *Management Today* (July 1999)

6 The popular slogan, stay close to your customers, appears not always to be robust advice.

Clayton M. Christensen (b. 1952) US writer. *The Innovator's Dilemma* (1997)

7 It is a company's customers who effectively control what it can and cannot do.

Clayton M. Christensen (b. 1952) US writer. *The Innovator's Dilemma* (1997)

8 As a creative retailer, my belief is simply that, if reasonable and intelligent people are offered products that are well made, well designed, work well, are of a decent quality and at a price they can afford, then they will like and buy them.

Terence Conran (b. 1931) British business executive, retailer, and founder of Habitat. Quoted in *The Adventure Capitalists* (Jeff Grout and Lynne Curry; 1998)

9 Customers are your future, representing new opportunities, ideas and avenues for growth.

Michael Dell (b. 1965) US chairman and CEO of Dell Computer Corporation. *Direct from Dell* (1996)

10 Profit in business comes from repeat customers; customers that boast about your product and service, and that bring friends with them.

W. Edwards Deming (1900–93) US consultant and author. *Out of the Crisis* (1984)

11 The only profit center is the customer.

Peter F. Drucker (b. 1909) US management consultant and academic. *Harvard Business Review* (January/February 1995)

12 There is only one valid definition of business: to create a customer.

Peter F. Drucker (b. 1909) US management consultant and academic. *The Practice of Management* (1954)

13 Helping someone personally is a better measure of success than picking a hot stock.

Grace Fey, US vice-president and director of Frontier Capital Management. Quoted in *Women of the Street* (Sue Herera; 1997)

14 What makes me *feel* more successful than picking stocks or any of that, is my client relationships.

Grace Fey, US vice-president and director of Frontier Capital Management. Quoted in *Women of the Street* (Sue Herera; 1997)

15 A manufacturer is not through with his customer when a sale is completed. He has then only started with his customer.

Henry Ford (1863–1947) US industrialist, car manufacturer, and founder of Ford Motor Company. *My Life and Work* (co-written with Samuel Crowther; 1922)

16 I come with the mindset of a customer.

Lou Gerstner (b. 1942) US chairman and CEO of IBM. *The Economist* (June 1998)

17 Whatever the business model, it doesn't matter what anybody else thinks if customers don't like it.

Paul Gratton (b. 1960) British CEO of Egg. *Sunday Times* (May 2000)

18 It has no God-given right to succeed if it does not give customers what they want.

Roger Holmes (b. 1960) British business executive. *Sunday Times* (September 2000)

19 You build an expertise around the customer, and that's an investment.

Rolf Hueppi (b. 1943) Swiss CEO of Zurich Insurance. *Wall Street Journal Europe* (June 1992)

20 I look in my closet, and if I need it, I design it. If it works for me, it works for the customer.

Donna Karan (b. 1948) US fashion designer. *Fortune* (Autumn-Winter 1993)

21 It's not just running a restaurant, it's being friends with your customers. It's a personal connection, very personal.

Mary Kelekis (b. 1925) Canadian restaurant owner. Quoted in *Relishing Taste and Tradition* (Helen Stein; 1997)

22 Customers provide you with the most accurate barometer of what's right and wrong.

Herb Kelleher (b. 1931) US businessman and founder of Southwest Airlines. *Industry Week* (8 January 1996)

23 At the Best Plants, the customer is king.

Theodore B. Kinni, US business author and editor. *America's Best* (1997)

24 There is far more involved in the relationship with customers than just providing good products and services. It is a question of personal identification, personal ethics and perhaps, a little more cynically, of personal self-esteem. This identification...rests on intangibles—on the elements that make up trust.

Mark Moody-Stuart (b. 1940) British chairman of Anglo American, and former chairman of Committee of Managing Directors Royal Dutch/Shell Group. Speech, St Paul's Cathedral, London. 'The Values of Sustainable Business in the Next Century' (12 July 1999)

25 The customer is never wrong.

César Ritz (1850–1918) Swiss hotel proprietor. 1908. Attrib.

26 We should never be allowed to forget that it is the customer who, in the end, determines how many people are employed and what sort of wages companies can afford to pay.

Alfred Robens (1910–99) British politician and chairman of the National Coal Board. *Observer* (1 May 1977)

27 The customer is always right.
Gordon Selfridge (1858–1947) British retailer. Quoted in *No Name on the Door* (A.H. Williams; 1957)

28 The customer will become so integrated into the production process that we will find it more and more difficult to tell just who is actually the consumer and the producer.
Alvin Toffler (b. 1928) US social commentator. *The Third Wave* (1980)

29 The key is to get into the stores and listen.
Sam M. Walton (1918–92) US entrepreneur and founder of Wal-Mart, Inc. *Wall Street Journal* (April 1982)

30 There aren't any categories of problems here. There's just one problem. Some of us aren't paying enough attention to our customers.
Thomas J. Watson Sr (1874–1956) US founder and president of IBM. Quoted in *In Search of Excellence* (Tom Peters and Robert Waterman; 1982)

DEBT

1 A debt may get mouldy, but it never decays.
Chinua Achebe (b. 1930) Nigerian novelist, poet, and essayist. *No Longer at Ease* (1960)

2 He who buys what he needs not, sells what he needs.
Anonymous. Japanese proverb.

3 If someone had told you four years ago that the national debt would be doubled in the next four years, you would have insisted on a saliva test for that person.
Dale Bumpers (b. 1925) US politician. *US News & World Report* (1984)

4 Think of all the energy you've wasted in your time looking for money to pay interest on your loans. If you'd used it on something else you might have turned the world upside down by now.
Anton Chekhov (1860–1904) Russian playwright and short-story writer. *The Cherry Orchard* (1904), Act 3

5 Bankruptcy or credit default is not an issue.
Bernie Ebbers (b. 1941) Canadian business executive. Said a few months before the bankruptcy of WorldCom. Press conference (February 2002)

6 Creditors have better memories than debtors.
Benjamin Franklin (1706–90) US politician, inventor, and journalist. The *Poor Richard's Almanack* series (1732–58) were originally published under the pseudonym Richard Saunders. *Poor Richard's Almanack* (1758)

7 Christmas is a time when kids tell Santa Claus what they want and adults pay for it. Deficits are when adults tell the government what they want—and their kids pay for it.
Richard D. Lamm (b. 1935) US politician. *US News & World Report* (1985)

8 I feel these days like a very large flamingo. No matter what way I turn, there is always a very large bill.
Joseph O'Connor (b. 1963) Irish journalist and novelist. *The Secret World of the Irish Male* (1994)

9 The debt is like a crazy aunt we keep down in the basement. All the neighbors know she's there, but nobody wants to talk about her.
H. Ross Perot (b. 1930) US entrepreneur, venture capitalist, and politician. *United We Stand: How We Can Take Back Our Country* (1992)

10 If I confess to you why I was so far behind you in these examples, you'd know why we have a budget deficit.
Ronald Reagan (b. 1911) US former president and actor. Said to a junior high school math class. Quoted in *US News & World Report* (1984)

11 Things continue in government unless you feel a crisis. In fact, we didn't have a crisis, so the deficit persisted.
Paul A. Volcker (b. 1927) US economist and banker. *Time* (1989)

12 At the rate we're borrowing from abroad, in the space of three years we will have wiped out all of the holdings we've built up overseas since the Second World War and become a debtor nation.
Paul A. Volcker (b. 1927) US economist and banker. *US News & World Report* (1984)

13 One must have some sort of occupation now-a-days. If I hadn't my debts I shouldn't have anything to think about.
Oscar Wilde (1854–1900) Irish writer and wit. *A Woman of No Importance* (1893), Act 1

DECISIONS

1 Good decisions come from wisdom. Wisdom comes from experience. Experience comes from bad decisions.
Anonymous. *Forbes* (10 August 1987)

2 You must avoid the investigation trap—you can't postpone tough decisions by studying them to death.
Percy Barnevik (b. 1941) Swedish former CEO of ABB. *Harvard Business Review* (March/April 1991)

3 We know what happens to people who stay in the middle of the road. They get run over.
Aneurin Bevan (1897–1960) British politician. *Observer* (6 December 1953)

4 DECIDE, v. i. To succumb to the preponderance of one set of influences over another set.
Ambrose Bierce (1842–?1914) US journalist and writer. *The Devil's Dictionary* (1911)

5 If we want people on the front lines of companies to be responsible for making good business decisions, they must have the same information that managers use to make good business decisions.
Kenneth Blanchard (b. 1939) US management theorist and author. *The 3 Keys to Empowerment* (co-written with John P. Carlos and Alan Randolph; 1999)

6 Every decision is liberating, even if it leads to disaster. Otherwise, why do so many people walk upright and with open eyes into their misfortune.

Elias Canetti (1905–94) British philosopher and writer. '1980', *The Secret Heart of the Clock: Notes, Aphorisms, Fragments 1973–85* (1991)

7 Knowing is different from doing and therefore theory must never be used as norms for a standard, but merely as aids to judgement.
Karl von Clausewitz (1780–1831) Prussian general and military strategist. *On War* (1831)

8 Decisions of the kind the executive has to make are not made well by acclamation. They are made well only if based on the clash of conflicting views...The first rule in decision-making is that one does not make a decision unless there is disagreement.
Peter F. Drucker (b. 1909) US management consultant and academic. *The Effective Executive* (1967), ch. 7

9 We should never allow ourselves to be bullied by an either-or. There is often the possibility of something better than either of these two alternatives.
Mary Parker Follett (1868–1933) US management thinker and author. *Dynamic Administration* (1941)

10 If businessmen always made the right decisions, business wouldn't be business.
J. Paul Getty (1892–1976) US entrepreneur, oil industry executive, and financier. *How to Be Rich* (1965)

11 You've got to take the bull by the teeth.
Samuel Goldwyn (1882–1974) US film producer. Quoted in *Goldwyn* (Arthur Marx; 1976)

12 A bad decision is when you know what to do and you don't do it.
Duncan Goodhew (b. 1957) British swimmer. Quoted in *Treasury of Investment Wisdom* (Bernice Cohen; 1999)

13 When it's time to make a decision about a person or problem...trust your intuition...act.
Bud Hadfield (b. 1923) US entrepreneur and founder of Kwik Kopy. *Wealth within Reach: Winning Strategies for Success from the Unconventional Wisdom of Bud Hadfield* (1995)

14 I believe that work is a combination of emotion and reason and you should never exclude how you feel from your decision-making process.
Tamara Ingram, British advertising executive. Quoted in *Management Today* (September 2001)

15 It's an unbelievable responsibility to influence decisions, shareholder value and, most important to me, people's careers and livelihoods.
Andrea Jung (b. 1958) US president of Avon Products. 'The 50 Most Powerful Women in American Business', *Fortune* (Patricia Sellers and Cora Daniels; October 1999)

16 People who are making decisions about the future often don't have access to some of the best ideas in the company, which may be at the periphery or at lower levels.
Rosabeth Moss Kanter (b. 1943) US management theorist, academic, and writer. Interview, *Strategy + Business* (July–September 1999)

17 Two basic values, autonomy and solidarity, serve as helpful prompters in any decision-making process.
György Konrád (b. 1933) Hungarian writer. *The Melancholy of Rebirth* (1995)

18 Business today is about making decisions amid ambiguity.
Geraldine Laybourne (b. 1947) US chairman of Oxygen Media. Quoted in 'Next Stop—The 21st Century', *Fast Company* (Lucy McCauley; 1999)

19 Now who is to decide between 'Let it be' and 'Force it'?
Katherine Mansfield (1888–1923) New Zealand short-story writer. *The Journal of Katherine Mansfield* (1927)

20 The velocity of decision making in government was extraordinarily slow. It took 18 to 24 months and 15 to 20 trips to Delhi to get a license to import computers.
Narayana Murthy (b. 1946) Indian founder and CEO of Infosys. *Forbes* (June 2000)

21 Decision making by consensus has been the subject of a great deal of research...evidence strongly suggests that a consensus approach yields more creative decisions and more effective implementation than does individual decision making.
William Ouchi (b. 1943) US writer. *Theory Z: How American Business Can Meet the Japanese Challenge* (1981)

22 What is important is not the decision itself but rather how committed and informed people are. The 'best' decisions can be bungled just as the 'worst' decisions can work just fine.
William Ouchi (b. 1943) US writer. *Theory Z: How American Business Can Meet the Japanese Challenge* (1981)

23 In America, business is going on faith. They're saying, hey this is for real and this is happening. I don't have to analyse this, I've made a decision.
John A. Roth (b. 1942) Canadian former president and CEO of Nortel Networks Corporation. *Sunday Times* (May 2000)

24 There is always a multitude of reasons both in favour of doing a thing and against doing it. The art of debate lies in presenting them; the art of life lies in neglecting ninety-nine hundreths of them.
Mark Rutherford (1831–1913) British novelist. *More Pages from a Journal* (1910)

25 A complex decision is like a great river, drawing from its many tributaries the innumerable premises of which it is constituted.
Herbert A. Simon (1916–2001) US political scientist and economist. *Administrative Behavior* (1947)

26 Many individuals and organisation units contribute to every large decision, and the very problem of centralisation and decentralisation is a problem of arranging the complex system into an effective scheme.
Herbert A. Simon (1916–2001) US political scientist and economist. *Administrative Behavior* (1947)

27 Advisers advise and ministers decide.
Margaret Thatcher (b. 1925) British former prime minister. Speech (October 1989)

28 I've learned one thing in politics. You don't take a decision until you have to.
Margaret Thatcher (b. 1925) British former prime minister. Quoted in *Diaries* (Alan Clark; 1994)

29 Nothing is impossible to those who act After wise counsel and careful thought.
Tiruvalluvar (*fl.* 1st century) Indian poet. *The Kural*, 462

30 Once a decision was made, I did not worry about it afterward.
Harry S. Truman (1884–1972) US president. *Memoirs* (1955), vol. 2, ch. 1

31 When people agree with me I always feel that I must be wrong.
Oscar Wilde (1854–1900) Irish writer and wit. 'The Critic as Artist' (1890)

32 One cool judgement is worth a thousand hasty councils.
Woodrow Wilson (1856–1924) US president. Speech (January 1916)

DELEGATING

1 I have never compared myself to my managers...although I have made some big financial decisions on my own and decided on new investments, I have never involved myself in managerial decisions.
Giovanni Agnelli (1921–2003) Italian business executive and president of Fiat. Quoted in *Interview on Modern Capitalism* (Arrigo Levi; 1983)

2 The finest plans are always ruined by the littleness of those who ought to carry them out, for the Emperor can actually do nothing.
Bertolt Brecht (1898–1956) German playwright and poet. *Mother Courage* (1939)

3 If you are having as much fun running a big corporation as you did running a piece of it, then you are probably interfering too much with the people who really make it happen.
James Burke (b. 1925) US CEO of Johnson & Johnson. *Fortune* (6 June 1988)

4 I've always thought that I had a great gift for being a beachcomber...if I could find someone who could do the work better than I could I would hire that man and take it easy myself.
J. Paul Getty (1892–1976) US entrepreneur, oil industry executive, and financier. 1973. Quoted in *Getty on Getty* (Somerset de Chair; 1989), ch. 1

5 When I arrange to put up a building, I don't try to become an expert judge of stones or other building materials.
Amadeo Giannini (1870–1949) US banker and founder of Bank of America. 'The Story of an Unusual Career', *Forbes* (November 1923)

6 Time span of discretion.
Elliot Jacques (b. 1917) Canadian psychologist and sociologist. Referring to the level of authority given to managers. *A General Theory of Bureaucracy* (1976)

7 You could not maintain any illusion of direct control over a general or provincial governor...You appointed him, you watched his chariot and baggage train disappear over the hill in a cloud of dust, and that was that.
Anthony Jay (b. 1930) British author and business consultant. Arguing that a key reason the Roman Empire grew so large and lasted so long was the delegation necessitated by poor communications. *Management Machiavelli* (1970)

8 Big things and little things are my job. Middle level management can be delegated.
Konosuke Matsushita (1894–1989) Japanese electronics executive, entrepreneur, and inventor. *Quest for Prosperity* (1988)

9 Written instructions are seldom adequate and personal involvement is essential.
David Packard (1912–96) US entrepreneur and co-founder of Hewlett-Packard. *The HP Way* (1995)

10 You establish some objectives for them, provide some incentive, and try not to direct the detailed way in which they do their work.
David Packard (1912–96) US entrepreneur and co-founder of Hewlett-Packard. *The HP Way* (1995)

11 I've got an ego and all that, but I know I need help. So I go and hire the very best people.
H. Ross Perot (b. 1930) US entrepreneur, venture capitalist, and politician. *Inc.* (January 1989)

12 My experience is that people who are really, really bright find it very difficult to delegate because they literally could do the job better themselves.
H. Ross Perot (b. 1930) US entrepreneur, venture capitalist, and politician. *Inc.* (January 1989)

13 Surround yourself with the best people you can find, delegate authority and don't interfere.
Ronald Reagan (b. 1911) US president and actor. Quoted in *Fortune* (September 1986)

14 Not the least among the qualities in a great king is a capacity to permit his ministers to serve him.
Cardinal Richelieu (1585–1642) French politician. *Testament Politique* (1641)

15 There is no indispensable man.
Franklin D. Roosevelt (1882–1945) US president. Campaign speech, New York City (3 November 1932)

16 He liked nobody to be in any way superior to him...he chose his ministers, not for their knowledge, but for their ignorance; not for their capacity, but for their want of it.
Duc de Saint-Simon (1675–1755) French writer and soldier. Referring to Louis XIV. *Memoires* (1694–1723), vol. 3

17 People complain that I cause too much havoc and don't intervene enough in times of crisis, but the day I intervene is the day I condemn the entire system.

Ricardo Semler (b. 1959) Brazilian business executive and president of Semco. 'The Mavericks', *Fortune* (June 1995)

18 Never learn to do anything. If you don't learn, you'll always find someone else to do it for you.
Mark Twain (1835–1910) US writer. Attrib.

19 I never hesitated to promote someone I didn't like.
Thomas J. Watson Jr (1914–93) US CEO of IBM. *Fortune* (August 1987)

DETAILS

1 It is the whole, not the detail, that matters.
Anonymous. German proverb.

2 He who purposes duly to manage any branch of economy should be well acquainted with the locality in which he undertakes to labour, and should be naturally clever, and by choice industrious and just.
Aristotle (384–322 BC) Greek philosopher and scientist. *Economics* (4th century BC)

3 When it comes to the minor affairs of life one has to go into a great deal of detail.
Honoré de Balzac (1799–1850) French writer. *The Vicar of Tours* (1832)

4 Genius (which means transcendent capacity of taking trouble first of all).
Thomas Carlyle (1795–1881) British historian and essayist. *Frederick the Great* (1858)

5 I recommend you to take care of the minutes for the hours will take care of themselves.
Lord Chesterfield (1694–1773) English statesman, orator, and letter writer. Letter to his son (November 1747)

6 Pedantry is the showy display of knowledge which crams our heads with learned lumber and takes out our brains to make room for it.
Charles Caleb Colton (?1780–1832) British clergyman and writer. *Lacon* (1820–22), vol. 1

7 Neglecting small things under the pretext of wanting to accomplish large ones is the excuse of a coward.
Alexandra David-Neel (1868–1969) French oriental scholar and explorer. *Quest* (May/June 1978)

8 It has long been an axiom of mine that the little things are infinitely the most important.
Arthur Conan Doyle (1859–1930) British writer and doctor. 1891. 'A Case of Identity', *The Adventures of Sherlock Holmes* (1892)

9 Practise yourself in little things.
Epictetus (?55–?135) Greek philosopher. *Discourses* (2nd century AD), bk 4

10 Leave no stone unturned.
Euripides (?484–?406 BC) Greek playwright. *Heraclidae* (?428 BC)

11 A handful of men have become very rich by paying attention to details that most others ignored.
Henry Ford (1863–1947) US industrialist, car manufacturer, and founder of Ford Motor Company. Attrib.

12 It was not the matter of the work, but the mind that went into it, that counted—and the man who was not content to do small things well would leave great things undone.
Ellen Glasgow (?1873–1945) US writer. *The Voice of the People* (1900)

13 The contribution which the human mind makes to work and business is very much one of picking up information from tiny, seemingly insignificant trifles, and relating them to new ideas or concepts.
John Harvey-Jones (b. 1924) British management adviser, author, and former chairman of ICI. *Managing to Survive* (1993)

14 A business is only as good as the sum of its parts, which means you can't afford to have weak parts.
Robert Heller (b. 1932) British management writer. *The Supermarketers* (1987)

15 However numerous your products, the company won't succeed unless each of them is treated with concentrated care.
Robert Heller (b. 1932) British management writer. *The Supermarketers* (1987)

16 A wise man recognizes the convenience of a general statement, but he bows to the authority of a particular fact.
Oliver Wendell Holmes (1809–94) US surgeon, teacher, and writer. *The Poet at the Breakfast-Table* (1872)

17 Pedantry is the dotage of knowledge.
Holbrook Jackson (1874–1948) British writer and critic. *Anatomy of Bibliomania* (1930), vol. 1

18 The art of being wise is the art of knowing what to overlook.
William James (1842–1910) US psychologist and philosopher. *The Principles of Psychology* (1890)

19 All knowledge is of itself of some value. There is nothing so minute or inconsiderable, that I would not rather know it than not.
Samuel Johnson (1709–84) British poet, lexicographer, essayist, and critic. 1775. Quoted in *The Life of Samuel Johnson* (James Boswell; 1791)

20 Particulars are not to be examined till the whole has been surveyed.
Samuel Johnson (1709–84) British poet, lexicographer, essayist, and critic. *The Plays of William Shakespeare* (1765), Preface

21 The whole premise of Oxygen is this grassroots movement that's trying to connect with the democratic landscape that the Web has provided, and to translate that into a TV network.
Geraldine Laybourne (b. 1947) US chairman of Oxygen Media. Quoted in '10 to Watch: Geraldine Laybourne', *The Standard* (Kenneth Li; 2000)

22 Look to the essence of a thing, whether it be a point of doctrine, of practice, or of interpretation.
Marcus Aurelius (121–180) Roman emperor. *Meditations* (2nd century AD), bk 8, sect. 22

23 God is in the details.
Ludwig Mies van der Rohe (1886–1969) German architect. *New York Times* (August 1969)

24 Trifles make the sum of human things,
And half our misery from our foibles spring.
Hannah More (1745–1833) British playwright and religious writer. *Sensibility* (1783)

25 I try to keep in touch with the details—you can't keep in touch with them all, but you've got to have a feel for what's going on.
Rupert Murdoch (b. 1931) US CEO of News Corporation. Attrib.

26 Things that are not of value singly are useful collectively.
Ovid (43 BC–AD 17) Roman poet. *Remedia Amoris (Cure for Love)* (early 1st century AD)

27 Effective visions are lived in details, not broad strokes.
Tom Peters (b. 1942) US management consultant and author. *Thriving on Chaos* (1987)

28 Who overrefines his argument brings himself to grief.
Petrarch (1304–74) Italian poet and scholar. 'To Laura in Life', canzone 11

29 Even a single hair casts its shadow.
Publilius Syrus (*fl.* 1st century BC) Roman writer. *Moral Sayings* (1st century BC)

30 Trifles make up the happiness or the misery of human life.
Alexander Smith (1830–67) Scottish poet and essayist. 'Men of Letters', *Dreamthorp* (1863)

31 Our life is frittered away by detail…Simplify, simplify.
Henry David Thoreau (1817–62) US writer. 'Where I Lived and What I Lived For', *Walden, or Life in the Woods* (1854)

32 There are three kinds of lies: lies, damned lies, and statistics.
Mark Twain (1835–1910) US writer. Attributed to Benjamin Disraeli. *Autobiography* (Albert Bigelow, ed.; 1924)

33 Whoever wants to accomplish great things must devote a lot of profound thought to details.
Paul Valéry (1871–1945) French poet and essayist. Attrib.

34 Think naught a trifle, though it small appear;
Small sands the mountain, moments make the year,
And trifles life.
Edward Young (1683–1765) English poet. *Love of Fame* (1728)

DETERMINATION

1 Miracles can be made, but only by sweating.
Giovanni Agnelli (1921–2003) Italian business executive and president of Fiat. *Corriere della Sera* (1994)

2 When the going gets tough the tough get going.
Anonymous. Associated with Joseph P. Kennedy.

3 If you think you can, you can. And if you think you can't, you're right.
Mary Kay Ash (1915–2001) US entrepreneur, business executive, and founder of Mary Kay Cosmetics. *New York Times* (20 October 1985)

4 Start with your own money and value your intuition. It's all about endurance in the beginning. Your dream and passion to succeed must be stronger than your fear of failure.
Terri Bowersock (b. 1956) US furniture company entrepreneur. Advice to would-be entrepreneurs. Quoted in 'Terri Bowersock: Furniture Franchiser', *Women to Watch*, *www.womenswire.com* (Teresa O'Neil; 1996)

5 Whatever I am engaged in I must push inordinately.
Andrew Carnegie (1835–1919) US industrialist and philanthropist. Personal memorandum (1868)

6 Most of the important things in the world have been accomplished by people who have kept on trying when there seemed to be no hope at all.
Dale Carnegie (1888–1955) US consultant and author. *How to Stop Worrying and Start Living* (1948)

7 Diligence is the mother of good fortune, and idleness, its opposite, never led to good intention's goal.
Miguel de Cervantes (1547–1616) Spanish novelist and playwright. *Don Quixote* (1615), pt 2, ch. 43

8 Charity is the power of defending that which we know to be indefensible. Hope is the power of being cheerful in circumstances which we know to be desperate.
G.K. Chesterton (1874–1936) British novelist, poet, and critic. *Heretics* (1905)

9 To gain that which is worth having, it may be necessary to lose everything else.
Bernadette Devlin (b. 1947) Irish politician. *The Price of My Soul* (1969), Preface

10 Only undefeated
Because we have gone on trying.
T.S. Eliot (1888–1965) British poet, dramatist, and critic. 1941. 'The Dry Salvages', *Four Quartets* (1943)

11 You have to believe in the impossible.
Howard Head (1914–91) US inventor of metal ski. *Sports Illustrated* (September 1980)

12 If I have to intervene to help British companies—I'll intervene—before breakfast, before lunch, before tea, and before dinner. And I'll get up the next morning and I'll start all over again.
Michael Heseltine (b. 1933) British politician and publisher. Referring to his job at the time as president of the Board of Trade. Speech, Conservative Party Conference (7 October 1992)

13 People are ambitious and unrealistic. They set targets for themselves that are higher than what you would set for them. And because they set them, they hit them.
Liisa Joronen (b. 1944) Finnish CEO of SOL (formerly Lindstrom). *Fast Company* (1997)

14 Few things are impossible of themselves; application to make them succeed fails us more often than the means.
François La Rochefoucauld (1613–80) French epigrammatist. *Reflections: or, Sentences and Moral Maxims* (1665)

15 If things were half as bad as some people persist in believing, I'd have retired with a bottle of Scotch and a pistol a long time ago.
Robert Maxwell (1923–91) British publisher, business executive, and politician. *Daily Mail* (June 1973)

16 I shall find a way or make one.
Robert Edwin Peary (1856–1920) US Arctic explorer. Inscription on an expedition hut (1902)

17 Perseverance is more prevailing than violence; and many things which cannot be overcome when they are together, yield themselves up when taken little by little.
Plutarch (?46–?120) Greek writer and philosopher. 'Sertorius', *Parallel Lives* (1st century AD), sect. 16

18 If you have great talents, industry will improve them: if you have but moderate abilities, industry will supply their deficiency.
Joshua Reynolds (1723–92) British painter. 11 December 1769. Quoted in *Discourses on Art* (R. Walk, ed.; 1975), no. 2

19 Perhaps there is no more important component of character than steadfast resolution. The boy who is going to make a great man...must make up his mind...to win in spite of a thousand repulses or defeats.
Theodore Roosevelt (1858–1919) US president. 'Character and Success', *Outlook* (31 March 1900)

20 I wish to preach, not the doctrine of ignoble ease, but the doctrine of the strenuous life, the life of toil and effort, of labor and strife.
Theodore Roosevelt (1858–1919) US president. 10 April 1899. 'The Strenuous Life', *The Strenuous Life: Essays and Addresses* (1900)

21 Fanaticism consists in redoubling your effort when you have forgotten your aim.
George Santayana (1863–1952) US philosopher, novelist, and poet. *The Life of Reason* (1905)

22 The more you can do, the greater should be your patience to endure.
Seneca (?4 BC–AD 65) Roman politician, philosopher, and writer. *The Troades* (1st century AD)

23 Battles in life are never won...Life's a continuous business, and so is success, and requires continuous effort.
Margaret Thatcher (b. 1925) British former prime minister. Quoted in *New York Times* (28 September 1989)

24 If I have accomplished anything in life, it is because I have been willing to work hard. I never yet started anything doubtingly, and I have always believed in keeping at things with a vim.
C.J. Walker (1867–1919) US business executive. The daughter of slaves, she was the first American woman to become a self-made millionaire. Quoted in 'Madam C.J. Walker, Historic Entrepreneur', *Women to Watch, womenswire.com* (Susan McHenry; 1995)

25 Success is to be measured not so much by the position that one has reached in life as by the obstacles which one has overcome while trying to succeed.
Booker T. Washington (1856–1915) US educator and political scientist. *Up from Slavery* (1901)

26 I fancy it is just as hard to do your duty when men are sneering at you as when they are shooting at you.
Woodrow Wilson (1856–1924) US president. Speech (1914)

27 Self-determination is not a mere phrase. It is an imperative principle of action, which statesmen will henceforth ignore at their peril.
Woodrow Wilson (1856–1924) US president. Speech to Congress (11 February 1918)

28 If you are capable of displaying energy, hold office, if not resign.
Zhou Ren (fl. 1st millennium BC) Chinese historiographer. 1st millennium BC. Quoted in *Analects* (6th–5th century BC)

DISCRIMINATION

1 We don't so much want to see a female Einstein become an assistant professor. We want a woman schlemiel to get promoted as quickly as a male schlemiel.
Bella Abzug (1920–98) US politician, lawyer, and campaigner. 1977. Quoted in *America Chronicle* (Lois Gordon and Alan Gordon; 1987)

2 The test for whether or not you can hold a job should not be the arrangement of your chromosomes.
Bella Abzug (1920–98) US politician, lawyer, and campaigner. *Bella!* (1972)

3 Economic empowerment of women is a key to advancement and not only for women. Economies which engage both genders in activity and decision making at all levels have stronger markets.
K.Y. Amoako, Ghanaian economist and executive secretary of the UN Economic Commission for Africa. 'Enhancing Productivity and Competitiveness: Positioning the SADC Region in the Global Marketplace' (February 1997)

4 What kind of nation is this...nation of silk knees, slender necks, narrow fingers, and ironic mouths which has established itself upon our boundaries?
Anonymous. A complaint about the growing number of women in the modern business office. *Fortune* (1935)

5 People come up to you at a party and say, 'Aren't you bright?' It isn't a compliment.
Anonymous. Said by a female director of a London investment bank. Quoted in *The Economist* (28 March 1992)

6 Our managers are all white, middle-aged men, and they promote in their own image.
Anonymous. Said by a woman in the financial services industry. Quoted in *The Economist* (28 March 1992)

7 The men are always playing their own macho games. It's not really the money they want—it's beating their colleagues by making that extra phone call at night.
Anonymous. A senior female banker on her male colleages and why women are still rare at the top of the profession. Quoted in *The Moneylenders: Bankers in a Dangerous World* (Anthony Sampson; 1981)

8 Join the union, girls, and together say Equal Pay for Equal Work.
Susan B. Anthony (1820–1906) US reformer and women's suffrage leader. *The Revolution* was the magazine of the women's suffrage movement in the United States. *The Revolution* (1868)

9 Make your employers understand that you are in their service as workers, not as women.
Susan B. Anthony (1820–1906) US reformer and women's suffrage leader. *The Revolution* was the magazine of the women's suffrage movement in the United States. *The Revolution* (1868)

10 Men their rights and nothing more; women their rights and nothing less.
Susan B. Anthony (1820–1906) US reformer and women's suffrage leader. *The Revolution* was the magazine of the women's suffrage movement in the United States. *The Revolution* (1868)

11 When you apply the word power to a man, it means strong and bold—very positive attributes. When you use it to describe a woman, it suggests bitchy, insensitive, hard.
Jill Barad (b. 1951) US CEO of Mattel. 'The 50 Most Powerful Women in American Business', *Fortune* (Patricia Sellers and Cora Daniels; October 1999)

12 The low wages at which women will work form the chief reason for employing them at all...A woman's cheapness is, so to speak, her greatest economic asset. She can be used to keep down the cost of production.
Bureau of Labor, US government department. Report on Conditions of Women and Child Wage-earners in the United States (1911), vol. 11

13 The first step in providing economic equality for women is to ensure a stable economy in which every person who wants to work, can work.
Jimmy Carter (b. 1924) US former president and business executive. Speech, Women's Agenda Conference, Washington, D.C. (2 October 1976)

14 Running a business here in the UK, particularly being a woman, is just far too big a deal. The point at which some woman starts up a business and nobody cares about it, that's when we'll all know we made it.
Barbara Cassani (b. 1960) US former CEO of Go. 'Mount Holyoke College: Barbara Cassani '82, Soaring to New Heights', *Vista* (2000)

15 There are twelve major forms of power. Seven are almost totally controlled by men...Money, the thirteenth power, can buy and control the twelve powers. It is a power sacred to most men—and foreign to most women.
Phyllis Chesler (b. 1940) US psychologist. *Women, Money, and Power* (co-written with Emily Jane Goodman; 1977)

16 I found that when I did as well as the men in the field, I got more credit for my work because I am a woman, which seems unfair.
Eugenie Clark (b. 1922) US biologist. Quoted in *Ms* (August 1979)

17 Women do two thirds of the world's work...Yet they earn only one tenth of the world's income and own less than one percent of the world's property. They are among the poorest of the world's poor.
Barber B. Conable Jr (b. 1923) US business executive and head of the World Bank. Said at the annual meeting of the World Bank and International Monetary Fund. *New York Times* (1986)

18 The feminist surge will crest when a lady named Arabella, flounces and ruffles and all, can rise to the top of a Fortune 500 corporation.
Alma Denny (b. 1912) US writer and educator. *New York Times* (30 August 1985)

19 It is difficult for minorities in general to get their input heard. Black managers must develop a strategy against racist resistance in order to impact the system.
Floyd Dickens Jr (b. 1940) US management consultant executive and author. *The Black Manager: Making it in the Corporate World* (co-written with Jacqueline B. Dickens; 1991), ch. 1

20 Many of the experiences, feelings, frustrations, and attitudes of minorities are shared by *all* managers...Minorities, however, share...an environment that is hostile to their attainment of success because of their lesser status...or because the norm demands the complete socialization of the minority.
Floyd Dickens Jr (b. 1940) US management consultant executive and author. *The Black Manager: Making it in the Corporate World* (co-written with Jacqueline B. Dickens; 1991), Introduction

21 Money speaks, but it speaks with a male voice.
Andrea Dworkin (b. 1946) US writer. *Pornography* (1981)

22 People assume you slept your way to the top. Frankly, I couldn't sleep my way to the middle.
Joni Evans (b. 1942) US publishing executive. Conference speech to female executives, referring to her start in publishing as a manuscript reader. *New York Times* (22 July 1986)

23 This fellow said to me, 'You know for a woman you make a lot of money. If I was you, I'd go back to my office and be happy just to have the job'.
Grace Fey, US vice-president and director of Frontier Capital Management. Quoted in *Women of the Street* (Sue Herera; 1997)

24 Business shouldn't be like sports, separating the men from the women.
Carly Fiorina (b. 1954) US president and CEO of Hewlett-Packard. Speech (October 2002)

25 Don't think of yourself as a woman in business.

Carly Fiorina (b. 1954) US president and CEO of Hewlett-Packard. 'The 50 Most Powerful Women in American Business', *Fortune* (Patricia Sellers and Cora Daniels; October 1999)

26 Unity not uniformity must be our aim. We attain unity only through variety. Differences must be integrated, not annihilated, nor absorbed.

Mary Parker Follett (1868–1933) US management thinker and author. *The New State* (1918)

27 A woman is handicapped by her sex, and handicaps society, either by slavishly copying the pattern of man's advance in the professions, or by refusing to compete with man at all.

Betty Friedan (b. 1921) US feminist writer. *The Feminine Mystique* (1963)

28 The male human being is thousands of years in advance of the female in economic status.

Charlotte Gilman (1860–1935) US feminist and writer. *Women and Economics* (1898)

29 I look forward to the day when we don't think in terms of a woman executive at all, but just an executive.

Ellen Gordon, US president of Tootsie Roll Industries. *Fortune* (1987)

30 If one is rich and one's a woman, one can be quite misunderstood.

Katharine Graham (1917–2001) US newspaper publisher and owner of *Washington Post*. 'The Power That Didn't Corrupt', *Ms.* (Jan Howard; 1974)

31 Organisations need talented women in their core jobs...because many will have the kinds of attitudes and attributes that the new flexible organisation will need. If they screen out the women they will handicap their futures.

Charles Handy (b. 1932) British business executive and author. *The Empty Raincoat: Making Sense of the Future* (1994), pt 3, ch. 10

32 If you want to push something...you're accused of being aggressive, and that's not supposed to be a good thing for a woman. If you get upset and show it, you're accused of being emotional.

Mary Harney (b. 1953) Irish politician. Attrib.

33 In countries as diverse as India and Japan, the USA and Latin America, we are seeing the emergence of a new, and very welcome, field of female talent. Highly trained, highly motivated and very involved in their work.

John Harvey-Jones (b. 1924) British management adviser, author, and former chairman of ICI. *Making it Happen* (1988)

34 Now I came to power and I said, 'Look, this is nonsense, we are great people, we Australians'. Employers are great blokes, workers are great blokes, farmers are great blokes—and I use the term blokes to encompass men and women.

Bob Hawke (b. 1929) Australian former prime minister. Quoted in 'Sayings of the Year', *Sydney Morning Herald* (31 December 1988)

35 Top jobs are designed for people with wives.

Lucy Heller (b. 1959) British business executive. Quoted in *The Economist* (28 March 1992)

36 Saying that a person cannot be kept out doesn't ensure that that person can get in, and more important, stay in.

Margaret Hennig (b. 1940) US business executive and writer. Discussing corporate responses to anti-discrimination legislation. *The Managerial Woman* (co-written with Anne Jardim; 1976)

37 Men don't have some special genetic coding that makes them better fit for playing the markets. It's simply a matter of education and knowledge.

Sue Herera (b. 1957) US journalist and author. *Women of the Street* (1997)

38 A new type of woman arises. She is called a career woman. A man is never a career man. That is his right and privilege. But the woman is called career woman because her 'career'...demands that she...even renounce normal life.

C.L.R. James (1901–89) Trinidadian critic, historian, and philosopher. 1943. Quoted in Letter to Constance Webb, *The C.L.R. James Reader* (Anna Grimshaw, ed.; 1992)

39 When women ask for equality, men take them to be demanding domination.

Elizabeth Janeway (b. 1913) US feminist and writer. *Man's World, Woman's Place* (1971)

40 This is a woman's industry. No man will vote our stock, transact our business, pronounce on woman's wages, supervise our factories. Give men whatever work is suitable but keep the governing power.

Amanda Theodosia Jones (1835–1914) US inventor, entrepreneur, and psychic. Jones founded the Women's Canning and Preserving Company after inventing a canning process. Address to employees of the Women's Canning and Preserving Company, Chicago, *A Psychic's Autobiography* (1910)

41 I remember how homogeneous corporations were when I first started working. I was often the first professional woman some of the men had ever seen.

Rosabeth Moss Kanter (b. 1943) US management theorist, academic, and writer. Interview, *Strategy + Business* (July–September 1999)

42 Men always try to keep women out of business so they won't find out how much fun it really is.

Vivien Kellems (1896–1975) US industrialist, feminist, and lecturer. Quoted in *Women Can Be Engineers* (Alice Goff; 1946)

43 There are very few jobs that actually require a penis or vagina. All other jobs should be open to everybody.

Florynce R. Kennedy (1916–2000) US lawyer and political activist. 'Freelancer with No Time to Write', *Writer's Digest* (February 1974)

44 Some authors use the feminine designations 'mother, daughter, sister' instead of 'father, son, brother'; but for some reason the masculine words seem more professional.

Donald E. Knuth (b. 1938) US computer programmer and writer. *The Art of Computer Programming: Fundamental Algorithms* (1995)

45 Men were expected to rise when women entered a room, and male language contained at least two vocabularies—one for exchanges between men—and one for men and women.

Angel Kwolek-Folland, US author. Referring to offices in the 1930s. *Engendering Business* (1994)

46 Women in business found themselves on the horns of a dilemma: To assert uniqueness was to deny what they shared with men as workers, but to insist on similarities...was to subvert the compelling cultural definitions of gender difference.

Angel Kwolek-Folland, US author. Referring to the early part of the 20th century. *Engendering Business* (1994)

47 Women's presence in the office work force challenged the Victorian ideal of separate public and private worlds for men and women.

Angel Kwolek-Folland, US author. Referring to the increasing number of women working in offices at the beginning of the 20th century. *Engendering Business* (1994)

48 Women are underserved and underestimated as consumers.

Geraldine Laybourne (b. 1947) US chairman of Oxygen Media. 'The 50 Most Powerful Women in American Business', *Fortune* (Patricia Sellers and Cora Daniels; October 1999)

49 I'm not concerned for women, but I'm concerned for business. If everyone leaves at once, we're going to have this void. Women won't be there to fill CEO-level posts.

Shelly Lazarus (b. 1949) US chairperson of Ogilvy & Mather Worldwide. Referring to the increasing tendency of American businesswomen to leave for family reasons. 'The 50 Most Powerful Women in American Business', *Fortune* (Patricia Sellers and Cora Daniels; October 1999)

50 I am a female. It's a mixed blessing. I sometimes wish I could be identified as a CEO of a major firm, not always as a 'female' CEO.

Bridget A. Macaskill (b. 1949) British non-executive director for J. Sainsburys, former president and CEO of Oppenheimer Funds. Quoted in *Women of the Street* (Sue Herera; 1997)

51 I look around me and I do not see many women who have reached the most senior levels with their husbands and children and outside lives intact.

Bridget A. Macaskill (b. 1949) British non-executive director for J. Sainsburys, former president and CEO of Oppenheimer Funds. Quoted in *Women of the Street* (Sue Herera; 1997)

52 For a woman to attain a high level in a male-dominated profession, she has to work twice as hard and/or be twice as smart.

Elizabeth MacKay, US investment strategist and managing director of Bear Stearns. Quoted in *Women of the Street* (Sue Herera; 1997)

53 We cannot, through ignorant prejudice, afford to under-use the talents and potential of half our citizens, merely because they are women.

Tom Mboya (1930–69) Kenyan politician. *The Challenge of Nationhood* (1970)

54 I think that I have three trouser suits to my name, but people think that when you wear them that's all you ever wear.

Mary McAleese (b. 1951) Irish president. Responding to reports that she had been criticised for wearing trouser suits on formal occasions. *Irish Times* (28 February 1998)

55 We need every human gift and cannot afford to neglect any gift because of artificial barriers of sex or race or class or national origin.

Margaret Mead (1901–78) US anthropologist. *Male and Female* (1949)

56 The legend of the jungle heritage and the evolution of man as a hunting carnivore has taken root in man's mind...He may even believe that equal pay will do something terrible to his gonads.

Elaine Morgan (b. 1920) Welsh playwright, screenwriter, and non-fiction author. *The Descent of Woman* (1972)

57 Gender took a back seat...and I became just part of the team. It was like a button was pressed: gender neutral.

Bernadette Murphy (b. 1934) US chief technical analyst of Kimelman & Baird LLC. Quoted in *Women of the Street* (Sue Herera; 1997)

58 Women...have a double responsibility. We must be achievers *and* we must make a significant difference.

Bernadette Murphy (b. 1934) US chief technical analyst of Kimelman & Baird LLC. Quoted in *Women of the Street* (Sue Herera; 1997)

59 Women's battle for financial equality has barely been joined, much less won. Society still traditionally assigns to woman the role of money-handler rather than money-maker, and our assigned specialty is far more likely to be home economics than financial economics.

Paula Nelson (b. 1944) US educator. *The Joy of Money* (1975)

60 I regard affirmative action as pernicious—a system that had wonderful ideals when it started but was almost immediately abused for the benefit of white middle-class women.

Camille Paglia (b. 1947) US academic, educator, and writer. April 1995. Interview, *Reason Magazine* (August–September 1995)

61 It's so much easier for men. They don't have to paint their nails for a meeting.

Eve Pollard (b. 1945) British journalist and newspaper editor. June 1995. Quoted in *Guardian* (30 December 1995)

62 What women don't want is just as important as what they do. They don't want to do business with an organization, a company, or a brand that condescends to them. That inconveniences them.

Faith Popcorn (b. 1947) US trend expert and founder of BrainReserve. *EVEolution* (2000), ch. 1

63 Women are opening businesses at twice the rate of men...Forty percent of businesses will be owned by women. Women are saying, 'I don't belong in this company. I'm sick of fighting this battle'.

Faith Popcorn (b. 1947) US trend expert and founder of BrainReserve. Interview, *phenomeNEWS* (1999)

64 It's still a man's world out there...I'd go to meetings and be one woman out of 30 men— you cope with whatever language and dirty jokes happen to be around at the time.

Pauline Portas (b. 1952) British entrepreneur. *Financial Times* (19 October 2000)

65 It's still harder for a woman to get up her own business than it is to get money for a new car, or certainly a new kitchen.

Anita Roddick (b. 1942) British entrepreneur and founder of The Body Shop. Quoted in *The Adventure Capitalists* (Jeff Grout and Lynne Curry; 1998)

66 Men are still clinging to the hope that women are powerless, because they haven't got much else to cling to.

Harriet Rubin (b. 1952) US author. 'Thank You Ma'am, May I Have Another?', *Fast Company* (1996)

67 We're good at sending people to diversity training, using politically correct language, and making sure we have people of color in our Annual Report photos. But...the deep-seated issues of intolerance and exclusivity go unexamined.

Raymond W. Smith (b. 1937) US chairman of Rothschild, Inc. and former chairman of Bell Atlantic Corporation. Speech (1 November 1995)

68 How do you get a girl to start thinking about a career early? That's really where it has to begin. And it has to begin with her parents. We're all conditioned to the kind of life we're expected to live by the time we're 5.

Jane Trahey (1923–2000) US copywriter and author. *Jane Trahey on Women and Power: Who's Got It? How to Get It?* (1977)

69 I am not a millionaire, but I hope to be one day, not because of the money, but because I could do so much then to help my race.

C.J. Walker (1867–1919) US business executive. Referring to her aspiration to be the first African American woman millionaire. *New York Times Magazine* (November 1917)

70 I am not merely satisfied in making money, for I am endeavoring to provide employment for hundreds of the women of my race.

C.J. Walker (1867–1919) US business executive. Referring to her aspiration to be the first African American woman millionaire. *New York Times Magazine* (November 1917)

71 I believe in push, and we must push ourselves.

C.J. Walker (1867–1919) US business executive. Referring to her aspiration to be the first African American woman millionaire. *New York Times Magazine* (November 1917)

72 The notion that by succeeding academically or later, by succeeding in any management,

you therefore destroy your 'femininity' is the most pervasive threat against women.

Mary Warnock (b. 1924) British philosopher and author. Speech, Institute of Directors, London (25 November 1985)

73 Do you know I'm black? Do you know I'm overweight? Are you sure you want me?

Oprah Winfrey (b. 1954) US talk show host, actor, and business executive. 'The 50 Most Powerful Women in American Business', *Fortune* (Patricia Sellers and Cora Daniels; October 1999)

74 The greatest contribution you can make to women's rights, is to be the absolute...best at what you do.

Oprah Winfrey (b. 1954) US talk show host, actor, and business executive. Quoted in *Oprah Winfrey Speaks* (Janet Lowe; 1998)

DOING BUSINESS IN AFRICA

1 If you look at Malaysian companies, they are not investing in Europe or the United States, they are investing in African countries, high-potential countries, where they can transfer their expertise.

Raphael Auphan, French business executive. Quoted in *International Herald Tribune* (4 November 1997)

2 We have long been told or made to believe that most of our economic ills derive from mismanagement or bad planning, inappropriate technology or prestige projects. I ask our critics: Is it not largely their responsibility? Have we not inherited their management techniques?

Madan Murlidas Dulloo (b. 1949) Mauritian lawyer and politician. Speaking of Africa's problems at the 21st summit of the Organization of African Unity, 1984. Quoted in *Squandering Eden: Africa at the Edge* (Mort Rosenblum and Doug Williliamson; 1987)

3 International finance is always looking for new opportunities. The challenge for Africa is not just to be attractive to traders and investors, but to offer opportunities which are more attractive than anywhere else in the world.

Peter Hain (b. 1950) British politician. Speech, Challenges for Governance in Africa Conference, Wilton Park, England (13 September 1999)

4 Here, in this realm of the spices, a 'market price' was being created—a set of fiscal frontiers within which to reach a consensus. It was the language of the stock exchange...and it was the bourse which had obviously imitated the ways of the souk.

Douglas Kennedy (b. 1955) British writer, journalist and playwright. Describing bartering for spices in the Casablanca souk. *Chasing Mammon: Travels in the Pursuit of Money* (1992)

5 We want to ensure that in the process of privatizing, we do not create greater room for control by those persons who already control the greater part of our economy.

Robert Mugabe (b. 1924) Zimbabwean president. Quoted in *Financial Times* (5 March 1997)

6 Africa's earth is rich, yet the products that come from above and below the soil continue to enrich, not Africans predominantly, but groups and individuals who operate to Africa's impoverishment.

Kwame Nkrumah (1909–72) Ghanaian president. *Neo-Colonialism* (1965)

7 Multinational organisations and those governments truly concerned about Africa should be directing all their efforts to creating and supporting a...policy of real diplomatic sticks and large economic carrots untainted by protectionism.

Nicky Oppenheimer (b. 1945) South African chairman of De Beers. Speech, Southern Africa Business Association, London (26 June 2000)

8 One of the principal reasons why genuine industrialization cannot easily be realized in Africa today is that the market for manufactured goods in any single African country is too small.

Walter Rodney (1942–80) Guyanese historian and political activist. *How Europe Underdeveloped Africa* (1972)

9 The circumstances of African trade with Europe were unfavorable to creating a consistent African demand for technology...when that demand was raised it was ignored or rejected by the capitalists.

Walter Rodney (1942–80) Guyanese historian and political activist. *How Europe Underdeveloped Africa* (1972)

DOING BUSINESS IN ASIA-PACIFIC

1 Given the economic growth and blossoming of billionaires in the region, Asia is likely to produce the world's first trillionaire.

Anonymous. Quoted in *Asia, Inc.* (September 1996)

2 Confronted with a fully developed world market, it is impossible for a country which cuts itself off and relies on the spontaneous role of its home market to catch up, let alone surpass the economically advanced countries.

Anonymous. Referring to China's industry and commerce. *Beijing Review* (2–8 November 1987)

3 Hard work is an Asian compulsion. In Hong Kong, people work hard to make a profit. In Tokyo, they work hard to impress their bosses. But in Singapore, we work hard to compete in the rat race.

Anonymous. Quoted in *Chasing Mammon: Travels in the Pursuit of Money* (Douglas Kennedy; 1992)

4 For the building of a new Japan
Let's put our mind and strength together,
Doing our best to promote production,
Sending our goods to the peoples of the world.

Anonymous. Matsushita Electrical Company anthem. Quoted in *Iemoto, the Heart of Japan* (F.L.K. Hsu; 1975)

5 Five Rules for Doing Business in China: 1. Think small—focus on one region at a time. 2. Skip the manager, talk to the clerk. 3. Study the side streets. 4. Get the goods to market. 5. Above all be flexible.

Anonymous. Quoted in *New York Times Magazine* (18 February 1996)

6 Live together like brothers and do business like strangers.

Anonymous. Arab proverb.

7 Experience has shown us that the trade of the East is the key to national wealth and influence.

Chester Alan Arthur (1829–86) US president. Message to the Senate (4 April 1882)

8 Bribes, backhanders and favours for 'cronies' are commonplace in business and government life in Southeast Asia.

James Bartholomew (b. 1950) British writer. *The World's Richest Man: The Sultan of Brunei* (1989)

9 The trade of the East has always been the richest jewel in the diadem of commerce. All nations, in all ages, have sought it; and those which obtained it, or even a share of it, attained the highest degree of opulence, refinement, and power.

Thomas Hart Benton (1782–1858) US politician. Speech in the Senate (1847)

10 A company's reputation does not necessarily follow it into India, which has been a closed market for so long that established global brands have no meaning for the Indian consumer.

Rajiv Desai, Indian journalist and public relations executive. *Indian Business Culture* (1999)

11 Indian businesses can be critical as partners at the time international firms are seeking to enter India.

Rajiv Desai, Indian journalist and public relations executive. *Indian Business Culture* (1999)

12 Indian businesses often appear to be weak partners...however, they are formidable opponents who can subvert the best-laid plans of international firms.

Rajiv Desai, Indian journalist and public relations executive. *Indian Business Culture* (1999)

13 *Swadeshi* is the doctrine that advocates restrictions on foreign investment with a view to protecting Indian business interests against those of international firms.

Rajiv Desai, Indian journalist and public relations executive. *Indian Business Culture* (1999)

14 This road of industrialisation was not planned in advance by theoreticians. Rather, it has been created by the peasants on the basis of their experience in real life.

Fei Xiaotong (b. 1910) Chinese social anthropologist. Comparing China's industrialisation favourably to that of the West, where modern industry had grown at the expense of the countryside. *Beijing Review* (1985), no. 21

15 In Japan, the best and brightest young people aspire to become bureaucrats, not businessmen, and there is intense competition for bureaucratic jobs.

Francis Fukuyama (b. 1952) US economist and writer. *Trust: The Social Virtues and the Creation of Prosperity* (1995)

16 Japan's...rapid rise from a predominantly agricultural society to a modern industrial power following the Meiji Restoration in 1868 is closely associated with the growth of the *zaibatsu*, the huge family-owned conglomerates like Mitsubishi and Sumitomo.

Francis Fukuyama (b. 1952) US economist and writer. *Trust: The Social Virtues and the Creation of Prosperity* (1995)

17 Never visit a Japanese company without tons of business cards. Basically, no 'meishi' (name cards) means no existence for you on this earth.

Mark Gauthier, US travel writer. *Making It in Japan: Work, Life, Leisure and Beyond* (1993)

18 Never 'tell it like it is' in company meetings. Speaking your mind and gushing out frank statements displays immaturity and is bad for group harmony.

Mark Gauthier, US travel writer. Advice to Westerners visiting Japan. *Making It in Japan: Work, Life, Leisure and Beyond* (1993)

19 Acts of marketing insanity such as the US firm that invested heavily in a campaign to sell cake mix to the Japanese—in profound and dismal ignorance of the fact that hardly any homes in Japan have ovens.

Robert Heller (b. 1932) British management writer. *The Supermarketers* (1987)

20 There is nothing Japan really wants to buy from foreign countries except, possibly, neckties with unusual designs.

Yoshihiro Inayama (1904–87) Japanese business executive. Quoted in 'Sayings of the Week', *Sydney Morning Herald* (3 August 1985)

21 Japan's strength and weakness—both—are its sense of national distinctiveness and superiority. This stimulates the Japanese to high levels of performance, but it also makes it hard for them to work with others as equal partners.

David S. Landes (b. 1924) US economic historian. *The Wealth and Poverty of Nations* (1998)

22 Old Asian commercial networks, for all their wealth and experience, yielded the juiciest transactions to foreign agency houses, and India's economic development from the late eighteenth century came to be shaped more by British imperial policy than by indigenous initiative.

David S. Landes (b. 1924) US economic historian. Referring to the legacy of such exploitative trading companies as the British East India Company. *The Wealth and Poverty of Nations* (1998)

23 For us the core of management is the art of mobilising and putting together the intellectual resources of all employees in the firm.

Konosuke Matsushita (1894–1989) Japanese electronics executive, entrepreneur, and inventor. Speaking to a visiting delegation of Western business people. Speech (May 1979)

24 The Japanese constantly pare down and reduce the complexity of products and ideas to the barest minimum...The influence of Zen and haiku poetry are often evident in the simplicity and utility of Japanese designs.

Akio Morita (1921–99) Japanese business executive. *Made in Japan* (1986)

25 Industry in India is not what industry is said to be in other parts of the world. It has its horrors; but...it does not dehumanize... Men handling new machines, exercising technical skills that to them are new, can also discover themselves as men, as individuals.

V.S. Naipaul (b. 1932) Trinidadian writer and winner of the 2001 Nobel Prize in Literature. *India: A Wounded Civilization* (1977)

26 Old India requires few tools, few skills, and many hands.

V.S. Naipaul (b. 1932) Trinidadian writer and winner of the 2001 Nobel Prize in Literature. *India: A Wounded Civilization* (1977)

27 Most Japanese corporations lack even an approximation of an organization chart.

Kenichi Ohmae (b. 1943) Japanese management consultant and theorist. 'The Myth and Reality of the Japanese Corporation', *Chief Executive* (Summer 1981)

28 I'm not going to rest until we're shipping cars to Japan.

H. Ross Perot (b. 1930) US entrepreneur, venture capitalist, and politician. *Forbes* (1986)

29 Japan is notoriously consensus oriented, and companies have a strong tendency to mediate differences among individuals rather than accentuate them. Strategy, on the other hand, requires hard choices.

Michael Porter (b. 1947) US strategist. *Harvard Business Review* (November–December 1996)

30 If England and France print linens with great elegance; if so many stuffs, formerly unknown in our climates, now employ our best artists, are we not indebted to India for all these advantages?

Guillaume Raynal (1713–96) French historian and philosopher. *The Philosophical and Political History of the Settlements and Trade of the Europeans in the East and West Indies* (1776), vol. 2

31 In Sydney, you're in Asia, but not of Asia. Basing your Asian operations in Sydney is like basing your American operations in Rio.

Donald Saunders, Australian business executive. *Asia Inc.* (December 1996)

32 Chinese managers and employees perceive that they have as many problems with foreign business representatives as the other way around.

Jan Selmer (b. 1942) Swedish academic and author. *International Management in China: Cross-cultural Issues* (Jan Selmer, ed.; 1998)

33 I founded Wang Laboratories...to show that Chinese could excel at things other than running laundries and restaurants.

An Wang (1920–90) US entrepreneur, business executive, electrical engineer, and founder of Wang Laboratories. *Boston Magazine* (December 1986)

34 It is not by force and violence that His Majesty intends to establish a commercial intercourse between his subjects and China; but by other conciliatory measures so strongly inculcated in all the instructions which you have received.

Arthur Wellesley Wellington (1769–1852) British general and statesman. Letter to Lord Napier (2 February 1835)

35 Foreign investing companies operating in China often face a choice between maintaining their standard of knowledge and expertise base with local Chinese partners.

Yanni Yan (b. 1958) Chinese business author and academic. 'Managerial and Organization—Learning in Chinese Firms', *China's Managerial Revolution* (Malcolm Warner, ed.; 1999)

DOING BUSINESS IN EUROPE

1 Lifestyles around Europe are converging, but tastes are not.

Nicholas Colchester (d. 1996) British author and journalist. *Europe Relaunched* (co-written with David Buchan; 1990)

2 No one can bring together a country that has 265 kinds of cheese.

Charles De Gaulle (1890–1970) French general and president. Said after an electoral setback in 1953. Quoted in *The Economist* (27 June 1992)

3 There are those who want an economic and monetary union so beautiful, so perfect, that it will never get started, it will never even be born.

Jacques Delors (b. 1925) French politician. Said while president of the European Commission. *Guardian* (14 September 1990)

4 The European companies that prosper will be those that re-create the European character and flair that Americans and Japanese never had, adding quality, reliability, and value.

Patrick Faure (b. 1946) French president of Renault-Sport. Quoted in *Fortune* (11 January 1993)

5 Italy is a poor country full of rich people.

Richard Gardner (b. 1927) US diplomat, lawyer, and educator. Quoted in *Observer* (16 August 1981)

6 Europe's strength is its diversity, not its uniformity.

John Harvey-Jones (b. 1924) British management adviser, author, and former chairman of ICI. Speech (1990)

7 I indispensably contributed to saving Eastern Europe.

Robert Maxwell (1923–91) British publisher, business executive, and politician. Quoted in *Guardian* (5 March 1990)

8 Europe has never existed. One must genuinely create Europe.

Jean Monnet (1888–1979) French diplomat and founder of European Community. Quoted in *The New Europeans* (Anthony Sampson; 1968)

9 The Common Market is a process, not a product.

Jean Monnet (1888–1979) French diplomat and founder of European Community. Quoted in *The New Europeans* (Anthony Sampson; 1968)

10 The American brand of democratic leadership doesn't work so well in Europe, where executives have a psychological need for more autocratic leadership.

David Ogilvy (1911–99) British advertising executive, founder and chairman of Ogilvy & Mather. *Ogilvy on Advertising* (1983)

11 It would not be in Britain's, or, I believe, Europe's interest to join the present half-baked system.

Alan Walters (b. 1926) British economist and government adviser. Referring to the European Monetary System. Quoted in *Financial Times* (30 December 1989)

12 Pound for pound, Sweden probably has more good managers than any other country.

Jack Welch (b. 1935) US former chairman and CEO of General Electric. *Financial Times* (1997)

DOING BUSINESS IN LATIN AMERICA

1 By combining better economic policies with a greater educational effort, per capita income in Latin America could be 20 percent higher within a decade and in two decades 50 percent higher than it would be without such strategies.

Anonymous. Inter-American Development Bank report, *Financial Times* (15 September 1997)

2 We may not be a tiger yet but we are already a jaguar.

Anonymous. Referring to the Chilean economy. Quoted in *Worth* (August 1995)

3 Since economies in the process of organization lack resources to dynamize themselves...it is right to accept the aid of all who want to run with us the risks of the marvelous adventure that is progress.

Roberto Campos (1917–2001) Brazilian politician and economist. Speech, Mackenzie University, São Paulo, Brazil (22 December 1966)

4 People complaining about Brazil's economy today don't have any perspective on how much better things have gotten.

Luiz Cezar Fernandes, Brazilian banker and founder of Brazilian investment bank Banco Pactual. Quoted in *Wall Street Journal* (17 May 1996)

5 The private sector needs more investment but also better wages, more jobs but also better productivity, better technology but also more training, better infrastructure but also more education.
Carlos Fuentes (b. 1928) Mexican writer. *A New Time for Mexico* (1994)

6 The United States is glad to manipulate cheap Mexican labor, chastising it in days of crisis, accepting it in boom times, and always maintaining the police fiction of an impregnable border.
Carlos Fuentes (b. 1928) Mexican writer. *A New Time for Mexico* (1994)

7 US capital is more tightly concentrated in Latin America itself; a handful of concerns control the overwhelming majority of investments.
Eduardo Galeano (b. 1940) Uruguayan writer and journalist. *Open Veins of Latin America* (1971), pt 2, ch. 5

8 Focusing on Latin America, there's no doubt that every country in the region is very awake to the opportunity of the Internet....Of all the regions the growth in information technology spending is number two, spending on Web commerce is predicted to be, just within three years, at over $10 billion.
Bill Gates (b. 1955) US entrepreneur, chairman and CEO of Microsoft. Speech, Enterprise Solutions Conference, Miami, Florida (21 March 2000)

9 Multinationals are no longer immune from violence in Mexico. I personally know of seven American chief executives that have looked at the wrong end of a weapon in Mexico.
Morton Palmer, US head of Palmer Associates security consultants. Quoted in *Wall Street Journal* (29 October 1996)

DOING BUSINESS IN NORTH AMERICA

1 If it's worth doing, California will do it to excess.
Anonymous. Comment on National Public Radio in the United States (1996)

2 America is still a place where most people react to seeing a man in a Ferrari by redoubling their own efforts to be able to afford one, rather than by trying to let down his tyres.
Anonymous. *The Economist* (3 January 1998)

3 It seems to be a law in American life that whatever enriches us anywhere except in the wallet inevitably becomes uneconomic.

Russell Baker (b. 1925) US journalist. *New York Times* (24 March 1968)

4 There is no business in America...which will not yield a fair profit if it receive the unremitting, exclusive attention, and all the capital of capable and industrious men.
Andrew Carnegie (1835–1919) US industrialist and philanthropist. Speech at Curry Commercial College, Pittsburgh, Pennsylvania. 'The Road to Business Success' (23 June 1885)

5 The United States is unusual among the industrial democracies in the rigidity of the system of ideological control—indoctrination, we might say—exercised through the mass media.
Noam Chomsky (b. 1928) US linguist and political activist. *Politics* (1979)

6 America needs a new approach to economics that will give new hope to our people and breathe new life into the American Dream.
Bill Clinton (b. 1946) US former president. *Putting People First: How We Can All Change America* (co-written with Al Gore; 1992)

7 Big business could do business anywhere.
Amadeo Giannini (1870–1949) US banker and founder of Bank of America. Referring to his strategy of opening local branches of the Bank of America. Quoted in *Biography of a Banker* (Marquis James and Bessie R. James; 1954)

8 Texaco is the quintessence of what is wrong with corporate America. We have a corporate welfare state in this country, which is why we can't compete.
Carl C. Icahn (b. 1936) US financier. One of the leading corporate raiders of the 1980s, Icahn made this statement during his unsuccessful bid to take over the major oil company. *Sunday Times* (5 June 1988)

9 Miami's single most important economic development agent turned out to be Fidel Castro.
Rosabeth Moss Kanter (b. 1943) US management theorist, academic, and writer. *World Class* (1995)

10 If there is anything of which American industry has a superfluity
It is green lights, know-how, initiative, and ingenuity.
Ogden Nash (1902–71) US humorist and writer. 1956. 'Ring Out the Old, Ring In the New, but Don't Get Caught In Between', *You Can't Get There from Here* (1957), 1: First Chime

11 European countries treat timber as a crop. We treat timber resources as if they were a mine.
Franklin D. Roosevelt (1882–1945) US president. Attrib.

12 With the supermarket as our temple and the singing commercial as our library, are we likely to fire the world with an irresistable vision of America's exalted purpose and inspiring way of life?
Adlai E. Stevenson (1900–65) US statesman and author. *Wall Street Journal* (1 June 1960)

E-COMMERCE

1 Stay one click ahead.
Anonymous. Sun Microsystems. Advertising slogan (September 2000)

2 The parking is easy, there are no checkout lines, we are open 24 hours a day, and we deliver right to your door.
Anonymous. Sales pitch of Salami.com, purveyors of Italian delicacies. Quoted in *Business Week* (23 September1996)

3 I am secretly looking forward to rediscovering the little pleasures of pre-electronic shopping: holding things in my hands, trying them on, and even taking them home with me after I have paid.
Anonymous. Quoted in *The Economist* (21 December 1996)

4 The web gives us more choices than before about how we weave society, how we choose, who and what we connect with.
Tim Berners-Lee (b. 1955) British computer scientist and founder of the World Wide Web. *Marketing* (June 2000)

5 I believe we can still be a footnote in the history of e-commerce.
Jeff Bezos (b. 1964) US founder and CEO of Amazon.com. *Sunday Telegraph* (July 2000)

6 It's hard to find things that won't sell online.
Jeff Bezos (b. 1964) US founder and CEO of Amazon.com. *Sunday Telegraph* (July 2000)

7 You'll see a growing differentiation between Internet companies working to build lasting companies and those working to build flash in the pan stocks.
Jeff Bezos (b. 1964) US founder and CEO of Amazon.com. *Sunday Telegraph* (July 2000)

8 The question is does India need dot coms? If you were to ask me this question, the answer is no, India needs infrastructure.
Subeer Bhatia (b. 1967) Indian IT entrepreneur and founder of Hotmail. *Business Week* (September 2000)

9 The Internet is an elite organization; most of the population of the world have never made a phone call.
Noam Chomsky (b. 1928) US linguist and political activist. *Observer* (February 1996)

10 The electronic highway is not merely open for business; it is relocating, restructuring, and literally redefining business in America.
Mary J. Cronin (b. 1947) US business author. *Doing More Business on the Internet* (1995)

11 I could see the Internet was going to be massive so clearly having your own identity seemed obvious.
Jason Drummond (b. 1969) British Internet entrepreneur. Referring to the practice of registering Internet domain names. *Sunday Times* (October 2000)

12 The future of retail is the integration of Internet and digital services with the retail network.
Charles Dunstone (b. 1964) British business executive and founder of Carphone Warehouse. *Digital Britain* (January 2000)

13 We believe that a customer should have a choice of different ways to shop.
Charles Dunstone (b. 1964) British business executive and founder of Carphone Warehouse. Referring to company policy of offering shoppers online sales, retail sales, or telesales. *Digital Britain* (January 2000)

14 The Internet supports a much faster turnover of employees due to different cultural influences...The Net changes the balance of power by valuing diversity over uniformity.
Esther Dyson (b. 1951) US knowledge entrepreneur and government adviser. Speech at the 4th Workshop on Inventing the Organisation of the 21st Century, Munich, Germany. 'The Future of Truth—The End of the "Official Story"' (February 1998)

15 We have to match the experience that consumers have when they go into a shopping centre.
Jon Florsheim (b. 1960) British Internet entrepreneur. *Marketing* (August 2000)

16 Thus, in the future, instead of buying bananas in a grocery store, you could go pick them off a tree in a virtual jungle.
Yasuhiro Fukushima (b. 1948) Japanese business executive. *Wired Asia* (June 2000)

17 Most discussions of how to make digital commerce more trustworthy have centered on...data security...however, there is the thornier problem of how to build trust in coworkers, clients, customers—people you will never see.
Francis Fukuyama (b. 1952) US economist and writer. 'Trust Still Counts in a Virtual World', *Forbes* (12 February 1996)

18 Fireflies throwing off sparks before the storm.
Lou Gerstner (b. 1942) US chairman and CEO of IBM. Referring to dot.com companies. *Sunday Times* (May 2000)

19 The storm that's arrived, the real disturbance, will be when the thousands and thousands of institutions that exist today seize the power and use it to transform themselves.
Lou Gerstner (b. 1942) US chairman and CEO of IBM. Referring to e-commerce. *Sunday Times* (May 2000)

20 How many people go to the Library of Congress to look through images?
Mark Getty (b. ?1978) US Internet entrepreneur. Referring to marketing of digital images via the Internet. *Sunday Times* (October 2000)

21 We're still at the lower slopes of this excitement and, at the moment, people are dazzled by the technological advances and possibilities.
Michael Grade (b. 1943) British television executive. Referring to new media. *Marketing* (June 2000)

22 The way we use the Internet to fight the giants is an afterthought to be honest.
Stelios Haji-Ioannou (b. 1967) Greek founder of EasyJet. *Revolution* (October 1999)

23 The government's job is to create the right economic climate to allow our e-commerce industries to flourish, but there is only so much we can do. The real hard work is down to business people across the country.
Patricia Hewitt (b. 1948) British government minister. *Digital Britain* (January 2000)

24 We have to take advantage of everything the technology and the new economy provide.
Nobuyuki Idei (b. 1937) Japanese chairman and CEO of Sony Corporation. *Forbes* (May 2000)

25 The Internet is this phenomenal and organized and democratic vehicle that's ideal for communicating with women.
Geraldine Laybourne (b. 1947) US chairman of Oxygen Media. 'The 50 Most Powerful Women in American Business', *Fortune* (Patricia Sellers and Cora Daniels; October 1999)

26 The Internet will eventually converge with television. I have the relationships with entertainment companies and big technology companies to pull this off.
Geraldine Laybourne (b. 1947) US chairman of Oxygen Media. 'The 50 Most Powerful Women in American Business', *Fortune* (Patricia Sellers and Cora Daniels; October 1999)

27 Brands like the Guardian and Guinness are so established that people have entrenched views. With lastminute.com you don't have that. Everyone's a potential triallist.
Carl Lyons (b. 1970) British marketing director of lastminute.com. *Marketing* (August 2000)

28 Marketing is marketing. It's easy to drape new media in magic but it comes down to whether it's a good business or not.
Carl Lyons (b. 1970) British marketing director of lastminute.com. *Marketing* (August 2000)

29 The web site needs to be as sticky as a currant bun.
Carolyn McCall (b. 1962) British managing director of Guardian Newspapers. *Marketing* (April 2000)

30 One of the most interesting aspects of the rapid growth of the Internet is how quickly some people have come to embrace it as an engine of entrepreneurial promise and wealth...It's the end-of-the-century gold rush.
Mark McCormack (1930–2003) US entrepreneur, founder and CEO of the International Management Group. *Staying Street Smart in the Internet Age: What Hasn't Changed about the Way We Do Business* (2000), Introduction

31 The next generation of E-markets will be open, global and based on E-business rules of engagement and interoperation. They include private E-business communities, open digital cooperatives, powerful market makers, electronic trading exchanges.
William (Walid) Mougayar, US consultant and management theorist. 'E-commerce? E-business? Who E-cares?', *Computerworld* (2 November 1998)

32 The new technology has put some truly sharp teeth in the long-standing effort to prevent

banks from adopting lending practices that deprive minority and low- and moderate-income neighborhoods of credit.
Ralph Nader (b. 1934) US lawyer and consumer-rights campaigner. 'Digital Democracy in Action', *Forbes* (12 February 1996)

33 The rush by marketers to establish World Wide Web sites at times resembled the Gold Rush that sent the 49ers west in search of riches.
Stan Rapp, US advertising executive and co-founder of Rapp Collins. *The New Maxi-Marketing* (co-written with Thomas L. Collins; 1995)

34 America has caught Internet fever.
John A. Roth (b. 1942) Canadian former president and CEO of Nortel Networks Corporation. *Sunday Times* (May 2000)

35 The phrase 'click, click you're dead' focuses the mind.
Martin Sorrell (b. 1945) British advertising executive. Interview (March 2000)

36 The web attacks traditional ways of doing things and elites, and this is very uncomfortable for traditional businesses to deal with.
Martin Sorrell (b. 1945) British advertising executive. *Marketing* (April 2000)

37 This is a group of tribes and I think the tribes have their value.
Martin Sorrell (b. 1945) British advertising executive. Referring to communities on the Internet. *Marketing* (April 2000)

38 If you sit down and you ask, 'Where is the value center, where is the economic engine for e-commerce?' I guarantee you it is not in cost reduction. Not even close. The economic engine is always in value.
Jay S. Walker, US entrepreneur and founder of Priceline.com, CEO of Walker Digital Corporation. Interview, *Strategy + Business* (January–March 2000)

39 We thought the creation and operation of websites was mysterious Nobel Prize stuff, the province of the wild-eyed and purple-haired.
Jack Welch (b. 1935) US former chairman and CEO of General Electric. *Sunday Times* (May 2000)

40 Any company, old or new, that does not see this technology as important as breathing could be on its last breath.
Jack Welch (b. 1935) US former chairman and CEO of General Electric. Referring to e-commerce. *Sunday Times* (May 2000)

41 Mankind now has a completely integrated financial and information marketplace capable of moving money and ideas to any place on this planet in minutes.
Walter Wriston (b. 1919) US banker. *Risk and Other Four Letter Words* (1986)

ECONOMICS

1 Economic growth may one day turn out to be a curse rather than a good, and under no conditions can it either lead to freedom or constitute a proof for its existence.

Hannah Arendt (1906–75) US political philosopher. *On Revolution* (1963)

2 Economists got away from really questioning how the world works, how decisions actually got made. If something doesn't conform to neoclassical models...people are not somehow behaving themselves properly.
W. Brian Arthur (b. 1945) US economist. Interview, *Strategy + Business* (April–June 1998)

3 If economics wants to understand the new economy, it not only has to understand increasing returns and the dynamics of instability. It also has to look at cognition itself, something we have never done before in economics
W. Brian Arthur (b. 1945) US economist. Interview, *Strategy + Business* (April–June 1998)

4 The invisible hand is not perfect. Indeed, the invisible hand is a little bit arthritic...I'm a believer in free markets, but I think we need to be less naïve. We need to accept that markets give us pretty good solutions, but occasionally they will lock in something inferior.
W. Brian Arthur (b. 1945) US economist. Interview, *Strategy + Business* (April–June 1998)

5 We're facing a danger that economics is rigorous deduction based upon faulty assumptions. Science after science gets that way from time to time. When it does, we're in real trouble
W. Brian Arthur (b. 1945) US economist. Interview, *Strategy + Business* (April–June 1998)

6 The modern history of economic theory is a tale of evasions of reality.
Thomas Balogh (1905–85) British economist. Referring to classical economics. *The Irrelevance of Conventional Economics* (1982)

7 Humanity seems bent on creating a world economy primarily based on goods that take no material form. In doing so, we may be eliminating any predictable connection between creators and a fair reward for the utility others may find in their works.
John Perry Barlow (b. 1947) US academic, lyricist, and writer. 'The Economy of Ideas', *Wired* (March 1994)

8 There is no inherent mechanism in our present system which can with certainty prevent competitive sectional bargaining for wages from setting up a vicious spiral of rising prices under full employment.
William Henry Beveridge (1879–1963) British economist and social reformer. *Full Employment in a Free Society* (1945)

9 ECONOMIST, n. A special (but not particular) kind of liar.
Ambrose Bierce (1842–?1914) US journalist and writer. *The Devil's Dictionary* (1911)

10 This is the generation that claims education, skills, and technology as the instruments of economic prosperity and personal fulfilment, not old battles between state and market.

Tony Blair (b. 1953) British prime minister. Quoted in *Financial Times* (30 May 1997)

11 A national economy, like an individual business...is the sum of the spiritual and mental qualities of its people, and its output of value will be only as strong as the values of society.
Warren T. Brookes (1929–91) US journalist and columnist. *The Economy in Mind* (1982)

12 Economics is a metaphysical rather than mathematical science in which intangible spiritual values and attitudes are at least as important as physical assets and morals more fundamental than the money supply.
Warren T. Brookes (1929–91) US journalist and columnist. *The Economy in Mind* (1982)

13 As the economy gets better, everything else gets worse.
Art Buchwald (b. 1925) US journalist. *Time* (31 January 1972)

14 Voodoo economics.
George Bush (b. 1924) US former president. Referring to the policies of Ronald Reagan. Remark (1980)

15 It's important for folks to understand that when there's more trade, there's more commerce.
George W. Bush (b. 1946) US president. Speech (April 2000)

16 Respectable Professors of the Dismal Science.
Thomas Carlyle (1795–1881) British historian and essayist. Referring to Political Economy (Economics) and its practitioners; a reputation that still survives. 'The Present Time', *Latter-day Pamphlets* (1850), no. 1

17 Here lies one who knew how to get around him men who were cleverer than himself.
Andrew Carnegie (1835–1919) US industrialist and philanthropist. Epitaph (1919)

18 Unlimited economic growth has the marvellous quality of stilling discontent while maintaining privilege. A fact that has not gone unnoticed among liberal economists.
Noam Chomsky (b. 1928) US linguist and political activist. *For Reasons of State* (1973), Introduction

19 It's the economy, stupid.
Bill Clinton (b. 1946) US former president. Slogan during the campaign of 1992. *New York Times* (2000)

20 The difference between buyers and sellers blurs to the point where both are in a web of economic, informational and emotional exchange.
Stan Davis (b. 1939) US business author. *Blur* (co-written with Christopher Meyer; 1998)

21 Corporate intentions and capabilities to create cross-national strategic alliances are affected by the ongoing structural changes of the global and regional economy.
Richard Drobnick (b. 1945) US academic. 'Economic Integration in the Pacific Rim', *Corporate Strategies in the Pacific Rim* (Denis Fred Simon, ed.; 1995)

22 I have no interest in celebrities. If all the superrich disappeared, the world economy would not even notice. The superrich are irrelevant to the economy.
Peter F. Drucker (b. 1909) US management consultant and academic. Quoted in 'Seeing Things as They Really Are', *Forbes* (Robert Lenzner and Stephen S. Johnson; 1987)

23 Everybody is always in favour of general economy and particular expenditure.
Anthony Eden (1897–1977) British prime minister. Quoted in 'Sayings of the Week', *Observer* (17 June 1956)

24 Economics is not a science in the sense that a policy can repeatedly be applied under similar conditions and will repeatedly produce similar results.
Millicent Fenwick (1910–92) US politician and writer. *Speaking Up* (1982)

25 Positive economics is in principle independent of any particular ethical position or normative judgement...In short, positive economics is or can be an 'objective' science.
Milton Friedman (b. 1912) US economist and winner of the 1976 Nobel Prize in Economics. *Essays in Positive Economics* (1953), pt 1, 1

26 The people are opposed to it. And who is being stupid in all of this, in my opinion, is the business community in Europe. They're not going to benefit from the euro, they're going to be harmed by it.
Milton Friedman (b. 1912) US economist and winner of the 1976 Nobel Prize in Economics. Referring to currency unification in Europe. *Forbes* (1997)

27 If freedom were not so economically efficient it certainly wouldn't stand a chance.
Milton Friedman (b. 1912) US economist and winner of the 1976 Nobel Prize in Economics. Quoted in 'Sayings of the Week', *Observer* (1 March 1987)

28 Economists may not know how to run the economy, but they know how to create shortages or gluts simply by regulating prices below the market, or artificially supporting them from above.
Milton Friedman (b. 1912) US economist and winner of the 1976 Nobel Prize in Economics. 1962. Attrib.

29 Neoclassical economics...has uncovered important truths about the nature of money and markets because its fundamental model of rational self-interested human behavior is correct about 80 percent of the time.
Francis Fukuyama (b. 1952) US economist and writer. *Trust: The Social Virtues and the Creation of Prosperity* (1995)

30 Virtually all economic activity in the contemporary world is carried out not by individuals but by organizations that require a high degree of social cooperation.
Francis Fukuyama (b. 1952) US economist and writer. *Trust: The Social Virtues and the Creation of Prosperity* (1995)

31 The attraction of power we take for granted in politics... But in economics...the thrust...is for pecuniary return, for money. And I have always felt that that denies in the economic world a very large part of the motivation.
J.K. Galbraith (b. 1908) US economist and diplomat. Interview, Conversations with History series, Institute of International Studies, University of California, Berkeley. 'Intellectual Journey: Challenging the Conventional Wisdom' (27 March 1986)

32 In economics, hope and faith coexist with great scientific pretension and also a deep desire for respectability.
J.K. Galbraith (b. 1908) US economist and diplomat. *New York Times Magazine* (June 1970)

33 The Affluent Society
J.K. Galbraith (b. 1908) US economist and diplomat. Book title. *The Affluent Society* (1958)

34 Monetary policy suffers from the unfortunate absence of any occult effect. It has long been clear that economic management...would be greatly facilitated if resort could occasionally be had to witchcraft.
J.K. Galbraith (b. 1908) US economist and diplomat. *The Affluent Society* (1958), ch. 16

35 Trickle-down theory—the less than elegant metaphor that if one feeds the horse enough oats, some will pass through to the road for the sparrows.
J.K. Galbraith (b. 1908) US economist and diplomat. *The Culture of Contentment* (1992)

36 There are three kinds of economist: Those who can count and those who can't.
Eddie George (b. 1939) British banker, governor of the Bank of England. *Observer* (1996)

37 Capital is a result of labor, and is used by labor to assist it in further production. Labor is the active and initial force, and labor is therefore the employer of capital.
Henry George (1839–97) US economist. *Progress and Poverty* (1879), bk 3, ch. 1

38 The new mixed economy looks...for a synergy between public and private sectors.
Anthony Giddens (b. 1938) British sociologist and author. *The Third Way: The Renewal of Social Democracy* (1998)

39 Unfortunately monetarism, like Marxism, suffered the only fate that for a theory is worse than death: it was put into practice.
Ian Gilmour (b. 1926) British politician. *Dancing with Dogma* (1992)

40 The volatility at the core of deregulated financial institutions makes a world economy that is organised as a system of free markets essentially unstable.
John Gray (b. 1948) British academic and writer. *False Dawn* (1998)

41 Institutions of the newer participants in global finance had not been tested, until recently...recent crises have underscored certain financial structure vulnerabilities that are not readily assuaged in the short run.

Alan Greenspan (b. 1926) US economist and chairman of US Federal Reserve Board. Speech to the Financial Crisis Conference, Council on Foreign Relations, New York. 'Global Challenges' (12 July 2000)

42 We may be in a rapidly evolving international financial system with all the bells and whistles of the so-called new economy. But the old-economy rules of prudence are as formidable as ever. We violate them at our own peril.

Alan Greenspan (b. 1926) US economist and chairman of US Federal Reserve Board. Speech to the Financial Crisis Conference, Council on Foreign Relations, New York. 'Global Challenges' (12 July 2000)

43 The recent period has been marked by a transformation to an economy that is more productive as competitive forces become increasingly intense and new technologies raise the efficiency of our businesses...While these tendencies were no doubt in train in the 'old', pre-1990s economy, they accelerated over the past decade as a number of technologies with their roots in the cumulative innovations of the past half-century began to yield dramatic economic returns.

Alan Greenspan (b. 1926) US economist and chairman of US Federal Reserve Board. Speech to the National Governors' Association 92nd Annual Meeting, State College, Pennsylvania. 'Structural Change in the New Economy' (11 July 2000)

44 History cannot be reduced to a set of statistics and probabilities.

Alan Greenspan (b. 1926) US economist and chairman of US Federal Reserve Board. Said in a speech on 14 October 1992. Quoted in *New York Times* (14 October 1992)

45 An economy that adds value through information, ideas, and intelligence—the Three I Economy—offers a way out of the apparent clash between material growth and environmemtal resources.

Charles Handy (b. 1932) British business executive and author. 'Trust and the Virtual Organization', *Harvard Business Review* (May–June 1991)

46 The market is a mechanism for sorting the efficient from the inefficient, it is not a substitute for responsibility.

Charles Handy (b. 1932) British business executive and author. *The Empty Raincoat: Making Sense of the Future* (1994), pt 1, ch. 1

47 Economists can be called the worldly philosophers for they sought to embrace in a scheme of philosophy the most worldly of man's activities—his drive for wealth.

Robert L. Heilbroner (b. 1919) US economist. *The Worldly Philosophers* (1953), Introduction

48 The eighties was an era when many companies were asset rich and cash poor.

Nicola Horlick (b. 1960) British fund manager. *Can You Have It All?* (1997)

49 Manufacturers...gradually shift their places, leaving those countries and provinces which they have already enriched, and flying to others, whither they are allured by the cheapness of provisions and labour.

David Hume (1711–76) Scottish philosopher and historian. 'Of Money', *Essays, Moral, Political, and Literary* (1754), pt 2, essay 3

50 Investment is not only volatile, it is the key motor of the economy's prosperity because it has a snowball effect.

Will Hutton (b. 1950) British author and newspaper editor. *The State We're In* (1995)

51 No less than war or statecraft, the history of Economics has its heroic ages.

Aldous Huxley (1894–1963) British novelist and essayist. *Collected Essays* (1958)

52 When future historians look back on our way of curing inflation...they'll probably compare it to bloodletting in the Middle Ages.

Lee Iacocca (b. 1924) US president of Ford Motor Company, chairman and CEO of Chrysler Corporation. *Fortune* (27 June 1983)

53 Observation of realities has never, to put it mildly, been one of the strengths of economic development.

Jane Jacobs (b. 1916) US urban theorist and social critic. *Cities and the Wealth of Nations* (1984)

54 Did you ever think that making a speech on economics is a lot like pissing down your leg? It seems hot to you but it never does to anyone else.

Lyndon Baines Johnson (1908–73) US president. Quoted in *A Life in our Times* (J.K. Galbraith; 1981)

55 We must have an economy that does not force the migrant worker's child to miss school in order to earn...just so the family can eat. That is the moral bankruptcy that trickle-down economics is all about.

Barbara Jordan (1936–96) US politician. Keynote address at the 1992 Democratic National Convention. 'Change: From What to What' (13 July 1992)

56 To take full advantage of the potential in e-business, leaders must lead differently, and people must work together differently. Let's call this new way of working e-culture—the human side of the global information era, the heart and soul of the new economy.

Rosabeth Moss Kanter (b. 1943) US management theorist, academic, and writer. 'How E-Smart Are You?', *World Link* (January–February 2000)

57 Good economics is good politics.

Paul Keating (b. 1944) Australian former prime minister. Quoted in *Sydney Morning Herald* (27 August 1988)

58 It is Enterprise which builds and improves the world's possessions...If Enterprise is afoot, Wealth accumulates whatever may be happening to Thrift; and if Enterprise is asleep, Wealth decays, whatever Thrift may be doing.

John Maynard Keynes (1883–1946) British economist. *A Treatise on Money* (1930)

59 The Economic Problem...the problem of want and poverty and the economic struggle between classes and nations, is nothing but a frightful muddle, a transitory and *unnecessary* muddle.
John Maynard Keynes (1883–1946) British economist. *Essays in Persuasion* (1932), Preface

60 The ideas of economists and political philosophers...are more powerful than is commonly understood. Indeed the world is ruled by little else. Practical men who believe themselves to be quite exempt from any intellectual influences, are usually the slaves of some defunct economist.
John Maynard Keynes (1883–1946) British economist. *The General Theory of Employment Interest and Money* (1936)

61 There are no intrinsic reasons for the scarcity of capital.
John Maynard Keynes (1883–1946) British economist. *The General Theory of Employment Interest and Money* (1936), ch. 24

62 The engine which drives enterprise is not thrift but profit.
John Maynard Keynes (1883–1946) British economist. Quoted in *Treasury of Investment Wisdom* (Bernice Cohen; 1999)

63 When the facts change, I change my mind.
John Maynard Keynes (1883–1946) British economist. Quoted in *Treasury of Investment Wisdom* (Bernice Cohen; 1999)

64 Economics is a subject that does not greatly respect one's wishes.
Nikita Sergeyevich Khrushchev (1894–1971) Soviet statesman. Attrib.

65 I have been...moved to wonder whether my job is a job or a racket, whether economists, and particularly economic theorists, may not be in the position that Cicero, citing Cato, ascribed to the augurs of Rome—that they should cover their faces or burst into laughter when they met on the street.
Frank H. Knight (1885–1972) US economist. 1950. *Essays on the History and Method of Economics* (1956)

66 Costs merely register competing attractions.
Frank H. Knight (1885–1972) US economist. *Risk, Uncertainty, and Profit* (1921)

67 Like nature, our economic system remains, in the long run, stable and rational...We welcome the inevitable seasons of nature, yet we are upset by the seasons of our economy! How foolish of us.
Jerzy Kosinski (1933–91) US novelist. *Being There* (1971)

68 The notion that economic life is a distinct realm, governed by immutable laws of narrow self-interest, is giving way to a much older notion: economic life is only one strand in the rich web of human relationships.
Frances Moore Lappé (b. 1944) US writer and activist on global isues. Speech to Vermont Businesses for Social Responsibility. 'Reweaving Business into the Social Fabric' (11 December 1997)

69 Today it's fashionable to talk about the New Economy, or the Information Economy, or the Knowledge Economy. But when I think about the imperatives of this market, I view today's economy as the Value Economy. Adding value has become more than just a sound business principle; it is both the common denominator and the competitive edge.
Arthur Levitt Jr (b. 1931) US author and former chairman of the US Securities and Exchange Commission. Speech to the Finance Conference 2000, Boston College, Boston, MA. 'The New Economy' (6 March 2000)

70 Monopoly is business at the end of its journey.
Henry Demarest Lloyd (1847–1903) US journalist and reformer. *Wealth Against Commonwealth* (1894)

71 It seems that nearly every American either has a share of federal spending or has a close relative who does.
Trent Lott (b. 1941) US senator. *US News & World Report* (1983)

72 Behind the screen of the ballot, the real holders of power...are the great industrial and monetary monopolies who own our national economic life.
Florence Luscomb (1887–1985) US campaigner for women's suffrage, architect, and pacifist. Attrib.

73 If a business can achieve high returns then it will accumulate more equity and it will have more leeway to reinvest on its own.
Minoru Makihara (b. 1930) Japanese president of Mitsubishi Corporation. Interview, *Strategy + Business* (Joel Kurtzman; January–March 1996)

74 Political work is the life-blood for all economic work.
Mao Zedong (1893–1976) Chinese revolutionary leader. *Quotations from Chairman Mao Tse Tung* (1976)

75 Political Economy or Economics is a study of mankind in the ordinary business of life.
Alfred Marshall (1842–1924) British economist. 1890. *Principles of Economics* (8th ed., 1920), vol. 1

76 A commodity appears, at first sight, a very trivial thing, and easily understood. Its analysis shows that is is, in reality, a very queer thing, abounding in metaphysical subtleties and theological niceties.
Karl Marx (1818–83) German political and economic philosopher. *Das Kapital* (1867), vol. 1

77 A nation is not in danger of financial disaster merely because it owes itself money.
Andrew William Mellon (1855–1937) US financier, industrialist, and public servant. 1933. Quoted in 'Sayings of Our Times', *Observer* (31 May 1953)

78 One speaks with great respect of economists, if only because they represent such a variety of opinions.
Robert Menzies (1894–1978) Australian prime minister. *Sydney Morning Herald* (14 March 1964)

79 I accept the proposition that there has been a significant improvement in underlying productivity growth in the United States, that it is very closely tied to improvements in information and communications technology, and that it is likely to spread around the world. But I resist the new economy label because it seems to encourage a disrespect for the old rules that could seriously undermine our success in taking advantage of the new opportunities.

Laurence H. Meyer (b. 1944) US economist and former member of the Board of Governors, US Federal Reserve System (1996–2002). Speech to the Boston Economics Club, Boston, MA. 'The New Economy Meets Supply and Demand' (6 June 2000)

80 So, is there a 'new economy'? The answer is: It depends. It depends on how you define new economy, and it depends on where you live.

Laurence H. Meyer (b. 1944) US economist and former member of the Board of Governors, US Federal Reserve System (1996–2002). Speech to the Boston Economics Club, Boston, MA. 'The New Economy Meets Supply and Demand' (6 June 2000)

81 There are broader and narrower definitions of the new economy. The narrow version defines the new economy in terms of two principal developments: first, an increase in the economy's maximum sustainable growth rate and, second, the spread and increasing importance of information and communications technology.

Laurence H. Meyer (b. 1944) US economist and former member of the Board of Governors, US Federal Reserve System (1996–2002). Speech to the Boston Economics Club, Boston, MA. 'The New Economy Meets Supply and Demand' (6 June 2000)

82 The broader interpretation that often seems to underlie the new economy label is that we are witnessing a more fundamental change in the paradigm. The old rules no longer apply. Throw out the NAIRU. Heck, throw out supply and demand. No limits, no business cycles.

Laurence H. Meyer (b. 1944) US economist and former member of the Board of Governors, US Federal Reserve System (1996–2002). Speech to the Boston Economics Club, Boston, MA. NAIRU equals non-accelerating-inflation rate of unemployment. 'The New Economy Meets Supply and Demand' (6 June 2000)

83 Political Economy as a branch of science is extremely modern; but the subject with which its enquiries are conversant has in all ages necessarily constituted one of the chief practical interests of mankind.

John Stuart Mill (1806–73) British economist and philosopher. 1848. *Principles of Political Economy, with Some of their Applications to Social Philosophy, 7th edition* (1871)

84 Everybody thinks of economics whether he is aware of it or not. In joining a political party or in casting his ballot, the citizen implicitly takes a stand upon essential economic theories.

Ludwig von Mises (1881–1973) US economist. *Human Action* (1949)

85 The market economy as such does not respect political frontiers. Its field is the world.

Ludwig von Mises (1881–1973) US economist. *Human Action* (1949)

86 Humans have trouble with economics, as you may have noticed, and not just because economic circumstances sometimes cause them to starve. Humans seem to have an innate inability to pay attention to economic principles.

P.J. O'Rourke (b. 1947) US humorist and journalist. *Eat the Rich* (1998), ch. 1

87 Economics is not an attempt to generalise human desires or human behaviour; but to generalise the phenomena of price.

Michael Oakeshott (1901–90) British philosopher and political theorist. Quoted in *Thinkers of Our Time: Oakeshott* (Robert Grant; 1990)

88 What we are left with is an overmanipulated economy that can't function normally.

Kenichi Ohmae (b. 1943) Japanese management consultant and theorist. Referring to Japanese economy. *Fortune* (December 1992)

89 Efforts to preserve all industries will lower the national standard of living.

Michael Porter (b. 1947) US strategist. *The Competitive Advantage of Nations* (1990)

90 One of the soundest rules to remember when making forecasts in the field of economics is that whatever is to happen is happening already.

Sylvia Porter (1913–91) US journalist and finance expert. Attrib.

91 A friend of mine was asked to a costume ball a short time ago. He slapped some egg on his face and went as a liberal economist.

Ronald Reagan (b. 1911) US former president and actor. *Speaking My Mind* (1990)

92 In a world where routine production is footloose...competitive advantage lies not in one-time breakthroughs but in continual improvements. Stable technologies get away.

Robert Reich (b. 1946) US economist and politician. *Tales of a New America* (1987)

93 Economics limps along with one foot in untested hypotheses and the other in untestable slogans.

Joan Robinson (1903–83) British economist. 'Metaphysics, Morals and Science', *Economic Philosophy* (1962)

94 The first essential for economists...is to...combat, not foster, the ideology which pretends that values which can be measured in terms of money are the only ones which count.

Joan Robinson (1903–83) British economist. 'What Are the Rules of the Game', *Economic Philosophy* (1962)

95 Unequal distribution of income is an excessively uneconomic method of getting the necessary saving done.

Joan Robinson (1903–83) British economist. *Essay on Marxian Economics* (1942)

96 The purpose of studying economics is not to acquire a set of ready-made answers to economic questions, but to learn to avoid being deceived by economists.

Joan Robinson (1903–83) British economist. *Marx, Marshall and Keynes* (1955)

97 This movement was the origin of the whole system of modern economic administration. It has revitalised the way of doing business all over the world.

John D. Rockefeller (1839–1937) US industrialist, philanthropist, and founder of Standard Oil. His assessment of the impact of the creation of Standard Oil. Quoted in *Frenzied Finance* (Thomas Lawson; 1906)

98 We have always known that heedless self-interest was bad morals; we know now that it is bad economics.

Franklin D. Roosevelt (1882–1945) US president. Second presidential inaugural address (20 January 1937)

99 A nobler economics...is not afraid to discuss spirit and conscience, moral purpose and the meaning of life, an economics that aims to educate and elevate people, not merely to measure their low-grade behaviour.

Theodore Roszak (1933–81) US historian, writer, and editor. Defining a humanistic economics. Quoted in *Small Is Beautiful* (E.F. Schumacher; 1973)

100 Economics is as much a study in fantasy and aspiration as in hard numbers—maybe more so.

Theodore Roszak (1933–81) US historian, writer, and editor. *The Making of a Counter Culture* (1995), Introduction

101 As in the instances of alchemy, astrology, witchcraft, and other such popular creeds, political economy, has a plausible idea at the root of it.

John Ruskin (1819–1900) British art critic and writer. 'The Roots of Honour', *Unto This Last* (1862)

102 The industrial era assumed the economy of scarcity, but now we have both the economy of scarcity and the economy of abundance: ideas are unlimited.

Charles M. Savage, US management consultant and theorist. Speech, 4th Workshop on Inventing the organisation of the 21st Century, Munich, Germany. 'Leadership & Management in the Knowledge Era' (February 1998)

103 The work of Smith is only a confused assemblage of the soundest principles of Political Economy, supported by luminous examples and by the most curious notions of statistics, mingled with instructive reflections.

Jean Baptiste Say (1767–1832) French political economist. Referring to Adam Smith's *The Wealth of Nations* (1776). *Traité d'économie politique* (1803)

104 Modern economic thinking...is peculiarly unable to consider the long term and to appreciate man's dependence on the natural world.

E.F. Schumacher (1911–77) British economist and conservationist. Speech, Blackpool, England. 'Clean Air and Future Energy' (19 October 1967)

105 Small is Beautiful

E.F. Schumacher (1911–77) British economist and conservationist. Book title. Referring to the importance of small-scale economics. *Small Is Beautiful* (1973)

106 The metal of economic theory is in Marx's pages immersed in such a wealth of steaming phrases as to acquire a temperature not naturally its own.

Joseph Alois Schumpeter (1883–1950) US economist and social theorist. *Capitalism, Socialism and Democracy* (1942)

107 The market economy succeeds not because some people's interests are suppressed and other people are kept out of the market, but because people gain individual advantage from it.

Amartya Sen (b. 1933) Indian economist and winner of the 1998 Nobel Prize in Economics. 'Humane Development', interview, *The Atlantic Monthly* (15 December 1999)

108 The generally accepted theory is that financial markets tend towards equilibrium, and...discount the future correctly. I operate using a different theory, according to which financial markets cannot possibly discount the future correctly because they do not merely discount the future; they help to shape it.

George Soros (b. 1930) US financier, entrepreneur, and philanthropist. Speech to the MIT Department of Economics, World Economy Laboratory Conference, Washington, D.C. 'The Theory of Reflexivity' (26 April 1994)

109 Studying economics is not a good preparation for dealing with it.

George Soros (b. 1930) US financier, entrepreneur, and philanthropist. *The Crisis of Global Capitalism* (1998)

110 Economic systems are not value-free columns of numbers based on rules of reason, but ways of expressing what varying societies believe is important.

Gloria Steinem (b. 1934) US entrepreneur, editor, and writer. *Moving Beyond Words* (1994)

111 One of the peculiarities of economics is that it still rests on a behaviorial assumption— rational utility maximization—that has long since been rejected by sociologists and psychologists.

Lester Thurow (b. 1938) US economist, management theorist, and writer. *Dangerous Currents* (1983)

112 Economists are always recommending the elimination of this or that 'market imperfection'...no astrophysicist recommends the elimination of planets that he does not like.

Lester Thurow (b. 1938) US economist, management theorist, and writer. Referring to how economists relate to economic realities. *Dangerous Currents* (1983)

113 Economics and ethics are not mutually exclusive.

Lionel Tiger (b. 1937) Canadian anthropologist. *The Manufacture of Evil* (1987)

114 Economics is a 'dismal science', we don't believe things are perfect, we don't believe there are free lunches. We believe there are trade-offs and costs and sacrifices.

Laura D'Andrea Tyson (b. 1947) US economist, academic, and chair of the Council of Economic Advisors and National

Economic Council (1993–96). Interview, Conversations with History series, Institute of International Studies, University of California, Berkeley. 'An Economist Goes to Washington' (14 January 1998)

115 Instead of investing in the goods as they pass between producer and consumer, as the merchant does, the businessman now invests in the processes of industry.

Thorstein Veblen (1857–1929) US economist and social scientist. *The Theory of Business Enterprise* (1904)

116 The corset is, in economic theory, substantially a mutilation, undergone for the purpose of lowering the subject's vitality and rendering her permanently and obviously unfit for work.

Thorstein Veblen (1857–1929) US economist and social scientist. *The Theory of the Leisure Class* (1899), ch. 7

117 There are only four ways to create value in the New Economy, and they're really simple: information, entertainment, convenience, and savings.

Jay S. Walker, US entrepreneur and founder of Priceline.com, CEO of Walker Digital Corporation. Interview, *Strategy + Business* (April–June 2000)

118 My views about economics are very simple. I think we know very little. We know some things, but our knowledge is limited...It is very important having humility in managing economics.

Alan Walters (b. 1926) British economist and government adviser. Interview, *Daily Mail* (28 July 1988)

119 It is not that pearls fetch a high price *because* men have dived for them; but on the contrary, men have dived for them because they fetch a high price.

Richard Whately (1787–1863) British archbishop and economist. *Introductory Lectures on Political Economy* (1832)

120 As long as capital—both human and money— can move toward opportunity, trade will not balance.

Walter Wriston (b. 1919) US banker. Speech (25 January 1993)

121 The first law of economics is that when the price goes up, consumption comes down. This is a divine law.

Ahmed Zaki Yamani (b. 1930) Saudi Arabian politician. Quoted in *Yamani* (Jeffrey Robinson; 1988)

EFFICIENCY

1 A business set up just to make money is rarely efficient, because it is not often intended to create wealth; it is only expected to make a fortune for certain people who occupy executive positions.

Sarah Tarleton Colvin, US nurse, campaigner for women's suffrage, and educationalist. *A Rebel in Thought* (1944)

2 I make no secret of the fact that I would rather lie on a sofa than sweep beneath it. But you have to be efficient if you're going to be lazy.

Shirley Conran (b. 1932) British designer, fashion editor, and author. 'The Reason Why', *Superwoman* (1975)

3 If the Wright brothers were alive today, Wilbur would have to fire Orvill to reduce costs.

Charles Horton Cooley (1864–1929) US sociologist. Quoted in *USA Today* (June 1994)

4 In an organization, doing is causing people to have a productivity that makes everything happen on time and profitably.

Philip B. Crosby (1926–2001) US business executive and author. *Running Things* (1986)

5 I believe there's an inverse correlation between the quality of the information you have and the amount of inventory you need. Most businesses tie up a tremendous amount of assets anticipating things that may not happen. If they had a system that was customer demand driven, they would be much more efficient.

Michael Dell (b. 1965) US chairman and CEO of Dell Computer Corporation. Speech to the Detroit Economic Club. 'Building a Competitive Advantage in an Internet Economy' (1 November 1999)

6 It is possible for a business venture to be an island of efficiency in a sea of sloth.

Indira Gandhi (1917–84) Indian prime minister. Speech (9 December 1967)

7 It is much more difficult to measure nonperformance than performance.

Harold S. Geneen (1910–97) US telecommunications entrepreneur and CEO of ITT. Referring to why managers sometimes accept underachievement. *Managing* (co-written with Alvin Moscow; 1984)

8 The worldwide movement towards fiscal rectitude and the creation of an economic environment which is transparent and rewards efficiency is no longer a matter of choice but one of necessity.

Deepak Lal (b. 1940) British political economist and author. *India in the World Economy* (1999)

9 Incompetence knows no barriers of time or place.

Laurence J. Peter (1919–90) Canadian academic and writer. *Why Things Go Wrong: The Peter Principle Revisited* (1984)

10 The pyramid, the chief organizational principle of the modern organization, turns a business into a traffic jam.

Ricardo Semler (b. 1959) Brazilian business executive and president of Semco. *Maverick!* (1993)

11 When two men always agree, one of them is unnecessary.

William Wrigley (1861–1932) US businessman and founder of Wrigley Company. *American Magazine* (March 1920)

EMPLOYEES

1 Empowerment: A magic wand management waves to help traumatized survivors of restructuring suddenly feel engaged, self-managed, and in control of their futures and their jobs.
Anonymous. *Fortune* (15 February 1995)

2 Employees may feel responsible for producing what is required of them, but they will not feel responsible for the way the situation is defined.
Chris Argyris (b. 1923) US academic and organisational behaviour theorist. *Flawed Advice and the Management Trap* (2000)

3 Twenty-first-century corporations will find it hard to survive...unless they get better work from their employees. This does not necessarily mean harder work or more work. What it does necessarily mean is employees who've learned to take active responsibility for their own behavior.
Chris Argyris (b. 1923) US academic and organisational behaviour theorist. 'Good Communication That Blocks Learning', *Harvard Business Review* (July–August 1994)

4 I don't think a manager can work with a person day in and day out and not develop some sort of personal relationship.
Mary Kay Ash (1915–2001) US entrepreneur, business executive, and founder of Mary Kay Cosmetics. *On People Management* (1984)

5 Don't be condescending to unskilled labor. Try it for a half a day first.
Brooks Atkinson (1894–1984) US critic and essayist. *Theatre Arts* (1956)

6 Perhaps the most important principle on which the economy of a manufactory depends is the division of labour among the people who perform the work.
Charles Babbage (1792–1871) British mathematician and inventor. *On the Economy of Machinery and Manufacture* (1832)

7 At nights and on weekends we cry out for human rights and freedom of speech, and then we go to work and become strategic and cautious about our every word for fear we will be seen as disloyal or uncommitted.
Peter Block (b. 1935) US writer. *Stewardship* (1993)

8 Many companies say they want to change, but they need to empower people below.
Marvin Bower (1903–2003) US CEO of McKinsey & Company. *The Will to Manage* (1966)

9 An art can only be learned in the workshop of those who are winning their bread by it.
Samuel Butler (1835–1902) British writer. *Erewhon* (1872)

10 The only irreplaceable capital an organization possesses is the knowledge and ability of its people. The productivity of that capital depends on how effectively people share their competence with those who can use it.
Andrew Carnegie (1835–1919) US industrialist and philanthropist. Quoted in *Intellectual Capital* (Thomas A. Stewart; 1997)

11 If your employer starts upon a course which you think will prove injurious, tell him so, protest, give your reasons, and stand to them unless convinced you are wrong. It is the young man who does this, that capital wants for a partner or for a son-in-law.
Andrew Carnegie (1835–1919) US industrialist and philanthropist. 'From Oakland: How to Succeed in Life', *The Pittsburgh Bulletin* (19 December 1903)

12 The inventory goes down the elevator every night.
Fairfax Cone (1903–77) US advertising executive. Quoted in *The Trouble with Advertising* (John O'Toole; 1981)

13 Having formal empowerment programs is a way of showing employees that management does not care about them.
Philip B. Crosby (1926–2001) US business executive and author. *Quality Is Still Free* (1996)

14 The paternalism of Pullman is the same as the self-interest of a slave-holder in his human chattels. You are striking to avert slavery and degradation.
Eugene V. Debs (1855–1926) US politician and trade union leader. 1894. *New York Times* (1999)

15 Few top executives can even imagine the hatred, contempt, and fury that has been created—not primarily among blue-collar workers who never had an exalted opinion of the 'bosses'—but among their middle management and professional people.
Peter F. Drucker (b. 1909) US management consultant and academic. Quoted in 'Seeing Things as They Really Are', *Forbes* (Robert Lenzner and Stephen S. Johnson; 1987)

16 The worker under capitalism was totally dependent on the machine. In the employee society the employee and the tools of production are interdependent.
Peter F. Drucker (b. 1909) US management consultant and academic. *Post-capitalist Society* (1993)

17 People are the lifeblood of any airline, and it is the people of BA who will deliver its future success.
Rod Eddington (b. 1950) Australian business executive and CEO of British Airways. *Marketing* (May 2000)

18 Although colleagues provide high-quality input to multisource processes, they often are insufficient as the only source.
Mark R. Edwards (b. 1949) US writer. *360 Degree Feedback* (co-written with Ann J. Ewen; 1996)

19 Naturally, the workers are perfectly free; the manufacturer does not force them to take his materials and his cards, but he says to them...'If you don't like to be frizzled in my frying-pan, you can take a walk into the fire.'
Friedrich Engels (1820–95) German social philosopher and political economist. *The Condition of the Working Class in England* (1844)

20 For any action whatsoever, an employee should receive orders from one superior only.
Henri Fayol (1841–1925) French business executive. *General and Industrial Management* (1916)

21 How come when I want a pair of hands I get a human being as well?
Henry Ford (1863–1947) US industrialist, car manufacturer, and founder of Ford Motor Company. *My Life and Work* (co-written with Samuel Crowther; 1922)

22 You should see some of the research people. If they were in sales they'd never get past the first base. Brilliant minds, but no social graces whatsoever.
Elaine Garzarelli (b. 1951) US CEO and president of Garzarelli Investment Management. Quoted in *Women of the Street* (Sue Herera; 1997)

23 Take our 20 best people away, and I will tell you that Microsoft would become an unimportant company.
Bill Gates (b. 1955) US entrepreneur, chairman and CEO of Microsoft. *Fortune* (November 1996)

24 We rely on skilled foreign workers for their math, science, and creative abilities as well as their cultural knowledge, which helps when localizing products for world markets.
Bill Gates (b. 1955) US entrepreneur, chairman and CEO of Microsoft. *New York Times Syndicate* (20 December 1995)

25 We can't run the business. We learned over twenty-five years ago to let the business run itself. Commitment, not authority, promotes results.
Wilbert Lee Gore (d. 1986) US founder of Goretex. Quoted in *A Passion for Excellence* (Tom Peters and Nancy Austin; 1985)

26 You can't treat your people like an expense item.
Andrew S. Grove (b. 1936) US entrepreneur, author, and chairman of Intel Corporation. Quoted in *In the Company of Giants* (Rama Dev Jager; 1997)

27 At the peak, we had 30,000 people working in these businesses. There was no way they could feel I was their boss.
Guy Hands (b. 1959) Zimbabwean CEO of Terra Firma Capital Partners. *Management Today* (October 1999)

28 There is practically no area of business where the difference between rhetoric and actuality is greater than in the handling of people.
John Harvey-Jones (b. 1924) British management adviser, author, and former chairman of ICI. *All Together Now* (1994)

29 I can charge a man's battery and then recharge it again. But it is only when he has his own generator that we can talk about motivation. He then needs no outside stimulation. He wants to do it.
Frederick Herzberg (1923–2000) US psychologist. *Harvard Business Review* (January–February 1968)

30 If you have someone on a job, use him. If you can't, get rid of him.
Frederick Herzberg (1923–2000) US psychologist. *Harvard Business Review* (January–February 1968)

31 KITA—Kick in the ass.
Frederick Herzberg (1923–2000) US psychologist. *Harvard Business Review* (January–February 1968)

32 One more time, how do you motivate?
Frederick Herzberg (1923–2000) US psychologist. *Harvard Business Review* (January–February 1968)

33 It seemed that the human being was forever debarred from rational understanding as to why they worked.
Frederick Herzberg (1923–2000) US psychologist. *Management Review* (1971)

34 True motivation comes from achievement, personal development, job satisfaction, and recognition.
Frederick Herzberg (1923–2000) US psychologist. *The Motivation to Work* (1959)

35 Start with good people, lay out the rules, communicate with your employees, motivate them and reward them. If you do all those things effectively you can't miss.
Lee Iacocca (b. 1924) US president of Ford Motor Company, chairman and CEO of Chrysler Corporation. On how to run a successful company. *Talking Straight* (1988)

36 The first and primary motive for setting up this company was to create a stable work environment where engineers who had a deep and profound appreciation for technology could work to their heart's content.
Masaru Ibuka (1908–97) Japanese co-founder and chief adviser of Sony Corporation. Referring to the origins of Sony. In 1958 Totsuko's brand label, Sony, was adopted as the company name. *Founding Prospectus of Tokyo Telecommunications Engineering Corporation (Totsuko)* (7 May 1946), Introduction

37 I'm completely convinced of the necessity of encouraging everybody to accept the maximum amount of personal responsibility and allowing them to have a say in every problem in which they can help.
Elliot Jacques (b. 1917) Canadian psychologist and sociologist. Radio broadcast (August 1997)

38 My friends, it is solidarity of labor we want. We do not want to find fault with each other, but to solidify our forces and say to each other: 'We must be together; our masters are joined together and we must do the same thing'.
Mother Jones (1830–1930) US trade union leader. 1902. Speaking before the Convention of the United Mine Workers of America, Indianapolis, Indiana. Quoted in *New York Times* (2000)

39 Security no longer comes from being employed. It comes from being employable.
Rosabeth Moss Kanter (b. 1943) US management theorist, academic, and writer. *Changing Workplace Alert* (1997)

40 If the employees aren't satisfied, they won't promote the product we need.
Herb Kelleher (b. 1931) US businessman and founder of Southwest Airlines. *Aviation Week and Space Technology* (March 1990)

41 The more time I spend with our people, the more I find out about our business.

Herb Kelleher (b. 1931) US businessman and founder of Southwest Airlines. *The Nation's Business* (October 1991)

42 I keep six honest serving men
(They taught me all I know)
Their names
are What and Why and When
And How and Where and Who.

Rudyard Kipling (1865–1936) British novelist, poet, and short-story writer. *Just So Stories* (1902)

43 At Koch, we have a new vision of employees. In this vision, employees don't have jobs; rather, they have a set of rights, responsibilities, and rewards that enable them to best contribute.

Charles G. Koch (b. 1935) US management theorist, author, chairman and CEO of Koch Industries. Speech, Kansas State University (4 March 1996)

44 The personnel in India are more versatile. They're simply more hungry for work.

Lycourgos Kyprianou (b. 1955) Greek Cypriot entrepreneur recently under investigation for fraud and insider dealing. *Forbes* (August 2000)

45 Capital is only the fruit of labour and could never have existed if labour had not first existed.

Abraham Lincoln (1809–65) US president. Speech (December 1861)

46 Labour is the superior of capital and deserves much the higher consideration.

Abraham Lincoln (1809–65) US president. Speech (December 1861)

47 In the United States, the shareholders are the owners. Period. They have the final say. But here...it is first the employees and then the shareholders. So if you think of who owns the company more broadly—as we do—then you are obliged to think from a longer-term point of view. I think that is an advantage.

Minoru Makihara (b. 1930) Japanese president of Mitsubishi Corporation. Interview, *Strategy + Business* (Joel Kurtzman; January–March 1996)

48 Always be smart enough to hire people brighter than yourself.

Caroline Marland (b. 1946) Irish former managing director of Guardian Newspapers. *Management Today* (September 1999)

49 The gravy train has hit the buffers.

Robert Maxwell (1923–91) British publisher, business executive, and politician. Referring to the newspaper print union strikes. *Daily Mirror* (November 1986)

50 I really like my staff. I try to give them room. I'm probably like Bill Clinton. I want everyone to like me so I say 'yes' all the time. But that's more useful in cable TV than I think it is in Washington.

Judy McGrath (b. 1952) US president of MTV. 'The Century's Business, Career, and Money Heroes', *Society and Politics* (2000)

51 We had better start admitting that the most important people in an organization are those who actually provide a service or make and add value to products, not those who administer the activity.

Rene C. McPherson (1924–96) US CEO of Dana Corporation. Quoted in 'Rene McPherson: GSB Deanship is his Way to Reinvest the System', *Stanford GSB* (Fall 1980–81)

52 Microsoft's only factory asset is the human ingredient.

Fred Moody (b. 1949) US journalist and author. *New York Times Magazine* (August 1991)

53 When I find an employee who turns out to be wrong for a job, I feel it is my fault because I made the decision to hire him.

Akio Morita (1921–99) Japanese business executive. Quoted in *In Search of European Excellence* (Robert Heller; 1997)

54 Japanese people tend to be much better adjusted to the notion of work as honourable.

Akio Morita (1921–99) Japanese business executive. *Made in Japan* (1986)

55 You can be totally rational with a machine. But, if you work with people, sometimes logic has to take a back seat to understanding.

Akio Morita (1921–99) Japanese business executive. *Made in Japan* (1986)

56 American managers are too little concerned about their workers.

Akio Morita (1921–99) Japanese business executive. 'Overhauling America's Business Management', *New York Times Magazine* (Steve Lohr; January 1981)

57 Human resources are the greatest assets of any company. You can raise tariffs or prevent MNCs from entering, but one can't stop the employees from leaving if they are dissatisfied.

Narayana Murthy (b. 1946) Indian founder and CEO of Infosys. 'Employee Satisfaction Crucial to Success', *Hindu Business Line* (2000)

58 If you were to hire household staff to cook, clean, drive, stoke the fire, and answer the door, can you imagine suggesting that they not talk to each other, not see what each other is doing, not coordinate their functions?

Nicholas Negroponte (b. 1943) US academic, co-founder and director of MIT Media Laboratory. Referring to the pressure on work relationships in an office. *Being Digital* (1995)

59 Many organizations view people as 'things' that are but one variable in the production equation.

David M. Noer (b. 1939) US writer and human resources consultant. *Healing the Wounds* (1993)

60 The root cause of layoff survivor sickness is a profound shift in the psychological employment contract that binds individual and organization.

David M. Noer (b. 1939) US writer and human resources consultant. *Healing the Wounds* (1993)

61 If each of us hires people who are smaller than we are, we shall become a company of dwarfs.

But if each of us hires people who are bigger than we are, we shall become a company of giants.

David Ogilvy (1911–99) British advertising executive, founder and chairman of Ogilvy & Mather. *Ogilvy on Advertising* (1983)

62 Japanese management keeps telling the workers that those at the frontier know the business best.

Kenichi Ohmae (b. 1943) Japanese management consultant and theorist. 'The Myth and Reality of the Japanese Corporation', *Chief Executive* (Summer 1981)

63 In a recession, people want to test me to see if I'm brave enough to have a lay-off. I'm willing to take that ridicule because it's paid off to hold on to our people.

Ken Olsen (b. 1926) US computer designer and founder of Digital Equipment Corporation. Speech (1982)

64 Corporations want singles—they work harder if they don't have family ties. They don't have to worry about being home in the evening or on weekends.

Yoko Ono (b. 1933) US artist and musician. Interview, *Playboy* (January 1981)

65 The one thing I know through experience...is that people don't know why they come to work until they don't have to come to work.

H. Ross Perot (b. 1930) US entrepreneur, venture capitalist, and politician. *Inc.* (January 1989)

66 You can't look the troops in the eye and say, 'It's been a bad year, we can't do anything for you', but then say, 'By the way, we're going to pay ourselves a $1 million bonus'.

H. Ross Perot (b. 1930) US entrepreneur, venture capitalist, and politician. Referring to his resignation from the General Motors Board in 1986 following GM's decision to freeze profit-sharing payments to workers while going ahead with executive bonus payments. Quoted in *Thriving on Chaos* (Tom Peters; 1987)

67 If future competitiveness depends on treating people as an important part of the institution, the least respectful thing I can imagine doing to a human being is asking him to urinate in a cup.

Tom Peters (b. 1942) US management consultant and author. Said in testimony before the California state legislature, 28 November 1993. *New York Times* (1993)

68 The average employee can deliver far more than his or her current job demands and far more than the terms 'employee empowerment', 'participative management', and 'multiple skills' imply.

Tom Peters (b. 1942) US management consultant and author. *The Tom Peters Seminar* (1994)

69 I think many people just work as a way of not confronting themselves.

Gerry Robinson (b. 1948) Irish chairman of Granada Television and chairman of the Arts Council of England. *Management Today* (April 1999)

70 The next phase of advanced capitalist expansion will hark back to Robert Owen's enlightened experiments...which proved at the very beginning of the Industrial Revolution that a major investment in employee morale more than paid for itself in productivity.

Theodore Roszak (1933–81) US historian, writer, and editor. *Person/Plant: The Creative Disintegration of Industrial Society* (1977), ch. 8

71 There was a nationwide strike—or as the newspapers of the day called it, 'a Workman's Holiday'—to campaign for an eight-hour workday.

Pete Seeger (b. 1919) US singer and songwriter. Referring to a strike in 1886. *Carry It On* (co-written with Bob Reiser; 1985)

72 I trust my employees. They're looking for success as much as I am.

Ricardo Semler (b. 1959) Brazilian business executive and president of Semco. 'The Mavericks', *Fortune* (June 1995)

73 I am a big believer in insight and insightful people are hard to find.

Ric Simcock (b. 1965) British advertising executive. *Marketing* (September 2000)

74 I felt the only way to turn things round was to get people to think like owners.

Jack Stack (b. 1951) US CEO of SRC Holdings Corp., former plant manager of International Harvester, and author. 'The Mavericks', *Fortune* (June 1995)

75 I needed to teach anyone who moved a broom or operated a grinder everything the bank lender knew. That way they could really understand how every nickel saved could make a difference.

Jack Stack (b. 1951) US CEO of SRC Holdings Corp., former plant manager of International Harvester, and author. 'The Mavericks', *Fortune* (June 1995)

76 Be ruthlessly meritocratic. If you are on top, you want people who will try and try again.

Dennis Stevenson (b. 1946) British company director. *Management Today* (April 1999)

77 Hardly a competent workman can be found who does not devote a considerable amount of time to studying just how slowly he can work and still convince his employer that he is going at a good pace.

F.W. Taylor (1856–1915) US engineer and author. *The Principles of Scientific Management* (1911)

78 The exact facts will have in this way been developed and they will constitute a series of laws which are destined to control the vast multitude of our daily personal acts which, at present, are the subjects of individual opinion.

F.W. Taylor (1856–1915) US engineer and author. *The Principles of Scientific Management* (1911)

79 You know as well as I do that a high-priced man has to do exactly as he is told from morning to night.

F.W. Taylor (1856–1915) US engineer and author. *The Principles of Scientific Management* (1911)

80 Get to know your people. What they do well, what they enjoy doing, what their weaknesses and strengths are, and what they want and need to get from their job.

Robert Townsend (b. 1920) US business executive and author. *Further Up the Organization* (1984)

81 Our philosophy is that management's role is simply to get the right people in the right places to do a job, and to encourage them to use their own inventiveness to accomplish the task at hand.
Sam M. Walton (1918–92) US entrepreneur and founder of Wal-Mart, Inc. 'Wal-Mart, the Model Disaster', *Dun's Business Month* (March 1982)

82 Our early emphasis on human relations was not motivated by altruism, but by the simple belief that if we respected our people and helped them to respect themselves, the company would make the most profit.
Thomas J. Watson Sr (1874–1956) US founder and president of IBM. Quoted in *A Business and Its Beliefs* (Thomas J. Watson Jr; 1963)

83 They (employees) have to feel the rewards that go with winning—in the soul as well as in the wallet.
Jack Welch (b. 1935) US former chairman and CEO of General Electric. Speech (November 1989)

84 I don't like the word empowerment. I think the word we're really talking about is involvement...We want everyone to have a say.
Jack Welch (b. 1935) US former chairman and CEO of General Electric. *Industry Week* (May 1994)

85 They are not the workers, nor are they the white-collar people in the usual, clerk, sense of the word. These people only work for the organisation. The ones I am talking about belong to it as well.
William Whyte (1914–2000) US author. *The Organization Man* (1956)

86 Most men are individuals no longer, so far as their business, its activities, or its moralities are concerned. They are not units but fractions.
Woodrow Wilson (1856–1924) US president. Speech (August 1910)

EMPLOYERS

1 Had the employers of past generations all of them dealt fairly with their employees there would have been no unions.
Stanley Baldwin (1867–1947) British prime minister. Speech to Parliament (10 November 1932)

2 Get as much as possible done first by your subordinates. Pardon small offences. Promote men of superior capacity.
Confucius (551–479 BC) Chinese philosopher, administrator, and writer. *Analects* (?500 BC)

3 To be dilatory about giving orders, but to expect absolute punctuality, that is called being a tormentor.
Confucius (551–479 BC) Chinese philosopher, administrator, and writer. *Analects* (?500 BC)

4 Many employers are mercenarily minded, obsessed only with determination to roll up profits regardless of the suicidal

consequences...without consciousness of their civic, social, patriotic responsibilities.
Bertie Charles Forbes (1880–1954) US publisher and writer. Quoted in *Forbes* (1974)

5 A good paymaster never wants workmen.
Thomas Fuller (1654–1734) English physician and writer. *Gnomologia* (1732), no. 168

6 I was extremely lucky that my first two bosses were people who believed in me as a person and felt that gender was totally irrelevant.
Nicola Horlick (b. 1960) British fund manager. *Can You Have It All?* (1997)

7 There could be no worse friend to labour than the benevolent, philanthropic employer...sooner or later he will be compelled to close.
Lord Leverhulme (1851–1925) British entrepreneur, philanthropist, and co-founder of Unilever. Quoted in *The History of Unilever* (Charles Wilson; 1951)

8 It might be said that it is the ideal of the employer to have production without employees and the ideal of the employee is to have income without work
E.F. Schumacher (1911–77) British economist and conservationist. Quoted in 'Sayings of the Week', *Observer* (4 May 1975)

9 Just as an employer should believe it is his duty to promote good human relations, so too should he see it as his duty to pursue the best possible relationship with the community.
Marcus Sieff (1913–2001) British president of Marks & Spencer. *Sieff on Management* (1990)

10 Companies...have a hard time distinguishing between the cost of paying people and the value of investing in them.
Thomas A. Stewart (b. 1948) US journalist and author. *Intellectual Capital* (1997)

11 Each employee should receive every day clear-cut definite instructions as to what he is to do and how he is to do it, and these instructions should be exactly carried out, whether they are right or wrong.
F.W. Taylor (1856–1915) US engineer and author. *The Principles of Scientific Management* (1911)

12 You want to be recognized for your intellectual achievement, not for the fact that a bunch of day traders took your stock to a price that may or may not represent the real value of the firm.
Jay S. Walker, US entrepreneur and founder of Priceline.com, CEO of Walker Digital Corporation. 'An Edison for a New Age?', *Forbes Global* (Dyan Machan; 1999)

ENTHUSIASM

1 A mediocre idea that generates enthusiasm will go further than a great idea that inspires no one.
Mary Kay Ash (1915–2001) US entrepreneur, business executive, and founder of Mary Kay Cosmetics. *On People Management* (1984)

2 It is unfortunate, considering that enthusiasm moves the world, that so few enthusiasts can be trusted to speak the truth.
Arthur James Balfour (1848–1930) British prime minister. Letter to Mrs Drew (1918)

3 A committee, of course, exists for the purpose of damping enthusiasms.
Stella Benson (1892–1933) British writer. *Living Alone* (1919)

4 I sell enthusiasm.
Silvio Berlusconi (b. 1936) Italian media entrepreneur and prime minister. 'Quotes of the Year', *Financial Times* (24 December 1988)

5 Nothing is so contagious as enthusiasm. It is the real allegory of the tale of Orpheus; it moves stones and charms brutes. It is the genius of sincerity and truth accomplishes no victories without it.
Edward Bulwer-Lytton (1803–73) British novelist and politician. In Greek mythology Orpheus was a musician who could move both the animate and the inanimate with his music. Quoted in *Dale Carnegie's Scrapbook* (Dorothy Carnegie, ed.; 1959)

6 Flaming enthusiasm, backed up by horse sense and persistence, is the quality that most frequently makes for success.
Dale Carnegie (1888–1955) US writer. *How to Win Friends and Influence People* (1936)

7 I get a tremendous charge out of business. I get the same sort of feeling that women must have when their babies pop out.
Terence Conran (b. 1931) British business executive, retailer, and founder of Habitat. *Daily Express* (24 April 1986)

8 Nothing great was ever achieved without enthusiasm.
Ralph Waldo Emerson (1803–82) US essayist, lecturer, and poet. 'Circles', *Essays: First Series* (1841)

9 People who never get carried away, should be.
Steve Forbes (b. 1947) US publishing executive. *Town and Country* (November 1976)

10 What did it for me? It wasn't my education or experience. It was my passion.
Andrea Jung (b. 1958) US president of Avon Products. 'The 50 Most Powerful Women in American Business', *Fortune* (Patricia Sellers and Cora Daniels; October 1999)

11 I've found that when it came to doing something I loved and fighting for it, things worked out. If you're going to kill yourself to develop something, you've got to enjoy it.
Jeanine Lobell (b. 1964) US entrepreneur, founder and CEO of Stila cosmetics. Quoted in 'Jeanine Lobell: Making It Up', *Women to Watch, womenswire.com* (Evelyn Sheinkopf; 1995)

12 We seriously undervalue the passion...a person brings to an enterprise. You can rent a brain, but you can't rent a heart.
Mark McCormack (1930–2003) US entrepreneur, founder and CEO of the International Management Group. *McCormack on Managing* (1985)

13 To business that we love we rise betime, And go to't with delight.
William Shakespeare (1564–1616) English poet and playwright. *Antony and Cleopatra* (1606–07), Act 4, Scene 4, ll. 20–21

14 When enthusiasm and commitment take root within a project, that project comes to life.
Robin Sieger, British business executive and author. *Natural Born Winners* (1999)

15 There is nothing so easy but that it becomes difficult when you do it reluctantly.
Terence (?190–159 BC) Roman comic playwright. *The Self-Tormenter* (163 BC), l. 805

16 If you don't have passion...you might as well give up...you have no chance of making it. Passion is the essence of life, and certainly the essence of success.
Donald J. Trump (b. 1946) US property developer. *Trump: The Art of the Comeback* (co-written with Kate Bohner; 1997)

17 Being good in business is the most fascinating kind of art.
Andy Warhol (1928–87) US artist and film maker. Quoted in *Observer* (1 March 1987)

ENTREPRENEURS

1 Dear, never forget one little point. It's my business. You just work here.
Elizabeth Arden (1884–1966) US entrepreneur and cosmetics manufacturer. Said to her husband. Quoted in *Miss Elizabeth Arden* (Alfred A. Lewis and Constance Woodworth; 1972)

2 The real challenge is creating an entrepreneurial atmosphere in what can easily amount to a big bureaucratic company.
Percy Barnevik (b. 1941) Swedish former CEO of ABB. Quoted in *In Search of European Excellence* (Robert Heller; 1997)

3 I want Britain to be a nation of entrepreneurs, a nation where talent and ability flourish.
Tony Blair (b. 1953) British prime minister. Said in a speech to Parliament on 15 May 1997. Quoted in *Financial Times* (1997)

4 I believe Mrs. Thatcher's emphasis on enterprise was right.
Tony Blair (b. 1953) British prime minister. *The Economist* (1999)

5 I found that everywhere articles, especially drugs, were being sold at ridiculously high prices...My idea was simply to buy tons where others bought hundredweights or less, thus buying more cheaply.
Jesse Boot (1850–1931) British entrepreneur and founder of Boots pharmacy chain. 1930. Reflecting on his early success in mass-marketing Epsom salts. Quoted in *Enlightened Entrepreneurs* (Ian Campbell Bradley; 1987), ch. 9

6 The truth is I started my own company because I could not fill out a job application.
Terri Bowersock (b. 1956) US furniture company entrepreneur. *Phoenix Business Journal* (1999)

7 I'm Richard Branson, I'm eighteen and I run a magazine that's doing something really useful for young people.
Richard Branson (b. 1950) British entrepreneur, business executive, and founder of the Virgin Group. Referring to his first business venture. Quoted in *Richard Branson, The Inside Story* (Mick Brown; 1988)

8 I understand small business growth. I was one.
George W. Bush (b. 1946) US president. Quoted in *New York Daily Times* (19 February 2000)

9 Masters of entrepreneurial judo.
Richard D'Aveni (b. 1950) US strategist. 'The Mavericks', *Fortune* (June 1995)

10 You can never be an entrepreneur if you're afraid to lose money. It's like being a pilot who is afraid of bad weather.
Peter de Savary (b. 1944) British entrepreneur. Quoted in *The Adventure Capitalists* (Jeff Grout and Lynne Curry; 1998)

11 Being an entrepreneur is about having the will and determination and not being frightened of getting it wrong.
Jason Drummond (b. 1969) British Internet entrepreneur. *Sunday Times* (October 2000)

12 I'm a dirt-under-the-nails serial entrepreneur.
Donna Dubinsky (b. 1955) US IT executive. 'Secrets of the Fastest-rising Stars', *Fortune* (Patricia Sellers; 2000)

13 First get in, then get rich, then get respectable.
Bernie Eccleston (b. 1930) British entrepreneur and CEO of Formula 1 motor racing. Referring to his success in developing Formula 1 motor racing. Quoted in *Formula 1, The Business of Winning* (Russell Hotten; 1998)

14 Our private enterprise is more private than enterprising.
Indira Gandhi (1917–84) Indian prime minister. Speech (5 December 1970)

15 No one can possibly achieve any real and lasting success or 'get rich' in business by being a conformist.
J. Paul Getty (1892–1976) US entrepreneur, oil industry executive, and financier. *International Herald Tribune* (10 January 1961)

16 Everything is always impossible before it works. That is what entrepreneurs are all about—doing what people have told them is impossible.
R. Hunt Greene (b. 1950) US venture capitalist. *Fortune* (27 May 1996)

17 I'm not an entrepreneur. I like rules too much and entrepreneurs break rules.
Guy Hands (b. 1959) Zimbabwean CEO of Terra Firma Capital Partners. *Management Today* (October 1999)

18 Successful entrepreneurs judge correctly the need for change, then do something about it.
James Edward Hanson (b. 1922) British business executive and entrepreneur. *Website* (2000)

19 Everything I do I love. An entrepreneur is a big artist.
Nicolas G. Hayek (b. 1928) Swiss entrepreneur and founder of SWATCH. *Sunday Times* (October 2000)

20 Entrepreneurs have no frontier other than their own ambition.
Robert Heller (b. 1932) British management writer. *Goldfinger* (1998)

21 I think the skills involved in putting together deals are crucial to a start-up. You need wide distribution and many partners.
Rob Herson (b. 1952) South African business executive. *Marketing* (July 2000)

22 Entrepreneurs are simply those who understand that there is little difference between obstacle and opportunity and are able to turn both to their advantage.
Victor Kiam (1926–2001) US CEO of Remington Corporation. 1990. Quoted in *East Valley Tribune* (2000)

23 I realised that if you built a New Age highway, you need it to be vibrant and dynamic. That can only happen if you have entrepreneurs taking risks.
Woon Toon King (b. 1967) Singaporean entrepreneur. *Forbes* (July 2000)

24 Around Britain, thousands of young people are working from bedrooms, workshops and run-down offices, hoping that they will come up with the next Hotmail or Netscape.
Charles Leadbetter, British government adviser, journalist, and author. Quoted in *Independent* (1999)

25 It sounds boring, but anything is easy to start—starting a novel, starting a business...it's keeping the thing going that is difficult.
Prue Leith (b. 1940) British cookery writer and business executive. Quoted in *The Adventure Capitalists* (Jeff Grout and Lynne Curry; 1998)

26 The entrepreneurial spirit is alive and well here but it's harder to get funding for your new business if you come from Leicestershire than if you went to Eton and are the son of some banker.
Isabel Maxwell (b. 1950) British president of CommTouch. Referring to United Kingdom. *Guardian* (22 July 2000)

27 Running a company is a constant process of breaking out of systems and challenging conditioned reflexes, of rubbing against the grain.
Mark McCormack (1930–2003) US entrepreneur, founder and CEO of the International Management Group. *What They Don't Teach You at Harvard Business School* (1984)

28 Just starting a company was a badge of courage, and the entrepreneur became an instant hero.
Regis McKenna (b. 1939) US marketing entrepreneur and chairman of The McKenna Group. Referring to high-technology industry entrepreneurs in 1990s. *Relationship Marketing* (1991)

29 The entrepreneur is...the most important player in the building of the global economy. So much so that big companies are decentralizing and reconstituting themselves as networks of entrepreneurs.
John Naisbitt (b. ?1929) US business executive and author. *Global Paradox* (1994)

30 I used to do a hell of a lot of cross selling. Before they knew it, they had spent a fortune.
Vijay Patel (b. 1950) Kenyan entrepreneur. *Sunday Times* (September 2000)

31 Where would the Rockefellers be today if old John D. had gone on selling short-weight kerosene…to widows and orphans instead of wisely deciding to mulct the whole country.
S.J. Perelman (1904–79) US humorist. Letter (25 October 1976)

32 Risk means not knowing if, or when, you can pay yourself, or anyone else. It means working without health and pension plans, regular promotions, and paid vacations.
Heather Robertson (b. 1942) Canadian author. *Taking Care of Business* (1997)

33 Success depends on having a product or a service that catches the consumer's imagination, although at first it may be that nobody but you has ever heard of it.
Heather Robertson (b. 1942) Canadian author. *Taking Care of Business* (1997)

34 Too much creative involvement can blind an entrepreneur to the hard reality of the bottom line.
Heather Robertson (b. 1942) Canadian author. *Taking Care of Business* (1997)

35 Three components make an entrepreneur: the person, the idea and the resources to make it happen.
Anita Roddick (b. 1942) British entrepreneur and founder of The Body Shop. *Body and Soul* (co-written with Russell Miller; 1991)

36 I wanted to set the world on fire and that would not come about through working for someone else in a nine-to-five job.
Ian Schrager (b. 1948) US entrepreneur. *Sunday Times* (May 2000)

37 It's better to be the head of a chicken than the tail of a cow.
Stan Shih (b. 1945) Taiwanese CEO of the Acer Group. Referring to a Taiwanese proverb and the preference of entrepreneurs for running their own small business. Quoted in *Giant Killers* (Geoffrey James; 1996)

38 As an entrepreneur, you have to go against the flow.
Reuben Singh (b. 1977) British entrepreneur and author. *Management Today* (September 1999)

39 Money isn't what motivates entrepreneurs; it is acknowledgement—a craving for your ideas to be acknowledged,
Reuben Singh (b. 1977) British entrepreneur and author. *Management Today* (September 1999)

40 The younger you are, the fewer responsibilities you have, the more prone you are to take risks and the more commitment you can put into your business.
Reuben Singh (b. 1977) British entrepreneur and author. *Management Today* (September 1999)

41 I am not a professional security analyst. I would rather call myself an insecurity analyst.
George Soros (b. 1930) US financier, entrepreneur, and philanthropist. *Soros on Soros* (1995)

42 To make it in any business, it's not enough to give 100 percent. If that's all you have in you, go work for someone else and give THEM 100 percent. You have to give 200 percent. That's how it happens.
Lise Watier (b. 1942) Canadian proprietor of a cosmetics chain. Quoted in *Looking Good* (Rosa Harris-Adler; 1997)

43 If you want to understand entrepreneurs, you have to study the psychology of the juvenile delinquent. They don't have the same anxiety triggers that we have.
Abraham Zaleznik (b. 1924) US psychologist. *US News & World Report* (October 1992)

44 They have no fear of failure. It's not part of their make-up.
Abraham Zaleznik (b. 1924) US psychologist. *US News & World Report* (October 1992)

EXCELLENCE

1 The sad truth is that excellence makes people nervous.
Shana Alexander (b. 1925) US writer and editor. 'Neglected Kids—the Bright Ones', *The Feminine Eye* (1967)

2 Striving for excellence motivates you; striving for perfection is demoralizing.
Harriet Beryl Braiker (b. 1948) US psychologist. *Type 'E' Woman: How to Overcome the Stress of Being Everything to Everybody* (1987)

3 Excellence is not an act but a habit. The things you do the most are the things you will do best.
Marva Collins (b. 1936) US educationalist. 'Marva Collins: Teaching Success in the City', *Message* (1987)

4 No one has a greater asset for his business than a man's pride in his work.
Mary Parker Follett (1868–1933) US management thinker and author. *Freedom and Co-ordination* (1949), ch. 2

5 Performance stands out like a ton of diamonds. Nonperformance can always be explained away.
Harold S. Geneen (1910–97) US telecommunications entrepreneur and CEO of ITT. *Managing* (co-written with Alvin Moscow; 1984)

6 There seems to be a certain healthy paranoia in companies that are great at change. They seem to say, 'O.K., we're doing well today, but we might not be doing well tomorrow, so we'd better be better at what we're doing, and we'd better try to destroy our own established model before somebody else does it for us'.
Rosabeth Moss Kanter (b. 1943) US management theorist, academic, and writer. Interview, *Strategy + Business* (July–September 1999)

7 The quality of your attention determines the quality of other people's thinking.

Nancy Kline (b. 1946) US author, educator, and consultant. *Time to Think* (1999)

8 The business world worships mediocrity. Officially we revere free enterprise, initiative, and individuality. Unofficially we fear it.
George Lois (b. 1931) US advertising executive. *The Art of Advertising* (1977)

9 You get the best out of others when you give the best of yourself.
Eugenio Montale (1896–1981) Italian poet. *Men and Rubber* (1926)

10 A specialist is someone who does everything else worse.
Ruggiero Ricci (b. 1918) US violinist. Quoted in *Daily Telegraph* (25 May 1990)

11 All things excellent are as difficult as they are rare.
Baruch Spinoza (1632–77) Dutch philosopher. *Ethica Ordine Geometrico Demonstrata* (1677), 5:8

12 If you don't do it excellently, don't do it at all. Because if it's not excellent, it won't be profitable or fun, and if you're not in business for fun or profit, what the hell are you doing there?
Robert Townsend (b. 1920) US business executive and author. *Further Up the Organization* (1984)

13 Good design is good business.
Thomas J. Watson Jr (1914–93) US CEO of IBM. *New York Times* (13 May 1990)

EXECUTIVES

1 Consultants eventually leave, which makes them excellent scapegoats for major management blunders.
Scott Adams (b. 1957) US cartoonist and humorist. *The Dilbert Principle* (1996)

2 Executives can get away with having a clean desk. For the rest of us, it looks like you're not working hard enough.
Scott Adams (b. 1957) US cartoonist and humorist. *The Dilbert Principle* (1996)

3 The biggest change in the workplace of the future will be the widespread realization that having one idiot boss is a much higher risk than having many idiot clients.
Scott Adams (b. 1957) US cartoonist and humorist. *The Dilbert Principle* (1996)

4 A molehill man is a pseudo-busy executive who comes to work at 9 a.m. and finds a molehill on his desk. He has until 5 p.m. to make this molehill into a mountain. An accomplished molehill man will often have his mountain finished before lunch.
Fred Allen (1894–1956) US comedian and satirist. *Treadmill to Oblivion* (1954)

5 I admire the capacity of American business executives to continually reinvent what they do; it shows they are never satisfied.
Anonymous. Said by a British member of parliament. *Hemispheres* (December 1996)

6 One lesson a man learns from Harvard Business School is that an executive is only as good as his health.
Jeffrey Archer (b. 1940) British novelist and politician. *Not a Penny More, Not a Penny Less* (1976)

7 When it comes to strategic underpinnings and what is broken and what needs to be fixed, those are the challenges that I love. I love looking for the holes.
Jill Barad (b. 1951) US CEO of Mattel. *BusinessWeek* (1997)

8 I don't play golf. I don't go to the men's room. I didn't have the ability to network the way men do. But I made myself visible.
Jill Barad (b. 1951) US CEO of Mattel. *Wall Street Journal* (1997)

9 The essential functions of the executive are first to provide the system of communication, second to promote the securing of essential efforts and, third, to formulate and define purpose.
Chester Barnard (1886–1961) US business executive and management theorist. *The Functions of the Executive* (1938)

10 In business, today the person at the top is seen as an integral part of the company's image, which is encouraged by the mass media. Much of my work is communicating internally and externally.
Percy Barnevik (b. 1941) Swedish former CEO of ABB. Interview, *Company Man: The Rise and Fall of Corporate Life* (Anthony Sampson; 1995), ch. 21

11 Their problem is that they play a lot of golf, which is right up there with heroin abuse as a killer of our nation's productivity. The only difference is that golf is more expensive.
Dave Barry (b. 1947) US humorist. Referring to executives. Interview, *Fortune* (7 July 1997)

12 Executives are like joggers. If you stop a jogger, he goes on running on the spot. If you drag an executive away from his business, he goes on running on the spot, pawing the ground, talking business.
Jean Baudrillard (b. 1929) French philosopher. *Cool Memories* (1987)

13 Lenin was greatly influenced by the scholarship of Marx, in much the same way as many contemporary business leaders are influenced by the works of leading economists and management scholars.
Warren Bennis (b. 1925) US educator and writer. *Beyond Leadership: Balancing Economics, Ethics and Ecology* (co-written with Jagdish Parikh and Ronnie Lessem; 1994)

14 Successful executives are great askers.
Warren Bennis (b. 1925) US educator and writer. *Beyond Leadership: Balancing Economics, Ethics and Ecology* (co-written with Jagdish Parikh and Ronnie Lessem; 1994)

15 I am a young executive. No cuffs than mine are cleaner;
I have a Slimline brief-case and I use the firm's Cortina.

John Betjeman (1906–84) British poet. 'The Executive', *A Nip in the Air* (1974)

16 If an executive does not have time for ostentatious spending, his wife or children will do it for him.

Jorge Luis Borges (1899–1986) Argentinian writer. 'On Thorstein Veblen's The Theory of the Leisure Class' (1985)

17 Other people set off firecrackers. We drop atomic bombs.

William Bourke (b. 1927) US executive vice-president of the Ford Motor Company. On forced resignation of company president Lee Iacocca. *New York Times* (1978)

18 Of one thing be certain: if a CEO is enthused about a particularly foolish acquisition, both his internal staff and his outside advisors will come up with whatever projections are needed to justify his stance. Only in fairy tales are emperors told that they are naked.

Warren Buffett (b. 1930) US entrepreneur and financier. Chairman's Letter to Shareholders (27 February 1998)

19 Some years back, a CEO friend of mine—in jest, it must be said—described the pathology of many big deals...With an impish look, he simply said: 'Aw, fellas, all the other kids have one'.

Warren Buffett (b. 1930) US entrepreneur and financier. Chairman's Letter to Shareholders (7 March 1995)

20 Captains of Industry

Thomas Carlyle (1795–1881) British historian and essayist. Book subtitle. *Past and Present* (1843), bk 4, ch. 4

21 When I've had a rough day, before I go to sleep I ask myself if there's anything more I can do right now. If there isn't, I sleep sound.

L.L. Colbert (1905–95) US chairman of Chrysler Corporation. *Newsweek* (1955)

22 I get many invitations but I only join the boards of companies where I admire the management and believe in the company.

Jill Ker Conway (b. 1934) Australian historian. *Financial Times* (October 2000)

23 For tired and harried executives, books are a balm for their worries.

Stuart Crainer, British business author. *Corporate Man to Corporate Skunk* (1997)

24 If executives could learn to get things right, and to quit wasting resources doing things over, then there would be work and jobs for all.

Philip B. Crosby (1926–2001) US business executive and author. *Quality Is Still Free* (1996)

25 All the guys I knew and loved when they were so young and cute have become the Establishment. Especially Mr. Gates.

Esther Dyson (b. 1951) US knowledge entrepreneur and government adviser. *Fortune* (1993)

26 Managerial skill can not be painted on the outside of executives—it has to go deeper than that.

Mary Parker Follett (1868–1933) US management thinker and author. *Freedom and Co-ordination* (ed. L. Urwick; 1949), ch. 2

27 Sometimes it is the men 'higher up' who most need revamping—and they themselves are the last to recognize it.

Henry Ford (1863–1947) US industrialist, car manufacturer, and founder of Ford Motor Company. *My Life and Work* (co-written with Samuel Crowther; 1922)

28 The nature of the job is you only hear problems—I guess that's what a CEO's job is.

William Clay Ford Jr (b. 1957) US business executive. Interview *Fortune* (November 2002)

29 The salary of the chief executive of the large corporation is not a market reward for achievement. It is frequently in the nature of a warm personal gesture by the individual to himself.

J.K. Galbraith (b. 1908) US economist and diplomat. *Annals of an Abiding Liberal* (1979)

30 It is practically impossible for a top management man, or even middle management, to be doing the degree and level of work that he should be doing and, at the same time, have a clean desk.

Harold S. Geneen (1910–97) US telecommunications entrepreneur and CEO of ITT. *Managing* (co-written with Alvin Moscow; 1984)

31 The worst disease which can afflict business executives in their work is not, as popularly supposed, alcoholism; it's egotism.

Harold S. Geneen (1910–97) US telecommunications entrepreneur and CEO of ITT. *Managing* (co-written with Alvin Moscow; 1984)

32 You can know a person by the kind of desk he keeps...If the president of a company has a clean desk...then it must be the executive vice president who is doing all the work.

Harold S. Geneen (1910–97) US telecommunications entrepreneur and CEO of ITT. *Managing* (co-written with Alvin Moscow; 1984)

33 It's time for IBM to perform and then talk, instead of talk and then perform.

Lou Gerstner (b. 1942) US chairman and CEO of IBM. *Fortune* (1993)

34 In business, the mystique of conformity is sapping the dynamic individualism that is the most priceless quality an executive or businessman can possess.

J. Paul Getty (1892–1976) US entrepreneur, oil industry executive, and financier. *How to Be Rich* (1965)

35 The successful executive—the leader, the innovator—is the exceptional man.

J. Paul Getty (1892–1976) US entrepreneur, oil industry executive, and financier. *How to Be Rich* (1965)

36 Many executives continue to believe that they are 'not in the technology business' and that they might just as well outsource their information technology needs. This is like an athlete saying that he is not in the strength business...these naysayers might as well say that they are not in the business of being in business.

J. William Gurley, US venture capitalist and journalist. *Above the Crowd: Productivity Paradox* (1997)

37 If you give top executives incentives based on profit, they may well apply the ½ x 2 x 3 rule. This will...result in a higher executive paycheck. But eventually it makes business unpopular and results in a lack of trust.

Charles Handy (b. 1932) British business executive and author. Speech at the Second Workshop on Inventing the Organization of the 21st Century, Munich, Germany. The ½ x 2 x 3 rule = half as many people, paid twice as well and producing three times the output results in profits. A CEO's formula for success as quoted by Handy. 'The Age of Paradox' (April 1996)

38 I always say to executives that they should go and see *King Lear*, because they'll be out there one day, wandering on the heath without a company car.

Charles Handy (b. 1932) British business executive and author. Interview, *The Times* (12 April 1989)

39 I think in every country that there is at least one executive who is scared of going crazy.

Joseph Heller (1923–99) US novelist. *Something Happened* (1974)

40 Executive: A man who can make quick decisions and is sometimes right.

Frank McKinney Hubbard (1868–1930) US humorist. *The Roycroft Dictionary* (1923)

41 The American people will find it hard...to accept a situation in which a tiny handful of steel executives whose pursuit of private power and profit exceeds their sense of public responsibility can show such utter contempt for the interests of 185 million Americans.

John F. Kennedy (1917–63) US president. Speech, April 11, 1962. Quoted in *Farewell America* (James Hepburn; 1968)

42 Regarded as a means, the businessman is tolerable. Regarded as an end, he is not so satisfactory.

John Maynard Keynes (1883–1946) British economist. *Essays in Persuasion* (1978)

43 Damn the great executives, the men of measured merriment, damn the men with careful smiles...oh, damn their measured merriment.

Sinclair Lewis (1885–1951) US writer and social critic. *Arrowsmith* (1925)

44 I can tell more about how someone is likely to react in a business situation from one round of golf than I can from a hundred hours of meetings.

Mark McCormack (1930–2003) US entrepreneur, founder and CEO of the International Management Group. *What They Don't Teach You at Harvard Business School* (1984)

45 Here's a dime. Call up both of them!

Andrew William Mellon (1855–1937) US financier, industrialist, and public servant. Mellon's response when Herbert Hoover asked for a nickel (5 cents) to call up a friend. Quoted in *Presidential Anecdotes* (Paul F. Boller Jr; 1981)

46 The chief executive...like a juggler keeps a number of projects in the air: periodically one

comes down, is given a new burst of energy, and is sent back into orbit.

Henry Mintzberg (b. 1939) Canadian academic and management theorist. 'The Manager's Job: Folklore and Fact', *Harvard Business Review* (July–August 1975)

47 The best leaders are apt to be found among those executives who have a strong component of unorthodoxy in their characters. Instead of resisting innovation, they symbolize it.

David Ogilvy (1911–99) British advertising executive, founder and chairman of Ogilvy & Mather. *Ogilvy on Advertising* (1983)

48 Beware the manager who proclaims to the world he is a long-termer, beginning today.

T. Boone Pickens (b. 1928) US oil company executive and financier. *Harvard Business Review* (May–June 1986)

49 Chief executives, who themselves own few shares of their companies, have no more feeling for the average stockholder than they do for baboons in Africa.

T. Boone Pickens (b. 1928) US oil company executive and financier. *Harvard Business Review* (May–June 1986)

50 The trouble with corporate America is that too many people with too much power live in a box (their home), travel the same road every day to another box (their office).

Faith Popcorn (b. 1947) US trend expert and founder of BrainReserve. *The Popcorn Report* (1991)

51 I believe that nicotine is not addictive.

Thomas Sandefur (1939–96) US head of Brown & Williamson. Said at the 1994 Congressional hearings on the tobacco industry. Quoted in *New York Times* (1997)

52 In retrospect, for a full-time chief executive to do what is almost a full-time job is extremely difficult.

Clive Thompson (b. 1943) British chairman of the Confederation of British Industry and former CEO of Rentokil. Referring to the position of CBI chairman, while acting as CEO of Rentokil. *Sunday Times* (October 2000)

53 Today's adaptive executives...must be experts not in bureaucracy, but in the co-ordination of ad-hocracy.

Alvin Toffler (b. 1928) US social commentator. *The Adaptive Corporation* (1985)

54 Nobody should be chief executive officer of anything for more than five or six years. By then he's stale, bored, and utterly dependent upon his own clichés.

Robert Townsend (b. 1920) US business executive and author. *Up the Organization* (1970)

55 All the president is is a glorified PR man who spends his life flattering, kissing, and kicking people to get them to do what they are supposed to do anyway.

Harry S. Truman (1884–1972) US president. Letter (November 1947)

56 People who eat white bread have no dreams.

Diana Vreeland (1903–89) US magazine editor. Quoted on *National Public Radio* (1997)

57 An overburdened, stretched executive is the best executive, because he or she doesn't have time to meddle, to deal in trivia, to bother people.
Jack Welch (b. 1935) US former chairman and CEO of General Electric. 'Quotes of the Year', *Financial Times* (30 December 1989)

58 To be vital, an organization has to repot itself, start again, get new ideas, renew itself. And I...should disappear from the company so my successor feels totally free.
Jack Welch (b. 1935) US former chairman and CEO of General Electric. Quoted in 'The Ultimate Manager', *Fortune* (22 November 1999)

59 From now on, choosing my successor is the most important decision I'll make. It occupies a considerable amount of thought almost every day.
Jack Welch (b. 1935) US former chairman and CEO of General Electric. 1991. Quoted in *The New GE* (Robert Slater; 1993)

60 Sure, I'm one of the fat cats. In fact, I'm the fattest cat, because I'm lucky enough to have this job.
Jack Welch (b. 1935) US former chairman and CEO of General Electric. *Wall Street Journal* (1997)

61 Not everyone is capable of being a CEO. It means you don't get to pal around with all your employees and that you leave the sorority/fraternity approach to life behind, and you take on a role that is, in some respects, lonely.
Ann Winblad (b. 1953) US venture capitalist. 'Women in the New Workplace', *BusinessWeek* (Mica Schneider; 2000)

62 It's something no one ever tells you. You're on and off airplanes all the time. It's a Texas wrestling match with a new team against you every night.
Walter Wriston (b. 1919) US banker. *New York Times* (1993)

EXPECTATIONS

1 Always do one thing less than you think you can do.
Bernard Baruch (1870–1965) US financier and economist. Referring to maintaining good health. *Newsweek* (28 May 1956)

2 Buy what's deliverable, not what could be.
Michael Bloomberg (b. 1942) US entrepreneur, business executive, and Mayor of New York. *Bloomberg by Bloomberg* (co-written with Matthew Winkler; 1997)

3 Unhappiness is best defined as the difference between our talents and our expectations.
Edward de Bono (b. 1933) British creative-thinking theorist, educator, and writer. Quoted in *Observer* (12 June 1997)

4 If you follow your passion, the money will follow. But if you chase the almighty dollar, you can easily lose that and end up with nothing.
Elizabeth MacKay, US investment strategist and managing director of Bear Stearns. Quoted in *Women of the Street* (Sue Herera; 1997)

5 In great endeavours the intention is enough.
Sextus Propertius (?50–15 BC) Roman poet. Attrib.

6 The loss that is unknown is no loss at all.
Publilius Syrus (*fl.* 1st century BC) Roman writer. *Moral Sayings* (1st century BC)

7 Expect nothing. Live frugally on surprise.
Alice Walker (b. 1944) US Pulitzer prize-winning writer and poet. *Expect Nothing* (1973)

EXPERIENCE

1 All experience is an arch, to build upon.
Henry Brooks Adams (1838–1918) US historian. *Education of Henry Adams* (1907)

2 Experience is a good teacher, but she sends in terrific bills.
Minna Antrim (1856–1950) US writer. *Naked Truth and Veiled Illusions* (1902)

3 Whenever you fall, pick up something.
Oswald Theodore Avery (1877–1955) US bacteriologist. Attrib.

4 EXPERIENCE, n. The wisdom that enables us to recognise as an undesirable old acquaintance the folly that we have already embraced.
Ambrose Bierce (1842–?1914) US journalist and writer. *The Devil's Dictionary* (1911)

5 Experience isn't interesting until it begins to repeat itself—in fact, till it does that, it hardly is experience.
Elizabeth Bowen (1899–1973) Irish writer. *The Death of the Heart* (1938), pt 1, ch. 1

6 Experience is a dim lamp, which only lights the one who bears it.
Louis-Ferdinand Céline (1894–1961) French author. Interview, *Writers at Work* (1967)

7 You cannot acquire experience by making experiments. You cannot create experience. You must undergo it.
Albert Camus (1913–60) French novelist and essayist. *Notebooks 1935–42* (1962)

8 To most men, experience is like the stern lights of a ship, which illumine only the track it has passed.
Samuel Taylor Coleridge (1772–1834) British poet. *Table Talk* (1836)

9 Circumstances? Life is circumstances.
Robert de Castella (b. 1957) Australian athlete and executive director of Focus on You. Quoted in *Running with the Legends* (Michael Sandrock; 1996)

10 Experientia does it—as papa used to say.
Charles Dickens (1812–70) British novelist. *David Copperfield* (1849–50), ch. 1

11 I try to avoid experience if I can. Most experience is bad.
E.L. Doctorow (b. 1931) US novelist. Interview, *Writers at Work* (1988)

12 We have been finely duped...full of courtesy, full of craft.

Maria Edgeworth (1767–1849) British writer. *The Parent's Assistant* (1796)

13 And the end of all our exploring
Will be to arrive where we started
And know the place for the first time.

T.S. Eliot (1888–1965) British poet, dramatist, and critic. 'Little Gidding', *Four Quartets* (1943)

14 You will find that you survive humiliation. And that's an experience of incalculable value.

T.S. Eliot (1888–1965) British poet, dramatist, and critic. *The Cocktail Party* (1950), Act 1, Scene 1

15 I do not see how any man can afford...to spare any action in which he can partake. Drudgery, calamity, exasperation, want, are instructors in eloquence and wisdom.

Ralph Waldo Emerson (1803–82) US essayist, lecturer, and poet. Speech to the Phi Beta Kappa Society, Cambridge Divinity College, Harvard. 'American Scholar' (31 August 1837)

16 Experience teaches you that the man who looks you straight in the eye, particularly if he adds a firm handshake, is hiding something.

Clifton Fadiman (1904–99) US editor and author. *Enter Conversing* (1962)

17 Experience teaches slowly, and at the cost of mistakes.

James Anthony Froude (1818–94) British historian. *Short Studies on Great Subjects* (1877)

18 In a human capital-intensive environment, all you bring to the table is your own intellectual property. You will not share this precious resource with others unless you trust them to reciprocate.

Francis Fukuyama (b. 1952) US economist and writer. 'Trust Still Counts in a Virtual World', *Forbes* (12 February 1996)

19 In the business world, everyone is paid in two coins: cash and experience. Take the experience first; the cash will come later.

Harold S. Geneen (1910–97) US telecommunications entrepreneur and CEO of ITT. *Managing* (co-written with Alvin Moscow; 1984)

20 Only the paranoid survive.

Andrew S. Grove (b. 1936) US entrepreneur, author, and chairman of Intel Corporation. The philosophy by which he runs his company, Intel Corporation. Attrib.

21 An expert is a man who knows some of the worst errors that can be made in the subject in question and who therefore understands how to avoid them.

Werner Heisenberg (1901–76) German physicist and philosopher. *The Part and the Whole* (1969)

22 A moment's insight is sometimes worth a life's experience.

Oliver Wendell Holmes (1809–94) US surgeon, teacher, and writer. *The Professor at the Breakfast-Table* (1860), ch. 10

23 Experience is never limited, and it is never complete; it is an immense sensibility, a kind of huge spider-web...suspended in the

chamber of consciousness, and catching every air-borne particle in its tissue.

Henry James (1843–1916) US novelist. 'The Art of Fiction', *Partial Portraits* (1888)

24 Mistakes are, after all, the foundation of truth, and if a man does not know what a thing *is*, it is at least an increase in knowledge if he knows what it is *not*.

Carl Gustav Jung (1875–1961) Swiss psychiatrist. 1951. 'Aion', *Collected Works* (William McGuire, ed.; 1959), vol. 19

25 Nothing ever becomes real till it is experienced...even a proverb is no proverb till your life has illustrated it.

John Keats (1795–1821) British poet. Letter to George and Georgiana Keats (19 March 1819)

26 Experience teaches
that it doesn't.

Norman MacCaig (1910–96) Scottish poet. 'A World of Difference' (1983)

27 My life has been a series of discoveries, of revelations and continues to be so.

John Makepeace (b. 1939) British furniture designer and manufacturer. Quoted in *Makepeace* (Jeremy Myerson; 1995)

28 The woman who seems to be thirty-five but whom I know to be sixty, is, to me, disquieting. A life should leave its traces, and the total lack of them is a negation of experience.

Marya Mannes (1904–90) US essayist and journalist. 'Of Time and the Woman', *Psychosomatics* (1968)

29 a man who is so dull
that he can learn only by personal experience
is too dull to learn
anything important by experience

Don Marquis (1878–1937) US journalist and humorist. 'Archy on this and that', *Archy Does His Part* (1935)

30 The only thing experience teaches us is that experience teaches us nothing.

André Maurois (1885–1967) French biographer and critic. Attrib.

31 We have learnt the hard way that we live in a 'show me' world where trust has to be earned and where statements of intent are no substitute for concrete action. But we also know that we can regain lost confidence and trust, through openness, a willingness to listen...and above all else, by taking positive steps to put our principles clearly into practice.

Mark Moody-Stuart (b. 1940) British chairman of Anglo American, and former chairman of Committee of Managing Directors Royal Dutch/Shell Group. Speech to the World Congress of the International Society of Business, Economics and Ethics, São Paolo, Brazil. Referring to the criticisms Shell has faced from environmental and human rights groups over its involvement in countries such as Nigeria. 'Putting Principles into Practice: The Ethical Challenge to Global Business' (19 July 2000)

32 Experience! Wise men do not need it. Experience! Idiots do not heed it.

Ogden Nash (1902–71) US humorist and writer. 'Experience to Let' (1940)

33 I have learned the novice can often see things that the expert overlooks.

Tom Peters (b. 1942) US management consultant and author. *Eupsychian Management* (1965)

34 I'd seen a lot of MBAs come down to the trading floors, and they were like sheep to the wolves...They think the world will function like this nice little model or equation and nothing's further from the truth.

Linda Raschke, US trader. Quoted in *Women of the Street* (Sue Herera; 1997)

35 Education is when you read the fine print; experience is what you get when you don't.

Pete Seeger (b. 1919) US singer and songwriter. Quoted in *Loose Talk* (L. Botts; 1980)

36 Men are wise in proportion, not to their experience, but to their capacity for experience.

George Bernard Shaw (1856–1950) Irish writer and critic. 'Maxims for Revolutionists', *Man and Superman* (1903)

37 I am putting old heads on young shoulders.

Muriel Spark (b. 1918) British novelist. *The Prime of Miss Jean Brodie* (1961)

38 Experientia docuit.

Cornelius Tacitus (?55–?120) Roman historian, orator, and politician. Experience has taught. More commonly quoted as: 'experientia docet' (experience teaches). *Histories* (?100), bk 5, ch. 6

39 We learned from everybody else's book and added a few pages of our own.

Sam M. Walton (1918–92) US entrepreneur and founder of Wal-Mart, Inc. 'The Hot Ticket in Retailing', *New York Times* (Isadore Barmash; July 1984)

40 Confidence is something rooted in the unpleasant, harsh aspects of life...it has its own momentum.The longer you are able to survive and succeed the better you are able further to survive and succeed.

An Wang (1920–90) US entrepreneur, business executive, electrical engineer, and founder of Wang Laboratories. *Current Biography* (January 1987)

41 Experience is the name everyone gives to their mistakes.

Oscar Wilde (1854–1900) Irish writer and wit. *Lady Windermere's Fan* (1892), Act 3

42 Hindsight is always 20–20.

Billy Wilder (1906–2001) US film director. Quoted in *Wit and Wisdom of the Moviemakers* (J.R. Columbo; 1979)

43 They have this wonderful process of learning from direct experience called 'After Action Review', in which everyone who was involved sits down and the three questions are: What happened? Why do you think it happened? And what can we learn from it? If you were...able to get those three questions as part

of your process, you could become a learning organization.

Walter Wriston (b. 1919) US banker. Referring to the Army as a learning organisation and as an example to business. Interview with Scott London, *US National Public Radio* (November 1996)

FAILURE

1 The payoff for failure is almost as much as for succeeding.

Anonymous. Referring to executive contracts negotiated by leading lawyers in the United States. Quoted in *BusinessWeek* (24 January 1994)

2 Lemons ripen faster than cherries.

Anonymous. Referring to the phrase 'lemons' applied to bad products or companies. Quoted in *Goldfinger* (Robert Heller; 1998)

3 Three failures denote uncommon strength. A weakling has not enough grit to fail thrice.

Minna Antrim (1856–1950) US writer. *At the Sign of the Golden Calf* (1905)

4 For every failure, there's an alternative course of action. You just have to find it. When you come to a roadblock, take a detour.

Mary Kay Ash (1915–2001) US entrepreneur, business executive, and founder of Mary Kay Cosmetics. *On People Management* (1984)

5 There are few things more dreadful than dealing with a man who knows he is going under, in his own eyes and in the eyes of others.

James Baldwin (1924–87) US writer. *The Price of the Ticket* (1985), Introduction

6 Ever tried. Ever failed. No matter. Try again. Fail again. Fail better.

Samuel Beckett (1906–89) Irish playwright, novelist, and poet. *Worstward Ho* (1983)

7 Accounting issues did not cause Enron's stock price to fall—it's failed business model did.

Joseph Berardino (b. 1951) US business executive. Quoted in *Guardian* (June 2002)

8 There's nothing the British like better than a bloke who comes from nowhere, makes it, and then gets clobbered.

Melvyn Bragg (b. 1939) British broadcaster and novelist. *Guardian* (23 September 1988)

9 A minute's success pays the failure of years.

Robert Browning (1812–89) British poet. 'Apollo and the Fates' (1886), st. 42

10 The first undertakers in all great attempts commonly miscarry, and leave the advantages of their losses to those that come after them.

Samuel Butler (1612–80) English poet. *Prose Observations* (1660–80)

11 In the built to flip world, the notion of investing persistent effort in order to build a great company seems, well, quaint, unnecessary, even stupid.

James Collins (b. 1958) US business thinker and author.

Referring to the short-term strategies of new-economy companies. 'Built to Flip', *Fast Company* (March 2000)

12 Doing is overrated, and success undesirable, but the bitterness of failure even more so.

Cyril Connolly (1903–74) British critic, essayist, and novelist. *The Unquiet Grave* (1944)

13 The benefits of many mergers have been lost during the integration phase.

Richard Corzone, British journalist. Quoted in *Treasury of Investment Wisdom* (Bernice Cohen; 1999)

14 When a business goes wrong, look only to the people who are running it.

Michael Dell (b. 1965) US chairman and CEO of Dell Computer Corporation. Quoted in *In the Company of Giants* (Rama Dev Jager; 1997)

15 The most common cause of executive failure is inability or unwillingness to change with the demands of a new position. The executive who keeps on doing what he has done successfully before is almost bound to fail.

Peter F. Drucker (b. 1909) US management consultant and academic. *The Effective Executive* (1967), ch. 3

16 I had a lot of successes, but what really made me fearless was my complete failure at Zidd-Davis. Once you've lived through that, you know you can survive, and you're not as scared...There's nothing to build confidence like real achievement, but also like real failure.

Esther Dyson (b. 1951) US knowledge entrepreneur and government adviser. Referring to her experience of being hired to start a newspaper, which flopped. Interview, *Reason Magazine* (November 1996)

17 Failing is good as long as it doesn't become a habit.

Michael Eisner (b. 1942) US chairman and CEO of the Disney Corporation. Speech (19 April 1996)

18 For everything you have missed, you have gained something else.

Ralph Waldo Emerson (1803–82) US essayist, lecturer, and poet. 'Compensation', *Essays: First Series* (1841)

19 If at first you don't succeed, try, try again. Then quit. No use being a damn fool about it.

W.C. Fields (1880–1946) US actor and comedian. Attrib.

20 The flaws of capitalism are people who don't know how to run businesses well. They waste capital. They wither it away.

Steve Forbes (b. 1947) US publishing executive. Interview, *Reason Magazine* (May 1991)

21 Microsoft is always just two years from failure.

Bill Gates (b. 1955) US entrepreneur, chairman and CEO of Microsoft. 1997. Quoted in *Goldfinger* (Robert Heller; 1998)

22 I think a man is a business failure who lets his family life interfere with his business record...business is no place for him.

J. Paul Getty (1892–1976) US entrepreneur, oil industry executive, and financier. 1973. Getty married five times. Quoted in *Getty on Getty* (Somerset de Chair; 1989), ch. 5

23 The very best takeovers are thoroughly hostile. I've never seen a really good company taken over. I've only seen bad ones.

James Goldsmith (1933–97) British entrepreneur, financier, and politician. *Financial Times* (21 March 1989)

24 Honorable errors do not count as failures...but as seeds for progress in the quintessential activity of correction.

Stephen Jay Gould (1941–2002) US geologist, palaeontologist, and philosopher of science. *Leonardo's Mountain of Clams and the Diet of Worms: Essays on Natural History* (1998)

25 It would have been cheaper to lower the Atlantic.

Lew Grade (1906–98) British entertainment entrepreneur. On the failure of his film *Raise the Titanic*. *Sun* (22 December 1987)

26 Too much money is a dangerous thing to deal with. And the point I'm saying is exponential— huge opportunities bring exponentially huge opportunities for failure as well.

Andrew S. Grove (b. 1936) US entrepreneur, author, and chairman of Intel Corporation. Speech, Los Angeles Times 3rd Annual Investment Strategies Conference, Los Angeles, California (22 May 1999)

27 Failing is a learning experience. It can be a gravestone or a stepping stone.

Bud Hadfield (b. 1923) US entrepreneur and founder of Kwik Kopy. *Wealth within Reach: Winning Strategies for Success from the Unconventional Wisdom of Bud Hadfield* (1995)

28 In the long run, failure was the only thing that worked predictably.

Joseph Heller (1923–99) US novelist. *Good as Gold* (1979)

29 The majority of men meet with failure because of their lack of persistence in creating new plans to take the place of those which fail.

Napoleon Hill (1883–1970) US motivational author. *Think and Grow Rich* (1937)

30 Our achievements speak for themselves. What we have to keep track of are our failures, discouragements, and doubts. We tend to forget the past difficulties, the many false starts, and the painful groping.

Eric Hoffer (1902–83) US philosopher. *Reflections on the Human Condition* (1973)

31 To me success can only be achieved through repeated failure and introspection. In fact, success represents 1 per cent of your work which results from the 99 per cent that is called failure.

Soichiro Honda (1906–91) Japanese entrepreneur, founder and president of Honda Corporation. Quoted in *Thriving on Chaos* (Tom Peters; 1988)

32 A failure is a man who has blundered, but is not able to cash in the experience.

Elbert Hubbard (1856–1915) US humorist. *Epigrams* (1905)

33 We don't publicize our failures. When something doesn't work don't leave the corpse lying around.

Kenneth Iverson (1925–2002) US industrialist, chairman and CEO of Nucor Corporation. Speech (5 February 1996)

34 There is no excuse. If they don't get the target, they don't get their bonus—we have no discussions.

Liisa Joronen (b. 1944) Finnish CEO of SOL (formerly Lindstrom). Interview in *The Winning Streak Mark II* (Walter Goldsmith and David Clutterbuck; 1997)

35 Failures, repeated failures, are finger posts on the road to achievement. The only time you don't fail is the last time you try something, and it works. One fails forward toward success.

Charles Franklin Kettering (1876–1958) US businessman and engineer. Quoted in *Reader's Digest* (May 1989)

36 When, in response to deteriorating business, a company blames outside forces or covers up its problems by changing its accounting methods or by using other tricks, it ensures failure.

Charles G. Koch (b. 1935) US management theorist, author, chairman and CEO of Koch Industries. 'Market-based Management', *Imprimis* (August 1996)

37 Failure is the foundation of success; success is the lurking place of failure.

Laozi (?570–?490 BC) Chinese philosopher, reputed founder of Daoism. *Daode Jing*

38 In their enterprises the people
Always ruin them when on the verge of success.
Be as careful at the end as at the beginning.
And there will be no ruined enterprises.

Laozi (?570–?490 BC) Chinese philosopher, reputed founder of Daoism. *Daode Jing*

39 How to Lose $100,000,000 and Other Valuable Information

Royal D. Little (1896–1989) US founder of Textron Corporation. Book title. *How to Lose $100,000,000 and Other Valuable Information* (1979)

40 In this business, by the time you realise you're in trouble, it's too late to save yourself.

Michael C. Lynch (b. 1946) Scottish historian. Referring to the volatility of the software business. Quoted in *Playboy* (1994)

41 It is not impossibilities which fill us with deepest despair, but possibilities which we have failed to realise.

Robert Mallet (1915–2002) French poet and playwright. *Apostilles: ou, L'Utile et le Futile* (1972)

42 If you aren't afraid to fail, then you probably don't care enough about success.

Mark McCormack (1930–2003) US entrepreneur, founder and CEO of the International Management Group. *What They Don't Teach You at Harvard Business School* (1984)

43 More strategies fail because they are overripe than because they are premature.

Kenichi Ohmae (b. 1943) Japanese management consultant and theorist. *The Mind of the Strategist* (1982)

44 Failures are like skinned knees—painful, but superficial.

H. Ross Perot (b. 1930) US entrepreneur, venture capitalist, and politician. Attrib.

45 If we do not succeed, then we run the risk of failure.

Dan Quayle (b. 1947) US former vice-president. 6 December 1989. Quoted in *Esquire* (August 1992)

46 Bankruptcy would be like stepping into a tepid bath and slashing your wrists: You might not feel yourself dying, but that's what would happen.

Felix Rohatyn (b. 1928) US investment company executive. *Wall Street Journal* (March 1985)

47 It is hard to fail; but it is worse never to have tried to succeed.

Theodore Roosevelt (1858–1919) US president. Speech, Hamilton Club, Chicago, Illinois. 'The Doctrine of the Strenuous Life' (10 April 1899)

48 At some point, we all have to decide how we are going to fail: by not going far enough, or by going too far. The only alternative for the most successful (maybe even the most fulfilled) people is the latter.

Harriet Rubin (b. 1952) US author. 'How Will You Fail?', *Fast Company* (1999)

49 It was not the power of the Spaniards that destroyed the Aztec Empire, but the disbelief of the Aztecs in themselves.

E.F. Schumacher (1911–77) British economist and conservationist. *Roots of Economic Growth* (1962)

50 You don't go broke making a profit.

Nicholas Shehadie (b. 1926) Australian sportsman and business executive. Quoted in 'Sayings of the Week', *Sydney Morning Herald* (26 March 1987)

51 You don't get any marks for trying...I'm not interested in any sophisticated reasons for failure.

Allen Sheppard (b. 1932) British chairman of Vizual Business Tools and former chairman of Grand Metropolitan. *Business* (August 1990)

52 The difference between failure and success is doing a thing nearly right and doing it exactly right.

Edward Emerson Simmons (1852–1931) US painter. Attrib.

53 I detest bankruptcy. To me it signifies failure—personal failure, corporate failure.

George Steinbrenner (b. 1930) US owner of the New York Yankees baseball team. *New York Times* (1992)

54 Key to creating wealth in the third industrial revolution is the willingness and ability to shut down the old and open up the new...This requires a high tolerance for failure.

Lester Thurow (b. 1938) US economist, management theorist, and writer. Speech, Sixth Workshop on Inventing the Organization of the 21st Century, Munich, Germany. 'Building Wealth in a Knowledge-Based Society' (February 2000)

55 An ill-planned scheme, though aided much, will go awry.

Tiruvalluvar (*fl.* 1st century) Indian poet. *The Kural*, 468

56 One of the most important tasks of a manager is to eliminate his people's excuses for failure.

Robert Townsend (b. 1920) US business executive and author. *Further Up the Organization* (1984)

57 It used to bug the hell out of me when I'd drop out of the bidding for something and then get a call from a reporter asking, 'So, Mr. Trump, how does it feel to get beat?'

Donald J. Trump (b. 1946) US property developer. *Trump: Surviving at the Top* (co-written with Charles Leerhsen; 1990)

58 Bankruptcy is a sacred state, a condition beyond conditions...attempts to investigate it are necessarily obscene like spiritualism. One knows only he has passed into it and lives beyond us, in a condition not ours.

John Updike (b. 1932) US novelist and critic. 'The Bankrupt Man', *Hugging the Shore* (1983)

59 There is no human failure greater than to launch a profoundly important endeavour and then leave it half done.

Barbara Ward (1914–81) British economist, journalist, and educator. *The Rich Nations and the Poor Nations* (1962)

60 When the rate of change outside exceeds the rate of change inside, the end is in sight.

Jack Welch (b. 1935) US former chairman and CEO of General Electric. *Inc.* (March 1995)

FOCUS

1 If railroads had understood they were in the transportation business instead of the steel-rail business, we'd all be flying on Union Pacific Airlines.

Anonymous. Quoted in *The Road Ahead* (Bill Gates, co-written with Nathan Myhrvold and Peter N. Rinearson; 1995)

2 Do not lose yourself in the work or in your ideas or plans or forget to keep yourself in constant touch with the true source.

Sri Aurobindo (1872–1950) Indian philosopher, mystic, and nationalist. Quoted in *Ethics in Management: Vedantic Perspectives* (S.K. Chakraborty; 1995)

3 It is better to do thine own duty, however lacking in merit, than to do that of another, even though efficiently.

Bhagavad Gita, Indian religious text. (?1st century BC)

4 Positive direction can have far reaching effects.

Jack Daniels (b. 1933) US athletics coach. *Daniels' Running Formula* (1998)

5 There are a lot of disadvantages—the pressure and the expectations, a lot of media attention. It is hard to concentrate and prepare without being distracted.

Robert de Castella (b. 1957) Australian athlete and executive director of Focus on You. Interview (1984)

6 Anything worth doing is worth doing to excess.

Edwin Land (1909–91) US inventor and founder of Polaroid Corporation. *Boston Globe* (March 1991)

7 When conscious activity is wholly concentrated on some one definite purpose, the ultimate result, for most people, is lack of balance accompanied by some form of nervous disorder.

Bertrand Russell (1872–1970) British philosopher and writer. Quoted in *Management by Objectives: An Integrated Approach* (S.K. Chakraborty; 1976)

8 Never waste your attention on matters that have nothing to do with your work...Remember that it is the family business that must not be neglected for a moment.

Mitsui Takafusa (1684–1748) Japanese merchant. Quoted in *Premodern Japan: A Historical Survey* (Mikiso Hane; 1991)

FORECASTING

1 Over the past 25 years, economic forecasters have missed four of the past five recessions.

Anonymous. *BusinessWeek* (30 September 1996)

2 The empires of the future are the empires of the mind.

Winston Churchill (1874–1965) British prime minister. Speech (September 1943)

3 In the mid 80s, Fortune magazine carried the prediction that, by the year 2010, North America would become the world's granary, the Pacific the world's manufacturing base and that Europe will become a discotheque. They could still be right.

Max Comfort, British business theorist. *Portfolio People* (1997)

4 Accountants and market researchers may be brilliant at examining and analysing facts about the past, but they have no forward vision.

Terence Conran (b. 1931) British business executive, retailer, and founder of Habitat. Quoted in *The Adventure Capitalists* (Jeff Grout and Lynne Curry; 1998)

5 By 2020, 80% of business profits and market value will come from that part of the enterprise that is built around info-business.

Stan Davis (b. 1939) US business author. *2020 Vision* (co-written with Bill Davidson; 1991)

6 There are two sorts of forecasters. Those who don't know and those who don't know they don't know.

J.K. Galbraith (b. 1908) US economist and diplomat. Quoted in *Treasury of Investment Wisdom* (Bernice Cohen; 1999)

7 The further ahead you forecast, the less well you do.

C.W.J. Granger (b. 1934) British economist. Quoted in *Fortune* (25 January 1996)

8 Forecast: to observe that which has passed, and guess it will happen again.

Frank McKinney Hubbard (1868–1930) US humorist. *The Roycroft Dictionary* (1923)

9 You...have to pick horses to ride for five to ten year periods because you don't want to be changing things.

Steve Jobs (b. 1955) US entrepreneur, co-founder and CEO of Apple Computer Company, and CEO of Pixar. Referring to spotting opportunities and trends. Quoted in 'Steve's Two Jobs', *Time* (Michael Krantz; 18 October 1999)

10 Oil-price forecasters make sheep seem like independent thinkers. There's no evidence that mineral prices rise over time. Technology always overwhelms depletion.

Michael C. Lynch (b. 1946) Scottish historian. Quoted in *BusinessWeek* (3 November 1997)

11 The future bears a resemblance to the past, only more so.

Faith Popcorn (b. 1947) US trend expert and founder of BrainReserve. *The Popcorn Report* (1991)

12 Most economists...are reluctant to make predictions, and those who make them are seldom accurate. The economy, like the human body, is a highly complex system whose workings are not thoroughly understood.

Alice M. Rivlin (b. 1931) US economist. *Reviving the American Dream* (1992)

13 I don't have time to get out the charts and show you how the world works.

Jim Rogers (b. 1935) US banker and management consultant. Quoted in *Treasury of Investment Wisdom* (Bernice Cohen; 1999)

14 Wall Street indexes predicted nine out of the last five recessions.

Paul Samuelson (b. 1915) US economist and winner of the 1970 Nobel Prize in Economics. *Newsweek* (19 September 1966)

15 Economists are about as useful as astrologers in predicting the future (and, like astrologers, they never let failure on one occasion diminish certitude on the next).

Arthur Schlesinger Jr (b. 1917) US historian, writer, and educator. Quoted in *New York Times* (15 April 1993)

16 Rehearsing the future.

Peter Schwartz, US consultant and author. Referring to the use of scenarios in forecasting. *The Art of the Long View* (1991)

17 In a crowded room, you only have to see one inch above everyone else to notice things that others will miss.

Jim Slater (b. 1929) British business executive and author. Quoted in *Treasury of Investment Wisdom* (Bernice Cohen; 1999)

GETTING STARTED

1 One sees great things from the valley; only small things from the peak.

G.K. Chesterton (1874–1936) British novelist, poet, and critic. *The Innocence of Father Brown* (1911)

2 Launching a start-up is tough in any country. In Mexico, it's something else.

Miguel Angel Davila (b. 1966) Mexican entrepreneur. *Forbes* (May 1998)

3 The challenge in a start-up is that you always have to spread your wings pretty far to see what will work.

Michael Dell (b. 1965) US chairman and CEO of Dell Computer Corporation. Quoted in *In the Company of Giants* (Rama Dev Jager; 1997)

4 We were all 25 years old, none of us had run a business and none of us had worked in retail. You can't get a much harder start.

Charles Dunstone (b. 1964) British business executive and founder of Carphone Warehouse. *Sunday Times* (June 2000)

5 I do know people who have got these life plans and if they haven't got there by 12 o'clock on Friday then they're going to resign.

Belinda Earl (b. 1961) British retail executive. *Sunday Times* (September 2000)

6 Each venture is a new beginning, a raid on the inarticulate.

T.S. Eliot (1888–1965) British poet, dramatist, and critic. 'East Coker', *Four Quartets* (1943)

7 It is kind of difficult to mess things up if you have the right people in the right place.

Tony Elliott (b. 1947) British publisher. *Sunday Times* (May 2000)

8 When I got my hands on Unit, I took the decision that I would be going nowhere fast if I just printed 500 copies to circulate around the university, so I printed 4000 copies.

Tony Elliott (b. 1947) British publisher. Referring to his transformation of a university magazine to a national publication. *Sunday Times* (May 2000)

9 I had this great urge...I had it the day I was born. Some may call it destiny. My parents and friends called it dismaying.

Dian Fossey (1932–85) US conservationist. *Gorillas in the Mist* (1983)

10 In a campaign, first you put up the façade, then you go around and build the building.

Newt Gingrich (b. 1943) US politician. *New Yorker* (October 1995)

11 To start a business and to run it successfully, you have to like people. You have to care about them.

Bud Hadfield (b. 1923) US entrepreneur and founder of Kwik Kopy. *Wealth Within Reach: Winning Strategies for Success from the Unconventional Wisdom of Bud Hadfield* (1995)

12 Give me six months to prove myself, then if you don't like what I'm doing, you can give me the shittiest job you've got.

Rob Herson (b. 1952) South African business executive. *Marketing* (July 2000)

13 He who has begun, has half done. Dare to be wise; begin!

Horace (65–8 BC) Roman poet and satirist. *Epistles* (?20 BC), bk 1, no. 2

14 An accidental business person.

Heather Killen (b. 1959) Australian Internet executive. *Fortune* (October 2000)

15 In business for yourself, not by yourself.

Ray Kroc (1902–84) US founder of McDonald's. Referring to franchising opportunities with McDonald's. Quoted in *McDonald's—Behind the Arches* (John F. Love; 1986)

16 Nothing in the world can take the place of persistence.

Ray Kroc (1902–84) US founder of McDonald's. Quoted in *The Fifties* (David Halberstan; 1993)

17 Really, I wanted to work in the movie business. But that was like saying I wanted to go to the moon.

Sherry Lansing (b. 1944) US chairman of Paramount Motion Picture Group. 'The 50 Most Powerful Women in American Business', *Fortune* (Patricia Sellers and Cora Daniels; October 1999)

18 If you are going to start a company, it takes so much energy that you'd better overcome your feeling of risk.

Michael C. Lynch (b. 1946) Scottish historian. Interview, *Fortune* (July 1998)

19 I can have a big say because I am the owner, the sole shareholder. I don't get involved in half measures.

Peter Mandelson (b. 1953) British politician. Referring to the Millennium Dome project. *Observer* (July 1997)

20 I have never avoided the influence of others. I would have considered this a cowardice and lack of sincerity toward myself.

Henri Matisse (1869–1954) French painter and sculptor. Interview (1907)

21 I always had to battle with that confidence thing...I was postponing or delaying the moment of truth.

Paul Merton (b. 1957) British comedian. *Observer* (October 2000)

22 We want to manage and grow our companies ourselves. If we give up 51 percent, we might as well get out of the business.

Sunil Mittal (b. 1948) Indian software entrepreneur. *Sunday Times* (May 2000)

23 The whole thing is fire, ready, aim and I love it.

Chris Moore (b. 1960) British marketing director of Domino's Pizza. Referring to dot.com businesses. *Marketing* (June 2000)

24 I think what we have in Portugal is perhaps what the Mexicans and the Africans have. We don't have a lot of facilities. We need to work very hard to get things done.

Rosa Mota (b. 1958) Portuguese athlete. Quoted in *Running with the Legends* (Michael Sandrock; 1996)

25 You do not have to be the son of a rich man to be an entrepreneur. Today kids are far more willing to take risks because they've seen high rewards.

Narayana Murthy (b. 1946) Indian founder and CEO of Infosys. *Forbes* (June 2000)

26 Launching your own business is like writing your own personal declaration of independence from the corporate beehive.

Paula Nelson (b. 1944) US educator. *The Joy of Money* (1975)

27 All we need is an old cigar box and someone to take notice.

Laurence Olivier (1907–89) British actor and director. Referring to acting. Interview (1986)

28 Poverty provided the hunger and I'm still hungry today. My glass is always half empty.

Vijay Patel (b. 1950) Kenyan entrepreneur. *Sunday Times* (September 2000)

29 I was scared of failing.

Pele (b. 1940) Brazilian footballer. Referring to his first professional football game. Press conference (1956)

30 Perhaps one of the greatest advantages I have is that I am not educated in the academic sense.

Jack Petchey (b. 1925) British investor. *Sunday Times* (September 2000)

31 Start small. If you can succeed with a few thousand pounds, then you can do much better with bigger sums.

Reuben Singh (b. 1977) British entrepreneur and author. *Management Today* (September 1999)

32 Remember that on day one, when you go in as the boss, you'll feel a mixture of exhilaration that you've made it and fatigue with all the effort.

Barbara Thomas (b. 1947) US banker. *Management Today* (October 1999)

33 I only started acting out of fearless ignorance and a side order of stupidity.

Uma Thurman (b. 1970) US actor. *Sunday Times* (October 2000)

34 The best thing I had going for me was my knowledge of women. I certainly didn't have much money...But I had respect in the market place I was entering—and that was better than a business degree.

Lise Watier (b. 1942) Canadian proprietor of a cosmetics chain. Quoted in *Looking Good* (Rosa Harris-Adler; 1997)

GLOBALISATION

1 The best course for our nation is not to curse globalization but to shape it, to make it work for America.

Madeleine Albright (b. 1937) US stateswoman and diplomat. Quoted in *Financial Times* (19 September 1997)

2 Staff should reflect the diversity of the company's user base.

Fabiola Arredondo (b. 1966) Spanish Internet executive. *Fortune* (October 2000)

3 Bosses tend to attract clusters of people from their own nationality around them.

Percy Barnevik (b. 1941) Swedish former CEO of ABB. *Financial Times* (October 1997)

4 Globalisation is a long-lasting competitive advantage...building a global company is not so easy to copy.

Percy Barnevik (b. 1941) Swedish former CEO of ABB. *Financial Times* (October 1997)

5 Global managers have exceptionally open minds. They respect how different countries do things.

Percy Barnevik (b. 1941) Swedish former CEO of ABB.
Harvard Business Review (March/April 1991)

6 Multidomestic competition.

Percy Barnevik (b. 1941) Swedish former CEO of ABB.
Referring to his company's policy of establishing strong local
companies around the world. Quoted in *Liberation
Management*. (Tom Peters; 1992)

7 At school we learned about going abroad to get
experience and prove that we are able to move
from one place to another.

Olivier Barre (b. 1970) French business executive. Referring
to multinational locations such as Dublin. *New York Times*
(October 2000)

8 When Sony's founder and chief executive,
Akio Morita, relocated to New York to build
the company's US operations, he sent the
most convincing message about Sony's
commitment to its overseas subsidiaries.

Christopher Bartlett (b. 1945) Australian business writer.
Managing Across Borders (co-written with Sumantra
Ghoshal; 1989)

9 Transnationals.

Christopher Bartlett (b. 1945) Australian business writer. The
term created by the authors to describe a new type of
international organisation. *Managing Across Borders*
(co-written with Sumantra Ghoshal; 1989)

10 As international companies begin to compete
with each other in the global marketplace, the
role of cross-cultural training becomes
increasingly important.

Rabi S. Bhagat (b. 1950) Indian business author.
'Cross-cultural Training in Organisational Contexts',
Handbook of Intercultural Training (co-edited with Dan
Landis, co-written with Kristin O. Prien; 1996)

11 Globalization requires that organizations
adopt a cross-cultural perspective to be
successful in accomplishing their goals in the
context of a global economy.

Rabi S. Bhagat (b. 1950) Indian business author.
'Cross-cultural Training in Organisational Contexts',
Handbook of Intercultural Training (co-edited with Dan
Landis, co-written with Kristin O. Prien; 1996)

12 One cannot separate the strategy involved in
the multinational mission from the human
resource strategy involved in placing the
international assignee.

Rabi S. Bhagat (b. 1950) Indian business author.
'Cross-cultural Training in Organisational Contexts',
Handbook of Intercultural Training (co-edited with Dan
Landis, co-written with Kristin O. Prien; 1996)

13 Globalisation such as it is today profits only
countries that have a material, technological
and technical basis. The globalisation towards
which we want to go is the globalisation that
excludes nobody.

Abdul Aziz Bouteflika (b. 1937) Algerian president. Speaking
in his role as Chairman of the Organization of African Unity
for 2000. Speech, UN Conference on Trade and
Development (UNCTAD) summit, Bangkok, Thailand
(19 February 2000)

14 Investing is a business that never tires. You
have to work with every known thing in the
world—the weather in Asia, or politics in East
Europe, or the scandal of an American
president.

Charles Brady (b. 1935) US investor. *Sunday Times*
(May 2000)

15 When we speak of the commerce with our
colonies, fiction lags after truth, invention is
unfruitful, and imagination cold and barren.

Edmund Burke (1729–97) British philosopher and politician.
On Conciliation with America (22 March 1775)

16 More and more of our imports are coming
from overseas.

George W. Bush (b. 1946) US president. Speech
(29 September 2000)

17 The Death of Distance

Frances Cairncross, British journalist and author. Book title.
Referring to the effects of increasing globalisation. *The
Death of Distance* (1997)

18 Provided that the City of London remains as it
is at present, the clearing house of the world.

Joseph Chamberlain (1836–1914) British prime minister.
Speech (January 1904)

19 We no longer live in a world of nations and
ideologies, Mr Beale. The world is a collage of
corporations inexorably determined by the
immutable by-laws of business. The world is a
business, Mr Beale.

Paddy Chayefsky (1923–81) US playwright and screenwriter.
Network (1976)

20 Lancashire merchants whenever they like
Can water the beer of a man in Klondike
Or poison the meat of a man in Bombay
And that is the meaning of Empire Day.

G.K. Chesterton (1874–1936) British novelist, poet, and
critic. *Songs of Education* (1922)

21 Environmental forces transcend borders and
oceans to threaten directly the health,
prosperity and jobs of American citizens.

Warren Christopher (b. 1925) US politician. Quoted in
Natural Capitalism (Paul Hawken, Amory B. Lovins, and
L. Hunter Lovins; 1999)

22 September 11th was the dark side of this new
age of global interdependence.

Bill Clinton (b. 1946) US former president. Speech
(18 December 2001)

23 If you are organised globally and understand
your business well enough...you can follow
the property cycle around the world.

Jill Ker Conway (b. 1934) Australian historian. *Financial
Times* (October 2000)

24 They have a great thing nationally that they
are trying to replicate abroad. In that
replication is the challenge.

Carlos Criado-Perez (b. 1952) Argentinian business
executive. *Sunday Times* (July 2000)

25 If global connectivity is the technological
breakthrough of our decade, then the outburst
of innovation is just beginning.

Mary J. Cronin (b. 1947) US business author. *Doing More
Business on the Internet* (1995)

26 Transnational corporations are powerful entities subject to regulation by Third World countries.
Rajani X. Desai, Indian political economist. *Arms of an Octopus: Siemens in India* (1990)

27 The Indian market has such long-term potential that no international company can take a narrow, short-term view.
Rajiv Desai, Indian journalist and public relations executive. *Indian Business Culture* (1999)

28 The BJP and its doctrine of *swadeshi* notwithstanding, multinational companies will continue to play an important role...the flow of international investment into India is likely to continue unabated.
Rajiv Desai, Indian journalist and public relations executive. The BJP is a Hindu nationalist political party in India. *Swadeshi* is a policy of protecting Indian business interests. *Indian Business Culture* (1999)

29 If the US and Japan cannot become partners, then there is a possibility that current trends could eventually make them enemies.
Richard Drobnick (b. 1945) US academic. 'Economic Integration in the Pacific Rim', *Corporate Strategies in the Pacific Rim* (Denis Fred Simon, ed.; 1995)

30 The economic integration of the Pacific region—which includes the United States, Canada, and Mexico—is occuring...the result of intra-regional capital flows, increased trade liberalization, and privatization trends.
Richard Drobnick (b. 1945) US academic. 'Economic Integration in the Pacific Rim', *Corporate Strategies in the Pacific Rim* (Denis Fred Simon, ed.; 1995)

31 Nationalism is an infantile sickness. It is the measles of the human race.
Albert Einstein (1879–1955) US physicist. Quoted in *The Human Side* (Helen Dukas and Banesh Hoffmann; 1979)

32 You should never underestimate the challenge of operating a multicultural business...As businesses are being intimately linked in the global economy, and as they partner with competitors...we become more and more reliant on each other.
William T. Esrey (b. 1940) US telecommunications entrepreneur, chairman and CEO of Sprint. Referring to Sprint's global alliance with Deutsche Telekom and France Telecom to form Global One. 'Leadership in the Next Century', *The Conference Board Challenge to Business: Industry Leaders Speak Their Minds* (Peter Krass and Richard E. Cavanagh, eds; 2000)

33 No nation was ever ruined by trade.
Benjamin Franklin (1706–90) US politician, inventor, and journalist. *Essays* (1730s)

34 Think globally, not locally.
Friends of the Earth, environmental campaign organisation. Slogan of the international environmental campaigning organisation Friends of the Earth. Slogan (1985)

35 The large corporation is here to stay. Those who would break it up and confine its operations within national boundaries are at war with history and circumstance. People

want large tasks performed...Large tasks require large organizations.
J.K. Galbraith (b. 1908) US economist and diplomat. *The Age of Uncertainty* (1977), ch. 9

36 There is certainly nothing competitive about a capitalism that today exports factories as well as merchandise and capital...this is a global industrial conglomeration by capitalism in the age of the multinational corporation.
Eduardo Galeano (b. 1940) Uruguayan writer and journalist. *Open Veins of Latin America* (1971), pt 2, ch. 2

37 Globalization can...be defined as the intensification of worldwide social relations which link distant realities in such a way that local happenings are shaped by events occurring many miles away and vice versa.
Anthony Giddens (b. 1938) British sociologist and author. *The Third Way: The Renewal of Social Democracy* (1998)

38 We are part of the community of Europe and we must do our duty as such.
William Ewart Gladstone (1809–98) British prime minister. Speech (April 1888)

39 A truly global economy is being created by the worldwide spread of new technologies, not by the spread of free markets...the result is not a universal free market but an anarchy of sovereign states, rival capitalisms and stateless zones.
John Gray (b. 1948) British academic and writer. *False Dawn* (1998)

40 The global market as it is presently organised does not allow the world's peoples to coexist harmoniously. It impels them to become rivals for resources while instituting no methods for conserving.
John Gray (b. 1948) British academic and writer. *False Dawn* (1998)

41 If the whole world operates as one big market, every employee will compete with every person in the world who is capable of doing the same job.
Andrew S. Grove (b. 1936) US entrepreneur, author, and chairman of Intel Corporation. *Fortune* (September 1995)

42 Globalisation is an opportunity. Well managed, it will help drive forward efforts to build prosperity and eliminate poverty. Badly managed it will increase the divide between rich and poor.
Peter Hain (b. 1950) British politician. Speech, Challenges for Governance in Africa Conference, Wilton Park, England (13 September 1999)

43 All things start in California and spread to New Jersey, then to London and then throughout Europe.
Stelios Haji-Ioannou (b. 1967) Greek founder of EasyJet. *Wall Street Journal* (December 1996)

44 In today's multicultural world, the truly reliable path to co-existence, to peaceful co-existence and creative co-operation must start from what is at the root of all cultures.
Václav Havel (b. 1936) Czech writer and president. Speech (1994)

45 In a global economy the challenges and changes are universal.
Robert Heller (b. 1932) British management writer. *In Search of European Excellence* (1997)

46 Merchants have no country. The mere spot they stand on does not constitute so strong an attachment as that from which they draw their gains.
Thomas Jefferson (1743–1826) US president. Letter to Horatio G. Spafford (17 March 1814)

47 Our key words now are globalisation, new products and business, and speed.
Tsutomu Kanai (b. 1929) Japanese chairman of Hitachi. *Fortune* (May 1996)

48 You can always buy something in English, you can't always sell something in English.
Rosabeth Moss Kanter (b. 1943) US management theorist, academic, and writer. *World Class* (1995)

49 Most powerful women...are only sporadically earthbound.
Heather Killen (b. 1959) Australian Internet executive. Referring to her frequent business travel by air. *Fortune* (October 2000)

50 Borders are not sacred; indeed, the best border is an inconspicuous one...As the border erodes, people who belong together will come together.
György Konrád (b. 1933) Hungarian writer. *The Melancholy of Rebirth* (1995)

51 Pan-Americanism is a grand sentiment over which to drink sweet champagne in Lima, Peru, or Santiago, anywhere, at the expense of the United States.
Stephen Leacock (1869–1944) Canadian humorist, essayist, economist, and historian. *While There Is Time* (1945)

52 Predictability: does the flap of a butterfly's wings in Brazil set off a tornado in Texas?
Edward N. Lorenz (b. 1917) US ethologist. Scientific paper (December 1979)

53 The time has now definitely come when every intelligent individual must learn to think globally, beyond the horizon of a narrow nationalist point of view.
Robert Maxwell (1923–91) British publisher, business executive, and politician. Preface to *Information USSR* (September 1962)

54 If only 50 or more people were doing for the country what I have been doing, there would not be a pay freeze or a balance of payments problem.
Robert Maxwell (1923–91) British publisher, business executive, and politician. Referring to his world trips to build an international scientific publishing business. Speech (December 1966)

55 The new electronic interdependence recreates the world in the image of a global village.
Marshall McLuhan (1911–80) Canadian sociologist and author. *The Gutenberg Galaxy* (1962)

56 These days Paris is a suburb of New York and vice-versa.
Jean-Marie Messier (b. 1956) French media owner. *Sunday Times* (September 2000)

57 We have combined BT's global expertise with a comprehensive local knowledge in this package.
Sunil Mittal (b. 1948) Indian software entrepreneur. Referring to international joint ventures. *Sunday Times* (May 2000)

58 Sustainable business has to navigate by more than one parameter. The demands of economics, of the environment and of contributing to a just society are all important for a global commercial enterprise to flourish. To neglect any one of them is to threaten the whole.
Mark Moody-Stuart (b. 1940) British chairman of Anglo American, and former chairman of Committee of Managing Directors Royal Dutch/Shell Group. Speech, St Paul's Cathedral, London. 'The Values of Sustainable Business in the Next Century' (12 July 1999)

59 All you need is the best product in the world, the most efficient production in the world and global marketing.
Akio Morita (1921–99) Japanese business executive. Quoted in *The Financial Times Handbook of Management* (Stuart Crainer, ed.; 1995)

60 In the eighteenth century, Voltaire said that every man had two countries: his own and France. In the twentieth century, that has come to be true of the US
Rupert Murdoch (b. 1931) US CEO of News Corporation. Speech (November 1989)

61 We're not going global because we want to or because of any megalomania, but because it's really necessary.
Rupert Murdoch (b. 1931) US CEO of News Corporation. *Worldbusiness* (1994)

62 India will become the country of choice...It's already starting to happen.
Narayana Murthy (b. 1946) Indian founder and CEO of Infosys. Referring to software development. *Forbes* (October 2000)

63 India missed the industrial revolution. Now for the first time, India has a clear competitive advantage in exports.
Narayana Murthy (b. 1946) Indian founder and CEO of Infosys. *Wired Asia* (June 2000)

64 Worldwide, IT companies embarking on the non-organic growth mode have understood the wisdom of mergers and acquisitions on the threshold of the Digital Age.
Narayana Murthy (b. 1946) Indian founder and CEO of Infosys. 'The Future Is Inorganic', *www.rediff.com* (1998)

65 The more the economies of the world integrate, the less important are the economies of countries and the more important are the economic contributions of individuals and individual economies.
John Naisbitt (b. ?1929) US business executive and author. *Global Paradox* (1994)

66 The world's trends point overwhelmingly toward political independence and self-rule on the one hand, and the formation of economic alliances on the other.
John Naisbitt (b. ?1929) US business executive and author. *Global Paradox* (1994)

67 The bigger the world economy, the more powerful its smallest player.
John Naisbitt (b. ?1929) US business executive and author. *Megatrends* (1982)

68 India Ceramics weds unique local skills and materials to advanced, foreign-origin production methods, and quality control.
Anat Napawan (b. 1953) Taiwanese business executive. *Forbes* (September 1998)

69 We cannot survive as a cheap labour platform for foreign-licenced products.
Anat Napawan (b. 1953) Taiwanese business executive. *Forbes* (September 1998)

70 We face neither East nor West; we face forward.
Kwame Nkrumah (1909–72) Ghanaian president. Speech (April 1960)

71 Region-states are economic units, not political ones, and they are anything but local...their primary linkage is with the global economy.
Kenichi Ohmae (b. 1943) Japanese management consultant and theorist. *Harvard Business Review* (January–February 1995)

72 The most successful Japanese consumer electronics companies send their product design engineers around the world for about six months each year to study the latest consumer needs and assess the competitive scene.
Kenichi Ohmae (b. 1943) Japanese management consultant and theorist. *Industry Week* (July 1985)

73 Today's global economic dance is no Strauss waltz. It's break dancing accompanied by street rap.
Tom Peters (b. 1942) US management consultant and author. *Liberation Management* (1992)

74 Strategy, policies and standards are set globally...but you still need local engagement skills.
Raoul Pinnell (b. 1951) British branding and marketing communications director of Shell International Petroleum. *Marketing* (June 2000)

75 Sometimes, I'm more in the air than I am in a country.
Raoul Pinnell (b. 1951) British branding and marketing communications director of Shell International Petroleum. Referring to the volume of business travel for a global marketing executive. *Marketing* (June 2000)

76 National and economic prosperity is created, not inherited.
Michael Porter (b. 1947) US strategist. *The Competitive Advantage of Nations* (1990)

77 We are always willing to be trade partners, but never trade patsies.
Ronald Reagan (b. 1911) US former president and actor. Speech (February 1987)

78 High Wage Economies can no longer depend on standardized mass production. Big Ideas...can be shipped in blueprints or electronic symbols anywhere on the globe
Robert Reich (b. 1946) US economist and politician. *Tales of a New America* (1987)

79 There is coming to be no such thing as an American corporation or an American industry. The American economy is but a region of the global economy.
Robert Reich (b. 1946) US economist and politician. *The Work of Nations* (1991)

80 We all of us, rich and poor, have to live with the insecurity caused by an out of control global casino with a built-in bias towards instability. Because it is instability that makes money for the money-traders.
Anita Roddick (b. 1942) British entrepreneur and founder of The Body Shop. Speech to the International Forum on Globalisation Teach-In, Seattle, Washington. 'Trading with Principles' (27 November 1999)

81 Europe is something happening; it's something we are trying to make.
Marjorie Scardino (b. 1947) US CEO of Pearson. *Fortune* (October 2000)

82 The new model is global in scale, an interdependent network.
John Sculley (b. 1939) US partner of Sculley Brothers, former president of Pepsi, and CEO of Apple Computers. *Harvard Business Review* (1991)

83 One of the greatest challenges to international business today is how to manage business operations across cultural boundaries.
Jan Selmer (b. 1942) Swedish academic and author. *International Management in China: Cross-cultural Issues* (Jan Selmer, ed.; 1998), Preface

84 Globalisation has in effect made the citizen disappear, and it has reduced the state into being a mere instrument of global capital.
Vandana Shiva (b. 1944) Indian academic. *Globalisation: Gandhi and Swadeshi* (2000)

85 Globalisation is not inevitable. There is not one but many alternatives to globalisation based on the rights of people rather than the rights of corporations, based on democracy rather than corporate rule.
Vandana Shiva (b. 1944) Indian academic. *Globalisation: Gandhi and Swadeshi* (2000)

86 Financial capital is better situated in the global system than industrial capital; once a plant has been built, moving it is difficult.
George Soros (b. 1930) US financier, entrepreneur, and philanthropist. *Atlantic Monthly* (January 1998)

87 All our clients want a common methodology in the marketplace. They want a common language to talk to one another.
Martin Sorrell (b. 1945) British advertising executive. *Financial Times* (March 1997)

88 If we want a vibrant, inclusive global economy there is no alternative...to finding some way between these two extremes. There is no alternative to the pursuit of policies and institutions that will make globalization work...for people.

Lawrence H. Summers (b. 1954) US president of Harvard University, economist, and politician. Referring to the 'false choice' between unfettered global capitalism and protectionism. Speech, School for Advanced International Studies, Washington, D.C. 'Rising to the Challenge of Global Economic Integration' (20 September 2000)

89 Does it really make sense to operate on all continents?

Keiji Tachikawa (b. 1939) Japanese IT executive. *Forbes* (May 2000)

90 We must not fall into the mistake of thinking that it is America that trades with Taiwan or Europe that trades with Asia. The truth is that it is American companies that trade with Taiwanese companies.

Margaret Thatcher (b. 1925) British former prime minister. *Far Eastern Economic Review* (2 September 1993)

91 This 'going into Europe' will not turn out to be the thrilling mutual exchange supposed. It is more like nine middle-aged couples with failing marriages meeting in a darkened bedroom in a Brussels hotel for a group grope.

E.P. Thompson (1924–93) British historian. *Sunday Times* (April 1975)

92 Management in a global environment is increasingly affected by cultural differences.

Fons Trompenaars (b. 1952) Dutch author and management consultant. *Riding the Waves of Culture* (1993)

93 Without establishing the appropriate networks in China, it will be virtually impossible to penetrate a market that is significantly different from that in the Western world.

Rosalie L. Tung (b. 1948) Canadian academic and business educator. *International Management in China: Cross-cultural Issues* (Jan Selmer, ed.; 1998)

94 Capital, technology, and ideas flow these days like quicksilver across national boundaries.

Robert H. Waterman Jr (b. 1936) US consultant and author. *The Frontiers of Excellence* (1994)

95 World peace through world trade.

Thomas J. Watson Sr (1874–1956) US founder and president of IBM. Quoted in *Going International* (Lennie Copeland; 1985)

96 Petrol is much more likely than wheat to be a cause of international conflict.

Simone Weil (1909–43) French philosopher and activist. *The Need for Roots* (1935)

97 What a country calls its vital economic interests are not the things that enable its citizens to live, but the things that enable it to make war.

Simone Weil (1909–43) French philosopher and activist. *The Need for Roots* (1935)

98 Ahead of us are Darwinian shakeouts in every major marketplace, with no losing prizes for the losing companies and nations.

Jack Welch (b. 1935) US former chairman and CEO of General Electric. Speech (1989)

99 If you find a way to get rid of the hierarchical nonsense and allow ideas to flourish, it doesn't matter if you're in Budapest or Beijing.

Jack Welch (b. 1935) US former chairman and CEO of General Electric. *Financial Times* (1 October 1997)

100 Most global corporations have three or four competitors, and you know who they are.

Jack Welch (b. 1935) US former chairman and CEO of General Electric. *Harvard Business Review* (September–October 1989)

101 The United States is just one part of a global marketplace today. There isn't any offshore anymore; it's all onshore.

Walter Wriston (b. 1919) US banker. *US News & World Report* (1987)

102 Sooner or later, we'll be part of the EU. We have to start establishing ourselves as a regional brand now.

Peter Zwack (b. 1928) Hungarian business executive. *Forbes* (April 2000)

GOALS AND OBJECTIVES

1 A good goal is like a strenuous exercise—it makes you stretch.

Mary Kay Ash (1915–2001) US entrepreneur, business executive, and founder of Mary Kay Cosmetics. *On People Management* (1984)

2 Goals too clearly defined can become blinkers.

Mary Catherine Bateson (b. 1939) US anthropologist. *Composing a Life* (1989)

3 Men do not live only by fighting evils. They live by positive goals, individual and collective, a vast variety of them, seldom predictable, at times incompatible.

Isaiah Berlin (1909–97) British philosopher. 'Political Ideas in the Twentieth Century', *Four Essays on Liberty* (1969)

4 Ah, but a man's reach should exceed his grasp, Or what's a heaven for?

Robert Browning (1812–89) British poet. 'Andrea del Sarto' (1855), l. 97

5 Make no effort to increase fortune, but spend the surplus each year for benevolent purposes. Cast aside business forever...get a thorough education.

Andrew Carnegie (1835–1919) US industrialist and philanthropist. Written in a New York hotel, the memorandum outlined his strategy for retiring from business in 1870, aged 35. In the event it was not until 1901 that he stopped actively acquiring wealth. Personal memorandum (1868)

6 When you meet someone better than yourself, turn your thoughts to becoming his equal. When you meet someone not as good as you are, look within and examine your own self.

Confucius (551–479 BC) Chinese philosopher, administrator, and writer. *Analects* (?500 BC)

7 Of all the things I've done, the most vital is coordinating the talents of those who work for us and pointing them towards a certain goal.
Walt Disney (1901–66) US entertainment entrepreneur and founder of the Walt Disney Company. Quoted in *The Disney Version* (Richard Schickel; 1968)

8 The great majority of executives tend to focus downward. They are occupied with efforts rather than with results...The effective executive focuses on contribution. He looks...outward towards goals.
Peter F. Drucker (b. 1909) US management consultant and academic. *The Effective Executive* (1967), ch. 3

9 I will build a motor car for the great multitude...constructed of the best materials...so low in price that no man making a good salary will be unable to own one.
Henry Ford (1863–1947) US industrialist, car manufacturer, and founder of Ford Motor Company. Quoted in 'The Businessmen of the Century', *Fortune* (22 November 1999)

10 Despair is the prize one pays for setting oneself an impossible aim.
Graham Greene (1904–91) British novelist. *The Heart of the Matter* (1948)

11 Only he who keeps his eye fixed on the far horizon will find his right road.
Dag Hammarskjöld (1905–61) Swedish politician, writer, and UN Secretary-General. *Markings* (Leif Sjöberg and W.H. Auden, tr.; 1964)

12 Our vision controls the way we think and, therefore, the way we act...the vision we have of our jobs determines what we do and the opportunities we see or don't see.
Charles G. Koch (b. 1935) US management theorist, author, chairman and CEO of Koch Industries. 'The Future of American Business' (March 1996)

13 The goal of a big business person should be to create a new organization that feels and operates like a smaller business, yet retains the resource advantages of big business.
John P. Kotter (b. 1947) US writer. *The New Rules* (1995)

14 It is my hope someday to build houses in which our work-people will be able to live...and in which they will learn that there is more enjoyment in life than in the mere going to and returning from work.
Lord Leverhulme (1851–1925) British entrepreneur, philanthropist, and co-founder of Unilever. On cutting the first sod at the site of his new Port Sunlight factory; Port Sunlight subsequently became the home for his model workers' community. Speech, Port Sunlight, near Liverpool, England (1888)

15 If you would hit the mark, you must aim a little above it;
Every arrow that flies feels the attraction of earth.
Henry Wadsworth Longfellow (1807–82) US poet. 'Elegaic Verse' (1880)

16 Commitment to objectives is a function of the rewards associated with their achievement.
Douglas McGregor (1906–64) US academic, educator, and management theorist. *The Human Side of Enterprise* (1960)

17 I believe a person of action...an administrator if you will, should put more weight on contemplation, should put more weight on establishing values in his mind, establishing goals and objectives for himself, for his organization and those he's associated with.
Robert S. McNamara (b. 1916) US politician and president of the World Bank. Interview, Conversations with History series, Institute of International Studies, University of California, Berkeley. 'A Life in Public Service' (16 April 1996)

18 In the foundation and development of a successful enterprise there must be a single-minded pursuit of financial profit.
C. Northcote Parkinson (1909–93) British political scientist and author. Quoted in *Famous Financial Fiascoes* (J. Train; 1995)

19 Like many businessmen of genius he learned that free competition was wasteful, monopoly efficient. And so he simply set about achieving that efficient monopoly.
Mario Puzo (1920–99) US novelist. Referring to Don Vito Corleone. *The Godfather* (1969), bk 3, ch. 14

20 If companies are in business solely to make money, you can't fully trust whatever else they do or say...The whole sense of fun is lost, the whole sense of play, of derring-do.
Anita Roddick (b. 1942) British entrepreneur and founder of The Body Shop. *Body and Soul* (co-written with Russell Miller; 1991)

21 If the business is to accomplish all that the Directors desire in combining social progress with commerical success, the entire body of workers must be animated by a common aim.
Joseph Rowntree (1836–1925) British confectionary entrepreneur, philanthropist, and social reformer. Editorial, *Cocoa Works Magazine* (1902)

22 There are two things to aim at in life: first, to get what you want; and, after that, to enjoy it. Only the wisest of mankind achieve the second.
Logan Pearsall Smith (1865–1946) British essayist and critic. 'Life and Human Nature', *Afterthoughts* (1931)

23 We can chart the path to the future clearly and wisely only when we know the path which has led to the present.
Adlai E. Stevenson (1900–65) US statesman and author. Speech, Richmond, Virginia (20 September 1952)

24 In an economy where for the first time jobs are looking for people...ensuring that no American is left behind is as much an economic as a moral imperative.
Lawrence H. Summers (b. 1954) US president of Harvard University, economist, and politician. Speech, Washington, D.C. 'Making the Right Choices for America's Long-term Prosperity' (19 September 2000)

25 In the 21st century, successful companies will need to develop new approaches for addressing key social and environmental concerns. They will need to develop new products and to identify new markets. They will need to work with others in developing innovative and creative solutions.

Jeroen Van der Veer (b. 1947) Dutch Advisory Director of Unilever, vice-chairman of the Royal Dutch/Shell Group, and president of Royal Dutch Petroleum Company. Speech, 'Earning the Licence to Grow' (26 November 1999)

26 There will always be those who argue that the role of business is purely the narrow pursuit of profit, regardless of the consequences. This view has been around since the 19th century...Today, it's a curiously outdated and old-fashioned view.

Jeroen Van der Veer (b. 1947) Dutch Advisory Director of Unilever, vice-chairman of the Royal Dutch/Shell Group, and president of Royal Dutch Petroleum Company. Speech, 'Earning the Licence to Grow' (26 November 1999)

27 Fulfillment is the nuts and bolts of any mail-order or online business.

Lillian Vernon (b. 1927) US entrepreneur and CEO of Lillian Vernon Corporation. 'Mentor FAQs', *Inc.* (2000)

28 The mantra of 'execute, execute, execute, speed, speed, speed' seems to preclude any consideration of what we are speeding toward. That's sort of like saying, 'Don't bother me with the facts—I'm busy executing them'.

Jay S. Walker, US entrepreneur and founder of Priceline.com, CEO of Walker Digital Corporation. Interview, *Strategy + Business* (January–March 2000)

29 Dreams have their place in management activity, but they need to be kept severely under control.

Arnold Weinstock (1924–2002) British managing director of General Electric Company. *Financial Times* (30 December 1989)

GOVERNMENTS

1 I will undoubtedly have to seek what is known as gainful employment, which I am glad to say does not describe holding public office.

Dean Acheson (1893–1971) US statesman. *Time* (December 1952)

2 The business of the Civil Service is the orderly management of decline.

William Armstrong (1915–80) British civil servant. 1973. Quoted in *Whitehall* (Peter Hennessey; 1990)

3 Governments of the Industrial World, you weary giants of flesh and steel, I come from Cyberspace...On behalf of the future, I ask you of the past to leave us alone...You have no sovereignty where we gather.

John Perry Barlow (b. 1947) US academic, lyricist, and writer. 'A Declaration of the Independence of Cyberspace' (8 February 1996)

4 It is with government as with medicine, its only business is the choice of evils. Every law is an evil, for every law is an infraction of liberty.

Jeremy Bentham (1748–1832) British philosopher, economist, and jurist. *Principles of Legislation* (1789)

5 The state is or can be master of money, but in a free society it is master of very little else.

William Henry Beveridge (1879–1963) British economist and social reformer. *Voluntary Action* (1948)

6 An effective antitrust enforcement program promotes innovation by, among other things, reducing barriers to entry. When antitrust enforcement is a reality, potential entrants have less reason to fear market exclusion by existing firms.

Anne K. Bingaman (b. 1943) US lawyer. Speech, University of Kansas Law School (19 September 1996)

7 There is most definitely a role for government in the innovative process. The market does not do everything well.

Anne K. Bingaman (b. 1943) US lawyer. Speech, University of Kansas Law School (19 September 1996)

8 The task of government policy is not to prejudge winners but to make sure that neither private nor public restraints narrow the potential sources of innovation.

Anne K. Bingaman (b. 1943) US lawyer. Speech, University of Kansas Law School (19 September 1996)

9 Where consumer desires are uncertain, and the technology is as yet undeveloped, we should not lose sight of our experience— governments generally do not do well at picking winners and losers from among competing technologies.

Anne K. Bingaman (b. 1943) US lawyer. Speech, University of Kansas Law School (19 September 1996)

10 The public policy questions raised by the growth of the new economy...may turn out to be much more profound than many have yet realised...helping people...is not about protection but empowerment. An economy based on knowledge is one where people are the greatest national resource.

Tony Blair (b. 1953) British prime minister. January 2000. Speech, World Economic Forum, Davos, Switzerland. Quoted in *World Link* (March/April 2000)

11 The problem in government with individual civil servants is that when they ask their boss...'What do you want to accomplish', they're told, 'Just don't mess things up'. Boy, that covers a lot of ground because things are already messed up.

Kenneth Blanchard (b. 1939) US management theorist and author. *Ken Blanchard's Profiles of Success* (1996)

12 This is a conflict without battlefields or beachheads, a conflict with opponents who believe they are invisible.

George W. Bush (b. 1946) US president. Referring to terrorist attacks on US, 11 September 2001. Speech (15 September 2001)

13 The only good government...is a bad one in a hell of a fright.

Joyce Cary (1888–1957) British writer. *The Horse's Mouth* (1944), ch. 32

14 Corruption can undermine government in major industrial countries as well as in developing countries. It destroys the wealth of industry for limited returns to the minority who perpetrate it.

Lynda Chalker (b. 1942) British politician. 'Public Sector Corruption from an International Perspective'. Speech, University of Glasgow, Scotland (19 February 1999)

15 Governments are facing more and more competition...they are losing power to multinational businesses, commercial organizations, and big media, as well as to small businesses that operate worldwide over the Net.
Esther Dyson (b. 1951) US knowledge entrepreneur and government adviser. Speech at the 4th Workshop on Inventing the Organisation of the 21st Century, Munich, Germany. 'The Future of Truth—The End of the "Official Story"' (February 1998)

16 If the government is big enough to give you everything you want, it is big enough to take away everything you have.
Gerald Ford (b. 1913) US former president. Quoted in *If Elected* (J.F. Parker; 1960)

17 Despite efforts by government throughout the years to prevent concentration in industry, the regulators are bringing us to the point where only the largest companies can survive.
Henry Ford (1919–87) US car manufacturer and CEO of Ford Motor Company. 'The High Cost of Regulation', *Newsweek* (20 March 1978)

18 There's only one place where inflation is made: that's in Washington.
Milton Friedman (b. 1912) US economist and winner of the 1976 Nobel Prize in Economics. 1977. Attrib.

19 We sense that our lives are shaped and that government is guided by the modern corporation....In the Age of Uncertainty the corporation is a major source of uncertainty. It leaves men wondering how and by whom and to what end they are ruled.
J.K. Galbraith (b. 1908) US economist and diplomat. *The Age of Uncertainty* (1977), ch. 9

20 If the government, usually the largest 'business' in any country, is a leader in the use of technology, it will automatically lift the country's technical skills and drive the move to an information market.
Bill Gates (b. 1955) US entrepreneur, chairman and CEO of Microsoft. *Business@the Speed of Thought* (co-written with Collins Hemingway; 1999)

21 Government has an essential role to play in investing in the human resources and infrastructure needed to develop an entrepreneurial culture.
Anthony Giddens (b. 1938) British sociologist and author. *The Third Way: The Renewal of Social Democracy* (1998)

22 Business has a clear interest in minimising government regulation. It is therefore counterproductive for managers to take the position that if something is not illegal it is not immoral.
Damian Grace (b. 1950) Australian academic. *Australian Problems and Cases* (1995)

23 This would, at a stroke, reduce the rise in prices, increase production and reduce unemployment.
Edward Heath (b. 1916) British prime minister. Referring to a government policy intended to deal with United Kingdom economic problems. Press release (June 1970)

24 If the mood of the country is for fiscal responsibility then let's get at that area of government which is the biggest waster of funds—the Defense Dept.
Elizabeth Holtzman (b. 1941) US politician. Quoted in *American Political Women* (E. Stineman; 1980)

25 You cannot extend the mastery of the Government over the daily working life of a people without at the same time making it the master of people's souls and thoughts.
Herbert Hoover (1874–1964) US president. Presidential campaign speech, New York (22 October 1928)

26 Laws for the regulation of trade should be most carefully scanned. That which hampers, limits, cripples, and retards must be done away with.
Elbert Hubbard (1856–1915) US humorist. *Notebook* (1927)

27 One of the things the government can't do is run anything. The only things our government runs are the post office and the railroads, and both of them are bankrupt.
Lee Iacocca (b. 1924) US president of Ford Motor Company, chairman and CEO of Chrysler Corporation. Remark (17 June 1973)

28 Willingness to accept direction from authorities makes guidance at successive stages of socio-economic and technological development possible.
Erdener Kaynak (b. 1947) Turkish business educator and author. *Global Business: Asia-Pacific Dimensions* (co-edited with Kam Hou-Lee; 1989)

29 It is a function of government to invent philosophies to explain the demands of its own convenience.
Murray Kempton (1917–97) US journalist. *America Comes of Middle Age* (1963)

30 With perfect citizens, any government is good.
Stephen Leacock (1869–1944) Canadian humorist, essayist, economist, and historian. 'The Unsolved Riddle of Social Justice' (1920)

31 Government has no other end but the preservation of property.
John Locke (1632–1704) English philosopher and political thinker. *Second Treatise on Civil Government* (1690)

32 Government could do better, it's not perfect, but I simply want to tell you, if you want to talk about competence, if you want to talk about dedication, it does at least as well as the private sector, and both could do better and both should do better.
Robert S. McNamara (b. 1916) US politician and president of the World Bank. Interview, Conversations with History series, Institute of International Studies, University of California, Berkeley. 'A Life in Public Service' (16 April 1996)

33 Truth is the glue that holds governments together. Compromise is the oil that makes governments go.
Karl Augustus Menninger (1893–1990) US psychiatrist. Speech, US House of Representatives (1973)

34 My government's number one priority is poverty reduction and we strongly believe that this can be achieved through an active and vibrant private sector.
Bakili Muluzi (b. 1943) Malawian president. Speech, Southern Africa Business Association, London (5 May 2000)

35 I think the government has an important role to play in the growth of the software industry as long as it becomes a catalyst and not a controlling authority.
Narayana Murthy (b. 1946) Indian founder and CEO of Infosys. Quoted in *www.rediff.com* (2000)

36 It is a popular delusion that the government wastes vast amounts of money through inefficiency and sloth. Enormous effort and elaborate planning are required to waste this much money.
P.J. O'Rourke (b. 1947) US humorist and journalist. *Parliament of Whores* (1991)

37 Japan took its success for granted. Now it does not really want to face, does not know how to face, the empty charade of subsidy and protection.
Kenichi Ohmae (b. 1943) Japanese management consultant and theorist. *Harvard Business Review* (May–June 1995)

38 Government, like dress, is the badge of lost innocence...man finds it necessary to surrender up a part of his property to furnish means for the protection of the rest.
Thomas Paine (1737–1809) British politician, philosopher, and writer. *Common Sense* (1776)

39 I draw my idea of the form of government from a principle in nature...that the more simple any thing is, the less liable it is to be disordered, and the easier repaired when disordered.
Thomas Paine (1737–1809) British politician, philosopher, and writer. *Common Sense* (1776)

40 The rulers of the state are the only ones who should have the privilege of lying, either at home or abroad.
Plato (?428–?347 BC) Greek philosopher. *The Republic* (?370 BC)

41 Government should be less concerned with economies than with measures necessary for the prosperity of the kingdom...great expenditures may cease to be excessive if they lead to an increase in wealth.
François Quesnay (1694–1774) French political economist. *General Rules for the Economic Government of an Agricultural Kingdom* (1757)

42 The only institution that can mortgage your future without your knowledge or consent: government securities...are promissory notes on future tax receipts, i.e., on your future production.
Ayn Rand (1905–82) US writer. *Philosophy: Who Needs It?* (1982)

43 One way to make sure crime doesn't pay would be to let the government run it.
Ronald Reagan (b. 1911) US former president and actor. Interview (1967)

44 And that, in my view, is what the whole controversy comes down to. Are you entitled to the fruits of your own labour, or does government have some presumptive right to spend and spend and spend?
Ronald Reagan (b. 1911) US former president and actor. *Speaking My Mind* (1990)

45 The Americans were not put on this earth to become managers of decline.
Ronald Reagan (b. 1911) US former president and actor. *Speaking My Mind* (1990)

46 We've polished up the American dream.
Ronald Reagan (b. 1911) US former president and actor. *Speaking My Mind* (1990)

47 Government does not solve problems; it subsidizes them.
Ronald Reagan (b. 1911) US former president and actor. 11 December 1972. Speech

48 Financial capital adapts much more easily to changed circumstances than do people. People often have the wrong skills, or no skills...or they're burdened with costs and responsibilities that make it hard for them to work. Government must be actively involved— helping them over the fence.
Robert Reich (b. 1946) US economist and politician. 'Under Construction', *World Link* (January/February 2000)

49 Cynics about government have much to be cynical about.
Alice M. Rivlin (b. 1931) US economist. *Reviving the American Dream* (1992)

50 Unemployment is a reproach to a democratic government.
Joan Robinson (1903–83) British economist. Quoted in 'What has become of the Keynsian Revolution?', *Essays on John Maynard Keynes* (Milo Keynes, ed.; 1975)

51 Governments can err. Presidents do make mistakes, but...better the occasional faults of a Government that lives in a spirit of charity than the consistent omissions of a Government frozen in the ice of its own indifference.
Franklin D. Roosevelt (1882–1945) US president. Speech accepting re-nomination for a second presidential term, Philadelphia (27 June 1936)

52 In a technocratic society political authority is based upon a mystique of scientific expertise. That is what supposedly guarantees the competence of the state and private corporations to keep an intricate industrial economy functioning.
Theodore Roszak (1933–81) US historian, writer, and editor. *Person/Plant: The Creative Disintegration of Industrial Society* (1977), Introduction

53 The most powerful force possessed by the individual citizen is her own government. Or governments because a multiplicity of levels means a multiplicity of strengths.
John Ralston Saul (b. 1947) Canadian writer. *The Unconscious Civilization* (1995)

54 A government which robs Peter to pay Paul can always depend on the support of Paul.
George Bernard Shaw (1856–1950) Irish writer and critic. *Everybody's Political What's What?* (1944)

55 There is no art which one government sooner learns of another than that of draining money from the pockets of the people.
Adam Smith (1723–90) British economist and philosopher. *An Inquiry into the Nature and Causes of the Wealth of Nations* (1776)

56 The advent of a new economy fundamentally changes the stakes involved in the choice of fiscal policy. In a world rich with investment opportunities...the importance of running a surplus and pursuing prudent policies becomes much, much greater.
Lawrence H. Summers (b. 1954) US president of Harvard University, economist, and politician. Speech, Washington, D.C. 'Making the Right Choices for America's Long-term Prosperity' (19 September 2000)

57 The administration (of a nation) must be entrusted to experts. We must not look upon these experts as grand presidents and ministers, but simply as our chauffeurs, as guards at the gate, as cooks, physicians, carpenters, or tailors.
Sun Yat-Sen (1866–1925) Chinese revolutionary leader. *The Three Principles of the People* (1924)

58 Trade and commerce, if they were not made of india-rubber, would never manage to bounce over obstacles which legislators are continually putting in their way.
Henry David Thoreau (1817–62) US writer. 'Resistance to Civil Government' (1849)

59 Government should focus on infrastructure investment, investment in human skills, and investment in generating the knowledge that creates new industries. The issue is not government, big or small, but investment versus consumption.
Lester Thurow (b. 1938) US economist, management theorist, and writer. *Reclaiming Prosperity: A Blueprint for Progressive Economic Reform* (1996), Preface

60 There is an important role for government in future economic success. It has to be the provider of the long-tailed social investments that underlie private economic success in an era of manmade brainpower industries.
Lester Thurow (b. 1938) US economist, management theorist, and writer. *Reclaiming Prosperity: A Blueprint for Progressive Economic Reform* (1996), Preface

61 You can't expect a viable economy if the only object of government policy is to be re-elected every four years.
Arnold Weinstock (1924–2002) British managing director of General Electric Company. *Independent* (20 December 1986)

GREED

1 Nothing defines human beings better than their willingness to do irrational things in the pursuit of phenomenally unlikely payoffs.
Scott Adams (b. 1957) US cartoonist and humorist. *The Dilbert Principle* (1996)

2 Some men turn every quality or art into a means of making money; this they conceive to be the end, and to the promotion of the end all things must contribute.
Aristotle (384–322 BC) Greek philosopher and scientist. *Politics* (4th century BC), bk 1

3 The fact that people will be full of greed, fear, or folly is predictable. The sequence is not predictable.
Warren Buffett (b. 1930) US entrepreneur and financier. *Channels* (1986)

4 Men who continue hoarding great sums all their lives, the proper use of which for the public ends would work good to the community, should be made to feel that the community, in the form of the state, cannot thus be deprived of its proper share. By taxing estates heavily at death the state marks its condemnation of the selfish millionaire's unworthy life.
Andrew Carnegie (1835–1919) US industrialist and philanthropist. 'Wealth', *North American Review* (June 1889)

5 The evils of our big businesses have not come because Americans are prone to cheat, because they want to get the better of their fellows, because their greed is inordinate, their ambition domineering. Individuals have not been to blame, but our whole system.
Mary Parker Follett (1868–1933) US management thinker and author. *The New State* (1918)

6 What kind of society isn't structured on greed?
Milton Friedman (b. 1912) US economist and winner of the 1976 Nobel Prize in Economics. *There's No Such Thing as a Free Lunch* (1975)

7 What is a man if he is not a thief who openly charges as much as he can for the goods he sells.
Mahatma Gandhi (1869–1948) Indian nationalist leader and philosopher. *Non-Violence in Peace and War* (1948)

8 My father said: 'You must never try to make all the money that's in a deal. Let the other fellow make some money too, because if you have a reputation for always making all the money...you won't make many deals'.
J. Paul Getty (1892–1976) US entrepreneur, oil industry executive, and financier. 1973–74. Referring to his father, George Franklin Getty, who was also a successful oil business executive. Quoted in *Getty on Getty* (Somerset de Chair; 1989), ch. 2

9 Greed is even more contagious than fear.
Bud Hadfield (b. 1923) US entrepreneur and founder of Kwik Kopy. *Wealth within Reach: Winning Strategies for Success from the Unconventional Wisdom of Bud Hadfield* (1995)

10 The Lord gave us farmers two hands so we could grab as much as we could with both of them.
Joseph Heller (1923–99) US novelist. *Catch 22* (1961)

11 Avarice, the spur of industry.
David Hume (1711–76) Scottish philosopher and historian. 'Of Civil Liberty', *Essays* (1741–42)

12 Greed—for lack of a better word—is good. Greed is right. Greed works.
Oliver Stone (b. 1946) US film director and screenwriter. From the film satirising some of the excesses of the 1980s. *Wall Street* (1987)

13 It is morally as bad not to care whether a thing is true or not, so long as it makes you feel good, as it is not to care how you got your money as long as you have got it.
Edwin Way Teale (1899–1980) US naturalist and writer. *Circle of the Seasons* (1953)

14 Many people have called me greedy because of the way I amassed real estate, companies, helicopters, planes, and yachts during the last several years. But what those critics don't know is that these same assets that excite me in the chase often, once they are acquired, leave me bored.
Donald J. Trump (b. 1946) US property developer. *Trump: Surviving at the Top* (co-written with Charles Leerhsen; 1990)

15 The point is that you can't be too greedy.
Donald J. Trump (b. 1946) US property developer. Quoted in *Trump: The Art of the Deal* (co-written with Tony Schwartz; 1987)

16 Money, big money (which is actually a relative concept) is always, under any circumstances, a seduction, a test of morals, a temptation to sin.
Boris Yeltsin (b. 1931) Russian former president. *The Struggle for Russia* (Catherine A. Fitzpatrick, tr.; 1994)

GROWTH

1 Is your company so small you have to do everything for yourself? Wait until you're so big that you can't. That's worse.
Michael Bloomberg (b. 1942) US entrepreneur, business executive, and Mayor of New York. *Bloomberg by Bloomberg* (co-written with Matthew Winkler; 1997)

2 Growth does not always lead a business to build on success. All too often it converts a highly successful business into a mediocre large business.
Richard Branson (b. 1950) British entrepreneur, business executive, and founder of the Virgin Group. Speech to the Institute of Directors, London. 'Growing Bigger While Still Staying Small' (May 1993)

3 The long-accepted goal of the enterprise as being profit-maximisation is surely and steadily being replaced by that of survival and growth objectives.
S.K. Chakraborty (b. 1957) Indian academic. *Management by Objectives: An Integrated Approach* (1976)

4 If you had asked me seven or eight years ago whether there is such a thing as a company that's growing too fast, I probably would have said no. All growth is good and you cannot grow a company too fast. But we learned that this is absolutely not true—there is a level of growth that is not only too fast but dangerous and deadly to a company.
Michael Dell (b. 1965) US chairman and CEO of Dell Computer Corporation. Speech to the Society of American Business Editors and Writers Technology Conference, Dallas. 'Maximum Speed: Lessons Learned from Managing Hypergrowth' (10 September 1998)

5 The strongest principle of growth lies in human choice.
George Eliot (1819–80) British novelist. *Daniel Deronda* (1876)

6 There are as many foolhardy ways to grow as there are to downsize.
Gary Hamel (b. 1954) US academic, business writer, and consultant. *Digital Britain* (January 2000)

7 The growth of a large business is merely a survival of the fittest.
John D. Rockefeller (1839–1937) US industrialist, philanthropist, and founder of Standard Oil. Quoted in *Our Benevolent Feudalism* (W.J. Ghent; 1902)

8 When you consider something 'ideal', you lose the opportunity to improve it.
Shoji Shiba (b. 1933) Japanese academic and author. Quoted in 'Toyota's Fresh Look at JIT [Just-In-Time]', *Financial Times* (10 September 1990)

9 I think you have to place bets and not predict growth rates.
Jack Welch (b. 1935) US former chairman and CEO of General Electric. *Leaders* (1993)

10 If you're interested in creating sustainable growth, sustainable productivity, sustainable morale, you can't do that through autocracy. You can work the numbers for a quarter or a half a year, you can drive people to exhaustion for a few months or a couple of years. But if you haven't focused on creating capacity in the organization, it will die through those efforts.
Walter Wriston (b. 1919) US banker. Interview with Scott London, *US National Public Radio* (November 1996)

HIRING AND FIRING

1 Restructuring: A simple plan instituted from above in which workers are right-sized, downsized, surplused, lateralized, or in the business jargon of the days of yore, fired.
Anonymous. *Fortune* (15 February 1995)

2 To downsize effectively you have to have empathy with the people who are losing their jobs…What you say to them has a lot to do with the attitude of the survivors: whether they see the company as a money-machine or keep their respect for it.
Percy Barnevik (b. 1941) Swedish former CEO of ABB. Interview, *Company Man: The Rise and Fall of Corporate Life* (Anthony Sampson; 1995), ch. 16

3 I believe you can go into any traditionally centralized corporation and cut its headquarters staff by 90 percent in one year.

Percy Barnevik (b. 1941) Swedish former CEO of ABB. *Harvard Business Review* (March/April 1991)

4 Downsizing has negative effects on companies. Early buyouts deplete the number of experienced, talented people, and multiple rounds of layoffs destroy employee commitment. Employees focus on keeping their jobs rather than on doing their best.

Kenneth Blanchard (b. 1939) US management theorist and author. 'Empowerment is the Key', *Quality Digest* (April 1996)

5 Employees throughout downsized companies do not have time to think about new growth opportunities. Nor are they inclined to suggest innovations because their implicit commitment contract with the company has been severed.

Kenneth Blanchard (b. 1939) US management theorist and author. 'Empowerment is the Key', *Quality Digest* (April 1996)

6 In the end we are all sacked and it's always awful. It is as inevitable as death following life. If you are elevated there comes a day when you are demoted.

Alan Clark (1928–99) British politician and diarist. Diary (21 June 1983)

7 We need people to really think about whether it's the fair and right thing to do...no one should lose a job for short-term considerations unnecessary for the long-term well-being of the profitable enterprise.

Bill Clinton (b. 1946) US former president. 4 March 1996. Referring to downsizing. Quoted in 'Bridging the Gap', *Online NewsHour* (20 March 1996)

8 Effective executives fill positions and promote on the basis of what a person can do. They do not make staffing decisions to minimize weaknesses but to maximize strength.

Peter F. Drucker (b. 1909) US management consultant and academic. *The Effective Executive* (1967), ch. 4

9 Two things to help keep one's job. First, let the boss think he's having his own way. Second, let him have it.

Sam Ewing (1920–2001) US author. Quoted in *Wall Street Journal* (4 December 1996)

10 Well sometimes you just don't like somebody.

Henry Ford (1919–87) US car manufacturer and CEO of Ford Motor Company. Referring to his reasons for sacking Lee Iacocca, then president of Ford, in 1978. Quoted in *Iacocca: An Autobiography* (Lee Iacocca; 1984)

11 Delayering and destaffing do not by themselves provide durable solutions to performance problems...Reduction of corporate overheads merely provides one-time relief and buys some time.

Sumantra Ghoshal (b. 1946) Indian academic and management theorist. 'Building the Entrepreneurial

Corporation', *The Financial Times Handbook of Management* (co-written with Christopher A. Bartlett; 1990)

12 The inexorable forces of competition and change catch up again with companies that restructure but do not revitalize, that cut people but do not fundamentally alter their ways of working.

Sumantra Ghoshal (b. 1946) Indian academic and management theorist. 'Building the Entrepreneurial Corporation', *The Financial Times Handbook of Management* (co-written with Christopher A. Bartlett; 1990)

13 There must be something wrong with a system where it pays to be sacked.

Jo Grimond (1913–93) British politician. Quoted in 'Sayings of the Week', *Observer* (1 May 1983)

14 If you have made someone redundant it is your responsibility to help them... You have removed the certainties from their life and your personal support and help is the least you can provide in return.

John Harvey-Jones (b. 1924) British management adviser, author, and former chairman of ICI. *All Together Now* (1994), ch. 10

15 People in the company are almost never fired...they are encouraged to retire early or are eased aside into hollow, insignificant positions with fake functions and no authority, where they are sheepish and unhappy for as long as they remain.

Joseph Heller (1923–99) US novelist. *Something Happened* (1974)

16 You do not get good people if you lay off half your workforce just because one year the economy isn't very good and then you hire them back.

Kenneth Iverson (1925–2002) US industrialist, chairman and CEO of Nucor Corporation. Speech (5 February 1996)

17 There was no question of appointing a man who was not fully trained...everything depended on his being the best man for the job before he set off. And so you took great care in selecting him.

Anthony Jay (b. 1930) British author and business consultant. *Management Machiavelli* (1970)

18 We had to lay some people off...every one that I had to do it personally, I thought, 'A lot of these fathers and mothers are going to have to...tell their families they just lost their jobs'. And I'd never really thought about that before.

Steve Jobs (b. 1955) US entrepreneur, co-founder and CEO of Apple Computer Company, and CEO of Pixar. Referring to his return to Apple and the impact on his outlook of being married and a father. Quoted in 'Steve's Two Jobs', *Time* (Michael Krantz; 18 October 1999)

19 Modern heretics are not burned at the stake. They are relegated to backwaters or pressured to resign.

Art Kleiner (b. 1954) US business writer. *The Age of Heretics* (1996)

20 Downsizing suddenly became news because for the first time, white-collar, college-educated workers were being fired in large numbers, even while skilled machinists and other blue-collar workers were in demand.
Paul R. Krugman (b. 1953) US economist. *New York Times Magazine* (30 September 1996)

21 'You're fired!' No other words can so easily and succinctly reduce a confident, self-assured executive to an insecure, groveling shred of his former self.
Frank P. Louchheim (b. 1923) US business executive. 'The Art of Getting Fired', *Wall Street Journal* (16 July 1984)

22 Handled creatively, getting fired allows an executive...to actually experience a sense of relief that he never wanted the job he has lost.
Frank P. Louchheim (b. 1923) US business executive. 'The Art of Getting Fired', *Wall Street Journal* (16 July 1984)

23 Recession isn't the fault of the workers. If management takes the risk of hiring them, we have to take the responsibility for them.
Akio Morita (1921–99) Japanese business executive. *Daily Telegraph* (24 February 1982)

24 There is ceasing to be the intimacy between masters and men...we scarcely know anything of men who have come into our service of late years because strangers negotiate most of the arrangements which are made.
Samuel Morley (1809–86) British textile entrepreneur, politician, and philanthropist. 1878. Quoted in *Enlightened Entrepreneurs* (Ian Campbell Bradley; 1987), ch. 3

25 I admit I have a reputation for firing editors, but the facts do not support it...I have only ever sacked one editor of *The Australian*—although I admit I sacked him twice.
Rupert Murdoch (b. 1931) US CEO of News Corporation. November 1972. Quoted in *Good Times, Bad Times* (Harold Evans; 1983)

26 Show me a man who enjoys firing people and I'll show you a charlatan or a sadist.
Tony O'Reilly (b. 1936) Irish executive chairman of Independent News & Media and former CEO of Heinz Corporation. Quoted in *BusinessWeek* (23 October 1987)

27 Nothing bad's going to happen to us. If we get fired, it's not failure; it's a midlife vocational assessment.
P.J. O'Rourke (b. 1947) US humorist and journalist. *Rolling Stone* (30 November 1989)

28 Instead of giving contracts to strangers, we decided we could just as well give contracts to our own employees. We would encourage them to leave...and start their own satellite enterprises.
Ricardo Semler (b. 1959) Brazilian business executive and president of Semco. 'Why My Former Employees Still Work For Me', *Harvard Business Review* (January/February 1994)

29 Fire the whole personnel department...Fire the whole purchasing department. They'd hire Einstein and then turn down his requisition for a blackboard.

Robert Townsend (b. 1920) US business executive and author. *Up the Organization* (1970)

30 Unless your company is too large (in which case, break it up into autonomous parts), have a one-girl people department, not a personnel department.
Robert Townsend (b. 1920) US business executive and author. *Up the Organization* (1970)

31 Trahey's Simple Rule: Would you hire you?
Jane Trahey (1923–2000) US copywriter and author. *Women in Advertising* (1979)

HONESTY

1 Unless the client could trust McKinsey, we could not work with them.
Marvin Bower (1903–2003) US CEO of McKinsey & Company. *The Will to Manage* (1966)

2 In recent years, probity has eroded. Many major corporations still play things straight, but a significant and growing number...have come to the view that it's okay to manipulate earnings to satisfy what they believe are Wall Street's desires...many CEOs think this kind of manipulation is not only okay, but actually their *duty*.
Warren Buffett (b. 1930) US entrepreneur and financier. Chairman's Letter to Shareholders, *Berkshire Hathaway 1998 Annual Report* (1 March 1999)

3 You only have to start a job of work to realise how few decent, honest folk there are about.
Anton Chekhov (1860–1904) Russian playwright and short-story writer. *The Cherry Orchard* (1904), Act 2

4 When dealing with complexity and uncertainty, trust and openness become critical.
David L. Dotlich (b. ?1950) US writer. *Action Learning* (co-written with James L. Noel; 1998)

5 If a man carefully examine his thoughts he will be surprised to find out how much he lives in the future.
Ralph Waldo Emerson (1803–82) US essayist, lecturer, and poet. Attrib.

6 Honour sinks where commerce long prevails.
Oliver Goldsmith (1730–74) British playwright, writer, and poet. *The Traveller* (1764)

7 Total commercial honesty always costs something, but total or partial dishonesty will cost more.
Robert Heller (b. 1932) British management writer. *The Supermarketers* (1987)

8 It has always been Enron's policy to be open with its accountants, Arthur Andersen.
Kenneth Lay (b. 1942) US business executive. Referring to Enron's accounting practices, which were later discredited. Quoted in *Guardian* (June 2002)

9 It is the weak and confused who worship the pseudo simplicities of brutal directness.
Marshall McLuhan (1911–80) Canadian sociologist and author. *The Mechanical Bride* (1951)

10 If a brand screws up, honesty with the customer is the best way to recapture support.
Michael Perry (b. 1934) British business executive. *Marketing* (March 2000)

11 Confronting reality—no matter how negative and depressing the process—is the first step towards coming to terms with it.
John Ralston Saul (b. 1947) Canadian writer. *The Unconscious Civilization* (1995)

12 Let those who follow me continue to build with the plumb of Honor, the level of Truth, and the Square of Integrity, Education, Courtesy, and Mutuality.
John Wanamaker (1838–1922) US businessman. 1910. Quoted in *New York Times* (1999)

13 Give me the abrasive guys. They'll tell the truth and they're tough.
Thomas J. Watson Jr (1914–93) US CEO of IBM. *Fortune* (February 1988)

IDEAS

1 Don't worry about people stealing an idea. If it's original, you will have to ram it down their throats.
Howard Aiken (1900–73) US computer engineer and mathematician. Quoted in *Portraits in Silicon* (Robert Slater; 1987)

2 Every man with an idea has at least two or three followers.
Brooks Atkinson (1894–1984) US critic and essayist. *Once Around the Sun* (1951)

3 One of the greatest pains to a human being is the pain of a new idea.
Walter Bagehot (1826–77) British economist and journalist. *Physics and Politics* (1872)

4 Ours is the age of substitutes; instead of language, we have jargon; instead of principles, slogans; and, instead of genuine ideas, bright ideas.
Eric Bentley (b. 1916) British writer. *New Republic* (December 1952)

5 In a restless, creative business with an emphasis on experiment and development, ideas are the lifeblood.
Richard Branson (b. 1950) British entrepreneur, business executive, and founder of the Virgin Group. Speech to the Institute of Directors, London. 'Growing Bigger While Still Staying Small' (May 1993)

6 I can't understand why people are frightened of new ideas. I'm frightened of the old ones.
John Cage (1912–92) US composer. Quoted in *Conversing with Cage* (1988)

7 Nothing is more dangerous than an idea, when you only have one idea.
Émile-August Chartier (1868–1951) French philosopher. *Propos sur la Religion* (1938)

8 By and large our culture is a culture of corpses—dead people. The whole thrust of our interface with thinking is in historical terms.

Edward de Bono (b. 1933) British creative-thinking theorist, educator, and writer. *International Management* (March 1988)

9 Ideas are a commodity. Execution of them is not.
Michael Dell (b. 1965) US chairman and CEO of Dell Computer Corporation. *Fortune* (1993)

10 The important thing is that a new idea should develop out of what is already there so that it soon becomes an old acquaintance.
Penelope Fitzgerald (1916–2000) British novelist and biographer. *The Gate of Angels* (1990)

11 Ideas do not rule the world. But it is because the world has ideas that it is not passively ruled by those who are its leaders or those who would like to teach it...what it must think.
Michel Foucault (1926–84) French philosopher. 'Les Reportages d'Idées', *Corriere della Sera* (12 November 1978)

12 All too often, executives expect every new idea or experiment to yield a big payoff. Such an expectation...makes a company overly conservative, and will quickly drain the portfolio of ideas and...of experiments of many interesting strategic options.
Gary Hamel (b. 1954) US academic, business writer, and consultant. Interview, *Barnes & Noble* (September 2000)

13 Ideas are useless unless used.
Theodore Levitt (b. 1925) US management theorist, writer, and editor. Article title, *Inc.* (February 1981)

14 Field theory is a method of analyzing causal relations and of building scientific constructs.
Kurt Lewin (1890–1947) US author. *Field Theory in Social Science: Selected Theoretical Papers* (D. Cartwright, ed.; 1951)

15 There is nothing so practical as a good theory.
Kurt Lewin (1890–1947) US author. *Field Theory in Social Science: Selected Theoretical Papers* (D. Cartwright, ed.; 1951)

16 An idea isn't responsible for the people who believe in it.
Don Marquis (1878–1937) US journalist and humorist. Attrib.

17 The newness of an idea matters less than its ease of use.
Mari Matsunaga (b. 1954) Japanese IT designer. *Fortune* (October 2000)

18 If new ideas are the lifeblood of any thriving organization...managers must learn to revere, not merely tolerate, the people who come up with the ideas.
Mark McCormack (1930–2003) US entrepreneur, founder and CEO of the International Management Group. *McCormack on Managing* (1985)

19 If you go through life convinced that your way is always best, all the new ideas in the world will pass you by.
Akio Morita (1921–99) Japanese business executive. *Made in Japan* (1986)

20 The most beautiful thing we can experience is the mysterious. It is the source of all true art and science.

William S. Paley (1901–90) US founder of Columbia Broadcasting Corporation. *What I Believe* (1930)

21 In the long run, no ideas, no information.
Theodore Roszak (1933–81) US historian, writer, and editor. *The Cult of Information* (1994)

22 Once the idea of inevitability is accepted the reality of inevitability is created.
Vandana Shiva (b. 1944) Indian academic. *Globalisation: Gandhi and Swadeshi* (2000)

23 Never dump a good idea on a conference table. It will belong to the conference.
Jane Trahey (1923–2000) US copywriter and author. *New York Times* (18 September 1977)

24 When an idea is not robust enough to stand expression in simple terms, it is a sign that it should be rejected.
Luc de Clapiers Vauvenargues (1715–47) French soldier and writer. *Reflections and Maxims* (1746)

25 You are always going to have people who copy things that work.
Jay S. Walker, US entrepreneur and founder of Priceline.com, CEO of Walker Digital Corporation. 'It's a Completely New Way of Buying', *BusinessWeek* (Diane Brady; 1999)

26 The only ideas that count are 'A' ideas. There is no second place. That means we have to get everybody in the organization involved. If you do that right, the best ideas will rise to the top.
Jack Welch (b. 1935) US former chairman and CEO of General Electric. 'GE Keeps These Ideas Coming', *Fortune* (Thomas A. Stewart; 1991)

27 Every really new idea looks crazy at first.
A.N. Whitehead (1861–1947) British philosopher and mathematician. *An Introduction to Mathematics* (1911)

28 Sometimes the first step is the hardest: coming up with an idea. Coming up with an idea should be like sitting on a pin—it should make you jump up and do something.
Kemmons Wilson (1913–2003) US entrepreneur, founder and chairman of Holiday Inn. 'What Makes for Success?', *Imprimis* (March 1997)

29 We're not awarding ideas awards. We're creating businesses.
Ann Winblad (b. 1953) US venture capitalist. *Wall Street Journal* (1999)

30 The only people in the whole world who can change things are those who can sell ideas.
Lois Wyse (b. 1926) US advertising executive and writer. *The Rosemary Touch* (1974)

IMAGE

1 We get business that we wouldn't get if I were an inanimate object.
Michael Bloomberg (b. 1942) US entrepreneur, business executive, and Mayor of New York. *Financial Times* (May 1997)

2 If you want to make money, hold your nose and go to Wall Street.
Warren Buffett (b. 1930) US entrepreneur and financier. *Newsday* (August 1991)

3 It was something you only spoke of in hushed tones. Advertising is a bit of an anathema.
Michael Bungey (b. 1940) British advertising executive. *Sunday Times* (August 2000)

4 Clothes are our weapons, our challenges, and our visible insult.
Angela Carter (1940–92) British novelist, short-story writer, and essayist. *Nothing Sacred* (1982)

5 It's very straightforward and it's very much part of who we are—that's why we chose a short word for our name.
Barbara Cassani (b. 1960) US former CEO of Go. Referring to Go, the budget airline. *Marketing* (August 2000)

6 There is an idea, broadly held on Wall Street, that names with X's are more memorable and tend to capture the attention of analysts. It is not held by us.
Clive Chajet (b. 1937) US management consultant. On advising clients about corporate name changes. 'How American Can Become Primerica', *New York Times* (Lisa Belkin; 1987)

7 Corporate identities must not be shortlived.
Clive Chajet (b. 1937) US management consultant. 'Why Corporate Identity Can't Be Designed', *The Manager* (David Uren; 2000)

8 They proactively protected the consumers. I don't think Bridgestone/Firestone has had as a priority nourishing their corporate image to withstand serious problems like this.
Clive Chajet (b. 1937) US management consultant. 'Delay in Tire-recall Decried', *The Topeka Capital-Journal* (Vicki Brown; 2000)

9 The best of us here have more rough than polished diamond.
Lord Chesterfield (1694–1773) English statesman, orator, and letter writer. Letter (November 1748)

10 Keep up appearances; there lies the test. The world will give thee credit for the rest.
Charles Churchill (1731–64) British curate and satirist. *Night* (1761)

11 Toughness doesn't have to come in a pinstripe suit.
Dianne Feinstein (b. 1933) US politician. *Time* (June 1984)

12 I am a Ford, not a Lincoln.
Gerald Ford (b. 1913) US former president. Speech (December 1973)

13 We don't know how to sell products based on performance. Everything we sell, we sell based on image.
Roberto Goizueta (1931–97) US CEO of Coca-Cola. *Wall Street Journal* (February 1997)

14 Our old stores looked like museums.
Farooq Kathwari (b. 1944) Indian entrepreneur and CEO of Ethan Allen. *Forbes* (April 1998)

15 Haute Couture should be fun, foolish, and almost unwearable.
Christian Lacroix (b. 1951) French couturier. *Observer* (December 1987)

16 If people don't want to listen to you, what makes you think they want to hear from your sweater.

Fran Lebowitz (b. 1950) US writer and columnist. *Metropolitan Life* (1978)

17 If you're in jazz and more than ten people like you, you're labelled commercial.

Herbie Mann (b. 1930) US musician. *Serious Music and All That Jazz* (1969)

18 They gave me star treatment when I was making a lot of money. But I was just as good when I was poor.

Bob Marley (1945–81) Jamaican musician. Quoted in *True Confessions* (Jon Winokar; 1992)

19 For exercise, I wind my watch.

Robert Maxwell (1923–91) British publisher, business executive, and politician. Quoted in *Time* (28 November 1988)

20 We in the free world can do great things. We proved it in Japan by changing the image of 'made in Japan' from something shoddy to something fine.

Akio Morita (1921–99) Japanese business executive. *Made in Japan* (1986)

21 I am the kind of writer that people think other people are reading.

V.S. Naipaul (b. 1932) Trinidadian writer and winner of the 2001 Nobel Prize in Literature. *Radio Times* (March 1979)

22 Things aren't always the way they seem from the outside.

Phil Nolan (b. 1953) British CEO of Eircom. *Sunday Times* (September 2000)

23 A hosiery queen masquerading as a food company.

Tony O'Reilly (b. 1936) Irish executive chairman of Independent News & Media and former CEO of Heinz Corporation. Referring to the diversification of the food company Sara Lee. *The Economist* (November 1992)

24 I didn't particularly care that I was the role model, but I thought it was important that somebody should be.

Sally Kristen Ride (b. 1951) US astronaut. Referring to being the first US woman in space. NASA press conference (1983)

25 I'm the beech tree. I chose it because of how strong the beech tree is, how beautiful its skin is, and how impenetrable it is.

Martha Stewart (b. 1942) US chairperson of Martha Stewart Living Omnimedia. Referring to a company organisation chart in which all managers are represented as trees. 'The 50 Most Powerful Women in American Business', *Fortune* (Patricia Sellers and Cora Daniels; October 1999)

26 My attempt not to be cast in a Hollywood niche definitely started hurting...I never seemed an obvious choice for anything.

Uma Thurman (b. 1970) US actor. *Sunday Times* (October 2000)

27 From leaders, we need clear, consistent and honest attention to the identity of the organization. Identity shows up in our actions, our visions, our relationships inside and out of the organization. Identity gets deepened as we do the work.

Walter Wriston (b. 1919) US banker. 'Don't Get Out of the Way!', *www.mgeneral.com* (1997)

IMAGINATION

1 Man is an imagining being.

Gaston Bachelard (1884–1962) French philosopher and scientist. *The Poetics of Reverie* (1969), ch. 2, sect. 10

2 The human imagination...has great difficulty in living strictly within the confines of a materialist practice or philosophy. It dreams, like a dog in its basket, of hares in the open.

John Berger (b. 1926) British novelist, essayist, and art critic. 'The Soul and the Operator', *Keeping a Rendezvous* (1992)

3 Mix your knowledge with imagination and mix both.

Clarence Birdseye (1886–1956) US businessman and founder of Birdseye. *American Magazine* (February 1951)

4 Live out of your imagination, not your history.

Arthur Bryan (b. 1923) British chairman of Josiah Wedgwood & Sons Ltd. *Seven Habits of Highly-Effective People* (1990)

5 The Fancy is indeed no other than a mode of memory emancipated from the order of time and space.

Samuel Taylor Coleridge (1772–1834) British poet. *Biographia Literaria* (1817), ch. 13

6 The imaginations which people have on one another are the solid facts of society.

Charles Horton Cooley (1864–1929) US sociologist. *Human Nature and the Social Order* (1902), ch. 3

7 Where there is no imagination there is no horror.

Arthur Conan Doyle (1859–1930) British writer and doctor. *A Study in Scarlet* (1887), ch. 5

8 What is the imagination? Only an arm or weapon of the interior energy; only the precursor of the reason.

Ralph Waldo Emerson (1803–82) US essayist, lecturer, and poet. 'Books', *Society and Solitude* (1870)

9 It would be a great mistake to confine your imagination to the way things have always been done. In fact, it would consign you to the mediocrity of the marketplace.

Harold S. Geneen (1910–97) US telecommunications entrepreneur and CEO of ITT. *Management* (co-written with Alvin Moscow; 1984), ch. 13

10 The moment a person forms a theory his imagination sees in every object only the traits which favor that theory.

Thomas Jefferson (1743–1826) US president. Letter to Charles Thompson (20 September 1787)

11 My imagination makes me human and makes me a fool; it gives me all the world and exiles me from it.

Ursula K. Le Guin (b. 1929) US author. 'Winged the Adventures on my Mind', *Harper's* (August 1990)

12 Imagine there's no heaven
It's easy if you try
No hell below us
Above us only sky
Imagine all the people
Living for today.
John Lennon (1940–80) British rock musician and songwriter. 'Imagine' (1971)

13 His imagination resembled the wings of an ostrich. It enabled him to run, though not to soar.
Thomas Babington Macaulay (1800–59) British politician and historian. Referring to John Dryden. 'John Dryden', *Essays and Biographies* (1828)

14 The capacity to exercise a relatively high degree of imagination, ingenuity, and creativity in the solution of organisational problems is widely, not narrowly, distributed in the population.
Douglas McGregor (1906–64) US academic, educator, and management theorist. *The Human Side of Enterprise* (1960)

15 Imagination is the voice of daring. If there is anything Godlike about God it is that. He dared to imagine everything.
Henry Miller (1891–1980) US writer. *Sexus* (1965), ch. 14

16 The life of nations no less than that of men is lived largely in the imagination.
Enoch Powell (1912–98) British politician. 1946. Epigraph. Quoted in *English Culture and the Decline of the Industrial Spirit, 1850–1980* (Martin J. Weiner; 1981)

17 Give me an ounce of civet, good apothecary, to sweeten my imagination.
William Shakespeare (1564–1616) English poet and playwright. *King Lear* (1605–06), Act 4, Scene 4, ll. 132–133

18 Tell me where is fancy bred.
Or in the heart or in the head?
How begot, how nourished?
William Shakespeare (1564–1616) English poet and playwright. *The Merchant of Venice* (1596–98), Act 3, Scene 2, ll. 63–65

19 I dream for a living.
Steven Spielberg (b. 1946) US film director. *Time* (July 1985)

20 The imagination is man's power over nature.
Wallace Stevens (1879–1955) US poet. 'Adagia', *Opus posthumous* (Samuel French Morse, ed.; 1957)

21 Skill without imagination is craftsmanship and gives us many useful objects such as wickerwork picnic baskets. Imagination without skill gives us modern art.
Tom Stoppard (b. 1937) British playwright and screenwriter. *Artist Descending a Staircase* (1988)

22 Imagination was given to man to compensate him for what he is not. A sense of humour was provided to console him for what he is.
Horace Walpole (1717–97) British writer. Quoted in 'The Artist', *A Kick in the Seat of the Pants* (Roger von Oech; 1986)

23 Imagination and fiction make up more than three quarters of our real life.
Simone Weil (1909–43) French philosopher and activist. *Gravity and Grace* (1952)

INDEPENDENCE

1 Never sing in chorus, if you want to be heard.
Jules Archibald (1856–1919) Australian journalist. Attrib.

2 Depend on none but yourself.
Charles V (1500–58) Spanish Holy Roman Emperor and King of Spain. Advice left in his papers for his son, King Philip II of Spain. Maxim (?1558)

3 Another lesson we've learned is that you can't follow the other guys. If you take the approach of saying, 'Competitor X has a good business, let's be just like them', that's not going to create a lot of value...It doesn't mean that we won't borrow good ideas from other companies when we see them, but we're not held to convention and we're not striving to be like other companies...We are building our own path.
Michael Dell (b. 1965) US chairman and CEO of Dell Computer Corporation. Speech to the Society of American Business Editors and Writers Technology Conference, Dallas. 'Maximum Speed: Lessons Learned from Managing Hypergrowth' (10 September 1998)

4 For an infant industry, protection is a legitimate demand, but infants must grow up one day.
Indira Gandhi (1917–84) Indian prime minister. Speech (10 April 1971)

5 Be an individualist—and an individual. You'll be amazed at how much faster you'll get ahead.
J. Paul Getty (1892–1976) US entrepreneur, oil industry executive, and financier. *How to Be Rich* (1965)

6 It's better to be a pirate than join the Navy.
Steve Jobs (b. 1955) US entrepreneur, co-founder and CEO of Apple Computer Company, and CEO of Pixar. 1983. Quoted in *West of Eden* (Frank Rose; 1989)

7 Companies gain the advantage of a network at a price; they become dependent on outsiders whose behaviour can affect them but who they do not control.
Rosabeth Moss Kanter (b. 1943) US management theorist, academic, and writer. 'How E-Smart Are You?', *World Link* (January–February 2000)

8 Private enterprise is the power...state control is the machine.
Stephen Leacock (1869–1944) Canadian humorist, essayist, economist, and historian. *While There Is Time* (1945)

9 We sometimes take for granted the freedom and power of independent thought and action. And only after it's been compromised, do we fully realize how fundamental it is to the pursuit of economic opportunity.
Arthur Levitt Jr (b. 1931) US author and former chairman of the US Securities and Exchange Commission. Speech to the New York University Center for Law and Business, New York City. 'Renewing the Covenant with Investors' (10 May 2000)

10 I would not join any club that would have me as a member.
Groucho Marx (1895–1977) US comedian and actor. Quoted in *Liberation Management* (Tom Peters; 1992)

11 I want to prevent as many men as possible from pretending that they have to do this or that because they must earn a living. *It is not true.*

Henry Miller (1891–1980) US writer. The book was based on Miller's five years' experience working for Western Union; he walked out of the job in 1925 declaring 'My own master now'. *Tropic of Capricorn* (1939)

12 We cannot work for others without working for ourselves.

Jean-Jacques Rousseau (1712–78) French philosopher and writer. *The Social Contract* (1762)

13 You know what happens when you are the servant of a corporation?...Your individuality is swallowed up in the individuality and purpose of a great organisation.

Woodrow Wilson (1856–1924) US president. *The New Freedom* (1913)

14 One of the things that my parents have taught me is never listen to other people's expectations. You should live your own life and live up to your own expectations, and those are the only things I really care about.

Tiger Woods (b. 1975) US golfer. Interview, *www.golf.com* (1999)

INDUSTRY

1 Science finds, industry applies, man conforms.

Anonymous. 1933. Subtitle of the guidebook to the Chicago World Fair.

2 In developing our industrial strategy for the period ahead, we have had the benefit of much experience. Almost everything has been tried at least once.

Tony Benn (b. 1925) British politician. Quoted in 'Sayings of the Week', *Observer* (17 March 1974)

3 It is an axiom, enforced by all the experience of the ages, that they who rule industrially will rule politically.

Aneurin Bevan (1897–1960) British politician. Quoted in *Aneurin Bevan* (Michael Foot; 1962), vol. 1

4 Man is a tool-using animal... Without tools he is nothing, with tools he is all.

Thomas Carlyle (1795–1881) British historian and essayist. *Sartor Resartus* (1834)

5 We do need a sense of urgency in our outlook in our regeneration of industry and enterprise, because otherwise what really worries me is that we are going to end up as a fourth-rate country and I don't want to see that.

Prince Charles (b. 1948) British prince. Speech, Edinburgh, *New Scotsman* (27 November 1985)

6 Our wages are lower, our holidays are shorter, our working hours are longer—simply because we produce less per man employed. Unless we put this right we risk becoming the peasants of the Western world.

Michael Clapham (1912–2002) British business executive. Quoted in 'Sayings of the Year', *Observer* (30 December 1973)

7 'Tis sweet to know that stocks will stand
When we with daisies lie,
That commerce will continue,
And trades as briskly fly.

Emily Dickinson (1830–86) US poet. Quoted in *The Poems of Emily Dickinson* (Thomas H. Johnson, ed.; 1955)

8 I cannot consent that the laws regulating the industry of a great nation should be made the shutttlecock of party strife.

Benjamin Disraeli (1804–81) British prime minister and novelist. Speech, House of Commons (11 February 1851)

9 The danger of the past was that men became slaves. The danger of the future is that men may become robots.

Erich Fromm (1900–80) US psychoanalyst and social philosopher. *The Sane Society* (1955)

10 In every rank, or great or small,
'Tis industry supports us all.

John Gay (1685–1732) English playwright and poet. *Fables: Second Series* (1738)

11 The task of industry is continuously, year on year, to make more and better things, using less of the world's resources.

John Harvey-Jones (b. 1924) British management adviser, author, and former chairman of ICI. *Making It Happen* (1988)

12 The difficulty is that we have an industrial base with so many characteristics of an industrial museum or of an industrial hospital.

Barry Owen Jones (b. 1932) Australian politician. Quoted in 'Sayings of the Week', *Sydney Morning Herald* (12 July 1986)

13 The high social costs of British industrialization reflect the shock of unpreparedness and the strange notion that wages and conditions of labor came from a voluntary agreement between free agents.

David S. Landes (b. 1924) US economic historian. Referring to industry's exploitation of the work force, especially of women and children during the nineteenth and early twentieth centuries. *The Wealth and Poverty of Nations* (1998)

14 In Canada and Australia trade has definitely tended to follow the flag.

H.J. Mackinder (1861–1947) British politician and geographer. *Britain and the British Seas* (1902)

15 My personal feeling is that the first markets for multimedia applications will be in the fields of education and business.

Minoru Makihara (b. 1930) Japanese president of Mitsubishi Corporation. Interview, *Strategy + Business* (Joel Kurtzman; January–March 1996)

16 Everywhere in the world the industrial regime tends to make the unorganized or unorganizable individual, the pauper, into the victim of a kind of human sacrifice offered to the gods of civilization.

Jacques Maritain (1882–1973) French philosopher. *Reflections on America* (1958)

17 In the pre-capitalist stages of society, commerce rules industry. The reverse is true of modern society.
Karl Marx (1818–83) German political and economic philosopher. *Das Kapital* (1895)

18 Consumption…is synonymous with use; and is, in fact, the great end and object of industry.
John Ramsay McCulloch (1789–1864) British statistician and political economist. *Principles of Political Economy* (1825)

19 The successful conduct of an industrial enterprise requires two quite distinct qualifications: fidelity and zeal.
John Stuart Mill (1806–73) British economist and philosopher. *Principles of Political Economy* (1848)

20 Industry is limited by capital.
John Stuart Mill (1806–73) British economist and philosopher. *Principles of Political Economy* (1848), bk 1, ch. 5

21 In place of 'industry', I suggest an alternative, more appropriate term: 'business ecosystem'. The term circumscribes the microeconomics of intense coevolution coalescing around innovative ideas.
James F. Moore (b. 1948) US writer and business consultant. *The Death of Competition* (1997)

22 We have created an industrial order geared to automation, where feeble-mindedness, native or acquired, is necessary for docile productivity in the factory; and where a pervasive neurosis is the final gift of the meaningless life which issues forth at the other end.
Lewis Mumford (1895–1990) US social thinker and writer. *The Conduct of Life* (1951)

23 The cost of the electronics in a modern car now exceeds the cost of its steel.
Nicholas Negroponte (b. 1943) US academic, co-founder and director of MIT Media Laboratory. *Being Digital* (1995)

24 Since the introduction of inanimate mechanism into British manufactories, man, with few exceptions, has been treated as a secondary and inferior machine; and far more attention has been given to perfect the raw materials of wood and metals than those of body and mind.
Robert Owen (1771–1858) British industrialist and social reformer. *A New View of Society* (1813)

25 Of course, certain industries will become redundant. But if you ask, 'Will Internet wash out print media?'—no, I don't think so.
Kerry Packer (b. 1937) Australian entrepreneur and chairman of Consolidated Press Holdings. 'There are More Advantages in India than in China', *Rediff* (Neena Haridas; 2000)

26 If we did not have such a thing as an airplane today, we would probably create something the size of NASA to make one.
H. Ross Perot (b. 1930) US entrepreneur, venture capitalist, and politician. *Newsweek* (1986)

27 It takes five years to develop a new car in this country. Heck, we won World War II in four years.
H. Ross Perot (b. 1930) US entrepreneur, venture capitalist, and politician. Quoted in *Thriving on Chaos* (Tom Peters; 1987)

28 People always want to call it 'the industry'. It's not an industry now. It was.
Otto Preminger (1906–86) US film producer and director. Referring to the film business. Interview *Films Illustrated* (January 1980)

29 It takes more than industry to industrialize.
W.W. Rostow (b. 1916) US economist. *The Stages of Economic Growth* (1960), ch. 3

30 Before the earth could become an industrial garbage can it had first to become a research laboratory.
Theodore Roszak (1933–81) US historian, writer, and editor. *Where the Wasteland Ends* (1972)

31 Properly, urban-industrialization must be regarded an experiment. And if the scientific spirit has taught us anything of value, it is that honest experiments may well fail.
Theodore Roszak (1933–81) US historian, writer, and editor. *Where the Wasteland Ends* (1972), Introduction

32 Life without industry is guilt, industry without art is brutality.
John Ruskin (1819–1900) British art critic and writer. *Lectures on Art* (1870)

33 I do not want the company to become a mass production line.
Sayyid Khalid bin Hamad bin Hamoud Al Bu Said (b. 1965) Omani entrepreneur. Referring to production of the world's most expensive perfume. *Forbes* (March 2000)

34 Rough, honest industry, and smiling peace, Thus plant, thus build, and give the land encrease.
Richard Savage (?1697–1743) English poet. *Of Public Spirit* (1736)

35 Modern industry seems to be inefficient to a degree that surpasses one's enduring powers of imagination. Its inefficiency therefore remains unnoticed.
E.F. Schumacher (1911–77) British economist and conservationist. *Small Is Beautiful* (1973)

36 The most striking thing about modern industry is that it requires so much and accomplishes so little.
E.F. Schumacher (1911–77) British economist and conservationist. *Small Is Beautiful* (1973)

37 The real problem is not whether machines think but whether men do.
B.F. Skinner (1904–90) US psychologist. *Contingencies of Reinforcement* (1969)

38 Any rigidity by an automobile manufacturer, no matter how large or how well established, is severely penalised in the market.
Alfred P. Sloan (1875–1966) US president of General Motors. *My Years with General Motors* (1964)

39 There is no resting place for an enterprise in a competitive economy.

Alfred P. Sloan (1875–1966) US president of General Motors. *My Years with General Motors* (1964)

40 This extraordinary metal, the soul of every manufacture, and the mainspring perhaps of civilised society.

Samuel Smiles (1812–1904) Scottish social reformer and writer. Referring to iron. *Men of Invention and Industry* (1884)

41 The City is a machine miraculously organized for extracting gold from the seas, airs, clouds, from barren lands, holds of ships, mines, plantations, cottage hearth-stones, trees and rock.

Christina Stead (1902–83) Australian writer. 'The Sensitive Goldfish', *The Salzburg Tales* (1934)

42 After all the maxims and systems of trade and commerce, a stander-by would think the affairs of the world were ridiculously contrived.

Jonathan Swift (1667–1745) Irish writer and satirist. *Thoughts on Various Subjects* (1711)

43 You can't spend your time trying to figure out why the market is what it is at any given moment, but there is a general belief that the Internet and the Information Revolution is a fundamental revolution.

Jay S. Walker, US entrepreneur and founder of Priceline.com, CEO of Walker Digital Corporation. 'It's a Completely New Way of Buying', *BusinessWeek* (Diane Brady; 1999)

44 Industry does nothing but produce scarce things.

Léon Walras (1834–1910) French economist. *Elements of Pure Economics* (1874–77), pt 1

45 The two sides of industry have traditionally always regarded each other in Britain with the greatest possible loathing, mistrust and contempt. They are both absolutely right.

Auberon Waugh (1939–2001) British writer and journalist. *Private Eye* (16 December 1983)

46 What will Britain's service industry be servicing when there is no hardware, when no wealth is actually being produced. We will be servicing presumably the product of wealth by others.

Arnold Weinstock (1924–2002) British managing director of General Electric Company. *International Management* (December 1985)

47 The industrial world is a spontaneous organization for transmuting what every man has into what he desires, wholly irrespective of what his desires may be.

Philip H. Wicksteed (1844–1927) US scholar and economist. *The Common Sense of Political Economy* (1933)

48 Industry is the root of all ugliness.

Oscar Wilde (1854–1900) Irish writer and wit. *Phrases and Philosophies for the Use of the Young* (1894)

49 For years I thought what was good for our country was good for General Motors and vice versa. The difference did not exist. Our

company is too big. It goes with the welfare of the country.

Charles E. Wilson (1890–1961) US politician and president of General Motors. Statement to US Senate committee, *New York Times* (24 February 1953)

INFORMATION

1 If you file your waste basket for 50 years, you have a public library.

Tony Benn (b. 1925) British politician. *Daily Telegraph* (March 1994)

2 I'd always rather err on the side of openness. But there's a difference between optimum and maximum openness, and fixing that boundary is a judgment call. The art of leadership is knowing how much information you're going to pass on.

Warren Bennis (b. 1925) US educator and writer. Interview, *Strategy + Business* (July–September 1997)

3 A Harvard professor told me that if there was no Gallup poll there'd be no Bill Clinton.

Jim Clifton (b. 1951) US CEO of Gallup. *Financial Times* (October 2000)

4 Our memories are card-indexes, consulted, and then put back in disorder by authorities whom we do not control.

Cyril Connolly (1903–74) British critic, essayist, and novelist. *The Unquiet Grave* (1944)

5 Yet another revolution has begun in the field of information systems. When it is over...users will completely control individual information systems.

John Dearden (b. 1919) US professor of accounting, planning, and control. 'The Withering Away of the IT Organization', *Sloan Management Review* (1987)

6 The first thing practically everyone must learn is to take information responsibly.

Peter F. Drucker (b. 1909) US management consultant and academic. Quoted in *Techno Vision* (C.B. Wang; 1994)

7 The fewer data needed, the better the information.

Peter F. Drucker (b. 1909) US management consultant and academic. *Management Tasks, Responsibilities and Practices* (1973)

8 We had the experience but missed the meaning.

T.S. Eliot (1888–1965) British poet, dramatist, and critic. 'The Dry Salvages', *Four Quartets* (1943)

9 C.R. England captures information on everything and recycles it back through the engine to improve performance.

Dan England (b. 1948) US CEO of C.R. England. 'The Mavericks', *Fortune* (June 1995)

10 We want to run this place like the cockpit of a jetliner, where you have hundreds of different instruments before you at all times and know exactly where you are.

Dan England (b. 1948) US CEO of C.R. England. 'The Mavericks', *Fortune* (June 1995)

11 It is a far, far better thing to have firm anchor in nonsense than to put out on the troubled sea of thought.
J.K. Galbraith (b. 1908) US economist and diplomat. *The Affluent Society* (1958)

12 I want no surprises.
Harold S. Geneen (1910–97) US telecommunications entrepreneur and CEO of ITT. *Managing* (co-written with Alvin Moscow; 1984)

13 The highest art of professional management requires the literal ability to smell a real fact from all others.
Harold S. Geneen (1910–97) US telecommunications entrepreneur and CEO of ITT. *Managing* (co-written with Alvin Moscow; 1984)

14 An individual without information cannot take responsibility; an individual who is given information cannot help but take responsibility.
Wilbert Lee Gore (d. 1986) US founder of Goretex. Quoted in *Thriving on Chaos* (Tom Peters; 1987)

15 Information networks straddle the world. Nothing remains concealed. But the sheer volume of information dissolves the information. We are unable to take it all in.
Günter Grass (b. 1927) German novelist and winner of the 1999 Nobel Prize in Literature. Interview, *New Statesman* (22 June 1990)

16 Most management books should not be tossed aside lightly; they should be hurled against the wall with great force.
Michael Hammer (b. 1948) US author and academic. *Hemispheres* (in-flight magazine for United Airlines) (December 1996)

17 Hoarding information or getting it first was one way managers in traditional companies expressed their power. But information blockages make the whole system less effective.
Rosabeth Moss Kanter (b. 1943) US management theorist, academic, and writer. 'How E-Smart Are You?', *World Link* (January–February 2000)

18 The more the data banks record about each one of us, the less we exist.
Marshall McLuhan (1911–80) Canadian sociologist and author. Interview, *Playboy* (March 1969)

19 While hard data may inform the intellect, it is largely soft data that generates wisdom.
Henry Mintzberg (b. 1939) Canadian academic and management theorist. *The Rise and Fall of Strategic Planning* (1994)

20 Most employees in portal companies are involved in the research, development... production and presentation of information. Most Fortune 1,000 companies are heavily dependent on physical products and process, this makes half their workforce obsolete.
William (Walid) Mougayar, US consultant and management theorist. 'What you can learn from the portals', *Computerworld* (31 August 1998)

21 I have direct knowledge. I don't have to call someone to ask a question.
Nancy Peretsman (b. 1955) US investment banker. *Forbes* (May 1999)

22 A wealth of information creates a poverty of attention.
Carl Shapiro (b. 1955) US academic and author. *Information Rules* (co-written with Hal L Varian; 1999)

23 Information is costly to produce, but cheap to reproduce.
Carl Shapiro (b. 1955) US academic and author. *Information Rules* (co-written with Hal L Varian; 1999)

24 Information is like an oyster. It has its greatest value when it is fresh.
Carl Shapiro (b. 1955) US academic and author. *Information Rules* (co-written with Hal L Varian; 1999)

25 Facts are available to everyone; it is interpretation and implementation that is key.
Ric Simcock (b. 1965) British advertising executive. *Marketing* (September 2000)

26 The biggest opportunity is harnessing our knowledge within the organisation to provide better solutions.
Martin Sorrell (b. 1945) British advertising executive. Interview (March 2000)

27 I am a seeker of the small facts, not the big explanation; a narrator, not a philosopher.
Barbara W. Tuchman (1912–89) US historian. Interview (1963)

28 Information is power. I see CNN as the democratization of information.
Ted Turner (b. 1938) US founder of Turner Broadcasting Systems. *Washington Post* (18 July 1988)

29 Information is a business in itself. It is also something that has made control impossible...you cannot get customers to accept prices in one place when they know there's a better deal elsewhere. It's a whole new world.
Walter Wriston (b. 1919) US banker. November 1985. Quoted in *The Financial Revolution: The Big Bang Worldwide* (Adrian Hamilton; 1986), ch. 2

30 The informated workplace, which may no longer be a place at all, is an arena through which information circulates, information to which intellectual effort is applied.
Shoshana Zuboff (b. 1951) US social scientist and author. *In the Age of the Smart Machine* (1988)

INITIATIVE

1 If offended, take the initiative to clear it up.
Stephen Covey (b. 1932) US writer and psychologist. *Thirty Methods of Influence* (1991)

2 Jelly-fish where their predecessors were masterful, they are slaves to their public relations departments.
Tony Crosland (1918–77) British politician. Reflecting on the lack of initiative of British corporate managers. *The Conservative Enemy* (1956)

3 TWIMBLE: I play it the company way
Where the company puts me, there I'll stay.
FINCH: But what is your point of view?
TWIMBLE: I have no point of view,
FINCH: Supposing the company thinks...
TWIMBLE: I think so too!

Frank Loesser (1910–69) US composer, lyricist, and librettist.
Song lyric. 'The Company Way', *How to Succeed in Business
without Really Trying* (1961)

4 The people who get on in this world are the
people who get up and look for the
circumstances they want, and, if they can't
find them, make them.

George Bernard Shaw (1856–1950) Irish writer and critic.
Mrs Warren's Profession (1893), Act 2

5 Brutally speaking, our scheme does not ask
any initiative in a man. We do not care for his
initiative.

F.W. Taylor (1856–1915) US engineer and author. *The
Principles of Scientific Management* (1911)

INNOVATION

1 A common mistake that people make when
trying to design something completely
foolproof is to underestimate the ingenuity of
complete fools.

Douglas Adams (1952–2001) British author. *Mostly
Harmless* (1992)

2 The easiest way to predict the future is to
invent it.

Anonymous. Xerox Research Center, Palo Alto, California
(1970)

3 Think outside the box.

Anonymous. Quoted in *Goldfinger* (Robert Heller; 1998)

4 The perpetual idea machine.

Anonymous. Referring to the research-led Thermo Electron
Corporation. *Research and Development* (November 1989)

5 If someone monopolizes the market for
personal finance software, are you going to go
after that company and dismantle it? I would
contend no. Because these temporary
monopolies are a prize for innovation. They're
the incentive for innovation.

W. Brian Arthur (b. 1945) US economist. Interview, *Strategy +
Business* (April–June 1998)

6 Science writers foresee the inevitable and,
although problems and catastrophes may be
inevitable, solutions are not.

Isaac Asimov (1920–92) US novelist, critic, and scientist.
Natural History (April 1975)

7 Machinery for producing any commodity in
great demand seldom actually wears out; new
improvements, by which the same operations
can be executed either more quickly or better,
generally supercede it long before that period
arrives.

Charles Babbage (1792–1871) British mathematician and
inventor. *On the Economy of Machinery and Manufacture*
(1832)

8 If I can make a deaf-mute talk, I can make
metal talk.

Alexander Graham Bell (1847–1922) US inventor. Referring
to the invention of the telephone. Quoted in *Concise
Dictionary of Great 20th Century Biographies* (Kathryn
Knox Soman, ed.; 1997)

9 Suppose I could program my computer to
create a space in which anything could be
linked to anything. There would be a single
global information space.

Tim Berners-Lee (b. 1955) British computer scientist and
founder of the World Wide Web. *Fortune* (October 2000)

10 Innovation, whether, in the form of improved
product quality and variety or production
efficiency that allows lower prices, is a
powerful engine for enhancing consumer
welfare. By prohibiting private restraints that
impede entry or mute rivalry, antitrust seeks
to create an economic environment in which
the entrepreneurial initiative that is the
hallmark of the US economy can flourish.

Anne K. Bingaman (b. 1943) US lawyer. Speech, University of
Kansas Law School (19 September 1996)

11 Doing the things we do now and doing them
better, cheaper and faster will take us so far.
But it will not take us far enough. We're going
to have to do new things in new ways.

Peter Bonfield (b. 1944) British former CEO of British
Telecom. Said at a British Telecom annual general meeting.
Remark (July 2000)

12 What makes this business difficult is that
grown ups have to solve children's problems.

Horst Brandstatter, German toy manufacturer and director of
Playmobil. Quoted in *Liberation Management* (Tom Peters;
1992)

13 The essence of science; ask an impertinent
question, and you are on the way to a
pertinent answer.

Jacob Bronowski (1908–74) Polish mathematician and
philosopher. *The Ascent of Man* (1973)

14 Innovation! One cannot be forever innovating.
I want to create classics.

Coco Chanel (1883–1971) French couturier. Quoted in *Coco
Chanel: Her Life, Her Secrets* (1971)

15 The word 'orthodoxy' not only no longer
means being right; it practically means being
wrong.

G.K. Chesterton (1874–1936) British novelist, poet, and
critic. *Heretics* (1905)

16 I don't think necessity is the mother of
invention—invention, in my opinion arises
directly from idleness, possibly also from
laziness. To save oneself trouble.

Agatha Christie (1891–1976) British novelist. *An
Autobiography* (1977)

17 Innovation is not just technical; it is also
organizational and managerial.

Stewart Clegg (b. 1947) Australian writer. 'Business Values
and Embryonic Industry: Lessons from Australia', *Whose
Business Values? Some Asian and Cross-Cultural
Perspectives* (Sally Stewart and Gabriel Donleavy, eds; 1995)

18 New markets open not only because of novel technologies; shifts in values and culture also are potent sources of innovation.
Stewart Clegg (b. 1947) Australian writer. 'Business Values and Embryonic Industry: Lessons from Australia', *Whose Business Values? Some Asian and Cross-Cultural Perspectives* (Sally Stewart and Gabriel Donleavy, eds; 1995)

19 The great discoveries are usually obvious.
Philip B. Crosby (1926–2001) US business executive and author. *Quality Is Free* (1979)

20 In science, the credit goes to the man who convinces the world, not to the man to whom the idea first occurs.
Francis Darwin (1848–1925) British botanist. *Eugenics Review* (April 1914)

21 One of the struggles many companies face is overcoming the desire to invent everything themselves. Even today, you see a lot of companies falling back on the idea that 'my baby's the most beautiful in the world and I'm not going to accept anybody else's'. This can get in the way of logical business thinking.
Michael Dell (b. 1965) US chairman and CEO of Dell Computer Corporation. Speech to the Society of American Business Editors and Writers Technology Conference, Dallas. 'Maximum Speed: Lessons Learned from Managing Hypergrowth' (10 September 1998)

22 Above all, innovation is not invention. It is a term of economics rather than of technology.
Peter F. Drucker (b. 1909) US management consultant and academic. Speech (April 1992)

23 The measure of innovation is its impact on the environment.
Peter F. Drucker (b. 1909) US management consultant and academic. Speech (April 1992)

24 Knowledge applied to existing processes, services and products is productivity; knowledge applied to the new is innovation.
Peter F. Drucker (b. 1909) US management consultant and academic. Interview, *Hot Wired* (Jul/Aug 1993)

25 The most successful innovators are the creative imitators, the number two.
Peter F. Drucker (b. 1909) US management consultant and academic. Interview, *Hot Wired* (August 1996)

26 Innovation is the specific instrument of entrepreneurship...the act that endows resources with a new capacity to create wealth.
Peter F. Drucker (b. 1909) US management consultant and academic. *Innovation and Entrepreneurship* (1985)

27 Knowledge-based innovation has the longest lead time of all innovations.
Peter F. Drucker (b. 1909) US management consultant and academic. *Innovation and Entrepreneurship* (1993)

28 Businessmen will have to learn to build and manage innovative organizations.
Peter F. Drucker (b. 1909) US management consultant and academic. *The Age of Discontinuity: Guidelines to Our Changing Society* (1969)

29 Everything that can be invented has been invented.
Charles H. Duell (1905–70) US commissioner of the US Office of Patents. 1899. Quoted in *Maxi Marketing* (Stan Rapp and Thomas L. Collins; 1995)

30 The basic idea is whether you have established structure and systems so that gadflies can challenge you.
Robert G. Eccles, US academic and business author. *Doing Deals: Investment Banking at Work* (co-written with Dwight B. Crane; 1988)

31 Reverse funnel effect.
Robert G. Eccles, US academic and business author. Referring to the flow of new ideas within an innovative company. *Doing Deals: Investment Banking at Work* (co-written with Dwight B. Crane; 1988)

32 Science is an edged tool, with which men play like children and cut their own fingers.
Arthur Eddington (1882–1944) British scientist. Quoted in *More Random Walks in Science* (R.L. Weber; 1982)

33 To invent, you need a good imagination and a pile of junk.
Thomas Edison (1847–1931) US inventor. Quoted in 'Building an Innovation Factory', *Harvard Business Review* (Andrew Hargadon and Robert I. Sutton; 2000)

34 Genius is one percent inspiration and ninety-nine percent perspiration.
Thomas Edison (1847–1931) US inventor. *Life* (1932)

35 The first rule of intelligent tinkering is to save all the parts.
Paul Ehrlich (b. 1932) US biologist. *Saturday Review* (June 1972)

36 It is easy to overlook the absence of appreciable advance in an industry. Inventions that are not made, like babies that are not born, are rarely missed.
J.K. Galbraith (b. 1908) US economist and diplomat. *The Affluent Society* (1958), ch. 9

37 The last thing IBM needs right now is a vision.
Lou Gerstner (b. 1942) US chairman and CEO of IBM. *Fortune* (1997)

38 No one can possibly achieve any real and lasting success or 'get rich' in business by being a conformist.
J. Paul Getty (1892–1976) US entrepreneur, oil industry executive, and financier. *International Herald Tribune* (1961)

39 Only a real lazybones can produce labour-saving inventions.
Günter Grass (b. 1927) German novelist and winner of the 1999 Nobel Prize in Literature. *The Tin Drum* (1959)

40 Science has lost its virgin purity, has become dogmatic instead of seeking for enlightenment, and has gradually fallen into the hands of traders.
Robert Graves (1895–1985) British poet, novelist, and classical scholar. Quoted in *Flawed Science, Damaged Human Life* (Bruno Friedman; 1969)

41 Innovation will always be a mixture of serendipity, genius, and sheer bull-mindedness. But while you can't bottle lightning, you can build lightning rods. Non-linear innovation can be legitimized, fostered, supported, and rewarded.
Gary Hamel (b. 1954) US academic, business writer, and consultant. Interview, *Barnes & Noble* (September 2000)

42 If they started by saying you have to prove to me this has a 90 percent chance of success, they'd never invest in anything.
Gary Hamel (b. 1954) US academic, business writer, and consultant. Referring to the attitude of investors to new product ideas. *Digital Britain* (January 2000)

43 A word beginning with X...the more we thought about it, the more we were ready to try it. And we got it into the dictionary.
John B. Hartnett (?1903–1982) US chairman of Xerox. Referring to the trademark Xerox. Quoted in obituary, *New York Times* (1982)

44 People are unlikely to know that they need a product which does not exist and the basis of market research in new and innovative products is limited in this regard.
John Harvey-Jones (b. 1924) British management adviser, author, and former chairman of ICI. *All Together Now* (1994)

45 I want to see an idea. I want to hold it and touch it.
Howard Head (1914–91) US inventor of the metal ski. *A Passion for Excellence* (Tom Peters and Nancy Austin; 1985)

46 The spark-gap is mightier than the pen. This is not the age of the pamphleteers, it is the age of the engineers.
Lancelot Hogben (1895–1975) British scientist. *Science for the Citizen* (1938)

47 It is the customary fate of new truths to begin as heresies and to end as superstitions.
Thomas Huxley (1825–95) British biologist. *Science and Culture* (1887)

48 Apple's the only company left in this industry that designs the whole widget. Hardware, software, developer relations, marketing. It turns out that that...is Apple's greatest strategic advantage...if you believe that there's still room for innovation in this industry.
Steve Jobs (b. 1955) US entrepreneur, co-founder and CEO of Apple Computer Company, and CEO of Pixar. Quoted in 'Steve's Two Jobs', *Time* (Michael Krantz; 18 October 1999)

49 You've got to change to excite.
Karl (Carl Williams) Kani (b. 1968) US fashion designer. 'The Players', *Fortune* (Eileen Gunn; April 1997)

50 You can innovate by not doing anything, if it's a conscious decision.
Herb Kelleher (b. 1931) US businessman and founder of Southwest Airlines. *International Organization and Dynamics* (Autumn 1994)

51 Our essential concept was that the role of industry is to sense a deep human need, then bring science and technology to bear on filling that need.
Edwin Land (1909–91) US inventor and founder of Polaroid Corporation. *BusinessWeek* (March 1981)

52 Very often the best way to find out whether something is worth making is to make it, distribute it and then to see, after the product has been around for a few years, whether it was worth the task.
Edwin Land (1909–91) US inventor and founder of Polaroid Corporation. *Physics Today* (June 1982)

53 Work only on problems that are manifestly important and seem to be nearly impossible to solve. That way you will have a natural market for your product and no competition.
Edwin Land (1909–91) US inventor and founder of Polaroid Corporation. *Physics Today* (January 1982)

54 A powerful new idea can kick around unused in a company for years, not because its merits are not recognised, but because nobody has assumed the responsibility for converting it from words to action.
Theodore Levitt (b. 1925) US management theorist, writer, and editor. 'Ideas Are Useless Unless Used', *Inc.* (February 1981)

55 There is no shortage of creative people in American business. The shortage is of innovators. All too often people believe that creativity leads to innovation. It doesn't.
Theodore Levitt (b. 1925) US management theorist, writer, and editor. 'Ideas Are Useless Unless Used', *Inc.* (February 1981)

56 The scarce people are the ones who have the know-how, energy, daring, and staying power to implement ideas...Since business is a 'get-things-done' institution, creativity without action-oriented follow-through is a barren form of behavior. In a sense it is irresponsible.
Theodore Levitt (b. 1925) US management theorist, writer, and editor. 'Ideas Are Useless Unless Used', *Inc.* (February 1981)

57 It is a good exercise for a research scientist to discard a pet hypothesis every day before breakfast.
Konrad Lorenz (1903–89) Austrian zoologist. *On Aggression* (1966)

58 I had a compulsive desire to understand how things were made. Perhaps that's why I took them apart.
John Makepeace (b. 1939) British furniture designer and manufacturer. Quoted in *Makepeace* (Jeremy Myerson; 1995)

59 Business demands innovation. There is a constant need to feel around the edges, but business schools, out of necessity, are condemned to teach the past.
Mark McCormack (1930–2003) US entrepreneur, founder and CEO of the International Management Group. *What They Don't Teach You at Harvard Business School* (1984)

60 Dewey, in reacting against passive print culture, was surf-boarding along the new electronic wave.
Marshall McLuhan (1911–80) Canadian sociologist and author. *The Gutenberg Galaxy* (1962)

61 We were not the victims of ancestor worship. We had the benefits of a fresh start.
Matthew Miller, US CEO of General Instruments. *New York Times* (12 July 1982)

62 I see true innovation to be made up of three elements which I call the three creativities. Creativity in technology of course, plus creativity in product planning and marketing as well.
Akio Morita (1921–99) Japanese business executive. Quoted in *How to Manage* (Ray Wild; 1995)

63 The public does not know what is possible, we do.
Akio Morita (1921–99) Japanese business executive. *Made in Japan* (1986)

64 Incrementalism is innovation's worst enemy. New concepts and big steps forward, in a very real sense, come from left field, from a mixture of people, ideas, backgrounds, and cultures that normally are not mixed.
Nicholas Negroponte (b. 1943) US academic, co-founder and director of MIT Media Laboratory. 'The Balance of Trade of Ideas', *Wired Magazine* (3 April 1995)

65 The wild, the absurd, the seemingly crazy: this kind of thinking is where new ideas come from...The people capable of such playful thought carry forward their childish qualities and childhood dreams, applying them in areas where most of us get stuck, victims of our adult seriousness. Staying a child isn't easy.
Nicholas Negroponte (b. 1943) US academic, co-founder and director of MIT Media Laboratory. 'Toys of Tomorrow', *Wired Magazine* (6 March 1998)

66 The best way to guarantee a steady stream of new ideas is to make sure that each person in your organization is as different as possible from the others. Under these conditions, and only these conditions, will people maintain varied perspectives and demonstrate their knowledge in different ways.
Nicholas Negroponte (b. 1943) US academic, co-founder and director of MIT Media Laboratory. 'Where Do New Ideas Come From', *Wired Magazine* (4 January 1996)

67 Slack allows innovative projects to be pursued because it buffers organizations from the uncertain success of these projects, fostering a culture of experimentation.
Nitin Nohria (b. 1962) US writer. *The Differentiated Network* (co-written with Sumantra Ghoshal; 1997)

68 Innovation typically occurs at the interface, requiring multiple disciplines. Thus the flexible Japanese organization has, now especially, become an asset.
Kenichi Ohmae (b. 1943) Japanese management consultant and theorist. 'The Myth and Reality of the Japanese Corporation', *Chief Executive* (Summer 1981)

69 By observing California's youngsters on roller skates, a Sony engineer came up with the concept of the Walkman.
Kenichi Ohmae (b. 1943) Japanese management consultant and theorist. *Industry Week* (July 1985)

70 Fashion is more usually a gentle progression of revisited ideas.
Bruce Oldfield (b. 1950) British fashion designer. *Independent* (September 1989)

71 Not a single, substantial, commercially-successful project had come from an adequately-funded team. They'd always come from the scrounging, scrapping, underfunded teams.
Ken Olsen (b. 1926) US computer designer and founder of Digital Equipment Corporation. Quoted in *A Passion for Excellence* (Tom Peters and Nancy Austin; 1985)

72 The driving force for the development of new products is not technology, not money, but the imagination of people.
David Packard (1912–96) US entrepreneur and co-founder of Hewlett-Packard. *The HP Way* (1995)

73 A butterfly is not more caterpillar or a better caterpillar or improved caterpillar: a butterfly is a different creature.
Richard Pascale (b. 1938) US academic and author. Referring to the process of new product development. 'The Reinvention Roller Coaster', *Harvard Business Review* (co-written with A. Athos and T. Goss; November–December 1993)

74 There are no such things as applied sciences, only applications of science.
Louis Pasteur (1822–95) French scientist. Address (September 1872)

75 In research, the horizon recedes as we advance, and is no nearer at sixty than it was at twenty.
Mark Pattison (1813–84) British author. *Isaac Casaubon* (1875)

76 Useful discoveries are best identified after the making of discoveries, rather than before.
John C. Polanyi (b. 1929) German scientist and author. Speech (June 1996)

77 Science must begin with myths and the criticism of myths.
Karl Raimund Popper (1902–94) British philosopher of science. Quoted in *British Philosophy in the Mid-Century* (C.A. Mace; 1957)

78 We may become the makers of our fate when we have ceased to pose as its prophets.
Karl Raimund Popper (1902–94) British philosopher of science. *The Open Society and its Enemies* (1945)

79 It is the tension between the scientist's laws and his own attempted breaking of them that powers the engines of science and makes it forge ahead.
W.V.O. Quine (1908–2000) US philosopher. *Quiddities* (1987)

80 In a small company, one person's hunch can be enough to launch a new product. In a big company, the same concept is likely to be buried in committee for months.
Al Ries (b. 1926) US advertising executive and chairman of Trout & Ries Advertising, Inc. *Marketing Warfare* (co-written with Jack Trout; 1986), ch. 10

81 We haven't got the money, so we've got to think.
Ernest Rutherford (1871–1937) British physicist. *Bulletin of the Institute of Physics* (1962)

82 For an idea ever to be fashionable is ominous, since it must afterwards always be old-fashioned.
George Santayana (1863–1952) US philosopher, novelist, and poet. *Winds of Doctrine* (1913)

83 Beyond a certain point, personal media such as telephones, computers, and planners aren't just functional objects anymore, they're fashion accessories.
Michael Schrage, US commentator on innovation. Quoted in *Liberation Management* (Tom Peters; 1992)

84 Implementers aren't considered bozos anymore.
John Sculley (b. 1939) US partner of Sculley Brothers, former president of Pepsi, and CEO of Apple Computers. Quoted in *Thriving on Chaos* (Tom Peters; 1987)

85 One possibility for difficulties innovating is that most people really don't care about innovation.
Peter Senge (b. 1947) US academic and author. 'The Practice of Innovation', *Leader to Leader* (1998)

86 Sometimes I think we'll see the day when you introduce a product in the morning and announce the end of its life at the end of the day.
Al Shugart (b. 1930) US entrepreneur and pioneer of disk drive technology. Quoted in *Goldfinger* (Robert Heller; 1998)

87 There are so many people involved and it requires such a tremendous effort to put something into effect that a new idea is likely to be considered insignificant in comparison with the effort that it takes to put it across.
Alfred P. Sloan (1875–1966) US president of General Motors. Quoted in *The Bigness Complex* (Walter Adams and James Brock; 1986)

88 Vision is the art of seeing things invisible.
Jonathan Swift (1667–1745) Irish writer and satirist. Attrib.

89 Discovery consists of seeing what everybody has seen and thinking what nobody has thought.
Albert Szent-Györgyi (1893–1986) US biochemist. 1925. Quoted in *The Scientist Speculates* (I.J. Good, ed.; 1962)

90 The artist brings something into the world that didn't exist before, and...he does it without destroying something else.
John Updike (b. 1932) US novelist and critic. Quoted in *Writers at Work* (George Plimpton, ed.; 1977)

91 Science means simply the aggregate of all the recipes that are always successful. The rest is literature.
Paul Valéry (1871–1945) French poet and essayist. *Moralités* (1932)

92 Basic research is what I am doing when I don't know what I am doing.
Wernher von Braun (1912–77) US rocket engineer. Quoted in *A Random Walk in Science* (R.L. Weber; 1973)

93 Our best ideas come from clerks and schoolboys.
Sam M. Walton (1918–92) US entrepreneur and founder of Wal-Mart, Inc. *Wall Street Journal* (April 1982)

94 The things I want to show are mechanical. Machines have less problems.
Andy Warhol (1928–87) US artist and film maker. Quoted in *Andy Warhol: In His Own Words* (Mike Wrenn; 1991)

95 Who the hell wants to hear actors talk?
Harry M. Warner (1881–1958) US film producer and head of Warner Brothers. Referring to introduction of sound movies. Quoted in *Maxi Marketing* (Stan Rapp and Thomas L. Collins; 1995)

96 The job for big companies, the challenge that we all face as bureaucrats, is to create an environment where people can reach their dreams—and they don't have to do it in a garage.
Jack Welch (b. 1935) US former chairman and CEO of General Electric. *Fortune* (May 1995)

97 Innovation is fostered by information gathered from new connections; from insights gained by journeys into other disciplines or places it arises from ongoing circles of exchange, where information is not just accumulated or stored, but created.
Meg Wheatley (b. 1941) US academic, management theorist, and president of the Berkana Institute. *Leadership and the New Science* (1992)

98 Everyone likes innovation until it affects himself, and then it's bad.
Walter Wriston (b. 1919) US banker. Quoted in 'Sayings of the Year', *Observer* (29 December 1974)

INTELLIGENCE

1 The brain is a wonderful organ. It starts working the moment you get up in the morning, and does not stop until you get into the office.
Robert Frost (1874–1963) US poet. Attrib.

2 A common core of personal and social abilities has proven to be the key ingredient in people's success: emotional intelligence.
Daniel Goleman (b. 1946) US behavioural scientist, journalist, and author. *Working with Emotional Intelligence* (1998)

3 All intellectual improvement arises from leisure.
Samuel Johnson (1709–84) British poet, lexicographer, essayist, and critic. Quoted in *Alexandra Stoddard's Book of Days* (Alexandra Stoddard; 1997)

4 Even in a hierarchy people can be equal as thinkers.
Nancy Kline (b. 1946) US author, educator, and consultant. *Time to Think* (1999)

5 Thinking is the endeavour to capture reality by means of ideas.
Jose Ortega y Gasset (1883–1955) Spanish author and philosopher. *The Dehumanization of Art* (1925)

6 Anti-intellectualism has long been the anti-Semitism of the businessman.

Arthur Schlesinger Jr (b. 1917) US historian, writer, and educator. *Partisan Review* (1953)

7 Intelligence...is really a kind of taste: taste in ideas.

Susan Sontag (b. 1933) US novelist and essayist. 1964. 'Notes on "Camp"', *Against Interpretation* (1966)

8 This is the age of intellectual capital, and the most valuable parts of jobs are the human tasks: sensing, judging, creating, building relationships.

Thomas A. Stewart (b. 1948) US journalist and author. 'Brain Power: Who Owns It...How They Profit From It', *Fortune* (1997)

9 Intellectual capital is the sum of everything everybody in a company knows that gives it a competitive edge.

Thomas A. Stewart (b. 1948) US journalist and author. *Intellectual Capital* (1997)

10 Intelligence becomes an asset when some useful order is created out of free-floating brainpower.

Thomas A. Stewart (b. 1948) US journalist and author. *Intellectual Capital* (1997)

INVESTMENT AND THE STOCK MARKET

1 A stockbroker is someone who takes all your money and invests it until it's gone.

Woody Allen (b. 1935) US actor, humorist, producer, and director. Quoted in *The Economist* (25 October 1997)

2 When Wall Street sneezes, London catches cold.

Anonymous. Quoted in *Treasury of Investment Wisdom* (Bernice Cohen; 1999)

3 The trend is your friend.

Anonymous. Referring to financial advice. Quoted in *Treasury of Investment Wisdom* (Bernice Cohen; 1999)

4 My advice to this investor is the same that I give to the young investors in my classes...Devote the same earnest attention to investing that $50,000 as you devoted to earning it.

Ivan Boesky (b. 1937) US financier convicted of insider dealing in 1987. Quoted in *Wall Street Journal* (2 January 1985)

5 Investing is an act of faith. We entrust our capital to corporate stewards in the faith—at least with the hope—that their efforts will generate high rates of return on our investments.

John Clifton Bogle (b. 1929) US investment analyst, founder and CEO of the Vanguard Group. *Common Sense on Mutual Funds: New Imperatives for the Intelligent Investor* (1999), ch. 1

6 The historical data support one conclusion with unusual force: *To invest with success, you must be a long-term investor.*

John Clifton Bogle (b. 1929) US investment analyst, founder and CEO of the Vanguard Group. *Common Sense on Mutual Funds: New Imperatives for the Intelligent Investor* (1999), ch. 1

7 Marketing has displaced management as the industry's chief principle, and expenditures on investment advisory services are dwarfed by expenditures on advertising and sales promotion.

John Clifton Bogle (b. 1929) US investment analyst, founder and CEO of the Vanguard Group. Referring to mutual funds. *John Bogle on Investing: The First 50 Years* (2000), Introduction

8 Blackest Panic Day of All. Record 16,410,000 shares traded. No bids at last prices. No bids— no bids.

John V. Bouvier Jr (1865–1948) US lawyer. 29 October 1929, 'Black Tuesday', marked the height of the crash on Wall Street that ushered in the Great Depression. Diary entry (29 October 1929)

9 Derivatives are financial weapons of mass destruction.

Warren Buffett (b. 1930) US entrepreneur and financier. *Berkshire Hathaway Annual Report* (2002)

10 Unfortunately the hangover from the market bubble may prove to be proportionate to the binge.

Warren Buffett (b. 1930) US entrepreneur and financier. *Berkshire Hathaway Annual Report* (2002)

11 It was a mass hallucination, by far the biggest in my lifetime.

Warren Buffett (b. 1930) US entrepreneur and financier. Referring to the market boom of dot.com company shares. Quoted in *Fortune* (October 2002)

12 Companies such as Coca-Cola and Gillette might well be labeled 'The Inevitables'...no sensible observer...questions that Coke and Gillette will dominate their fields worldwide for an investment lifetime...Obviously many companies in high-tech businesses will grow much faster than will 'The Inevitables'. But I would rather be certain of a good result than hopeful of a great one.

Warren Buffett (b. 1930) US entrepreneur and financier. Chairman's Letter to Shareholders (28 February 1997)

13 If you aren't willing to own a stock for ten years, don't even think about owning it for ten minutes.

Warren Buffett (b. 1930) US entrepreneur and financier. Chairman's Letter to Shareholders (28 February 1997)

14 If you expect to be a net saver during the next five years, should you hope for a higher or lower stock market?...Many investors get this one wrong...Only those who will be sellers of equities in the near future should be happy at seeing stocks rise.

Warren Buffett (b. 1930) US entrepreneur and financier. Chairman's Letter to Shareholders (27 February 1998)

15 In assessing risk, a beta purist will disdain examining what a company produces, what its competitors are doing...What he treasures is the price history of its stock. In contrast, we...seek whatever information will further

our understanding of the company's business. After we buy a stock we would not be disturbed if markets closed for a year or two.
Warren Buffett (b. 1930) US entrepreneur and financier. Chairman's Letter to Shareholders (7 March 1995)

16 Smile when you read a headline that says 'Investors lose as market falls'. Edit it in your mind to 'Disinvestors lose as market falls—but investors gain'. Though writers often forget this truism, there is a buyer for every seller and what hurts one necessarily helps the other.
Warren Buffett (b. 1930) US entrepreneur and financier. Chairman's Letter to Shareholders (27 February 1998)

17 The true investor *welcomes* volatility...a wildly fluctuating market means that irrationally low prices will periodically be attached to solid businesses.
Warren Buffett (b. 1930) US entrepreneur and financier. Chairman's Letter to Shareholders (7 March 1995)

18 What an investor needs is the ability to correctly evaluate selected businesses. Note that word 'selected': You don't have to be an expert on every company, or even many. You only have to be able to evaluate companies within your circle of competence. The size of that circle is not very important; knowing its boundaries, however, is vital.
Warren Buffett (b. 1930) US entrepreneur and financier. Chairman's Letter to Shareholders (28 February 1997)

19 Why potential buyers even look at projections prepared by sellers baffles me...I never give them a glance, but instead keep in mind the story of the man with an ailing horse. Visiting the vet, he said: 'Can you help me? Sometimes my horse walks just fine and sometimes he limps'. The vet's reply was pointed: 'No problem—when he's walking fine, sell him'.
Warren Buffett (b. 1930) US entrepreneur and financier. Chairman's Letter to Shareholders (1 March 1996)

20 Your goal as an investor...to purchase, at a rational price, a part interest in an easily-understandable business whose earnings are virtually certain to be materially higher...years from now. Over time, you will find only a few companies that meet these standards—so when you see one...buy a meaningful amount of stock.
Warren Buffett (b. 1930) US entrepreneur and financier. Chairman's Letter to Shareholders (28 February 1997)

21 The truly big investment idea can usually be explained in a short paragraph. We like a business with enduring competitive advantages that is run by able and owner-oriented people. When these attributes exist, and when we can make purchases at sensible prices, it is hard to go wrong.
Warren Buffett (b. 1930) US entrepreneur and financier. Explaining Berkshire Hathaway's investment principles. Chairman's Letter to Shareholders (7 March 1995)

22 I don't pay attention to what the stock does. If the business does well, the stock eventually follows.
Warren Buffett (b. 1930) US entrepreneur and financier. *BusinessWeek* (1994)

23 Buy stocks like you buy your groceries, not like you buy your perfume.
Warren Buffett (b. 1930) US entrepreneur and financier. *Fortune* (9 March 1992)

24 A group of lemmings looks like a pack of individuals compared with Wall Street when it gets a concept in its teeth.
Warren Buffett (b. 1930) US entrepreneur and financier. Quoted in *Treasury of Investment Wisdom* (Bernice Cohen; 1999)

25 Business is all about putting out money today to get a whole lot back later.
Warren Buffett (b. 1930) US entrepreneur and financier. Quoted in *Treasury of Investment Wisdom* (Bernice Cohen; 1999)

26 Never speculate...if you have savings, invest them in solid securities, lands, or property. The man who gambles upon the exchanges is in the condition of the man who gambles at the gaming table. He rarely, if ever, makes a permanent success.
Andrew Carnegie (1835–1919) US industrialist and philanthropist. The sixth of his rules of business success. 'From Oakland: How to Succeed in Life', *The Pittsburgh Bulletin* (19 December 1903)

27 Too many companies, especially large ones, are driven more and more narrowly by the need to ensure that investors get good quarterly returns and to justify executives' high salaries. Too often, this means that they view most employees as costs.
Hillary Clinton (b. 1947) US lawyer, politician, and former first lady. *It Takes a Village* (1996)

28 London's preoccupation is one for returns rather than maintaining capital. Still less is the City concerned with sustaining British industry.
Ralf Dahrendorf (b. 1929) British sociologist. *On Britain* (1982)

29 While...economic elements and fundamentals are underlying the market, the next 10 percent move in the market...is going to be driven by psychology.
Gail Dudack (b. 1948) US managing director and chief investment strategist of UBS Securities Ltd. Quoted in *Women of the Street* (Sue Herera; 1997)

30 There is no human feeling to the US securities markets and sometimes no discernible evidence of human intelligence either. But they work.
Robert J. Eaton (b. 1940) US motor industry executive and engineer. Speech (18 March 1996)

31 Contacts with economists take years to develop, and then you've got to know the biases of those economists.
Elaine Garzarelli (b. 1951) US CEO and president of Garzarelli Investment Management. Quoted in *Women of the Street* (Sue Herera; 1997)

32 Good moves are anticipatory. That's why when things look great you sell; when things look horrible you buy.

Elaine Garzarelli (b. 1951) US CEO and president of Garzarelli Investment Management. Quoted in *Women of the Street* (Sue Herera; 1997)

33 If risky investments turn out poorly—as risky investments are wont to do on occasion—governments or international financial institutions should not endeavor to shield investors from loss. This is as it should be, since investors earn premiums to compensate for the risks of such investments.

Alan Greenspan (b. 1926) US economist and chairman of US Federal Reserve Board. Speech to the Financial Crisis Conference, Council on Foreign Relations, New York. 'Global Challenges' (12 July 2000)

34 Private capital markets are the fundamental building block of the capitalist system of resource allocation across activities and over time. Such markets can function properly only if investors bear the costs of their bad decisions and bad luck and reap the benefits of their good decisions and good luck.

Alan Greenspan (b. 1926) US economist and chairman of US Federal Reserve Board. Speech to the Financial Crisis Conference, Council on Foreign Relations, New York. 'Global Challenges' (12 July 2000)

35 Market share is gained and lost at times of technology breaks. This is the mother of all technology breaks...So the opportunity to try and bet on the horse that's going to get ahead is very, very tempting. At the same time, the ability to discriminate between one choice and another choice in this very noisy investment environment is becoming very difficult.

Andrew S. Grove (b. 1936) US entrepreneur, author, and chairman of Intel Corporation. Speech, Los Angeles Times 3rd Annual Investment Strategies Conference, Los Angeles, California (22 May 1999)

36 This is a challenging time to be a participant and a challenging time to be an investor also, because what you have in front of you is the wholesale reengineering of the US and, for that matter, the global gross domestic product delivery.

Andrew S. Grove (b. 1936) US entrepreneur, author, and chairman of Intel Corporation. Speech, Los Angeles Times 3rd Annual Investment Strategies Conference, Los Angeles, California (22 May 1999)

37 The public may be willing to forgive us for mistakes in judgment but it will not forgive us for mistakes in motive.

Robert W. Haack (1917–92) US president of New York Stock Exchange. *Wall Street Journal* (17 October 1967)

38 Knowledge resides in the heads of people. Shareholders cannot own it since owning people is not considered moral. It is also not practical. Acquisitions of intellectual capital firms therefore often fail.

Charles Handy (b. 1932) British business executive and author. Speech at the Second Workshop on Inventing the Organization of the 21st Century, Munich, Germany. 'The Age of Paradox' (April 1996)

39 Only a fool holds out for the top dollar.

Joseph P. Kennedy (1888–1969) US entrepreneur, government official, and diplomat. Following this bearish maxim, Kennedy offloaded his stock during the speculative frenzy of summer 1929. During the subsequent market collapse he famously pursued a strategy of selling stocks short. By 1930 he was estimated to be worth $100 million compared with some $8 million before the Great Crash. Quoted in *The Edge of Chaos: Financial Booms, Bubbles, Crashes and Chaos* (Bernice Cohen; 1997), pt 1, ch. 2

40 Professionals and speculators are not primarily concerned with making superior long-term forecasts but with foreseeing changes in the conventional basis of valuation a short time ahead of the general public.

John Maynard Keynes (1883–1946) British economist. *The General Theory of Employment Interest and Money* (1936)

41 Speculators may do no harm as bubbles on the steady stream of enterprise. But the position is serious when enterprise becomes the bubble on the whirl-pool of speculation.

John Maynard Keynes (1883–1946) British economist. *The General Theory of Employment Interest and Money* (1936)

42 Investors don't like uncertainty. When there's uncertainty, they always think that there's another shoe to fall. There is no other shoe to fall.

Kenneth Lay (b. 1942) US business executive. Referring to concerns about the later-bankrupt Enron. Quoted in *BusinessWeek* (14 December 2001)

43 It is not the pace of technology or the brilliance of innovation that guarantees the success of our markets, but rather an unyielding commitment to quality...Quality, at its broadest and most basic level, is the protection of the investor interest. This principle reaffirms a simple and salient truth—markets exist by the grace of investors.

Arthur Levitt Jr (b. 1931) US author and former chairman of the US Securities and Exchange Commission. Speech to the Columbia Law School, New York City. 'Dynamic Markets, Timeless Principles' (23 September 1999)

44 We should never lose sight of the underlying essence of a market—a place where buyers and sellers come together. Every other feature—whether crafted by tradition or technology—exists only to serve that primary purpose.

Arthur Levitt Jr (b. 1931) US author and former chairman of the US Securities and Exchange Commission. Speech to the Columbia Law School, New York City. 'Dynamic Markets, Timeless Principles' (23 September 1999)

45 At its most basic level, a market represents an agreement between two people. For that market to sustain long-term health, those two people must honor that agreement. They must trust each other...you can have all the technology and global forces you want, but it's useless if basic trust does not exist.

Arthur Levitt Jr (b. 1931) US author and former chairman of the US Securities and Exchange Commission. Speech to the Securities Industry Association Annual Meeting, Boca Raton, Florida. 'Meeting the Challenges of a 21st Century Marketplace' (6 November 1998)

46 For most individuals, the stock market is best used for investing, not trading...On-line trading may be quick and easy; on-line investing requires old-fashioned elbow grease like researching a company or making the time to appreciate the level of risk. I'm often surprised by investors who spend more time deciding what movie they'll rent than on which stock to buy.

Arthur Levitt Jr (b. 1931) US author and former chairman of the US Securities and Exchange Commission. Speech to the National Press Club. 'Plain Talk about On-line Investing' (4 May 1999)

47 I'm concerned that some of the basic but important fundamentals of investing are being lost on investors. Or, even worse, simply ignored. Unless investors truly understand both the opportunities and the risks of today's market, too many may fall victim to their own wishful thinking.

Arthur Levitt Jr (b. 1931) US author and former chairman of the US Securities and Exchange Commission. Speech to the Finance Conference 2000, Boston College, Boston, MA. 'The New Economy' (6 March 2000)

48 If past is prologue, many new companies rushing to market today will not be around for the long haul, perhaps not even a few years from now. Investors today cannot fall prey to an urge that tells them it's okay to suspend good judgment and invest with their eyes closed and their fingers crossed.

Arthur Levitt Jr (b. 1931) US author and former chairman of the US Securities and Exchange Commission. Speech to the Finance Conference 2000, Boston College, Boston, MA. 'The New Economy' (6 March 2000)

49 More and more, Americans are investing in our stock markets...Standing in line at the supermarket or the hardware store, you're as likely to hear about the Nasdaq's performance as you are Monday night's football score.

Arthur Levitt Jr (b. 1931) US author and former chairman of the US Securities and Exchange Commission. Speech to the Finance Conference 2000, Boston College, Boston, MA. 'The New Economy' (6 March 2000)

50 Much of today's activity highlights an important difference between trading and investing. Trading is buying in the belief that the stock price will rise—regardless of what the buyer actually thinks it's worth... Investing for the long term means focusing on the fundamentals that make up a solid company...no matter how revolutionary change is.

Arthur Levitt Jr (b. 1931) US author and former chairman of the US Securities and Exchange Commission. Speech to the Finance Conference 2000, Boston College, Boston, MA. 'The New Economy' (6 March 2000)

51 Successful investors, through good times and bad, focus a vigilant eye on managing risk. Periods of promise and prosperity are not an excuse for us to let our guard down. In fact, it's times like these when we need to raise it even higher.

Arthur Levitt Jr (b. 1931) US author and former chairman of the US Securities and Exchange Commission. Speech to the Finance Conference 2000, Boston College, Boston, MA. 'The New Economy' (6 March 2000)

52 These are not easy times. Pressures proliferate. Responsibilities overlap. Objectives run counter to each other. Demands often are at cross-purposes. But, investors, regardless, continue to value companies that achieve value through honesty and hard work.

Arthur Levitt Jr (b. 1931) US author and former chairman of the US Securities and Exchange Commission. Speech, Directors' College, Stanford Law School, Stanford University, California (22 March 1999)

53 If investors lose faith in the integrity of our markets' prices, they will go elsewhere. If investors believe that they are not receiving high quality financial information, they will go elsewhere. If they believe that their interests are being placed secondary for any reason whatsoever, they will go elsewhere.

Arthur Levitt Jr (b. 1931) US author and former chairman of the US Securities and Exchange Commission. Speech, Economic Club of Washington, Washington, D.C. (6 April 2000)

54 Investors today commit capital because they have confidence in the quality and the integrity of America's markets. That faith does more than fuel markets—it makes markets possible. In many respects, the dynamism of our market system depends on integrity, professionalism, and the public confidence they inspire.

Arthur Levitt Jr (b. 1931) US author and former chairman of the US Securities and Exchange Commission. Speech, Economic Club of Washington, Washington, D.C. (6 April 2000)

55 We are living in a time when investors are increasingly able to shift their capital in and out of markets cheaply and easily...the road to restoring lost confidence is a long one indeed. As those of you with a bit of gray hair know well, no market has a divine right to the savings of America's investors.

Arthur Levitt Jr (b. 1931) US author and former chairman of the US Securities and Exchange Commission. Speech, Economic Club of Washington, Washington, D.C. (6 April 2000)

56 Never invest in any ideas you can't illustrate with a crayon.

Peter Lynch (b. 1944) US fund manager. *Beating the Street* (1993)

57 We told you that the time would come when the master would become impersonal, and that powers that have nothing to do with industry would control industry—the powers of gambling with credit.

Ramsay MacDonald (1866–1937) British prime minister. Speech, Llandudno, Wales (7 October 1930)

58 Women actually do quite well on Wall Street because so much of this business is intuitive.

Elizabeth MacKay, US investment strategist and managing director of Bear Stearns. Quoted in *Women of the Street* (Sue Herera; 1997)

59 We do advise in no uncertain terms that you take advantage of the present high prices.

Charles Merrill (1885–1956) US stockbroker, co-founder of Merrill Lynch & Co. Summer 1929. Letter to customers sent before the October 1929 Great Crash on Wall Street. Quoted in 'Main Street Broker', *Time 100: Heroes and Inspirations* (December 1999)

60 I do not really understand the stock market.

Narayana Murthy (b. 1946) Indian founder and CEO of Infosys. Quoted in *www.rediff.com* (2000)

61 I can calculate the motions of heavenly bodies, but not the madness of people.

Isaac Newton (1642–1727) English mathematician and physicist. Referring to his losses having bought South Sea shares. Quoted in *Treasury of Investment Wisdom* (Bernice Cohen; 1999)

62 Management have been allowed to act like owners. But it is the stockholders who own companies, not managements and the stockholders are just beginning to realise it.

T. Boone Pickens (b. 1928) US oil company executive and financier. Interview, *Sunday Times* (1 December 1985)

63 Make your company stock a consumer product. When consumers buy stock in your company, they'll never buy a competitive product. You've linked their financial future to yours.

Faith Popcorn (b. 1947) US trend expert and founder of BrainReserve. 'Q&A with Faith Popcorn', *www.brainreserve.com* (1999)

64 The stock market is just like a sieve...through the holes...the little investors go. They pick themselves up, do something to get some more money, and then...away they go again.

Will Rogers (1879–1935) US actor, columnist, and humorist. 'Battling Wall Street', *Tulsa Daily World* (10 November 1929)

65 Never invest your money in anything that eats or needs repainting.

Billy Rose (1899–1966) US theatrical impresario and composer. *New York Post* (26 October 1957)

66 'Wall Street', runs the sinister old gag, 'is a street with a river at one end and a graveyard at the other'. This is striking, but incomplete. It omits the kindergarten in the middle.

Fred Schwed (1901–66) US author. *Where Are The Customers' Yachts?* (1940)

67 It's important to understand that investing is in no way an intellectual pursuit in which 'research', 'information', and 'business degrees' are more important than common sense, greed control, discipline, and experience.

Steven R. Selengut (b. 1945) US investment manager and founder of Sanco Services. *A Millionaire's Secret Investment Strategy* (1999)

68 Volatility is more a function of what's reported in the media than the actual fundamentals of companies and economics. And this is precisely what creates the opportunity for profit!

Steven R. Selengut (b. 1945) US investment manager and founder of Sanco Services. *A Millionaire's Secret Investment Strategy* (1999)

69 A crash does not come knocking at the front door by appointment.

Jim Slater (b. 1929) British business executive and author. Quoted in *Treasury of Investment Wisdom* (Bernice Cohen; 1999)

70 As few people know very much about Zulus, anyone who takes the trouble to study them can become an expert.

Jim Slater (b. 1929) British business executive and author. Referring to his 'Zulu Principle' for investment. Quoted in *Treasury of Investment Wisdom* (Bernice Cohen; 1999)

71 They seldom pretend to understand anything of the business of the company...but receive contentedly such half yearly or yearly dividends, as the directors think proper to make them.

Adam Smith (1723–90) British economist and philosopher. Referrring to stockholders in joint-stock companies. *An Inquiry into the Nature and Causes of the Wealth of Nations* (1776), bk 5, ch. 1, pt 3, article 1

72 Financial markets...resent any kind of government interference but they hold a belief deep down that if conditions get really rough the authorities will step in.

George Soros (b. 1930) US financier, entrepreneur, and philanthropist. *The Crisis of Global Capitalism* (1998)

73 The stock market adopts a thesis and tests it; when it fails, as it usually does, it tries out another...that is what produces market fluctuations.

George Soros (b. 1930) US financier, entrepreneur, and philanthropist. *The Crisis of Global Capitalism* (1998)

74 It's not whether you are right or wrong that's important, but how much money you make when you're right and how much you lose when you're wrong.

George Soros (b. 1930) US financier, entrepreneur, and philanthropist. Quoted in *Treasury of Investment Wisdom* (Bernice Cohen; 1999)

75 The City has one rule which it always obeys even in the face of social prejudice: 'If there is money in it we must move in'.

Gerald Sparrow (1903–88) British business executive and writer. *How to Become a Millionaire* (1960), ch. 8

76 The City has persuaded itself—it is cardinal doctrine—that what is good for the City is good for Britain.

Gerald Sparrow (1903–88) British business executive and writer. *How to Become a Millionaire* (1960), ch. 8

77 There should be some professional exam for these analysts. Most of the time they talk through their backsides.

Alan Sugar (b. 1947) British entrepreneur, founder and chairman of Amstrad electronics company. Referring to stock market analysts. Quoted in *The Amstrad Story* (David Thomas; 1990)

78 Property and stock market crashes...litter the history of capitalism. But at the same time there is no evidence that anyone has ever

been successful in preventing such a crash.
Lester Thurow (b. 1938) US economist, management theorist, and writer. 'Barking up the Wrong Tree', *www.lthurow.com* (2 November 1999)

79 Some of the greatest investors I have ever known invest by instinct, rather than research, study, or hard work. If you look back over history, this is the way the greatest fortunes have been built.
Donald J. Trump (b. 1946) US property developer. *Trump: The Art of the Comeback* (co-written with Kate Bohner; 1997)

80 Sometimes your best investments are the ones you don't make.
Donald J. Trump (b. 1946) US property developer. Quoted in *Trump: The Art of the Deal* (co-written with Tony Schwartz; 1987)

81 October. This is one of the peculiarly dangerous months to speculate in stocks. The others are July, January, September, April, November, May, March, June, December, August, and February.
Mark Twain (1835–1910) US writer. Quoted in *The Edge of Chaos: Financial Booms, Bubbles, Crashes and Chaos* (Bernice Cohen; 1997)

82 The stock price is not really interesting at all. The stock price is a lot like the weather. You could walk outside and it could be raining, it could be snowing, there could be a hurricane. I don't control the weather.
Jay S. Walker, US entrepreneur and founder of Priceline.com, CEO of Walker Digital Corporation. Quoted in 'Idea Man', *The Standard* (Todd Woody; 1999)

83 The only reason to invest in the market is because you think you know something others don't.
R. Foster Winans (b. 1948) US journalist and author. *Newsweek* (1 December 1986)

84 I don't invest in anything I don't understand—it makes more sense to buy TV stations than oil wells.
Oprah Winfrey (b. 1954) US talk show host, actor, and business executive. Quoted in *Oprah Winfrey Speaks* (Janet Lowe; 1998)

85 On Wall Street he and a few others—how many?—three hundred, four hundred, five hundred?—had become precisely that...Masters of the Universe.
Tom Wolfe (b. 1931) US novelist and journalist. *The Bonfire of the Vanities* (1987), ch. 1

86 A broker is a man who takes your fortune and runs it into a shoestring.
Alexander Woollcott (1887–1943) US journalist and writer. Quoted in *Alexander Woollcott* (S. Hopkins Adams; 1945), ch. 13

JOBS

1 It is just a job. Grass grows, birds fly, waves pound the sand. I beat people up.
Muhammad Ali (b. 1942) US boxer. Quoted in *New York Times* (6 April 1977)

2 You ask me what I do. Well, actually, you know,
I'm partly a liaison man and partly P.R.O.
Essentially I integrate the export drive
And basically I'm viable from ten o'clock till five.
John Betjeman (1906–84) British poet. 'The Executive', *A Nip in the Air* (1974)

3 People change their coping techniques when they are unable to change the conditions of their jobs easily, and they must live with a job that is either too demanding or not demanding enough.
Rabi S. Bhagat (b. 1950) Indian business author. *Human Stress and Cognition in Organisations* (co-edited and co-written with Terry A. Beehr; 1985), Conclusion

4 Today's organization is rapidly being transformed from a structure built out of jobs to a field of work needing to be done...jobs are rigid solutions to an elastic problem...and...are going the way of the dinosaur.
William Bridges (b. 1933) US transition management thinker. *Jobshift: How to Prosper in a Workplace without Jobs* (1994)

5 I don't think anybody yet has invented a pastime that's as much fun, or keeps you as young, as a good job.
Frederick Hudson Ecker (1867–1964) US insurance executive and chairman of Metropolitan Life. Quoted in his obituary. *New York Times* (20 March 1964)

6 It is at least conceivable that the 21st century business environment will be so fluid that it defies analysis, forcing executives to fall back upon hunch, or instinct.
John Elkington (b. 1949) British author and ecologist. *Cannibals with Forks* (1997)

7 In the past, business was the employer of all those who wanted to work. In the future, there will be lots of customers, but not lots of jobs.
Charles Handy (b. 1932) British business executive and author. *The Empty Raincoat: Making Sense of the Future* (1994)

8 Editor: A person employed on a newspaper whose business is to separate the wheat from the chaff and see that the chaff is printed.
Elbert Hubbard (1856–1915) US humorist. 1903. Quoted in *New York Times* (2000)

9 'Oh brave new world', said Robyn, 'where only the managing directors have jobs'.
David Lodge (b. 1935) British novelist and critic. *Nice Work* (1968)

10 You don't need to interpret tea leaves stuck in a cup
To understand that people who work sitting down get paid more than those people who work standing up.
Ogden Nash (1902–71) US humorist and writer. 'Will Consider Situation', *The Face Is Familiar* (1940)

11 Ninety percent of our jobs are in jeopardy, and corporations are in the middle of unprecedented change. If we simply do the job our bosses want us to do, we may soon find ourselves without any marketable skills.

Tom Peters (b. 1942) US management consultant and author. 'The Ominous Prediction of Tom Peters', *Small Manufacturing SIG Newsletter* (Ira Smolowitz; 2000)

12 I'd got to the point where the salary was quite exciting and the car was either a BMW or a Mercedes, but there was no job satisfaction.

Pauline Portas (b. 1952) British entrepreneur. *Financial Times* (19 October 2000)

13 I think it takes more courage to get up every morning and go to a job that's killing you...more rewards go to the person who does what he or she loves because you do such a better job at it.

Harriet Rubin (b. 1952) US author. *www.tompeters.com* (2000)

JUDGEMENTS

1 It takes little talent to see clearly what lies under one's nose, a good deal of it to know in what direction to point that organ.

W.H. Auden (1907–73) US poet. *The Dyers Hand* (1963)

2 We made a professional judgement about the appropriate accounting treatment that turned out to be wrong.

Joseph Berardino (b. 1951) US business executive. Referring to Enron's accounting practices. Submission to a hearing on Enron (12 December 2002)

3 Your representative owes you, not his industry only, but his judgement; and he betrays instead of serving you if he sacrifices it to your opinion.

Edmund Burke (1729–97) British philosopher and politician. Speech, Bristol, United Kingdom (3 November 1774)

4 Power in a corporation becomes residual and dwells in the background. It is the ability to exercise nice matters of judgment.

Oliver Lyttelton Chandos (1893–1972) British statesman and industrialist. *Memoirs of Lord Chandos: An Unexpected View from the Summit* (1963)

5 I leave this rule for others when I'm dead. Be always sure you're right—then go ahead.

Davy Crockett (1786–1836) US frontiersman, pioneer, and politician. His motto in the war of 1812. *Autobiography* (1834)

6 A man with a surplus can control circumstances, but a man without a surplus is controlled by them, and often has no opportunity to exercise judgment.

Harvey Firestone (1868–1938) US founder of Firestone Tire and Rubber. Quoted in *The Arizona Republic* (2000)

7 When you're caught in the turbulence of a strategic inflection point, the sad fact is that instinct and judgment are all you've got to guide you through.

Andrew S. Grove (b. 1936) US entrepreneur, author, and chairman of Intel Corporation. Attrib.

8 There are more pompous, arrogant, self-centered mediocre...people running corporate America...their judgments and misjudgments have made me rich.

Joseph D. Jamail Jr (b. 1925) US lawyer. Referring to the $10.5 billion settlement he won for Pennzoil against Texaco. *New York Times* (21 November 1985)

9 A community that endures a contemptible law is itself contemptible.

Alfred G. Stephens (1865–1933) Australian journalist and literary critic. *Bookfellow* (1 March 1912)

10 Hindsight gives everyone perfect vision.

Chris Wright (b. 1944) British entrepreneur and music promoter. Quoted in *The Adventure Capitalists* (Jeff Grout and Lynne Curry; 1998)

KNOWLEDGE

1 Applying knowledge to knowledge in business only really begins when we reflect on the learning and knowledge component of the work itself.

Verna Allee (b. 1949) US writer and consultant. *The Knowledge Evolution* (1997)

2 Strategic advantage lies in the leverage of knowledge.

Robert Buckman (b. 1937) US chairman of Buckman Laboratories. Speech (1992)

3 We could have over 520 brains connected in real time across time and space available for any problem.

Robert Buckman (b. 1937) US chairman of Buckman Laboratories. Speech (1992)

4 An expert is one who knows more and more about less and less.

Nicholas Murray Butler (1862–1947) US academic. *Speed* (1901)

5 I...understand the importance of maintaining a balance between information, knowledge, and meaning. Remember what Thoreau said about news: 'If it's important enough, it'll reach you'.

James Champy (b. 1942) US business executive. Quoted in *Forbes* (22 September 1997)

6 Knowledge may give weight, but accomplishments add lustre, and many more people see than weigh.

Lord Chesterfield (1694–1773) English statesman, orator, and letter writer. Letter (1756)

7 The use of knowledge is not easily restricted and bounded.

Diane Coyle, British economist and journalist. *The Weightless World* (1997)

8 To know all is not to forgive all. It is to despise everybody.

Quentin Crisp (1908–99) British writer. *The Naked Civil Servant* (1968)

9 We live in an economy where knowledge, not buildings and machinery, is the chief resource and where knowledge-workers make up the

biggest part of the work force. Until well into the 20th century, most workers were manual workers. Today...40% of our total work force, are knowledge-workers.
Peter F. Drucker (b. 1909) US management consultant and academic. Discussing the rapid expansion of continuing education generally, and online education in particular. 'Putting More Now into the Internet', *www.Forbes.com* (15 March 2000)

10 I find more and more executives less and less well informed about the outside world, if only because they believe that the data on the computer printouts are ipso facto information.
Peter F. Drucker (b. 1909) US management consultant and academic. Quoted in 'Seeing Things as They Really Are', *Forbes* (Robert Lenzner and Stephen S. Johnson; 1987)

11 The single greatest challenge facing managers in the developed countries of the world is to raise the productivity of knowledge and service works.
Peter F. Drucker (b. 1909) US management consultant and academic. *Harvard Business Review* (November/December 1991)

12 This challenge, which will dominate the management agenda for the next several decades, will ultimately determine the competitive performance of companies.
Peter F. Drucker (b. 1909) US management consultant and academic. Referring to the management of knowledge. *Harvard Business Review* (November/December 1991)

13 Knowledge is the only meaningful resource today.
Peter F. Drucker (b. 1909) US management consultant and academic. *Post-capitalist Society* (1993)

14 Proficient is defined with one word: skilled. In order to become skilled you must have more than knowledge, you need to apply that information.
Jac Fitz-Enz (b. 1948) US writer. *How to Measure Human Resources Management* (1995)

15 The conventional wisdom.
J.K. Galbraith (b. 1908) US economist and diplomat. *The Affluent Society* (1958)

16 And still they gazed, and still the wonder grew, That one small head could carry all he knew.
Oliver Goldsmith (1730–74) British playwright, writer, and poet. *The Deserted Village* (1770)

17 What is it that breathes fire into the equations and makes a universe for them to describe?
Stephen Hawking (b. 1942) British scientist and author. *A Brief History of Time* (1988)

18 Knowledge is proportionate to being. You know in virtue of what you are.
Aldous Huxley (1894–1963) British novelist and essayist. *Time Must Have a Stop* (1944)

19 If this capsule history of our progress teaches us anything, it is that man, in his quest for knowledge and progress, is determined and cannot be deterred.
John F. Kennedy (1917–1963) US president. Referring to the US space programme. Speech (13 September 1962)

20 Companies, like people, cannot be skillful at everything. Therefore, core capabilities both advantage and disadvantage a company.
Dorothy Leonard, US academic and business author. *Wellsprings of Knowledge* (1995)

21 Knowledge building for an organization occurs by combining people's distinct individualities with a particular set of activities.
Dorothy Leonard, US academic and business author. *Wellsprings of Knowledge* (1995)

22 I agree completely with my son James when he says 'Internet is like electricity. The latter lights up everything, while the former lights up knowledge'. Frankly, I don't want to be left behind. In fact, I want to be here before the action starts.
Kerry Packer (b. 1937) Australian entrepreneur and chairman of Consolidated Press Holdings. 'There are More Advantages in India Than in China', *Rediff* (Neena Haridas; 2000)

23 Real education must ultimately be limited to one who INSISTS on knowing, the rest is mere sheep-herding.
Ezra Pound (1885–1972) US poet, critic, editor, and translator. *ABC of Reading* (1960)

24 The person who knows 'how' will always have a job. The person who knows 'why' will always be his boss.
Diane Ravitch (b. 1938) US educationalist and academic. *Time* (17 June 1985)

25 What our competitive and careerist knowledge industry has produced already hopelessly exceeds our ability to make graceful use of it.
Theodore Roszak (1933–81) US historian, writer, and editor. *Where the Wasteland Ends* (1972)

26 The demands for new knowledge and skills will be constant, no longer a value added element, but the essential factor in determining organizational survival.
Meg Wheatley (b. 1941) US academic, management theorist, and president of the Berkana Institute. 'The Future of Workplace Learning and Performance', *Training and Development* (1994)

LAWYERS

1 Organised business is a thing of law; and the law is always hard and unrelenting toward the weak.
Henry Ward Beecher (1813–87) US clergyman and reformer. *Proverbs from Plymouth Pulpit* (1887)

2 Lawyers are the only persons in whom ignorance of the law is not punished.
Jeremy Bentham (1748–1832) British philosopher, economist, and jurist. Attrib.

3 Woe unto you, lawyers! for ye have taken away the key of knowledge: ye entered not in yourselves, and them that were entering in ye hindered.
Bible. Luke 11:52

4 LAWYER, n. One skilled in circumvention of the law.

Ambrose Bierce (1842–?1914) US journalist and writer. *The Devil's Dictionary* (1911)

5 A client is fain to hire a lawyer to keep from the injury of other lawyers.

Samuel Butler (1612–80) English poet. *Prose Observations* (1660–80)

6 Doctors are just the same as lawyers; the only difference is that lawyers merely rob you, whereas doctors rob you and kill you, too.

Anton Chekhov (1860–1904) Russian playwright and short-story writer. *Ivanov* (1887), Act 1

7 When the meek inherit the earth, lawyers will be there to work out the deal.

Sam Ewing (1920–2001) US author. Quoted in *Wall Street Journal* (22 May 1997)

8 As in law so in war, the longest purse finally wins.

Mahatma Gandhi (1869–1948) Indian nationalist leader and philosopher. Lecture to the Bombay Provincial Conference (17 September 1917)

9 There is no better way of exercising the imagination than the study of law. No poet ever interpreted nature as freely as a lawyer interprets truth.

Jean Giraudoux (1882–1944) French diplomat, novelist, and playwright. *Tiger at the Gates* (1935)

10 You might as well try to employ a boa constrictor as a tape-measure as to go to a lawyer for legal advice.

Oliver St John Gogarty (1878–1957) Irish poet and novelist. *Tumbling in the Hay* (1939)

11 Unnecessary laws are not good laws but traps for money.

Thomas Hobbes (1588–1679) English philosopher and political theorist. *Leviathan, or, The Matter, Form, and Power of a Commonwealth Ecclesiastical and Civil* (1651), pt 2, ch. 26

12 To a lawyer facts were there to be challenged. All facts. The more self-evident a fact might appear to the layman, the more vigorously must the conscientious lawyer contest it.

John Le Carré (b. 1931) British novelist. *Single and Single* (1999)

13 The Law is a sort of hocus-pocus science that smiles in yer face while it picks yer pocket.

Charles Macklin (?1697–1797) Irish actor and dramatist. *Love à la Mode* (?1759), Act 2, Scene 1

14 Lawyers are like rhinoceroses: thick-skinned, short-sighted, and always ready to charge.

David Mellor (b. 1949) British politician and broadcaster. 'Question Time', BBC Television (3 December 1992)

15 No brilliance is needed in the law. Nothing but common sense, and relatively clean finger nails.

John Mortimer (b. 1923) British lawyer, dramatist, and writer. *A Voyage Round My Father* (1970)

16 To me the law seems like a sort of maze through which a client must be led to safety; a collection of reefs, rocks and underwater harzards through which he or she must be piloted.

John Mortimer (b. 1923) British lawyer, dramatist, and writer. *Clinging to the Wreckage* (1982), ch. 7

17 Trying to control corporate power and abuse by American corporate law has proven about as effective as drinking coffee with a fork.

Ralph Nader (b. 1934) US lawyer and consumer-rights campaigner. Quoted in *The Times* (23 October 1976)

18 A lawyer with his briefcase can steal more than a hundred men with guns.

Mario Puzo (1920–99) US novelist. *The Godfather* (1969)

19 Laws are like spider's webs: if some poor weak creature come up against them, it is caught; but a bigger one can break through and get away.

Solon (?638–?559 BC) Athenian statesman, legislator, and poet. Quoted in 'Solon', *Parallel Lives* (Plutarch 1st century AD)

20 It is not entirely accidental that corporate lawyers in the United States are often called 'hired guns'...From the smallest commercial litigation to the multibillion dollar lawsuit...law marks force—which implies the potential application of violence.

Alvin Toffler (b. 1928) US social commentator. *Powershift* (1990), pt 2, ch. 4

21 Always remember...that when you go into an attorney's office door, you will have to pay for it, first or last.

Anthony Trollope (1815–82) British novelist. *The Last Chronicle of Barset* (1867), vol. 1, ch. 20

LEADERSHIP

1 Strong men can accomplish a lot, even with poor organisation, but weakness at the top cannot be overcome by the best.

Dean Acheson (1893–1971) US statesman. *Present at the Creation* (1969)

2 Leadership is about a sense of direction...It's knowing what the next step is.

John Adair (b. 1933) British management theorist. Interview, *Director* (November 1988)

3 Dear Lord...Give me the mysterious something which will enable me at all times satisfactorily to explain policies, rules, regulations...even when they have never been explained to me.

Anonymous. Quoted in 'A Leader's Prayer', *Understanding Organisations* (Charles Handy; 1976), pt 1, ch. 4

4 Teach me to smile if it kills me. Make me a better leader...by helping develop larger and greater qualities of understanding, tolerance, sympathy, wisdom, perspective, equanimity, mind-reading, and second sight.

Anonymous. Quoted in 'A Leader's Prayer', *Understanding Organisations* (Charles Handy; 1976), pt 1, ch. 4

5 The speed of the leader is the speed of the gang.
Mary Kay Ash (1915–2001) US entrepreneur, business executive, and founder of Mary Kay Cosmetics. *Mary Kay* (1981)

6 Finding the right balance of hierarchical looseness versus control is a central task of leadership in the boundaryless organization.
Ron Ashkenas (b. 1950) US writer. *The Boundaryless Organization* (co-written with Dave Ulrich, Todd Jick, and Steve Kerr; 1995)

7 Leadership is interpersonal influence, exercised in a situation and directed, through the communication process, toward the attainment of a specified goal or goals.
Lionel J. Beaulieu (b. 1950) US writer. *CD-22, Florida Cooperative Extension Service* (1992)

8 At a rehearsal I let the orchestra play as they like. At the concert I make them play as I like.
Thomas Beecham (1879–1961) British conductor. Quoted in *Sir Thomas Beecham* (Neville Cardew; 1961)

9 I think consensus is a poor substitute for leadership.
Charlotte Beers (b. 1935) US advertising executive and former under secretary of state for public diplomacy and public affairs in the US government. *Fortune* (August 1996)

10 A faith is something you die for; a doctrine is something you kill for; there is all the difference in the world.
Tony Benn (b. 1925) British politician. *Observer* (April 1989)

11 Social architects.
Warren Bennis (b. 1925) US educator and writer. Referring to business leaders. 'Why Leaders Can't Lead', *Amacom* (1976)

12 Empowerment is the collective effort of leadership.
Warren Bennis (b. 1925) US educator and writer. *An Invented Life* (1993)

13 Leadership can be felt throughout an organization. It gives pace and energy to the work and empowers the workforce.
Warren Bennis (b. 1925) US educator and writer. *An Invented Life* (1993)

14 Leaders walk their talk; in true leaders there is no gap between the theories they espouse and their practice.
Warren Bennis (b. 1925) US educator and writer. *Business* (October 1990)

15 The capacity to create a compelling vision and translate it into action and sustain it.
Warren Bennis (b. 1925) US educator and writer. His definition of leadership. Quoted in *Director* (April 1991)

16 The leader...is the translator, facilitator, the articulating point between the group's genius, who is doing great things, producing big and innovative ideas, and the public, the market.
Warren Bennis (b. 1925) US educator and writer. Referring to the role of leaders in 'Great Groups', his concept of the exceptional groups thrown up in business and elsewhere. Great Groups achieve tremendous successes, often with very limited resources. Interview, *Strategy + Business* (July– September 1997)

17 Leaders articulate and define what has previously remained implicit or unsaid, then they invent images, metaphors, and models that provide a focus for new attention.
Warren Bennis (b. 1925) US educator and writer. *Leaders* (1985)

18 Leaders are the most results-oriented individuals in the world, and results get attention.
Warren Bennis (b. 1925) US educator and writer. *Leaders: The Strategies for Taking Charge* (co-written with Burt Nanus; 1997)

19 Managers are people who do things right and leaders are people who do the right things.
Warren Bennis (b. 1925) US educator and writer. *Leaders: The Strategies for Taking Charge* (co-written with Burt Nanus; 1997)

20 Leaders are almost like midwives of ideas. They really understand what is going on. You know when you come to them with an idea, they aren't going to just say, 'Well, that's nice, and maybe we can use that'.
Warren Bennis (b. 1925) US educator and writer. Interview, *Strategy + Business* (July–September 1997)

21 Leaders configure the context while managers surrender to it.
Warren Bennis (b. 1925) US educator and writer. 'Managing the Dream', *Training Management* (1990)

22 The manager does things right; the leader does the right thing.
Warren Bennis (b. 1925) US educator and writer. 'Managing the Dream', *Training Management* (1990)

23 Whatever a great man does, others imitate. People conform to the standards he has set.
Bhagavad Gita, Indian religious text (?1st century BC)

24 The art of leadership is saying no, not yes. It is very easy to say yes.
Tony Blair (b. 1953) British prime minister. *Daily Mail* (October 1994)

25 I don't do plumbing.
Christopher Bland (b. 1938) British media executive and chairman of BT. Referring to his single-mindedness. *Management Today* (July 1999)

26 Discrimination is the capacity to discern what is important.
Warren Blank (b. 1945) US writer. *The 9 Natural Laws of Leadership* (1995)

27 Followers are allies who represent the necessary opposite side of the leadership coin.
Warren Blank (b. 1945) US writer. *The 9 Natural Laws of Leadership* (1995)

28 I'm the boss. I'm allowed to yell.
Ivan Boesky (b. 1937) US financier convicted of insider dealing in 1987. Quoted in *Den of Thieves* (James B. Stewart; 1991)

29 A fanatic is a great leader who is just entering the room.
Heywood Broun (1888–1939) US journalist. *New York World* (February 1928)

30 Managing change is about leading change.
Shona L. Brown (b. 1966) Canadian writer. *Competing on the Edge* (co-written with Kathleen M. Eisenhardt; 1998)

31 Leadership, unlike naked power wielding is thus inseparable from followers' needs and goals.
James MacGregor Burns (b. 1918) US political scientist. *Leadership* (1978)

32 The crisis of leadership today is the mediocrity or irresponsibility of so many of the men and women in power.
James MacGregor Burns (b. 1918) US political scientist. *Leadership* (1978)

33 The fundamental process is an elusive one; it is in large part to make conscious what lies unconscious among followers.
James MacGregor Burns (b. 1918) US political scientist. *Leadership* (1978)

34 The leadership approach tends often unconsciously to be elitist; it projects heroic figures against the shadowy figures background of drab, powerless masses.
James MacGregor Burns (b. 1918) US political scientist. *Leadership* (1978)

35 Transformational leadership is dynamic leadership in the sense that the leaders throw themselves into a relationship with followers who will feel elevated by it and often become more active themselves.
James MacGregor Burns (b. 1918) US political scientist. *Leadership* (1978)

36 The hierarchical manager of yesterday ran the Industrial Age company with 'Yes Sir! Yes Sir'...When you're running an Information Age company, you've got to allow a lot of dissent.
Bill Campbell (b. 1940) US CEO of Intuit Corporation. Quoted in *Giant Killers* (Geoffrey James; 1996)

37 If your role is leader, then you should try to simplify things and help other people understand things when they are complicated.
Barbara Cassani (b. 1960) US former CEO of Go. *Management Today* (August 1999)

38 Effective leadership...including 'values for becoming', besides just 'skills for doing'...seems to demand continuous reflection and integral assimilation by a true leader.
S.K. Chakraborty (b. 1957) Indian academic. *Ethics in Management: Vedantic Perspectives* (1995)

39 If a leader were...to assume the role of a teacher (which also implies study) on a regular basis, he would be spurred to internalize and project higher values more deeply and genuinely than if the job were delegated to other specialists.
S.K. Chakraborty (b. 1957) Indian academic. *Ethics in Management: Vedantic Perspectives* (1995)

40 Leaders with unruly, lowly minds will project and create turbulent and contaminated environments in their spheres of action.
S.K. Chakraborty (b. 1957) Indian academic. *Ethics in Management: Vedantic Perspectives* (1995)

41 All leadership, management or vision will be useless if it becomes static.
Paul Corrigan (b. 1948) British author. *Shakespeare on Management* (1999)

42 The leader is not just a scorekeeper. He is responsible for creating something new and better.
Bill Creech (b. 1958) US commanding general of US Air Force Tactical Air Command. 'Creech's Laws' (1984)

43 The rot starts at the top.
W. Edwards Deming (1900–93) US consultant and author. Lecture (1983)

44 The basic cause of sickness in American industry and resulting unemployment is the failure of top management to manage.
W. Edwards Deming (1900–93) US consultant and author. *Out of the Crisis* (1992)

45 Drive out fear, so that everyone may work effectively for the company.
W. Edwards Deming (1900–93) US consultant and author. *Quality, Productivity, and Competitive Position* (1982)

46 Because recruiting new leaders is difficult (if not impossible), it is important to use a process to transform the people whom companies already have in place.
David L. Dotlich, US writer. *Action Learning* (co-written with James L. Noel; 1998)

47 Leadership is all hype. We've had three great leaders in this century—Hitler, Stalin, and Mao.
Peter F. Drucker (b. 1909) US management consultant and academic. *Fortune* (February 1994)

48 They have a particular drive, a desire to bring order out of chaos, or if something is too cosy, to create chaos in order to bring change.
Michael Owen Edwardes (b. 1930) British company executive. On leaders. Quoted in *The New Elite* (Berry Ritchie and Walter Goldsmith; 1987)

49 I'll tell you what leadership is. It's persuasion and conciliation, and education, and patience.
Dwight David Eisenhower (1890–1969) US general and president. Quoted in *Handbook of Leadership* (R.M. Stogdill; 1974)

50 I believe absolutely in one man having one vision for the way something should be done.
Chris Evans (b. 1966) British broadcaster and media executive. *Management Today* (July 1999)

51 In the early days, it was easy to lead by example. Now it has to be done by structured education and training.
Tom Farmer (b. 1940) British chairman and CEO of Kwik-Fit. *Digital Britain* (January 2000)

52 I think you have a rocket up your ass and I want to point it in the right direction.
Harry E. Figgie Jr, US founder of Figgie International. Exemplifying Figgie's aggressive management style. Quoted in *Dangerous Company* (James O'Shea and Charles Madigan; 1997)

53 Challenge the mind and capture the heart.
Carly Fiorina (b. 1954) US president and CEO of
Hewlett-Packard. *Forbes* (October 2000)

54 A company is an organic, living, breathing
thing, not just an income sheet and balance
sheet. You have to lead it with that in mind.
Carly Fiorina (b. 1954) US president and CEO of
Hewlett-Packard. 'Secrets of the Fastest Rising Stars',
Fortune (Patricia Sellers; 2000)

55 We want worked out a relationship between
leader and led which will give each the
opportunity to make creative contributions to
the situation.
Mary Parker Follett (1868–1933) US management thinker
and author. *Dynamic Administration* (1941)

56 Drive thy business, let not that drive thee.
Benjamin Franklin (1706–90) US politician, inventor, and
journalist. The *Poor Richard's Almanack* series (1732–58)
were originally published under the pseudonym Richard
Saunders. *Poor Richard's Almanack* (1758)

57 Leaders who understand their organizations
can articulate the negatives as well as the
positives of their organizations.
Jay R. Galbraith (b. 1950) US writer. *Designing
Organizations* (1995)

58 Passionate leadership won't succeed if
contradictory signals are sent out.
Bill Gates (b. 1955) US entrepreneur, chairman and CEO of
Microsoft. Speech (September 1996)

59 Leadership is practiced, not so much in words
as in attitude and in actions.
Harold S. Geneen (1910–97) US telecommunications
entrepreneur and CEO of ITT. Quoted in *Business Studies*
(2000)

60 My philosophy is to stay as close as possible to
what's happening. If I can't solve something,
how the hell can I expect my managers to?
Harold S. Geneen (1910–97) US telecommunications
entrepreneur and CEO of ITT. *New York Times* (23
November 1997)

61 The meek shall inherit the earth, but not the
mineral rights.
J. Paul Getty (1892–1976) US entrepreneur, oil industry
executive, and financier. Quoted in *The Great Getty* (Robert
Lenzner; 1985)

62 Isolation deprives leaders of new ideas.
Doris Helen Kearns Goodwin (b. 1943) US writer and history
educator. 'Lessons of Presidential Leadership', *Leader to
Leader* (1998)

63 The art of leadership is to mobilize people to
care about the tasks ahead.
Doris Helen Kearns Goodwin (b. 1943) US writer and history
educator. 'Lessons of Presidential Leadership', *Leader to
Leader* (1998)

64 The grab for a quick killing is the mark of the
worst kind of leadership, for it places
immediate profit above the long-term interest
of the organization and can lead ultimately
only to disaster.
Crawford H. Greenewalt (d. 1993) US president of DuPont.
'A Philosophy of Business Leadership', *The Conference

*Board Challenge to Business: Industry Leaders Speak
Their Minds* (Peter Krass and Richard E. Cavanagh, eds;
2000)

65 A leader is one who ventures and takes the
risks of going out ahead to show the way and
whom others follow, voluntarily, because they
are persuaded that the leader's path is the
right one—for them, probably better than they
could devise for themselves.
Robert Greenleaf (1904–90) US director of Management
Research for AT&T and author. 'Servant: Retrospect and
Prospect', *The Power of Servant Leadership* (Larry Spears,
ed.; 1998)

66 The best test, and most difficult to administer,
is: Do those served grow as persons? Do they,
while being served, become healthier, wiser,
freer, more autonomous, more likely
themselves to become servants?
Robert Greenleaf (1904–90) US director of Management
Research for AT&T and author. 'Servant: Retrospect and
Prospect', *The Power of Servant Leadership* (Larry Spears,
ed.; 1998)

67 Never look down to test the ground before
taking your next step; only he who keeps his
eye fixed on the far horizon will find his right
road.
Dag Hammarskjöld (1905–61) Swedish politician, writer, and
UN Secretary-General. *Markings* (Leif Sjöberg and W.H.
Auden, tr.; 1964)

68 Managers have been brought up on a diet of
power, divide and rule. they have been
pre-occupied with authority, rather than
making small things happen.
Charles Handy (b. 1932) British business executive and
author. *The Age of Unreason* (1989)

69 He who wields the knife never wears the
crown.
Michael Heseltine (b. 1933) British politician and publisher.
New Society (February 1986)

70 Everyone is capable of exercising effective
leadership in roles that carry leadership
accountability, so long as they value the role.
Elliot Jacques (b. 1917) Canadian psychologist and
sociologist. *Executive Leadership* (1991)

71 Leadership competence…is a matter
fundamentally of competence in the specific
role that carries the leadership accountability.
Elliot Jacques (b. 1917) Canadian psychologist and
sociologist. *Executive Leadership* (1991)

72 In the language of the industrial leader,
quality is primarily a business problem, not a
technical problem.
Joseph M. Juran (b. 1904) US business thinker. 1981. 'The
Two Worlds of Quality Control', *www.juran.com* (2000)

73 By empowering others, a leader does not
decrease his power, instead he may increase
it—especially if the whole organization
performs better.
Rosabeth Moss Kanter (b. 1943) US management theorist,
academic, and writer. *Men and Women of the Corporation*
(1997)

74 Leadership is not about being nice. It's about being right and being strong.
Paul Keating (b. 1944) Australian former prime minister. Quoted in *Time* (1995)

75 I think leadership is valuing the time you spend with your people more than anything else you do.
Herb Kelleher (b. 1931) US businessman and founder of Southwest Airlines. *Computer World* (September 1998)

76 There are a hundred roads to Rome; the important thing is to get there, not to use the same road.
Herb Kelleher (b. 1931) US businessman and founder of Southwest Airlines. *International Organization and Dynamics* (Autumn 1994)

77 Without some element of leadership, the many at the bottom will be paralyzed with choices.
Kevin Kelly (b. 1958) US executive editor of Wired magazine. *New Rules for the New Economy: 10 Radical Strategies for a Connected World* (1998)

78 Leaders must invoke an alchemy of great vision. Those leaders who do not are ultimately judged failures, even though they may be popular at the moment.
Henry Kissinger (b. 1923) US diplomat. *Time* (October 1980)

79 The task of the leader is to get people from where they are to where they have not been.
Henry Kissinger (b. 1923) US diplomat. *Time* (October 1980)

80 The difference between a leader and a boss is the difference between good and bad management.
Joe Klock (b. 1949) US writer. *Like Klockwork: The Whimsy, Wit, and (Sometime) Wisdom of a Key Largo Curmudgeon* (1995)

81 Good leaders make people feel they're at the heart of things, not at the periphery.
Fred Kofman, US writer. *Leaders* (co-written with Burt Nanus; 1985)

82 Leaders today sometimes appear to be an endangered species.
Fred Kofman, US writer. *On Becoming a Leader* (1998)

83 When the effective leader is finished with his work, the people say it happened naturally.
Laozi (?570–?490 BC) Chinese philosopher, reputed founder of Daoism. *Daode Jing*

84 For what I'm doing, you have to be scrappy and partner with a variety of companies.
Geraldine Laybourne (b. 1947) US chairman of Oxygen Media. 'The 50 Most Powerful Women in American Business', *Fortune* (Patricia Sellers and Cora Daniels; October 1999)

85 Men like to issue orders. They like to feel powerful.
Shelly Lazarus (b. 1949) US chairperson of Ogilvy & Mather Worldwide. 'The 50 Most Powerful Women in American Business', *Fortune* (Patricia Sellers and Cora Daniels; October 1999)

86 The genius of a good leader is to leave behind him a situation which common sense, without the grace of genius, can deal with successfully.

Walter Lippmann (1889–1974) US political commentator, editor, and writer. 'Roosevelt Has Gone', *New York Herald Tribune* (14 April 1945)

87 He ought above all things to keep his men well organised and drilled to follow incessantly the chase.
Niccolò Machiavelli (1469–1527) Italian historian, statesman, and political philosopher. *The Prince* (1513)

88 He that would govern others, first should be the master of himself.
Philip Massinger (1583–1640) English playwright. *The Bondman* (1624)

89 The tail tracks the head. If the head moves fast the tail will keep up the same pace. If the head is sluggish, the tail will drop.
Konosuke Matsushita (1894–1989) Japanese electronics executive, entrepreneur, and inventor. *Quest for Prosperity* (1988)

90 Professionals require little direction and supervision. What they do require is protection and support.
Henry Mintzberg (b. 1939) Canadian academic and management theorist. 'Covert Leadership: Notes on Managing Professionals', *Harvard Business Review* (1998)

91 A leader has to be one of two things: he either has to be a brilliant visionary himself, a truly creative strategist, in which case he can do what he likes and get away with it; or else he has to be a true empowerer who can bring out the best in others.
Henry Mintzberg (b. 1939) Canadian academic and management theorist. Quoted in *The Drama of Leadership* (Patricia Pitcher; 1997)

92 Modern business leadership has been generally characterised by the capacity to create large organisations, but by failure in knowing what to do with them.
James Mooney (1884–1957) US business executive. *Onward Industry* (co-written with Alan Reiley; 1931)

93 The most effective leader is the one who satisfies the psychological needs of his followers.
David Ogilvy (1911–99) British advertising executive, founder and chairman of Ogilvy & Mather. *Ogilvy on Advertising* (1983)

94 A chairman who never wanders about his agency becomes a hermit, out of touch with his staff.
David Ogilvy (1911–99) British advertising executive, founder and chairman of Ogilvy & Mather. *Principles of Management* (1968)

95 Our problem today is that the tools are there but our vision is limited.
Richard Pascale (b. 1938) US academic and author. *The Art of Japanese Management* (co-written with Anthony Athos; 1981)

96 Suppose somebody says, look, Ross, I'm very busy. What's the most important thing you can tell me about leadership? I'd say, 'Just treat people the way you'd want to be treated'.

H. Ross Perot (b. 1930) US entrepreneur, venture capitalist, and politician. *Inc.* (January 1989)

97 You have a responsibility to shape the vision of a company, and you know whatever process you choose will determine ultimately the well-being of the organization.
Eckhard Pfeiffer (b. 1941) German CEO of Compaq Corporation. Quoted in *Giant Killers* (Geoffrey James; 1996)

98 The leader must know, must know that he knows, and must be able to make it abundantly clear to those about him that he knows.
Clarence B. Randall (1891–1967) US industrialist and government adviser. *Making Good in Management* (1964)

99 To grasp and hold a vision, that is the very essence of successful leadership—not only on the movie set where I learned it, but everywhere.
Ronald Reagan (b. 1911) US former president and actor. 1994. Attrib.

100 What we need is not a saviour or a guru, but an active movement, so that people work together to understand local difficulties. I'm not saying this is the final answer. There is no final answer for anything.
Reg Revans (1907–2003) British academic. Interview, *Financial Times* (Stuart Crainer; 1996)

101 Leadership, above all, consists of telling the truth, unpalatable though it may be. It is better to go down with the truth on one's lips than to rise high by innuendo and doubletalk.
Alfred Robens (1910–99) British politician and chairman of the National Coal Board. Speech, Institute of Directors' Annual Convention (7 November 1974)

102 Do not delegate an assignment and then attempt to manage it yourself—you will make an enemy of the overruled subordinate.
Wess Roberts (b. 1946) US writer. *Leadership Secrets of Attila the Hun* (1991)

103 Do not expect everyone to agree with you...Do not consider all opponents to be enemies.
Wess Roberts (b. 1946) US writer. *Leadership Secrets of Attila the Hun* (1991)

104 The more your team comes together, the more I think you really want to withdraw.
Jack Rowell (b. 1937) British rugby captain and coach. Quoted in *The Adventure Capitalists* (Jeff Grout and Lynne Curry; 1998)

105 I learned more about managing people when I was captain of the rugby team than when I was working for Procter & Gamble, because you didn't pay them—they had to respect your leadership, otherwise you were in a fix.
Jack Rowell (b. 1937) British rugby captain and coach. Referring to the English national rugby team. Quoted in *The Adventure Capitalists* (Jeff Grout and Lynne Curry; 1998)

106 Legend is the missing ingredient in leadership—although you often see it in women.
Harriet Rubin (b. 1952) US author. 'We Won't See Great

Leaders Until We See Great Women Leaders. As Role Models, Men Are Going Flat', *Fast Company* (2000)

107 Because I was president in the good times, I had to be president in the most difficult times.
Juan Antonio Samaranch (b. 1920) Spanish president of the International Olympic Committee. Referring to his refusal to stand down after a series of crises. *Sunday Times* (September 2000)

108 If a group's survival is threatened because elements of its culture have become maladapted, it is ultimately the function of leadership to recognize and do something about the situation.
Edgar H. Schein (b. 1928) US writer. *Organizational Culture and Leadership* (1992)

109 The new leaders face new tests such as how to lead in this idea-intensive, interdependent network environment.
John Sculley (b. 1939) US partner of Sculley Brothers, former president of Pepsi, and CEO of Apple Computers. Attrib.

110 I try to create an environment in which others make decisions. Success means not making them myself.
Ricardo Semler (b. 1959) Brazilian business executive and president of Semco. *Maverick!* (1993)

111 To be mission-based means that those in positions of authority are not the source of authority.
Peter Senge (b. 1947) US academic and author. 'The Practice of Innovation', *Leader to Leader* (1998)

112 No one in the past 30 years has had a more profound impact on thinking about leadership than Robert Greenleaf.
Peter Senge (b. 1947) US academic and author. *Synchronicity: The Inner Path of Leadership* (Joseph Jaworski; 1996), Introduction

113 The secret of a leader lies in the tests he has faced over the whole course of his life and the habit of action he develops in meeting those tests.
Gail Sheehy (b. 1937) US journalist and author. 'Gorbachev', *Looking for Mikhail Gorbachev* (1991)

114 A loose grip around the throat.
Allen Sheppard (b. 1932) British chairman of Vizual Business Tools and former chairman of Grand Metropolitan. Referring to his personal management style. Quoted in *The Adventure Capitalists* (Jeff Grout and Lynne Banks; 1998)

115 Leadership is the process of achieving a dream together, especially when that dream seems impossible to achieve.
Stan Shih (b. 1945) Taiwanese CEO of the Acer Group. Quoted in *Giant Killers* (Geoffrey James; 1996)

116 I have never issued an order since I have been the operating head of the corporation.
Alfred P. Sloan (1875–1966) US president of General Motors. Referring to the benefits of decentralised management. 'The Most Important Things I Learned About Management', *System* (August 1924)

117 Administrators are cheap and easy to find and cheap to keep. Leaders—risk takers: they are in very short supply. And ones with vision are pure gold.

Raymond W. Smith (b. 1937) US chairman of Rothschild Inc. and former chairman of Bell Atlantic Corporation. Speech (1 August 1988)

118 Consensus is the negation of leadership.

Margaret Thatcher (b. 1925) British former prime minister. Quoted in *Woodbury Reports Archives* (June 1997)

119 Most people in big companies are administered, not led. They are treated as personnel, not people.

Robert Townsend (b. 1920) US business executive and author. *Further Up the Organization* (1984)

120 The first lesson is: To hell with centralized strategic planning. If you don't have a good leader, it's all nothing; it's just a bunch of papers flying around.

Robert Townsend (b. 1920) US business executive and author. 'Townsend's Third Degree in Leadership', *The Conference Board Challenge to Business: Industry Leaders Speak Their Minds* (Peter Krass and Richard E. Cavanagh, eds; 2000)

121 A leader is a man who has the ability to get other people to do what they don't want to do and like it.

Harry S. Truman (1884–1972) US president. Quoted in *Leadership Is Not a Bowler Hat* (P. Prior; 1977)

122 You just have to be the kind of guy to get people to do things.

Donald J. Trump (b. 1946) US property developer. *US News & World Report* (April 1987)

123 I am a leader by default, only because nature does not allow a vacuum.

Desmond Tutu (b. 1931) South African Archbishop, former head of the South African Council of Churches, and winner of the 1984 Nobel Peace Prize. *Christian Science Monitor* (20 December 1984)

124 If we're going to run this business on viscera, it's going to be my viscera.

Thomas J. Watson Jr (1914–93) US CEO of IBM. Quoted in *CEO* (Harry Levinson and Stuart Rosenthal; 1984)

125 Simplicity is an indispensable element of a leader's most important functions.

Jack Welch (b. 1935) US former chairman and CEO of General Electric. Speech (November 1989)

126 The leader's unending responsibility must be to remove every detour, every barrier to ensure that vision is first clear, and then real,

Jack Welch (b. 1935) US former chairman and CEO of General Electric. Speech (November 1989)

127 It is ours to win with—if we can shift gears from decades of controlling things to a decade of liberty—turning people loose to dream, dare, and win.

Jack Welch (b. 1935) US former chairman and CEO of General Electric. *Leaders* (1993)

128 Power wasn't even part of my vocabulary.

Oprah Winfrey (b. 1954) US talk show host, actor, and business executive. 'The 50 Most Powerful Women in American Business', *Fortune* (Patricia Sellers and Cora Daniels; October 1999)

129 If you're trying to create a healthy organization, one that can sustain itself over time, simply legislating and dictating behavior and outcomes doesn't work at all.

Walter Wriston (b. 1919) US banker. Interview with Scott London, *US National Public Radio* (November 1996)

LEARNING

1 A spirit of national masochism prevails, encouraged by an effete corps of impudent snobs who characterize themselves as intellectuals.

Spiro Agnew (1918–96) US vice-president. *New York Times* (1969)

2 The lessons of the past are ignored and obliterated in a contemporary antagonism known as the generation gap.

Spiro Agnew (1918–96) US vice-president. *New York Times* (1969)

3 In the Middle Ages, the rich tried to buy immortality by building cathedrals. These days they set up business schools instead.

Anonymous. *The Economist* (20 July 1996)

4 People no more buy management books for their insights into epistemology than they read *Playboy* for the essays by John Updike.

Anonymous. *The Economist* (31 May 1997)

5 Individual learning is a necessary but insufficient condition for organizational learning.

Chris Argyris (b. 1923) US academic and organisational behaviour theorist. *Organizational Learning: A Theory of Action Perspective* (co-written with Donald A. Schon; 1978)

6 The learning person looks forward to failure or mistakes. The worst problem in leadership is basically early success.

Warren Bennis (b. 1925) US educator and writer. Quoted in *Guide to the Management Gurus* (C. Kennedy; 1998)

7 Learning and performance will become one and the same thing. Everything you say about learning will be about performance. People will get the point that learning is everything.

Peter Block (b. 1935) US writer. 'The Future of Workplace Learning and Performance', *Training and Development* (1994)

8 Example is the school of mankind, and they will learn at no other.

Edmund Burke (1729–97) British philosopher and politician. *Two Letters on the Proposals for Peace with the Regicide Directory* (1796)

9 Learning how to learn is life's most important skill.

Tony Buzan (b. 1942) US author. *Lessons from the Art of Juggling: How to Achieve Your Full Potential in Business, Learning, and Life* (co-written with Michael J. Gelb; 1997)

10 When you are Mind Mapping, you are not only practising and exercising your fundamental memory powers and your information processing, networking, and organising capabilities; you are also...helping you manifest your own genius!

Tony Buzan (b. 1942) US author. *The History of Memory Techniques Leading to Mind Maps* (2000)

11 Your brain is, indeed, a supreme example of, and is the ultimate, Internet.

Tony Buzan (b. 1942) US author. *The Human Brain and the Global Brain* (2000)

12 Education is simply the soul of a society as it passes from one generation to another.

G.K. Chesterton (1874–1936) British novelist, poet, and critic. Attrib.

13 For the bold new world of the 21st century...every adult American must be able to keep on learning for a lifetime.

Bill Clinton (b. 1946) US former president. State of the Union address. (2 February 1997)

14 He who learns but does not think is lost. He who thinks but does not learn is in great danger.

Confucius (551–479 BC) Chinese philosopher, administrator, and writer. *Analects* (?500 BC)

15 Once a company has adapted to a new environment, it is no longer the organization it used to be; it has evolved. That is the essence of learning.

Arie De Geus (b. 1938) Dutch writer. 'The Living Company', *Harvard Business Review* (1997)

16 Back in 1989 Dell made a massive mistake relating to inventory, and now we're regarded as the best in our industry in inventory. The answer is not having a brilliant conception of all the best ideas before you start a business, but rather learning from your mistakes and not repeating them—and making sure that those lessons are passed along as the organization continues to grow.

Michael Dell (b. 1965) US chairman and CEO of Dell Computer Corporation. Speech to the Society of American Business Editors and Writers Technology Conference, Dallas. 'Maximum Speed: Lessons Learned from Managing Hypergrowth' (10 September 1998)

17 Our schools must preserve and nurture the yearning for learning that everyone is born with.

W. Edwards Deming (1900–93) US consultant and author. Quoted in *Woodbury Reports Archives* (February 1998)

18 Organizational learning style is a function of how organizations learn.

Anthony DiBella, US writer and consultant. *How Organizations Learn* (co-written with Edwin C. Nevis; 1998)

19 To engage in the learning cycle, some firms move their employees instead of their knowledge.

Anthony DiBella, US writer and consultant. *How Organizations Learn* (co-written with Edwin C. Nevis; 1998)

20 It took more than 200 years...for the printed book to create the modern school. It won't take nearly that long for the big change.

Peter F. Drucker (b. 1909) US management consultant and academic. Quoted in 'Seeing Things as They Really Are', *Forbes* (Robert Lenzner and Stephen S. Johnson; 1987)

21 Intellectual integrity...the ability to see the world as it is, not as you want it to be.

Peter F. Drucker (b. 1909) US management consultant and academic. Interview, *Forbes* (1987)

22 We should not provide universal access to the Internet. I'd rather provide universal good education so that people could afford universal access—but could have the individual choice of whether to pay for it and how much to buy.

Esther Dyson (b. 1951) US knowledge entrepreneur and government adviser. *Atlantic Online* (1994)

23 I think I'd rather have an English major than an economics major.

Michael Eisner (b. 1942) US chairman and CEO of the Disney Corporation. Speech (June 1994)

24 I'm not an educator...I'm a learner.

Bill Gates (b. 1955) US entrepreneur, chairman and CEO of Microsoft. *The Road Ahead* (co-written with Nathan Myhrvold and Peter N. Rinearson; 1995)

25 Emotional intelligence is a different way of being smart.

Daniel Goleman (b. 1946) US behavioural scientist, journalist, and author. 'On Emotional Intelligence: A Conversation with Daniel Goleman', *Educational Leadership* (John O'Neil; 1996)

26 Lifelong learners take risks. Much more than others, these men and women push themselves out of their comfort zones and try new ideas.

Bob Guccione (b. 1930) US magazine publisher. *Leading Change* (1996)

27 In a time of drastic change, it is the learners who inherit the future. The learned usually find themselves equipped to live in a world that no longer exists.

Eric Hoffer (1902–83) US philosopher. *Reflections on the Human Condition* (1973)

28 It is the true nature of mankind to learn from mistakes, not from example.

Fred Hoyle (1915–2001) British astronomer. *Into Deepest Space* (1974)

29 The purpose of a university is to make students safe for ideas—not ideas safe for students.

Clark Kerr (b. 1911) US educator. Quoted in *Arizona Republic* (1999)

30 True learning begins with unlearning.

Fred Kofman, US writer. *On Becoming a Leader* (1998)

31 Government can legislate but unless the leaders in the children's world step up and support quality educational shows, there will be absolutely no change.

Geraldine Laybourne (b. 1947) US chairman of Oxygen Media. 'It Takes Three to Tango', *www.childrennow.org/media* (2000)

32 The process of maturing is an art to be learned, an effort to be sustained. By the age of

fifty you have made yourself what you are, and if it is good, it is better than your youth.
Marya Mannes (1904–90) US essayist and journalist. *More in Anger* (1958)

33 When students are separated from the influence of destructive peer relations and dysfunctional environments...they have the opportunity to assess their current system of operation without the reinforcement of that system.
Phil Muir, US field director of the Aspen Achievement Academy. *Aspen Trails* (Fall 1994)

34 The most important thing I would learn in school was that almost everything I would learn in school would be utterly useless.
Joseph O'Connor (b. 1963) Irish journalist and novelist. *The Secret World of the Irish Male* (1994)

35 To understand is to perceive patterns.
Yoko Ono (b. 1933) US artist and musician. *Historical Inevitability* (1954)

36 Even though they had won Nobel prizes, they were willing to acknowledge that things could be going on elsewhere. They asked questions.
Reg Revans (1907–2003) British academic. *Action Learning* (1979)

37 The essence of action learning is to become better acquainted with the self by trying to observe what one may actually do, to trace the reasons for attempting it and the consequences of what one seemed to be doing.
Reg Revans (1907–2003) British academic. Interview, *Financial Times* (Stuart Crainer; 1996)

38 All men who have turned out worth anything have had the chief hand in their own education.
Walter Scott (1771–1832) Scottish novelist and poet. Letter to J.G. Lockhart (August 1825)

39 Over the long run, superior performance depends on superior learning.
Peter Senge (b. 1947) US academic and author. 'The Leader's New Work: Building Learning Organizations', *Sloan Management Review* (1990)

40 Often the most effective facilitators in learning processes are not professional trainers but line managers themselves.
Peter Senge (b. 1947) US academic and author. 'Leading Learning Organizations', *Training and Development* (1996)

41 Modern mind has become more and more calculating. The calculative exactness of practical life which the money economy has brought about corresponds to the ideal of natural science.
Georg Simmel (1858–1918) German sociologist and philosopher. Quoted in *The Sociology of Georg Simmel* (Kurt H. Wolff; 1950)

42 Education is what survives when what has been learned has been forgotten.
B.F. Skinner (1904–90) US psychologist. *New Scientist* (21 May 1964)

43 Tedium is never a useful teaching tool.
Earl Stevens, US expert on home schooling. *Electronic Forum on Unschooling* (May 1994)

44 The illiterate of the year 2000 will not be the individual who cannot read and write, but the one who cannot learn, unlearn, and relearn.
Alvin Toffler (b. 1928) US social commentator. Quoted in *Peak Learning—A Master Course in Learning how to Learn* (Ronald Gross; 1991)

45 Never let formal education get in the way of your learning.
Mark Twain (1835–1910) US writer. Quoted in *Jump Start Your Brain* (Doug Hall; 1996)

46 Learning is a willingness to let one's ability and attitude change in response to new ideas, information, and experiences.
Peter B. Vaill (b. 1935) US writer. *Learning as a Way of Being* (1996)

47 Learn from the best while they're good and move on.
Robert H. Waterman Jr (b. 1936) US consultant and author. *The Frontiers of Excellence* (1994)

48 We would not knowingly hire anyone in our company that wasn't 'boundaryless', that wasn't open to an idea from anywhere, that wasn't excited about a learning environment.
Jack Welch (b. 1935) US former chairman and CEO of General Electric. *Washington Post* (1997)

49 Education is an admirable thing, but it is well to remember from time to time that nothing that is worth knowing can be taught.
Oscar Wilde (1854–1900) Irish writer and wit. *Intentions* (1891)

50 Many organizations are now trying to walk under the banner of 'The Learning Organization', realizing that knowledge is our most important product...But the only place that I've seen it is in the Army. As one colonel said, 'We realized a while ago that it's better to learn than be dead'.
Walter Wriston (b. 1919) US banker. Interview with Scott London, *US National Public Radio* (November 1996)

51 What I observe in our business organizations— even in our public institutions—is that after a crisis or breakdown, or after something worked really well, we don't get together and say, 'Okay, what do we each think happened, and what can we learn from it?' We either take credit for it, or, if it's an error, we try to bury it as fast as we can and move on.
Walter Wriston (b. 1919) US banker. Interview with Scott London, *US National Public Radio* (November 1996)

52 Learning is not compulsory, neither is survival.
Peter Zwack (b. 1928) Hungarian business executive. *Out of the Crisis* (1982)

LIMITATIONS

1 The aim of science is not to open the door to infinite wisdom, but to set a limit to infinite error.
Bertolt Brecht (1898–1956) German playwright and poet. *The Life of Galileo* (1939)

2 If you limit a company by its structure or by the people in the company, you will, by definition, limit the full potential of that business. It sounds basic, but a lot of companies don't follow the idea that the structure should be last and not first.
Michael Dell (b. 1965) US chairman and CEO of Dell Computer Corporation. Speech to the Society of American Business Editors and Writers Technology Conference, Dallas. 'Maximum Speed: Lessons Learned from Managing Hypergrowth' (10 September 1998)

3 Bromidic though it may sound, some questions don't have answers, which is a terribly difficult lesson to learn.
Katharine Graham (1917–2001) US newspaper publisher and owner of *Washington Post*. 'The Power That Didn't Corrupt', *Ms.* (Jane Howard; 1974)

4 In some circumstances, a refusal to be defeated is a refusal to be educated.
Margaret Halsey (1910–97) US writer. *No Laughing Matter* (1977)

5 In vulgar usage, progress has come to mean limitless movement in space and time, accompanied, necessarily, by an equally limitless command of energy: culminating in limitless destruction.
Lewis Mumford (1895–1990) US social thinker and writer. *The Pentagon of Power* (1970)

6 The danger is that people can fall in love with the business they're in and get mesmerised by it. As a result, they don't actually see the business.
Allen Sheppard (b. 1932) British chairman of Vizual Business Tools and former chairman of Grand Metropolitan. Quoted in *The Adventure Capitalists* (Jeff Grout and Lynne Banks; 1998)

7 There is no limit to what a man can do or where he can go if he doesn't mind who gets the credit.
Robert W. Woodruff (1889–1985) US CEO of Coca-Cola. Sign on Robert Woodruff's desk.

LISTENING

1 Good listeners, like precious gems, are to be treasured.
Walter Anderson (b. 1944) US writer. *The Confidence Course: Seven Steps to Self-Fulfillment* (1998)

2 Management and the business firm will be better served if the various fights were converted into a reconciliation process which will identify the conditions under which the respective modes become appropriate for success.
Igor Ansoff (1918–2002) US author and academic. *The New Corporate Strategy* (1988)

3 Sometimes listening itself may not be enough—some people must be prodded if you are to find out what they're thinking.
Mary Kay Ash (1915–2001) US entrepreneur, business executive, and founder of Mary Kay Cosmetics. *On People Management* (1984)

4 Wisdom comes with talking less frivolously and listening more seriously. The latter implies a learning attitude; the former assumes an air of omniscience that does not exist.
S.K. Chakraborty (b. 1957) Indian academic. *Management by Objectives: An Integrated Approach* (1976)

5 We listen to what our employees want and it shows up in everything from the layout of our offices to the benefits and amenities.
Raul Fernandez (b. 1966) Mexican IT entrepreneur. *Washingtonian* (November 1999)

6 I have often heard that the outstanding man is he who thinks deeply about a problem, and the next is he who listens carefully to advice.
Livy (59 BC–AD 17) Roman historian. *History of Rome* (26 BC–AD 15)

7 I think we have to lead people by being good listeners. That is to say, we lead in a company such as ours by drawing out ideas from people…We can't simply issue commands.
Minoru Makihara (b. 1930) Japanese president of Mitsubishi Corporation. Interview, *Strategy + Business* (Joel Kurtzman; January–March 1996)

8 In the industrial age, the CEO sat on the top of the hierarchy and didn't have to listen to anybody…In the information age, you have to listen to the ideas of people regardless of where they are in the organization.
John Sculley (b. 1939) US partner of Sculley Brothers, former president of Pepsi, and CEO of Apple Computers. *Nation's Business Today* (1987)

LOSING

1 I never thought of losing, but now that it's happened, the only thing is to do it right. That's my obligation to all the people who believe in me. We all have to take defeats in life.
Muhammad Ali (b. 1942) US boxer. Said after losing his first fight to Ken Norton, 31 March 1973. Quoted in *New York Times* (1973)

2 'Tis better to have fought and lost,
Than never to have fought at all.
Arthur Hugh Clough (1819–61) British poet. 'Peschiera', *Poems* (1862)

3 It's a lot more fun winning. It hurts to lose.
Robert Dole (b. 1923) US politician. *Daily Telegraph* (November 1996)

4 Take care to sell your horse before he dies. The art of life is passing losses on.
Robert Frost (1874–1963) US poet. 'The Ingenuities of Debt', *Steeple Bush* (1947)

5 For me coming second is the same as coming last.

Lew Grade (1906–98) British entertainment entrepreneur. Interview, *You Magazine* (25 October 1987)

6 I think there's going to be a lot of losers. There's no question that if you took a snapshot of the economy today and a snapshot of the economy five years from now, the lineup of participants are going to be very different. But just the same way as...the PC industry swept in and the semiconductor industry swept in, if I mention the starters, a lot of people would say 'Who?' A lot of the high fliers today are going to be 'Who?'

Andrew S. Grove (b. 1936) US entrepreneur, author, and chairman of Intel Corporation. Speech, Los Angeles Times 3rd Annual Investment Strategies Conference, Los Angeles, California (22 May 1999)

7 A remembered pain can lead to revenge psychology...They'll get back at you some day when you need them.

Frederick Herzberg (1923–2000) US psychologist. *The Motivation to Work* (1959)

8 There is nothing worse than a battle won except a battle lost.

Arthur Wellesley Wellington (1769–1852) British general and statesman. Letter to Philip von Neumann (11 January 1821)

LOYALTY

1 Total loyalty is possible only when fidelity is emptied of all concrete content, from which changes of mind might naturally arise.

Hannah Arendt (1906–75) US political philosopher. *The Origins of Totalitarianism* (1951)

2 Almost all our relationships begin and most of them continue as forms of mutual exploitation.

W.H. Auden (1907–73) US poet. *The Dyers Hand* (1963)

3 What job is worth the enormous psychic cost of following a leader who values loyalty in the narrowest sense.

Warren Bennis (b. 1925) US educator and writer. *On Becoming a Leader* (1989)

4 In extending and exploring my own horizons, I have not deserted my country. It is possible to transcend nationality but very few people are entirely disenthralled from political events.

Conrad Black (b. 1944) Canadian newspaper proprietor and business executive. *A Life in Progress* (1993)

5 Today professionalism is almost a byword for loyalty towards personal mercenary aims. Yet no great achievement is ever possible without a focus of loyalty which transcends the individual self.

S.K. Chakraborty (b. 1957) Indian academic. *Management by Values: Towards Cultural Congruence* (1991)

6 A useless piece of plastic.

Carlos Criado-Perez (b. 1952) Argentinian business executive. Referring to retailer Safeway's customer loyalty card which was dropped by the author. *Sunday Times* (July 2000)

7 Make yourself necessary to someone.

Ralph Waldo Emerson (1803–82) US essayist, lecturer, and poet. *The Conduct of Life* (1860)

8 Good customers are an asset which, when well managed and served, will return a handsome lifetime income stream for the company.

Philip Kotler (b. 1931) US marketing management thinker. *Marketing Management* (1967)

9 The future will be a future of more and more intensified relationships, especially in industrial marketing, but also increasingly in frequently-purchased consumer goods.

Theodore Levitt (b. 1925) US management theorist, writer, and editor. *Marketing Imagination* (1993)

10 Demand sincerity.

Arthur Lydiard (b. 1917) New Zealand athletics coach. *Running to the Top* (co-written with Garth Gilmour; 1995)

11 There's a significant shift away from mere spontaneity...we want to be a regular part of people's lives.

Carl Lyons (b. 1970) British marketing director of lastminute.com. Referring to lastminute.com's efforts to build repeat business. *Marketing* (August 2000)

12 What I want is men who will support me when I am in the wrong.

Lord Melbourne (1779–1848) British prime minister. 1839. Quoted in *Lord M* (David Cecil; 1954), vol. 2

13 Forget loyalty. Or at least loyalty to one's corporation. Try loyalty to your Rolodex—your network—instead.

Tom Peters (b. 1942) US management consultant and author. *The Economist* (1996)

14 GM reportedly has 14 million GM credit card holders being contacted, questioned, tabulated, tracked, and romanced each month when the credit card statement is delivered.

Stan Rapp, US advertising executive and co-founder of Rapp Collins. *The New Maxi-Marketing* (co-written with Thomas L. Collins; 1995)

15 Partisanship is our great curse. We too readily assume that everything has two sides and that it is our duty to be on one or the other.

James Harvey Robinson (1863–1936) US historian and educator. *The Mind in the Making* (1921)

16 The need for a form of enterprise which could command trust and loyalty...was only one facet of a broader need: the rising world of trade needed a moral system.

Nathan Rosenberg (b. 1927) US economist. *How the West Grew Rich: The Economic Transformation of the Industrial World* (co-written with L.E. Birdzell Jr; 1986)

17 Increasingly our society does not see social obligation as the primary obligation of the individual. The primary obligation is loyalty to the corporation.

John Ralston Saul (b. 1947) Canadian writer. *The Unconscious Civilization* (1995)

18 The marathon is my only girlfriend. I give her everything I have.

Toshihiko Seko (b. 1956) Japanese athlete. Quoted in *Running with the Legends* (Michael Sandrock; 1996)

19 Loyalty programmes will turn conventional markets into lock-in markets.

Carl Shapiro (b. 1955) US academic and author. *Information Rules* (co-written with Hal L. Varian; 1999)

20 All of our long-term suppliers are very profitable.

Marcus Sieff (1913–2001) British president of Marks & Spencer. Quoted in *The Winning Streak* (David Clutterbuck and Walter Goldsmith; 1984)

21 The primary rule of business success is loyalty to your employer. That's all right as a theory. What is the matter with loyalty to yourself?

Mark Twain (1835–1910) US writer. 1901. Quoted in *East Valley Tribune* (2000)

22 Loyalty saves the wear and tear of making daily decisions as to what is best to do.

Thomas J. Watson Sr (1874–1956) US founder and president of IBM. Quoted in *Think* (William Rogers; 1972)

23 I walk into all these organizations, and I'm always puzzled when I realize that people still want to be there. Most people really want to love their organizations. We need that level of commitment...Yet organizations have done very little to deserve that kind of staying-power.

Walter Wriston (b. 1919) US banker. Interview with Scott London, *US National Public Radio* (November 1996)

LUCK

1 After hard work, the biggest determinant is being in the right place at the right time.

Michael Bloomberg (b. 1942) US entrepreneur, business executive, and Mayor of New York. *Newsweek* (4 August 1997)

2 All good fortune is a gift of the gods and you don't win the favour of the ancient gods by being good but by being bold.

Anita Brookner (b. 1928) British novelist and art historian. Quoted in *Writers at Work* (1988)

3 We must believe in luck. For how else can we explain the success of those we don't like?

Jean Cocteau (1889–1963) French poet, novelist, dramatist, and film director. Attrib.

4 What we call luck is the inner man externalized. We make things happen to us.

Robertson Davies (1913–95) Canadian novelist, playwright, and essayist. *What's Bred in the Bone* (1985)

5 The man who glories in his luck may be overthrown by destiny.

Euripides (?484–?406 BC) Greek playwright. *The Suppliant Women* (?421 BC)

6 It is a great skill to know how to guide your luck even while waiting for it.

Baltasar Gracián (1601–58) Spanish writer and priest. Attrib.

7 With all due respect to Microsoft and Intel, there is no substitute for being in the right place at the right time.

Andrew S. Grove (b. 1936) US entrepreneur, author, and chairman of Intel Corporation. *Fortune* (June 1993)

8 Some folk want their luck buttered.

Thomas Hardy (1840–1928) British novelist and poet. *The Mayor of Casterbridge* (1886)

9 It is on disaster that good fortune perches; it is beneath good fortune that disaster crouches.

Laozi (?570–?490 BC) Chinese philosopher, reputed founder of Daoism. *Daode Jing*

10 I think a lot more decisions are made on serendipity than people think. Things come across their radar screens and they jump at them.

Jay W. Lorsch (b. 1932) US sociologist. *Wall Street Journal* (1 October 1984)

11 Where observation is concerned, chance favours only the prepared mind.

Louis Pasteur (1822–95) French scientist. Address (December 1854)

MANAGEMENT

1 The conventional definition of management is getting work done through people, but real management is developing people through work.

Hasan Abedi (1922–95) Pakistani banker and president of the Bank of Credit and Commerce International, Luxembourg. *Leaders* (July 1984)

2 We are beginning to recognize that it is more important to organize the unorganized than to argue about who will get the workers when they are organized.

Morton Bahr (b. 1926) US trade union leader and president of the Communications Workers of America. *New York Times* (1986)

3 Ultimately, the job of the manager is to get ordinary people to create extraordinary results.

Christopher Bartlett (b. 1945) Australian business writer. *The Individualised Corporation* (co-written with Sumantra Ghoshal; 1997)

4 Whips and chains are no longer an alternative for corporate management.

Warren Bennis (b. 1925) US educator and writer. *Fortune* (February 1994)

5 Either I can't manage this place or it's unmanageable.

Warren Bennis (b. 1925) US educator and writer. Quoted in *The Leadership Challenge* (Barry Posner and James Kouzes; 1987)

6 A common mistake about the image of a manager is that they must be loud, flamboyant, and a great drinker...This is wrong. In any company, if you look hard enough, you will find quiet modest people who manage teams with great personal success.

Gerald M. Blair (b. 1959) US writer. *What Makes a Great Manager* (2000)

7 The first steps to becoming a really great manager are simply common sense; but common sense is not very common.

Gerald M. Blair (b. 1959) US writer. *What Makes a Great Manager* (2000)

8 Managers should work for their people...and not the reverse.

Kenneth Blanchard (b. 1939) US management theorist and author. *Leadership and the One Minute Manager* (2000)

9 Many labor problems have spirit issues at their core, with lack of respect being perhaps the biggest.

Kenneth Blanchard (b. 1939) US management theorist and author. 'The Gift of the Goose', *Quality Digest* (December 1997)

10 A good manager is a man who isn't worried about his own career but rather the careers of those who work for him.

H.S.M. Burns (1900–71) British oil industry executive, geophysicist, and president of Shell Oil Company. Quoted in *Men at the Top* (Osborn Elliott; 1959)

11 Mr. Morgan buys his partners; I grow my own.

Andrew Carnegie (1835–1919) US industrialist and philanthropist. Referring to the banker J. Pierpont Morgan. Quoted in *Life of Andrew Carnegie* (B.J. Hendrick; 1932)

12 Don't criticize, condemn, or complain; give honest and sincere appreciation; and arouse in the other person an eager want.

Dale Carnegie (1888–1955) US consultant and author. Attrib.

13 Ego-management is a critical tonic for vitalizing organizational transformation.

S.K. Chakraborty (b. 1957) Indian academic. *Ethics in Management: Vedantic Perspectives* (1995)

14 In large organizations, middle managers serve the purpose of relaying information up and down—orders down, numbers up. But with the new information technologies and more efficient forms of work, their purpose dwindles.

James Champy (b. 1942) US business executive. Quoted in *New York Times* (7 January 1996)

15 If multicultural management is to become a reality in the fastest possible time, then skills adequate to the management of diversity must become a central component of management education.

Stewart Clegg (b. 1947) Australian writer. 'Business Values and Embryonic Industry: Lessons from Australia', *Whose Business Values? Some Asian and Cross-Cultural Perspectives* (Sally Stewart and Gabriel Donleavy, eds; 1995)

16 Two of the great myths circulating now are that Heinz's beans are the best and that I can get more out of men than they have inside them.

Brian Clough (b. 1935) British football player and manager. Quoted in *Observer* (15 November 1975)

17 Responsibility without control is at the core of management.

Paul Corrigan (b. 1948) British author. *Shakespeare on Management* (1999)

18 The problem for managers is that they have to take responsibility for their part in the organization, but they have to do so in a context that they can never completely control.

Paul Corrigan (b. 1948) British author. *Shakespeare on Management* (1999)

19 Refrain from saying the unkind or negative thing.

Stephen Covey (b. 1932) US writer and psychologist. *Thirty Methods of Influence* (1991)

20 Management today is reactive behaviour. You put your hand on a hot stove and yank it off. A cat would know to do as much.

W. Edwards Deming (1900–93) US consultant and author. Quoted in *BusinessWeek* (10 January 1994)

21 The role of management is always to identify the weakest links, support them and strengthen them.

Ron Dennis (b. 1949) British entrepreneur and Formula 1 motor racing team owner. Quoted in *The Adventure Capitalists* (Jeff Grout and Lynne Curry; 1998)

22 Basic assumptions about reality are the paradigms of a social science, such as management.

Peter F. Drucker (b. 1909) US management consultant and academic. *Management Challenges for the 21st Century* (1999)

23 Professional management today sees itself often in the role of a judge who says 'yes' or 'no' to ideas as they come up...A top management that believes its job is to sit in judgment will inevitably veto the new idea. It is always 'impractical'.

Peter F. Drucker (b. 1909) US management consultant and academic. *The Age of Discontinuity: Guidelines to Our Changing Society* (1969)

24 There's a rule that says if you can't run this business, buy another one.

Peter F. Drucker (b. 1909) US management consultant and academic. Interview, *Time* (1990)

25 All activities to which industrial undertakings give rise can be divided into the following six activities—technical, commercial, financial, security, accounting, managerial.

Henri Fayol (1841–1925) French business executive. *General and Industrial Management* (1916)

26 There is no merit in sowing dissension among subordinates; any beginner can do it.

Henri Fayol (1841–1925) French business executive. *General and Industrial Management* (1916)

27 To manage is to forecast and plan, to organise, to command, to co-ordinate, and to control.

Henri Fayol (1841–1925) French business executive. *General and Industrial Management* (1916)

28 Managers in all too many American companies do not achieve the desired results because nobody makes them do it.
Harold S. Geneen (1910–97) US telecommunications entrepreneur and CEO of ITT. *Managing* (co-written with Alvin Moscow; 1984)

29 Managers must manage.
Harold S. Geneen (1910–97) US telecommunications entrepreneur and CEO of ITT. *Managing* (co-written with Alvin Moscow; 1984)

30 The moment you let avoiding failure become your motivator, you're down the path of inactivity.
Roberto Goizueta (1931–97) US CEO of Coca-Cola. *Fortune* (May 1997)

31 When I'm in London, the focus is on corporate governance things rather than motivating people to be brilliant—which is what the day job is.
Paul Gratton (b. 1960) British CEO of Egg. *Sunday Times* (May 2000)

32 Management is the study of how things get done.
Robert Greenleaf (1904–90) US director of Management Research for AT&T and author. *The Servant as Leader* (1970)

33 Management is more fun, more creative, more personal, more political and more intuitive than any textbook.
Charles Handy (b. 1932) British business executive and author. *Gods of Management* (1986)

34 Management by trust, empathy, and forgiveness sounds good. It also sounds soft. It is in practice tough. Organizations based on trust have, on occasion, to be ruthless.
Charles Handy (b. 1932) British business executive and author. *Harvard Business Review* (November–December 1992)

35 An attack upon the trade unionists in this country Australia and upon cost structure in this country is no excuse...for management not getting off their sometimes lazy butt.
Bob Hawke (b. 1929) Australian former prime minister. Quoted in *Sydney Morning Herald* (12 July 1986)

36 Nobody is sure anymore who really runs the company (not even the people who are credited with running it), but the company does run.
Joseph Heller (1923–99) US novelist. *Something Happened* (1974)

37 Hey boys, I've got a shotgun at your heads. I've got thousands of jobs at 17 bucks an hour. I've got none at 20. So you better come to your senses.
Lee Iacocca (b. 1924) US president of Ford Motor Company, chairman and CEO of Chrysler Corporation. *Iacocca: An Autobiography* (1984)

38 The real impediment to producing a higher-quality product more efficiently isn't

the workers, union or nonunion, it's management.
Kenneth Iverson (1925–2002) US industrialist, chairman and CEO of Nucor Corporation. Quoted in *Thriving on Chaos* (Tom Peters; 1987)

39 No matter how lofty you are in your department, the responsibility for what your lowliest assistant is doing is yours.
Bessie Rowland James (1895–1974) US journalist and author. Quoted in *Adlai's Almanac* (H. Schuman, ed.; 1952)

40 Managers should not have to choose between financial and operational measures. We have found that senior executives can provide a clear performance target or focus attention on the critical areas of the business.
Robert Kaplan (b. 1940) US accounting educator. *Harvard Business Review* (January–February 1992)

41 Timing; originality; forcefulness; a gift for self-promotion and perhaps above all else, the ability to encapsulate memorably what others recognize as true...are the hallmarks of the modern management guru.
Carol Kennedy (b. 1952) British business executive, editor, and author. *Guide to the Management Gurus* (1991)

42 You can be a captain of industry with a brilliant track record at turning companies around and...still not rank as a true guru.
Carol Kennedy (b. 1952) British business executive, editor, and author. *Guide to the Management Gurus* (1991)

43 Alignment is not about the management of quality. It is about the quality of management.
George Labovitz (b. 1940) US writer, consultant, and CEO of Organizational Dynamics, Inc. *The Power of Alignment* (co-written with Victor Rosansky; 1997)

44 If one is on the spot, disorders are seen as they spring up, and one can quickly remedy them; but if one is not at hand, they are heard of only when they are great and then one can no longer remedy them.
Niccolò Machiavelli (1469–1527) Italian historian, statesman, and political philosopher. *The Prince* (1513)

45 I am the proprietor. I am the boss...There can only be one boss and that is me.
Robert Maxwell (1923–91) British publisher, business executive, and politician. July 13, 1984. Speech to trade union leaders. Quoted in *Maxwell: The Outsider* (Tom Bower; 1988)

46 The process of developing heterogeneous resources must be continuous; it is never completed.
Douglas McGregor (1906–64) US academic, educator, and management theorist. *The Human Side of Enterprise* (1960)

47 A tough manager may never look outside his own factory walls or be conscious of his partnership in a wider world.
Robert Menzies (1894–1978) Australian prime minister. 1954. First William Queale Memorial Lecture, *Wit and Wisdom of Robert Menzies* (1982)

48 The key managerial processes are enormously complex and mysterious, drawing on the vaguest of information and using the least articulated of mental processes.
Henry Mintzberg (b. 1939) Canadian academic and management theorist. *Harvard Business Review* (July–August 1976)

49 Professional management is an invention that produced gain in organizational efficiency so great that it eventually destroyed organizational effectiveness.
Henry Mintzberg (b. 1939) Canadian academic and management theorist. *Mintzberg on Management* (1989)

50 Society has become unmanageable as a result of management.
Henry Mintzberg (b. 1939) Canadian academic and management theorist. *Mintzberg on Management* (1989)

51 Men love to organise.
James Mooney (1884–1957) US business executive. *Onward Industry* (co-written with Alan Reiley; 1931)

52 Highly centralized management can suffocate the innovative energies of individuals in the subsidiary units.
Nitin Nohria (b. 1962) US writer. *The Differentiated Network* (co-written with Sumantra Ghoshal; 1997)

53 They anchor themselves in the stomach of the business.
James O'Shea, US author, journalist, and editor. Referring to the tendency of management consultancies to form dependent relationships with clients. *Dangerous Company* (co-written with Charles Madigan; 1997)

54 We have a technique at Hewlett-Packard for helping managers and supervisors know their people and understand the work their people are doing...Management by Walking About.
David Packard (1912–96) US entrepreneur and co-founder of Hewlett-Packard. *The HP Way* (1995)

55 A great many American managers are influenced by beliefs, assumptions, and perceptions about management that unduly constrain them.
Richard Pascale (b. 1938) US academic and author. *The Art of Japanese Management* (co-written with Anthony Athos; 1981)

56 A couple of hours in a hot kitchen can teach you as much about management as the latest books on reengineering or total quality management.
Tom Peters (b. 1942) US management consultant and author. 'The Way the Cookie Crumbles' (1995)

57 He not only conducts his version of Beethoven and Bach, but scores it as he goes along.
Tom Peters (b. 1942) US management consultant and author. Referring to the management style of Cable Network News. *Liberation Management* (1992)

58 Our fixation with financial measures leads us to downplay or ignore less tangible non-financial measures.
Tom Peters (b. 1942) US management consultant and author. *Thriving in Chaos* (1987)

59 Managers should be getting everybody from the top of the human organization to the bottom doing things that make the business successful.
Bill Reffitt (b. 1946) US writer. Quoted in 'Linking the People with the Strategic Needs of Business', *Organizational Dynamics* (Randall S. Schuler; 1992)

60 If management is people, management must become humanagement.
Jonas Ridderstråle, Swedish academic and author. *Funky Business* (co-written with Kjell Nordström; 2000)

61 Controlled unreasonableness.
Gerry Robinson (b. 1948) Irish chairman of Granada Television and chairman of the Arts Council of England. Referring to his personal management style. *Management Today* (April 1999)

62 The great body of managers...spend their whole careers climbing up inside one great Leviathan, with little contact with anyone outside.
Anthony Sampson (b. 1926) British author and journalist. *The Anatomy of Britain* (1962)

63 I don't think anyone can manage Apple.
John Sculley (b. 1939) US partner of Sculley Brothers, former president of Pepsi, and CEO of Apple Computers. *Fortune* (1996)

64 One useful starting point for all managers is to look at their time for thinking.
Peter Senge (b. 1947) US academic and author. *The Fifth Discipline: The Art and Practice of the Learning Organization* (1990)

65 And I think one of the powers of fad surfing is that it really is a kind of managerial prozac. It allows managers to say, I am doing something therefore I am managing and leading.
Eileen C. Shapiro, US business consultant and author. Radio interview. 'The Consultants: Fad Surfers of Globalisation' (3 August 1997)

66 The consultants are the thinkers and the strategists. And the managers have the most bizarre job.
Eileen C. Shapiro, US business consultant and author. Radio interview. 'The Consultants: Fad Surfers of Globalisation' (3 August 1997)

67 Thinking must be the hardest job in the world. What people want to do is outsource it to a mantra or a methodology like re-engineering.
Eileen C. Shapiro, US business consultant and author. *Fad Surfing in the Boardroom* (1998)

68 At best we live by homely proverbs, at worst we live by pompous inanities.
Herbert A. Simon (1916–2001) US political scientist and economist. *Administrative Behavior* (1947)

69 Management—the collective effort of intelligence, experience, and imagination.
Alfred P. Sloan (1875–1966) US president of General Motors. *Adventures of a White Collar Man* (1941)

70 If we had the means to review and judge the effectiveness of operations, we could safely leave the prosecution of these operations to the men in charge of them.

Alfred P. Sloan (1875–1966) US president of General Motors. *My Years with General Motors* (1964)

71 Of all business activities, 99% are routine...The entire 100% can be handled by managing the 1% of exceptions.

Alfred P. Sloan (1875–1966) US president of General Motors. 'The Most Important Things I Learned About Management', *System* (August 1924)

72 The only report we ask from all of our units is one page a month.

Alfred P. Sloan (1875–1966) US president of General Motors. 'The Most Important Things I Learned About Management', *System* (August 1924)

73 Traditional management structures were devised when information was a scarce commodity, so that knowledge about how to run the business could be communicated layer by layer.

Raymond W. Smith (b. 1937) US chairman of Rothschild Inc. and former chairman of Bell Atlantic Corporation. Speech (17 October 1995)

74 Managing is getting paid for home runs someone else hits.

Casey Stengel (?1890–1975) US baseball player and manager. Attrib.

75 Bad administration, to be sure, can destroy good policy; but good administration can never save bad policy.

Adlai E. Stevenson (1900–65) US statesman and author. Speech, Los Angeles (11 September 1952)

76 When the rats are running for cover, you must ensure that, as captain, you know what they are doing.

Dennis Stevenson (b. 1946) British company director. *Management Today* (April 1999)

77 This blight is management—the dreaded four Ms, male, middle class, middle-aged and mediocre.

Janet Street-Porter (b. 1946) British broadcaster. Referring to television management in the United Kingdom. MacTaggart Lecture, Edinburgh Television Festival, Scotland (August 1995)

78 First the gathering in on the part of management of all the knowledge...in the heads of the workmen; second, the scientific selection and progressive development of the workmen; third, the bringing together of the science and...the trained men; and fourth, the constant cooperaton which always occurs between the management and the workmen.

F.W. Taylor (1856–1915) US engineer and author. Taylor's four principles of 'scientific management', the basis of Henry Ford's mass-production revolution. Testimony to the House of Representatives, US Congress (1912)

79 It is always easier to talk about change than to make it. It is easier to consult than to manage.

Alvin Toffler (b. 1928) US social commentator. *The Adaptive Corporation* (1985)

80 'Top' management is supposed to be a tree full of owls...hooting when management heads

into the wrong part of the forest. I'm still unpersuaded they even know where the forest is.

Robert Townsend (b. 1920) US business executive and author. *Further up the Organization* (1984)

81 I started wondering if any of the American management techniques I was brainwashed with in eight years of the best business education money could buy would apply in the Netherlands or indeed in the rest of the world.

Fons Trompenaars (b. 1952) Dutch author and management consultant. *Riding the Waves of Culture* (1993)

82 Chinese management has its roots in ancient thinking and practices...it is characterized by teamwork, orientation around relationships, and multi-level regulations.

Zhong-Ming Wang, Chinese academic and business author. 'Management in China', *Management in Asia Pacific* (Malcolm Warner, ed.; 2000)

83 The formal Chinese accounting system was established around 475–221 BC and functioned primarily as a performance evaluation system, with indicators for promotion and demotion.

Zhong-Ming Wang, Chinese academic and business author. 'Management in China', *Management in Asia Pacific* (Malcolm Warner, ed.; 2000)

84 I want to begin with what I think is the most important factor: our respect for the individual. This is a simple concept, but in IBM it occupies a major portion of management time.

Thomas J. Watson Jr (1914–93) US CEO of IBM. *A Business and Its Beliefs* (1963)

85 A manager is an assistant to his men.

Thomas J. Watson Sr (1874–1956) US founder and president of IBM. Quoted in *Father, Son & Co.: My Life at IBM and Beyond* (Thomas J. Watson Jr and Peter Petre; 1990)

86 Frightened, nervous managers use thick, convoluted planning books and busy slides filled with everything they've known since childhood.

Jack Welch (b. 1935) US former chairman and CEO of General Electric. *Harvard Business Review* (September–October 1989)

87 People always overestimate how complex business is. This isn't rocket science; we've chosen one of the world's more simple professions.

Jack Welch (b. 1935) US former chairman and CEO of General Electric. *Harvard Business Review* (September–October 1989)

88 Insecure managers create complexity.

Jack Welch (b. 1935) US former chairman and CEO of General Electric. Quoted in *In Search of European Excellence* (Robert Heller; 1997)

89 One of the most important things about being a good manager is to rule with a heart. You have to know the business, but you also have to know what's at the heart of the business and that's people.

Oprah Winfrey (b. 1954) US talk show host, actor, and business executive. Quoted in *The Uncommon Wisdom of Oprah Winfrey* (Bill Adler; 1997)

90 You have to surround yourself with people you trust, and people that are good. But they also have to be people who will tell the emperor you have no clothes.

Oprah Winfrey (b. 1954) US talk show host, actor, and business executive. Quoted in *The Uncommon Wisdom of Oprah Winfrey* (Bill Adler; 1997)

91 The manager's job is to thrive in a chaotic world he cannot control. He is at last reconciled to being, openly, an intermediary.

Theodore Zeldin (b. 1933) British academic, author, and historian. *An Intimate History of Humanity* (1994)

MARKETING

1 One of the primary objectives of a market analysis is to determine the attractiveness of a market to current and potential participants.

David A. Aaker (b. 1938) US business executive and vice-chairman of Prophet Brand Strategy. *Developing Business Strategies* (1998)

2 Strategic market management is a system designed to help management both precipitate and make strategic decisions, as well as create strategic vision.

David A. Aaker (b. 1938) US business executive and vice-chairman of Prophet Brand Strategy. *Developing Business Strategies* (1998)

3 Focus Groups are people who are selected on the basis of their inexplicable free time and their common love of free sandwiches.

Scott Adams (b. 1957) US cartoonist and humorist. *The Dilbert Principle* (1996)

4 Half the sponsors don't know if their money is wasted or not; the other half do it in order not to be left out.

Anonymous. Quoted in *Formula 1, The Business of Winning* (Russell Hotten; 1998)

5 Retailers estimate that the Nike Inc. line of shoes with Michael Jordan's name rings up more than $100 million per year.

Anonymous. *Wall Street Journal* (23 September 1997)

6 The importance of collecting data for the purpose of enabling the manufacturer to ascertain how many additional customers he will acquire by a given reduction in the price of the article he makes cannot be too strongly pressed.

Charles Babbage (1792–1871) British mathematician and inventor. *On the Economy of Machinery and Manufacture* (1832)

7 In good times, people want to advertise; in bad times, they have to.

Bruce Barton (1886–1967) US advertising executive and author. *Town and Country* (1955)

8 Christmas is the Disneyfication of Christianity.

Don Cupitt (b. 1934) British theologian. *Independent* (December 1996)

9 You see yourself as a good product that sits on a shelf and sells well, and people make a lot of money out of you.

Diana (1961–97) British princess. Referring to her treatment by the media. BBC interview (1995)

10 Marketing is not a function, it is the whole business seen from the customer's point of view.

Peter F. Drucker (b. 1909) US management consultant and academic. Quoted in *Business Studies* (Ian Marcouse *et al.*; 2000)

11 Investor relations is about stock marketing.

Utz Felcht (b. 1947) German chairman of Degussa. *Sunday Times* (October 2000)

12 If you don't enjoy consuming it, you can't work in it.

Michael Grade (b. 1943) British television executive. *Marketing* (June 2000)

13 Success should not be measured by earnings per share, but by market share.

Bruce Henderson (1915–92) US consultant and founder Boston Consulting Group. Quoted in *Dangerous Company* (James O'Shea and Charles Madigan; 1997)

14 Our challenge is to stand out from the crowd when the crowd has much more money than you. Ideas are relatively cheap to have.

Dave Hieatt (b. 1965) British founder of anti-corporate marketing agency. *Marketing* (October 2000)

15 Marketing takes a day to learn. Unfortunately, it takes a lifetime to master.

Philip Kotler (b. 1931) US marketing management thinker. *Marketing Management* (1967)

16 Your company does not belong in any market where it cannot be the best.

Philip Kotler (b. 1931) US marketing management thinker. *Marketing Management* (1967)

17 In financial institutions...salesmen were not just people who pushed a product. They were 'virile', 'manly men' engaged in an important public calling.

Angel Kwolek-Folland, US author. *Engendering Business* (1994)

18 The man who whispers down a well
About the goods he has to sell
Will not make as many dollars
As the man who climbs the tree and hollers!

Lord Leverhulme (1851–1925) British entrepreneur, philanthropist, and co-founder of Unilever. Leverhulme was a consummate salesman, pioneering US mass-marketing techniques in Britain. Quoted in *Enlightened Entrepreneurs* (Ian Campbell Bradley; 1987), ch. 10

19 Not since John D. Rockefeller sent free kerosene lamps to China has the oil industry done anything really outstanding to create a demand for its product.

Theodore Levitt (b. 1925) US management theorist, writer, and editor. 'Marketing Myopia', *Harvard Business Review* (September–October 1975)

20 The meek shall inherit the earth, but they'll never increase market share.
William G. McGowan (1927–92) US business executive. Quoted in *The Master Marketer* (Christopher Ryan; 1993)

21 Most large markets evolve from niche markets.
Regis McKenna (b. 1939) US marketing entrepreneur and chairman of The McKenna Group. *Harvard Business Review* (September–October 1988)

22 Marketing should focus on market creation, not market share.
Regis McKenna (b. 1939) US marketing entrepreneur and chairman of The McKenna Group. *The Regis Touch* (1986)

23 Every marketer should be on the road half the time. You get that sixth sense only by spending time in the marketplace.
Regis McKenna (b. 1939) US marketing entrepreneur and chairman of The McKenna Group. Quoted in *Thriving on Chaos* (Tom Peters; 1987)

24 Music is spiritual. The music business is not.
Van Morrison (b. 1945) Irish musician. *The Times* (July 1990)

25 We feel the spear of the marketplace in our back.
Tony O'Reilly (b. 1936) Irish executive chairman of Independent News & Media and former CEO of Heinz Corporation. *Fortune* (9 April 1990)

26 Manufacturers who don't test their products incur the colossal cost (and disgrace) of having their products fail on a national scale instead of dying inconspicuously and economically in test markets.
David Ogilvy (1911–99) British advertising executive, founder and chairman of Ogilvy & Mather. *Confessions of an Advertising Man* (1963)

27 Anyone can build market share and, if you set your prices low enough, you can get the whole damn market.
David Packard (1912–96) US entrepreneur and co-founder of Hewlett-Packard. *The HP Way* (1995)

28 They're exactly the demographics I'm looking for.
Manuel Perluondo (b. 1967) Cuban entrepreneur. *Forbes* (February 1999)

29 Marketing goes wrong when it is perceived by companies as a bolt-on activity.
Michael Perry (b. 1934) British business executive. *Marketing* (March 2000)

30 One of the qualities I always seek in marketing people is curiosity.
Raoul Pinnell (b. 1951) British branding and marketing communications director of Shell International Petroleum. *Marketing* (June 2000)

31 But markets today are moving targets. The only way to hit them is to launch your business like a cruise missile.
Harry V. Quadracci (1936–2002) US entrepreneur and founder of Quad Graphics. *Success* (June 1988)

32 Cents-off coupons have proliferated like the progeny of sex-starved rabbits.
Stan Rapp, US advertising executive and co-founder of Rapp Collins. *The New Maxi-Marketing* (co-written with Thomas L. Collins; 1995)

33 Welcome to the new age of datamation—a whole new way to move the prospect to making a purchase, using different strokes for different folks.
Stan Rapp, US advertising executive and co-founder of Rapp Collins. *The New Maxi-Marketing* (co-written with Thomas L. Collins; 1995)

34 The USP almost lifts itself out of the ruck and wings its way to some corner of the mind.
Rosser Reeves (1910–84) US advertising executive. Referring to the Unique Selling Proposition. *Reality in Advertising* (1986)

35 The company is moving from product marketing to audience marketing.
Oliver Roll (b. 1966) British marketing executive. *Marketing* (July 2000)

36 A society in which consumption has to be artificially stimulated in order to keep production going is a society founded on trash and waste, and such a society is a house built on sand.
Dorothy L. Sayers (1893–1957) British author. *Creed or Chaos* (1947)

37 No one wins a sales promotion war.
Don E. Schultz (b. 1934) US author, advertising executive, and academic. *Sales Promotion Management* (co-written with William Robinson; 1982)

38 Marketing strategy is a series of integrated actions leading to a sustainable competitive advantage.
John Sculley (b. 1939) US partner of Sculley Brothers, former president of Pepsi, and CEO of Apple Computers. Quoted in *Business Studies* (Ian Marcouse et al.; 2000)

39 No great marketing decisions have ever been made on qualitative data.
John Sculley (b. 1939) US partner of Sculley Brothers, former president of Pepsi, and CEO of Apple Computers. Quoted in *The Intuitive Manager* (Roy Rowan; 1986)

40 We know every dollar added to the cost means more than one dollar added to the consumer price. We know a higher consumer price means fewer consumer sales.
Alfred P. Sloan (1875–1966) US president of General Motors. 'The Most Important Things I Learned About Management', *System* (August 1924)

41 The media industry has only started to take marketing seriously over the past five years and has failed to understand their brands in a business context.
Vijay Solanki (b. 1969) Kenyan marketing executive. *Marketing* (August 2000)

42 They don't understand that the cold face of the marketing business is about bringing in cash, not just about having big ad campaigns.
Vijay Solanki (b. 1969) Kenyan marketing executive. *Marketing* (August 2000)

43 The mass market has split into ever-multiplying, ever-changing sets of micromarkets that demand a continually expanding range of options.
Alvin Toffler (b. 1928) US social commentator. *Powershift* (1990)

44 Don't focus on the mink, but what's in it.
Jane Trahey (1923–2000) US copywriter and author. 1969. Speaking about her famous advertising campaign for Blackglama fur. Quoted in *New York Times* (2000)

45 The shelf life of the modern hardback writer is somewhere between the milk and the yoghurt.
Calvin Trillin (b. 1935) US writer and journalist. *Sunday Times* (June 1991)

46 In Australia, it's all about sales tomorrow and how to appeal to this huge, generic target audience.
Trish Wadley (b. 1962) Australian marketing director. 'Independently Minded', *Independent* (Poppy Brech; 2000)

47 Don't sell the steak; sell the sizzle. It is the sizzle that sells the steak and not the cow, although the cow is, of course, mighty important.
Elmer Wheeler (1903–68) US writer. *Principles of Salesmanship* (?1936), no. 1

48 Every product has some element of service, and every service some element of product.
Aubrey Wilson, British marketing consultant and author. *New Directions in Marketing* (1991)

49 There's no business without show business.
Michael J. Wolf, US consultant and author. *The Entertainment Economy* (1999)

MEDIA

1 TV—a clever contraption derived from the words Terrible Vaudeville—we call it a medium because nothing's well done.
Goodman Ace (1899–1982) US humorist. Letter to Groucho Marx (1967)

2 I'm all in favour of free expression, provided it's kept strictly under control.
Alan Bennett (b. 1934) British playwright. *Forty Years On* (1969)

3 There is not one shred of evidence that the Internet has had any downward influence on North American or European newspaper circulation.
Conrad Black (b. 1944) Canadian newspaper proprietor and business executive. Press conference (March 2000)

4 Newspapers...remain powerful outlets for advertising and information (and political influence)...literacy and the printed word are not as out of fashion as many have feared.
Conrad Black (b. 1944) Canadian newspaper proprietor and business executive. *A Life in Progress* (1993)

5 Someone once described the information business as exactly the opposite of sex. When it's good, it's still lousy.
Michael Bloomberg (b. 1942) US entrepreneur, business executive, and Mayor of New York. *New York Times* (November 1993)

6 A continuous clash of egomaniacal monsters, wasting more energy than dinosaurs and pouring rivers of money into the sand.
Robert Bolt (1924–95) British screenwriter and dramatist. Referring to the movie industry. *Sunday Times* (June 1961)

7 The market will pay better to entertain than educate.
Warren Buffett (b. 1930) US entrepreneur and financier. AGM speech (1986)

8 If you look at the entire chain of entities— studio, networks, stations, cable channels, cable operations, Internet distribution—you have to be strong in as many of them as you can.
Peter Chernin (b. 1953) US chief operating officer of News Corporation, chairman and CEO of the Fox Group. *Forbes* (June 1998)

9 We're in the attention getting business.
Peter Chernin (b. 1953) US chief operating officer of News Corporation, chairman and CEO of the Fox Group. *Forbes* (June 1998)

10 Journalism largely consists of saying 'Lord Jones dead' to people who never knew that Lord Jones was alive.
G.K. Chesterton (1874–1936) British novelist, poet, and critic. *The Wisdom of Father Brown* (1914)

11 Literature is the art of writing something that wll be read twice; journalism what will be read once.
Cyril Connolly (1903–74) British critic, essayist, and novelist. *Enemies of Promise* (1938)

12 Television thrives on unreason and unreason thrives on television.
Robin Day (1923–2000) British broadcaster. *Grand Inquisition* (1989)

13 The British Press is always looking for stuff to fill the space between their cartoons.
Bernadette Devlin (b. 1947) Irish politician. 1970. Attrib.

14 Music you can see and pictures you can hear.
Walt Disney (1901–66) US entertainment entrepreneur and founder of the Walt Disney Company. Quoted in *New York Times* (May 1992)

15 The first time a rat saved a sinking ship.
Greg Dyke (b. 1947) British television executive. Referring to the puppet Roland Rat, whose popularity saved a failing television programme. Quoted in *The Adventure Capitalists* (Jeff Grout and Lynne Curry; 1998)

16 I realised that the only successful people in TV would be those who recognised that it was just a small part of the leisure industry.
Noel Edmonds (b. 1948) British broadcaster and media executive. 1987. Quoted in *Noel Edmonds* (Alison Bowyer; 1999)

17 We live in an anonymous world where people are desperate for their fifteen minutes of fame.
Noel Edmonds (b. 1948) British broadcaster and media executive. 1998. Quoted in *Noel Edmonds* (Alison Bowyer; 1999)

18 As a publisher, we've not done acquisitions.
Duncan Edwards (b. 1964) British publishing executive.
Marketing (July 2000)

19 Scale in publishing is increasingly important.
Duncan Edwards (b. 1964) British publishing executive.
Marketing (July 2000)

20 What I love about magazines is that an individual can change the destiny of an entire business.
Duncan Edwards (b. 1964) British publishing executive.
Marketing (July 2000)

21 The most important thing we've done with this company is to stay away from emotional investments in over-priced media assets.
Michael Eisner (b. 1942) US chairman and CEO of the Disney Corporation. *Forbes* (January 1987)

22 The music industry is toast. It has been completely overtaken by events and can do nothing about it.
Shaun Fanning (b. 1981) US software entrepreneur. Referring to music downloads on the Internet. *Sunday Times* (May 2000)

23 Is there enough creativity to go around? No, there never has been.
Michael Grade (b. 1943) British television executive. Referring to the rapid development of new media. *Marketing* (June 2000)

24 Success in journalism can be a form of failure.
Graham Greene (1904–91) British novelist. *New Statesman* (May 1968)

25 When I started out, people were afraid of parish priests. Now they're afraid of newspaper editors.
Michael D. Higgins (b. 1941) Irish politician. 1997. Attrib.

26 Some day we'll call it personal broadcasting.
Nobuyuki Idei (b. 1937) Japanese chairman and CEO of Sony Corporation. *Forbes* (May 2000)

27 Blood sport is brought to its ultimate refinement in the gossip columns.
Bernard Ingham (b. 1932) British politician. Speech (February 1986)

28 The media...is like an oil painting. Close up, it looks like nothing on earth. Stand back and you get the drift.
Bernard Ingham (b. 1932) British politician. Speech (February 1990)

29 Television is simultaneously blamed, often by the same people, for worsening the world and for being powerless to change it.
Clive James (b. 1939) Australian writer and broadcaster. *Glued to the Box* (1981)

30 Freedom of the press is guaranteed only to those who own one.
A.J. Liebling (1904–63) US journalist. *The Wayward Press* (1960)

31 Television brought the brutality of war into the comfort of the living room. Vietnam was lost in the living rooms of America—not the battlefields of Vietnam.
Marshall McLuhan (1911–80) Canadian sociologist and author. *Montreal Gazette* (May 1975)

32 The medium is the message.
Marshall McLuhan (1911–80) Canadian sociologist and author. *Understanding Media* (1964)

33 Whenever I see a newspaper, I think of the poor trees. As trees they provide beauty, shade and shelter. But, as paper, all they provide is rubbish.
Yehudi Menuhin (1916–99) British musician. Interview (1982)

34 It's like a bug that bites you and gets in your bloodstream.
Paul Merton (b. 1957) British comedian. Referring to films. *Observer* (October 2000)

35 I am not realising a dream to become a media mogul. I am realising my dream of creating a truly global media company.
Jean-Marie Messier (b. 1956) French media owner. *Sunday Times* (September 2000)

36 A good newspaper, I suppose, is a nation talking to itself.
Arthur Miller (b. 1915) US dramatist. *Observer* (November 1961)

37 Information is the most valuable commodity in the world today and this business is about giving people access to information that is relevant to their lives.
James Murdoch (b. 1973) Australian chief executive and chairman of Star TV. *Forbes* (July 1998)

38 I don't give a damn what the media critics say. It's what your readers say. If you haven't got any readers, you're only talking to yourself.
Rupert Murdoch (b. 1931) US CEO of News Corporation. Quoted in *Good Times, Bad Times* (Harold Evans; 1983)

39 The power of the press is very great but not so great as the power of suppresion.
Lord Northcliffe (1865–1922) British newspaper proprietor. *Daily Mail* (1918)

40 I've been lonely for the active question and answer sessions only the Irish media can provide.
Denis O'Brien (b. 1958) Irish telecommunications entrepreneur. *Sunday Times* (October 2000)

41 Not only is this the first live televised war, it's also the first war ever covered by sober journalists.
P.J. O'Rourke (b. 1947) US humorist and journalist. Referring to the Gulf War. *Give War a Chance* (1992)

42 Television has made dictatorship impossible, but democracy unbearable.
Shimon Peres (b. 1923) Israeli former prime minister. *Financial Times* (January 1995)

43 The revolution people are talking about is one of form rather than substance.

Michael Perry (b. 1934) British business executive. Referring to new electronic media. *Marketing* (March 2000)

44 For a politician to complain about the press is like a ship's captain complaining about the sea.
Enoch Powell (1912–98) British politician. *Guardian* (December 1984)

45 Government always tends to want, not a really free press, but a managed and well-conducted one.
Lord Radcliffe (1899–1977) British lawyer. 1967. Quoted in *What the Papers Never Said* (Peter Hennessey; 1983)

46 I think editors are excellent marketers. They know their audience and produce copy to appeal to them—they just don't call it marketing.
David Robinson (b. 1959) Australian marketing executive. *Marketing* (June 2000)

47 No self-respecting fish would be wrapped in a Murdoch newspaper.
Mike Royko (1932–97) US journalist. *Chicago Sun Times* (1984)

48 In the rarefied air of the media, a single misstep separates sitting on top of the world from standing in the unemployment line.
Harriet Rubin (b. 1952) US author. 'Success and Excess', *Fast Company* (1998)

49 Television;. The word is half Greek, half Latin. No good can come of it.
C.P. Scott (1846–1932) British editor. Quoted in *The BBC's First Fifty Years* (Asa Briggs; 1985)

50 In a world full of audio-visual marvels, may words matter to you and be full of magic.
Geoffrey Smith (b. 1926) British journalist. Letter (July 1987)

51 Freedom of the press in Britain means freedom to print such of the proprietor's prejudices as the advertisers don't object to.
Hannen Swaffer (1879–1962) British journalist. Quoted in *Swaff* (Tom Driberg; 1974)

52 The newspaper and magazine business is an intellectual brothel from which there is no escape.
Leo Tolstoy (1828–1910) Russian novelist. Quoted in *Wit and Wisdom* (Charlotte Bingham; 1982)

53 A critic is a man who knows the way but can't drive the car.
Kenneth Tynan (1927–80) British critic. *New York Times* (January 1966)

54 No first world country has ever managed to eliminate so entirely from its media all objectivity—much less dissent.
Gore Vidal (b. 1925) US novelist and critic. Referring to the United States. *A View from the Diner's Club* (1991)

55 News is what a chap who doesn't care much about anything wants to read.
Evelyn Waugh (1903–66) British novelist. *Scoop* (1938)

56 I hate television. I hate it as much as peanuts. But I can't stop eating peanuts.
Orson Welles (1915–85) US actor and film director. *New York Herald Tribune* (October 1956)

57 Journalism—an ability to meet the challenge of filling the space.
Rebecca West (1892–1983) British writer and journalist. *New York Herald Tribune* (April 1956)

58 In the old days men had the rack. Now they have the Press.
Oscar Wilde (1854–1900) Irish writer and wit. *Fortnightly Review* (February 1891)

59 Television contracts the imagination and radio expands it.
Terry Wogan (b. 1938) Irish broadcaster. *Observer* (December 1984)

MEETINGS

1 A conference is a gathering of important people who, singly, can do nothing but together can decide that nothing can be done.
Fred Allen (1894–1956) US comedian and satirist. W.M. Martin was the president of the New York Stock Exchange. Letter to W.M. Martin (25 January 1940)

2 There were board meetings when my wife was doing needlepoint, one sister was addressing Christmas cards, and another didn't bother to attend.
Barry Bingham (b. 1933) US journalist and editor. Referring to the breakdown of the family media business. *Fortune* (1986)

3 I find that no matter how long a meeting goes on, the best ideas always come during the final five minutes, when people drop their guard and I ask them what they really think.
Michael Eisner (b. 1942) US chairman and CEO of the Disney Corporation. *International Management* (April 1988)

4 No grand idea was ever born in a conference, but a lot of foolish ideas have died there.
F. Scott Fitzgerald (1896–1940) US writer. *The Crack-Up* (1945)

5 Meetings are a great trap. Soon you find yourself trying to get agreement and then the people who disagree come to think they have a right to be persuaded…However, they are indispensable when you don't want to do anything.
J.K. Galbraith (b. 1908) US economist and diplomat. *Ambassador's Journal* (1969), ch. 5

6 In a good meeting there is a momentum that comes from the spontaneous exchange of fresh ideas and produces extraordinary results. That momentum depends on the freedom permitted the participants.
Harold S. Geneen (1910–97) US telecommunications entrepreneur and CEO of ITT. *Fortune* (15 October 1984)

7 Whoever invented the meeting must have had Hollywood in mind. I think they should consider giving Oscars for meetings: Best Meeting of the Year, Best Supporting Meeting, Best Meeting Based on Material from Another Meeting.

William Goldman (b. 1931) US screenwriter and novelist. *Adventures in the Screen Trade* (1983), ch. 2

8 Meetings—bodies in the same room—are but the most obvious, and a somewhat antiquated, example of the sense in which work is shared.
Daniel Goleman (b. 1946) US behavioural scientist, journalist, and author. *Emotional Intelligence* (1996)

9 What is a committee? A group of the unwilling, picked from the unfit, to do the unnecessary.
Richard Harkness (1907–77) US radio and television journalist. *New York Herald Tribune* (1960)

10 Don't try to manage from any board of directors—or any other kind of meeting.
Robert Heller (b. 1932) British management writer. *The Super Managers* (1984), ch. 9

11 A committee is a thing which takes a week to do what one good man can do in an hour.
Elbert Hubbard (1856–1915) US humorist. Quoted in 'Cooperation', *All About Success* (Peter Potter; 1988)

12 A manager's ability to turn meetings into a thinking environment is probably an organization's greatest asset.
Nancy Kline (b. 1946) US author, educator, and consultant. *Time to Think* (1999)

13 I love meetings with suits...because I know they had a really boring week and I walk in there with my orange velvet leggings and drop popcorn in my cleavage and then fish it out and eat it.
Madonna (b. 1958) US singer and actor. Quoted in *Vanity Fair* (April 1991)

14 I don't know the statistics, but I'm willing to guess that the executives of corporate America spend 70 to 80 percent of their time in meetings. I do know that most of those meetings...are 70 to 80 percent posturing and leveling...The posturing is gratuitous, and the leveling is better done elsewhere. This alone would enhance US productivity far more than any trade agreement.
Nicholas Negroponte (b. 1943) US academic, co-founder and director of MIT Media Laboratory. 'Get a Life?', *Wired Magazine* (3 September 1995)

15 Outside of traffic, there is nothing that has held this country back as much as committees.
Will Rogers (1879–1935) US actor, columnist, and humorist. Quoted in *Will Rogers, His Life and Times* (Richard M. Ketchum; 1973)

16 There is no better place in the world to find out the shortcomings of each other than a conference.
Will Rogers (1879–1935) US actor, columnist, and humorist. Quoted in *Will Rogers, His Life and Times* (Richard M. Ketchum; 1973)

17 The length of a meeting rises with the number of people present and the productiveness of a meeting falls with the square of the number of people present.

Eileen Shanahan (1924–2001) US journalist and author. *Times Talk* (1963)

18 My life has been a meeting...one long meeting. Even on the few committees I don't yet belong to, the agenda winks at me when I pass.
Gwyn Thomas (1913–81) Welsh dramatist and writer. *The Keep* (1961)

19 When committees gather, each member is necessarily an actor, uncontrollably acting out the part of himself, reading the lines that identify him, asserting his identity.
Lewis Thomas (1913–93) US academic, physician, and writer. 'On Committees', *The Medusa and the Snail* (1979)

20 A meeting is an arrangement whereby a large number of people gather together, some to say what they really do not think, some not to say what they really do.
Vladimir Voinovich (b. 1932) Russian novelist. *The Life and Extraordinary Adventures of Private Ivan Chonkin* (1969), pt 2, ch. 6

21 Any committee that is the slightest use is a committee of people who are too busy to want to sit on it for a second longer than they have to.
Katharine Whitehorn (b. 1926) British journalist. 'Are You Sitting Comfortably?', *Observations* (1970)

22 I know, of course, how important it is not to keep a business engagement if one wants to retain any sense of the beauty of life.
Oscar Wilde (1854–1900) Irish writer and wit. Said by Cecily. *The Importance of Being Earnest* (1895), Act 2

MISTAKES

1 When new industries become phenomenons, a lot of investors bet on the wrong companies...decades ago, it was de rigueur to use 'Motors' in the name, just as everybody uses 'dot-com' today...the parallel is interesting.
Jeff Bezos (b. 1964) US founder and CEO of Amazon.com. 'Bezos on Buffet', *Fortune* (22 November 1999)

2 The kinds of people we employ are not afraid of taking risks. If someone mucks up, they don't get a bollocking from me. They know they've mucked up and they redouble their efforts.
Richard Branson (b. 1950) British entrepreneur, business executive, and founder of the Virgin Group. Interview, *ASAP* (27 February 1997)

3 Every great mistake has a halfway moment, a split second when it can be recalled and perhaps remedied.
Pearl S. Buck (1892–1973) US writer. *What America Means to Me* (1943)

4 Common sense always speaks too late...it is the little man in a grey suit who never makes a mistake in addition. But it's always somebody else's money he's adding up.

Raymond Chandler (1888–1959) US writer. *Playback* (1958), ch. 14

5 Don't argue for other people's weaknesses. Don't argue for your own. When you make a mistake, admit it, correct it, and learn from it— immediately.
Stephen Covey (b. 1932) US writer and psychologist. *The 7 Habits of Highly Effective People* (1989)

6 Some mistakes cost money, others have a more personal cost.
Peter de Savary (b. 1944) British entrepreneur. Quoted in *The Adventure Capitalists* (Jeff Grout and Lynne Curry; 1998)

7 Among all forms of mistake, prophecy is the most gratuitous.
George Eliot (1819–80) British novelist. *Middlemarch* (1871–72)

8 If all else fails, immortality can always be achieved by a spectacular mistake.
J.K. Galbraith (b. 1908) US economist and diplomat. Attrib.

9 We have to be willing to forge out our own path, make our own mistakes and learn from our own mistakes, and from the mistakes go on to achievement.
Indira Gandhi (1917–84) Indian prime minister. Speech (25 October 1969)

10 The Internet was not always the top priority in Microsoft's strategy. Its arrival changed our business and became the biggest unplanned event we've ever had to respond to.
Bill Gates (b. 1955) US entrepreneur, chairman and CEO of Microsoft. *Business@the Speed of Thought* (co-written with Collins Hemingway; 1999)

11 Mistakes are a fact of life
It is the response to error that counts.
Nikki Giovanni (b. 1943) US poet. 'Of Liberation', *Black Feeling/Black Talk/Black Judgment* (1970)

12 Man errs as long as he strives.
Johann Wolfgang von Goethe (1749–1832) German poet, playwright, novelist, and scientist. *Faust* (1808), pt 1

13 Walking on the eggs will smash the eggs.
Barry Hearn (b. 1948) British sports promoter. Referring to the ease of making mistakes. Quoted in *The Adventure Capitalists* (Jeff Grout and Lynne Banks; 1998)

14 Error is just as important a condition of life as truth.
Carl Gustav Jung (1875–1961) Swiss psychiatrist. *Psychological Reflections* (Jolande Jacobi, ed.; 1953)

15 I've always been able to make erroneous decisions very quickly.
Herb Kelleher (b. 1931) US businessman and founder of Southwest Airlines. *The Nation's Business* (October 1991)

16 It is a good thing to make mistakes so long as you're found out quickly.
John Maynard Keynes (1883–1946) British economist. Attrib.

17 There is no harm in being sometimes wrong, especially if one is promptly found out.
John Maynard Keynes (1883–1946) British economist. *Essays in Biography* (1963)

18 A mistake is an event, the full benefit of which has not yet been turned to your advantage.
Edwin Land (1909–91) US inventor and founder of Polaroid Corporation. Personal maxim. Quoted in *The Fifth Discipline: The Art and Practice of the Learning Organization* (Peter M. Senge; 1990)

19 Conceal a flaw, and the world will imagine the worst.
Martial (?40–?104) Roman poet and epigrammist. *Epigrams* (?87), bk 3, 42

20 By failing to grasp the critical issues, too many senior managers today impose great anxiety on themselves and their subordinates, whose efforts end in failure and frustration.
Kenichi Ohmae (b. 1943) Japanese management consultant and theorist. *The Mind of the Strategist* (1982), ch. 2

21 Give me fruitful error any time, full of seeds, bursting with its own corrections.
Vilfredo Pareto (1848–1923) Italian economist and sociologist. *Mind and Society* (1916)

22 You can't live life without an eraser.
Tom Peters (b. 1942) US management consultant and author. *The Circle of Innovation* (1998)

23 The man who makes no mistakes does not usually make anything.
E.J. Phelps (1822–1900) US diplomat. Speech, Mansion House, London (24 January 1899)

24 A man should never be ashamed to own he has been in the wrong, which is but saying, in other words, that he is wiser to-day than he was yesterday.
Alexander Pope (1688–1744) English poet. *Thoughts on Various Subjects* (1741)

25 The mistakes of the great, promulgated along with the discoveries of their genius, are apt to work havoc.
Erwin Schrödinger (1887–1961) Austrian physicist. *Nature and the Greeks* (1954)

26 A life spent making mistakes is not only more honourable but more useful than a life spent doing nothing.
George Bernard Shaw (1856–1950) Irish writer and critic. *The Doctor's Dilemma* (1906)

27 We often discover what *will* do, by finding out what will not do; and probably he who never made a mistake never made a discovery.
Samuel Smiles (1812–1904) Scottish social reformer and writer. *Self-Help* (1859), ch. 11

28 Errors using inadequate data are much less than those using no data at all.
Julia Stone, US business executive. Quoted in *In Mathematical Circles* (H. Eves; 1969)

29 The only people who never make mistakes are those who have never taken a decision.
Jack Straw (b. 1946) British politician. *Observer* (May 1999)

30 Use missteps as stepping stones to deeper understanding and greater achievement.
Susan L. Taylor (b. 1946) US journalist and editor. Quoted in *My Soul Looks Back, 'Less I Forget* (Dorothy Winbush Riley; 1995)

31 We are built to make mistakes, coded for error.
Lewis Thomas (1913–93) US academic, physician, and writer. 'To Err is Human', *The Medusa and the Snail* (1979)

32 A mistake is simply another way of doing things.
Luc de Clapiers Vauvenargues (1715–47) French soldier and writer. Quoted in *Washington Post* (January 1988)

33 My own success was attended by quite a few failures along the way. But I refused to make the biggest mistake of all: worrying too much about making mistakes.
Kemmons Wilson (1913–2003) US entrepreneur, founder and chairman of Holiday Inn. Speech, Hillsdale College, Hillsdale, Michigan (September 1996)

MODERATION

1 If I cannot get men who steer a middle course to associate with, I would far rather have the impetuous and hasty. For the impetuous at any rate assert themselves.
Confucius (551–479 BC) Chinese philosopher, administrator, and writer. *Analects* (?500 BC)

2 To be overbearing when one has wealth and position
Is to bring calamity upon oneself.
Laozi (?570–?490 BC) Chinese philosopher, reputed founder of Daoism. *Daode Jing*, IX

3 The extreme inequality and uncertainty of a tax assess in this manner can be compensated only by its extreme moderation.
Adam Smith (1723–90) British economist and philosopher. Referring to tax based on estimation. *An Inquiry into the Nature and Causes of the Wealth of Nations* (1776)

4 Candour and generosity, unless tempered by moderation, lead to ruin.
Cornelius Tacitus (?55–?120) Roman historian, orator, and politician. *Histories* (?100), bk 3

5 Moderation is a fatal thing, Lady Hunstanton. Nothing succeeds like excess.
Oscar Wilde (1854–1900) Irish writer and wit. *A Woman of No Importance* (1893), Act 3

MONEY

1 Numbers written on restaurant bills within the confines of restaurants do not follow the same mathematical laws as numbers written on any other piece of paper in any other part of the universe.
Douglas Adams (1952–2001) British author. *Life, the Universe and Everything* (1986)

2 What troubles me is not that movie stars run for office, but that they find it easy to get elected. It should be difficult. It should be difficult for millionaires, too.
Shana Alexander (b. 1925) US writer and editor. *Life* (1966)

3 Money is better than poverty, if only for financial reasons.
Woody Allen (b. 1935) US actor, humorist, producer, and director. 'The Early Essays', *Without Feathers* (1976)

4 It does seem the more you get the more you spend. It is rather like being on a golden treadmill.
Charles Allsop (b. 1940) US commodities broker. Remark (December 1988)

5 The almighty dollar is the only object of worship.
Anonymous. *Philadelphia Public Ledger* (2 December 1836)

6 When money speaks, the truth keeps silent.
Anonymous

7 Getting money is like digging with a needle; spending it is like water soaking into sand.
Anonymous. Japanese proverb.

8 Money has no legs, but it runs.
Anonymous. Japanese proverb.

9 Money alone is the ruling principle of the world.
Anonymous. Latin proverb.

10 With money in your pocket, you are wise and you are handsome and you sing well too.
Anonymous. Yiddish proverb.

11 When money is once parted with, it can never return.
Jane Austen (1775–1817) British novelist. *Sense and Sensibility* (1811), vol. 1, ch. 2

12 Money, of course, is never just money. It's always something else, and it's always something more, and it always has the last word.
Paul Auster (b. 1947) US novelist, short-story writer, and poet. *Hand to Mouth* (1997)

13 Money is like muck, not good except it be spread.
Francis Bacon (1561–1626) English philosopher and statesman. 'Of Seditions and Troubles', *Essays* (1597–1625)

14 Money, it turned out, was exactly like sex: you thought of nothing else if you didn't have it and thought of other things if you did.
James Baldwin (1924–87) US writer. 'Black Boy Looks at the White Boy', *Esquire* (May 1961)

15 Money speaks sense in a language all nations understand
Aphra Behn (1640–89) English novelist and playwright. *The Rover* (1681), pt 2, 1

16 How they love money...They adore money! Holy money! Beautiful money!...people were feeble-minded about everything except money.
Saul Bellow (b. 1915) US novelist. *Seize the Day* (1956), ch. 2

17 For the love of money is the root of all evil: which while some coveted after, they have erred from the faith, and pierced themselves through with many sorrows.
Bible. I Timothy 6:10

18 MONEY, n. A blessing that is of no advantage to us excepting when we part with it.
Ambrose Bierce (1842–?1914) US journalist and writer. *The Devil's Dictionary* (1911)

19 When money talks, few are deaf.
Earl Derr Biggers (1884–1933) US novelist and playwright. *Charlie Chan in Honolulu* (1938)

20 Whether he admits it or not, a man has been brought up to look at money as a sign of his virility, a symbol of his power, a bigger phallic symbol than a Porsche.
Victoria Billings (b. 1945) US journalist and author. *The Womansbook* (1974)

21 We all need money, but there are degrees of desperation.
Anthony Burgess (1917–93) British novelist, critic, and composer. Interview, *The Face* (December 1984)

22 It's clearly a budget. It's got a lot of numbers in it.
George W. Bush (b. 1946) US president. Quoted in *Reuters* (5 May 2000)

23 It has been said that the love of money is the root of all evil. The want of money is so quite as truly.
Samuel Butler (1835–1902) British writer. *Erewhon* (1872), ch. 20

24 Money can only be the useful drudge of things immeasurably higher than itself. Exalted beyond this, as it sometimes is, it remains Caliban still and still plays the beast.
Andrew Carnegie (1835–1919) US industrialist and philanthropist. Address, at the presentation of the Carnegie Library, Pittsburgh, Pennsylvania (5 November 1895)

25 Dollar making is not necessarily business.
Andrew Carnegie (1835–1919) US industrialist and philanthropist. 1920. Attrib.

26 That realm cannot be rich whose coin is poor or base.
William Cecil (1520–98) English statesman. Said at the time of the reform of the English coinage. Attrib.

27 Fireworks are the best fun you can have spending money.
Terence Conran (b. 1931) British business executive, retailer, and founder of Habitat. *Evening Standard* (July 5 1989)

28 Annual income twenty pounds, annual expenditure nineteen nineteen six, result happiness. Annual income twenty pounds, annual expenditure twenty pounds ought and six, result misery.
Charles Dickens (1812–70) British novelist. *David Copperfield* (1849–50), ch. 12

29 Money and goods are certainly the best of references.
Charles Dickens (1812–70) British novelist. *Our Mutual Friend* (1864–65), bk 1, ch. 4

30 Finance is an art. And it represents the operations of the subtlest of the intellectuals and of the egoists.
Theodore Dreiser (1871–1945) US novelist and journalist. *The Financier* (1912)

31 Business? It's quite simple. It's other people's money.
Alexandre Dumas (1824–95) French playwright and novelist. *La Question d'argent* (1857), Act 11, Scene 7

32 Money doesn't talk, it swears.
Bob Dylan (b. 1941) US singer. Song lyric. 'It's Alright Ma, I'm Only Bleeding' (1965)

33 Money, which represents the prose of life, and which is hardly spoken of in parlors without an apology, is, in its effects and laws, as beautiful as roses.
Ralph Waldo Emerson (1803–82) US essayist, lecturer, and poet. 'Nominalist and Realist', *Essays: Second Series* (1844)

34 There are only two fools in this world. One is the millionaire who thinks that by hoarding money he can somehow accumulate real power, and the other is the penniless reformer who thinks that if only he can take the money away from one class and give it to another, all the world's ills will be cured.
Henry Ford (1863–1947) US industrialist, car manufacturer, and founder of Ford Motor Company. *My Life and Work* (co-written with Samuel Crowther; 1922)

35 If money is your hope for independence, you will never have it.
Henry Ford (1863–1947) US industrialist, automobile manufacturer, and founder of Ford Motor Company. *My Life and Work* (co-written with Samuel Crowther; 1922)

36 Money is like an arm or a leg, use it or lose it.
Henry Ford (1863–1947) US industrialist, automobile manufacturer, and founder of Ford Motor Company. Interview (November 1931)

37 Remember that time is money.
Benjamin Franklin (1706–90) US politician, inventor, and journalist. *Advice to a Young Tradesman* (1748)

38 If you'd know the value of money, go and borrow some.
Benjamin Franklin (1706–90) US politician, inventor, and journalist. The *Poor Richard's Almanack* series (1732–58) were originally published under the pseudonym Richard Saunders. *Poor Richard's Almanack* (1754)

39 She had a powerful regard for money—I suppose because we never had any.
Brian Friel (b. 1929) Irish writer. *The Diviner* (1982)

40 He that payeth beforehand shall have his work ill done.
Thomas Fuller (1654–1734) English physician and writer. *Gnomologia* (1732)

41 I've always had a place for every dollar that came in. I've never seen the day where I could say that I felt rich. Generally you have to worry about paying the bills.
J. Paul Getty (1892–1976) US entrepreneur, oil industry executive, and financier. Interview, *Evening Standard* (11 February 1974)

42 My hardest job has been to keep from being a millionaire.
Amadeo Giannini (1870–1949) US banker and founder of Bank of America. *American* magazine (January 1931)

43 Money itch is a bad thing. I never had that trouble.
Amadeo Giannini (1870–1949) US banker and founder of Bank of America. Quoted in 'America's Banker', *Time 100: Heroes and Inspirations* (December 1999)

44 Once one has got the money habit, it is extremely difficult to kick it.
Godfrey Golzen (1930–2001) British business writer. 'The Money Junkies', *Smart Moves* (co-written with Andrew Gardner; 1990)

45 And what we men of business should remember is that art, philosophy and religion can and should...be made to pay. And it's pay or perish in this world.
Harley Granville-Barker (1877–1946) British actor, manager, and playwright. *The Madras House* (1910)

46 These companies have money thrown at them. And that's good, but it's also dangerous. It's good because it allows them to do big things, and it is dangerous because companies who have too much money don't have the market discipline of learning to operate with the money that they bring in as part of their business...and developing a pattern or focusing that that discipline brings.
Andrew S. Grove (b. 1936) US entrepreneur, author, and chairman of Intel Corporation. Referring to the rush to invest in dot.com companies during the late 1990s. Speech, Los Angeles Times 3rd Annual Investment Strategies Conference, Los Angeles, California (22 May 1999)

47 Accountants are the witch-doctors of the modern world and willing to turn their hands to any kind of magic.
Charles Eustace Harman (1894–1970) British judge. Speech (February 1964)

48 Money is certainly too dangerous an instrument to leave to the fortuitous expediency of politicians.
Friedrich August von Hayek (1899–1992) British economist. *Choice in Currency* (1976)

49 If possible honestly, if not, somehow, make money.
Horace (65–8 BC) Roman poet and satirist. *Epistles* (?20 BC), bk 1, no. 1, l. 66

50 Money is to the fore now. It is the romance, the poetry of our age.
William Dean Howells (1837–1920) US novelist, journalist, editor, and critic. *The Rise of Silas Lapham* (1885)

51 Money is not, properly speaking, one of the subjects of commerce...It is none of the wheels of trade: it is the oil which renders the motion of the wheels more smooth and easy.
David Hume (1711–76) Scottish philosopher and historian. 'Of Money', *Essays, Moral, Political, and Literary* (1754), pt 2, essay 3

52 The instinct of acquisitiveness has more perverts, I believe, than the instinct of sex. At any rate, people seem to me odder about money than about even their amours.
Aldous Huxley (1894–1963) British novelist and essayist. *Point Counter Point* (1928), ch. 22

53 We all know how the size of sums of money appear to vary in a remarkable way according as they are paid in or out.
Julian Huxley (1887–1975) British biologist and writer. *Essays of a Biologist* (1923)

54 That's the American way. If little kids don't aspire to make money like I did, what the hell good is this country?
Lee Iacocca (b. 1924) US president of Ford Motor Company, chairman and CEO of Chrysler Corporation. Referring to his $20 million plus pay package in a period when the company was encouraging pay restraint among workers. Quoted in *Thriving on Chaos* (Tom Peters; 1987)

55 The almighty dollar, that great object of universal devotion throughout our land.
Washington Irving (1783–1859) US writer and diplomat. *Wolfert's Roost* (1855)

56 Men are more often bribed by their loyalties and ambitions than money.
Robert H. Jackson (1892–1954) US jurist. United States v. Wunderlich (1951)

57 Money's a horrid thing to follow, but a charming thing to meet.
Henry James (1843–1916) US novelist. *The Portrait of a Lady* (1881), ch. 35

58 Lenin was right. There is no subtler, no surer means of overturning the existing basis of society than to debauch the currency.
John Maynard Keynes (1883–1946) British economist. *Economic Consequences of the Peace* (1919)

59 The moral problem of our age is concerned with the love of money.
John Maynard Keynes (1883–1946) British economist. *Essays in Persuasion* (1925)

60 Give the Germans five deutschmarks and they will save it. But give the British £5 and they will borrow £25 and spend it.
John Major (b. 1943) British former prime minister. Said while Chancellor of the Exchequer. Interview, *Daily Express* (28 May 1990)

61 There is nothing so habit forming as money.
Don Marquis (1878–1937) US journalist and humorist. Attrib.

62 Money is like a sixth sense without which you cannot make a complete use of the other five.
W. Somerset Maugham (1874–1965) British novelist, short-story writer, and dramatist. *Of Human Bondage* (1915)

63 Money is a poor man's credit card.
Marshall McLuhan (1911–80) Canadian sociologist and author. Quoted in *Maclean's* (June 1971)

64 You've heard money talking? Did you understand the message?
Marshall McLuhan (1911–80) Canadian sociologist and author. *The Mechanical Bride* (1951)

65 In an industrial society capital is a scarce resource, but in today's information society there's plenty of capital.
Michael R. Milken (b. 1946) US investment banker and financial entrepreneur. 'A Chat with Michael Milken', *Forbes* (13 July 1987)

66 To mistake money for wealth, is the same sort of error as to mistake the highway which may be the easiest way of getting to your house or lands, for the house and lands themselves.
John Stuart Mill (1806–73) British economist and philosopher. 1848. *Principles of Political Economy, with Some of their Applications to Social Philosophy, 7th edition* (1871)

67 Money couldn't buy you friends but you got a better class of enemy.
Spike Milligan (1918–2002) Irish comedian and writer. *Puckoon* (1963)

68 Americans relate all effort, all work, and all of life itself to the dollar.
Nancy Mitford (1904–73) British novelist and biographer. *Noblesse Oblige: An Enquiry into the Identifiable Characteristics of the English Aristocracy* (co-written with A.S.C. Ross; 1956)

69 I'm not in Wall Street for my health.
J.P. Morgan (1837–1913) US financier. Quoted in *Treasury of Investment Wisdom* (Bernice Cohen; 1999)

70 Money is like manure. If you spread it around, it does a lot of good, but if you pile it up in one place, it stinks like hell.
Clint W. Murchison (1885–1969) US entrepreneur, oil industry executive, and financier. Quoted by his son Clint Murchison Jr. *Time* (16 June 1961)

71 A credit card is a money tool, not a supplement to money. The failure to make this distinction has 'supplemented' many a poor soul right into bankruptcy.
Paula Nelson (b. 1944) US educator. *The Joy of Money* (1975)

72 Americans want action for their money. They are fascinated by its self-reproducing qualities if it's put to work.
Paula Nelson (b. 1944) US educator. *The Joy of Money* (1975), ch. 15

73 There's only one thing to do with loose change of course. Tighten it.
Flann O'Brien (1911–66) Irish writer. *The Best of Myles* (1968)

74 To make money, you have to spend money. But if you are going to make money, you have to make it with love.
Yoko Ono (b. 1933) US artist and musician. Interview, *Playboy* (January 1981)

75 Expenditure rises to meet income.
C. Northcote Parkinson (1909–93) British political scientist and author. *The Law and the Profits* (1960)

76 All money nowadays seems to be produced with a homing instinct for the Treasury.
Prince Philip (b. 1921) British consort of Queen Elizabeth II. Quoted in *Observer* (26 May 1963)

77 Money never remains just coins and pieces of paper. Money can be translated into the beauty of living, a support in misfortune, an education, or future security. It also can be translated into a source of bitterness.
Sylvia Porter (1913–91) US journalist and finance expert. *Sylvia Porter's Money Book* (1975), ch. 1

78 I finally know what distinguishes man from the other beasts: financial worries.
Jules Renard (1864–1910) French writer. 1910. *Journal* (1877–1910)

79 There is no such thing as a paper loss. A paper loss is a very real loss.
Jim Rogers (b. 1935) US banker and management consultant. Quoted in *Treasury of Investment Wisdom* (Bernice Cohen; 1999)

80 Money is the seed of money. The first guinea is sometimes more difficult to aquire than the second million.
Jean-Jacques Rousseau (1712–78) French philosopher and writer. *Discourse Upon the Origin and Foundation of the Inequality Among Mankind* (1754)

81 My boy...always try to rub up against money, for if you rub up against money long enough, some of it may rub off on you.
Damon Runyon (1884–1946) US writer and journalist. 'A Very Honorable Guy', *Runyon on Broadway* (1950)

82 Money that bears no relationship to reality is imaginary. It is pure inflation.
John Ralston Saul (b. 1947) Canadian writer. *The Unconscious Civilization* (1995)

83 It is a curious and terrible thing, but for some reason it is easier for a man to raise a thousand dollars for a margin call than it is for him to raise the price of supper if he is starving.
Fred Schwed (1901–66) US author. *Where Are The Customers' Yachts?* (1940)

84 Money makes a man laugh.
John Selden (1584–1654) English jurist, antiquary, and politician. mid-17th century. *Table Talk* (1689)

85 He that wants money, means, and content, is without three good friends.
William Shakespeare (1564–1616) English poet and playwright. *As You Like It* (1599), Act 3, Scene 2, l. 25

86 The universal regard for money is the one hopeful fact in our civilization.
George Bernard Shaw (1856–1950) Irish writer and critic. *Major Barbara* (1905), Preface

87 The substitution of monetary values for all other values is pushing society toward a dangerous disequilibrium.
George Soros (b. 1930) US financier, entrepreneur, and philanthropist. *The Crisis of Global Capitalism* (1998)

88 Pennies don't fall from heaven. They have to be earned on earth.
Margaret Thatcher (b. 1925) British former prime minister. Quoted in 'Sayings of the Week', *Observer* (18 November 1979)

89 It is not wisdom to lose the capital For the sake of the interest.
Tiruvalluvar (fl. 1st century) Indian poet. *The Kural*, 463

90 Nobody who has wealth to distribute ever omits himself.
Leon Trotsky (1879–1940) Russian revolutionary leader and Marxist theorist. Quoted in 'Sayings of the Week', *Observer* (1937)

91 It's not how much you earn, it's how much you owe.

Ted Turner (b. 1938) US founder of Turner Broadcasting Systems. Speech (1986)

92 I've been learning how to give. It's something you have to keep working on, because people like money the way they do their homes and their dogs.

Ted Turner (b. 1938) US founder of Turner Broadcasting Systems. *New York Times* (20 September 1997)

93 The powerful have money, and money is the master of everything in a state.

Voltaire (1694–1778) French writer, philosopher, and reformer. *Dictionnaire Philosophique* (1764)

94 One lady friend of mine asked me…'What do you love most?' That's how I started painting money.

Andy Warhol (1928–87) US artist and film maker. Referring to the inspiration for his dollar sign paintings. *The Andy Warhol Diaries* (P. Hackett, ed.; 1989)

95 Money should circulate like rain water.

Thornton Wilder (1897–1975) US playwright and novelist. Spoken by Mrs Levi. *The Matchmaker* (1954), Act 1

96 The venture industry doesn't like to see new venture capitalists because it means more competition. There is always more money than deals.

Ann Winblad (b. 1953) US venture capitalist. *www.womenswire.com* (Soledad O'Brien; 2000)

97 If money is your motivation, forget it.

Oprah Winfrey (b. 1954) US talk show host, actor, and business executive. Quoted in *Oprah Winfrey Speaks* (Janet Lowe; 1998)

MOTIVATION

1 I do not love the money. What I do love is the getting of it…What other interest can you suggest to me? I do not read. I do not take part in politics. What can I do?

Philip D. Armour (1832–1901) US business executive. Quoted in *Forbes* (26 October 1987)

2 The opportunities for distinction, prestige, personal power, and the attainment of dominating positions are much more important than material rewards in the development of…commercial organizations.

Chester Barnard (1886–1961) US business executive and management theorist. *Organization and Management* (1948)

3 Motivation, really moving people to do something, needs emotion.

Paul Corrigan (b. 1948) British author. *Shakespeare on Management* (1999)

4 It is only when a person has his own generator that we can talk about motivation. He then needs no outside stimulation. He wants to do it.

Frederick Herzberg (1923–2000) US psychologist. *Harvard Business Review* (January–February 1968)

5 A reward once given becomes a right.

Frederick Herzberg (1923–2000) US psychologist. *The Motivation to Work* (1959)

6 If you want to do something because you want a house or a Jaguar, that's movement. It's not motivation.

Frederick Herzberg (1923–2000) US psychologist. *The Motivation to Work* (1959)

7 The more a person can do, the more can motivate them.

Frederick Herzberg (1923–2000) US psychologist. *The Motivation to Work* (1959)

8 No longer directed by other emotions, I work the way a cow grazes.

Käthe Kollwitz (1867–1945) German painter and graphic artist. April 1910. Diary entry. *Diaries and Letters* (Hans Kollwitz, ed.; 1955)

9 Women are naturally good motivators, good at juggling different projects and issues at the same time, and more cooperative rather than aggressive and confrontational.

Bridget A. Macaskill (b. 1949) British non-executive director for J. Sainsburys, former president and CEO of Oppenheimer Funds. Quoted in *Women of the Street* (Sue Herera; 1997)

10 The common wisdom is that…managers have to learn to motivate people. Nonsense. Employees bring their own motivation.

Tom Peters (b. 1942) US management consultant and author. *A Passion for Excellence* (co-written with Nancy Austin; 1985)

11 If a man is producing nothing, nobody can be the worse for a reduction of his incentive to produce.

George Bernard Shaw (1856–1950) Irish writer and critic. 'Socialism and Superior Brains', *Fortnightly Review* (April 1894)

12 If you don't understand what makes people tick, they won't tick.

Robert Swan (b. 1956) British explorer and environmentalist. Quoted in *Management Today* (September 2001)

13 If you have an olive, you want an olive tree. You want a little more. You want the whole tree.

Ted Turner (b. 1938) US founder of Turner Broadcasting Systems. *New York Times* (November 1996)

14 It's part of my strong feeling for the necessity of constant change, for keeping people a little off balance.

Sam M. Walton (1918–92) US entrepreneur and founder of Wal-Mart, Inc. *Made in America* (co-written with John Huey; 1992)

15 Almost every kind of fanfare was tried to create enthusiasm.

Thomas J. Watson Sr (1874–1956) US founder and president of IBM. Quoted in *A Business and Its Beliefs* (Thomas J. Watson Jr; 1963)

NEGOTIATION

1 This is about negotiations, but the answer to that question is 'No'.
David Andrews (b. 1935) Irish politician. When asked if the Irish government would compromise on North-South political bodies, during talks on the future of Northern Ireland. 'This Week They Said', *Irish Times* (11 April 1998)

2 We believe that negotiation is a game which must result in winners and losers. The anxiety we experience...ranks negotiation right after a visit to the dentist...anxiety will disappear when you recognize that both sides can have their needs met.
Ed Brodow, US consultant, author, and actor. *Negotiate with Confidence* (1996)

3 The only way a working man can get anything is by collective bargaining, and by saying , 'If you don't give us a raise, not only will I quit but we will all quit and tie up your business'; that is the only way he can do it.
Clarence Darrow (1857–1938) US lawyer. Testimony before the US Senates Commission on Industrial Relations (1915)

4 Some of them think they have me by the balls, but their hands aren't big enough.
Bernie Eccleston (b. 1930) British entrepreneur and CEO of Formula 1 motor racing. Referring to negotiations with Formula 1 racing teams, when planning to float Formula 1 on the Stock Exchange. Quoted in *Formula 1, The Business of Winning* (Russell Hotten; 1998)

5 Industrial relations are like sexual relations. It's better between consenting parties.
Vic Feather (1908–76) British trade union leader. *Guardian* (8 August 1976)

6 Necessity never made a good bargain.
Benjamin Franklin (1706–90) US politician, inventor, and journalist. The *Poor Richard's Almanack* series (1732–58) were originally published under the pseudonym Richard Saunders. *Poor Richard's Almanack* (1735)

7 Diplomacy is the art of letting someone else have your way.
David Frost (b. 1939) British broadcaster. Attrib.

8 It's a well-known proposition that you know who's going to win a negotiation: it's he who pauses the longest.
Robert Holmes à Court (1937–90) Australian entrepreneur. *Sydney Morning Herald* (24 May 1986)

9 Let us never negotiate out of fear. But let us never fear to negotiate.
John F. Kennedy (1917–63) US president. Presidential inaugural speech (20 January 1961)

10 When you're negotiating for a 35 hour week, remember they have only just got 66 hours in Taiwan, and you're competing with Taiwan.
Victor Kiam (1926–2001) US CEO of Remington Corporation. *Daily Express* (12 June 1981)

11 A negotiator should observe everything. You must be part Sherlock Holmes, part Sigmund Freud.
Victor Kiam (1926–2001) US CEO of Remington Corporation. *Going For It* (1986)

12 Large scale collective bargaining...a seductive name for bilateral monopoly...means either adjudication of conflicts in terms of power, or deadlock and stoppages.
Frank H. Knight (1885–1972) US economist. *Freedom and Reform* (1947), ch. 13

13 The harder a guy negotiates with us about equity, the better CEO he is likely to be.
Henry R. Kravis (b. ?1944) US investor, co-founder of Kohlberg Kravis Roberts. Quoted in *Merchants of Debt* (George Anders; 1992)

14 Never corner an opponent, and always assist him to save his face...Avoid self-righteousness like the devil—there is nothing so self-blinding.
Basil Henry Liddell Hart (1895–1970) British military historian and strategist. *Deterrent or Defence* (1960)

15 If you have to boil down your negotiating attitude to two things you can do a lot worse than *question everything* and *think big*.
Mark McCormack (1930–2003) US entrepreneur, founder and CEO of the International Management Group. *McCormack on Negotiating* (1995)

16 Anger can be an effective negotiating tool, but only as a calculated act, never as a reaction.
Mark McCormack (1930–2003) US entrepreneur, founder and CEO of the International Management Group. *What They Don't Teach You at Harvard Business School* (1984)

17 Make a suggestion or assumption and let them tell you you're wrong. People also have a need to feel smarter than you are.
Mark McCormack (1930–2003) US entrepreneur, founder and CEO of the International Management Group. *What They Don't Teach You at Harvard Business School* (1984)

18 It's a crunch moment when you are in negotiations. You suddenly see an opening in the hedge and dive through it even if you get scratched.
Len Murray (b. 1922) British trade union leader. Interview, *Observer* (2 September 1984)

19 Never apologize and never explain—it's a sign of weakness.
Frank S. Nugent (1908–65) US screenwriter. Spoken by John Wayne. *She Wore a Yellow Ribbon* (1949)

20 The talent of insinuating is more useful than that of persuading, because you can insinuate to everybody and you can almost never persuade anybody.
Cardinal de Retz (1613–79) French prelate and politician. *Mémoires du Cardinal de Retz* (1660–79)

21 To know how to dissimulate is the knowledge of kings.
Cardinal Richelieu (1585–1642) French politician. *Testament Politique* (1641)

22 Place a higher priority on discovering what a win looks like for the other person.
Harvey Robbins, US writer on business psychology. *TransCompetition* (co-written with Michael Finley; 1998)

23 Never make concessions.
Gertrude Stein (1874–1946) US author. Attrib. *Independent Magazine* (1995)

24 Be careful, be cautious, do not rush into negotiations...be careful what you give away now, you may wish you had not done so should in future the balance of forces turn in your favour.
Oliver Tambo (1917–93) South African political leader. 1991. Advice on negotiating with the apartheid-supporting South African government. Quoted in *Mandela: The Authorised Biography* (Anthony Sampson; 2000)

25 My style of dealmaking is quite simple and straightforward. I just keep pushing and pushing to get what I'm after.
Donald J. Trump (b. 1946) US property developer. *Time* (January 1989)

26 He knew the precise psychological moment when to say nothing.
Oscar Wilde (1854–1900) Irish writer and wit. *The Picture of Dorian Gray* (1891), ch. 2

27 The single and most dangerous word to be spoken in business is 'no'. The second most dangerous word is 'yes'. It is possible to avoid saying either.
Lois Wyse (b. 1926) US advertising executive and writer. *Company Manners* (1987)

28 When money is at stake, never be the first to mention sums.
Ahmed Zaki Yamani (b. 1930) Saudi Arabian politician. Quoted in *Yamani* (Jeffrey Robinson; 1988)

29 The current structure of a joint venture imposed by foreign investing companies tends to concentrate upon how an individual joint venture's internal management system is vertically integrated into the foreign corporate structure.
Yanni Yan (b. 1958) Chinese business author and academic. 'Managerial and Organization—Learning in Chinese Firms', *China's Managerial Revolution* (Malcolm Warner, ed.; 1999)

30 If you choose to be a negotiator, you eliminate worry about whether you deserve to be successful.
Theodore Zeldin (b. 1933) British academic, author, and historian. *An Intimate History of Humanity* (1994)

31 The trouble about bargaining...is that when one loses in a particular competitive negotiation, one's chances of winning the next negotiation are frequently diminished.
Theodore Zeldin (b. 1933) British academic, author, and historian. *An Intimate History of Humanity* (1994)

OBSTACLES

1 The biggest obstacle to professional writing is the necessity for changing a typewriter ribbon.
Robert Benchley (1889–1945) US humorist. Quoted in *Chips off the Old Benchley* (1949)

2 Terrorist attacks can shake the foundations of our biggest buildings, but they cannot touch the foundations of America.
George W. Bush (b. 1946) US president. Referring to terrorist attacks on US, 11 September 2001. Address to the Nation (2001)

3 These acts shatter steel, but they cannot dent the steel of America's resolve.
George W. Bush (b. 1946) US president. Referring to terrorist attacks on US, 11 September 2001. Address to the Nation (2001)

4 To believe there is no way out of the present crisis for capitalism is an error. No situation is ever absolutely hopeless.
Vladimir Ilich Lenin (1870–1924) Russian revolutionary leader and political theorist. Speech (1917)

5 Every obstacle yields to stern resolve.
Leonardo Da Vinci (1452–1519) Italian artist and inventor. *Notebooks* (1508–18)

OFFICE POLITICS

1 A memorandum is written not to inform the reader but to protect the writer.
Anonymous. *Wall Street Journal* (8 September 1977)

2 Whenever I ask individuals...what leads them to play political games in organizations, they respond that that's human nature and the nature of organizations. We are the carriers of defensive routines, and organizations are the hosts.
Chris Argyris (b. 1923) US academic and organisational behaviour theorist. *Strategy, Change, and Defensive Routines* (1985)

3 To be honest with you, if I'd known the sour look I was going to get from the head of our department I wouldn't have gone to the office at all.
Nikolay Gogol (1809–52) Russian novelist and playwright. *Diary of a Madman* (1835)

4 Men are troublesome. They complain about trifles a woman wouldn't notice. The office boys...complain that the temperature of the building is too hot or too cold...If they have a slight headache, they stay at home.
Clara Lanza (1859–1939) US journalist. 'Women Clerks in New York', *Cosmopolitan* (1891)

5 There are but two means of locomotion to the top. Either people must like you so much that they push you there, or you, yourself, are so good that you push yourself there.
Gerald Sparrow (1903–88) British business executive and writer. *How to Become a Millionaire* (1960), ch. 2

6 You can play too much at corporate politics. Just say, 'I may lose my job, but I will try to do the best I can'.
Dennis Stevenson (b. 1946) British company director. *Management Today* (April 1999)

OPINIONS

1 Freedom is the by-product of economic surplus.
Aneurin Bevan (1897–1960) British politician. Quoted in *Aneurin Bevan* (Michael Foot; 1962), vol. 1, ch. 3

2 I enjoy the fact that I am creating a climate of opinion.

Jan Brown, New Zealand public relations executive. *Marketing* (September 2000)

3 Laissez-faire, supply and demand—one begins to be weary of all that. Leave all to egotism, to ravenous greed of money, of pleasure, of applause—it is the gospel of despair.

Thomas Carlyle (1795–1881) British historian and essayist. *Past and Present* (1843)

4 Few people do business well who do nothing else.

Lord Chesterfield (1694–1773) English statesman, orator, and letter writer. Letter (7 August 1749)

5 One never repents of having spoken too little but often of having spoken too much.

Philippe de Commines (?1445–?1511) French historian and politician. *Mémoires* (1524)

6 I would rather a thousand times be a free soul in jail than to be a sycophant and coward in the streets...If it had not been for the men and women who, in the past, have had the moral courage to go to jail, we would still be in the jungles.

Eugene V. Debs (1855–1926) US politician and trade union leader. Speech, Canton, Ohio (16 June 1918)

7 Power and machinery, money and goods are useful only as they set us free to live.

Henry Ford (1863–1947) US industrialist, car manufacturer, and founder of Ford Motor Company. 1923. *My Life and Work* (co-written with Samuel Crowther; 1922)

8 After all, the three major sources of apartments are death, divorce, and transfer.

Cornelius Gallagher (b. 1921) US real estate executive. *New York Times* (1985)

9 Business is many things, the least of which is the balance sheet. It is a fluid, ever changing, living thing, sometimes building to great peaks, sometimes falling to crumbled lumps.

Harold S. Geneen (1910–97) US telecommunications entrepreneur and CEO of ITT. *Managing* (co-written with Alvin Moscow; 1984)

10 The soul of a business is a curious alchemy of needs, desires, greed, and gratifications mixed together with selflessness, sacrifices, and personal contributions far beyond material rewards.

Harold S. Geneen (1910–97) US telecommunications entrepreneur and CEO of ITT. *Managing* (co-written with Alvin Moscow; 1984)

11 It is not asset stripping...I prefer to think of it as unbundling...The businesses have been stifled under a bureaucracy and we would be liberating them.

James Goldsmith (1933–97) British entrepreneur, financier, and politician. Defending himself against accusations of asset stripping. 'Quotes of the Year', *Financial Times* (30 December 1989)

12 Much as we talk about Internet companies today, in five years' time there won't be any Internet companies. All companies will be Internet companies or they will be dead.

Andrew S. Grove (b. 1936) US entrepreneur, author, and chairman of Intel Corporation. Speech, Los Angeles Times 3rd Annual Investment Strategies Conference, Los Angeles, California (22 May 1999)

13 I didn't go to high school, and I didn't go to grade school either. Education, I think, is for refinement and is probably a liability.

H.L. Hunt (1889–1974) US entrepreneur, oil industry executive, and founder of Hunt Oil. '60 Minutes', CBS Television (1 April 1969)

14 All men are created equal...they are endowed by their Creator with inalienable rights...among these are Life, Liberty, and the pursuit of happiness.

Thomas Jefferson (1743–1826) US president. Declaration of Independence (4 July 1776)

15 Leonardo da Vinci was a great artist and a great scientist. Michelangelo knew how to cut stone at the quarry. Edwin Land at Polaroid once said, 'I want Polaroid to stand at the intersection of art and science', and I've never forgotten that.

Steve Jobs (b. 1955) US entrepreneur, co-founder and CEO of Apple Computer Company, and CEO of Pixar. Referring to the relationship between technology and the arts. Quoted in 'Steve's Two Jobs', *Time* (Michael Krantz; 18 October 1999)

16 Business is like sex. When it's good, it's very, very good; when it's not so good, it's still good.

George Katona (1901–81) US academic and business analyst. *Wall Street Journal* (9 April 1969)

17 Injustice anywhere is a threat to justice everywhere.

Martin Luther King (1929–68) US clergyman and civil rights leader. Attrib.

18 Confusion blast all mercantile transactions, all traffick, exchange of commodities...between nations, all the consequent civilisation and wealth...and rot the very firs of the forest that look so romantic alive, and die into desks.

Charles Lamb (1775–1834) British essayist. 1815. Letter to William Wordsworth. Lamb worked as an East India Company clerk for 33 years (1792–1825). He was one of the first to document life as a 'company man' through his essays and letters. Quoted in *The Life of Charles Lamb* (E.V. Lucas; 1921)

19 I like to stand on line, buy my popcorn, and see a picture with the people.

Sherry Lansing (b. 1944) US chairman of Paramount Motion Picture Group. Quoted in *Arizona Republic* (2000)

20 The rise of ownership by workers offers another glimmer of what economic life might look like based on the emerging understanding that most human beings...are capable of insight, common sense, and intrinsic motivation.

Frances Moore Lappé (b. 1944) US writer and activist on global isues. Speech to Vermont Businesses for Social Responsibility. 'Reweaving Business into the Social Fabric' (11 December 1997)

21 Love your neighbour is not merely sound Christianity; it is good business.

David Lloyd-George (1863–1945) British prime minister. Quoted in 'Sayings of the Week', *Observer* (20 February 1921)

22 Holidays are often overrated disturbances of routine, costly and uncomfortable, and they usually need another holiday to correct their ravages.
E.V. Lucas (1868–1938) British writer and editor. Attrib.

23 Perhaps the most revolting character that the United States ever produced was the Christian business man.
H.L. Mencken (1880–1956) US journalist, essayist, and critic. *Minority Report—H.L. Mencken's Notebook* (1956)

24 If electronic business rules could transcend particular entities, we would have open emarkets...first, we must work on developing a critical mass of businesses that are organically dependent on electronic markets.
William (Walid) Mougayar, US consultant and management theorist. 'Emarkets: Many Choices, No Excuses', *Business 2.0* (October 1998)

25 Perhaps the nirvana of the Net economy is one in which any business would have an equal chance of competing anywhere in the world by adhering to known electronic business rules of engagement.
William (Walid) Mougayar, US consultant and management theorist. 'Emarkets: Many Choices, No Excuses', *Business 2.0* (October 1998)

26 Monopoly is a terrible thing, till you have it.
Rupert Murdoch (b. 1931) US CEO of News Corporation. *The New Yorker* (1979)

27 It's not that I don't have opinions, rather that I'm not paid to think aloud.
Yitzhak Navon (b. 1921) Israeli former president. Quoted in *Observer* (16 January 1983)

28 We do not live to think, but, on the contrary, we think in order that we may succeed in surviving.
Jose Ortega y Gasset (1883–1955) Spanish author and philosopher. *Partisan Review* (December 1949)

29 No advance in wealth, no softening of manners, no reform or revolution has ever brought human equality a millimetre nearer.
George Orwell (1903–50) British novelist, critic, and essayist. *Nineteen Eighty-Four* (1949), pt 2, ch. 9

30 Given the natural differences between human beings, equality is an ethical aspiration that cannot be realised without recourse either to despotism or to an act of fraternity.
Octavio Paz (1914–98) Mexican writer. Attrib.

31 It's a no win situation, like judging a beauty contest; whoever gets it thinks they deserve it and the others think you are an idiot.
Gerry Robinson (b. 1948) Irish chairman of Granada Television and chairman of the Arts Council of England. Referring to the problems of awarding Arts Council grants. *Management Today* (April 1999)

32 The fact that an opinion has been widely held is no evidence whatever that it is not utterly absurd.

Bertrand Russell (1872–1970) British philosopher and writer. *Marriage and Morals* (1929)

33 We're a me-me-me generation. We're borrowing the savings of every nation in the world. We're...piling up a big tab. Now, I may think we're too big to have a run on us. You may think that. But it's possible that God does not.
Paul Samuelson (b. 1915) US economist and winner of the 1970 Nobel Prize in Economics. Interview, 'The "New" Economy?' (Online NewsHour; 13 January 2000)

34 Comment is free but facts are sacred.
C.P. Scott (1846–1932) British editor. *Manchester Guardian* (May 1922)

35 If I want to voice my opinion, I can give it to you now or later. But it's just another opinion.
Ricardo Semler (b. 1959) Brazilian business executive and president of Semco. 'The Mavericks', *Fortune* (June 1995)

36 Public opinion is a weak tyrant compared with our own private opinion.
Henry David Thoreau (1817–62) US writer. *Walden, or Life in the Woods* (1854)

37 Prosperity or egalitarianism—you have to choose. I favour freedom—you never achieve real equality anyway: you simply sacrifice prosperity for an illusion.
Mario Vargas Llosa (b. 1936) Peruvian novelist, playwright, and essayist. *Independent on Sunday* (5 May 1991)

38 All business sagacity reduces itself in the last analysis to a judicious use of sabotage.
Thorstein Veblen (1857–1929) US economist and social scientist. *An Inquiry into the Nature of Peace and the Terms of its Perpetuation* (1917)

39 The more opinions you have, the less you see.
Wim Wenders (b. 1945) German film director and producer. Quoted in *Evening Standard* (25 April 1990)

OPPORTUNITY

1 A wise man will make more opportunities than he finds.
Francis Bacon (1561–1626) English philosopher and statesman. 'Of Ceremonies and Respects', *Essays* (1597–1625)

2 Only through curiosity can we discover opportunities, and only through gambling can we take advantage of them.
Clarence Birdseye (1886–1956) US businessman and founder of Birdseye. *American Magazine* (February 1951)

3 Many leading business people...are revelling in the opportunity to put new ranges on the market with 'eco-friendly' flashes and a 20 per cent mark up.
John Button (b. 1933) Australian politician. Referring to the market's response to the growing demand for environmentally friendly products. *The Times* (22 September 1989)

4 We do not make very full value of the opportunities provided by technology because we prefer critical to constructive thinking, argument to design.

Edward de Bono (b. 1933) British creative-thinking theorist, educator, and writer. 'Away with the Gang of Three', *Guardian* (25 January 1997)

5 There's an underutilized work force of well-qualified women who want to work part time. We've created job opportunities that allow parents to balance work and family life.

Gun Denhart (b. 1945) US mail-order entrepreneur, founder and chairwoman of Hanna Andersson. Referring to women in the workplace. Quoted in 'Gun Denhart: Mail-order Maven', *Women to Watch*, *www.womenswire.com* (Stephanie Irving; 1996)

6 Next to knowing when to seize an opportunity, the most important thing in life is to know when to forgo an advantage.

Benjamin Disraeli (1804–81) British prime minister and novelist. *The Infernal Marriage* (1834)

7 As an investor in small companies, I don't care how rich Microsoft is. I care about what my opportunities are.

Esther Dyson (b. 1951) US knowledge entrepreneur and government adviser. *Wall Street Journal* (1997)

8 As entrepreneurs, we have to remember the importance of building bridges...to new opportunities. Those links should reach out to all sorts of folks: artists, engineers, teachers, business owners, writers, elders, singles, couples.

Gladys E. Edmunds, US travel company entrepreneur. 'Building Bridges to Prosperity', *USA Today* (9 August 2000)

9 The distinction between past, present, and future is only an illusion.

Albert Einstein (1879–1955) US physicist. Letter (March 1955)

10 Don't fight forces; use them.

R. Buckminster Fuller (1895–1983) US inventor, architect, and philosopher. *Shelter* (1932)

11 Opportunities are not offered; they must be wrested and worked for. And this calls for perseverance and tenacity, determination and courage.

Indira Gandhi (1917–84) Indian prime minister. Speech (16 November 1968)

12 In an increasingly non-linear economy, incremental change is not enough—you have to build a capacity for strategy innovation, one that increases your ability to recognize new opportunities.

Gary Hamel (b. 1954) US academic, business writer, and consultant. Interview, *Strategy + Business* (October–December 1997)

13 One way of building private foresight out of public data is looking where others aren't...if you want to see the future, go to an industry confab and get the list of what was talked about. Then ask, 'What did people never talk about?' That's where you're going to find opportunity.

Gary Hamel (b. 1954) US academic, business writer, and consultant. Interview, *Strategy + Business* (October–December 1997)

14 The opportunities for future growth are everywhere. Seeing the future has nothing to do with speculating about what might happen. Rather, you must understand the revolutionary potential of what is already happening.

Gary Hamel (b. 1954) US academic, business writer, and consultant. Interview, *Strategy + Business* (October–December 1997)

15 Seize opportunity by the forelock and see where it leads you.

Armand Hammer (1898–1990) US industrialist, philanthropist, founder and CEO of Occidental Petroleum. *Witness to History* (1987)

16 When nobody wants something, that creates an opportunity.

Carl C. Icahn (b. 1936) US financier. Referring to buying into Texaco when it was in trouble. *Fortune* (5 November 1990)

17 I look for vectors going in time. What's changing, what are the trends? What windows have just opened and what windows are closing?

Steve Jobs (b. 1955) US entrepreneur, co-founder and CEO of Apple Computer Company, and CEO of Pixar. Quoted in 'Steve's Two Jobs', *Time* (Michael Krantz; 18 October 1999)

18 Pleasure disappoints, possibility never. And what wine is so sparkling, what so fragrant, what so intoxicating—as possibility?

Søren Kierkegaard (1813–55) Danish philosopher. *Either/Or* (1843), vol. 1

19 Companies worry too much about the cost of doing something. They should worry about the cost of not doing it.

Philip Kotler (b. 1931) US marketing management thinker. *Marketing Management* (1967)

20 Opportunities are usually disguised as hard work, so most people don't recognise them.

Ann Landers (1918–2002) US columnist. Attrib.

21 One can present people with opportunities. One cannot make them equal to them.

Rosamond Lehmann (1901–90) British novelist. *The Ballad and the Source* (1944)

22 In our business, the windows of opportunity open and close with dazzling rapidity...I constantly have to remind people to seize the moment.

Mark McCormack (1930–2003) US entrepreneur, founder and CEO of the International Management Group. *McCormack on Managing* (1985)

23 An unsuccessful manager blames failure on his obligations; the effective manager turns them to his own advantage. A speech is a chance to lobby...a visit to an important customer a chance to extract trade information.

Henry Mintzberg (b. 1939) Canadian academic and management theorist. 'The Manager's Job: Folklore and Fact', *Harvard Business Review* (July–August 1975)

24 The man who loses his opportunity loses himself.

George Moore (1852–1933) Irish novelist, poet, playwright, and critic. *The Bending of the Bough* (1900)

25 You can't pick cherries with your back to the tree.

J.P. Morgan (1837–1913) US financier. Attrib.

26 E-commerce, E-business, or whatever else you may want to call it is a means to an end. The objectives, as with IT, are to improve or exploit unique business propositions.

William (Walid) Mougayar, US consultant and management theorist. 'E-commerce? E-business? Who E-cares?', *Computerworld* (2 November 1998)

27 The man who is denied the opportunity of taking decisions of importance begins to regard as important the decisions he is allowed to take.

C. Northcote Parkinson (1909–93) British political scientist and author. *Parkinson's Law: The Pursuit of Progress* (1958)

28 Equal opportunity means everyone will have a fair chance at becoming incompetent.

Laurence J. Peter (1919–90) Canadian academic and writer. *Why Things Go Wrong: The Peter Principle Revisited* (1984)

29 While we stop to think, we often miss an opportunity.

Publilius Syrus (*fl.* 1st century BC) Roman writer. *Moral Sayings* (1st century BC), no. 185

30 Grab a chance and you won't be sorry for a might have been.

Arthur Ransome (1884–1967) British writer and journalist. *We Didn't Mean to Go to Sea* (1937)

31 AT&T invented the cellular telephone, but saw no future in it. It takes entrepreneurs, who are angels of destruction, to take advantage of things which the inventor cannot or does not see.

Lester Thurow (b. 1938) US economist, management theorist, and writer. Speech, Sixth Workshop on Inventing the Organization of the 21st Century, Munich, Germany. 'Building Wealth in a Knowledge-Based Society' (February 2000)

ORDER

1 Chaos often breeds life, when order breeds habit.

Henry Brooks Adams (1838–1918) US historian. *Education of Henry Adams* (1907)

2 That man is a creature who needs order yet yearns for change is the creative contradiction at the heart of the laws which structure his conformity and define his deviancy.

Freda Adler (b. 1934) US writer, educator, and criminologist. *Sisters in Crime* (1975)

3 Order means light and peace, inward liberty and free command over oneself; order is power... Order is man's greatest need, and his true well-being.

Henri-Frédéric Amiel (1821–81) Swiss poet and philosopher. 15 December 1859. *Journal intime* (1883–84)

4 Set thine house in order.

Bible. Isaiah 38:1

5 Order is a lovely thing;
On disarray it lays its wing,
Teaching simplicity to sing.

Anna Hempstead Branch (1875–1937) US poet and social worker. 'The Monk in the Kitchen', *American Poetry 1671–1928* (Conrad Aiken, ed.; 1929)

6 Order is the shape upon which beauty depends.

Pearl S. Buck (1892–1973) US writer. 'The Home-maker', *To My Daughters, With Love* (1967)

7 Good order is the foundation of all good things.

Edmund Burke (1729–97) British philosopher and politician. *Reflections on the Revolution in France* (1790)

8 It is meritorious to insist on forms; religion and all else naturally clothes itself in forms. Everywhere the formed world is the only habitable one.

Thomas Carlyle (1795–1881) British historian and essayist. *On Heroes, Hero-Worship and the Heroic in History* (1841)

9 Large organisation is loose organisation. Nay, it would be almost as true to say that organisation is always disorganisation.

G.K. Chesterton (1874–1936) British novelist, poet, and critic. 'The Bluff of the Big Shops', *Outline of Sanity* (1926)

10 At the point where order and chaos most closely resemble one another, there exists the greatest possibility for broadening the human capacity to adapt to instability and uncertainty.

Daryl R. Conner (b. 1946) US management author. *Leading at the Edge of Chaos* (1998)

11 The desire for order is the only order in the world.

Georges Duhamel (1884–1966) French writer. *The Pasquier Chronicles* (1933)

12 There is a rage to organize which is the sworn enemy of order.

Georges Duhamel (1884–1966) French writer. *Vie des Martyrs* (1917)

13 Exactness and neatness in moderation is a virtue, but carried to extremes narrows the mind.

François de Salignac de la Mothe-Fénelon (1651–1715) French theologian and writer. *Télémaque* (1699)

14 I tell you, sir, the only safeguard of order and discipline in the modern world is a standardized worker with interchangeable parts. That would solve the entire problem of management.

Jean Giraudoux (1882–1944) French diplomat, novelist, and playwright. *The Madwoman of Chaillot* (1945)

15 Everything which is properly *business* we must keep separate from *life*. Business requires earnestness and method; life must have a freer handling.

Johann Wolfgang von Goethe (1749–1832) German poet, playwright, novelist, and scientist. *Elective Affinities* (1809)

16 It is best to do things systematically, since we are only human, and disorder is our worst enemy.

Hesiod (*fl.* 800 BC) Greek poet. *Works and Days* (8th century BC)

17 There is a quality even meaner than outright ugliness or disorder, and this meaner quality is the dishonest mask of pretended order, achieved by ignoring or suppressing the real order that is struggling to exist and to be served.

Jane Jacobs (b. 1916) US urban theorist and social critic. *The Death and Life of Great American Cities* (1961)

18 Order and simplification are the first steps towards the mastery of a subject.

Thomas Mann (1875–1955) German writer. *The Magic Mountain* (1924)

19 Confusion is a word we have invented for an order which is not understood.

Henry Miller (1891–1980) US writer. 'Interlude', *Tropic of Capricorn* (1939)

20 Excess of severity is not the path to order. On the contrary, it is the path to the bomb.

John Morley (1838–1923) British politician and writer. *Recollections* (1917)

21 Order marches with weighty and measured strides; disorder is always in a hurry.

Bonaparte Napoleon I (1769–1821) French emperor. *Maxims* (1804–15)

22 There's a certain amount of disorder that has to be reorganized.

William S. Paley (1901–90) US founder of Columbia Broadcasting Corporation. On his return as CBS chairman after his retirement. *Boston Globe* (1986)

23 Life creates order, but order does not create life.

Antoine de Saint-Exupéry (1900–44) French writer and aviator. *Letter to a Hostage* (1942)

24 Diversity is intimately linked to the possibility of self-organization.

Vandana Shiva (b. 1944) Indian academic. *Globalisation: Gandhi and Swadeshi* (2000)

25 It is not until a creature begins to manage its environment that nature is thrown into disorder.

Clifford Simak (1904–88) US writer. *Shakespeare's Planet* (1976)

26 A place for everything and everything in its place. Order is wealth.

Samuel Smiles (1812–1904) Scottish social reformer and writer. *Thrift* (1875)

27 A. A violent order is disorder; and
B. A great disorder is an order.
These two things are one.

Wallace Stevens (1879–1955) US poet. 'Connoisseur of Chaos', *Notes Toward a Supreme Fiction* (1942)

28 Since we cannot hope for order let us withdraw with style from the chaos.

Tom Stoppard (b. 1937) British playwright and screenwriter. *Lord Malaquist and Mr Moon* (1966)

29 Method is good in all things. Order governs the world. The Devil is the author of confusion.

Jonathan Swift (1667–1745) Irish writer and satirist. 26 October 1710. Letter to Stella. *Journal to Stella* (1766–68)

30 How very much do they err who consider the absence of order and method as implying greater liberty or removing a sense of restraint.

Charlotte Elizabeth Tonna (1790–1846) British writer and educator. *Personal Recollections* (1841), Letter 4

31 As order is heavenly, where quiet is had,
So error is hell, or a mischief as bad.

Thomas Tusser (1524–80) English writer. 'Huswifery Admonitions', *A Hundreth Good Poynts Huswifery* (1561)

32 Have a place for everything and keep the thing somewhere else. This is not advice, it is merely custom.

Mark Twain (1835–1910) US writer. *Notebook* (1935)

33 Order always weighs on the individual. Disorder makes him wish for the police or for death. These are two extreme circumstances in which human nature is not at ease.

Paul Valéry (1871–1945) French poet and essayist. Quoted in *Letters* (Montesquieu; 1926), Preface

34 If disorder is the rule with you, you will be penalized for installing order.

Paul Valéry (1871–1945) French poet and essayist. *Tel Quel* (1941–43)

35 Filing is concerned with the past; anything you actually need to see again has to do with the future.

Katharine Whitehorn (b. 1926) British journalist. *Sunday Best* (1976)

ORGANISATIONS

1 A tiny and closed fraternity of privileged men, elected by no one, and enjoying a monopoly sanctioned and licensed by government.

Spiro Agnew (1918–96) US vice-president. Referring to network news divisions. Television address (13 November 1969)

2 If factories are wanting, let it be remembered that the closet-philosopher is unfortunately too little acquainted with the admirable arrangements of the factory.

Charles Babbage (1792–1871) British mathematician and inventor. *On the Economy of Machinery and Manufacture* (1832)

3 The arrangements which ought to regulate the interior economy of a manufactory are founded on principles of deeper root than may have been supposed.

Charles Babbage (1792–1871) British mathematician and inventor. *On the Economy of Machinery and Manufacture* (1832)

4 Lured by tax concessions and a climate like northern California's, dozens of multinational companies had moved into the business park that now employed over ten thousand people. The senior managements were...a new elite of administrators, énarques and scientific entrepreneurs.

J.G. Ballard (b. 1930) British novelist. Referring to new techno-parks/development zones, such as Sophia-Antipolis, in southern France. *Super-Cannes* (2000), ch. 1

5 Denying the authority of an organization communication is a threat to the interests of all individuals who derive a net advantage from their connection with the organization.

Chester Barnard (1886–1961) US business executive and management theorist. *Organization and Management* (1948)

6 You can build a lasting competitive edge through the excellence of your organisation structure.

Percy Barnevik (b. 1941) Swedish former CEO of ABB. Presentation to World Economic Forum (January 1997)

7 Our task is to create organizations we believe in and to do it as an offering, not a demand.

Peter Block (b. 1935) US writer. *Stewardship* (1993)

8 We are still unbelievably regulated.

Peter Bonfield (b. 1944) British former CEO of British Telecom. *Sunday Times* (July 2000)

9 Some are born great, some achieve greatness, and some hire public relations officers.

Daniel J. Boorstin (b. 1914) US Pulitzer-prize-winning historian. *The Image* (1961)

10 More cohesion is needed rather than hierarchy.

Marvin Bower (1903–2003) US CEO of McKinsey & Company. *Eurobusiness* (February 1995)

11 Network of leaders.

Marvin Bower (1903–2003) US CEO of McKinsey & Company. Referring to the unique structure of McKinsey. *The Will to Manage* (1966)

12 Cultural competence refers to the ability to be able to harness and use culturally diverse myths, symbols, rituals, norms, and ideational symbols creatively to add to an organisation's activities.

Stewart Clegg (b. 1947) Australian writer. 'Business Values and Embryonic Industry: Lessons from Australia', *Whose Business Values? Some Asian and Cross-Cultural Perspectives* (Sally Stewart and Gabriel Donleavy, eds; 1995)

13 For any organization to survive, it must have distinctive competence.

Stewart Clegg (b. 1947) Australian writer. 'Business Values and Embryonic Industry: Lessons from Australia', *Whose Business Values? Some Asian and Cross-Cultural Perspectives* (Sally Stewart and Gabriel Donleavy, eds; 1995)

14 In the knowledge economy, bureaucracy will increasingly be replaced by adhocracy, a holding unit that co-ordinates the work of numerous temporary workers.

Richard Crawford, US investment banker. *In the Era of Human Capital* (1991)

15 The collapsible corporation.

Richard Crawford, US investment banker. *In the Era of Human Capital* (1991)

16 Even the best leaders get submerged and stymied in organisations that are highly centralised and highly consolidated.

Bill Creech (b. 1958) US commanding general of US Air Force Tactical Air Command. Quoted in *A Passion for Excellence* (Tom Peters and Nancy Austin; 1985)

17 Connected individuals and their knowledge, not the corporation, are becoming the key organising unit.

Stan Davis (b. 1939) US business author. *Blur* (co-written with Christopher Meyer; 1998)

18 Instead of vertical integration, we have a kind of virtual integration that is taking hold. It shows up in the efficiency of companies. Our company, for example, has a return on invested capital of roughly 290 per cent which...is significantly above our cost of capital...This says there is a fair bit of competitive power in a model like this.

Michael Dell (b. 1965) US chairman and CEO of Dell Computer Corporation. Speech to the Canadian Club of Toronto, Canada. 'Leadership in the Internet Economy' (7 April 2000)

19 There are a lot of companies around that need to be restructured and split up, that never had a justification for being.

Peter F. Drucker (b. 1909) US management consultant and academic. Interview, *Time* (1990)

20 The chief weakness in business organization is lack of coordination.

Mary Parker Follett (1868–1933) US management thinker and author. Lecture, New York (10 December 1926)

21 If neighborhood organization is one among many methods of getting things, then it is not of great value; if, however, it is going to bring about a different mental life, it will give us an open mind, a flexible mind, a cooperative mind, then it is the greatest movement of our time.

Mary Parker Follett (1868–1933) US management thinker and author. *The New State* (1918)

22 Top executives know that they have to shift to a talent-based, flat structure, but don't know what to do with all the entitled, middle-aged managers they have.

Yasuhiro Fukushima (b. 1948) Japanese business executive. *Wired Asia* (June 2000)

23 In the future the optimal form of industrial organization will be neither small companies nor large ones but network structures that share the advantages of both.

Francis Fukuyama (b. 1952) US economist and writer. *Trust: The Social Virtues and the Creation of Prosperity* (1995)

24 Variety, change, and speed are the determinants in the choice of the new organizational structure.

Jay R. Galbraith (b. 1950) US writer. *Designing Organizations* (1995)

25 Every company has two organizational structures: The formal one is written on the charts; the other is the everyday relationships of the men and women in the organization.

Harold S. Geneen (1910–97) US telecommunications entrepreneur and CEO of ITT. *Managing* (co-written with Alvin Moscow; 1984)

26 You can only stumble if you're moving.

Roberto Goizueta (1931–97) US CEO of Coca-Cola. *Fortune* (May 1995)

27 Highly-adaptive, informal networks move diagonally and eliptically, skipping entire functions to get things done.

Daniel Goleman (b. 1946) US behavioural scientist, journalist, and author. *Emotional Intelligence* (1996)

28 Developing a sound and healthy organisation requires understanding the environment as much as understanding the organisation.

Gary Hamel (b. 1954) US academic, business writer, and consultant. *Competing for the Future* (co-written with C.K. Prahalad; 1994)

29 Neither Stalinist bureaucracy nor Silicon Valley provide an optimal ecosystem.

Gary Hamel (b. 1954) US academic, business writer, and consultant. *Competing for the Future* (co-written with C.K. Prahalad; 1994)

30 It is sobering to reflect on the extent to which the structure of our business has been dictated by the limitations of the file folder.

Michael Hammer (b. 1948) US author and academic. *Re-engineering the Corporation* (co-written with James Champy; 1993)

31 It's a gross distortion of nature to conceive of corporations as if they were Newtonian machines—an error which has brought about bureaucracies, alienating work...it is a complement to human nature to build networks.

Charles M. Hampden-Turner (b. 1934) British economist and management theorist. 'Living in a World of Paradox: from Chaos to Self-Organization in the Knowledge Economy' (February 1998)

32 Organisations have their essential core of jobs and people surrounded by an open and flexible space which they fill with flexible workers and flexible supply contracts.

Charles Handy (b. 1932) British business executive and author. *The Empty Raincoat: Making Sense of the Future* (1994)

33 The shamrock organisation.

Charles Handy (b. 1932) British business executive and author. Referring to a three-part structure of core staff, suppliers, and peripheral staff. *The Future of Work* (1984)

34 In large-scale diversified multi-product companies, it was impractical for sector management to be familiar in depth with each business, each product, each competitor segment, and each unit's implied strategy.

Bruce Henderson (1915–92) US consultant and founder Boston Consulting Group. Quoted in *Competing against Time* (George Stall Jr and Thomas M. Hunt; 1990)

35 There was little real judgement possible at the corporate level.

Bruce Henderson (1915–92) US consultant and founder Boston Consulting Group. Quoted in *Competing against Time* (George Stall Jr and Thomas M. Hunt; 1990)

36 Well-ventilated, well-lighted, and sanitarily kept workrooms, rest-rooms and other creature comforts provided in factories, stores, and office buildings are largely the results of women's presence in industry.

Edith Johnson (1891–1954) US writer and educator. *To Women of the Business World* (1923)

37 Women's presence...has done more, I believe, than labor's strikes and struggles to shorten the working day, and improve the conditions under which work is performed.

Edith Johnson (1891–1954) US writer and educator. *To Women of the Business World* (1923)

38 The whole ecosystem is here so I'm so much closer to the decision makers.

Woon Toon King (b. 1967) Singaporean entrepreneur. Referring to his decision to relocate a high-tech business from Asia to California. *Forbes* (July 2000)

39 History consists of the tracks made by strategy and includes the risks players take, whether they win or lose.

György Konrád (b. 1933) Hungarian writer. *The Melancholy of Rebirth* (1995)

40 Like magnetism, alignment is a force. It coalesces and focuses an organization and moves it forward.

George Labovitz (b. 1940) US writer, consultant, and CEO of Organizational Dynamics, Inc. *The Power of Alignment* (co-written with Victor Rosansky; 1997)

41 The organization exists to restrict and channel the range of individual actions and behaviors into a predictable and knowable routine.

Theodore Levitt (b. 1925) US management theorist, writer, and editor. 'Creativity Is Not Enough', *Harvard Business Review* (1963)

42 Without organizations, there would be chaos and decay.

Theodore Levitt (b. 1925) US management theorist, writer, and editor. 'Creativity Is Not Enough', *Harvard Business Review* (1963)

43 An organisation should be outstanding in its performance if it has competent personnel, if it has leadership which develops highly effective groups and uses the overlapping group form of structure.

Rensis Likert (1903–81) US psychologist. *New Patterns of Management* (1961)

44 Authoritarian organisations tend to develop dependent people and few leaders. Participative organisations tend to develop emotionally and socially mature persons capable of effective interaction, initiative, and leadership.

Rensis Likert (1903–81) US psychologist. *New Patterns of Management* (1961)

45 If there is a single assumption that pervades conventional organizational theory, it is that authority is the central, indispensable means of managerial control.

Douglas McGregor (1906–64) US academic, educator, and management theorist. *The Human Side of Enterprise* (1960)

46 It is no more possible to create an organisation today which will be a full, effective application of this theory than it was to build an atomic power plant in 1945.
Douglas McGregor (1906–64) US academic, educator, and management theorist. *The Human Side of Enterprise* (1960)

47 The introduction of a new grammar, not just new words, is the key to organizational transformation.
Michael D. McMaster (b. 1943) US writer. *The Intelligence Advantage* (1996)

48 The new theory of organization relates to a corporation as though it has characteristics of its own, such as intelligence, ability to learn, and a culture.
Michael D. McMaster (b. 1943) US writer. *The Intelligence Advantage* (1996)

49 Hotels are a wonderful business. They have been around since year zero when Jesus' parents tried to get into a hotel and couldn't.
David Michels (b. 1946) British CEO of Hilton Hotels. *Sunday Times* (September 2000)

50 There have been seven directors or acting directors in six years. That's not an organisation. That's an institutional collapse.
Daniel P. Moynihan (b. 1927) US politician. Referring to the problems of managing the CIA. *Independent on Sunday* (March 1997)

51 Changing the formal organization is sometimes the most effective way to influence the informal operating environment.
David A. Nadler (b. 1948) US author and organisational behaviour specialist. *Competing by Design* (co-written with Michael A. Tushman; 1997)

52 The last remaining source of truly sustainable competitive advantage lies in what we've come to describe as organizational capabilities.
David A. Nadler (b. 1948) US author and organisational behaviour specialist. *Competing by Design* (co-written with Michael A. Tushman; 1997)

53 Small companies right down to the individual can beat big bureaucratic companies ten times out of ten.
John Naisbitt (b. ?1929) US business executive and author. *Megatrends* (1982)

54 The pyramid inside companies is being flattened by IT.
Masahiro Noilia (b. 1939) Japanese business executive. *Wired Asia* (June 2000)

55 It would give us flexibility because it is very unusual to find a company with one asset on its balance sheet that is worth £12 billion.
Phil Nolan (b. 1953) British CEO of Eircom. Referring to gas pipelines. *Sunday Times* (September 2000)

56 In Japan, organizations and people in the organization are synonymous.

Kenichi Ohmae (b. 1943) Japanese management consultant and theorist. 'The Myth and Reality of the Japanese Corporation', *Chief Executive* (Summer 1981)

57 Nobody knows how Honda is organized, except that it uses lots of project teams and is quite flexible.
Kenichi Ohmae (b. 1943) Japanese management consultant and theorist. 'The Myth and Reality of the Japanese Corporation', *Chief Executive* (Summer 1981)

58 The full organization—the proposal boxes, quality circles and the like—looks organized and entrepreneurial as opposed to mechanical and bureaucratic.
Kenichi Ohmae (b. 1943) Japanese management consultant and theorist. 'The Myth and Reality of the Japanese Corporation', *Chief Executive* (Summer 1981)

59 I realised that talent would get me as far as middle management, but beyond that point it would become a matter of politics and currying favour with bosses.
Masahiro Origuchi (b. 1962) Japanese business executive. *Wired Asia* (June 2000)

60 The professional service firm—with its obsession on clients and projects—must be the new organizational model.
Tom Peters (b. 1942) US management consultant and author. 'Work Matters!' movement manifesto, *www.tompeters.com* (September 1999)

61 Women are becoming enormously successful... They're running their businesses on what we call a familial model, a family, instead of a hierarchical top-down military model. They work with, not over or for.
Faith Popcorn (b. 1947) US trend expert and founder of BrainReserve. Interview, *phenomeNEWS* (1999)

62 The newest technologies (flexible manufacturing, faster computers, and better telecommunications) have reduced the optimum size of any business.
Michael Porter (b. 1947) US strategist. *The Economist* (January 1990)

63 In our complex industrial society, no business enterprise can succeed without sharing the burdens of the problems of other enterprises
Ayn Rand (1905–82) US writer. *Atlas Shrugged* (1957), pt 1, ch. 3

64 The core corporation is...increasingly a façade, behind which teems an array of decentralised groups and subgroups continuously contracting with similarly diffuse working units all over the world.
Robert Reich (b. 1946) US economist and politician. *The Work of Nations* (1991)

65 Disconnected organizations spawn workaholism, a grim breed of estranged loners, running out the clock and avoiding one another.
Harvey Robbins, US writer on business psychology. *TransCompetition* (co-written with Michael Finley; 1998)

66 It's like breaking up a family row as an outsider.

Gerry Robinson (b. 1948) Irish chairman of Granada
Television and of the Arts Council of England. Referring to
committee disputes. *Management Today* (April 1999)

67 The working of great institutions is mainly the
result of a vast mass of routine, petty malice,
self interest, carelessness, and sheer mistake.
Only a residual fraction is thought.
George Santayana (1863–1952) US philosopher, novelist,
and poet. *The Crime of Galileo* (1958)

68 I believe that crisis really tends to help
develop the character of an organization.
John Sculley (b. 1939) US partner of Sculley Brothers, former
president of Pepsi, and CEO of Apple Computers. Quoted in
Fortune (1998)

69 Large, centralized organizations foster
alienation like stagnant ponds breed algae.
Ricardo Semler (b. 1959) Brazilian business executive and
president of Semco. *Maverick!* (1993)

70 We talk about organisations in terms not
unlike those used by an Ubongi medicine man
to discuss diseases.
Herbert A. Simon (1916–2001) US political scientist and
economist. *Administrative Behavior* (1947)

71 Bringing the two together is like having a
brake and an accelerator in the car. You can't
have one without the other.
Reuben Singh (b. 1977) British entrepreneur and author.
Referring to a scheme to introduce entrepreneurs to the
traditional management structure of established companies.
Management Today (September 1999)

72 Decentralisation or not, an industrial
corporation is not the mildest form of
organisation...I never minimised the
administrative power of the chief executive.
Alfred P. Sloan (1875–1966) US president of General Motors.
My Years with General Motors (1964)

73 Everything possible starts in the organization
from the bottom.
Alfred P. Sloan (1875–1966) US president of General Motors.
'The Most Important Things I Learned About Management',
System (August 1924)

74 Whatever the country, whatever the culture,
whatever the time, when you become a big
enough organization, you start to collapse and
slow down.
Masayoshi Son (b. 1943) Taiwanese CEO of Softbank
Corporation. Quoted in *Giant Killers* (Geoffrey James;
1996)

75 Corporate America is so hierarchical.
Martha Stewart (b. 1942) US chairperson of Martha Stewart
Living Omnimedia. 'The 50 Most Powerful Women in
American Business', *Fortune* (Patricia Sellers and
Cora Daniels; October 1999)

76 In the past the man was first. In the future the
system will be first.
F.W. Taylor (1856–1915) US engineer and author. *The
Principles of Scientific Management* (1911)

77 It can take just as much effort to run a small
company as a much larger one.
Barbara Thomas (b. 1947) US banker. *Management Today*
(October 1999)

78 The new system takes us a giant step beyond
mass production towards increasing
customization, beyond mass marketing and
distribution towards niches and
micromarketing.
Alvin Toffler (b. 1928) US social commentator. *Powershift*
(1990)

79 The new systems will challenge all the old
executive turfs, the hierarchies, the sexual role
divisions, the departmental barriers of the
past.
Alvin Toffler (b. 1928) US social commentator. *The Third
Wave* (1980)

80 If you have to have a policy manual, publish
the Ten Commandments.
Robert Townsend (b. 1920) US business executive and
author. *Up the Organization* (1970)

81 Fairly short shelf life of chief executives in
plcs.
Tony Trahar (b. 1950) South African CEO of Anglo American.
Sunday Times (May 2000)

82 Developing a sound and healthy organisation
requires understanding the environment as
much as understanding the organisation.
Kees van der Heijden, Dutch writer and consultant.
Scenarios (1996)

83 We're controlled by ideas and norms that have
outlived their usefulness, that are only ghosts
but have as much influence on our behavior as
if they were alive.
Robert H. Waterman Jr (b. 1936) US consultant and author.
Adhocracy (1993)

84 The basic philosophy of an organization has
far more to do with its achievements than do
technological or economic resources,
organizational structure, innovation and
timing.
Thomas J. Watson Jr (1914–93) US CEO of IBM. *A Business
and Its Beliefs* (1963)

85 For a large organisation to be effective, it must
be simple.
Jack Welch (b. 1935) US former chairman and CEO of
General Electric. Quoted in *In Search of European
Excellence* (Robert Heller; 1997)

86 The things we fear most in organizations—
fluctuations, disturbances, imbalances—need
not be signs of impending disorder that will
destroy us. Instead, fluctuations are the
primary source of creativity.
Meg Wheatley (b. 1941) US academic, management
theorist, and president of the Berkana Institute. *Leadership
and the New Science* (1992)

87 It's a hostile world out there, and
organizations, or we who create them, survive
only because we build crafty and smart—
smart enough to defend ourselves from the
natural forces of destruction.
Meg Wheatley (b. 1941) US academic, management
theorist, and president of the Berkana Institute. *Leadership
and the New Science Revised* (1999)

88 The Organization Man.
William Whyte (1914–2000) US author. Book title. *The Organization Man* (1956)

89 The trouble with organizing a thing is that pretty soon folks get to paying more attention to the organization than to what they're organized for.
Laura Ingalls Wilder (1867–1957) US novelist. *Little Town on the Prairie* (1941)

90 We are all caught up in a great economic system which is heartless. The modern corporation is not engaged in business as an individual. When we deal with it we deal with an...immaterial piece of society.
Woodrow Wilson (1856–1924) US president. *The New Freedom* (1913)

91 In organizations where people trust and believe in each other, they don't get into regulating and coercing behaviors. They don't need a policy for every mistake...people in these trusting environments respond with enormous commitment and creativity.
Walter Wriston (b. 1919) US banker. 'Don't Get Out of the Way!', *www.mgeneral.com* (1997)

ORIGINALITY

1 The true is inimitable, the false untransformable.
Robert Bresson (1907–99) French film director. '1950–58: The Real', *Notes on the Cinematographer* (1975)

2 The ideas I stand for are not mine. I borrowed them from Socrates. I swiped them from Chesterfield. I stole them from Jesus. And I put them in a book. If you don't like their rules, whose would you use?
Dale Carnegie (1888–1955) US consultant and author. Referring to his book, *How to Win Friends and Influence People* (1936). *Newsweek* (1955)

3 Keep on the lookout for novel ideas that others have used successfully. Your idea has to be original only in its adaption to the problem you're working on.
Thomas Edison (1847–1931) US inventor. Quoted in *A Kick in the Seat of the Pants* (Roger von Oech; 1986)

4 Anyone who attempts anything original in the world must expect a bit of ridicule.
Alberto Juantorena (b. 1950) Cuban athlete and businessman. Quoted in *Quick Frozen Foods* (March 1960)

5 Original thought is like original sin: both happened before you were born to people you could not have possibly met.
Fran Lebowitz (b. 1950) US writer and columnist. *Social Studies* (1981)

6 New opinions are always suspected, and usually opposed, without any other reason but because they are not already common.
John Locke (1632–1704) English philosopher and political thinker. *Essay Concerning Human Understanding* (1690), Dedicatory epistle

PEOPLE AND RELATIONSHIPS

1 Nobody knew why he wanted to go to the expense of a telephone. You could hear his voice from the ferry building to Twin Peaks.
Anonymous. Said by a colleague, referring to Amadeo Peter Giannini, US founder of the Bank of America. 'The Story of an Unusual Career', *Forbes* (November 1923)

2 If Thomas Edison had gone to business school, we would all be reading by larger candles.
Anonymous. Quoted in *What They Don't Teach You at Harvard Business School* (Mark H. McCormack; 1984)

3 Propose to an Englishman any principle, or any instrument, however admirable, and you will observe that the whole effort of the English mind is directed to find a difficulty, a defect, or an impossibility in it.
Charles Babbage (1792–1871) British mathematician and inventor. Referring to the British inability to support inventors. Quoted in *The Code Book* (Simon Singh; 1999)

4 We have got to take the gloves off and have a bare-knuckle fight on some of the things we have to do, because we have to have an effective and prosperous industry.
Terence Norman Beckett (b. 1923) British business executive. Said as director-general of the CBI (Confederation of British Industry). Speech, CBI Conference (1981)

5 When people are in unfamiliar environments and when they behave in unpredictable ways, they are likely to lose control.
Rabi S. Bhagat (b. 1950) Indian business author. 'Cross-cultural Training in Organisational Contexts', *Handbook of Intercultural Training* (co-edited with Dan Landis, co-written with Kristin O. Prien; 1996)

6 Everyone has peak performance potential. You just need to know where they are coming from and meet them there.
Kenneth Blanchard (b. 1939) US management theorist and author. *Leadership and the One Minute Manager* (2000)

7 Everyone is a potential winner. Some people are disguised as losers, don't let their appearances fool you.
Kenneth Blanchard (b. 1939) US management theorist and author. *The One Minute Manager* (1993)

8 The best minute I spend is the one I invest in people.
Kenneth Blanchard (b. 1939) US management theorist and author. *The One Minute Manager* (1993)

9 Develop the business around the people; build it, don't buy it; and, then, be the best.
Richard Branson (b. 1950) British entrepreneur, business executive, and founder of the Virgin Group. Speech to the Institute of Directors, London. 'Growing Bigger While Still Staying Small' (May 1993)

10 Distinguish between the person and the behavior or performance.
Stephen Covey (b. 1932) US writer and psychologist. *Thirty Methods of Influence* (1991)

11 Involve people in meaningful projects.
Stephen Covey (b. 1932) US writer and psychologist. *Thirty Methods of Influence* (1991)

12 Years ago I recognized my kinship with all living things, and I made up my mind that I was not one bit better than the meanest on the earth. I said then and I say now, that while there is a lower class, I am in it.

Eugene V. Debs (1855–1926) US politician and trade union leader. Statement to the Court after being convicted for violating the Sedition Act, Cleveland, Ohio (18 September 1918)

13 Edison didn't invent the light bulb...Edison invented the electric industry.

Peter F. Drucker (b. 1909) US management consultant and academic. Interview, *Hot Wired* (August 1996)

14 There is no more inflammatory issue than large-scale immigration, especially from countries of different cultures and religions.

Peter F. Drucker (b. 1909) US management consultant and academic. *Management Challenges for the 21st Century* (1999)

15 It is given to few persons to transform a people in a generation. Yet this was done by the late Madam C. J. Walker.

W.E.B. Du Bois (1868–1963) US historian and politician. 1919. Quoted in *Madam C. J. Walker* (M.C. Brown; 1996)

16 People are now becoming the most expensive optional component of the production process and technology is becoming the cheapest.

Michael Dunkerley, British author. *The Jobless Economy* (1996)

17 The genius of any slave system is found in the dynamics which isolate slaves from each other, obscure the reality of a common condition, and make united rebellion against the oppressor inconceivable.

Andrea Dworkin (b. 1946) US feminist writer. *Our Blood* (1976)

18 No organizational action has more power for motivating employee behavior change than feedback from credible work associates.

Mark R. Edwards (b. 1949) US writer. *360 Degree Feedback* (co-written with Ann J. Ewen; 1996)

19 A woman may see things that somebody who's just crunching numbers may not. It's almost as if women have a more general, macro view.

Grace Fey, US vice-president and director of Frontier Capital Management. Quoted in *Women of the Street* (Sue Herera; 1997)

20 A normalizing society is the historical outcome of a technology of power centred on life.

Michel Foucault (1926–84) French philosopher. *The History of Sexuality* (1976)

21 The glad hand is alright in sunshine, but it's the helping hand on a dark day that folks remember to the end of time.

Amadeo Giannini (1870–1949) US banker and founder of Bank of America. 'The Citizen' (October 1926)

22 Just look at him. He runs his company with five people in an office the size of a closet.

Katharine Graham (1917–2001) US newspaper publisher and owner of *Washington Post*. Referring to Warren Buffett. *US News & World Report* (1986)

23 I want to make people feel intensively alive. I'd rather have them against me than indifferent.

Martha Graham (1894–1991) US dancer and choreographer. Interview (1960)

24 Bill Gates follows somebody's tail lights for a while then zooms past. Soon there will be no tail lights left.

Andrew S. Grove (b. 1936) US entrepreneur, author, and chairman of Intel Corporation. *BusinessWeek* (June 1994)

25 Most individuals, by the time they reach maturity, have built up an array of concepts which they use to interpret the data they observe.

Charles Handy (b. 1932) British business executive and author. *Understanding Organisations* (1993)

26 We are self-activating organisms, and can, to some degree, control our own destiny and our own responses to pressures...we can select our goals and choose the paths toward them.

Charles Handy (b. 1932) British business executive and author. *Understanding Organisations* (1993)

27 Every falling-away from species virtue, every crime against one's own nature, every evil act, every one without exception records itself in our unconscious, and makes us despise ourselves.

Abraham Maslow (1908–70) US behavioural psychologist. *Toward a Psychology of Being* (1968)

28 Ordinary people may not understand the meaning of democracy but they've a passionate regard for fair play.

Robert Maxwell (1923–91) British publisher, business executive, and politician. Quoted in *Maxwell* (Joe Haines; 1988)

29 We don't have the slightest idea of what people are going to buy.

Rupert Murdoch (b. 1931) US CEO of News Corporation. *BusinessWeek* (March 1994)

30 You're useless in business with just an academic background. You're also useless if you spend too much time in the military.

Ken Olsen (b. 1926) US computer designer and founder of Digital Equipment Corporation. Quoted in *In the Company of Giants* (Rama dev Jager; 1997)

31 Resentment or grudges do no harm to the person against whom you hold these feelings but every day and every night of your life, they are eating at you.

Norman Vincent Peale (1898–1993) US religious leader. *Positive Thinking Every Day* (1995)

32 The excellent companies treat the rank and file as the root source of quality and productivity gain.

Tom Peters (b. 1942) US management consultant and author. *In Search of Excellence: Lessons from America's Best-Run Companies* (co-written with Robert H. Waterman Jr; 1988)

33 Successful organizations understand the importance of implementation, not just

strategy, and, moreover, recognize the crucial role of their people in this process.
Jeffrey Pfeffer (b. 1946) US writer. *The Human Equation* (1998)

34 The essence of high performance work arrangements is reliance on all organizational members for their ideas, intelligence, and commitment to making the organization successful.
Jeffrey Pfeffer (b. 1946) US writer. *The Human Equation* (1998)

35 Human capital grows two ways: When the organization uses more of what people know and when more people know more stuff that is useful to the organization.
Thomas A. Stewart (b. 1948) US journalist and author. 'Brain Power: Who Owns It...How They Profit from It', *Fortune* (1997)

36 I was adopted myself. I know the importance of what family means. There are so many kids out there in foster care who don't have a permanent home. You lose your childhood so fast. You realize how important it is to have that home.
Dave Thomas (1932–2002) US founder of Wendy's. 'Dave Thomas' Beef: 'Nobody Thinks about It'', *BusinessWeek* (2000)

37 By a career-resilient workforce, we mean a group of employees who not only are dedicated to the idea of continuous learning but also stand ready to reinvent themselves to keep pace with change.
Robert H. Waterman Jr (b. 1936) US consultant and author. 'Toward a Career-Resilient Workforce', *Harvard Business Review* (co-written with J.H. Waterman and B.A. Collard; 1994)

38 The point of work-out is to give people better jobs. When people see that their ideas count, their dignity is raised. Instead of feeling numb, like robots, they feel important.
Jack Welch (b. 1935) US former chairman and CEO of General Electric. 'Jack Welch's Lessons for Success', *Fortune* (Noel Tichy and Stratford Sherman; 1993)

39 We cannot hide behind our boundaries, or hold onto the belief that we can survive alone.
Meg Wheatley (b. 1941) US academic, management theorist, and president of the Berkana Institute. *Leadership and the New Science Revised* (1999)

PERFECTION

1 The perfection preached in the Gospels never yet built an empire. Every man of action has a strong dose of egotism, pride, hardness, and cunning
Charles De Gaulle (1890–1970) French general and president. Quoted in *New York Times Magazine* (12 May 1968)

2 Perfect numbers, like perfect people, are very rare.
René Descartes (1596–1650) French philosopher and mathemetician. Quoted in *Mathematical Circles Squared* (H. Eves; 1972)

3 The delusion that you're perfect—or that if you just do the right thing, things will always work out OK—makes you resistant to change and fearful of failure...you'd rather not discover that you're imperfect, that maybe what you were doing was wrong. The more people can go through those discoveries the better.
Esther Dyson (b. 1951) US knowledge entrepreneur and government adviser. Interview, *Reason Magazine* (November 1996)

4 Perfection can be a fetish.
Bernard Leach (1887–1979) British potter. *The Potter's Challenge* (1976)

5 Perfection of planned layout is achieved only by institutions on the point of collapse.
C. Northcote Parkinson (1909–93) British political scientist and author. *Parkinson's Law: The Pursuit of Progress* (1958)

6 The indefatigable pursuit of an unattainable perfection...is what alone gives a meaning to our life on this unavailing star.
Logan Pearsall Smith (1865–1946) British essayist and critic. 'Art and Letters', *Afterthoughts* (1931)

7 An environment which calls for perfection is not likely to be easy. But aiming for it is always good for progress.
Thomas J. Watson Jr (1914–93) US CEO of IBM. *A Business and Its Beliefs* (1963)

PERSISTENCE

1 I just love it when people say I can't do something.
David Andrews (b. 1935) Irish politician. Quoted in *CNN: The Inside Story* (Hank Whittemore; 1990)

2 You can eat an elephant one bit at a time.
Mary Kay Ash (1915–2001) US entrepreneur, business executive, and founder of Mary Kay Cosmetics. *Mary Kay* (1981)

3 What's the difference between a guy in the bighouse and the average guy you pass on the street? The guy in the bighouse is a Loser who tried.
Charles Bukowski (1920–94) US poet, novelist, and essayist. *Notes of a Dirty Old Man* (1969)

4 We must just KBO.
Winston Churchill (1874–1965) British prime minister. 1941. KBO stands for 'Keep Buggering On'. Quoted in *Finest Hour* (Martin Gilbert; 1983)

5 Nothing in the world can take the place of persistence. Talent will not; nothing is more common than unsuccessful men of talent. Genius will not; unrewarded genius is almost a proverb. Education will not; the world is full of educated derelicts. Persistence and determination are omnipotent.
Calvin Coolidge (1872–1933) US president. Quoted at his memorial service (1933). Attrib.

6 One never notices what has been done; one can only see what remains to be done.
Marie Curie (1867–1934) French physicist. Letter to her brother (18 March 1894)

7 The secret of success is constancy to purpose.
Benjamin Disraeli (1804–81) British prime minister and novelist. Speech (24 June 1872)

8 Go the extra mile.
Napoleon Hill (1883–1970) US motivational author. *Think and Grow Rich* (1937)

9 Great works are performed not by strength but by perseverance.
Samuel Johnson (1709–84) British poet, lexicographer, essayist, and critic. *Rasselas, Prince of Abyssinia* (1759)

10 A terrace nine storeys high
Rises from a handful of earth;
A journey of a thousand miles
Starts from beneath one's feet.
Laozi (?570–?490 BC) Chinese philosopher, reputed founder of Daoism. *Daode Jing*, LXIV

11 Irresolute men are sometimes very persistent in their undertakings, because if they give up their designs they would have to make a second resolution.
Giacomo Leopardi (1798–1837) Italian poet and scholar. 'Sayings of Filippo Ottonieri', *Essays, Dialogues, and Thoughts* (1827)

12 What I want people to know, as they look at this building and its treasures, is that they are the creations...of hard, plodding work within the reach of all those who wish to make the necessary sacrifice.
Lord Leverhulme (1851–1925) British entrepreneur, philanthropist, and co-founder of Unilever. On the official opening of the art gallery at Port Sunlight. Speech, Port Sunlight, near Liverpool, England (1922)

13 Defeat doesn't finish a man—quit does. A man is not finished when he's defeated. He's finished when he quits.
Richard Milhous Nixon (1913–94) US president. July 1969. Quoted in *Before the Fall* (William Safire; 1975), pt 3, ch. 4

14 There are no secrets to success: don't waste time looking for them. Success is the result of perfection, hard work, learning from failure, loyalty to those for whom you work, and persistence.
Colin Powell (b. 1937) US military leader and politician. *Colin Powell* (1989)

15 There is nothing which persevering effort and unceasing and diligent care cannot overcome.
Seneca (?4 BC–AD 65) Roman politician, philosopher, and writer. 'Epistle 50', *De Lucilium* (AD 64), sect. 6

16 'Tis known by the name of perseverance in a good cause,—and of obstinacy in a bad one.
Laurence Sterne (1713–68) British novelist and humorist. *The Life and Opinions of Tristram Shandy, Gentleman* (1759–67), bk 1, ch. 17

17 It's dogged as does it. It ain't thinking about it.
Anthony Trollope (1815–82) British novelist. *The Last Chronicle of Barset* (1867), vol. 1, ch. 61

18 We're gonna stay on until the end of the world. And when that day comes we'll cover it, play 'Nearer My God to Thee' and sign off.
Ted Turner (b. 1938) US founder of Turner Broadcasting Systems. Referring to his ambitions for the then fledgling Cable News Network. Quoted in *The Corporate Warriors* (Douglas K. Ramsey; 1988)

19 Remember, a person who wins success may have been counted out many times before. He wins because he refuses to give up.
Kemmons Wilson (1913–2003) US entrepreneur, founder and chairman of Holiday Inn. Speech, Hillsdale College, Hillsdale, Michigan (September 1996)

PERSONAL GROWTH

1 There's nothing methodises a man but business.
Fanny Burney (1752–1840) British writer. *Cecilia* (1782), vol. 3

2 Every day, in every way, I am getting better and better.
Émile Coué (1857–1926) French psychotherapist. Formula inscribed in his sanatorium. His prescription was one of autosuggestion. Attrib.

3 The return from your work must be the satisfaction which that work brings you and the world's need of that work. With this, life is heaven, or as near heaven as you can get. Without this, with work which you despise, which bores you, and which the world does not need this life is hell.
W.E.B. Du Bois (1868–1963) US historian and politician. Said on his 90th birthday. 'To His Newborn Great-Grandson' (1958)

4 Business pressures are good for the soul: when it has unburdened itself of them, it plays all the more fully and enjoys life.
Johann Wolfgang von Goethe (1749–1832) German poet, playwright, novelist, and scientist. Attrib.

5 Nothing seems to support the habits that promote personal growth more than continuous, humanistic goals.
Bob Guccione (b. 1930) US magazine publisher. *Leading Change* (1996)

6 The mind is enlarged and elevated by mere purposes, though they end as they begin by airy contemplation.
Samuel Johnson (1709–84) British poet, lexicographer, essayist, and critic. Letter to Hester Thrale (29 November 1783)

7 Freedom is a more complex and delicate thing than force. It is not as simple to live under as force is.
Thomas Mann (1875–1955) German writer. Attrib.

8 You don't learn to hold your own by standing on guard, but by attacking, and getting well hammered yourself.
George Bernard Shaw (1856–1950) Irish writer and critic. *Getting Married* (1908)

PLANNING

1 If you are planning for one year, plant rice. If you are planning for ten years plant trees. If you are planning for 100 years plant people.
Anonymous. Indian proverb.

2 Which of you, intending to build a tower, sitteth not down first, and counteth the cost?
Bible. Luke 14:28

3 The success of a project will depend critically upon the effort, care, and skill you apply in its initial planning.
Gerald M. Blair (b. 1959) US writer. *Planning a Project* (2000)

4 Central planning didn't work for Stalin or Mao, and it won't work for an entrepreneur either.
Michael Bloomberg (b. 1942) US entrepreneur, business executive, and Mayor of New York. *Bloomberg on Bloomberg* (co-written with Matthew Winkler; 1997)

5 Managers who extensively plan the future get the timing wrong.
Shona L. Brown (b. 1966) Canadian writer. *Competing on the Edge* (co-written with Kathleen M. Eisenhardt; 1998)

6 Preparation is everything. Noah did not start building the ark when it was raining.
Warren Buffett (b. 1930) US entrepreneur and financier. Attrib.

7 You can never plan the future by the past.
Edmund Burke (1729–97) British philosopher and politician. Letter to a member of the National Assembly (1791)

8 There was no business plan, no model. It was just guts.
Peter Chernin (b. 1953) US chief operating officer of News Corporation, chairman and CEO of the Fox Group. Referring to the planning style of News Corporation. *Forbes* (June 1998)

9 To be practical, any plan must take account of the enemy's power to frustrate it.
Karl von Clausewitz (1780–1831) Prussian general and military strategist. *On War* (1831)

10 Basing our happiness on our ability to control everything is futile.
Stephen Covey (b. 1932) US writer and psychologist. *First Things First: To Live, To Love, To Learn, To Leave a Legacy* (1994)

11 In preparing for battle I have always found that plans are useless, but planning is indispensible.
Dwight David Eisenhower (1890–1969) US general and president. Quoted in 'Krushchev', *Six Crises* (Richard Nixon; 1962)

12 Hindsight is good, foresight is better; but second sight is best of all.
Evan Esar (1899–1995) US humorist. Attrib.

13 You need to plan the way a fire department plans: it cannot anticipate where the next fire will be, so it has to shape an energetic and efficient team that is capable of responding to the unanticipated as well as to any ordinary event.

Andrew S. Grove (b. 1936) US entrepreneur, author, and chairman of Intel Corporation. *Only the Paranoid Survive: How to Exploit the Crisis Points That Challenge Every Company and Career* (1996), Preface

14 Although strategic planning is billed as a way of becoming more future oriented, most managers...will admit that their strategic plans reveal more about today's problems than tomorrow's opportunities.
Gary Hamel (b. 1954) US academic, business writer, and consultant. 'Strategic Intent', *Harvard Business Review* (co-written with C.K. Prahalad; May–June 1989)

15 An Act of God was defined as something which no reasonable man could have expected.
A.P. Herbert (1890–1971) British writer and politician. *Uncommon Law* (1935)

16 Incomes policy alone as a way to ablate inflation caused by excessive money supply is like trying to stop water coming out of a leaky hose without turning off the tap.
Keith Joseph (1918–94) British politician. Speech, Preston, England (5 September 1974)

17 I never had a business plan—though I did have the background in makeup artistry—and I simply started finding the labs, developing formulas, putting together a color palette and designing packaging.
Jeanine Lobell (b. 1964) US entrepreneur, founder and CEO of Stila cosmetics. 'Jeanine Lobell, A Fresh Face', *www.womenswire.com* (Evelyn Sheinkopf; 2000)

18 Today, if someone showed me a five-year plan, I'd toss out the pages detailing Years Three, Four, and Five as pure fantasy...Anyone who thinks he or she can evaluate business conditions five years from now, flunks.
Mark McCormack (1930–2003) US entrepreneur, founder and CEO of the International Management Group. *Staying Street Smart in the Internet Age: What Hasn't Changed about the Way We Do Business* (2000), Introduction

19 When we are planning for posterity, we ought to remember that virtue is not heredity.
Thomas Paine (1737–1809) British politician, philosopher, and writer. *Common Sense* (1776)

20 The beginning is the most important part of any work.
Plato (?428–?347 BC) Greek philosopher. *The Republic* (?370 BC), bk 2, sect. 377

21 Planning is as natural to the process of success as its absence is to the process of failure.
Robin Sieger, British business executive and author. *Natural Born Winners* (1999)

22 Planning ahead is a matter of class. The rich and even the middle class plan for future generations, but the poor can plan ahead only a few weeks or days.
Gloria Steinem (b. 1934) US entrepreneur, editor, and writer. 'The Time Factor', *Ms.* (March 1980)

23 The general who wins a battle makes many calculations...here the battle is fought. The general who loses a battle makes but few calculations beforehand. Thus do many calculations lead to victory, and few to defeat.

Sun Tzu (*fl.* 500 BC) Chinese military theorist. 500 BC. *The Art Of War* (Lionel Giles, tr.; 1910)

24 Whoever is first in the field and awaits the coming of the enemy, will be fresh for the fight; whoever is second in the field and has to hasten to battle will arrive exhausted.

Sun Tzu (*fl.* 500 BC) Chinese military theorist. 500 BC. *The Art Of War* (Lionel Giles, tr.; 1910)

25 Even the seemingly 'hardest' models and data are frequently based on 'soft' assumptions, especially when these concern human affairs.

Alvin Toffler (b. 1928) US social commentator. *Powershift* (1990)

26 If we had had more time for discussion we should probably have made a great many more mistakes.

Leon Trotsky (1879–1940) Russian revolutionary leader and Marxist theorist. Referring to discussions of the Soviet Communist Party's Central Committee about the Red Army. *My Diary* (1930), ch. 36

27 Scenario planning distinguishes itself from other more traditional approaches to strategic planning through its explicit approach towards ambiguity and uncertainty in the strategic question.

Kees van der Heijden, Dutch writer and consultant. *Scenarios* (1996)

28 The wisest prophets make sure of the event first.

Horace Walpole (1717–97) British writer. Letter to Thomas Walpole (19 February 1785)

29 I can read a lot of plans in 45 minutes. It gets my adrenaline rising. And it helps prepare me for spotting good investment areas.

Ann Winblad (b. 1953) US venture capitalist. *Wall Street Journal* (1999)

30 A lot of companies...find planning more interesting than getting out a salable product.

Ed Wrapp, US academic. *Dunn's Review* (September 1980)

31 Planning is good, but not if it excludes the opportunity to be able to take chances when they come up.

Chris Wright (b. 1944) British entrepreneur and music promoter. Quoted in *The Adventure Capitalists* (Jeff Grout and Lynne Curry; 1998)

POWER

1 Power tends to corrupt and absolute power corrupts absolutely.

Lord Acton (1834–1902) British historian. Letter to Bishop Mandell Creighton (5 April 1887)

2 A friend in power is a friend lost.

Henry Brooks Adams (1838–1918) US historian. *Education of Henry Adams* (1907)

3 Power always thinks it has a great soul and vast views beyond the comprehension of the weak, and that it is doing God's service, when it is violating His laws.

John Adams (1735–1826) US president. Letter to Thomas Jefferson (2 February 1814)

4 Power is not only what you have but what the enemy thinks you have.

Saul Alinsky (1909–72) US activist. 'Tactics', *Rules for Radicals* (1971)

5 Power tires only those who do not have it.

Giulio Andreotti (b. 1919) Italian prime minister of Italy. Reply to question about how he remained in power so long. Quoted in *Independent on Sunday* (5 April 1992)

6 Whosoever owns the river bank owns the fish.

Anonymous. Russian proverb.

7 I was allowed to ring the bell for five minutes until everyone was in assembly. It was the beginning of power.

Jeffrey Archer (b. 1940) British novelist and politician. Referring to his experience at school. Quoted in *Daily Telegraph* (16 March 1988)

8 It is a strange desire to seek power, and to love liberty or to seek power over others, and to lose power over one's self.

Francis Bacon (1561–1626) English philosopher and statesman. 'Of Great Place', *Essays* (1597–1625)

9 Men in great place are thrice servants: servants of the sovereign or state; servants of fame; and servants of business.

Francis Bacon (1561–1626) English philosopher and statesman. 'Of Great Place', *Essays* (1597–1625)

10 But the relationship of morality and power is a very subtle one. Because ultimately power without morality is no longer power.

James Baldwin (1924–87) US writer. 4 November 1971. *A Dialogue* (1973)

11 Where the people possess no authority, their rights obtain no respect.

George Bancroft (1800–91) US statesman and historian. 'To the Workingmen of Northampton', *Boston Courier* (22 October 1834)

12 You carry forever the fingerprint that comes from being under someone's thumb.

Nancy Banks-Smith (b. 1929) British journalist. *Guardian* (30 January 1991)

13 He did not care in which direction the car was travelling, so long as he remained in the driver's seat.

Max Beaverbrook (1879–1964) British newspaper owner and politician. Referring to Lloyd George. *New Statesman* (14 June 1963)

14 The purpose of getting power is to be able to give it away.

Aneurin Bevan (1897–1960) British politician. Quoted in *Aneurin Bevan* (Michael Foot; 1962), vol. 1, ch. 1

15 The strongest poison ever known
Came from Caesar's laurel crown.

William Blake (1757–1827) British poet, painter, engineer, and artist. 'Auguries of Innocence' (1803?)

16 Those who have been once intoxicated with power and have derived any kind of emolument from it, even though but for one year, never can willingly abandon it. They may be distressed in the midst of all their power; but they will never look to anything but power for their relief.
Edmund Burke (1729–97) British philosopher and politician. Letter to a member of the National Assembly (19 January 1791)

17 The greater the power, the more dangerous the abuse.
Edmund Burke (1729–97) British philosopher and politician. Speech on the Middlesex election (1771)

18 Power intoxicates men. It is never voluntarily surrendered. It must be taken from them.
James F. Byrnes (1879–1972) US politician. Quoted in *New York Times* (15 May 1956)

19 The less people know about what is really going on, the easier it is to wield power and authority.
Prince Charles (b. 1948) British prince. Quoted in 'Sayings of the Week', *Observer* (2 March 1975)

20 In order to be influential a man must be by nature straightforward and a lover of right.
Confucius (551–479 BC) Chinese philosopher, administrator, and writer. *Analects* (?500 BC)

21 You have more control and less ambiguity today than you are likely to have for the rest of your life.
Daryl R. Conner (b. 1946) US management author. *Managing at the Speed of Change* (1993)

22 The need to exert power, when thwarted in the open fields of life, is the more likely to assert itself in trifles.
Charles Horton Cooley (1864–1929) US sociologist. *Human Nature and the Social Order* (1902), ch. 5

23 Why should I run for Mayor when I'm already King?
Walt Disney (1901–66) US entertainment entrepreneur and founder of the Walt Disney Company. Responding to Ray Bradbury's suggestion that he run for Mayor of Los Angeles. Quoted in *Listener* (7 October 1982)

24 Power has only one duty—to secure the social welfare of the People.
Benjamin Disraeli (1804–81) British prime minister and novelist. *Sybil* (1845), bk 4, ch. 4

25 I repeat...that all power is a trust—that we are accountable for its exercise—that, from the people, and for the people, all springs, and all must exist.
Benjamin Disraeli (1804–81) British prime minister and novelist. *Vivian Grey* (1826), bk 6, ch. 7

26 All empire is no more than power in trust.
John Dryden (1631–1700) English poet and playwright. *Absalom and Achitophel* (1680), pt 1, l. 411

27 In the councils of government we must guard against the acquisition of unwarranted influence, whether sought or unsought, by the military-industrial complex. The potential for the disastrous rise of misplaced power exists and will persist.
Dwight David Eisenhower (1890–1969) US general and president. Farewell address (17 January 1961)

28 Power ceases in the instant of repose.
Ralph Waldo Emerson (1803–82) US essayist, lecturer, and poet. 'Self-Reliance', *Essays: First Series* (1841)

29 Life is a search after power.
Ralph Waldo Emerson (1803–82) US essayist, lecturer, and poet. 'Power', *The Conduct of Life* (1860)

30 Power is the ability to change things.
Carly Fiorina (b. 1954) US president and CEO of Hewlett-Packard. 'Secrets of the Fastest Rising Stars', *Fortune* (Patricia Sellers; 2000)

31 Men of power have no time to read; yet the men who do not read are unfit for power.
Michael Foot (b. 1913) British politician and writer. *Debts of Honour* (1980)

32 Power is not an institution, and not a structure; neither is it a certain strength we are endowed with; it is the name that one attributes to a complex strategical situation in a particular society.
Michel Foucault (1926–84) French philosopher. *The History of Sexuality* (1976), vol. 1, pt 4, ch. 2

33 In the United States, though power corrupts, the expectation of power paralyzes.
J.K. Galbraith (b. 1908) US economist and diplomat. *New York* (15 November 1971)

34 'Power may be at the end of a gun', but sometimes it's also at the end of the shadow or the image of a gun.
Jean Genet (1910–86) French playwright and novelist. Referring to a quotation by Mao Zedong. *Prisoner of Love* (1986), pt 1

35 You must either conquer and rule or serve and lose, suffer or triumph, be the anvil or the hammer.
Johann Wolfgang von Goethe (1749–1832) German poet, playwright, novelist, and scientist. *Der Gross-Cophta* (1791), bk 2

36 Power is neither male nor female.
Katharine Graham (1917–2001) US newspaper publisher and owner of *Washington Post*. Quoted in *Company Man: the Rise and Fall of Corporate Life* (Anthony Sampson; 1995), ch. 19

37 In the general course of human nature, a power over a man's substance amounts to a power over his will.
Alexander Hamilton (1757–1804) US lawyer and politician. *The Federalist* (1787)

38 My speciality is omniscience.
Charles Haughey (b. 1925) Irish former prime minister. Attrib.

39 The exercise of power is determined by thousands of interactions between the world of the powerful and that of the powerless, all the more so because these worlds are never divided by a sharp line; everyone has a small part of himself in both.

Václav Havel (b. 1936) Czech writer and president. *Disturbing the Peace* (1990), ch. 5

40 Those in possession of absolute power can not only prophesy and make their prophecies come true, but they can also lie and make their lies come true.
Eric Hoffer (1902–83) US philosopher. *The Passionate State of Mind* (1955)

41 The great secret of power is never to will to do more than you can accomplish.
Henrik Ibsen (1828–1906) Norwegian playwright. Attrib.

42 An honest man can feel no pleasure in the exercise of power over his fellow citizens.
Thomas Jefferson (1743–1826) US president. Letter to John Melish (13 January 1813)

43 I hope our wisdom will grow with our power, and teach us, that the less we use our power the greater it will be.
Thomas Jefferson (1743–1826) US president. Letter to Thomas Leiper (12 June 1815)

44 My opinion is, that power should always be distrusted, in whatever hands it is placed.
William Jones (1746–94) British jurist, linguist, and orientalist. Letter to Lord Althorp (5 October 1782)

45 Power is the ability to get things done.
Rosabeth Moss Kanter (b. 1943) US management theorist, academic, and writer. *Getting It All Together: Communes Past, Present, Future* (1996)

46 In the past, those who foolishly sought power by riding on the back of the tiger ended up inside.
John F. Kennedy (1917–63) US president. Presidential inaugural speech (20 January 1961)

47 Whenever you're sitting across from some important person, always picture him sitting there in a suit of long red underwear. That's the way I always operated in business.
Joseph P. Kennedy (1888–1969) US entrepreneur, government official, and diplomat. Quoted in *No Final Victories* (Lawrence O'Brien; 1974)

48 The cyclone derives its power from a calm centre. So does a person.
Brendan Kennelly (b. 1936) Irish poet and academic. *The Power of Positive Thinking* (1972)

49 Four things greater than all things are,— Women and Horses and Power and War.
Rudyard Kipling (1865–1936) British novelist, poet, and short-story writer. 'The Ballad of the King's Jest' (1891)

50 Power is the ultimate aphrodisiac.
Henry Kissinger (b. 1923) US diplomat. *New York Times* (19 January 1971)

51 We should keep silent about those in power; to speak well of them almost implies flattery; to speak ill of them while they are alive is dangerous, and when they are dead is cowardly.
Jean de La Bruyère (1645–96) French essayist and moralist. 'Of Great Nobles', *Characters or Manners of the Age* (1688)

52 The stronger man's argument is always the best.
Jean de La Fontaine (1621–95) French writer and poet. 'The Wolf and the Lamb', *Fables* (1668), bk 1, fable 10

53 The important thing about power is to make sure you don't have to use it.
Edwin Land (1909–91) US inventor and founder of Polaroid Corporation. *BusinessWeek* (March 1981)

54 What is hateful are not rebels but the men, who, having the enjoyment of power, do not discharge the duties of power; they are the men who, having the power to redress wrongs, refuse to listen to the petitioners that are sent to them.
Wilfrid Laurier (1841–1919) Canadian politician. Speech, House of Commons (16 March 1886)

55 The vaster the power gained, the vaster the appetite for more.
Ursula K. Le Guin (b. 1929) US author. *The Lathe of Heaven* (1971)

56 The quality of the will to power is, precisely, growth. Achievement is its cancellation. To be, the will to power must increase with each fulfillment, making the fulfillment only a step to a further one.
Ursula K. Le Guin (b. 1929) US author. *The Lathe of Heaven* (1971), ch. 9

57 I claim not to have controlled events, but confess plainly that events have controlled me.
Abraham Lincoln (1809–65) US president. Letter to A.G. Hodges (4 April 1864)

58 Power? It's like a dead sea fruit. When you achieve it, there's nothing there.
Harold Macmillan (1894–1986) British prime minister. Quoted in *The New Anatomy of Britain* (Anthony Sampson; 1971)

59 Power never takes a back step—only in the face of more power.
Malcolm X (1925–65) US black consciousness leader. *Malcolm X Speaks* (1965)

60 Every Communist must grasp the truth. 'Political power grows out of the barrel of a gun'.
Mao Zedong (1893–1976) Chinese revolutionary leader. Speech to Central Committee, Communist Party (6 November 1938)

61 Being chairman of the Senate Commerce Committee is like being a mosquito in a nudist colony.
John McCain (b. 1936) US senator. Quoted in *Fortune* (March 2003)

62 Wielding that sort of influence is easier when one controls tremendous sums of money.
Carl McCall (b. 1935) US former Comptroller of New York State. Referring to the achievements of African Americans in business. 'The Players', *Fortune* (Eileen Gunn; April 1997)

63 A man comes into a great hotel and says, I am a messenger. Who is this man? He disappears walking, there is no noise, nothing. Maybe he will never come back, maybe he will never deliver the message, But a man who rides up on a great machine, this man exists. He will be given messages.

Arthur Miller (b. 1915) US dramatist. *A View from the Bridge* (1955), Act 1

64 The power of kings and magistrates is nothing else, but what only is derivative, transformed and committed to them in trust from the people to the common good of them all, in whom the power yet remains fundamentally, and cannot be taken from them, without a violation of their natural birthright.

John Milton (1608–74) English poet. *The Tenure of Kings and Magistrates* (1649)

65 Not necessity, not desire—no, the love of power is the demon of men. Let them have everything—health, food, a place to live, entertainment—they are and remain unhappy and low-spirited; for the demon waits and waits and will be satisfied.

Friedrich Nietzsche (1844–1900) German philosopher. *Daybreak* (1881)

66 Power is not a means, it is an end. One does not establish a dictatorship in order to safeguard a revolution; one makes the revolution in order to establish the dictatorship.

George Orwell (1903–50) British novelist, critic, and essayist. Said by O'Brien to Winston Smith. *Nineteen Eighty-Four* (1949), pt 3, ch. 3

67 Power-worship blurs political judgement because it leads, almost unavoidably, to the belief that present trends will continue. Whoever is winning at the moment will always seem to be invincible.

George Orwell (1903–50) British novelist, critic, and essayist. 'Second Thoughts on James Burnham', *Shooting an Elephant* (1950)

68 God must have loved the People in Power, for he made them so very like their own image of him.

Kenneth Patchen (1911–72) US poet. Quoted in *Guardian* (1 February 1972)

69 Great men can't be ruled.

Ayn Rand (1905–82) US writer. *The Fountainhead* (1943)

70 The least one can say about power is that a vocation for it is suspicious.

Jean Rostand (1894–1977) French biologist and writer. 1939. 'A Biologist's Thoughts', *The Substance of Man* (1962), ch. 10

71 The new source of power is not money in the hands of the few, but information in the hands of many.

W.W. Rostow (b. 1916) US economist. *Megatrends* (1982)

72 Women have so much power that even hearing the word power frightens them.

Harriet Rubin (b. 1952) US author. *www.tompeters.com* (2000)

73 The megalomaniac differs from the narcissist by the fact that he wishes to be powerful

rather than charming, and seeks to be feared rather than loved. To this type belong many lunatics and most of the great men of history.

Bertrand Russell (1872–1970) British philosopher and writer. *The Conquest of Happiness* (1930), ch. 1

74 The man who is activated by love of power is more apt to inflict pain than to permit pleasure.

Bertrand Russell (1872–1970) British philosopher and writer. Attrib.

75 We cannot all be masters.

William Shakespeare (1564–1616) English poet and playwright. *Othello* (1602–04), Act 1, Scene 1, l. 43

76 The good want power, but to weep barren tears.
The powerful goodness want: worse need for them.
...And all best things are thus confused with it.

Percy Bysshe Shelley (1792–1822) British poet. *Prometheus Unbound* (1819), l. 625

77 Power like a desolating pestilence
Pollutes whate'er it touches.

Percy Bysshe Shelley (1792–1822) British poet. *Queen Mab* (1813), pt 3

78 Power can be taken but not given. The process of the taking is empowerment in itself.

Gloria Steinem (b. 1934) US entrepreneur, editor, and writer. 'Far from the Opposite Shore', *Ms.* (July 1978)

79 Power corrupts, but lack of power corrupts absolutely.

Adlai E. Stevenson (1900–65) US statesman and author. Referring to Lord Acton's quotation about power corrupting and absolute power corrupting absolutely. Quoted in *Observer* (January 1963)

80 In the new organisation, power flows from expertise, not position.

Thomas Stewart (b. 1948) US journalist and author. *Intellectual Capital* (1997)

81 One still strong man in a blatant land,
Whatever they call him, what care I,
Aristocrat, democrat, autocrat—one
Who can rule and dare not lie.

Alfred Tennyson, Lord (1809–92) British poet. *Maud* (1855), pt 1, st. 5

82 I shan't be pulling the levers there but I shall be a very good back-seat driver.

Margaret Thatcher (b. 1925) British former prime minister. Referring to the appointment of John Major as prime minister. *Independent* (27 November 1990)

83 You don't have power if you surrender all your principles—you have office.

Ron Todd (b. 1927) British trade union leader. Quoted in *Daily Telegraph* (17 June 1988)

84 Go for an interview when you feel dead-ended. If someone calls you at 9:30 a.m. to set the time for your luncheon date and you want to say 'Right now', it's time to get out your contact list and set up some interviews.

Jane Trahey (1923–2000) US copywriter and author. *Jane Trahey on Women and Power: Who's Got It? How to Get It?* (1977)

85 I have, I fear, confused power with greatness.

Stewart L. Udall (b. 1920) US politician and conservationist. Commencement speech at Dartmouth College (1965)

86 Powerful men in particular suffer from the delusion that human beings have no memories. I would go so far as to say that the distinguishing trait of powerful men is the psychotic certainty that people forget acts of infamy as easily as their parents' birthdays.

Stephen Vizinczey (b. 1933) Hungarian novelist and critic. 'Commentary on a Poem', *Horizon* (October 1976)

87 Alexander at the head of the world never tasted the fine pleasure that boys of his own age have enjoyed at the head of a school.

Horace Walpole (1717–97) British writer. Letter (6 May 1736)

88 The appetite for power, even for universal power, is only insane when there is no possibility of indulging it; a man who sees the possibility opening before him and does not try to grasp it, even at the risk of destroying himself and his country, is either a saint or a mediocrity.

Simone Weil (1909–43) French philosopher and activist. 1939. 'Cold War Policy in 1939', *Selected Essays* (Richard Rees, ed.; 1962)

89 The good old rule
Sufficeth them, the simple plan,
that they should take, who have the power,
And they should keep who can.

William Wordsworth (1770–1850) British poet. 'Rob Roy's Grave' (1803), st. 9

90 When a system of national currencies run by a central bank is transformed into a global electronic marketplace driven by currency traders, power changes hands.

Walter Wriston (b. 1919) US banker. 1993. Said in a speech on 25 January 1993. Quoted in *The Arizona Republic* (1999)

PRACTICE

1 A thing may look specious in theory yet be ruinous in practice; a thing may look evil in theory, and yet be in practice excellent.

Edmund Burke (1729–97) British philosopher and politician. Speaking for the prosecution at the impeachment of Warren Hastings, former govenor-general of India. Speech, House of Commons (19 February 1788)

2 Just having a great Web site is only one step in a company thinking of itself as an Internet company. You also have to change all the processes inside your company to be digital. The people at the desk...the knowledge workers, need to work in a different way.

Bill Gates (b. 1955) US entrepreneur, chairman and CEO of Microsoft. Speech, Enterprise Solutions Conference, Miami, Florida (21 March 2000)

3 I set a rule that people weren't allowed to send good news unless they sent around an equal amount of bad news. We had to get a balanced picture. In fact, I kind of favored just hearing about the accounts we were losing because...bad news is generally more actionable than good news.

Bill Gates (b. 1955) US entrepreneur, chairman and CEO of Microsoft. Speech, Microsoft's Second Annual CEO Summit, Seattle, Washington (28 May 1998)

4 The essence of a company like Intel is execution and strategy. Intel, looked at in another way, is a three-legged stool. One leg is technology—design and silicon technology—another leg is manufacturing, and the third leg is marketing. Whenever Intel did well it was because the three legs were equal. Whenever one of those legs was shorter than the others, we wobbled.

Andrew S. Grove (b. 1936) US entrepreneur, author, and chairman of Intel Corporation. Interview, *Upside Magazine* (12 October 1997)

5 Having a large business is not against the law. Achieving it in violation of fairly specifically prescribed codes of behavior is. So we don't worry about the grand concept of it. We don't worry about being big, we worry about not being big enough. But we are worried about playing by the rules—not just the letter of the law, but the spirit of the law.

Andrew S. Grove (b. 1936) US entrepreneur, author, and chairman of Intel Corporation. On the Antitrust Division of the Department of Justice's investigation into the practices of dominant industry players such as Intel and Microsoft. Interview, *Upside Magazine* (12 October 1997)

6 Most of our organization tends to be arranged on the assumption that people cannot be trusted...that sort of attitude creates a paraphernalia of systems, checkers, and checkers checking checkers—expensive and deadening.

Charles Handy (b. 1932) British business executive and author. 'Trust and the Virtual Organization', *Harvard Business Review* (May–June 1991)

7 Intellectual honesty and truth are at a minimum in command systems...The creation of knowledge grinds to a halt, and progress ceases. This is as true for command-based business organizations as for political regimes.

Charles G. Koch (b. 1935) US management theorist, author, chairman and CEO of Koch Industries. 'The Future of American Business' (March 1996)

8 Unless we believe that the expert in any particular job is most often the person performing it, we shall forever limit the potential of that person, in terms of both his own contributions to the organization and his own personal development.

Rene C. McPherson (1924–96) US CEO of Dana Corporation. 'The People Principle', *Leaders* (January–March 1980)

9 I think that business practices would improve immeasurably if they were guided by 'feminine' principles—qualities like love and care and intuition.

Anita Roddick (b. 1942) British entrepreneur and founder of The Body Shop. *Body and Soul* (co-written with Russell Miller; 1991)

10 Forget socialism, capitalism, just-in-time deliveries, salary surveys, and the rest...concentrate on building organizations that accomplish that most difficult of all challenges: to make people look forward to coming to work in the morning.
Ricardo Semler (b. 1959) Brazilian business executive and president of Semco. *Maverick!* (1993)

11 Companies...have a hard time distinguishing between the cost of paying people and the value of investing in them.
Thomas A. Stewart (b. 1948) US journalist and author. *Intellectual Capital* (1997)

PRAISE

1 Sandwich every bit of criticism between two layers of praise.
Mary Kay Ash (1915–2001) US entrepreneur, business executive, and founder of Mary Kay Cosmetics. Attrib.

2 There are two things people want more than sex and money—recognition and praise.
Mary Kay Ash (1915–2001) US entrepreneur, business executive, and founder of Mary Kay Cosmetics. Attrib.

3 The worst mistake a boss can make is not to say 'Well done'.
John Ashcroft (b. 1948) British business executive. *Sunday Telegraph Magazine* (5 June 1988)

4 Congratulations offer more potential than cash. The amount of available cash is limited, but managers have an unlimited supply of congratulations. It's important to pay people fairly, but managers also should heap on congratulations and feed people's souls.
Kenneth Blanchard (b. 1939) US management theorist and author. 'The Gift of the Goose', *Quality Digest* (December 1997)

5 Why do people focus...on cash rewards?...we seldom create opportunities to congratulate each other. It's hard to imagine union leaders storming into a meeting, smashing their fists on the desk and demanding, 'We want more congratulations!'
Kenneth Blanchard (b. 1939) US management theorist and author. 'The Gift of the Goose', *Quality Digest* (December 1997)

6 An industrial worker would sooner have a £5 note but a country man must have praise.
Ronald Blythe (b. 1922) British writer. *Akenfield: Portrait of an English Village* (1969)

7 Watch how a man takes praise and there you have the measure of him.
Thomas Burke (1886–1945) British writer. *T.P.'s Weekly* (8 June 1928)

8 The advantage of doing one's praising for oneself is that one can lay it on so thick and in exactly the right places.
Samuel Butler (1835–1902) British writer. *The Way of All Flesh* (1903), ch. 24

9 It is essential to condemn what must be condemned, but swiftly and firmly. On the other hand, one should praise at length what still deserves to be praised.
Albert Camus (1913–60) French novelist and essayist. *Resistance, Rebellion, and Death* (Justin O'Brien, tr.; 1961)

10 Slight attentions or a kind word to the humble often bring back reward as great as it is unlooked for...I am indebted to these trifles for some of the happiest attentions and the most pleasing incidents of my life.
Andrew Carnegie (1835–1919) US industrialist and philanthropist. *Autobiography* (1920)

11 I praise loudly, I blame softly.
Catherine the Great (1729–96) Russian empress. Letter (23 August 1794)

12 You cannot love an employee into creativity, although you can...avoid his dissatisfactions with the way you treat him.
Frederick Herzberg (1923–2000) US psychologist. *Work and the Nature of Man* (1966), ch. 6

13 There's nothing more demoralizing than having nobody notice good performance...the successful culture is one that provides constant recognition and applause. At the same time, it breeds a restless dissatisfaction that keeps you challenging yourself to a higher and higher performance.
Rosabeth Moss Kanter (b. 1943) US management theorist, academic, and writer. Interview, *Strategy + Business* (July–September 1999)

14 People ask you for criticism but they only want praise.
W. Somerset Maugham (1874–1965) British novelist, short-story writer, and dramatist. *Of Human Bondage* (1915)

15 Damn with faint praise, assent with civil leer, And, without sneering, teach the rest to sneer.
Alexander Pope (1688–1744) English poet. 'An Epistle to Dr Arbuthnot' (1735)

16 I will praise any man that will praise me.
William Shakespeare (1564–1616) English poet and playwright. *Antony and Cleopatra* (1606–07), Act 2, Scene 6, l. 90

17 Good fortune brings success, but it is endeavour that deserves praise.
Marcus Terentius Varro (116–27 BC) Roman scholar. *Rerum Divinarum* (47 BC), bk 14

18 Very few people in the world can be relied upon to work without praise or recognition.
Varindra Tarzie Vittachi (1921–93) Sri Lankan writer and deputy director of Unicef. *The Brown Sahib* (1962)

PRINCIPLES

1 It is easier to fight for one's principles than to live up to them.
Alfred Adler (1870–1937) Austrian psychologist and psychiatrist. Quoted in *Alfred Adler* (Phyllis Bottome; 1939)

2 Either lead, follow, or get out of the way.

Anonymous. Sign on the desk of broadcasting executive Ted Turner. *Fortune* (5 January 1987)

3 PRINCIPLE, n. A thing which too many people confuse with interest.

Ambrose Bierce (1842–?1914) US journalist and writer. *The Devil's Dictionary* (1911)

4 It is better to be defeated on principle than to win on lies.

Arthur Calwell (1896–1973) Australian politician. Attrib.

5 This, then, is held to be the duty of the man of wealth: first, to set an example of modest unostentatious living...to provide moderately for the legitimate wants of those dependent upon him; and, after doing so, to consider all surplus revenues...as trust funds which he is strictly bound as a matter of duty to administer in the manner...best calculated to produce the most beneficial results for the community.

Andrew Carnegie (1835–1919) US industrialist and philanthropist. Summing up his philosophy. *The Gospel of Wealth* (1889)

6 Human beings possess the potential to be educated for values.

S.K. Chakraborty (b. 1957) Indian academic. *Management by Values: Towards Cultural Congruence* (1991)

7 Influence, position and wealth are not given for nothing and we must try to use them as we would wish at the last we had done.

Jeremiah James Colman (1830–98) British food industry executive. 1856. Quoted in *Enlightened Entrepreneurs* (Ian Campbell Bradley; 1987), ch. 5

8 Here's the rule for bargains: 'Do other men, for they would do you'. That's the true business precept.

Charles Dickens (1812–70) British novelist. *Martin Chuzzlewit* (1843–44), ch. 11

9 The principle of maximum diversity operates both at the physical and at the mental level. It says that the laws of nature and the initial conditions are such as to make the universe as interesting as possible.

Freeman Dyson (b. 1923) US physicist. *Infinite in All Directions* (1988)

10 Management principles aim at the success of associations and at the satisfying of economic interests...The principle is the lighthouse fixing the bearings but it can only serve those who already know the way into port.

Henri Fayol (1841–1925) French business executive. *General and Industrial Management* (1916)

11 Resolve to perform what you ought. Perform without fail what you resolve.

Benjamin Franklin (1706–90) US politician, inventor, and journalist. The fourth of his 13 precepts for moral living. *Benjamin Franklin's Autobiography* (1793), pt 2

12 Principles always become a matter of vehement discussion when practice is at an ebb.

George Gissing (1857–1903) British novelist. *Private Papers of Henry Ryecroft* (1903)

13 Important principles may and must be inflexible.

Abraham Lincoln (1809–65) US president. Said during his last public address. Speech, Washington, D.C. (11 April 1865)

14 I don't believe in principles. Principles are only excuses for what we want to think or what we want to do.

Compton Mackenzie (1883–1972) British novelist and broadcaster. *The Adventures of Sylvia Scarlett* (1918)

15 Better service for the customer is for the good of the public, and this is the true purpose of enterprise.

Konosuke Matsushita (1894–1989) Japanese electronics executive, entrepreneur, and inventor. *Quest for Prosperity* (1988)

16 You can't learn too soon that the most useful thing about a principle is that it can always be sacrificed to expediency.

W. Somerset Maugham (1874–1965) British novelist, short-story writer, and dramatist. *The Circle* (1921)

17 Companies cannot deliver lasting change in isolation. Just as at the company level, we need a framework of clear principles to guide individual actions, so at the national and international level, we need a common ethical framework to inform and to guide the conduct of global business.

Mark Moody-Stuart (b. 1940) British chairman of Anglo American, and former chairman of Committee of Managing Directors Royal Dutch/Shell Group. Speech to the World Congress of the International Society of Business, Economics and Ethics, São Paolo, Brazil. 'Putting Principles into Practice: The Ethical Challenge to Global Business' (19 July 2000)

18 It may seem an obvious point but principles do not embed themselves in the minds of staff. To be effective, they have to be lived. It's one thing to sign up for a set of principles, quite another to ensure that they are implemented and embedded in our corporate culture.

Mark Moody-Stuart (b. 1940) British chairman of Anglo American, and former chairman of Committee of Managing Directors Royal Dutch/Shell Group. Speech to the World Congress of the International Society of Business, Economics and Ethics, São Paolo, Brazil. 'Putting Principles into Practice: The Ethical Challenge to Global Business' (19 July 2000)

19 Avoid having your ego so close to your position that, when your position fails, your ego goes with it.

Colin Powell (b. 1937) US military leader and politician. Kept on his desk at the Pentagon. Attrib.

20 The man who accepts the laissez-faire doctrine would allow his garden to grow wild so that roses might fight it out with the weeds and the fittest might survive.

John Ruskin (1819–1900) British art critic and writer. Attrib.

21 The Great Principles on which we will build this Business are as everlasting as the Pyramids.
Gordon Selfridge (1858–1947) British retailer. Preliminary announcement, opening of Selfridge's store, London. (1909)

22 What is important is our open-mindedness, our trust in our employees and distrust of dogma. We are neither socialist nor purely capitalist, but we take the best of these failed systems and others to re-organize work.
Ricardo Semler (b. 1959) Brazilian business executive and president of Semco. *Maverick!* (1993)

23 I'm very sympathetic to the view that the economy should spend more time in dealing with the predicament of people who are thrown into turmoil when things go wrong.
Amartya Sen (b. 1933) Indian economist and winner of the 1998 Nobel Prize in Economics. Interview, *NewsHour, Online Focus* (PBS; 15 October 1998)

24 Business doesn't have to choose between making profit and protecting the environment, between economic success and ethical responsibility, between satisfying the customer and meeting the demands of other stakeholders. In other words, we don't have to make a choice between profits and principles
Jeroen Van der Veer (b. 1947) Dutch Advisory Director of Unilever, vice-chairman of the Royal Dutch/Shell Group, and president of Royal Dutch Petroleum Company. Speech, 'Earning the Licence to Grow' (26 November 1999)

PRIORITIES

1 First things first, second things never.
Shirley Conran (b. 1932) British designer, fashion editor, and author. *Superwoman* (1975)

2 The one predominant duty is to find one's work and do it.
Charlotte Gilman (1860–1935) US feminist and writer. *The Living of Charlotte Perkins Gilman* (1935)

3 My #1 job here at Apple is to make sure that the top 100 people are A+ players. And everything else will take care of itself. If the top 50 people are right, it just cascades down throughout the whole organization.
Steve Jobs (b. 1955) US entrepreneur, co-founder and CEO of Apple Computer Company, and CEO of Pixar. Quoted in 'Steve's Two Jobs', *Time* (Michael Krantz; 18 October 1999)

4 Setting the direction of the company has become one of my priorities...Before the bubble economy burst, the direction was automatic...we are now finding ourselves in a much more competitive world. It is also a world that is rapidly changing and that requires a lot of thought as to the company's overall direction
Minoru Makihara (b. 1930) Japanese president of Mitsubishi Corporation. Interview, *Strategy + Business* (Joel Kurtzman; January–March 1996)

5 Managing intellectual assets has become the single most important task of business.
Thomas A. Stewart (b. 1948) US journalist and author. *Intellectual Capital* (1997)

6 The priority in life is to keep an eye on the business and not to get lured into the high social life with groupie-type poseurs who wish to be seen with the new blue-eyed boy.
Alan Sugar (b. 1947) British entrepreneur, founder and chairman of Amstrad electronics company. Speech, City University Business School, London (April 1987)

PROBLEMS

1 The problem when solved will be simple.
Anonymous. Sign on the wall of the General Motors' research laboratory at Dayton, Ohio. Quoted in *Positioning: The Battle for Your Mind* (Al Ries and Jack Trout; 1981)

2 Settle one difficulty and you keep a hundred others away.
Anonymous. Chinese proverb.

3 If anything can go wrong, it will.
Anonymous. 1950s. Murphy's Law.

4 Managers who are skilled communicators may also be good at covering up real problems.
Chris Argyris (b. 1923) US academic and organisational behaviour theorist. *Harvard Business Review* (1986)

5 Threat is dealt with by defensive reasoning...This in turn, produces learning systems in organizations that are actually against understanding how to deal with threatening issues so they can be eliminated.
Chris Argyris (b. 1923) US academic and organisational behaviour theorist. *Strategy, Change and Defensive Routines* (1985), ch. 12

6 The problem of our age is the administration of wealth, so that the ties of brotherhood may still bind together the rich and poor in harmonious relationship.
Andrew Carnegie (1835–1919) US industrialist and philanthropist. *The Gospel of Wealth* (1889)

7 Crisis situations are usually unanticipated sudden developments, originating either within or outside the organisation...if these could be managed within the framework of normal practice they would not be crises after all.
S.K. Chakraborty (b. 1957) Indian academic. *Management by Objectives: An Integrated Approach* (1976)

8 It isn't that they can't see the solution. It is that they can't see the problem.
G.K. Chesterton (1874–1936) British novelist, poet, and critic. *The Scandal of Father Brown* (1935)

9 You're either part of the solution or part of the problem.
Eldridge Cleaver (1935–98) US civil rights activist. Speech, San Francisco (1968)

10 A gentleman can withstand hardships; it is only the small man who, when submitted to them, is swept off his feet.
Confucius (551–479 BC) Chinese philosopher, administrator, and writer. *Analects* (?500 BC)

11 It is characteristic of all deep human problems that they are not to be approached without some humor and some bewilderment.
Freeman Dyson (b. 1923) US physicist. *Disturbing the Universe* (1979)

12 We must bear in mind that the statistical relationships we work with, embodied in our econometric models, are only loose approximations of the underlying reality...Some fog always obstructs our vision, but when the structure of the economy is changing, the fog is considerably denser than at other times.
Roger W. Ferguson Jr (b. 1951) US economist, vice-chairman of the Federal Reserve Board. On the problems facing the Federal Reserve Board in deciding policy. Speech, New Economy Forum, Haas School of Business, University of California, Berkeley, California. 'Conversation with Leaders of the "New Economy"' (9 May 2000)

13 What is the answer to the question? The problem. How is the problem resolved? By displacing the question...We must think problematically rather than question and answer dialectically.
Michel Foucault (1926–84) French philosopher. 'Theatrum Philosophicum', *Language, Counter-Memory, Practice* (1977)

14 In solving our problems, we should beware of creating worse ones.
Indira Gandhi (1917–84) Indian prime minister. Speech (10 February 1969)

15 Yesterday's success formula is often today's obsolete dogma...We must continually challenge the past so that we can renew ourselves each day.
Sumantra Ghoshal (b. 1946) Indian academic and management theorist. 'Rebuilding Behavioral Context: A Blueprint for Corporate Renewal', *Sloan Management Review* (co-written with Christopher A. Bartlett; Winter 1996)

16 All professional men are handicapped by not being allowed to ignore things which are useless.
Johann Wolfgang von Goethe (1749–1832) German poet, playwright, novelist, and scientist. *Maxims and Reflections* (1819)

17 If you see a bandwagon, it's too late.
James Goldsmith (1933–97) British entrepreneur, financier, and politician. Quoted in *The Risk Takers* (Jeffrey Robinson; 1985)

18 In my experience the worst thing you can do to an important problem is to discuss it.
Simon Gray (b. 1936) British playwright. *Otherwise Engaged* (1975), Act 2

19 If key aspects of the business shift around you, the very process of genetic selection that got you and your associates where you are might retard your ability to recognize the new trends. A sign of this might be that all of a sudden some people 'don't seem to get it'....When they don't get it or you don't get it, it may not be because of encroaching age; it may be because the 'it' has changed around you.
Andrew S. Grove (b. 1936) US entrepreneur, author, and chairman of Intel Corporation. Referring to the signs of an approaching strategic inflection point. *Only the Paranoid Survive: How to Exploit the Crisis Points That Challenge Every Company and Career* (1996), ch. 6

20 My argument is that companies are often blind, and that it is a genetic problem, making blinders a bigger challenge than mere inefficiency. Blindness can even affect an entire industry because most companies in an industry are blind in the same way.
Gary Hamel (b. 1954) US academic, business writer, and consultant. Interview, *Strategy + Business* (October–December 1997)

21 I've spent 30 years going round factories. When you know something's wrong, nine times out of ten it's the management...people aren't being led right. And bad leaders invariably blame the people.
John Harvey-Jones (b. 1924) British management adviser, author, and former chairman of ICI. Interview, *Daily Telegraph* (24 March 1990)

22 Problems can only be solved by the people who have them. You have to try and coax them and love them into seeing ways in which they can help themselves.
John Harvey-Jones (b. 1924) British management adviser, author, and former chairman of ICI. On his approach as a 'Mr Fix-It' for troubled businesses. *Independent on Sunday* (11 March 1990)

23 We live in an information economy. The problem is that information's usually impossible to get, at least in the right place, at the right time.
Steve Jobs (b. 1955) US entrepreneur, co-founder and CEO of Apple Computer Company, and CEO of Pixar. Interview, 'The Next Insanely Great Thing', *Wired Magazine* (February 1996)

24 Problems are only opportunities in work clothes.
Henry J. Kaiser (1882–1967) US industrialist. Quoted in obituary, *New York Times* (24 August 1967)

25 Problems are the price of progress. Don't bring me anything but trouble. Good news weakens me.
Charles Franklin Kettering (1876–1958) US businessman and engineer. Quoted in *Strategy + Business* (1997)

26 The greatest risk lies in not knowing what you don't know. In a fast changing marketplace such as the Internet, this trap seems to be so open and so wide.
William (Walid) Mougayar, US consultant and management theorist. Referring to the challenge to managers of traditional industries of the new economy. *Opening Digital Markets* (1997), Introduction to 2nd edition

27 Difficulties, opposition, criticism—these things are meant to be overcome, and there is a special joy in facing them and coming out on top.

Vijaya Lakshmi Pandit (1900–90) Indian diplomat. Quoted in *The Envoy Extraordinary* (Vera Brittain; 1965)

28 We resort too often to the unhelpful practice of trying to solve a problem with larger doses of capital.

H. Ross Perot (b. 1930) US entrepreneur, venture capitalist, and politician. Speech to the Detroit Economic Club, Detroit, Michigan (January 1987)

29 Traditional business defaults to the familiar; it's easy, comfortable, and bonus-building to rely on old business models, outdated templates, yesterday's strategies.

Faith Popcorn (b. 1947) US trend expert and founder of BrainReserve. *EVEolution* (2000), ch. 1

30 Every solution of a problem raises new unsolved problems.

Karl Raimund Popper (1902–94) British philosopher of science. *Conjectures and Refutations* (1963)

31 Beware of the danger signals that flag problems: silence, secretiveness, or sudden outburst.

Sylvia Porter (1913–91) US journalist and finance expert. Attrib.

32 No business enterprise can succeed without sharing the burden of the problems of other enterprises.

Ayn Rand (1905–82) US writer. *Atlas Shrugged* (1957), pt 1, ch. 3

33 I need problems. A good problem makes me come alive.

Tiny Rowland (1917–98) British entrepreneur, co-CEO and managing director of Lonrho. *Sunday Times* (4 March 1990)

34 'My door is always open—bring me your problems'. This is guaranteed to turn on every whiner, lackey, and neurotic on the property.

Robert F. Six (1907–86) US airline executive. Quoted in *Money Talks* (Robert W. Kent, ed.; 1986)

35 The problems of this world are only truly solved in two ways: by extinction or duplication.

Susan Sontag (b. 1933) US novelist and essayist. *I, Etcetera* (1978)

36 One must think until it hurts. One must worry a problem in one's mind until it seems there cannot be another aspect of it that hasn't been considered.

Roy Herbert Thomson (1894–1976) British media entrepreneur, founder and chairman of the Thomson Organisation. *After I Was Sixty* (1975)

37 The worst possible thing...was to lie dead in the water with any problem. Solve it, solve it quickly...If you solved it wrong, it would come back and slap you in the face, and then you could solve it right.

Thomas J. Watson Jr (1914–93) US CEO of IBM. Quoted in 'The Businessmen of the Century', *Fortune* (22 November 1999)

PROCRASTINATION

1 Tomorrow is often the busiest day of the week.

Anonymous. Spanish proverb.

2 By and by never comes.

St Augustine (354–430) Numidian Doctor of the Church and theologian. *The Confessions* (?400), bk 8, ch. 5, sect. 12

3 Nothing is worse than procrastination. When I look at 10 decisions I failed to make, there will be nine of them where I delayed.

Percy Barnevik (b. 1941) Swedish former CEO of ABB. *New York Times* (May 1990)

4 No task is a long one but the task on which one dare not start. It becomes a nightmare.

Charles Baudelaire (1821–67) French poet and critic. *My Heart Laid Bare* (1869)

5 We know what happens to people who stay in the middle of the road. They get run over.

Aneurin Bevan (1897–1960) British politician. *Observer* (9 December 1953)

6 How long halt ye between two opinions?

Bible. I Kings 18:21

7 She felt weary and careworn, in the way one often does before the big job of work is tackled; that sense of premature or projected exhaustion that is the breeding-ground of all procrastination.

William Boyd (b. 1952) British novelist and scriptwriter. *Brazzaville Beach* (1990)

8 He who hesitates is poor.

Mel Brooks (b. 1926) US film director, actor, and screenwriter. Said by the failed Broadway producer Max Bailystock (Zero Mostel) to his tax accountant Leo Bloom (Gene Wilder). *The Producers* (1968)

9 Business neglected is business lost.

Daniel Defoe (1660–1731) English novelist and journalist. *The Complete English Tradesman* (1726), vol. 1

10 Most executives have learned that what one postpones, one actually abandons...timing is a most important element in the success of any effort. To do five years later what would have been smart to do five years earlier, is almost a sure recipe for frustration and failure.

Peter F. Drucker (b. 1909) US management consultant and academic. *The Effective Executive* (1967), ch. 5

11 Procrastination brings loss; delay danger.

Desiderius Erasmus (?1466–1536) Dutch writer, scholar, and humanist. 'Adolescens', *Colloquia* (1518)

12 Lose no Time. Be always employ'd in something useful. Cut off all unnecessary Actions.

Benjamin Franklin (1706–90) US politician, inventor, and journalist. The sixth of his 13 precepts for moral living. *Benjamin Franklin's Autobiography* (1793), pt 2

13 A wrong decision isn't forever; it can always be reversed. The losses from a delayed decision *are* forever; they can never be retrieved.
J.K. Galbraith (b. 1908) US economist and diplomat. *A Life in Our Times* (1981)

14 Most companies don't die because they are wrong; most die because they don't commit themselves. They fritter away their momentum and their valuable resources while attempting to make a decision. The greatest danger is in standing still.
Andrew S. Grove (b. 1936) US entrepreneur, author, and chairman of Intel Corporation. *Only the Paranoid Survive: How to Exploit the Crisis Points That Challenge Every Company and Career* (1996), ch. 8

15 In delay there is advantage.
Herodotus (?484–?425 BC) Greek historian. *History* (?455 BC), bk 7, ch. 10

16 Pusillanimity disposeth men to irresolution, and consequently to lose the occasions and fittest opportunities of action.
Thomas Hobbes (1588–1679) English philosopher and political theorist. *Leviathan, or, The Matter, Form, and Power of a Commonwealth Ecclesiastical and Civil* (1651), pt 1, ch. 11

17 While we're talking, envious time is fleeing: seize the day, put no trust in the future.
Horace (65–8 BC) Roman poet and satirist. *Odes* (24–23 BC), bk 1, no. 11, l. 7

18 Make up your mind to act decidedly and take the consequences. No good is ever done in this world by hesitation.
Thomas Huxley (1825–95) British biologist. *Aphorisms and Reflections* (Henrietta A. Huxley, ed.; 1907)

19 There is no more miserable human being than the one in whom nothing is habitual but indecision.
William James (1842–1910) US psychologist and philosopher. *The Principles of Psychology* (1890), ch. 10

20 Procrastination is epidemic. The number of people who finish projects three weeks ahead of time you can count on one hand.
Jeffrey P. Kahn (b. 1953) US psychiatrist. Quoted in *Wall Street Journal* (7 May 1996)

21 If I had eight hours to chop down a tree, I'd spend six sharpening the axe.
Abraham Lincoln (1809–65) US president. Attrib.

22 Delays breed dangers.
John Lyly (?1554–1606) English writer and dramatist. *Euphues: The Anatomy of Wit* (1578)

23 procrastination is the
art of keeping
up with yesterday
Don Marquis (1878–1937) US journalist and humorist. *certain maxims of archie* (1927)

24 Far from being the thief of Time, procrastination is the king of it.
Ogden Nash (1902–71) US humorist and writer. 'Long Live Delays' (1940)

25 To plan carefully is the safest delay.
Publilius Syrus (*fl.* 1st century BC) Roman writer. *Moral Sayings* (1st century BC), no. 151

26 Nothing is so devastating as indecision and nothing is so futile.
Bertrand Russell (1872–1970) British philosopher and writer. *The Conquest of Happiness* (1930)

27 Defer no time; delays have dangerous ends.
William Shakespeare (1564–1616) English poet and playwright. *Henry VI, Part One* (1592), Act 3, Scene 3, l. 16

28 Make me a beautiful word for doing things tomorrow; for that surely is a great and blessed invention.
George Bernard Shaw (1856–1950) Irish writer and critic. *Back to Methuselah* (1921)

29 The time for hesitation is past—let us act!
Sophocles (?496–406 BC) Greek tragedian. *Electra* (?430-?415 BC)

30 My rule is always to do the business of the day in the day.
Arthur Wellesley Wellington (1769–1852) British general and statesman. Quoted in *Notes of Conversations with the Duke of Wellington* (Philip Henry Stanhope; 1888)

31 Procrastination is the thief of time.
Edward Young (1683–1765) English poet. *The Complaint, or Night Thoughts on Life, Death, and Immortality* (1742–45)

PRODUCTIVITY

1 The best balance of morale for employee productivity can be described this way: happy, but with low self-esteem.
Scott Adams (b. 1957) US cartoonist and humorist. *The Dilbert Principle* (1996)

2 Idleness is only the refuge of weak minds.
Lord Chesterfield (1694–1773) English statesman, orator, and letter writer. Letter to his son (July 1749)

3 Dispatch is the soul of business, and nothing contributes more to Dispatch than Method.
Lord Chesterfield (1694–1773) English statesman, orator, and letter writer. Letter to his son (5 February 1750)

4 To obtain the most from a man's energy it is necessary to increase the effect without increasing the fatigue.
Augustin Colomb (1736–1806) French scientist. *Observations* (1791)

5 Producing is more important than possessing.
Simone de Beauvoir (1908–86) French writer. *Les Belles Images* (1966)

6 Thanks to him, we have increased the productivity of manual work 3% to 4% compounded—which is 50-fold—and on that achievement rests all the prosperity of the modern world.
Peter F. Drucker (b. 1909) US management consultant and academic. Referring to Frederick W. Taylor, who inspired Henry Ford's mass-production revolution. Quoted in 'The Businessman of the Century', *Fortune* (22 November 1999)

7 Because we don't have as many people pounding out manufactured goods as we once did, many fallaciously conclude our productivity has withered.
Malcolm Forbes (1919–90) US publisher. *Forbes* (1988)

8 Management productivity is a more appropriate term than labor productivity. Improved productivity means less human sweat, not more.
Henry Ford (1919–87) US car manufacturer and CEO of Ford Motor Company. Speech, *US News & World Report* (March 1959)

9 Production not being the sole end of human existence, the term unproductive does not necessarily imply any stigma.
John Stuart Mill (1806–73) British economist and philosopher. *Principles of Political Economy* (1848)

10 Creation comes before distribution—or there will be nothing to distribute.
Ayn Rand (1905–82) US writer. *The Fountainhead* (1943)

11 In an industrial society which confuses work and productivity, the necessity of producing has always been an enemy of the desire to create.
Raoul Vaneigem (b. 1934) Belgian philosopher. *The Revolution of Everyday Life* (1967)

PRODUCTS

1 In the era of globalization, plants tend to be focused in terms of product, robotized in terms of technology, and diversified in terms of markets served.
Paul W. Beamish (b. 1953) Canadian academic and author. *International Management* (1990)

2 Junk is the ideal product—the ultimate merchandise. No sales talk necessary. The client will crawl through a sewer and beg to buy.
William S. Burroughs (1914–97) US novelist. *The Naked Lunch* (1959)

3 Treating processes holistically means that much more is being included under the umbrella of product development.
Dan Dimancescu (b. 1943) US consultant and writer. *World-class New Product Development* (co-written with Kemp Dwenger; 1996)

4 I have no use for a motor car which has more spark plugs than a cow has teats.
Henry Ford (1863–1947) US industrialist, car manufacturer, and founder of Ford Motor Company. *My Life and Work* (co-written with Samuel Crowther; 1922)

5 We in the US have a problem or, if you will, an opportunity to break away from technological traditions and to find really new and better ways of making products for the markets of the world.
Henry Ford (1919–87) US car manufacturer and CEO of Ford Motor Company. Speech (1964)

6 It is duality of design we're concerned with, not just how it looks, but how it works and how the two inter-relate.
Rawdon Glover (b. 1968) British marketing executive. *Marketing* (June 2000)

7 A successful product merely gives us a head start in the race.
John Harvey-Jones (b. 1924) British management adviser, author, and former chairman of ICI. *Managing to Survive* (1993)

8 You just don't understand. Go find a car and saw the top off the darn thing.
Lee Iacocca (b. 1924) US president of Ford Motor Company, chairman and CEO of Chrysler Corporation. Referring to his wish to see a quick prototype of a new convertible car. Quoted in *Thriving on Chaos* (Tom Peters; 1987)

9 Both Apple and Pixar...Their product is pure intellectual property. Bits on a disk.
Steve Jobs (b. 1955) US entrepreneur, co-founder and CEO of Apple Computer Company, and CEO of Pixar. Quoted in 'Steve's Two Jobs', *Time* (Michael Krantz; 18 October 1999)

10 My theory is that good furniture could be priced so that the man with a flat wallet could be attracted to it.
Ingvar Kamprad (b. 1926) Swedish business executive and founder of IKEA. *Forbes* (August 2000)

11 A product is anything that can be offered to a market for attention, acquisition, use, or consumption.
Philip Kotler (b. 1931) US marketing management thinker. *Marketing Management* (1967)

12 Every company should work hard to obsolete its own product line before its competitors do.
Philip Kotler (b. 1931) US marketing management thinker. *Marketing Management* (1967)

13 If you can't smell it, you can't sell it.
Estée Lauder (b. 1908) US entrepreneur and cosmetics executive. Interview (1976)

14 All products must be seen as experiments.
Regis McKenna (b. 1939) US marketing entrepreneur and chairman of The McKenna Group. *Relationship Marketing* (1991)

15 The important product comparisons come from people in the marketplace.
Regis McKenna (b. 1939) US marketing entrepreneur and chairman of The McKenna Group. *The Regis Touch* (1986)

16 Twenty four out of twenty five new products never get out of test markets.
David Ogilvy (1911–99) British advertising executive, founder and chairman of Ogilvy & Mather. *Confessions of an Advertising Man* (1963)

17 The engineers do the marketing in a less quantified and less sophisticated way, but move right into product design.
Kenichi Ohmae (b. 1943) Japanese management consultant and theorist. Quoted in *Thriving on Chaos* (Tom Peters; 1987)

18 There is no reason for any individual to have a computer in their home.
Ken Olsen (b. 1926) US computer designer and founder of Digital Equipment Corporation. 1977. Quoted in *The Experts Speak* (Christopher Cerse and Victor Navasky; 1984)

19 It's not just a concept, but the way that concept is executed that is important.
I.M. Pei (b. 1917) US architect. Interview (1979)

20 Average sales reflect oil prices.
Sayyid Khalid bin Hamad bin Hamoud Al Bu Said (Al Bu Said) (b. 1965) Omani entrepreneur. Referring to production of the world's most expensive perfume. *Forbes* (March 2000)

PROFITS

1 Profit is like health, necessary but not the reason why we live.
Anonymous. Statement by the London-based St Luke's Advertising Agency. *Management Today* (April 1999)

2 Where profit is, loss is hidden nearby.
Anonymous. Japanese proverb.

3 Clearly, we're a not-for-profit company.
Jeff Bezos (b. 1964) US founder and CEO of Amazon.com. Referring to Amazon.com's failure to go into profit. *Sunday Telegraph* (July 2000)

4 Undue profits are not made; there are no esoteric tricks that enable arbitrageurs to outwit the system.
Ivan Boesky (b. 1937) US financier convicted of insider dealing in 1987. *Merger Mania* (1985)

5 Civilisation and profits go hand in hand.
Calvin Coolidge (1872–1933) US president. Speech (November 1920)

6 The blur of business has created a new economic model in which returns increase, rather than diminish.
Stan Davis (b. 1939) US business author. *Blur* (co-written with Christopher Meyer; 1998)

7 The idea of making workers share in profits is a very attractive one…But the practical formula for such sharing has not yet been found.
Henri Fayol (1841–1925) French business executive. *General and Industrial Management* (1916)

8 The idea that commerce and profit may actually be pulling in the same direction is difficult for some people to accept.
Henry Ford (1919–87) US car manufacturer and CEO of Ford Motor Company. Speech (1 July 1969)

9 No good entrepreneur should wish to sacrfice long-term interest for the sake of short-term profits.
Indira Gandhi (1917–84) Indian prime minister. Remark (14 March 1970)

10 You borrow money at a certain rate and invest it at a higher rate and pocket the difference. It's that simple.
Roberto Goizueta (1931–97) US CEO of Coca-Cola. Quoted in *Fortune* (October 1997)

11 Because business equates success or failure with profitability, the superficial conclusion is that profit is the sole objective…the difficult decisions…are those involving the conditions under which profit may be realized.
Crawford H. Greenewalt (d. 1993) US president of DuPont. 'A Philosophy of Business Leadership', *The Conference Board Challenge to Business: Industry Leaders Speak Their Minds* (Peter Krass and Richard E. Cavanagh, eds; 2000)

12 Profit has to be a means to other ends rather than an end in itself.
Charles Handy (b. 1932) British business executive and author. *The Empty Raincoat: Making Sense of the Future* (1994)

13 You've made a mistake. You forgot the little brackets on the bottom line.
Cathy Hughes (b. ?1947) US broadcasting executive. Referring to her company's first year in profit. *Forbes* (September 1999)

14 The bottom line is in heaven.
Edwin Land (1909–91) US inventor and founder of Polaroid Corporation. Shareholder meeting (1977)

15 I just never got involved with the cash flow thing. My attitude was creativity will see me through.
Adrienne Landau (b. 1950) US fashion designer. *Forbes* (October 2000)

16 Company directors always have to prove that things are going better. They are judged like politicians, only worse, because elections are held every three months.
André Leysen (b. 1927) French chairman of Agfa-Gevaert. Quoted in *Euromanagement* (H. Bloom, R. Claori, and P. de Woot; 1998)

17 Short-term can be terminal.
Mark McCormack (1930–2003) US entrepreneur, founder and CEO of the International Management Group. Referring to error of commitment to short-term profitability. *What They Don't Teach You at Harvard Business School* (1984)

18 When a company's profits slip, its position is tarnished. People are reluctant to buy from companies in financial trouble.
Regis McKenna (b. 1939) US marketing entrepreneur and chairman of The McKenna Group. *Relationship Marketing* (1992)

19 We could have shown higher profits, but we've always put our profits back into starting things. We don't get credit for these until they start to turn in a profit.
Rupert Murdoch (b. 1931) US CEO of News Corporation. *Forbes* (June 1998)

20 Overhead is something that creeps in. It's not something that overtakes you overnight.
David Packard (1912–96) US entrepreneur and co-founder of Hewlett-Packard. *The HP Way* (1995)

21 If there is excitement in their lives, it is contained in the figures on the profit and loss sheet. What an indictment.
Anita Roddick (b. 1942) British entrepreneur and founder of The Body Shop. Referring to companies run by accountants. *Body and Soul* (co-written with Russell Miller; 1991)

22 My argument is: keep the bloody bottom line at the bottom. That's where it should be.
Anita Roddick (b. 1942) British entrepreneur and founder of The Body Shop. Quoted in *The Adventure Capitalists* (Jeff Grout and Lynne Curry; 1998)

23 Profits are the lifeblood of the economic system, the magic elixir upon which progress and all good things depend ultimately. But one man's lifeblood is another man's cancer.
Paul Samuelson (b. 1915) US economist and winner of the 1970 Nobel Prize in Economics. Speech, Forum of European and American Economists, Harvard University, Cambridge, Massachusetts, Quoted in *Time* (16 August 1976)

24 No manufacturing company will ever do well if they are concerned only with calculating profits.
Shoichiro Toyoda (b. 1925) Japanese chairman of Toyota Motor Corporation. Quoted in *How to Manage* (Ray Wild; 1995)

25 I've always believed in cash flow rather than stated profits, because when you state profits you've got to pay 50% to the government.
Ted Turner (b. 1938) US founder of Turner Broadcasting Systems. *Broadcasting* (August 1987)

PROGRESS

1 It is not only by the questions we have answered that progress will be measured, but also by those we are still asking.
Freda Adler (b. 1934) US writer, educator, and criminologist. *Sisters in Crime* (1975)

2 Like the agricultural age of the past and our industrial age of the present, an emerging information age is now filled with questions calling for leadership in development.
K.Y. Amoako, Ghanaian economist and executive secretary of the UN Economic Commission for Africa. Speech, Africa Development Forum, Addis Ababa, Ethiopia (25 October 1999)

3 Notions of property, value, ownership, and the nature of wealth itself are changing more fundamentally than at any time since the Sumerians first poked cuneiform into wet clay and called it stored grain...few people are aware of the enormity of this shift and fewer of them are lawyers or public officials.
John Perry Barlow (b. 1947) US academic, lyricist, and writer. Former songwriter for the Grateful Dead, Barlow was the first to use William Gibson's science-fiction term 'cyberspace' to describe the global electronic social space. 'The Economy of Ideas', *Wired* (March 1994)

4 It's the same each time with progress. First they ignore you, then they say you're mad, then dangerous, then there's a pause and you can't find anyone who disagrees with you.
Tony Benn (b. 1925) British politician. Quoted in *Observer* (6 October 1991)

5 Men will not be content to manufacture life; they will want to improve on it.
J.D. Bernal (1901–71) Irish physicist. *The World, the Flesh and the Devil* (1929)

6 We have stopped believing in progress. What progress that is!
Jorge Luis Borges (1899–1986) Argentinian writer. *Borges et Borges* (1969)

7 All progress is based upon a universal innate desire on the part of every organism to live beyond its income.
Samuel Butler (1835–1902) British writer. 'Life', *Notebooks* (H. Festing-Jones, ed.; 1912)

8 As enunciated today 'progress' is simply a comparative of which we have not settled the superlative.
G.K. Chesterton (1874–1936) British novelist, poet, and critic. *Heretics* (1905)

9 pity this busy monster, manunkind,
not. Progress is a comfortable disease.
e.e. cummings (1894–1962) US poet and painter. *1 x 1* (1944), no. 14

10 What we call progress is the exchange of one nuisance for another nuisance.
Havelock Ellis (1859–1939) British psychologist. Attrib.

11 Society never advances. It recedes as fast on one side as it gains on the other. Society acquires new arts, and loses old instincts.
Ralph Waldo Emerson (1803–82) US essayist, lecturer, and poet. 'Self-Reliance', *Essays: First Series* (1841)

12 That is the trouble with prosperity—it hides the defects of a business.
Harvey Firestone (1868–1938) US founder of Firestone Tire and Rubber. *Men and Rubber* (co-written with Samuel Crowther; 1926)

13 Growth is like creativity, it doesn't go along very neat, precise plans. You get clogged highways before you figure out a way to open up capacity. You get pollution before you figure out a way to fight it.
Steve Forbes (b. 1947) US publishing executive. Interview, *Reason Magazine* (May 1991)

14 When you give people new tools, breakthrough communication tools, it has a transformational effect. The last time anything this dramatic happened you'd have to go back to the beginning of the Industrial Age.
Bill Gates (b. 1955) US entrepreneur, chairman and CEO of Microsoft. Speech, Government Leaders Conference, Seattle, Washington (4 April 2000)

15 The world is not changing because computer operators have replaced clerk-typists, but because the human struggle to survive and prosper now depends on an entirely new source of wealth. It is information, knowledge applied to work to create value.
Bill Gates (b. 1955) US entrepreneur, chairman and CEO of Microsoft. Speech, Manhattan Institute, New York City (2 December 1998)

16 The growing technical prowess of nations such as India unnerves some people...who fear a loss of jobs and opportunities. I think these fears are misplaced. Economics is not a zero-sum game.
Bill Gates (b. 1955) US entrepreneur, chairman and CEO of Microsoft. *New York Times Syndicate* (8 April 1997)

17 So long as all the increased wealth which modern progress brings goes but to build up great fortunes, to increase luxury and make sharper the contrast between the House of Have and the House of Want, progress is not real and cannot be permanent.
Henry George (1839–97) US economist. *Progress and Poverty* (1879)

18 'Progress' involves the systematic substitution of the technosphere or manmade world for the biosphere or natural world.
Edward Goldsmith (b. 1928) British ecologist. 'Biospheric Ethics', *The Future of Progress* (Helena Norberg-Hodge, Peter Goering, and Steven Gorelick, eds; 1992)

19 The revolution that has destroyed the traditional corporation began with efforts to improve it.
Michael Hammer (b. 1948) US author and academic. *Beyond Re-engineering* (1996)

20 We were not destined to be empty raincoats, nameless numbers on a payroll...If that is to be its price, economic progress is an empty promise.
Charles Handy (b. 1932) British business executive and author. Quoted in *BusinessWeek* (4 April 1994)

21 If economic progress means that we become anonymous cogs in some great machine, then progress is an empty promise.
Charles Handy (b. 1932) British business executive and author. *The Empty Raincoat: Making Sense of the Future* (1994)

22 One of the remarkable features of the communications revolution is the way in which the tools of that revolution...have empowered small business and dismantled many of the market barriers and the costs involved in world-wide information seeking.
John Winston Howard (b. 1939) Australian prime minister. Speech, Tokyo, Japan (19 September 1996)

23 You have to invest in thinking through the architecture of things.
Steve Jobs (b. 1955) US entrepreneur, co-founder and CEO of Apple Computer Company, and CEO of Pixar. Quoted in 'Steve's Two Jobs', *Time* (Michael Krantz; 18 October 1999)

24 To go fast, row slowly.
Brendan Kennelly (b. 1936) Irish poet and academic. *The Power of Positive Thinking* (1972)

25 Changes are not without cost. It produces reactionaries that fight to block progress. We have found it possible to minimize resistance by establishing a culture based on core values.
Charles G. Koch (b. 1935) US management theorist, author, chairman and CEO of Koch Industries. Speech, Kansas State University (4 March 1996)

26 Progress is mostly the product of rogues.
Tom Peters (b. 1942) US management consultant and author. *Liberation Management* (1992)

27 I think economics is about passion. Economic progress, whether it is a two-person coffee shop or whether it is Netscape, is about people with brave ideas. Because it is brave to mortgage the house when you've got two kids to start a coffee shop.
Tom Peters (b. 1942) US management consultant and author. Interview, *Reason Magazine* (October 1997)

28 How we feel about the evolving future tells us who we are as individuals and as a civilization: Do we search for stasis—a regulated, engineered world? Or do we embrace dynamism—a world of constant creation, discovery, and competition?
Virginia Postrel (b. 1960) US editor and author. *The Future and Its Enemies: The Growing Conflict over Creativity, Enterprise, and Progress* (1998)

29 Tap the energy of the anarchist and he will be the one to push your company ahead.
Anita Roddick (b. 1942) British entrepreneur and founder of The Body Shop. *Body and Soul* (co-written with Russell Miller; 1991)

30 The test of our progress is not whether we add more to the abundance of those who have much; it is whether we provide enough for those who have too little.
Franklin D. Roosevelt (1882–1945) US president. Second presidential inaugural address (20 January 1937)

31 Every advance in civilisation has been denounced as unnatural while it was recent.
Bertrand Russell (1872–1970) British philosopher and writer. 'An Outline of Intellectual Rubbish', *Unpopular Essays* (1950)

32 Progress, far from consisting in change, depends on retentiveness. Those who cannot remember the past are condemned to repeat it.
George Santayana (1863–1952) US philosopher, novelist, and poet. *The Life of Reason* (1905)

33 The reasonable man adapts himself to the world; the unreasonable one persists in trying to adapt the world to himself. Therefore all progress depends on the unreasonable man.
George Bernard Shaw (1856–1950) Irish writer and critic. 'Reason', *Maxims for Revolutionists* (1905)

34 The tendency of mechanical and scientific invention is not so much to diminish employment as to change its character.
Herbert Sidebotham (1872–1940) British journalist and author. 'Like Madam's Hat', *The Sense of Things* (1938)

35 An involuntary return to the point of departure is, without doubt, the most disturbing of all journeys.
Iain Sinclair (b. 1943) British author. 'Riverside Opportunities', *Downriver* (1991)

36 It depends entirely upon the image of you that people have in their minds whether you will climb the ladder slowly, painfully, or with a rapidity that will surprise—and appal—your friends.
Gerald Sparrow (1903–88) British business executive and writer. *How to Become a Millionaire* (1960), ch. 2

37 Progress, therefore, is not an accident but a necessity...a part of nature.
Herbert Spencer (1820–1903) British social theorist. *Social Statics* (1851), pt 1, ch. 2

PUBLICITY

1 A Company for carrying on an undertaking of Great Advantage, but no one to know what it is.
Anonymous. Overconfidence in the company led to the 'South Sea Bubble', a frenzy of speculation that ended in collapse. South Sea Company prospectus (1711)

2 Silence is the virtue of fools.
Francis Bacon (1561–1626) English philosopher and statesman. *De Dignitate et Augmentis Scientiarium* (1640)

3 There's no such thing as bad publicity except your own obituary.
Brendan Behan (1923–64) Irish playwright and author. Quoted in *My Brother Brendan* (Dominic Behan; 1965)

4 The price of justice is eternal publicity.
Arnold Bennett (1867–1931) British novelist, playwright, and essayist. *The Title* (1918)

5 Celebrity gets in the way of a reasonable life.
Tim Berners-Lee (b. 1955) British computer scientist and founder of the World Wide Web. *Fortune* (October 2000)

6 The celebrity is a person who is well-known for his well-knowness.
Daniel J. Boorstin (b. 1914) US Pulitzer-prize-winning historian. *The Image* (1961)

7 PR cannot overcome things that shouldn't have been done.
Harold Burson (b. 1921) US business executive and founder of Burson-Marsteller Public Relations. *USA Today* (7 June 1993)

8 A Parliament speaking through reporters to Buncombe and the 27 millions, mostly fools.
Thomas Carlyle (1795–1881) British historian and essayist. *Latter-day Pamphlets* (1850)

9 Private enterprise has no press agent. Government does.
Milton Friedman (b. 1912) US economist and winner of the 1976 Nobel Prize in Economics. *Economic Myths and Public Opinion* (1976)

10 I'm not a headline kind of guy.
Lou Gehrig (1903–41) US baseball player. Referring to publicity given to other famous sports personalities. Press statement (1925)

11 There's got to be some way of stopping the word of mouth on this picture.
Samuel Goldwyn (1882–1974) US film producer. Quoted in *Which Reminds Me* (Tony Randall and Michael Mindlin; 1990)

12 With publicity comes humiliation.
Tama Janowitz (b. 1957) US author. Quoted in *International Herald Tribune* (8 September 1992)

13 It's always dangerous to give interviews.
Steve Jobs (b. 1955) US entrepreneur, co-founder and CEO of Apple Computer Company, and CEO of Pixar. *Wall Street Journal* (September 1996)

14 What I'm really against is the hype of fashion. I think it's a poison to the business.
Donna Karan (b. 1948) US fashion designer. *Style* (August 2000)

15 I didn't want any attention before I went...I deliberately kept a low profile because then I could quietly go about my business and do what I knew I could do best.
Lorraine Moller (b. 1955) New Zealand athlete. Press conference (1992)

16 Many people expect many things from me. It's a big responsibility. Everyone is looking at me.
Noureddine Morceli (b. 1970) Algerian athlete. Quoted in *Running with the Legends* (Michael Sandrock; 1996)

17 You can't shame or humiliate modern celebrities. What used to be called shame and humiliation is now called publicity.
P.J. O'Rourke (b. 1947) US humorist and journalist. *Give War a Chance* (1992)

18 I must have fame.
Robert Edwin Peary (1856–1920) US Arctic explorer. Letter (1887)

19 I always have a spare pair of pants underneath.
Pele (b. 1940) Brazilian footballer. Referring to fans' habits of ripping off Pele's sports kit for souvenirs. Interview (1968)

20 I'm devastated when I get bad reviews. I taught a lot of that shit but every wound is fatal.
Tom Peters (b. 1942) US management consultant and author. Quoted in *Corporate Man to Corporate Skunk* (Stuart Crainer; 1997)

21 It was a weird experience. The ultimate American experience. From being a black-suited management consultant to having a double page spread in *People*.
Tom Peters (b. 1942) US management consultant and author. Quoted in *Corporate Man to Corporate Skunk* (Stuart Crainer; 1997)

22 The worst tragedy that could have befallen me was my success. I knew right away that I was through, cast out.
Jonas Salk (1914–95) US medical researcher. Referring to other scientists' reactions to publicity surrounding his discovery of a polio vaccine. Interview (1992)

23 This famous store needs no name on the door.
Gordon Selfridge (1858–1947) British retailer. Referring to the fact that Selfridge removed the name from his famous London store in 1925. Quoted in *No Name on the Door* (A.H. Williams; 1957)

24 We must try to find ways to starve the terrorist and the hijacker of the oxygen of publicity on which they depend.

Margaret Thatcher (b. 1925) British former prime minister. Speech (July 1985)

QUALITY

1 More will mean worse.

Kingsley Amis (1922–95) British novelist and poet. *Encounter* (July 1960)

2 Standards are always out of date. That's what makes them standards.

Alan Bennett (b. 1934) British playwright. *Forty Years On* (1969)

3 The funny thing is better TV shows don't cost that much more than lousy TV shows.

Warren Buffett (b. 1930) US entrepreneur and financier. *Channels* (November 1986)

4 Quality has to be caused, not controlled.

Philip B. Crosby (1926–2001) US business executive and author. *Quality Is Free* (1979)

5 Quality Is Free

Philip B. Crosby (1926–2001) US business executive and author. Book title. *Quality Is Free* (1979)

6 People all over the world think that it is the factory worker that causes problems. He is not your problem...He is not allowed to do it because the management wants figures, more products, and never mind the quality.

W. Edwards Deming (1900–93) US consultant and author. Lecture (1983)

7 Don't just make it and try to sell it. But redesign it and then bring the process under control with ever-increasing quality.

W. Edwards Deming (1900–93) US consultant and author. *Out of the Crisis* (1992)

8 Quality is characteristic of a product or service that helps somebody and which has a market.

W. Edwards Deming (1900–93) US consultant and author. *Out of the Crisis* (1992)

9 We have learned to live in a world of mistakes and defective products as if they were necessary to life. It is time a adapt to a new philosophy in America.

W. Edwards Deming (1900–93) US consultant and author. *Out of the Crisis* (1992)

10 Henry Ford made great automobiles, but his Model T was not a quality car.

W. Edwards Deming (1900–93) US consultant and author. *San Jose Mercury News* (April 1987)

11 A little neglect may breed mischief...for want of a nail the shoe was lost.

Benjamin Franklin (1706–90) US politician, inventor, and journalist. The *Poor Richard's Almanack* series (1732–58) was originally published under the pseudonym Richard Saunders. *Poor Richard's Almanack* (1758)

12 The quality of a society will be judged by what the least privileged in it achieves.

Robert Greenleaf (1904–90) US director of Management Research for AT&T and author. 'Old Age: The Ultimate Test of the Spirit', *The Power of Servant Leadership* (Larry Spears, ed.; 1998)

13 Quality is remembered long after the price is forgotten.

Gucci family, Italian. Business slogan.

14 In broad terms, quality planning consists of developing the products and processes required to meet the customer's needs.

Joseph M. Juran (b. 1904) US business thinker. *Planning for Quality* (1988)

15 A road map, an invariable sequence of steps.

Joseph M. Juran (b. 1904) US business thinker. Referring to quality processes. *Planning for Quality* (1988)

16 Quality is not a program that can be simply imposed on an operation; instead it is a way of operating that permeates a business and the thinking of its employees.

Theodore B. Kinni, US business author and editor. *America's Best* (1997)

17 The subtle accumulation of nuances, a hundred things done a little better.

Henry Kissinger (b. 1923) US diplomat. Quoted in *In Search of Excellence* (Tom Peters and Robert H. Waterman; 1982)

18 Pride should consist in doing your job in the best possible manner.

Jawaharlal Nehru (1889–1964) Indian prime minister. Quoted in *Glorious Thoughts of Nehru* (N.B. Sen; 1964)

19 In the industrial age, you competed on price and, at the moment, you compete on quality, but quality is not enough to distinguish you. Quality does not give you an advantage.

Andrew Neil (b. 1949) British publisher and broadcaster. *Marketing* (October 2000)

20 Caring about what you are doing is considered either unimportant or taken for granted.

Robert M. Pirsig (b. 1928) US author. *Zen and the Art of Motorcycle Maintenance* (1974)

21 Quality is a direct experience independent of and prior to intellectual abstraction.

Robert M. Pirsig (b. 1928) US author. *Zen and the Art of Motorcycle Maintenance* (1974)

22 Quality is not a thing. It is an event.

Robert M. Pirsig (b. 1928) US author. *Zen and the Art of Motorcycle Maintenance* (1974)

23 That's the classical mind at work, runs fine inside but looks dingy on the surface.

Robert M. Pirsig (b. 1928) US author. *Zen and the Art of Motorcycle Maintenance* (1974)

24 What the hell is quality? What is it...need we ask anyone to tell us these things?

Robert M. Pirsig (b. 1928) US author. *Zen and the Art of Motorcycle Maintenance* (1974)

25 The voice is so special, you have to guard it with care, to let nothing disturb it.

Leontyne Price (b. 1927) US opera singer. *Opera News* (1985)

26 Quality control was treated as a fad here, but it's been part of the Japanese business philosophy for decades. That's why they laugh at us.

Peter Senge (b. 1947) US academic and author. *The Fifth Discipline: The Art and Practice of the Learning Organization* (1990)

27 People can be trusted so checks can be eliminated.

Marcus Sieff (1913–2001) British president of Marks & Spencer. Marks & Spencer operating principles (1982)

28 Sensible approximation—the price of perfection is prohibitive.

Marcus Sieff (1913–2001) British president of Marks & Spencer. Marks & Spencer operating principles (1982)

29 I and each of my executives make it a hard and fast point to visit a minimum of 40 suppliers a year.

Marcus Sieff (1913–2001) British president of Marks & Spencer. Speech (1982)

30 If we can't find better (tomatoes), we shouldn't be in the business.

Marcus Sieff (1913–2001) British president of Marks & Spencer. *Don't Ask the Price, George* (1987)

REPUTATION

1 Morgan, Morgan, the Great Financial Gorgon!

Anonymous. Referring to US banker J.P. Morgan. Popular song (1900)

2 You know what the difference is between a dead skunk and a dead banker on the road? There's skid marks by the skunk.

Anonymous. Quoted in *Final Harvest: An American Tragedy* (Andrew H. Malcolm; 1986)

3 Doing business with Alan Bond is like wrestling with a pig. You both get sprayed with mud and the pig loves it.

Anonymous. An anonymous Texan banker on Bond's famously aggressive business strategy. *Sunday Times* (12 February 1989)

4 In business a reputation for keeping absolutely to the letter and spirit of an agreement, even when it is unfavorable, is the most precious of assets, although it is not entered on the balance sheet.

Oliver Lyttelton Chandos (1893–1972) British statesman and industrialist. *Memoirs of Lord Chandos: An Unexpected View from the Summit* (1963)

5 I find it rather easy to portray a businessman. Being bland, rather cruel and incompetent comes naturally to me.

John Cleese (b. 1939) British comedian, actor, and writer. Referring to appearing in industrial training videos. *Newsweek* (15 June 1987)

6 When people come to write my obituary, I hope they will recognise that I had a vision of how retailing would change and that it happened as I said it would.

Terence Conran (b. 1931) British business executive, retailer, and founder of Habitat. *Financial Times* (18 February 1989)

7 You can't build a reputation on what you are going to do.

Henry Ford (1863–1947) US industrialist, car manufacturer, and founder of Ford Motor Company. Quoted in *Woodbury Reports Archives* (December 1994)

8 I would most like to be remembered for bringing emphasis to an economic structure in which the characteristic organization is the great corporation rather than the competitive enterprise and of seeing economic life as a bipolar phenomenon.

J.K. Galbraith (b. 1908) US economist and diplomat. Interview, Conversations with History series, Institute of International Studies, University of California, Berkeley. 'Intellectual Journey: Challenging the Conventional Wisdom' (27 March 1986)

9 Everything he says is horse shit and hot air.

Armand Hammer (1898–1990) US industrialist, philanthropist, founder and CEO of Occidental Petroleum. Referring to US financier and corporate raider T. Boone Pickens. *Sunday Times Magazine* (1 December 1985)

10 It is the unpleasant and unacceptable face of capitalism, but one should not suggest that the whole of British industry consists of practices of this kind.

Edward Heath (b. 1916) British prime minister. Referring to Lonrho, which had operated a tax-avoidance scheme involving the payment of directors' fees into foreign bank accounts. Speech, House of Commons (15 May 1973)

11 Your legacy should be that you made it better than it was when you got it.

Lee Iacocca (b. 1924) US president of Ford Motor Company, chairman and CEO of Chrysler Corporation. *Talking Straight* (1988)

12 If a guy is over 25 percent jerk, he's in trouble. And Henry was 95 percent.

Lee Iacocca (b. 1924) US president of Ford Motor Company, chairman and CEO of Chrysler Corporation. Referring to Henry Ford II. Said in a speech to market analysts in Detroit. Quoted in *Time* (1 April 1985)

13 I am just a hoary old bastard who wants to win.

Ian McGregor (1912–98) British chairman of the National Coal Board. *Observer* (11 March 1984)

14 In business we cut each others' throats, but now and then we sit around the same table and behave—for the sake of the ladies.

Aristotle Onassis (1906–75) Greek shipowner and financier. *Sunday Times* (16 March 1969)

15 I consider that I am a revolutionary socialist.

Tiny Rowland (1917–98) British entrepreneur, co-CEO and managing director of Lonrho. Quoted in *My Life with Tiny* (Richard Hall; 1987)

16 Of course being called the acceptable face of capitalism would be equally insulting.

Tiny Rowland (1917–98) British entrepreneur, co-CEO and managing director of Lonrho. May 1973. Responding to Prime Minister Edward Heath's description of Lonrho as the 'unacceptable face of capitalism'. Quoted in *The Risk Takers* (Jeffrey Robinson; 1985)

17 Reputation, reputation, reputation—O, I ha' lost my reputation, I ha' lost the immortal part of myself, and what remains is bestial!

William Shakespeare (1564–1616) English poet and playwright. *Othello* (1602–04), Act 2, Scene 3, ll. 256–258

18 The purest treasure mortal times afford
Is spotless reputation; that away
Men are but gilded loam or painted clay.

William Shakespeare (1564–1616) English poet and playwright. *Richard II* (1595), Act 1, Scene 1, ll. 177–179

19 The world is not unkind, and reprobates are worse than their reputations.

Logan Pearsall Smith (1865–1946) British essayist and critic. *Afterthoughts* (1931)

20 There was worlds of reputation in it, but no money.

Mark Twain (1835–1910) US writer. *A Connecticut Yankee in King Arthur's Court* (1889), ch. 9

21 I'm not retiring because I'm old and tired. I'm retiring because an organization has had 20 years of me. My success will be determined by how well my successor grows it in the next 20 years.

Jack Welch (b. 1935) US former chairman and CEO of General Electric. Referring to his planned retirement on 31 December 2000. Quoted in 'The Ultimate Manager', *Fortune* (22 November 1999)

22 But I'm merely a simple Bedouin.

Ahmed Zaki Yamani (b. 1930) Saudi Arabian politician. Yamani masterminded the OPEC pricing strategy that brought huge returns to producers but ultimately precipitated the oil crisis of the 1970s. Interview, *Newsweek* (20 December 1973)

RESEARCH

1 A consultant is a person who takes your money and annoys your employees while tirelessly searching for the best way to extend the consulting contract.

Scott Adams (b. 1957) US cartoonist and humorist. *The Dilbert Principle* (1996)

2 While I acknowledge that an occasional natural monopoly may arise, and that enormous economies of scale may inevitably reduce rivalry to a few in some markets, I remain skeptical about any general policy of eschewing rivalry in favor of collaborative research and development.

Anne K. Bingaman (b. 1943) US lawyer. Speech, University of Kansas Law School (19 September 1996)

3 The function of the expert is not to be more right than other people, but to be wrong for more sophisticated reasons.

David Butler (b. 1924) British psephologist. Quoted in *Observer* (1969)

4 Market research can be not just misleading, but disastrous for people who work on instinct.

Terence Conran (b. 1931) British business executive, retailer, and founder of Habitat. Quoted in *The Adventure Capitalists* (Jeff Grout and Lynne Curry; 1998)

5 The ultimate goal of all research is not objectivity, but truth.

Helen Deutsch (1884–1982) US psychiatrist. *The Psychology of Women* (1944–45)

6 Facts are the most important thing in business. Study facts and do more than is expected of you.

Frederick Hudson Ecker (1867–1964) US insurance executive and chairman of Metropolitan Life. Quoted in his obituary. *New York Times* (20 March 1964)

7 Like mushrooms, they look enticing, but their nutritional value can be suspect. Some are even poisonous.

Harold S. Geneen (1910–97) US telecommunications entrepreneur and CEO of ITT. Referring to management consultancy concepts. *The Synergy Myth* (co-written with Brent Bowers; 1997)

8 The way to do research is to attack the facts at the point of greatest astonishment.

Celia Green (b. 1935) US psychophysicist. *The Decline and Fall of Science* (1977)

9 My fundamental belief is that if a company wants to see the future, 80 percent of what it is going to have to learn will be from outside its own industry.

Gary Hamel (b. 1954) US academic, business writer, and consultant. Interview, *Strategy + Business* (October–December 1997)

10 Most of the information we use now is obtained free…and there is no way of knowing anymore whether the information on which we base our own information for distribution is true or false. But that doesn't seem to matter; all that matters is that the information comes from a reputable source.

Joseph Heller (1923–99) US novelist. *Something Happened* (1974)

11 People in the Market Research Department…are not expected to change reality but merely to find it if they can and suggest ingenious ways of disguising it…converting whole truths into half truths and half truths into whole ones.

Joseph Heller (1923–99) US novelist. *Something Happened* (1974)

12 Research! A mere excuse for idleness; it has never achieved, and will never achieve any results of the slightest value.

Benjamin Jowett (1817–93) British theologian and scholar. Quoted in *Unforgotten Years* (Logan Pearsall Smith; 1939)

13 I don't like to hire consultants. They're like castrated bulls: all they can do is advise.

Victor Kiam (1926–2001) US CEO of Remington Corporation. *Going for It* (1986)

14 The trouble with research is that it tells you what people were thinking about yesterday, not tomorrow. It's like driving a car using a rearview mirror.

Bernard Loomis (b. 1923) US business executive. *International Herald Tribune* (1985)

15 If politics is the art of the possible, research is surely the art of the soluble. Both are immensely practical-minded affairs.

Peter Medawar (1915–87) British zoologist and immunologist. *New Statesman* (1964)

16 We don't believe in market research for a new product unknown to the public. So we never do any.
Akio Morita (1921–99) Japanese business executive. Referring to his rejection of in-house engineers' concerns regarding lack of research into his idea for the Sony Walkman. *Made in Japan* (1986)

17 As large, high-tech corporations around the world reengineer themselves by downsizing and rightsizing, the first casualty is basic research. And with good reason. The uncertainty, the risk-reward ratio, and the sheer expense come at too high a price for a cost-conscious society, which includes belt-tightening managers and nearsighted shareholders.
Nicholas Negroponte (b. 1943) US academic, co-founder and director of MIT Media Laboratory. 'Where Do New Ideas Come From', *Wired Magazine* (4 January 1996)

18 Many of the essentials of a fertile, creative environment are anathema to an orderly, well-run organization. In fact, the concept of 'managing research' is an oxymoron.
Nicholas Negroponte (b. 1943) US academic, co-founder and director of MIT Media Laboratory. 'Where Do New Ideas Come From', *Wired Magazine* (4 January 1996)

19 Some people use research like a drunkard uses a lamp-post: for support not illumination.
David Ogilvy (1911–99) British advertising executive, founder and chairman of Ogilvy & Mather. Ogilvy's advocacy of the importance of sound research reflected the experience gained during his early career selling George Gallup's innovative sampling techniques to Hollywood studios. Quoted in 'Anatomies of Desire: David Ogilvy', BBC Radio 4 (4 September 2000)

20 Research is always incomplete.
Mark Pattison (1813–84) British author. *Isaac Casaubon* (1875)

21 Scenarios are the most powerful vehicles I know for challenging our mental models about the world and lifting the blinkers that limit our creativity and resourcefulness.
Peter Schwartz, US consultant and author. *The Art of the Long View* (1991)

22 There have always been a considerable number of pathetic people who busy themselves examining the last thousand numbers which have appeared on a roulette wheel, in search of some repeating pattern. Sadly enough, they have usually found it.
Fred Schwed (1901–66) US author. *Where Are the Customers' Yachts?* (1940)

23 They are the people who borrow your watch to tell you what time it is and then walk off with it.
Robert Townsend (b. 1920) US business executive and author. Referring to consultants. *Up the Organization* (1970)

24 We don't spend $20,000 on formal market research to predict a product's success. We use space in our catalog to do the same thing. At the worst, the product bombs...we lose a few thousand dollars.

Lillian Vernon (b. 1927) US entrepreneur and CEO of Lillian Vernon Corporation. Speech. 'The Entrepreneur and the Professional Manager: Getting the Best of Both Worlds' (1998)

RESPONSIBILITY

1 Patriotism is a lively sense of collective responsibility. Nationalism is a silly cock crowing on a dunghill.
Richard Aldington (1892–1962) British poet and novelist. *The Colonel's Daughter* (1931)

2 CORPORATION, n. An ingenious device for obtaining profit without individual responsibility.
Ambrose Bierce (1842—?1914) US journalist and writer. *The Devil's Dictionary* (1911)

3 Perhaps it is better to be irresponsible and right than to be responsible and wrong.
Winston Churchill (1874–1965) British prime minister. Party political broadcast, London (26 August 1950)

4 Each man the architect of his own fate.
Claudius Caecus (*fl.* 300 BC) Roman statesman. Quoted in *De Civitate* (Sallust), sect. 1

5 There is no right to strike against the public safety by anybody, anywhere, any time.
Calvin Coolidge (1872–1933) US president. Telegram (September 1919)

6 I'm not wild about accepting responsibility without authority. Why should my people be?
Bill Creech (b. 1958) US commanding general of US Air Force Tactical Air Command. 'Creech's Laws' (1984)

7 We must earn true respect and equal rights from any men by accepting responsibility.
Amelia Earhart (1898–1937) US aviator. Speech (1935)

8 Responsibility is what awaits outside the Eden of Creativity.
Nadine Gordimer (b. 1923) South African novelist and short-story writer. October 12, 1984. Lecture, University of Michigan, *The Tanner Lectures on Human Values* (Sterling M. McMurrin, ed.; 1985)

9 Whatever you blame, that you have done yourself.
Georg Groddeck (1866–1934) German psychoanalyst. *The Book of the It* (1923), Letter 14

10 It matters not how strait the gate,
How charged with punishments the scroll,
I am the master of my fate:
I am the captain of my soul.

W.E. Henley (1849–1903) British poet and playwright. *Invictus* (1888), st. 4

11 Only aim to do your duty, and mankind will give you credit where you fail.
Thomas Jefferson (1743–1826) US president. *The Rights of British America* (1774)

12 Our privileges can be no greater than our obligations. The protection of our rights can endure no longer than the performance of our responsibilities.

John F. Kennedy (1917–63) US president. Speech (18 May 1963)

13 We are responsible for actions performed in response to circumstances for which we are not responsible.

Allan Massie (b. 1938) British author. 'Etienne', *A Question of Loyalties* (1989), pt 3, ch. 22

14 Accuse not Nature, she hath done her part; Do thou but thine.

John Milton (1608–74) English poet. *Paradise Lost* (1667), bk 8, l. 561

15 We can believe what we choose. We are answerable for what we choose to believe.

John Henry Newman (1801–90) British theologian. Letter to Mrs Froude (27 June 1848)

16 There are plenty of recommendations on how to get out of trouble cheaply and fast. Most of them come down to the same thing. Deny your responsibility.

Nancy Peretsman (b. 1955) US investment banker. Speech (September 1967)

17 You become responsible, forever, for what you have tamed. You are responsible for your rose.

Antoine de Saint-Exupéry (1900–44) French writer and aviator. *The Little Prince* (1943), ch. 21

18 To be a man is...to be responsible. It is to feel shame at the sight of what seems to be unmerited misery. It is to take pride in a victory won by one's comrades.

Antoine de Saint-Exupéry (1900–44) French writer and aviator. *Wind, Sand and Stars* (1939), ch. 2, sect. 2

19 When one does nothing, one believes oneself responsible for everything.

Jean-Paul Sartre (1905–80) French philosopher, playwright, and writer. *The Condemned of Altona* (1959), pt 1

20 Study how a society uses its land, and you can come to pretty reliable conclusions as to what its future will be.

E.F. Schumacher (1911–77) British economist and conservationist. *Small Is Beautiful* (1973)

21 Madness in great ones must not unwatched go.

William Shakespeare (1564–1616) English poet and playwright. Said by Claudius. *Hamlet* (1601), Act 3, Scene 1

22 Men at some time are masters of their fates;
The fault, dear Brutus, is not in our stars,
But in ourselves, that we are underlings.

William Shakespeare (1564–1616) English poet and playwright. *Julius Caesar* (1599), Act 1, Scene 2

23 Liberty means responsibility.

George Bernard Shaw (1856–1950) Irish writer and critic. *Maxims for Revolutionists* (1905)

24 It is impossible to get the measure of what an individual can accomplish unless the responsibility is given him.

Alfred P. Sloan (1875–1966) US president of General Motors. 'Modern Ideas of the Big Business World', *Work* (October 1926)

25 The salvation of mankind lies only in making everything the concern of all.

Aleksander Solzhenitsyn (b. 1918) Russian author and winner of the 1970 Nobel Prize in Literature. Nobel lecture (1970)

26 For Man is man and master of his fate.

Lord Alfred Tennyson (1809–92) British poet. 'The Marriage of Geraint', *Idylls of the King* (1859), l. 355

27 A burden in the bush is worth two on your hands.

James Thurber (1894–1961) US writer and cartoonist. 'The Hunter and the Elephant', *Fables for Our Times* (1943)

28 Human beings were held accountable long before there were corporate bureaucracies. If the knight didn't deliver, the king cut off his head.

Alvin Toffler (b. 1928) US social commentator. 'Breaking with Bureaucracy', *Across the Board* (February 1991)

29 The buck stops here.

Harry S. Truman (1884–1972) US president. Sign on his desk while president. Quoted in *Presidential Anecdotes* (Paul F. Boiler; 1981)

30 I don't know whether you fellows ever had a load of hay fall on you, but when they told me yesterday what had happened, I felt like the moon, the stars, and all the planets had fallen on me.

Harry S. Truman (1884–1972) US president. April 1944. Said on succeeding Franklin D. Roosevelt as president. Attrib.

31 People are responsible for their opinions, but Providence is responsible for their morals.

William Butler Yeats (1865–1939) Irish poet and playwright. Quoted in *Edward Marsh, Patron of the Arts* (Christopher Hassall; 1959), ch. 6

RISK TAKING

1 By definition, risk-takers often fail. So do morons. In practice it's difficult to sort them out.

Scott Adams (b. 1957) US cartoonist and humorist. *The Dilbert Principle* (1996)

2 Comin' in on a wing and a prayer.

Harold Adamson (1906–80) US songwriter. Song title. Referring to the phrase used by a pilot about to crash land, later adopted for general use. 'Comin' in on a wing and a prayer' (1943)

3 Don't subcontract your soul.

Anonymous. Referring to trends in outsourcing in Federal Express. Quoted in *Liberation Management* (Tom Peters; 1992)

4 If a man will begin with certainties, he shall end in doubts; but if he will be content to begin with doubts, he shall end in certainty.

Francis Bacon (1561–1626) English philosopher and statesman. *Advancement of Learning* (1605)

5 We are pioneers and the history of pioneers is not that good.

Jeff Bezos (b. 1964) US founder and CEO of Amazon.com. *Sunday Telegraph* (July 2000)

6 Never is there just one cockroach in the kitchen.

Warren Buffett (b. 1930) US entrepreneur and financier. Annual report (1989)

7 We will continue to ignore political and economic forecasts, which are an expensive distraction for many investors...we have usually made our best purchases when apprehensions about some macro event were at a peak. Fear is the foe of the faddist, but the friend of the fundamentalist.

Warren Buffett (b. 1930) US entrepreneur and financier. Chairman's Letter to Shareholders (7 March 1995)

8 Risk comes from not knowing what you are doing.

Warren Buffett (b. 1930) US entrepreneur and financier. Quoted in *Treasury of Investment Wisdom* (Bernice Cohen; 1999)

9 I guess one was using logic in an area where emotion played the biggest part.

Michael Bungey (b. 1940) British advertising executive. *Sunday Times* (August 2000)

10 Genius has been described as a supreme capacity for taking trouble.

Samuel Butler (1835–1902) British writer. *Notebooks* (H. Festing-Jones, ed.; 1912)

11 Take a chance! All life is a chance. The man who goes the furthest is generally the one who is willing to do and dare.

Dale Carnegie (1888–1955) US consultant and author. Attrib.

12 Regulation is not an easy billet in London because you are riding a tiger, really.

Howard Davies (b. 1951) British chairman of the Financial Services Authority. Referring to proposed changes to the regulation of financial services. *Sunday Times* (July 2000)

13 It's important not to be too emotional. You just go and roll with the punches.

Robert de Castella (b. 1957) Australian athlete and executive director of Focus on You. Press conference (1990)

14 Dealmaking beats working. Dealmaking is exciting and fun, and working is grubby.

Peter F. Drucker (b. 1909) US management consultant and academic. Interview, *Time* (1990)

15 If you are scared to go to the brink you are lost.

John Foster Dulles (1888–1959) US statesman. *Life* (16 January 1956)

16 In skating over thin ice, our safety is in our speed.

Ralph Waldo Emerson (1803–82) US essayist, lecturer, and poet. *The Conduct of Life* (1860)

17 A desperate disease requires a dangerous remedy.

Guy Fawkes (1570–1606) English conspirator. Referring to the attempted destruction of Parliament. Speech (November 1605)

18 The lesson I learnt was not to think small.

Lynn Forrester (b. 1955) US business executive. *Sunday Times* (June 2000)

19 A little blindness is necessary when you undertake risk.

Bill Gates (b. 1955) US entrepreneur, chairman and CEO of Microsoft. Remark (November 1997)

20 There are one hundred men seeking security to one able man who is willing to risk his fortune.

J. Paul Getty (1892–1976) US entrepreneur, oil industry executive, and financier. Quoted in *The Great Getty* (Robert Lenzner; 1985)

21 We became uncompetitive by not being tolerant of mistakes.

Roberto Goizueta (1931–97) US CEO of Coca-Cola. *Fortune* (May 1995)

22 You can try anything as long as it is above the waterline.

Wilbert Lee Gore (d. 1986) US founder of Goretex. Referring to risks that would not affect the integrity of the business. Quoted in *Thriving on Chaos* (Tom Peters; 1987)

23 Markets operate under uncertainty. It is therefore crucial to market performance that participants manage their risks properly...To the extent that policymakers are unable to anticipate or evaluate the types of complex risks that the newer financial technologies are producing, the answer, as it always has been...less debt, more equity, and hence a larger buffer against adversity.

Alan Greenspan (b. 1926) US economist and chairman of US Federal Reserve Board. Speech to the Financial Crisis Conference, Council on Foreign Relations, New York. 'Global Challenges' (12 July 2000)

24 I am a risk taker but only within rules. I just like the support that an organisation gives, combined with the freedom to express myself.

Guy Hands (b. 1959) Zimbabwean CEO of Terra Firma Capital Partners. *Management Today* (October 1999)

25 We sort out all the hygiene factors, get all the control and risks battened down, then look for the sizzle.

Guy Hands (b. 1959) Zimbabwean CEO of Terra Firma Capital Partners. *Management Today* (October 1999)

26 Being in front merely gives one the right to try harder. It means that you are setting the pace which every competitor has to follow.

John Harvey-Jones (b. 1924) British management adviser, author, and former chairman of ICI. *All Together Now* (1994)

27 If we are to be more prosperous we need more millionaires and more bankrupts.

Keith Joseph (1918–94) British politician. Maiden speech to the House of Lords (19 February 1988)

28 Go around asking a lot of damn-fool questions and taking chances.

Alberto Juantorena (b. 1950) Cuban athlete and businessman. Quoted in *American Magazine* (February 1951)

29 There are risks and costs to a program of action. But they are far less than the long-range risks and costs of comfortable inaction.

John F. Kennedy (1917–63) US president. Speech to Americans for Democratic Action (12 May 1961)

30 A lot of people criticize Formula 1 as an unnecessary risk. But what would life be like if we only did what is necessary?

Niki Lauda (b. 1949) Austrian racing driver and founder of Lauda-Air. Quoted in *Treasury of Investment Wisdom* (Bernice Cohen; 1999)

31 The sea does not reward those who are too anxious, too greedy, or too impatient... Patience, patience, patience, is what the sea teaches.

Anne Morrow Lindbergh (1906–2001) US writer. *Gift from the Sea* (1955)

32 Unless you're running scared all the time, you're gone.

Michael C. Lynch (b. 1946) Scottish historian. Quoted in *Playboy* (1994)

33 I have not become the Publisher to stand by and watch MGN commit suicide.

Robert Maxwell (1923–91) British publisher, business executive, and politician. Referring to the threat of print union strikes to viability of MGN (Mirror Group Newspapers). *Daily Mail* (April 1985)

34 We must win respect for daring and courage and have the ability which all good editors must have to make enemies.

Robert Maxwell (1923–91) British publisher, business executive, and politician. *Sunday Citizen* (June 1967)

35 Sometimes you have to pay a high price for an opportunity.

Rupert Murdoch (b. 1931) US CEO of News Corporation. *Forbes* (June 1998)

36 I hope one of you is picking up the cheque because I lost $1.2 billion today.

Rupert Murdoch (b. 1931) US CEO of News Corporation. 1987. Referring to the 1987 stock market crash. Quoted in *Forbes* (June 1998)

37 If I have seen further, it is by standing on the shoulders of giants.

Isaac Newton (1642–1727) English mathematician and physicist. Letter to Robert Hooke (5 February 1675)

38 I pick the jockeys, and the jockeys pick the horses and ride 'em.

H. Ross Perot (b. 1930) US entrepreneur, venture capitalist, and politician. Quoted in *The NeXT Big Thing* (Randall Stross; 1993)

39 You must somehow steer between the Scylla of humility and the Charybdis of foolhardiness.

Stan Rapp, US advertising executive and co-founder of Rapp Collins. *The New Maxi-Marketing* (co-written with Thomas L. Collins; 1995)

40 Risk is what an entrepreneur eats for breakfast. It's what she slips into bed with at night. If you have no appetite for this stuff, or no ability to digest it, then get out of the game right now.

Heather Robertson (b. 1942) Canadian author. *Taking Care of Business* (1997)

41 To be a leader in this new economy, you have to love risk—which means patterning your life on the heroic, not on the strategic. Acting boldly is better than acting knowingly.

Harriet Rubin (b. 1952) US author. 'How Will You Fail?', *Fast Company* (1999)

42 The easy way out usually leads back in.

Peter Senge (b. 1947) US academic and author. *The Fifth Discipline: The Art and Practice of the Learning Organization* (1990)

43 We couldn't afford to miss the computer revolution.

Stan Shih (b. 1945) Taiwanese CEO of the Acer Group. *Forbes* (September 1998)

44 I am cautious about going against the herd. I am liable to be trampled on.

George Soros (b. 1930) US financier, entrepreneur, and philanthropist. Quoted in *Treasury of Investment Wisdom* (Bernice Cohen; 1999)

45 You don't go to a poker table with no money in your pocket.

Barbara Thomas (b. 1947) US banker. *Management Today* (October 1999)

SELLING

1 There's a sucker born every minute.

P.T. Barnum (1810–91) US showman and circus entrepreneur. Attrib.

2 A best-seller is a book which somehow sold well simply because it was selling well.

Daniel J. Boorstin (b. 1914) US Pulitzer-prize-winning historian. *The Image* (1961)

3 In epochs when the cash payment has become the sole nexus of man to man.

Thomas Carlyle (1795–1881) British historian and essayist. *Critical and Miscellaneous Essays* (1838)

4 Rather than comparing war to art, we could more accurately compare it to commerce, which is also a conflict of interests and activities.

Karl von Clausewitz (1780–1831) Prussian general and military strategist. *On War* (1831)

5 Do You Sincerely Want to Be Rich?

Bernard Cornfeld (1927–95) US business executive. Title of book on sales techniques. *Do You Sincerely Want to Be Rich?* (1971)

6 The person who agrees with everything you say either isn't paying attention or else plans to sell you something.

Sam Ewing (1920–2001) US author. Quoted in *Reader's Digest* (1989)

7 Retail has been described as selling things which don't come back to customers who do.

Tom Farmer (b. 1940) British chairman and CEO of Kwik-Fit. Quoted in *How to Manage* (Ray Wild; 1995)

8 If you pump up your salesforce at a meeting and tell them, 'The most important goal is to make customers happy', you can't go back the next day and say, 'Your quota just doubled so go out there and sell twice as much'.

Bill Gates (b. 1955) US entrepreneur, chairman and CEO of Microsoft. Speech (September 1996)

9 We sell sex. It is never going to go out of style.

Bob Guccione (b. 1930) US magazine publisher. *Wall Street Journal* (1996)

10 Inequality of knowledge is the key to a sale.

Deil O. Gustafson (1932–99) US real estate executive. *Newsweek* (1974)

11 Keeping dreams alive and trying to make them come true is crucial in the watch business. We're in the business of selling emotional products.

Nicolas G. Hayek (b. 1928) Swiss entrepreneur and founder of SWATCH. *Sunday Times* (October 2000)

12 When the product is right, you don't have to be a great marketer.

Lee Iacocca (b. 1924) US president of Ford Motor Company, chairman and CEO of Chrysler Corporation. 1991. Quoted in *Wall Street Journal* (1999)

13 Unless you're in the trenches every day, you don't understand what issues are coming up.

Farooq Kathwari (b. 1944) Indian entrepreneur and CEO of Ethan Allen. *Forbes* (April 1998)

14 I just knew, even though I had not yet named the technique, that a gift with a purchase was very appealing.

Estée Lauder (b. 1908) US entrepreneur and cosmetics executive. Referring to the idea of giving a free gift with a purchase. *Estée: A Success Story* (1985)

15 If you don't sell, it's not the product that's wrong, it's you.

Estée Lauder (b. 1908) US entrepreneur and cosmetics executive. 'As Gorgeous As It Gets', *New Yorker* (Kennedy Fraser; 1986)

16 When you stop talking, you've lost your customer. When you turn your back, you've lost her.

Estée Lauder (b. 1908) US entrepreneur and cosmetics executive. 'As Gorgeous As It Gets', *New Yorker* (Kennedy Fraser; 1986)

17 A man's success in business today turns upon his power of getting people to believe he has something that they want.

Gerald Stanley Lee (1862–1944) US academic and writer. *Crowds* (1913)

18 If you don't listen, you don't sell anything.

Caroline Marland (b. 1946) Irish former managing director of Guardian Newspapers. *Management Today* (September 1999)

19 I reckon the most important thing about selling is to give people what they think they want.

Caroline Marland (b. 1946) Irish former managing director of Guardian Newspapers. *Management Today* (September 1999)

20 It is quite true that man lives by bread alone— when there is no bread. But what happens to man's desires when there is plenty of bread and when his belly is chronically filled?

Abraham Maslow (1908–70) US behavioural psychologist. *Motivation and Personality* (1954)

21 Hierarchy of needs.

Abraham Maslow (1908–70) US behavioural psychologist. Referring to Maslow's classification of needs as a basis for selling and motivating. *Motivation and Personality* (1954)

22 Don't sell customers goods they are attracted to. Sell them goods that will benefit them.

Konosuke Matsushita (1894–1989) Japanese electronics executive, entrepreneur, and inventor. *Quest for Prosperity* (1988)

23 A salesman has got to dream, boy, it comes with the territory.

Arthur Miller (b. 1915) US dramatist. *Death of a Salesman* (1949)

24 For a salesman, there is no rock bottom to the life.

Arthur Miller (b. 1915) US dramatist. *Death of a Salesman* (1949)

25 He's a man way out there in the blue, riding on a smile and a shoestring.

Arthur Miller (b. 1915) US dramatist. *Death of a Salesman* (1949)

26 Our sales representatives are like race car drivers. They can't succeed without incredible co-operation from the support team back at HQ.

Doug Nelson (b. 1944) US regional vice-president of Altria Group Inc. (formerly Philip Morris). 'The Mavericks', *Fortune* (June 1995)

27 It's having a relationship with a community whereby you can give them more control over their lives by trading with them.

Anita Roddick (b. 1942) British entrepreneur and founder of The Body Shop. Quoted in *The Adventure Capitalists* (Jeff Grout and Lynne Curry; 1998)

28 Don't ask the price it's a penny.

Marcus Sieff (1913–2001) British president of Marks & Spencer. Referring to the origins of Marks & Spencer, where every product was priced at one penny. *Don't Ask the Price, George* (1987)

29 The propensity to trade, barter and exchange...is common to all men and is to be found in no other race of animals.

Adam Smith (1723–90) British economist and philosopher. *An Inquiry into the Nature and Causes of the Wealth of Nations* (1776)

30 To found a great empire for the sole purpose of raising up a people of customers may at first sight appear a project fit only for a nation of shopkeepers.

Adam Smith (1723–90) British economist and philosopher. *An Inquiry into the Nature and Causes of the Wealth of Nations* (1776)

31 I have heard of a man who had a mind to sell his house, and therefore carried a piece of brick in his pocket, which he showed as a pattern to encourage purchasers.

Jonathan Swift (1667–1745) Irish writer and satirist. *The Drapier's Letters* (1724)

32 You have to love the products if you are going to sell them.

Barbara Thomas (b. 1947) US banker. *Management Today* (October 1999)

33 I didn't realize it then, but everything I ever needed to know about selling I was learning at my kitchen table: I was learning how to identify, find, and keep customers.

Lillian Vernon (b. 1927) US entrepreneur and CEO of Lillian Vernon Corporation. 'Make Someone Happy—Your Customer', *Inc.* (1998)

34 Selling, in short, is the core of any business, no more so than in catalog retailing, where an entrepreneur's relationship is entwined directly with the customer.

Lillian Vernon (b. 1927) US entrepreneur and CEO of Lillian Vernon Corporation. 'Make Someone Happy—Your Customer', *Inc.* (1998)

35 I like to dress egos.

Gianni Versace (1946–97) Italian fashion designer. Quoted in *Guardian* (July 1997)

36 People do not buy much from a man who fails to command their respect.

William Wrigley (1861–1932) US businessman and founder of Wrigley Company. 'The Lowdown on Salesmanship', *American Magazine* (Neil M. Clark; October 1929)

37 Real salesmen stick until the buyer has used up his last 'No'.

William Wrigley (1861–1932) US businessman and founder of Wrigley Company. 'The Lowdown on Salesmanship', *American Magazine* (Neil M. Clark; October 1929)

38 The art of salesmanship can be stated in four words: Believing something and convincing others.

William Wrigley (1861–1932) US businessman and founder of Wrigley Company. 'The Lowdown on Salesmanship', *American Magazine* (Neil M. Clark; October 1929)

SERVICE

1 A man without a smiling face must not open a shop.

Anonymous. Chinese proverb.

2 As soon as I spend time with the people who deliver our service, or the customers, I feel rejuvenated and can come back to anything.

Barbara Cassani (b. 1960) US former CEO of Go. Referring to Go, the budget airline. *Marketing* (August 2000)

3 How can you bring prices down to below people's wildest dreams and surprise them with the service and the way the whole experience feels.

Barbara Cassani (b. 1960) US former CEO of Go. Referring to Go, the budget airline. *Marketing* (August 2000)

4 I like the way we work really hard behind the scenes to make it look easy up front.

Barbara Cassani (b. 1960) US former CEO of Go. Referring to Go, the budget airline. *Marketing* (August 2000)

5 That's what I say about restaurants—the back part is manufacturing, the front part is retailing, the theatre is what holds the whole thing together.

Terence Conran (b. 1931) British business executive, retailer, and founder of Habitat. Quoted in *The Adventure Capitalists* (Jeff Grout and Lynne Curry; 1998)

6 The decision to do that extra bit must be embedded in the company's culture.

Tom Farmer (b. 1940) British chairman and CEO of Kwik-Fit. *Management Today* (July 1999)

7 In the best institutions, promises are kept, no matter what the cost in agony and overtime.

David Ogilvy (1911–99) British advertising executive, founder and chairman of Ogilvy & Mather. *Confessions of an Advertising Man* (1963)

8 Electronic shopping doesn't mean we still won't want to get out of the house on a Saturday afternoon. The digital age may not mean errands but more away-from-home entertainment.

Nancy Peretsman (b. 1955) US investment banker. 'Smarter than Herbert's Dog', *Forbes Global* (Dyan Machan; 1999)

9 I would advise young companies, particularly the small dot.com companies, to pay close attention to their service levels.

Lillian Vernon (b. 1927) US entrepreneur and CEO of Lillian Vernon Corporation. 'Mentor FAQs', *Inc.* (2000)

10 In time, good service became almost a reflex in IBM.

Thomas J. Watson Jr (1914–93) US CEO of IBM. *A Business and Its Beliefs* (1963)

SINCERITY

1 The only work that spiritually purifies us is that which is done without personal motives.

Sri Aurobindo (1872–1950) Indian philosopher, mystic, and nationalist. Quoted in *Ethics in Management: Vedantic Perspectives* (S.K. Chakraborty; 1995)

2 Private sincerity is a public welfare.

Cyrus Augustus Bartol (1813–1900) US clergyman. 'Individualism', *Radical Problems* (1872)

3 Men are always sincere. They change sincerities, that's all.

Tristan Bernard (1866–1947) French novelist and dramatist. *Ce que l'on dit aux Femmes* (1922), Act 3

4 Nobody speaks the truth when there's something they must have.

Elizabeth Bowen (1899–1973) Irish writer. *The House in Paris* (1935)

5 Few people would not be the worse for complete sincerity.

F.H. Bradley (1846–1924) British philosopher. *Collected Essays* (1935)

6 We ought to see far enough into a hypocrite to see even his sincerity.

G.K. Chesterton (1874–1936) British novelist, poet, and critic. *Heretics* (1905)

7 Hold faithfulness and sincerity as first principles.

Confucius (551–479 BC) Chinese philosopher, administrator, and writer. *Analects* (?500 BC)

8 He that trades in jest...will certainly break in earnest.
Daniel Defoe (1660–1731) English novelist and journalist. *The Complete English Tradesman* (1726), vol. 1, letter 5

9 There is no wisdom like frankness.
Benjamin Disraeli (1804–81) British prime minister and novelist. *Sybil* (1845)

10 Managing a business requires a great deal of frankness and openness and you actually lead by being very honest with people.
Michael Owen Edwardes (b. 1930) British company executive. Quoted in 'Sayings of the Week', *Observer* (19 June 1983)

11 Every man alone is sincere.
Ralph Waldo Emerson (1803–82) US essayist, lecturer, and poet. 'Friendship', *Essays, First Series* (1841)

12 Profound sincerity is the only basis of talent as of character.
Ralph Waldo Emerson (1803–82) US essayist, lecturer, and poet. 'Natural History of Intellect', *Essays: First Series* (1841)

13 Sincerity is the highest compliment you can pay.
Ralph Waldo Emerson (1803–82) US essayist, lecturer, and poet. *Journals* (1836)

14 Use no hurtful deceit; think innocently and justly and, if you speak, speak accordingly.
Benjamin Franklin (1706–90) US politician, inventor, and journalist. *Autobiography* (1793)

15 The true hypocrite is the one who ceases to perceive his deception, the one who lies with sincerity.
André Gide (1869–1951) French novelist and essayist. *The Counterfeiters* (1926)

16 The secret of success is sincerity: once you can fake that, you've got it made.
Jean Giraudoux (1882–1944) French diplomat, novelist, and playwright. Quoted in *Murphy's Law, Book Two* (A. Bloch; 1980)

17 Some of the worst men in the world are sincere and the more sincere they are the worse they are.
Lord Hailsham (1907–90) British politician. Quoted in 'Sayings of the Week', *Observer* (7 January 1968)

18 Sincerity has to do with the connexion between our words and thoughts, and not between our beliefs and actions.
William Hazlitt (1778–1830) British essayist and journalist. 'On Cant and Hypocrisy', *London Weekly Review* (6 December 1828)

19 That's what show business is—sincere insincerity.
Benny Hill (1925–92) British comedian. Quoted in 'Sayings of the Week', *Observer* (12 June 1977)

20 Don't be 'consistent', but be simply *true*.
Oliver Wendell Holmes (1809–94) US surgeon, teacher, and writer. *The Professor at the Breakfast-Table* (1860)

21 It is always the best policy to speak the truth, unless of course you are an exceptionally good liar.
Jerome K. Jerome (1859–1927) British humorist and writer. *The Idler* (February 1892)

22 Civility is not a sign of weakness, and sincerity is always subject to proof.
John F. Kennedy (1917–63) US president. Presidential inaugural speech (20 January 1961)

23 Nothing in all the world is more dangerous than sincere ignorance and conscientious stupidity.
Martin Luther King (1929–68) US clergyman and civil rights leader. *Strength to Love* (1963)

24 Sincerity is an opening of the heart, found in very few people. What we usually see is merely a cunning deceit to gain another's confidence.
François La Rochefoucauld (1613–80) French epigrammatist. *Reflections: or, Sentences and Moral Maxims* (1665)

25 Weak people cannot be sincere.
François La Rochefoucauld (1613–80) French epigrammatist. *Reflections: or, Sentences and Moral Maxims* (5th ed.; 1678)

26 No man can produce great things who is not thoroughly sincere in dealing with himself.
James Russell Lowell (1819–91) US poet and diplomat. 'Rousseau and the Sentimentalists', *Among My Books* (1870)

27 The only conclusive evidence of a man's sincerity is that he gave *himself* for a principle.
James Russell Lowell (1819–91) US poet and diplomat. 'Rousseau and the Sentimentalists', *Among My Books* (1870)

28 Sincerity is impossible unless it pervade the whole being, and the pretense of it saps the very foundation of character.
James Russell Lowell (1819–91) US poet and diplomat. 'Pope', *Political Essays* (1888)

29 It's never what you say, but how
You make it sound sincere.
Marya Mannes (1904–90) US essayist and journalist. 'Controverse', *But Will It Sell?* (1955–64)

30 Never esteem anything as of advantage to you that will make you break your word or lose your self-respect.
Marcus Aurelius (121–180) Roman emperor. *Meditations* (2nd century AD), bk 3, sect. 7

31 The great man does not think beforehand of his words that they may be sincere, nor of his actions that they may be resolute—he simply speaks and does what is right.
Mencius (?371–289 BC) Chinese philosopher, reformer, and teacher. *Works* (James Legge, tr.; 1861–86), bk 4, 2:11

32 A man must not always tell all, for that were folly; but what a man says should be what he thinks.
Michel Eyquem de Montaigne (1533–92) French essayist and moralist. *Essays* (1580–88)

33 The great enemy of clear language is insincerity. When there is a gap between one's real and one's declared aims, one turns as it were instinctively to long words and exhausted idioms, like a cuttlefish squirting ink.
George Orwell (1903–50) British novelist, critic, and essayist. 'Politics and the English Language', *Shooting an Elephant* (1950)

34 In their declamations and speeches they made use of words to veil and muffle their design.
Plutarch (746—?120) Greek writer and philosopher. Referring to the Sophists. 'On Hearing', *Morals* (1st century AD)

35 It is undoubtedly true that some people mistake sycophancy for good nature, but it is equally true that many more mistake impertinence for sincerity.
George Dennison Prentice (1802–70) US newspaperman and editor. *Prenticeana* (1860)

36 We find it easy to believe that praise is sincere: why should anyone lie in telling us the truth?
Jean Rostand (1894–1977) French biologist and writer. *De la vanité* (1925)

37 He preferred to be, rather than to seem, virtuous.
Sallust (86—?35 BC) Roman historian and politician. *The Catiline War* (1st century BC), sect. 54

38 The way I see it, it doesn't matter what you believe just so you're sincere.
Charles M. Schulz (1922–2000) US cartoonist. *Go Fly a Kite, Charlie Brown* (1963)

39 Let us say what we feel, and feel what we say; let speech harmonize with life.
Seneca (?4 BC–AD 65) Roman politician, philosopher, and writer. *Letters to Lucilius* (1st century AD)

40 Men should be what they seem;
Or those that be not, would they might seem none!
William Shakespeare (1564–1616) English poet and playwright. *Othello* (1602–04), Act 3, Scene 3

41 It is dangerous to be sincere unless you are also stupid.
George Bernard Shaw (1856–1950) Irish writer and critic. *Man and Superman* (1903)

42 For sincerity is a jewel which is pure and transparent, eternal and inestimable.
Christopher Smart (1722–71) British poet. 1758–63. *Jubilate Agno* (William Force Stead, ed.; 1939)

43 Be suspicious of your sincerity when you are the advocate of that upon which your livelihood depends.
John Lancaster Spalding (1840–1916) US writer and clergyman. *Thoughts and Theories of Life and Education* (1897)

44 One's belief that one is sincere is not so dangerous as one's conviction that one is right. We all feel we are right; but we felt the same twenty years ago and today we know we weren't always right.

Igor Stravinsky (1882–1971) US composer. *Conversations with Igor Stravinsky* (1959)

45 Always be sincere, even if you don't mean it.
Harry S. Truman (1884–1972) US president. Attrib.

46 When in doubt tell the truth.
Mark Twain (1835–1910) US writer. *Following the Equator* (1897)

47 If you tell the truth you don't have to remember anything.
Mark Twain (1835–1910) US writer. *Notebooks* (1935)

48 A little sincerity is a dangerous thing, and a great deal of it is absolutely fatal.
Oscar Wilde (1854–1900) Irish writer and wit. 'The Critic as Artist' (1890)

49 In matters of grave importance, style, not sincerity, is the vital thing.
Oscar Wilde (1854–1900) Irish writer and wit. Said by Gwendolen. *The Importance of Being Earnest* (1895), Act 3

50 Everyone says he's sincere, but everyone isn't sincere. If everyone was sincere who says he's sincere there wouldn't be half so many insincere ones in the world and there would be lots, lots, lots more really sincere ones!
Tennessee Williams (1911–83) US playwright. *Camino Real* (1953), Block 12

51 It is not the crook in modern business that we fear, but the honest man who does not know what he is doing.
Owen D. Young (1874–1962) US lawyer and corporate executive. Attrib.

SPEECHES

1 The best orator is one who can make men see with their ears.
Anonymous. Arab proverb.

2 Listening to a speech by Chamberlain is like paying a visit to Woolworth's: everything in its place and nothing above sixpence.
Aneurin Bevan (1897–1960) British politician. Quoted in *Aneurin Bevan* (Michael Foot; 1962), vol. 1

3 The speeches of one that is desperate, which are as wind.
Bible. Job 6:26

4 I do not object to people looking at their watches when I am speaking. But I strongly object when they start shaking them to make sure they are still going.
William Norman Birkett (1883–1962) British barrister and judge. Quoted in *Observer* (30 October 1960)

5 I take the view...that if you cannot say what you are going to say in twenty minutes you ought to go away and write a book about it.
Lord Brabazon of Tara (1884–1964) British aviator and politician. Quoted in *Hansard* (21 June 1955)

6 An orator is a man who says what he thinks and feels what he says.
William Jennings Bryan (1860–1925) US lawyer and politician. Quoted in *The Peerless Leader* (Paxton Pattison Hibben; 1929)

7 The Orator persuades and carries all with him, he knows not how; the Rhetorician can prove that he ought to have persuaded and carried all with him.
Thomas Carlyle (1795–1881) British historian and essayist. 'Characteristics', *Critical and Miscellaneous Essays* (1839)

8 Pay especial attention to speaking in public.
Andrew Carnegie (1835–1919) US industrialist and philanthropist. Carnegie was himself a consummate orator. Private memo to himself (December 1868)

9 Grasp the subject, the words will follow.
Cato the Elder (234–149 BC) Roman statesman, writer, and orator. Quoted in *Ars Rhetorica* (Caius Julius Victor; 4th century)

10 And adepts in the speaking trade
Keep a cough by them ready made.
Charles Churchill (1731–64) British curate and satirist. *The Ghost* (1763)

11 He is one of those orators of whom it was well said, 'Before they get up, they do not know what they are going to say; when they are speaking, they do not know what they are saying; and when they have sat down, they do not know what they have said'.
Winston Churchill (1874–1965) British prime minister. Referring to Lord Charles Beresford (1846–1919). Quoted in *Hansard* (20 December 1912)

12 Nothing is so unbelievable that oratory cannot make it acceptable.
Cicero (106–43 BC) Roman orator and statesman. *Paradoxa Stoicorum* (?46 BC)

13 Eloquence is the language of nature, and cannot be learned in the schools; but rhetoric is the creature of art, which he who feels least will most excel in.
Charles Caleb Colton (?1780–1832) British clergyman and writer. *Lacon* (1825)

14 If you don't say anything you won't be called on to repeat it.
Calvin Coolidge (1872–1933) US president. Attrib.

15 Prepare your heart and mind before you prepare your speech.
Stephen Covey (b. 1932) US writer and psychologist. *Thirty Methods of Influence* (1991)

16 I will sit down now, but the time will come when you will hear me.
Benjamin Disraeli (1804–81) British prime minister and novelist. Maiden speech, House of Commons (1837)

17 An orator is the worse person to tell a plain fact.
Maria Edgeworth (1767–1849) British writer. *Harrington* (1817)

18 All the great speakers were bad speakers at first.
Ralph Waldo Emerson (1803–82) US essayist, lecturer, and poet. 'Power', *The Conduct of Life* (1860)

19 Public speaking is like the winds of the desert: it blows constantly without doing any good.
King Faisal (1905–75) Saudi Arabian prime minister and monarch. 1945. When, as Saudi Arabian foreign minister and delegate at the inauguration of the UN, he was asked why he was the only one not to have given a speech. Quoted in *Karsh: A 50-year Retrospective* (Yousef Karsh; 1983)

20 Think before you speak is criticism's motto; speak before you think is creation's.
E.M. Forster (1879–1970) British writer. 'Raison d'être of Criticism', *Two Cheers for Democracy* (1951)

21 I absorb the vapour and return it as a flood.
William Ewart Gladstone (1809–98) British prime minister. Referring to public speaking. Quoted in *Some Things That Matter* (Lord Riddell; 1927)

22 I feel like Zsa Zsa Gabor's fifth husband. I know what I'm supposed to do but I don't know if I can make it interesting.
Al Gore (b. 1948) US vice-president. Said on being twenty-third speaker at a political dinner. Quoted in *Today* (1 March 1989)

23 Oratory is dying; a calculating age has stabbed it to the heart with innumerable dagger-thrusts of statistics.
W. Keith Hancock (1898–1988) Australian academic. *Australia* (1930)

24 An orator can hardly get beyond commonplaces: if he does he gets beyond his hearers.
William Hazlitt (1778–1830) British essayist and journalist. *The Plain Speaker* (1826)

25 If no thought
your mind does visit,
make your speech
not too explicit.
Piet Hein (1905–96) Danish poet and scientist. 'The Case for Obscurity', *Crooks* (1966)

26 Speak clearly, if you speak at all;
Carve every word before you let it fall.
Oliver Wendell Holmes (1809–94) US surgeon, teacher, and writer. 'A Rhymed Lesson' (1848)

27 Speeches measured by the hour die within the hour.
Thomas Jefferson (1743–1826) US president. Letter to David Harding (20 April 1824)

28 Oratory is the power of beating down your adversary's arguments, and putting better in their place.
Samuel Johnson (1709–84) British poet, lexicographer, essayist, and critic. 8 May 1781. Quoted in *The Life of Samuel Johnson* (James Boswell; 1791)

29 Talking and eloquence are not the same: to speak, and to speak well, are two things. A fool may talk, but a wise man speaks.
Ben Jonson (1572–1637) English playwright and poet. *Timber, or Discoveries* (1640)

30 Whereas logic is the art of demonstrating truth, eloquence is the gift of winning over people's hearts and minds so that you may inspire them and persuade them in whatever way you choose.
Jean de La Bruyère (1645–96) French essayist and moralist. *Characters or Manners of the Age* (1688)

31 We oftener say things because we can say them well, than because they are sound and reasonable.
Walter Savage Landor (1775–1864) British poet. 'Marcus Tullius and Quintus Cicero', *Imaginary Conversations of Greeks and Romans* (1853)

32 Eloquence lies as much in the tone of the voice, in the eyes, and in the speaker's manner, as in his choice of words.
François La Rochefoucauld (1613–80) French epigrammatist. *Reflections: or, Sentences and Moral Maxims* (1665)

33 The finest eloquence is that which gets things done; the worst is that which delays them.
David Lloyd-George (1863–1945) British prime minister. Speech, Paris Peace Conference (1919)

34 The object of oratory is not truth, but persuasion.
Thomas Babington Macaulay (1800–59) British politician and historian. *The Athenian Orators* (1824)

35 The most popular speaker is the one who sits down before he stands up.
John Pentland Mahaffy (1839–1919) Irish educator and scholar. Quoted in *Mahaffy* (W.B. Stanford and R.B. McDowell; 1971)

36 Everyone may speak truly, but to speak logically, prudently, and adequately is a talent few possess.
Michel Eyquem de Montaigne (1533–92) French essayist and moralist. *Essays* (1580–88)

37 What orators lack in depth, they make up in length.
Charles-Louis de Secondat Montesquieu (1689–1755) French political philosopher. *Persian Letters* (1721)

38 The mark of a true politician is that he is never at a loss for words because he is always half-expecting to make a speech.
Richard Milhous Nixon (1913–94) US president. 'The Campaign of 1960', *Six Crises* (1962)

39 A speech is poetry and cadence, rhythm, imagery, sweep! A speech reminds us that words, like children, have the power to make dance the dullest beanbag of a heart.
Peggy Noonan (b. 1950) US author and presidential speechwriter. *What I Saw at the Revolution* (1990)

40 Oratory is just like prostitution: you must have little tricks.
Vittorio Emanuele Orlando (1860–1952) Italian statesman. Quoted in *Time* (8 December 1952)

41 I never failed to convince an audience that the best thing they could do was to go away.
Thomas Love Peacock (1785–1866) British writer and satirist. *Crotchet Castle* (1831)

42 Where judgment has wit to express it, there's the best orator.
William Penn (1644–1718) English colony builder. *Some Fruits of Solitude* (1693)

43 His speeches are like cypress trees; they are tall and comely, but bear no fruit.
Phocion (?402–318 BC) Athenian general and politician. Quoted in 'Phocion', *Parallel Lives* (Plutarch; 1st century AD)

44 Rhetoric is the art of ruling the minds of men.
Plato (?428–?347 BC) Greek philosopher. Attrib.

45 What is the short meaning of this long speech?
Friedrich Schiller (1759–1805) German dramatist. *The Piccolomini* (1799), Act 1, Scene 2

46 Even the most timid man can deliver a bold speech.
Seneca (?4 BC–AD 65) Roman politician, philosopher, and writer. *Letters to Lucilius* (1st century AD)

47 Brevity is the soul of wit.
William Shakespeare (1564–1616) English poet and playwright. Said by Polonius, who did not follow his own advice. *Hamlet* (1601), Act 2, Scene 2

48 I am no orator, as Brutus is;
But, as you know me all, a plain, blunt man,
That love my friend.
William Shakespeare (1564–1616) English poet and playwright. *Julius Caesar* (1599), Act 3, Scene 2

49 I would be loath to cast away my speech, for besides that it is excellently well penned, I have taken great pains to con it.
William Shakespeare (1564–1616) English poet and playwright. *Twelfth Night* (1601), Act 1, Scene 5

50 It is terrible to speak well and be wrong.
Sophocles (?496–406 BC) Greek tragedian. *Electra* (?430–?415 BC)

51 I fear I cannot make an amusing speech. I have just been reading a book which says that 'all geniuses are devoid of humour'.
Stephen Spender (1909–95) British poet and editor. Speech, Cambridge Union debate (January 1938)

52 The relationship of the toastmaster to the speaker should be the same as that of the fan to the fan dancer. It should call attention to the subject without making any particular effort to cover it.
Adlai E. Stevenson (1900–65) US statesman and author. Quoted in *The Stevenson Wit* (Bill Adler; 1966)

53 In oratory the greatest art is to hide art.
Jonathan Swift (1667–1745) Irish writer and satirist. *A Critical Essay upon the Faculties of the Mind* (1709)

54 One may discover a new side to his most intimate friend when for the first time he hears him speak in public. The longest intimacy could not foretell how he would behave then.
Henry David Thoreau (1817–62) US writer. Entry for 6 February 1841, *Journal* (1906)

55 Well-timed silence hath more eloquence than speech
Martin Farquhar Tupper (1810–89) British writer. *Proverbial Philosophy* (1838–42), 1st series

56 It usually takes me more than three weeks to prepare a good impromptu speech.
Mark Twain (1835–1910) US writer. Attrib.

57 The keenness of his sabre was blunted by the difficulty with which he drew it from the scabbard; I mean, the hesitation and ungracefulness of his delivery took off from the force of his arguments.

Horace Walpole (1717–97) British writer. 1755. Referring to Henry Fox (1705–74). *Memoires of the Last Ten Years of the Reign of George II* (1822)

58 If I am to speak for ten minutes, I need a week for preparation; if fifteen minutes, three days; if half an hour, two days; if an hour, I am ready now.

Woodrow Wilson (1856–1924) US president. Quoted in *The Wilson Era* (Josephus Daniels; 1946)

STATISTICS

1 Thou shalt not sit
With statisticians nor commit
A social science.

W.H. Auden (1907–73) US poet. 'Under Which Lyre' (1946), st. 27

2 Like dreams, statistics are a form of wish fulfilment.

Jean Baudrillard (b. 1929) French philosopher. *Cool Memories* (1987)

3 Statistics are the triumph of the quantitative method and the quantitative method is the victory of sterility and death.

Hilaire Belloc (1870–1953) British writer and politician. *Silence of the Sea* (1941)

4 Employing data bases and statistical skills, academics compute with precision the 'beta' of a stock...then build arcane investment and capital-allocation theories around this calculation. In their hunger for a single statistic to measure risk they forget a fundamental principle: It is better to be approximately right than precisely wrong.

Warren Buffett (b. 1930) US entrepreneur and financier. Chairman's Letter to Shareholders (7 March 1995)

5 The state of statistical control is...the goal of all experimentation.

W. Edwards Deming (1900–93) US consultant and author. Referring to inferences. Quoted in *Statistical Method from the Viewpoint of Quality Control* (W.A. Shewhart; 1939)

6 There are three kinds of lies: lies, damned lies, and statistics.

Benjamin Disraeli (1804–81) British prime minister and novelist. Attrib.

7 Statistical figures referring to economic events are historical data. They tell us what happened in a nonrepeatable case.

Ludwig von Mises (1881–1973) US economist. *Human Action* (1949)

8 The average family exists only on paper and its average budget is a fiction, invented by statisticians for the convenience of statisticians.

Sylvia Porter (1913–91) US journalist and finance expert. *Sylvia Porter's Money Book* (1975)

9 There are two kinds of statistics, the kind you look up and the kind you make up.

Rex Stout (1886–1975) US writer. *Death of a Doxy* (1966)

STRATEGY

1 Reengineering: The principal slogan of the Nineties, used to describe any and all corporate strategies.

Anonymous. *Fortune* (15 February 1995)

2 Vision: Top management's heroic guess about the future, easily printed on mugs, T-shirts, posters, and calendar cards.

Anonymous. *Fortune* (15 February 1995)

3 You shouldn't mix up the long-term business opportunities with the occasional shoot-out. These things will happen.

Percy Barnevik (b. 1941) Swedish former CEO of ABB. *Fortune* (November 1993)

4 You can be very bold as a theoretician. Good theories are like good art. A practitioner has to compromise.

Warren Bennis (b. 1925) US educator and writer. *The Director* (October 1988)

5 Grand business plans are all very well, but nothing beats dipping your toe in the water.

Karan Bilimoria (b. 1962) Indian entrepreneur and founder of Cobra. *Sunday Times* (October 2000)

6 At Berkshire, our carefully-crafted acquisition strategy is simply to wait for the phone to ring. Happily, it sometimes does so, usually because a manager who sold to us earlier has recommended to a friend that he think about following suit.

Warren Buffett (b. 1930) US entrepreneur and financier. Chairman's Letter to Shareholders, *Berkshire Hathaway 1999 Annual Report* (1 March 2000)

7 To keep such adaptability while still keeping the initiative, the best way is to operate along a line which offers alternative objectives.

Karl von Clausewitz (1780–1831) Prussian general and military strategist. *On War* (1831)

8 Swing for hits, not home runs.

Michael Dell (b. 1965) US chairman and CEO of Dell Computer Corporation. *Direct from Dell* (1996)

9 I believe that you have to understand the economics of a business before you have a strategy, and you have to understand your strategy before you have a structure. If you get these in the wrong order, you will probably fail.

Michael Dell (b. 1965) US chairman and CEO of Dell Computer Corporation. Speech to the Society of American Business Editors and Writers Technology Conference, Dallas. 'Maximum Speed: Lessons Learned from Managing Hypergrowth' (10 September 1998)

10 Winning races gives you a great deal of satisfaction from playing a part in the strategy.

Ron Dennis (b. 1949) British entrepreneur and Formula 1 motor racing team owner. Referring to the teamwork in preparation for Formula 1 motor racing. Quoted in *The Adventure Capitalists* (Jeff Grout and Lynne Curry; 1998)

11 Long-range planning does not deal with future decisions. It deals with the future of present decisions.

Peter F. Drucker (b. 1909) US management consultant and academic. *Managing in Turbulent Times* (1980)

12 Our mission tritely is to change the world.

Donna Dubinsky (b. 1955) US IT executive. *Forbes* (October 2000)

13 BA wants to be big in Europe. It is after all our own backyard.

Rod Eddington (b. 1950) Australian business executive and CEO of British Airways. *Marketing* (May 2000)

14 Strategy must attract, win, and retain end-customers and distribution channel members, as well as suppliers or vendors.

Liam Fahey (b. 1951) British writer and consultant. *Competitors* (1999)

15 My aim in management has always been to lay foundations that will make a club successful for years or even decades.

Alex Ferguson (b. 1941) Scottish footballer and manager. *Managing My Life* (1999)

16 We're still trying to put the brakes on a freight train. We've got to stop it before we can turn it round.

William Clay Ford Jr (b. 1957) US business executive. Interview, *Fortune* (November 2002)

17 A large part of my mantra is about getting there before somebody takes it away from you.

Lynn Forrester (b. 1955) US business executive. *Sunday Times* (June 2000)

18 You have to understand what clients are thinking, what the consensus is and when to go against the consensus.

Elaine Garzarelli (b. 1951) US CEO and president of Garzarelli Investment Management. Quoted in *Women of the Street* (Sue Herera; 1997)

19 I haven't spent any time setting goals. I'm spending my time trying to understand our competitive position and how we're serving customers.

Lou Gerstner (b. 1942) US chairman and CEO of IBM. *Fortune* (May 1993)

20 I buy when other people are selling.

J. Paul Getty (1892–1976) US entrepreneur, oil industry executive, and financier. *International Herald Tribune* (1961)

21 The secret isn't counting the beans, it's growing more beans.

Roberto Goizueta (1931–97) US CEO of Coca-Cola. *Fortune* (November 1995)

22 The role of takeovers is to improve unsatisfactory companies and to allow healthy companies to grow strategically by acquisitions.

James Goldsmith (1933–97) British entrepreneur, financier, and politician. Quoted in *International Herald Tribune* (16 November 1989)

23 Columbus didn't have a business plan when he discovered America.

Andrew S. Grove (b. 1936) US entrepreneur, author, and chairman of Intel Corporation. *New Yorker* (April 1994)

24 A question that often comes up at times of strategic transformation is, should you pursue a highly focused approach, betting everything on one strategic goal, or should you hedge?...Mark Twain hit it on the head when he said, 'Put all of your eggs in one basket and WATCH THAT BASKET'.

Andrew S. Grove (b. 1936) US entrepreneur, author, and chairman of Intel Corporation. *Only the Paranoid Survive: How to Exploit the Crisis Points That Challenge Every Company and Career* (1996), ch. 8

25 Without an appropriate vision, a transformation effort can easily dissolve into a list of confusing, incompatible and time-consuming projects that go in the wrong direction or nowhere at all.

Bob Guccione (b. 1930) US magazine publisher. *Leading Change* (1996)

26 Whatever you shoot is dead for a while before it starts to stink. The same goes for strategies. How many organizations carry this dead thing around with them, unaware of its irrelevancy until it is too late?

Gary Hamel (b. 1954) US academic, business writer, and consultant. Lecture, 'Pronking and Surviving in the Age of Gazelles' (26 October 1999)

27 We like to believe we can break strategy down to Five Forces or Seven Ss. But you can't. Strategy is extraordinarily emotional and demanding.

Gary Hamel (b. 1954) US academic, business writer, and consultant. *Competing for the Future* (co-written with C.K. Prahalad; 1994)

28 Creative strategies seldom emerge from the annual planning ritual. The starting point for next year's strategy is almost always this year's strategy...the company sticks to what it knows, even though the real opportunities may be elsewhere.

Gary Hamel (b. 1954) US academic, business writer, and consultant. 'Strategic Intent', *Harvard Business Review* (co-written with C.K. Prahalad; May–June 1989)

29 Brains are becoming the core of organisations—other activities can be contracted out.

Charles Handy (b. 1932) British business executive and author. Interview (February 1994)

30 Observe due measure, for right timing is in all things the most important factor.

Hesiod (*fl.* 800 BC) Greek poet. *Works and Days* (8th century BC)

31 Are we going to be a services power? The double cheeseburger or the mayo kings of the world.

Lee Iacocca (b. 1924) US president of Ford Motor Company, chairman and CEO of Chrysler Corporation. *Fortune* (July 1986)

32 To stay ahead, you must have your next idea waiting in the wings.

Rosabeth Moss Kanter (b. 1943) US management theorist, academic, and writer. *Men and Women of the Corporation* (1977)

33 The balanced scorecard is not a way of formalising strategy. It's a way of understanding and checking what you have to do throughout the organisation to make your strategy work.

Robert Kaplan (b. 1940) US accounting educator. The 'balanced scorecard', created by Robert Kaplan and David Norton, is a means of measuring performance in key areas. *Financial Times* (April 1997)

34 There is only one winning strategy. It is to carefully define the target market and direct a superior offering to that target market.

Philip Kotler (b. 1931) US marketing management thinker. Interview, *The Events & Awards Managers of Asia and Hamlin-Iturralde Corporation* (1999)

35 What business are we in?

Theodore Levitt (b. 1925) US management theorist, writer, and editor. Referring to the short-sighted view of US companies. 'Marketing Myopia', *Harvard Business Review* (September–October 1975)

36 Differentiation is a distancing designed to reduce the price sensitivity of the offering.

Shiv S. Mathur (b. 1927) British writer. *Creating Value* (co-written with Alfred Kenyon; 1997)

37 The task of business strategy is to make the business more valuable by a specific route: that of targeting profitable customers.

Shiv S. Mathur (b. 1927) British writer. *Creating Value* (co-written with Alfred Kenyon; 1997)

38 If the system does the thinking, the thought must be detached from the action, strategy from operations and ostensible thinkers from doers.

Henry Mintzberg (b. 1939) Canadian academic and management theorist. *The Rise and Fall of Strategic Planning* (1994)

39 Mould-breaking strategies grow initially like weeds, they are not cultivated like tomatoes in a hothouse.

Henry Mintzberg (b. 1939) Canadian academic and management theorist. *The Rise and Fall of Strategic Planning* (1994)

40 Strategy is not the consequence of planning but the opposite, its starting point.

Henry Mintzberg (b. 1939) Canadian academic and management theorist. *The Rise and Fall of Strategic Planning* (1994)

41 Strategy making is an immensely complex process involving the most sophisticated, subtle, and at times subconscious of human cognitive and social processes.

Henry Mintzberg (b. 1939) Canadian academic and management theorist. *The Rise and Fall of Strategic Planning* (1994)

42 Be nice to people on your way up because you'll meet 'em on your way down.

Wilson Mizner (1876–1933) US hotelier, screenwriter, and

wit. Quoted in *The Legendary Mizners* (Alva Johnston; 1953)

43 It's much overstated that there has been some grand world plan for News Corporation. We have really been much more opportunistic than that.

Elisabeth Murdoch (b. 1968) Australian film and television executive. Referring to the management style of her father, Rupert Murdoch. *Forbes* (July 1998)

44 In business as on the battlefield, the object of strategy is to bring about the condition most favorable to one's own side.

Kenichi Ohmae (b. 1943) Japanese management consultant and theorist. *The Mind of the Strategist* (1982)

45 The strategist's method is very simply to challenge the prevailing assumptions with a single question: Why?

Kenichi Ohmae (b. 1943) Japanese management consultant and theorist. *The Mind of the Strategist* (1982)

46 The essence of strategy is not the structure of a company's products and markets, but the dynamics of its behaviour.

Tom Peters (b. 1942) US management consultant and author. *Liberation Management* (1992)

47 Competitive strategy is about being different. It means deliberately choosing a different set of activities to deliver a unique mix of values.

Michael Porter (b. 1947) US strategist. *Harvard Business Review* (November–December 1996)

48 The most successful computer companies will be those that buy computers rather than build them. The strategic goal should be to create persistent value in computing from software.

Andy Rappaport, US start-up expert and consultant. 'The Computerless Computer Company', *Harvard Business Review* (co-written with Shmuel Halevi; July/August 1991)

49 We try to picture what the products will be and then say, what technology should we be working on today to help us get there?

John Sculley (b. 1939) US partner of Sculley Brothers, former president of Pepsi, and CEO of Apple Computers. *Inc.* magazine (1988)

50 The prevailing wisdom is that markets are always right. I take the opposite position. I assume that markets are always wrong.

George Soros (b. 1930) US financier, entrepreneur, and philanthropist. *Soros on Soros* (1995)

51 Successful companies move quickly in and out of products, markets, and sometimes even entire businesses.

George Stalk (b. 1951) US author. 'Competing on Capabilities', *Harvard Business Review* (co-written with Philip Eras and Lawrence Shulman; March/April 1992)

52 The essence of a strategy is not the structure of a company's products and markets, but the dynamics of its behaviour.

George Stalk (b. 1951) US author. 'Competing on Capabilities', *Harvard Business Review* (co-written with Philip Eras and Lawrence Shulman; March/April 1992)

53 Starting companies is very hard and time-consuming. You want to keep those to a minimum.
Jay S. Walker, US entrepreneur and founder of Priceline.com, CEO of Walker Digital Corporation. Quoted in 'Idea Man', *The Standard* (Todd Woody; 1999)

54 Strategies that succeed are organic. They evolve. They wrap themselves around problems, challenges, and opportunities, make progress and move on.
Robert H. Waterman Jr (b. 1936) US consultant and author. *The Frontiers of Excellence* (1994)

55 By a progressive, I do not mean a man who is ready to move, but a man who knows where he is going when he moves.
Woodrow Wilson (1856–1924) US president. Speech (1919)

56 Our business is company creation.
Ann Winblad (b. 1953) US venture capitalist. 'The 50 Most Powerful Women in American Business', *Fortune* (Patricia Sellers and Cora Daniels; October 1999)

STRESS

1 At a certain speed, the speed of light, you lose even your shadow. At a certain speed, the speed of information, things lose their sense.
Jean Baudrillard (b. 1929) French philosopher. 'The Gulf War Did Not Take Place', *The Gulf War Did Not Take Place* (1995)

2 One is more likely...to perceive a situation of overload when one has many things demanded...than when fewer things are demanded.
Rabi S. Bhagat (b. 1950) Indian business author. *Human Stress and Cognition in Organisations* (co-edited and co-written with Terry A. Beehr; 1985), Introduction

3 People can place demands upon themselves that create uncertainty.
Rabi S. Bhagat (b. 1950) Indian business author. *Human Stress and Cognition in Organisations* (co-edited and co-written with Terry A. Beehr; 1985), Introduction

4 If you want to avoid worry, do what Sir William Osler did: Live in 'day-tight compartments'. Don't stew about the futures. Just live each day until bedtime.
Dale Carnegie (1888–1955) US consultant and author. *How to Stop Worrying and Start Living* (1948)

5 Brain cells create ideas. Stress kills brain cells. Stress is not a good idea.
Doug Hall (b. 1959) US business writer. *Jump Start Your Brain* (1996)

6 I try to only worry about things I have control over.
Steve Nash (b. 1974) Canadian basketball player who plays in the United States. 'Stevie Wonder', *FastBreak Magazine* (Brian Bujdos; April 1998)

7 What the banker sighs for, the meanest clown may have—leisure and a quiet mind.
Henry David Thoreau (1817–62) US writer. Entry for 18 January 1841, *Journal* (1906)

8 The trouble with being in the rat race is that even if you win, you're still a rat.
Lily Tomlin (b. 1939) US comedian and actor. Quoted in *Slowing Down in a Speeded Up World* (Adair Lara; 1994)

SUCCESS

1 I've had enough success for two lifetimes. My success is talent put together with hard work and luck.
Kareem Abdul-Jabbar (b. 1947) US basketball player. *Star* (1986)

2 Tis not in mortals to command success But we'll do more, Sempronius, we'll deserve it.
Joseph Addison (1672–1719) English statesman and author. *Cato* (1713)

3 Eighty percent of success is showing up.
Woody Allen (b. 1935) US actor, humorist, producer, and director. Quoted in *In Search of Excellence* (Thomas J. Peters and Robert H. Waterman; 1982)

4 Making a success of the job at hand is the best step toward the kind you want.
Bernard Baruch (1870–1965) US financier and economist. *Arizona Republic* (2000)

5 There are two golden rules for an orchestra: start together and finish together. The public doesn't give a damn what happens in between.
Thomas Beecham (1879–1961) British conductor. Quoted in *Beecham Stories* (H.J. Atkins and A. Newman; 1978)

6 The test of a first-rate work, and a test of your sincerity in calling it a first-rate work, is that you finish it.
Arnold Bennett (1867–1931) British novelist, playwright, and essayist. *Things That Have Interested Me* (1921–25)

7 The toughest thing about success is that you've got to keep on being a success.
Irving Berlin (1888–1989) US composer and songwriter. Quoted in *Theater Arts* (1958)

8 Only positive consequences encourage good future performance.
Kenneth Blanchard (b. 1939) US management theorist and author. *Putting the One Minute Manager to Work* (1992)

9 There aren't a lot of us, so there are no cubby holes.
Bruce R. Bond (b. 1946) US CEO of ANS Communications. Referring to achievements of African Americans in business. 'The Players', *Fortune* (Eileen Gunn; April 1997)

10 The conduct of a losing party never appears right: at least it never can possess the only infallible criterion of wisdom to vulgar judgements—success.
Edmund Burke (1729–97) British philosopher and politician. Letter to a member of the National Assembly (1791)

11 The certainty of success in many destroys, in all weakens, its charm: the bashful excepted, to whom it gives courage; and the indolent, to whom it saves trouble.
Fanny Burney (1752–1840) British writer. *Cecilia* (1782)

12 If you want to succeed, double your failure rate.
Samuel Butler (1835–1902) British writer. *Men-Minutes-Money* (1934)

13 The process of succeeding can be seen as a series of trials in which your vision constantly guides you toward your target while in your actual performance you are regularly slightly off target. Success in any area requires constantly readjusting.
Tony Buzan (b. 1942) US author. *Lessons from the Art of Juggling: How to Achieve Your Full Potential in Business, Learning, and Life* (co-written with Michael J. Gelb; 1997)

14 It takes years to make an overnight success.
Eddie Cantor (1892–1964) US entertainer. Quoted in *Treasury of Investment Wisdom* (Bernice Cohen; 1999)

15 A man may be concerned in the management of more than one business enterprise, but they should all be of the one kind, which he understands. The great successes of life are made by concentration.
Andrew Carnegie (1835–1919) US industrialist and philanthropist. 'From Oakland: How to Succeed in Life', *The Pittsburgh Bulletin* (19 December 1903)

16 What is the philosophical foundation of the enterprise? That the most competent, the most able, the most audacious will triumph.
Fidel Castro (b. 1927) Cuban president. Interview, *Playboy* (Lee Lockwood; January 1967)

17 Good business practices can ultimately weaken a great firm.
Clayton M. Christensen (b. 1952) US writer. Referring to over-dependence on established products at the expense of innovation. *The Innovator's Dilemma* (1997)

18 The great north-east migration.
Clayton M. Christensen (b. 1952) US writer. Referring to the shape of a graph line for an innovative company. *The Innovator's Dilemma* (1997)

19 The man of virtue makes the difficulty to be overcome his first business, and success only a subsequent consideration.
Confucius (551–479 BC) Chinese philosopher, administrator, and writer. *Analects* (?500 BC)

20 The more volatile the market, the quicker an organization's success formula becomes obsolete.
Daryl R. Conner (b. 1946) US management author. *Leading at the Edge of Chaos* (1998)

21 Whom the gods wish to destroy they first call promising.
Cyril Connolly (1903–74) British critic, essayist, and novelist. *Enemies of Promise* (1938)

22 When you struggle hard and lose money, you're a hero. When you start making money you become a capitalist swine.
Terence Conran (b. 1931) British business executive, retailer, and founder of Habitat. Quoted in *The Risk Takers* (Jeffrey Robinson; 1985)

23 No one has all the answers to success.
Jack Daniels (b. 1933) US athletics coach. *Daniels' Running Formula* (1998)

24 I am doomed to an eternity of compulsive work. No set goal achieved satisfies. Success only breeds a new goal. The golden apple devoured has seeds. It is endless.
Bette Davis (1908–89) US actor. *The Lonely Life* (1962)

25 To be successful you have to be lucky, or a little mad, or very talented, or to find yourself in a rapid-growth field.
Edward de Bono (b. 1933) British creative-thinking theorist, educator, and writer. *Tactics: The Art and Science of Success* (1984)

26 You can only raise individual performance by elevating that of the entire system.
W. Edwards Deming (1900–93) US consultant and author. Quoted in *In Search of European Excellence* (Robert Heller; 1997)

27 The secret of success is constancy to purpose.
Benjamin Disraeli (1804–81) British prime minister and novelist. Speech, House of Commons (June 24, 1870)

28 No other area offers richer opportunities for successful innovation than the unexpected success.
Peter F. Drucker (b. 1909) US management consultant and academic. *Innovation and Entrepreneurship* (1993)

29 If you look after the customers and look after the people who look after the customers, you should be successful.
Charles Dunstone (b. 1964) British business executive and founder of Carphone Warehouse. *Sunday Times* (June 2000)

30 She knows there's no success like failure and that failure's no success at all.
Bob Dylan (b. 1941) US singer. Song lyric. 'Love Minus Zero, No Limits' (1965)

31 Success is made of 99 percent failure.
James Dyson (b. 1947) British entrepreneur. *Management Today* (July 1999)

32 In Latin countries, in Catholic countries, a successful person is a sinner.
Umberto Eco (b. 1932) Italian novelist and semiotician. *International Herald Tribune* (14 December 1988)

33 The real measure of success is the number of experiments that can be crowded into 24 hours.
Thomas Edison (1847–1931) US inventor. Quoted in 'Building an Innovation Factory', *Harvard Business Review* (Andrew Hargadon and Robert I. Sutton; 2000)

34 The sums are so large I can't regard them with any more seriousness than the person who fills in the pools coupon and sticks it in the post.
Noel Edmonds (b. 1948) British broadcaster and media executive. From 1986. Referring to the possibility of a lucrative US TV contract. Quoted in *Noel Edmonds* (Alison Bowyer; 1999)

35 The secret of the truly successful...is that they learned early in life how *not* to be busy.
Barbara Ehrenreich (b. 1941) US writer, sociologist, and feminist. 1985. 'The Cult of Busyness', *The Worst Years of Our Lives* (1991)

36 If A is a success in life, then A equals x plus y plus z. Work is x; y is play; and z is keeping your mouth shut.

Albert Einstein (1879–1955) US physicist. Quoted in *Observer* (15 January 1950)

37 Success is relative: It is what we can make of the mess we have made of things.

T.S. Eliot (1888–1965) British poet, dramatist, and critic. *The Family Reunion* (1939)

38 The most important attribute of successful people is not that they always succeed, but that they respond to failure by coming back and redoubling their efforts.

Mary Farrell (b. 1956) US managing director of PaineWebber. Quoted in *Women of the Street* (Sue Herera; 1997)

39 In order to win at some of the big ones, you will always lose at others along the way.

Ranulph Fiennes (b. 1944) British explorer. *Observer* (October 2000)

40 There is no glass ceiling. My gender is interesting, but it is not the story here.

Carly Fiorina (b. 1954) US president and CEO of Hewlett-Packard. 'The Century's Business, Career, and Money Sheroes', *Society and Politics* (2000)

41 A big man has no time really to do anything but just sit and be big.

F. Scott Fitzgerald (1896–1940) US writer. *This Side of Paradise* (1920)

42 Our outlook is narrowed, our activity is restricted, our chances of business success largely diminished when our thinking is constrained within the limits of what has been called an either-or situation.

Mary Parker Follett (1868–1933) US management thinker and author. *Dynamic Administration* (1941)

43 Those who invest only to get rich will fail. Those who invest to help others will probably succeed.

Art Fry, US entrepreneur and inventor of Post-it notes. Interview, *The Empty Raincoat: Making Sense of the Future* (Charles Handy; 1994)

44 Without vassal loyalty, or abject vassal fear, the monopolist's sleep can never be secure.

Joseph Furphy (1843–1912) Australian journalist, novelist, and poet. *Such Is Life* (1903)

45 Just fragmenting an organization does not create conditions sufficient for success.

Lou Gerstner (b. 1942) US chairman and CEO of IBM. *Fortune* (May 1993)

46 The truly successful businessman is essentially a dissenter, a rebel who is seldom if ever satisfied with the status quo.

J. Paul Getty (1892–1976) US entrepreneur, oil industry executive, and financier. *How to Be Rich* (1965)

47 If you can actually count your money then you are not a really rich man.

J. Paul Getty (1892–1976) US entrepreneur, oil industry executive, and financier. Quoted in *The Pendulum Years* (Bernard Levin; 1970)

48 I have worked without thinking of myself. This is the largest factor in whatever success I have attained.

Amadeo Giannini (1870–1949) US banker and founder of Bank of America. Quoted in 'America's Banker', *Time 100: Heroes and Inspirations* (December 1999)

49 For a writer, success is always temporary, success is only a delayed failure. And it is incomplete.

Graham Greene (1904–91) British novelist. *A Sort of Life* (1971)

50 I believe in the value of paranoia. Business success contains the seeds of its own destruction. The more successful you are, the more people want a chunk of your business and then another chunk and then another until there is nothing left.

Andrew S. Grove (b. 1936) US entrepreneur, author, and chairman of Intel Corporation. *Only the Paranoid Survive: How to Exploit the Crisis Points That Challenge Every Company and Career* (1996), Preface

51 I think making a name for yourself is a wrong objective...I would prefer to look for ways where you can make maximum contribution, and that depends on two things: clearly what your skills are and, less clearly, what the activities that you truly enjoy are. By choosing occupations that you can get excited about you are likely to do your best work.

Andrew S. Grove (b. 1936) US entrepreneur, author, and chairman of Intel Corporation. Interview, *WebChat Broadcasting System* (7 October 1996)

52 No one is ever in doubt when a business is in overdrive...the whole business begins to hum. Problems cease to be problems and are viewed as opportunities.

John Harvey-Jones (b. 1924) British management adviser, author, and former chairman of ICI. *All Together Now* (1994), ch. 2

53 If you do anything just for the money you don't succeed.

Barry Hearn (b. 1948) British sports promoter. *Sunday Telegraph* (10 April 1988)

54 Success is power; because it maketh reputation of wisdom, or good fortune; which makes men either fear him or rely on him.

Thomas Hobbes (1588–1679) English philosopher and political theorist. *Leviathan: or, The Matter, Form, and Power of a Commonwealth Ecclesiastical and Civil* (1651)

55 Never fear the want of business. A man who qualifies himself well for his calling, never fails of employment.

Thomas Jefferson (1743–1826) US president. Letter to Peter Carr (22 June 1792)

56 My luxury is to work, not spend money.

Mehmet Kanbur (b. 1948) Turkish entrepreneur. *Forbes* (October 1999)

57 Paul Keating: 'This is the great coming of age of Australia. This is the golden age of economic change'. Interviewer: 'How much credit do you take?' Paul Keating: 'Oh, a very large part'.

Paul Keating (b. 1944) Australian former prime minister. Interview on Channel 9, Australian TV (18 September 1987)

58 To succeed, you have to have confidence in yourself and your product. You have to love what you're doing, and you have to care about your customers.
Mary Kelekis (b. 1925) Canadian restaurant owner. Quoted in *Relishing Taste and Tradition* (Helen Stein; 1997)

59 You gotta think; you gotta work; you gotta know what's going on. You have to go forward.
Mary Kelekis (b. 1925) Canadian restaurant owner. Quoted in *Relishing Taste and Tradition* (Helen Stein; 1997)

60 The shortest and the best way to make your fortune is to let people see clearly that it is in their interests to promote yours.
Jean de La Bruyère (1645–96) French essayist and moralist. 'Of the Gifts of Fortune', *Characters or Manners of the Age* (1688)

61 I think we've blown up everything we can blow up.
Sherry Lansing (b. 1944) US chairman of Paramount Motion Picture Group. Referring to the failure of high-budget action films. *New York Times* (1997)

62 Observing your own and your competitor's successes and failures makes your inner business voice more sure and vivid.
Estée Lauder (b. 1908) US entrepreneur and cosmetics executive. *Estée: A Success Story* (1985)

63 The conduct of successful business merely consists in doings things in a very simple way, doing them regularly, and never neglecting to do them.
Lord Leverhulme (1851–1925) British entrepreneur, philanthropist, and co-founder of Unilever. Speech, Liverpool University (1922)

64 It's a little bit like the landed gentry—you may be sitting on a couple of hundred extremely valuable acres and, on paper, you are worth x amount of money, but you can't spend it.
Wayne Lockner (b. 1958) British Internet entrepreneur. *Sunday Times* (May 2000)

65 To me it is just a relative statement of where I am compared to my peers in business.
Wayne Lockner (b. 1958) British Internet entrepreneur. Referring to the paper value of Internet millionaires. *Sunday Times* (May 2000)

66 By always being optimistic, by having self-confidence...you will *succeed*.
Orison Swett Marden (1848–1924) US author. *The Young Man Entering Business* (1903)

67 Brits seem to envy people who are successful, somehow they feel that they did it underhandedly, that it's not quite right or that they must have got a pot of money from somewhere. Instead of envying they should be saying well done.
Isabel Maxwell (b. 1950) British president of CommTouch. *Guardian* (22 July 2000)

68 I suffer no slings and arrows. I just sail on. That's the secret of success in life.

Robert Maxwell (1923–91) British publisher, business executive, and politician. *Observer* (24 June 1990)

69 When you own one million shares of stock, you don't have to picket.
Carl McCall (b. 1935) US former Comptroller of New York State. Referring to the achievements of African Americans in business. 'The Players', *Fortune* (Eileen Gunn; April 1997)

70 Perhaps the fundamental principle for success in the digital age is to think network.
Gerry McGovern (b. 1962) Irish consultant and author. *The Caring Economy* (1999)

71 For a long time, people kept saying MTV wouldn't last, but it has and it is always changing.
Judy McGrath (b. 1952) US president of MTV. 'The 50 Most Powerful Women in American Business', *Fortune* (Patricia Sellers and Cora Daniels; October 1999)

72 How to Succeed in Business without Really Trying
Shepherd Mead (b. 1914) US advertising executive and writer. Book title. *How to Succeed in Business without Really Trying* (1952)

73 A restaurant is great if there are people queuing to get into it. It doesn't matter what the critics say.
David Michels (b. 1946) British CEO of Hilton Hotels. *Sunday Times* (September 2000)

74 My dad...always encouraged me to develop my mind. 'With a trained mind you can do anything'...He told me to challenge the world and take advantage of it.
Bernadette Murphy (b. 1934) US chief technical analyst of Kimelman & Baird LLC. Quoted in *Women of the Street* (Sue Herera; 1997)

75 The bottom line that determines success for either a man or a woman is: 'Can you make money?' That, in essence makes gender less relevant.
Bernadette Murphy (b. 1934) US chief technical analyst of Kimelman & Baird LLC. Quoted in *Women of the Street* (Sue Herera; 1997)

76 To be successful you definitely have to stand out, no matter who you are. You have to make a noticeable difference.
Bernadette Murphy (b. 1934) US chief technical analyst of Kimelman & Baird LLC. Quoted in *Women of the Street* (Sue Herera; 1997)

77 I've always realised that if I'm doing well at business I'm cutting some other bastard's throat.
Kerry Packer (b. 1937) Australian entrepreneur and chairman of Consolidated Press Holdings. *Daily Mail* (1 November 1988)

78 A major reason for the superiority of the Japanese is their managerial skill.
Richard Pascale (b. 1938) US academic and author. *The Art of Japanese Management* (co-written with Anthony Athos; 1981)

79 To burn always with this hard, gem-like flame, to maintain this ecstasy, is success in life.
Walter Pater (1839–94) British author and critic. *Studies in the History of the Renaissance* (1873)

80 Fortune knocks once, but misfortune has much more patience.

Laurence J. Peter (1919–90) Canadian academic and writer. *The Peter Principle: Why Things Always Go Wrong* (co-written with Raymond Hull; 1969)

81 If at first you don't succeed, you may be at your level of incompetence.

Laurence J. Peter (1919–90) Canadian academic and writer. *The Peter Principle: Why Things Always Go Wrong* (co-written with Raymond Hull; 1969)

82 Success is the final place at the level of incompetence.

Laurence J. Peter (1919–90) Canadian academic and writer. *The Peter Principle: Why Things Always Go Wrong* (co-written with Raymond Hull; 1969)

83 If I'd gotten this much success in Hollywood, I never would have left.

Ronald Reagan (b. 1911) US former president and actor. Speech (January 1981)

84 To succeed you have to believe in something with such a passion that it becomes a reality.

Anita Roddick (b. 1942) British entrepreneur and founder of The Body Shop. *Body and Soul* (co-written with Russell Miller; 1991)

85 If you want to succeed you should strike out on new paths rather than travel the worn paths of accepted success.

Anita Roddick (b. 1942) British entrepreneur and founder of The Body Shop. Quoted in *The World's Best Thoughts on Life and Living* (Eugene Raudsepp, ed.; 1981)

86 The acquisition of wealth is not in the least the only test of success. After a certain amount of wealth has been accumulated, the accumulation of more is of very little consequence from the standpoint of success.

Theodore Roosevelt (1858–1919) US president. 'Character and Success', *Outlook* (31 March 1900)

87 People who are successful simply want it more than people who are not.

Ian Schrager (b. 1948) US entrepreneur. *Sunday Times* (May 2000)

88 The secret of success is concentration...Taste everything a little, look at everything a little; but live for one thing.

Olive Schreiner (1855–1920) South African novelist and social critic. *The Story of an African Farm* (1883)

89 The organisations that will truly excel in the future will be the organisations that discover how to tap people's commitment and capacity to learn at all levels.

Peter Senge (b. 1947) US academic and author. *The Fifth Discipline: The Art and Practice of the Learning Organization* (1990)

90 Positive feedback makes the strong grow stronger and the weak grow weaker.

Carl Shapiro (b. 1955) US academic and author. *Information Rules* (co-written with Hal L. Varian; 1999)

91 You only succeed when you are in survival mode.

Reuben Singh (b. 1977) British entrepreneur and author. *Management Today* (September 1999)

92 Those who believe in our ability do more than stimulate us. They create for us an atmosphere in which it becomes easier to succeed.

John Lancaster Spalding (1840–1916) US writer and clergyman. *Aphorisms and Reflections: Conduct, Culture and Religion* (1901)

93 If we want to be part of the financial mainstream, more of us have to go out and build these institutions.

Marianne Camille Spraggins (b. 1946) US president and CEO of ALICIA, former CEO of WR Lazard. Referring to achievements of African Americans in business. 'The Players', *Fortune* (Eileen Gunn; April 1997)

94 Only through growth do we become part of the real economic deal.

Marianne Camille Spraggins (b. 1946) US president and CEO of ALICIA, former CEO of WR Lazard. Referring to achievements of African Americans in business. 'The Players', *Fortune* (Eileen Gunn; April 1997)

95 There's nothing wrong with people trying, but no one has a right to succeed because they think they are clever.

Alan Sugar (b. 1947) British entrepreneur, founder and chairman of Amstrad electronics company. *Marketing* (May 2000)

96 I shall be like that tree, I shall die at the top.

Jonathan Swift (1667–1745) Irish writer and satirist. Quoted in *Works of Swift* (Sir Walter Scott, ed.; 1814)

97 Success, in my view, is the willingness to strive for something you really want.

Fran Tarkenton (b. 1940) US American football player and management consultant. Quoted in *Like Klockwork: The Whimsy, Wit, and (sometime) Wisdom of a Key Largo Curmudgeon* (Joe Klock; 1995)

98 God doesn't require us to succeed; he only requires that you try.

Mother Teresa (1910–97) Albanian missionary. Quoted in *Rolling Stone* (December 1992)

99 We believe that a sustainable and successful company can only be built on the solid foundations of economic success. But in the long-term, that economic success depends on improvements in our financial, environmental *and* social performance.

Jeroen Van der Veer (b. 1947) Dutch Advisory Director of Unilever, vice-chairman of the Royal Dutch/Shell Group, and president of Royal Dutch Petroleum Company. Speech, 'Earning the Licence to Grow' (26 November 1999)

100 It is not enough to succeed. Others must fail.

Gore Vidal (b. 1925) US novelist and critic. December 1976. Attrib.

101 You cannot be a success in any business without believing that it is the greatest business in the world...You have to put your heart in the business and the business in your heart.

Thomas J. Watson Sr (1874–1956) US founder and president of IBM. Quoted in *IBM: Colossus in Transition* (Robert Sobel; 1981)

102 Success is a science; if you have the conditions, you get the result.

Oscar Wilde (1854–1900) Irish writer and wit. Letter (1883)

103 A living is made, Mr Kemper, by selling something that everybody needs at least once a year...And a million is made producing something that everybody needs every day.
Thornton Wilder (1897–1975) US playwright and novelist. Spoken by Horace Vandergelder. *The Matchmaker* (1954), Act 1

104 A good completion takes a long time; a bad completion cannot be changed.
Zhuangzi (369?–286? BC) Chinese philosopher. 4th century BC. *Basic Writings* (Burton Watson, tr.; 1964)

TALENT

1 There is no such thing as great talent without great will-power.
Honoré de Balzac (1799–1850) French writer. *La Muse du Département* (1843)

2 A formal and orderly conception of the whole is rarely present, perhaps even rarely possible, except to a few men of exceptional genius.
Chester Barnard (1886–1961) US business executive and management theorist. *The Functions of the Executive* (1938)

3 Too many companies believe people are interchangeable. Truly gifted people never are. They have unique talents. Such people cannot be forced into roles they are not suited for, nor should they be.
Warren Bennis (b. 1925) US educator and writer. *Organizing Genius: The Secrets of Creative Collaboration* (co-written with Patricia Ward Biederman; 1998)

4 An idea can turn to dust or magic, depending on the talent that rubs against it.
William Bernbach (1911–82) US advertising executive. *New York Times* (6 October 1982)

5 All our talents increase in the using, and every faculty, both good and bad, strengthens by exercise.
Anne Brontë (1820–49) British novelist and poet. *The Tenant of Wildfell Hall* (1848)

6 Talent is cheaper than table salt. What separates the talented individual from the successful one is a lot of hard work.
Stephen King (b. 1947) US writer. Quoted in *Independent on Sunday* (19 March 1996)

7 The world is filled with unsuccessful men of talent.
Ray Kroc (1902–84) US founder of McDonald's. Quoted in *The Fifties* (David Halberstam; 1993)

8 Timing and arrogance are decisive factors in the successful use of talent.
Marya Mannes (1904–90) US essayist and journalist. *Out of My Time* (1971)

9 This is the age of time and talent.
Jonas Ridderstråle, Swedish academic and author. *Funky Business* (co-written with Kjell Nordström; 2000)

10 The system is producing a horde of managers with demonstrable talents...The tragedy is...these talented performers run for cover when grubby operating decisions must be made and often fail miserably when they are charged with earning a profit, getting things done, and moving the organization forward.
Ed Wrapp, US academic. *Dunn's Review* (September 1980)

TARGETS

1 Focus on operational positions where you have responsibility for profit and loss. That way it's easy to measure whether you're doing a good job.
Fabiola Arredondo (b. 1966) Spanish Internet executive. *Fortune* (October 2000)

2 Satisfactory under-performance is a far greater problem than a crisis.
Christopher Bartlett (b. 1945) Australian business writer. *The Individualised Corporation* (co-written with Sumantra Ghoshal; 1997)

3 Stretch and discipline are the yin and yang of business.
Christopher Bartlett (b. 1945) Australian business writer. *The Individualised Corporation* (co-written with Sumantra Ghoshal; 1997)

4 My vision was to provide advice on managing to top executives and to do it with the professional standards of a leading law firm.
Marvin Bower (1903–2003) US CEO of McKinsey & Company. *The Will to Manage* (1966)

5 You never reach the promised land. You can march towards it.
James Callaghan (b. 1912) British former prime minister. Television interview (July 1978)

6 The struggle itself towards the heights is enough to fill a human heart.
Albert Camus (1913–60) French novelist and essayist. *The Myth of Sisyphus* (1942)

7 By looking on each engagement as a part of a series...the commander is always on the high road to his goal.
Karl von Clausewitz (1780–1831) Prussian general and military strategist. *On War* (1831)

8 We build four of them a year—it's my job to sell four a year.
Robert Clifford (b. 1943) Australian business executive. Referring to the production of luxury yachts. *Australian Financial Review* (September 2000)

9 I have a feeling there is just about one more good flight left in my system.
Amelia Earhart (1898–1937) US aviator. Referring to her attempted round-the-world flight. Press conference (1937)

10 A minor invention every ten days and a big thing every six months.
Thomas Edison (1847–1931) US inventor. Press conference (1876)

11 Our view was, if we could measure it, we could manage it.
Dan England (b. 1948) US CEO of C.R. England. 'The Mavericks', *Fortune* (June 1995)

12 Ten yearly forecasts—revised every five years.
Henri Fayol (1841–1925) French business executive. *General and Industrial Management* (1916)

13 The most successful leader of all is one who sees another picture not yet actualized.
Mary Parker Follett (1868–1933) US management thinker and author. *Dynamic Administration* (1941)

14 Our policy is to reduce the price, extend the operations and improve the article.
Henry Ford (1863–1947) US industrialist, car manufacturer, and founder of Ford Motor Company. *My Life and Work* (co-written with Samuel Crowther; 1922)

15 The art of reaching business targets is not to aim at the impossible, but to aim at the championship level.
Charles Forte (b. 1908) British founder of Forte restaurants and hotels. Quoted in 'The Making of Fortes', *Management Today* (Robert Heller; September 1969)

16 Real artists ship.
Steve Jobs (b. 1955) US entrepreneur, co-founder and CEO of Apple Computer Company, and CEO of Pixar. *New York Times* (October 1992)

17 Double machine performance at every price point every year.
Theodore Levitt (b. 1925) US management theorist, writer, and editor. *Only the Paranoid Survive* (1996)

18 The goals on which hope are based have to be realistic.
Arthur Lydiard (b. 1917) New Zealand athletics coach. *Running to the Top* (co-written with Garth Gilmour; 1995)

19 I treat everything as a learning experience; then you become detached from the result and more interested in the experience itself.
Lorraine Moller (b. 1955) New Zealand athlete. Quoted in *Running with the Legends* (Michael Sandrock; 1996)

20 I can't stand working and not seeing results.
Chris Moore (b. 1960) British marketing director of Domino's Pizza. *Marketing* (June 2000)

21 My responsibilities are to get Australia right and get our stats here in order. I don't spend much time worrying about the future.
Lachlan Murdoch (b. 1972) Australian deputy chief operating officer of News Corporation. *Forbes* (July 1998)

22 Think nothing done while aught remains to do.
Samuel Rogers (1763–1855) British poet. *Human Life* (1819)

23 To take currants and sultanas beyond the fruitcake.
Barbara Thomas (b. 1947) US banker. Referring to transformation of a food company. *Management Today* (October 1999)

24 Man belongs where he wants to go—and he'll do plenty well when he gets out there.
Wernher von Braun (1912–77) US rocket engineer. Referring to space. *Time* (February 1958)

25 We also demand our place in the sun.
Bernhard Heinrich von Bülow (1849–1929) German politician. Speech (December 1897)

TAXES

1 It is better to tax 25 per cent of something than 60 per cent of nothing.
Johannes Bjelke-Petersen (b. 1911) Australian politician. Quoted in 'Sayings of the Week', *Sydney Morning Herald* (6 July 1985)

2 Writing checks to the IRS that include strings of zeros does not bother me...Overall, we feel extraordinarily lucky to have been dealt a hand in life that enables us to write large checks to the government rather than one requiring the government to regularly write checks to us—say, because we are disabled or unemployed.
Warren Buffett (b. 1930) US entrepreneur and financier. 'IRS' stands for Internal Revenue Service. Chairman's Letter to Shareholders, *Berkshire Hathaway 1998 Annual Report* (1 March 1999)

3 To tax and to please, no more than to love and to be wise, is not given to men.
Edmund Burke (1729–97) British philosopher and politician. *On American Taxation* (1775)

4 Read my lips: no new taxes.
George Bush (b. 1924) US former president. His promise made during the 1988 presidential campaign, which he later broke. *New York Times* (19 August 1988)

5 Tax laws also benefit those who have the best lobbying efforts...and the larger the corporations are, the smaller proportion they pay in taxes.
Jimmy Carter (b. 1924) US former president and business executive. Interview, *Playboy* (November 1976)

6 It was as true as...taxes. And nothing's truer than taxes.
Charles Dickens (1812–70) British novelist. *David Copperfield* (1849–50)

7 The hardest thing in the world to understand is income tax.
Albert Einstein (1879–1955) US physicist. Attrib.

8 President Herbert Hoover returned his salary to government. His idea caught on and now we're all doing it.
Sam Ewing (1920–2001) US author. Referring to taxation. Quoted in *Wall Street Journal* (23 July 1996)

9 It has been said that one man's loophole is another man's livelihood...this is not fair, because the loophole-livelihood of those who are reaping undeserved benefits can be the economic noose of those...paying more than they should.
Millicent Fenwick (1910–92) US politician and writer. *Speaking Up* (1982)

10 Taxes are a barrier to progress, and they punish rather than reward success.
Steve Forbes (b. 1947) US publishing executive. 'The Moral Case for the Flat Tax', *Imprimis* (October 1996)

11 Taxes are not simply a means of raising revenue; they are also...the price we pay for the privilege of working, the price we pay for being productive, and the price we pay for being innovative and successful.
Steve Forbes (b. 1947) US publishing executive. 'The Moral Case for the Flat Tax', *Imprimis* (October 1996)

12 But in this world nothing can be said to be certain, except death and taxes.
Benjamin Franklin (1706–90) US politician, inventor, and journalist. Letter to Jean-Baptiste Le Roy (13 November 1789)

13 Inflation is one form of taxation that can be imposed without legislation.
Milton Friedman (b. 1912) US economist and winner of the 1976 Nobel Prize in Economics. *Observer* (22 September 1974)

14 The best taxes are such as are levied upon consumptions, especially those of luxury...They seem, in some measure, voluntary; since a man may chuse how far he will use the commodity which is taxed.
David Hume (1711–76) Scottish philosopher and historian. 1752. 'Of Taxes', *Essays, Moral, Political, and Literary* (1754), pt 2, essay 8

15 Sex and taxes are in many ways the same. Tax does to cash what males do to genes. It dispenses assets among the population as a whole.
Steve Jones (b. 1944) British geneticist. Speech, London (25 January 1997)

16 Under the hypnosis of war hysteria, with a pusillanimous Congress rubber-stamping every whim of the White House, we passed the withholding tax. We appointed ourselves so many policemen and with this club in our hands, we set out to collect a tax from every hapless individual who received wages from us.
Vivien Kellems (1896–1975) US industrialist, feminist, and lecturer. 1952. Quoted in 'The Greedy Hand: How Taxes Drive Americans Crazy and What To Do About It', *Denver Post* (Amity Shlaes; 1999)

17 The avoidance of taxes is the only pursuit that still carries any reward.
John Maynard Keynes (1883–1946) British economist. Attrib.

18 Patrick Henry railed against taxation without representation. He should see it with representation.
Saul Landau (b. 1936) US filmmaker and writer. *New York Times* (1995)

19 The apportionment of taxes...is an act which seems to require the most exact impartiality; yet there is, perhaps, no legislative act in which greater opportunity and temptation are given to a predominant party to trample on the rules of justice.
James Madison (1751–1836) US president. *The Federalist* (1788), no. 10

20 Logic and taxation are not always the best of friends.
James C. McReynolds (1862–1946) US jurist. Sonneborn Bros. v. Cureton (1923)

21 Death and taxes and childbirth! There's never any convenient time for any of them.
Margaret Mitchell (1900–49) US author. *Gone with the Wind* (1936)

22 I don't think that meals have any business being deductible. I'm for separation of calories and corporations.
Ralph Nader (b. 1934) US lawyer and consumer-rights campaigner. *Wall Street Journal* (July 1985)

23 Taxes will eventually become a voluntary process, with the possible exception of real estate—the one physical thing that does not move easily and has computable value...wait until that's all there is left to tax, when the rest of the things we buy and sell come from everywhere, anywhere, and nowhere.
Nicholas Negroponte (b. 1943) US academic, co-founder and director of MIT Media Laboratory. Referring to the prospects for taxing Internet commerce. 'Taxing Taxes', *Wired Magazine* (6 May 1998)

24 Taxation without representation is tyranny.
James Otis (1725–83) US lawyer and politician. February 1761. According to tradition and a note in the papers of President John Adams this legendary phrase was used by Otis in the Massachusetts Superior Court, Boston. Attrib.

25 The British parliament has no right to tax the Americans...Taxation and representation are inseparably united. God hath joined them; no British parliament can put them asunder.
Charles Pratt (1714–94) British politician. Speech, House of Lords (December 1765)

26 A snare and a delusion.
Donald T. Regan (b. 1918) US politician. Referring to the flat tax. An old expression. *US News & World Report* (1984)

27 Income tax has made more liars out of the American people than golf.
Will Rogers (1879–1935) US actor, columnist, and humorist. *The Illiterate Digest* (1924)

28 No taxation without respiration.
Bob Schaffer (b. 1962) US politician. Referring to phasing out estate tax. *Time* (4 August 1997)

29 To tax and to please is no more given to man than to love and be wise.
John Simon (1873–1954) British foreign secretary and chancellor of the exchequer. Budget speech, House of Commons, Parliament (25 April 1938)

30 The accountants have told me that I can have one foot in Jersey, my left earlobe in the Isle of Man, and my right foot in Zurich and pay little or no tax, but...I will not be running away to the South of France.
Alan Sugar (b. 1947) British entrepreneur, founder and chairman of Amstrad electronics company. *Guardian* (29 March 1984)

TEAMS

1 One man can be a crucial ingredient on a team, but one man cannot make a team.
Kareem Abdul-Jabbar (b. 1947) US basketball player. *Star* (1986)

2 Team-building exercises come in many forms but they all trace their roots back to the prison system.
Scott Adams (b. 1957) US cartoonist and humorist. *The Dilbert Principle* (1996)

3 Team player: An employee who substitutes the thinking of the herd for his/her own good judgment.
Anonymous. *Fortune* (15 February 1995)

4 A team is like a baby tiger given to you at Christmas. It does a wonderful job of keeping the mice away for about 12 months, and then it starts to eat your kids.
Anonymous. Quoted in *Fortune* (19 February 1996)

5 A team is not a bunch of people with job titles, but a congregation of individuals, each of whom has a role that is understood by other members.
Meredith Belbin (b. 1926) British psychologist and training expert. *Team Roles at Work* (1993)

6 Empowered teams can say 'no' to the status quo...Teams will replace the hierarchy in the private sector. In government, teams can get a lot more done at a lower cost to the taxpayer
Kenneth Blanchard (b. 1939) US management theorist and author. *Ken Blanchard's Profiles of Success* (1996)

7 Teamwork is a constant balancing act between self-interest and group interest.
Susan Campbell (b. 1946) US lecturer and author. *From Chaos to Confidence* (1995)

8 There are two important factors in building a self-motivated team of people—the opportunity to learn through increased effort and trust in the management to give the utmost support.
Tom Farmer (b. 1940) British chairman and CEO of Kwik-Fit. *Management Today* (July 1999)

9 Dividing enemy forces to weaken them is clever, but dividing one's own team is a grave sin against the business.
Henri Fayol (1841–1925) French business executive. *General and Industrial Management* (1916)

10 Self-deception operates both at the level of the individual mind, and in the collective awareness of the group. To belong to a group of any sort, the tacit price of membership is to agree not to notice one's own feelings of uneasiness and misgiving, and certainly not to question anything that challenges the group's way of doing things.
Daniel Goleman (b. 1946) US behavioural scientist, journalist, and author. *Vital Lies, Simples Truths: The Psychology of Self-Deception* (1996)

11 The people we get along with, trust, feel simpatico with, are the strongest links in our networks.
Daniel Goleman (b. 1946) US behavioural scientist, journalist, and author. *Working with Emotional Intelligence* (1998)

12 A good team is a great place to be, exciting, stimulating, supportive, successful. A bad team is horrible, a sort of human prison.
Charles Handy (b. 1932) British business executive and author. *Inside Organisations* (1999)

13 A camel is a horse invented by a committee.
Alec Issigonis (1906–88) British engineer. Quoted in *Guardian* (14 January 2001)

14 High-performing companies increasingly believe that teams, rather than business units or individuals, are the basic building blocks of a succesful organisation.
Anthony Jay (b. 1930) British author and business consultant. Quoted in *Management Teams—Why They Succeed* (R. Meredith Belbin; 1984)

15 It is not the individual but the team that is the instrument of sustained and enduring success in management.
Anthony Jay (b. 1930) British author and business consultant. Quoted in *Management Teams—Why They Succeed* (R. Meredith Belbin; 1984)

16 You've got to figure out a way to manage the complexity of large projects yet still allow your core teams to focus on the essentials.
Steve Jobs (b. 1955) US entrepreneur, co-founder and CEO of Apple Computer Company, and CEO of Pixar. Quoted in 'Steve's Two Jobs', *Time* (Michael Krantz; 18 October 1999)

17 Teams are now the primary force of organizations. They are worth cultivating at their core. Their core is the *mind* of each team member.
Nancy Kline (b. 1946) US author, educator, and consultant. *Time to Think* (1999)

18 The desire to stand well with one's fellows, the so-called human instinct of association, easily outweighs the merely individual interest.
Elton Mayo (1880–1949) US psychologist. *The Human Problems of an Industrial Civilization* (1933)

19 Seek to understand each others' problems and develop a sense of responsibility for each other through working in small groups.
Reg Revans (1907–2003) British academic. *Action Learning* (1979)

20 People don't want to be left out of teams. You don't threaten them or anything like that.
Jack Rowell (b. 1937) British rugby captain and coach. Quoted in *The Adventure Capitalists* (Jeff Grout and Lynne Curry; 1998)

21 To function as a group, the individuals who come together must establish a system of communication and a language that permits interpretation of what is going on.
Edgar H. Schein (b. 1928) US writer. *Organizational Culture and Leadership* (1992)

22 People can be themselves only in small comprehensible groups.
E.F. Schumacher (1911–77) British economist and conservationist. *Small Is Beautiful* (1973)

23 A team of dragons doesn't need a head.
Stan Shih (b. 1945) Taiwanese CEO of the Acer Group. *Forbes* (September 1998)

24 To create human capital, a company needs to foster teamwork, communities of practice, and other social forms of learning.
Thomas A. Stewart (b. 1948) US journalist and author. 'Brain Power: Who Owns It...How They Profit From It', *Fortune* (1997)

25 Male bonding.
Lionel Tiger (b. 1937) Canadian anthropologist. *Men in Groups* (1969)

26 A team-oriented incentive system with group responsibility is...more effective in reducing team conflict and facilitating morale, cooperation, and productivity in Chinese organizations.
Zhong-Ming Wang, Chinese academic and business author. 'Team Conflict Management', *International Management in China: Cross-Cultural Issues* (Jan Selmer, ed.; 1998)

27 Team management has been considered as the Chinese approach to enhance collective culture at work.
Zhong-Ming Wang, Chinese academic and business author. 'Team Conflict Management', *International Management in China: Cross-Cultural Issues* (Jan Selmer, ed.; 1998)

28 Building a team is extremely challenging in software.
Ann Winblad (b. 1953) US venture capitalist. 'Coaching in the Software Industry Play-offs', *Red Herring* (1997)

29 You can't play the game without all the players on the court...The teams must be assembled quickly and play as a unit almost from the start. Failure to recruit a strong, cohesive team means a losing season.
Ann Winblad (b. 1953) US venture capitalist. 'Coaching in the Software Industry Play-offs', *Red Herring* (1997)

TECHNOLOGY

1 Technology is our word for something that doesn't work yet.
Douglas Adams (1952–2001) British author. *Sunday Times* (June 2000)

2 Today's portable net technology is at the Kitty Hawk stage. But with things moving at Internet speed, we can expect Concorde to be along shortly.
Douglas Adams (1952–2001) British author. *Sunday Times* (June 2000)

3 The classic development questions need to be reformulated for a 21st century economy... Will the poor continue to be left behind, will the wealth of information be hoarded by an elite?
K.Y. Amoako, Ghanaian economist and executive secretary of the UN Economic Commission for Africa. Speech, Africa

Development Forum, Addis Ababa, Ethiopia (25 October 1999)

4 Fantasy romps.
Anonymous. Referring to virtual reality. Quoted in *Goldfinger* (Robert Heller; 1998)

5 Official designs are aggressively neuter, The Puritan work of an eyeless computer.
John Betjeman (1906–84) British poet. *The Newest Bath Guide* (1974)

6 Science, engineering and technology are fundamental drivers in the economy of the future, providing the foundation for business growth and overall improvement in the quality of life.
Mark Birrell (b. 1958) Australian politician. 'Investing in Innovation', *Business Links* (July 1999)

7 Technology is so much fun but we can drown in our technology. The fog of information can drive out knowledge.
Daniel J. Boorstin (b. 1914) US Pulitzer-prize-winning historian. *New York Times* (1983)

8 Dotcom will become in our corporate language like Inc. or Co. or Corp.—a generic way of describing a company, in this case a company that does business on the Internet.
Clive Chajet (b. 1937) US management consultant. 'Names Outlast Stocks of Internet Firms', *New Jersey Star-Ledger* (Beth Fitzgerald; 1999)

9 Any sufficiently advanced technology is indistinguishable from magic.
Arthur C. Clarke (b. 1917) British science fiction writer. *The Lost Worlds of 2001* (1972)

10 If the automobile had followed the same development as the computer, a Rolls Royce would cost $100, get a million miles per gallon, and explode once a year, killing everyone inside.
Robert X. Cringley, US journalist and author. *Infoworld* (6 March 1969)

11 For many businesses, the Internet is still a technology in search of a strategy.
Mary J. Cronin (b. 1947) US business author. Attrib.

12 Technology will move so fast that unfortunately, or fortunately for me, you will be required to buy a new phone quite often.
Charles Dunstone (b. 1964) British business executive and founder of Carphone Warehouse. *Management Today* (August 1999)

13 It's like if you want to buy a car. Would you want to get an engine from BMW, a chassis from Jaguar, windscreen wipers from Ford?
Larry D. Ellison (b. 1945) US CEO of Oracle Corporation. Referring to integrated software suites. *Forbes* (October 2000)

14 One might be tempted to think that technological change is just a straight, upward trajectory...a very simple message would be to be prepared to lead as we have in the 1990s, but at a much faster pace. That would be very bad advice, indeed.

William T. Esrey (b. 1940) US telecommunications entrepreneur, chairman and CEO of Sprint. 'Leadership in the Next Century', *The Conference Board Challenge to Business: Industry Leaders Speak Their Minds* (Peter Krass and Richard E. Cavanagh, eds; 2000)

15 Clearly, there is great potential to improve efficiency using Internet-based e-commerce strategies such as electronic marketplaces and business-to-business supply chain management. But no one really knows how big those productivity gains will be, how long they will take to be realized, and who will be the ultimate beneficiaries.

Roger W. Ferguson Jr (b. 1951) US economist, vice-chairman of the Federal Reserve Board. Speech, New Economy Forum, Haas School of Business, University of California, Berkeley, California.'Conversation with Leaders of the "New Economy"' (9 May 2000)

16 The Internet has attracted the most attention as a symbol of the new economy. It clearly improves communication, collapsing time and space, but are we overstating the potential benefits of this one, admittedly stunning, innovation? Does the Internet have the potential to *continuously* improve business processes, as some enthusiasts argue, and if it does, what conditions are required to achieve that?

Roger W. Ferguson Jr (b. 1951) US economist, vice-chairman of the Federal Reserve Board. Speech, New Economy Forum, Haas School of Business, University of California, Berkeley, California.'Conversation with Leaders of the "New Economy"' (9 May 2000)

17 People were sceptical about the new technology. They wanted it to be de-risked.

Jon Florsheim (b. 1960) British Internet entrepreneur. *Marketing* (August 2000)

18 Broadband is like a narcotic. Once you have it, you won't be able to give it up.

Lynn Forrester (b. 1955) US business executive. *Sunday Times* (June 2000)

19 Technology — the knack of so arranging the world that we need not experience it.

Max Frisch (1911–91) Swiss author. *Homo Faber* (1957)

20 Automation does not make optimism obsolete.

Keith Funston (1910–92) US president of New York Stock Exchange. Address, George Peabody College for Teachers, Vanderbilt University, Nashville (11 March 1964)

21 The imperatives of technology and organization...are what determines the shape of economic society.

J.K. Galbraith (b. 1908) US economist and diplomat. *The New Industrial State* (1967)

22 The web workstyle will change the boundaries of business...because the ability to use the electronic marketplace to reach outside...will allow you to do things that you would have done internally in the past. Technology is driving the trend for the average-sized organization to be much smaller.

Bill Gates (b. 1955) US entrepreneur, chairman and CEO of Microsoft. Speech, Manhattan Institute, New York City (2 December 1998)

23 The world of business is still very, very paper-oriented...Although they may use personal computers...most of the information they work with ends up on paper...Well, all of that will go away. It will simply be a series of bits that are transmitted, and then automatically categorized.

Bill Gates (b. 1955) US entrepreneur, chairman and CEO of Microsoft. Speech, Manhattan Institute, New York City (2 December 1998)

24 It is important to step back from an industry that is full of people announcing new widgets every day—faster widgets, smaller widgets, more widgets.

Lou Gerstner (b. 1942) US chairman and CEO of IBM. *Fortune* (November 1993)

25 A new organization of matter is building up: the technosphere or world of material goods and technological devices: or the surrogate world.

Edward Goldsmith (b. 1928) British ecologist. *The Great U-Turn* (1988)

26 Technologies such as electronic mail are not just part and parcel of the way European companies operate. It is largely incidental to the way managers work.

Andrew S. Grove (b. 1936) US entrepreneur, author, and chairman of Intel Corporation. *Financial Times* (January 1997)

27 We live in an age in which the pace of technological change is pulsating ever faster, causing waves that spread outward toward all industries. This increased rate of change will have an impact on you, no matter what you do for a living. It will bring new competition from new ways of doing things, from corners that you don't expect.

Andrew S. Grove (b. 1936) US entrepreneur, author, and chairman of Intel Corporation. *Only the Paranoid Survive: How to Exploit the Crisis Points That Challenge Every Company and Career* (1996), Preface

28 The trouble is that all-encompassing though information technology may be, it will always convey facts and numbers...what it does not convey is perception, belief and motivation.

John Harvey-Jones (b. 1924) British management adviser, author, and former chairman of ICI. *Managing to Survive* (1993)

29 The thing with high-tech is that you always end up using scissors.

David Hockney (b. 1937) British artist. *Observer* (July 1994)

30 We bet the company on that basic technology and, in 23 years, nobody else has been able to match it.

Masaru Ibuka (1908–97) Japanese co-founder and chief adviser of Sony Corporation. *Fortune* (February 1992)

31 Apple and Pixar are the same in that...they both deliver a product that has immense technology underpinnings and yet they both strive to say you don't need to know anything about this technology in order to use it.

Steve Jobs (b. 1955) US entrepreneur, co-founder and CEO of Apple Computer Company, and CEO of Pixar. Quoted in 'Steve's Two Jobs', *Time* (Michael Krantz; 18 October 1999)

32 Apple has always been, and I hope it will always be, one of the premier bridges between mere mortals and this very difficult technology.

Steve Jobs (b. 1955) US entrepreneur, co-founder and CEO of Apple Computer Company, and CEO of Pixar. Quoted in 'Steve's Two Jobs', *Time* (Michael Krantz; 18 October 1999)

33 Technology has nothing to do with the corporate world. I don't see technology and the corporate world as being necessarily intertwined, any more than art and the corporate world are intertwined.

Steve Jobs (b. 1955) US entrepreneur, co-founder and CEO of Apple Computer Company, and CEO of Pixar. Quoted in 'Steve's Two Jobs', *Time* (Michael Krantz; 18 October 1999)

34 An important technology first creates a problem and then solves it.

Alan Kay (b. 1940) US entrepreneur and personal computer developer. Quoted in *Reengineering the Corporation* (Michael Hammer and James Champy; 1993)

35 The last man standing in an increasingly unhealthy industry.

Ashok Kumar (b. 1964) Indian investment analyst. Referring to the performance of the IT industry. *Forbes* (September 2000)

36 Since the worker has been reduced to a machine, the machine can confront him as a competitor.

Karl Marx (1818–83) German political and economic philosopher. 1844. Quoted in *Karl Marx* (Francis Wheen; 1999)

37 Gutenberg made everyone a reader. Xerox makes everybody a publisher.

Marshall McLuhan (1911–80) Canadian sociologist and author. *Guardian* (June 1977)

38 When this circuit learns your job, what are you going to do?

Marshall McLuhan (1911–80) Canadian sociologist and author. *The Medium Is the Message* (1967)

39 The acceleration of technological progress has created an urgent need for a counter ballast— for high-touch experience.

John Naisbitt (b. ?1929) US business executive and author. *Megatrends* (1982)

40 It is almost genetic in its nature, in that each generation will become more digital than the preceding one.

Nicholas Negroponte (b. 1943) US academic, co-founder and director of MIT Media Laboratory. *Being Digital* (1995)

41 Like a force of nature, the digital age cannot be denied or stopped. It has four very powerful qualities that will result in its ultimate triumph: decentralizing, globalizing, harmonizing, and empowering.

Nicholas Negroponte (b. 1943) US academic, co-founder and director of MIT Media Laboratory. *Being Digital* (1995)

42 Machines need to talk easily to one another in order to better serve people.

Nicholas Negroponte (b. 1943) US academic, co-founder and director of MIT Media Laboratory. *Being Digital* (1995)

43 One way to look at the future being digital is to ask if the quality of one medium can be transposed to another.

Nicholas Negroponte (b. 1943) US academic, co-founder and director of MIT Media Laboratory. *Being Digital* (1995)

44 We believe technology in itself does not make a business. Useful applications that utilise technology do.

Sandy Oh (b. 1971) Malaysian investment banker. *Business Week* (September 2000)

45 Thanks to lateral technology, a one-person global business is both technically feasible and a practical reality.

W.W. Rostow (b. 1916) US economist. *Megatrends* (1982)

46 High tech is embedded in the texture of industrial history; it needs to be planned into existence.

Theodore Roszak (1933–81) US historian, writer, and editor. *The Cult of Information* (1994)

47 If computerized information services have any natural place in a democratic society, it is in the public library.

Theodore Roszak (1933–81) US historian, writer, and editor. *The Cult of Information* (1994)

48 The hard-pressed weavers of Northern England who rallied around the mythical General Ludd appear to have had no grudge against technology in and of itself; their grievance was with those who used machines to lower wages or eliminate jobs.

Theodore Roszak (1933–81) US historian, writer, and editor. *The Cult of Information* (1994)

49 If the technocratic class often invokes technology, it is because these inanimate objects can take on a trajectory of their own and so cover for the manager's inability to give leadership.

John Ralston Saul (b. 1947) Canadian writer. *The Unconscious Civilization* (1995)

50 The technology of mass production is inherently violent, ecologically damaging, self-defeating in terms of non-renewable resources, and stultifying for the human person.

E.F. Schumacher (1911–77) British economist and conservationist. *Small Is Beautiful* (1973)

51 Anybody who runs a successful high tech company has to be an eternal optimist, has to be able to take big risks.

John Sculley (b. 1939) US partner of Sculley Brothers, former president of Pepsi, and CEO of Apple Computers. *Fortune* (July 1993)

52 If we hadn't put a man on the moon, there wouldn't be a Silicon Valley today.

John Sculley (b. 1939) US partner of Sculley Brothers, former president of Pepsi, and CEO of Apple Computers. *US News & World Report* (1992)

53 At the beginning of the 21st century six new technologies—micro-electronics, computers, telecommunications, new man-made materials, robotics, and biotechnology—are interacting to create a new and very different economic world.

Lester Thurow (b. 1938) US economist, management theorist, and writer. *Building Wealth: New Rules for Individuals, Companies, and Countries in a Knowledge-Based Economy* (1999), Prologue

54 The possession of technological know-how and the adoption of suitable strategies ultimately will determine the firm's ability to survive and indeed flourish in China in the long run.

Rosalie L. Tung (b. 1948) Canadian academic and business educator. *International Management in China: Cross-cultural Issues* (Jan Selmer, ed.; 1998)

55 Like the anthropologist returning home from a foreign culture, the voyager in virtuality can return home to a real world better equipped to understand its artifices.

Sherry Turkle (b. 1948) US sociologist. *Life on the Screen* (1995)

56 We've all heard that a million monkeys banging on one million typewriters will eventually reproduce the entire works of Shakespeare. Now, thanks to the Internet, we know this is not true.

Robert Wilensky (b. 1951) US academic. *Mail on Sunday* (February 1997)

57 Everyone basically told us, 'Software is a stupid thing to invest in because the assets walk out of the door at night'.

Ann Winblad (b. 1953) US venture capitalist. 'The 50 Most Powerful Women in American Business', *Fortune* (Patricia Sellers and Cora Daniels; October 1999)

58 If it keeps up, man will atrophy all his limbs but the push-button finger.

Frank Lloyd Wright (1867–1959) US architect. Referring to advances in technology. *New York Times Magazine* (1953)

59 Satellites are no respecters of ideology.

Walter Wriston (b. 1919) US banker. *The Twilight of Sovereignty* (1992)

TIME MANAGEMENT

1 I love deadlines. I especially like the whooshing sound they make as they go flying by.

Douglas Adams (1952–2001) British author. *The Hitchhiker's Guide to the Galaxy* (1979)

2 The number of operations performed in a given time may frequently be counted when the workman is quite unconscious that any person is observing him.

Charles Babbage (1792–1871) British mathematician and inventor. *On the Economy of Machinery and Manufacture* (1832)

3 I've never seen a job being done by a five-hundred person engineering team that couldn't be done better by fifty people.

C. Gordon Bell (b. 1934) US inventor and computer pioneer. *Spectrum* (February 1989)

4 Worthwhile success is impossible in a forty hour week.

Clarence Birdseye (1886–1956) US businessman and founder of Birdseye. *American Magazine* (February 1951)

5 The key is not in spending time, but using it.

Arthur Bryan (b. 1923) British chairman of Josiah Wedgwood & Sons Ltd. *First Things First* (1994)

6 The best way to fill time is to waste it.

Marguerite Duras (1914–96) French novelist and screenwriter. *Practicalities* (1987)

7 It's not the hours you put in your work that count, it's work you put in the hours.

Sam Ewing (1920–2001) US author. Quoted in *Reader's Digest* (September 2000)

8 We are speeding up our lives and working harder in a futile attempt to buy the time to slow down and enjoy it.

Paul Hawken (b. ?1946) US entrepreneur and business author. *The Ecology of Commerce* (1993)

9 Do not wait; the time will never be just right.

Napoleon Hill (1883–1970) US motivational author. *Think and Grow Rich* (1937)

10 City people try to buy time...whereas country people are prepared to kill time, although both try to cherish in their mind's eye the notion of a better life ahead.

Edward Hoagland (b. 1932) US novelist, essayist, and naturalist. 'The Ridge-Slope Fox and the Knife-Thrower', *Harper's Magazine* (January 1977)

11 In government it is order that matters; In action it is timeliness that matters.

Laozi (?570–?490 BC) Chinese philosopher, reputed founder of Daoism. *Daode Jing*, VIII

12 He who would make serious use of his life must always act as though he had a long time to live and must schedule his time as though he were about to die.

Émile Littré (1801–81) French philosopher and lexicographer. *Dictionnaire de la Langue Française* (1863–73)

13 The clock not the steam engine is the key machine of the modern industrial age.

Lewis Mumford (1895–1990) US social thinker and writer. *Technics and Civilization* (1934)

TRAINING

1 Most trainers are well-intentioned individuals and provide training with a plethora of individual-level interventions designed to help the individual adjust to his or her role in the overseas context. More often than not,

these...are at odds with the overall
organizational strategy.
Rabi S. Bhagat (b. 1950) Indian business author.
'Cross-cultural Training in Organisational Contexts',
Handbook of Intercultural Training (co-edited with Dan
Landis, co-written with Kristin O. Prien; 1996)

2 It takes less time to put up a factory than to
train men of competence to run it.
Indira Gandhi (1917–84) Indian prime minister. Speech
(13 April 1968)

3 In the digital age you need to make knowledge
workers out of every employee possible.
Bill Gates (b. 1955) US entrepreneur, chairman and CEO of
Microsoft. *Business@the Speed of Thought* (co-written with
Collins Hemingway; 1999)

4 I see nothing to suggest that the
trends...toward increased demand for
conceptual skills in our workforce will end.
The rapidity of innovation and the
unpredictability of the directions it may take
imply a need for considerable investment in
human capital.
Alan Greenspan (b. 1926) US economist and chairman of US
Federal Reserve Board. Speech to the National Governors'
Association 92nd Annual Meeting, State College,
Pennsylvania. 'Structural Change in the New Economy'
(11 July 2000)

5 There is too much education altogether.
William S. Paley (1901–90) US founder of Columbia
Broadcasting Corporation. *The World As I See It* (1949)

6 Education and training are decisive, and the
single greatest long-term leverage point
available to all levels of government.
Michael Porter (b. 1947) US strategist. *The Competitive
Advantage of Nations* (1990)

7 I must say that acting was good training for the
political life that lay ahead of us.
Nancy Reagan (b. 1921) US actor and former first lady.
Nancy (1980)

8 I used to always say, 'I never went to business
school and I never read a business book'. But
now I think maybe I should have read a few.
Oprah Winfrey (b. 1954) US talk show host, actor, and
business executive. Quoted in *Oprah Winfrey Speaks*
(Janet Lowe; 1998)

TRAVEL

1 They say travel broadens the mind; but you
must have the mind.
G.K. Chesterton (1874–1936) British novelist, poet, and
critic. 'The Shadow of the Shark' (1921)

2 A man who leaves home to mend himself and
others is a philosopher; but he who goes from
country to country, guided by a blind impulse
of curiosity, is a vagabond.
Oliver Goldsmith (1730–74) British playwright, writer, and
poet. *The Citizen of the World* (1762)

3 In the Middle Ages, people were tourists
because of their religion, whereas now they
are tourists because tourism is their religion.
Robert Runcie (1921–2000) British archbishop. Speech
(December 1988)

4 Travel is glamorous only in retrospect.
Paul Theroux (b. 1941) US travel writer. Quoted in *Observer*
(7 October 1979)

5 Commuter—one who spends his life
In riding to and from his wife;
A man who shaves and takes a train,
And then rides it back to shave again.
E.B. White (1899–1985) US writer. 'The Commuter' (1982)

VALUE

1 Nothing that costs only a dollar is worth
having.
Elizabeth Arden (1884–1966) US entrepreneur and
cosmetics manufacturer. Quoted in *In Cosmetics the Old
Mystique Is No Longer Enough* (Eleanore Carruth; 1973)

2 Trust and similar values...have real, practical,
economic value; they increase the efficiency
of the system, enable you to produce more
goods or more of whatever values you hold in
high esteem.
Kenneth Joseph Arrow (b. 1921) US economist. *The Limits
of Organization* (1973)

3 Real riches are the riches possessed inside.
Bertie Charles Forbes (1880–1954) US publisher and writer.
Quoted in *Forbes* (1973)

4 Time waste differs from material waste in that
there can be no salvage.
Henry Ford (1863–1947) US industrialist, car manufacturer,
and founder of Ford Motor Company. *My Life and Work*
(co-written with Samuel Crowther; 1922)

5 The way I was raised, if something wasn't
tough it was not a valuable or enriching
experience.
Lynn Forrester (b. 1955) US business executive. *Sunday
Times* (June 2000)

6 The value of a thing is the amount of laboring
or work that its possession will save the
possessor.
Henry George (1839–97) US economist. *The Science of
Political Economy* (1897)

7 Value is the most invisible and impalpable of
ghosts.
William Stanley Jevons (1835–82) British economist and
mathematician. *Investigations on Currency and Finance*
(1884)

8 Value depends entirely on utility.
William Stanley Jevons (1835–82) British economist and
mathematician. *Theory of Political Economy* (1871)

9 You've no future unless you add value and
create projects.
Rosabeth Moss Kanter (b. 1943) US management theorist,
academic, and writer. Interview (1989)

10 Creating value is an inherently cooperative
process, capturing value is inherently
competitive.
Barry J. Nalebuff, US author. *Co-opetition* (co-written with
Adam M. Brandenburger; 1997)

11 Stop competing on price; compete on value. Deliver total consumer solutions, rather than just your piece of the solution.

Faith Popcorn (b. 1947) US trend expert and founder of BrainReserve. 'Q&A with Faith Popcorn', *www.brainreserve.com* (1999)

12 Unless your ideas are ridiculed by experts, they are worth nothing.

Reg Revans (1907–2003) British academic. *Action Learning* (1979)

13 If a commodity were in no way useful—in other words, if it could in no way contribute to our gratification—it would be destitute of exchangeable value.

David Ricardo (1772–1823) British economist. Referring to the factors determining the price of a product; one of the first summaries of the modern view of price making, the interplay of supply and demand. *Principles of Political Economy and Taxation* (1817)

14 My job is to help people see what I see. If it's of value, fine. And, if it's not of value, then at least I've done what I can do.

Jonas Salk (1914–95) US medical researcher. Referring to his development of the Salk vaccine for polio. Interview (1992)

WAGES

1 Draw your salary before spending it.

George Ade (1866–1944) US humorist. 'The People's Choice', *Forty Modern Fables* (1901)

2 Be content with your wages.

Bible. Luke 3:14

3 The labourer is worthy of his hire.

Bible. Luke 10:7

4 A fair day's wages for a fair day's work: it is as just a demand as governed men ever made of governing.

Thomas Carlyle (1795–1881) British historian and essayist. *Past and Present* (1843)

5 The progress of human society consists...in...the better and better apportioning of wages to work.

Thomas Carlyle (1795–1881) British historian and essayist. *Past and Present* (1843), bk 1, ch. 3

6 By this time two years I can so arrange all my business as to secure at least 50,000 per annum. Beyond this never earn—make no effort to increase fortune, but spend the surplus each year for benovelent purposes

Andrew Carnegie (1835–1919) US industrialist and philanthropist. Carnegie's spelling was not always very good—'benovelent'—and, indeed, he gave financial backing to the Simplified Spelling Board. Private memo to himself (December 1868)

7 Whatever your wages are, save a little. Live within your means. The heads of stores, farms, banks...insurance companies, mills and factories are not seeking capital; they are seeking brains and business habits. The man who saves...has given the surest indication of the qualities which every employer is seeking for.

Andrew Carnegie (1835–1919) US industrialist and philanthropist. The fifth of his rules of business success. 'From Oakland: How to Succeed in Life', *The Pittsburgh Bulletin* (19 December 1903)

8 Not a penny off the pay; not a minute on the day.

A.J. Cook (1885–1931) British trade union leader. Said during the General Strike (1926)

9 It is determined, in the last result, by the consumer, without regard to the needs or expectations of the worker.

Peter F. Drucker (b. 1909) US management consultant and academic. Referring to the worker's wage. *Management* (1974)

10 In every work a reward added makes the pleasure twice as great.

Euripides (?484–?406 BC) Greek playwright. *Rhesus* (?450 BC)

11 Anything that promises to pay too much can't help being risky.

Dorothy Fisher (1879–1958) US writer. *The Deepening Storm* (1930)

12 Industry must manage to keep wages high and prices low. Otherwise it will limit the number of its customers. One's own employees should be one's best customers.

Henry Ford (1863–1947) US industrialist, car manufacturer, and founder of Ford Motor Company. Quoted in *The American Treasury 1455–1955* (Clifton Fadiman, ed.; 1955)

13 Men work but slowly, that have poor wages.

Thomas Fuller (1654–1734) English physician and writer. *Gnomologia* (1732), no. 3407

14 The income men derive from producing things of slight consequence is of great consequence. The production reflects the low marginal utility of the goods to society. The income reflects the high total utility of a livelihood to a person.

J.K. Galbraith (b. 1908) US economist and diplomat. *The Affluent Society* (1958), ch. 21

15 It is but a truism that labor is most productive where its wages are largest. Poorly paid labor is inefficient labor, the world over.

Henry George (1839–97) US economist. *Progress and Poverty* (1879), bk 9

16 Dr __ well remembered that he had a salary to receive, and only forgot that he had a duty to perform.

Edward Gibbon (1737–94) British historian. *Memoirs of My Life* (1796)

17 When employers are forced to pay high wages for low-productivity jobs, they attract a glut of applicants who can best be sorted out by credentials. Bricklayers, toll-booth personnel, building workers and truck drivers have all often been required to have high-school diplomas.

George Gilder (b. 1939) US economist. *Wealth and Poverty* (1981)

18 Already today, no matter what you do, the money you receive is more and more likely to track the recognition that comes to you for doing what you do. If there is nothing very special about your work, no matter how hard you apply yourself you won't get noticed, and that increasingly means you won't get paid much either.

Michael Goldhaber (b. 1942) US physicist, academic, and author. 'Attention Shoppers!', *Wired Magazine* (December 1997)

19 We're overpaying him, but he's worth it.

Samuel Goldwyn (1882–1974) US film producer. Attrib.

20 My task accomplished and the long day done, My wages taken, and in my heart Some late lark singing ...

W.E. Henley (1849–1903) British poet and playwright. 'In Memoriam Margaritae Sororis', *Echoes* (1889)

21 The theory of the determination of wages in a free market is simply a special case of the general theory of value. Wages are the price of labour.

John Richard Hicks (1904–89) British economist. *The Theory of Wages* (1932), pt 1

22 In the not too distant future the notion of the annual pay increase must become as exceptional as it was novel a generation ago.

Geoffrey Howe (b. 1926) British politician. Quoted in 'Sayings of the Week', *Observer* (24 October 1982)

23 All wages are based primarily on productive power. Anything else would be charity.

Elbert Hubbard (1856–1915) US humorist. *Notebook* (1927)

24 The Americans are such stupid creatures that if we make their employers deduct our loot from the cash or cheque they receive, they will never know the difference...but if they actually have the money in their hands before they pay us, even such dumb brutes might see what we are doing and might get ideas.

Vivien Kellems (1896–1975) US industrialist, feminist, and lecturer. Quoted in *American Heroine* (Revilo P. Oliver; 1989)

25 The most un-American phrase in our modern vocabulary is 'take-home pay'.

Vivien Kellems (1896–1975) US industrialist, feminist, and lecturer. *Toil, Taxes, and Trouble* (1952)

26 Each in his place, by right, not grace, Shall rule his heritage— The men who simply do the work For which they draw the wage.

Rudyard Kipling (1865–1936) British novelist, poet, and short-story writer. 'The Wage-Slaves' (1903)

27 Wages ought not to be insufficient to support a frugal and well-behaved wage-earner.

Leo XIII (1810–1903) Italian pontiff. *Rerum novarum* (15 May 1891)

28 I don't care how hard money is Ez long ez mine's paid punctooal.

James Russell Lowell (1819–91) US poet and diplomat. *The Biglow Papers, First Series* (1848)

29 As we know well, price policies and wage control policies do not succeed; they just create a dam which, when it bursts, creates something worse than existed before.

Harold Macmillan (1894–1986) British prime minister. Speech, House of Lords (23 January 1985)

30 Wages are determined by the bitter struggle between capitalist and worker.

Karl Marx (1818–83) German political and economic philosopher. *Early Writings* (T.B. Bottomore, ed.; 1963)

31 The bad workmen who form the majority of the operatives in many branches of industry are decidedly of the opinion that bad workmen ought to receive the same wages as good.

John Stuart Mill (1806–73) British economist and philosopher. *On Liberty* (1859)

32 As a general view, remuneration by fixed salaries does not in any class of functionaries produce the maximum amount of zeal.

John Stuart Mill (1806–73) British economist and philosopher. *Principles of Political Economy* (1848)

33 The efficiency of industry may be expected to be great, in proportion as the fruits of industry are insured to the person exerting it.

John Stuart Mill (1806–73) British economist and philosopher. *Principles of Political Economy* (1848)

34 Economy: cutting down other people's wages.

J.B. Morton (1893–1979) British writer and humorist. Attrib.

35 It is an economic axiom as old as the hills that goods and services can be paid for only with goods and services.

Albert Jay Nock (1870–1945) US author. *Memoirs of a Superfluous Man* (1943)

36 Large consumption is at the basis of saving in manufacture, and hence high wages contribute their share to progress.

Thomas Brackett Reed (1839–1902) US politician. Speech in the House of Representatives (1 November 1894)

37 There is no way of keeping profits up but by keeping wages down.

David Ricardo (1772–1823) British economist. *On Protection to Agriculture* (1820)

38 Wages should be left to the fair and free competition of the market, and should never be controlled by the interference of the legislature.

David Ricardo (1772–1823) British economist. *Principles of Political Economy and Taxation* (1817)

39 I worked for a menial's hire. Only to learn, dismayed, That any wage I had asked of life, Life would have paid.

Jessie Belle Rittenhouse (1869–1948) US poet and literary critic. Quoted in *A Book of Living Poems* (William R. Bowlin, ed.; 1934)

40 No business which depends for existence on paying less than living wages to its workers has any right to continue in this country...by living wages I mean more than a bare subsistence level—I mean the wages of decent living.
Franklin D. Roosevelt (1882–1945) US president. Address (1933)

41 Entrepreneurial profit...is the expression of the value of what the entrepreneur contributes to production in exactly the same sense that wages are the value expression of what the worker 'produces'. It is not a profit of exploitation any more than are wages.
Joseph Alois Schumpeter (1883–1950) US economist and social theorist. *The Theory of Economic Development* (1934)

42 He is well paid that is well satisfied.
William Shakespeare (1564–1616) English poet and playwright. *The Merchant of Venice* (1596–98), Act 4, Scene 1

43 The price of ability does not depend on merit but on supply and demand.
George Bernard Shaw (1856–1950) Irish writer and critic. 'Socialism and Superior Brains', *Fortnightly Review* (April 1894)

44 Masters are always and everywhere in a sort of tacit, but constant and uniform, combination, not to raise the wages above their actual rate.
Adam Smith (1723–90) British economist and philosopher. *An Inquiry into the Nature and Causes of the Wealth of Nations* (1776)

45 Wages are the measure of dignity that society puts on a job.
Johnnie Tillmon (1926–95) US welfare rights activist. 'Welfare is a Woman's Issue', *The First Ms Reader* (Francine Klagsbrun, ed.; 1972)

46 If you do things by the job, you are perpetually driven: the hours are scourges. If you work by the hour, you gently sail on the stream of Time, which is always bearing you on to the haven of Pay, whether you make any effort or not.
Charles Dudley Warner (1829–1900) US writer. *My Summer in a Garden* (1871)

47 Bonuses, as well as salaries, reward the finding and sharing of ideas even more than their origination.
Jack Welch (b. 1935) US former chairman and CEO of General Electric. Interview in *The Winning Streak Mark II* (Walter Goldsmith and David Clutterbuck; 1997)

48 When a man says he wants to work, what he means is that he wants wages.
Richard Whately (1787–1863) British archbishop and economist. Quoted in *Principles of Political Economy* (Henry Sidgwick; 1883)

49 The trouble with the profit system has always been that it was highly unprofitable to most people.
E.B. White (1899–1985) US writer. *One Man's Meat* (1942)

50 There is no rate of pay at which a United States pick-and-shovel laborer can live which is low enough to compete with the work of a steam shovel as an excavator.
Norbert Wiener (1894–1964) US mathematician. *Cybernetics, or Control and Communication in the Animal and the Machine* (1948)

51 One man's wage increase is another man's price increase.
Harold Wilson (1916–95) British prime minister. Speech, Blackburn, Lancashire (8 January 1970)

WEALTH

1 I bet you're all wondering what it's like to be a billionaire? It's disappointing really.
David Andrews (b. 1935) Irish politician. Speech (1997)

2 The rich would have to eat money, but luckily the poor provide food.
Anonymous. Russian proverb.

3 A man who has a million dollars is as well off as if he were rich.
John Jacob Astor (1763–1848) US entrepreneur and financier. Attrib.

4 Riches are a good handmaid, but the worst mistress.
Francis Bacon (1561–1626) English philosopher and statesman. 'The Antitheta of Things', *De Dignitate et Augmentis Scientiarum* (1623), bk 6, ch. 3, pt 3

5 Riches are for spending.
Francis Bacon (1561–1626) English philosopher and statesman. 'Of Expense', *Essays* (1597–1625)

6 It is easier for a camel to go through the eye of a needle, than for a rich man to enter into the kingdom of God.
Bible. Matthew 19:24

7 It is the interest of the commercial world that wealth should be found everywhere.
Edmund Burke (1729–97) British philosopher and politician. Letter (23 April 1778)

8 I have known millionaires starving for lack of the nutriment which alone can sustain all that is human in man, and I know workmen...who revel in luxuries beyond the power of those millionaires to reach. It is the mind that makes the body rich. There is no class so pitiably wretched as that which possesses money and nothing else.
Andrew Carnegie (1835–1919) US industrialist and philanthropist. Address, at the presentation of the Carnegie Library, Pittsburgh, Pennsylvania (5 November 1895)

9 Not evil, but good, has come to the race from the accumulation of wealth by those who have the ability and energy that produce it.
Andrew Carnegie (1835–1919) US industrialist and philanthropist. 'Wealth', *North American Review* (June 1889)

10 Rich men should be thankful for one inestimable boon. They have it in their power

during their lives to busy themselves in organizing benefactions from which the masses of their fellows will derive lasting advantage, and thus dignify their own lives.
Andrew Carnegie (1835–1919) US industrialist and philanthropist. 'Wealth', *North American Review* (June 1889)

11 The man who dies rich dies disgraced.
Andrew Carnegie (1835–1919) US industrialist and philanthropist. 'Wealth', *North American Review* (June 1889)

12 Today, it's enough to pull together a good story, to implement the rough draft of an idea, and—presto—instant wealth.
James Collins (b. 1958) US business thinker and author. 'Built to Flip', *Fast Company* (March 2000)

13 Prosperity is only an instrument to be used, not a deity to be worshipped.
Calvin Coolidge (1872–1933) US president. Speech, Boston, Massachusetts (11 June 1928)

14 The Rich aren't like us—they pay less taxes.
Peter De Vries (1910–93) US novelist and short-story writer. *Washington Post* (30 July 1989)

15 The secret point of money and power in America is neither the things that money can buy nor power for power's sake...but absolute personal freedom, mobility, privacy.
Joan Didion (b. 1934) US novelist, screenwriter, and journalist. *7000 Romaine, Los Angeles* (1967)

16 The public mind is polluted with economic fancies: a depraved desire that the rich may become richer without the interference of industry and toil.
Benjamin Disraeli (1804–81) British prime minister and novelist. Speech, House of Commons (15 May 1846)

17 Enterprises are paid to create wealth, not control costs.
Peter F. Drucker (b. 1909) US management consultant and academic. *Harvard Business Review* (January/February 1995)

18 We are the poorest rich people we know.
Charles Dunstone (b. 1964) British business executive and founder of Carphone Warehouse. Referring to the reality of being a 'paper millionaire'. *Management Today* (August 1999)

19 There are many excuses for the persons who made the mistake of confounding money and wealth. Like many others they mistook the sign for the thing signified.
Millicent Fawcett (1847–1929) British female suffrage leader. *Political Economy for Beginners* (1870)

20 Let me tell you about the very rich. They are different from you and me.
F. Scott Fitzgerald (1896–1940) US writer. Said to Ernest Hemingway. He replied: 'Yes, they have more money'. 'Rich Boy', *All the Sad Young Men* (1926)

21 You don't have to worry if somebody says 'Gee that guy's a nut'. If you have enough money, they say 'Gee that guy's eccentric'.
Malcolm Forbes (1919–90) US publisher. Quoted in Obituary, *Daily Telegraph* (26 February 1990)

22 In every well-governed state wealth is a sacred thing; in democracies it is the only sacred thing.
Anatole France (1844–1924) French novelist. *Penguin Island* (1908)

23 At the level at which entrepreneurs like Henry Ford, Andrew Carnegie, or Ted Turner operate, consumption is not a meaningful motive...money is more a symbol of their ability as entrepreneurs rather than a means to acquire goods.
Francis Fukuyama (b. 1952) US economist and writer. *The End of History and the Last Man* (1991)

24 Wealth is not without its advantages and the case to the contrary, although it has often been made, has never proved widely persuasive.
J.K. Galbraith (b. 1908) US economist and diplomat. *The Affluent Society* (1958), ch. 1

25 In the affluent society, no useful distinction can be made between luxuries and necessities.
J.K. Galbraith (b. 1908) US economist and diplomat. *The Affluent Society* (1958)

26 There are three ways by which an individual can get wealth—by work, by gift, and by theft. And, clearly, the reasons why the workers get so little is that the beggars and thieves get so much.
Henry George (1839–97) US economist. *Social Problems* (1883)

27 It's hard to make money in business; it's very difficult...and if your reward is relatively great, that's the way nature works. I don't see it's any more extraordinary for a man in business to accumulate a large fortune than a man in politics to attain high office.
J. Paul Getty (1892–1976) US entrepreneur, oil industry executive, and financier. April 1974. Quoted in *Getty on Getty* (Somerset de Chair; 1989), ch. 2

28 If you can count your money you don't have a billion dollars.
J. Paul Getty (1892–1976) US entrepreneur, oil industry executive, and financier. Quoted in *The Great Getty* (Robert Lenzner; 1985)

29 The higher our income, the more resources we control and the more havoc we wreak.
Paul Carter Harrison (b. 1936) US dramatist. *Guardian* (May 1992)

30 Desire of riches, covetousness: a name used always in signification of blame, because men contending for them are displeased with one another's attaining them.
Thomas Hobbes (1588–1679) English philosopher and political theorist. *Leviathan, or, The Matter, Form, and Power of a Commonwealth Ecclesiastical and Civil* (1651), pt 1, ch. 6

31 Few rich men own their own property. The property owns them.
Robert Green Ingersoll (1833–99) US lawyer and writer. Address to the McKinley League, New York City (29 October 1896)

32 Sir, the insolence of wealth will creep out.

Samuel Johnson (1709–84) British poet, lexicographer, essayist, and critic. Quoted in *The Life of Samuel Johnson* (James Boswell; 1791), vol. 3

33 There's nothing surer,
The rich get richer and the poor get poorer,
In the meantime, in between time,
Ain't we got fun?

Gus Kahn (1886–1941) US songwriter. 'Ain't We Got Fun?' (1921)

34 Money you haven't earned is not good for you.

Robert Maxwell (1923–91) British publisher, business executive, and politician. Quoted in *Time* (28 November 1988)

35 Most rich people just shop.

Robert Maxwell (1923–91) British publisher, business executive, and politician. Quoted in *Time* (28 November 1988)

36 Writers on Political Economy profess to...investigate the nature of Wealth, and the laws of its production and distribution: including the operation of all the causes by which...human beings are made prosperous or the reverse.

John Stuart Mill (1806–73) British economist and philosopher. 1848. *Principles of Political Economy, with Some of their Applications to Social Philosophy* (7th ed.; 1871)

37 I am rich beyond the dreams of avarice.

Edward Moore (1712–57) British writer. *The Gamester* (1753), Act 2

38 Prosperity has no fixed limits. It is not a finite substance to be diminished by division. On the contrary, the more of it that other nations enjoy, the more each nation will have for itself.

Henry Morgenthau Jr (1891–1967) US politician and publisher. Speech, United Nations Monetary and Financial Conference, Bretton Woods, New Hampshire (July 1944)

39 I don't know what we have. It becomes so complex that you need to have ten accountants working for two years to find out what you have.

Yoko Ono (b. 1933) US artist and musician. Interview, *Playboy* (January 1981)

40 Short of genius, a rich man cannot imagine poverty.

Charles Pierre Péguy (1873–1914) French writer. 'Socialism and the Modern World', *Basic Verities* (1943)

41 Money can be translated into the beauty of living, a support in misfortune, an education, or future security. It can also be translated into a source of bitterness.

Sylvia Porter (1913–91) US journalist and finance expert. *Sylvia Porter's Money Book* (1975)

42 Having money is rather like being a blond. It is more fun but not vital.

Mary Quant (b. 1934) British fashion designer. Quoted in *Observer* (2 November 1986)

43 There are men who gain from their wealth only the fear of losing it.

Antoine Rivarol (1753–1801) French journalist. 1802. *L'Esprit de Rivarol* (1808)

44 Recognition of the falsity of material wealth as the standard of success goes hand in hand with the abandonment of the false belief that public office and high position are to be valued only by...personal profit.

Franklin D. Roosevelt (1882–1945) US president. Presidential inaugural address (4 March 1933)

45 As long as there are rich people in the world, they will be desirous of distinguishing themselves from the poor.

Jean-Jacques Rousseau (1712–78) French philosopher and writer. *Discours sur l'Économie Politique* (1758)

46 Any considerable amount of wealth most often proves a curse than a blessing...I know how easy it is to acquire expensive habits which, so far from increasing the real richness and fullness of life, add to its burden.

Joseph Rowntree (1836–1925) British confectionary entrepreneur, philanthropist, and social reformer. 1907. Memorandum to his children. Quoted in *Enlightened Entrepreneurs* (Ian Campbell Bradley; 1987)

47 The enormous increase of wealth which has come to the country since the introduction of machinery has not been all that evenly distributed...and the share of the great body of workers has been inadequate.

Joseph Rowntree (1836–1925) British confectionary entrepreneur, philanthropist, and social reformer. 1907. Rowntree was a pioneer in the introduction of minimum wage rates and employee pensions in Britain. Memorandum to his children. Quoted in *Enlightened Entrepreneurs* (Ian Campbell Bradley; 1987)

48 The writings which we (verbally) esteem as divine...declare woe to the rich, and blessing to the poor. Where upon we forthwith investigate a science of becoming rich as the shortest road to national prosperity

John Ruskin (1819–1900) British art critic and writer. 1860. 'Qui Judicatis Terram', *Unto This Last* (1862)

49 What is really desired, under the name of riches, is essentially, power over men...this power...is in direct proportion to the poverty of the men over whom it is exercised, and in inverse proportion to the number of persons who are as rich as ourselves.

John Ruskin (1819–1900) British art critic and writer. 'The Veins of Wealth', *Unto This Last* (1862)

50 Prosperity tries the souls even of the wise.

Sallust (86–?35 BC) Roman historian and politician. *Bellum Catilinae* (?41 BC), ch. 11

51 Wealth is like sea-water; the more we drink, the thirstier we become; the same is true of fame.

Arthur Schopenhauer (1788–1860) German philosopher. 'What a Man Has', *Parerga and Paralipomena* (1851)

52 An attitude to life which seeks fulfilment in the single-minded pursuit of wealth—in short, materialism—does not fit into this world, because it contains within itself no limiting principle, while the environment in which it is placed is strictly limited.

E.F. Schumacher (1911–77) British economist and conservationist. *Small Is Beautiful* (1973)

53 Finding wealth an intolerable burden is the mark of an unstable mind.

Seneca (?4 BC–AD 65) Roman politician, philosopher, and writer. Letter to Lucilius, *Epistulae ad Lucilium* (AD 63–64), Letter 5

54 But, whiles I am a beggar, I will rail
And say there is no sin but to be rich;
And being rich, my virtue then shall be
To say there is no vice but beggary.

William Shakespeare (1564–1616) English poet and playwright. *King John* (1591–98), Act 2, Scene 1, ll. 594–597

55 I am a Millionaire. That is my religion.

George Bernard Shaw (1856–1950) Irish writer and critic. *Major Barbara* (1907)

56 Idiots are always in favour of inequality of income (their only chance of eminence), and the truly great in favour of equality.

George Bernard Shaw (1856–1950) Irish writer and critic. *The Intelligent Woman's Guide to Socialism and Capitalism* (1928)

57 There is no fixed road to wealth, and goods do not stay with the same master forever.

Sima Qian (?145–?86 BC) Chinese historian. Attrib.

58 Wealth flows to those with ability as the spokes of a wheel converge upon the axle, but it slips like a smashed tile through the hands of incompetent men.

Sima Qian (?145–?86 BC) Chinese historian. Attrib.

59 With the greater part of rich people, the chief enjoyment of riches consists in the parade of riches...In their eyes the merit of an object...is greatly enhanced by its scarcity.

Adam Smith (1723–90) British economist and philosopher. *An Inquiry into the Nature and Causes of the Wealth of Nations* (1776)

60 Wealth I would have, but wealth by wrong procure/I would not; justice, e'en if slow, is sure.

Solon (?638–?559 BC) Athenian statesman, legislator, and poet. Quoted in 'Solon', *Parallel Lives* (Plutarch 1st century AD)

61 It is not the level of prosperity that makes for happiness but the kinship of heart to heart.

Aleksander Solzhenitsyn (b. 1918) Russian author and winner of the 1970 Nobel Prize in Literature. *Cancer Ward* (1968), pt 1

62 The millionaires are a product of natural selection...the naturally selected agents of society for certain work. They get high wages and live in luxury, but the bargain is a good one for society.

William Graham Sumner (1840–1910) US economist and sociologist. Sumner was the leading US advocate of Herbert Spencer's Social Darwinism, 'the survival of the fittest'. *The Challenge of Facts and Other Essays* (Albert Galloway Keller, ed.; 1914)

63 A society which reverences the attainment of riches as the supreme felicity will naturally be disposed to regard the poor as damned... if only to justify itself for making their life a hell.

Richard Tawney (1880–1962) British economic historian and social critic. *Religion and the Rise of Capitalism* (1926), ch. 4, sect. 4

64 Industrialized communities neglect the very objects for which it is worth while to acquire riches in their feverish preoccupation with the means by which riches can be acquired.

Richard Tawney (1880–1962) British economic historian and social critic. *The Acquisitive Society* (1921)

65 Superfluous wealth can buy superfluities only.

Henry David Thoreau (1817–62) US writer. *Walden, or Life in the Woods* (1854), Conclusion

66 The only way to create tremendous wealth is in the midst of an industrial revolution. It is then that you have the opportunity to do old things in new ways...never before conceived.

Lester Thurow (b. 1938) US economist, management theorist, and writer. Speech, Sixth Workshop on Inventing the Organization of the 21st Century, Munich, Germany. 'Building Wealth in a Knowledge-Based Society' (February 2000)

67 The old foundations of success are gone...The world's wealthiest man, Bill Gates, owns nothing tangible: no land, no gold or oil, no factories...For the first time in history the world's wealthiest man owns only knowledge.

Lester Thurow (b. 1938) US economist, management theorist, and writer. *Building Wealth: New Rules for Individuals, Companies, and Countries in a Knowledge-Based Economy* (1999), Prologue

68 The more good I do, the more money has come in. You have to learn to give. You're not born to give. You're born selfish.

Ted Turner (b. 1938) US founder of Turner Broadcasting Systems. Following his decision to donate US$1 billion to the United Nations over a decade. Interview with Larry King, *CNN* (19 September 1997)

69 When I got my statement in January, I was worth $2.2 billion. Then I got another statement in August that said I was worth $3.2 billion. So I figure it's only nine months' earnings, who cares?

Ted Turner (b. 1938) US founder of Turner Broadcasting Systems. Referring to his decision to donate US$1 billion to the United Nations over a decade. Speech, United Nations Association-USA, Marriott Marquis Hotel, New York, *CNN* (19 September 1997)

70 Purchasing power is a licence to purchase power.

Raoul Vaneigem (b. 1934) Belgian philosopher. *The Revolution of Everyday Life* (1967)

71 The most successful people are those who take pride in their work, pride in their family...It is great to attain wealth, but money is really just one way—and hardly the best way—to keep score.

Kemmons Wilson (1913–2003) US entrepreneur, founder and chairman of Holiday Inn. Referring to the measures of success. 'What Makes for Success?', *Imprimis* (March 1997)

72 Even a rich man is sad if he has no ideals. He may try to hide his sadness from himself and others, but his efforts only make him sadder still.

Yevgeny Aleksandrovich Yevtushenko (b. 1933) Russian poet. *A Precocious Autobiography* (1963)

WINNERS AND WINNING

1 Champions aren't made in gyms. Champions are made from something they have deep inside them—a desire, a dream, a vision. They have to have the skill, and the will. But the will must be stronger than the skill.

Muhammad Ali (b. 1942) US boxer. *The Greatest* (1975)

2 Usually I like more of a challenge. It was a very easy run.

Said Aouita (b. 1960) Moroccan athlete. Referring to his victory at the Los Angeles Olympics. Press conference (1984)

3 If someone breaks my world records, it won't bother me. It gives me a reason to train even harder.

Said Aouita (b. 1960) Moroccan athlete. Quoted in *Running with the Legends* (Michael Sandrock; 1996)

4 Treat a horse like a woman and a woman like a horse. And they'll both win for you.

Elizabeth Arden (1884–1966) US entrepreneur and cosmetics manufacturer. Quoted in *Miss Elizabeth Arden* (Alfred A. Lewis and Constance Woodworth; 1972)

5 I hope I can prove to be the exception to the rule that good guys always finish last.

Arthur Ashe (1943–93) US tennis player. Alluding to Leo Durocher's remark 'Nice guys. Finish last'. Speech at an award ceremony (1964)

6 When you cross the tape, you feel like you were always training for something, and now I was there.

Arturo Barrios (b. 1962) US athlete. 1989. Quoted in *Running with the Legends* (Michael Sandrock; 1996)

7 He who owns the most when he dies, wins.

Ivan Boesky (b. 1937) US financier convicted of insider dealing in 1987. *The Times* (20 November 1986)

8 It's a bit like being a racehorse—you like to win.

Charles Brady (b. 1935) US investor. *Sunday Times* (May 2000)

9 If you want to be a champion, you have to train like a contender.

Linford Christie (b. 1960) British athlete. Quoted in *The Contenders* (Richard Dale and Colin Cameron; 1994)

10 A victory without danger is a triumph without glory.

Pierre Corneille (1606–84) French playwright. *Le Cid* (1636)

11 Run with your head the first two thirds of a race and with your heart the final one third.

Jack Daniels (b. 1933) US athletics coach. *Daniels' Running Formula* (1998)

12 We all get more practice winning than losing, so it is important to be a good loser, as it is to be a graceful winner.

Jack Daniels (b. 1933) US athletics coach. *Daniels' Running Formula* (1998)

13 To run well, you have to run with a passion. If that is quenched, you can't do it.

Robert de Castella (b. 1957) Australian athlete and executive director of Focus on You. Quoted in *Running with the Legends* (Michael Sandrock; 1996)

14 The important thing in life is not the victory but the contest; the essential thing is not to have won, but to have fought well.

Pierre de Coubertin (1863–1937) French founder of the modern Olympic Games. Speech (July 1908)

15 A business' flexibility in adapting to change and market dynamics will mark the winners and losers in this fast-changing Internet Age. Flexibility is a tight pairing of speed and agility. Linking businesses together using information is at the center of value creation in the Internet Age.

Michael Dell (b. 1965) US chairman and CEO of Dell Computer Corporation. Speech to the Windows 2000 Deployment Conference, San Francisco. 'The Foundation of E-Business' (15 February 2000)

16 Winning is achieving every single goal you set for the people to achieve. Our objective is to be the best at everything, not just winning Grand Prix.

Ron Dennis (b. 1949) British entrepreneur and Formula 1 motor racing team owner. Quoted in *The Adventure Capitalists* (Jeff Grout and Lynne Curry; 1998)

17 Nice guys. Finish last.

Leo Durocher (1905–91) US baseball player and manager. 6 July 1946. Referring to the New York Giants baseball team. Quoted in *Nice Guys Finish Last* (1975)

18 It can be construed as arrogance or big-headedness. It's not. It's just that I'm not scared of all the things other people are scared of.

Chris Evans (b. 1966) British broadcaster and media executive. *Management Today* (July 1999)

19 To learn from the failures and to keep going.

Ranulph Fiennes (b. 1944) British explorer. *Observer* (October 2000)

20 I am not afraid to take steps to become the biggest and best on the block.

Lynn Forrester (b. 1955) US business executive. *Sunday Times* (June 2000)

21 A man of action forced into a state of thought is unhappy until he can get out of it.

John Galsworthy (1867–1933) British novelist and playwright. *Maid in Waiting* (1932)

22 Nobody has ever built a stake in one of my companies without my approval.

Donald Gordon (b. 1930) South African financier. *Sunday Times* (June 2000)

23 Winning is fun. And, for most of us, making a real contribution is pleasing to the soul.

Bob Guccione (b. 1930) US magazine publisher. *Leading Change* (1996)

24 If you think you can win, you can win.
William Hazlitt (1778–1830) British essayist and journalist. 'On Great and Little Things', *Literary Remains* (1836)

25 Winning is everything. The only ones who remember you when you come second are your wife and your dog.
Damon Hill (b. 1960) British Formula 1 racing driver. *Sunday Times* (December 1994)

26 The key to success for Sony and to everything in business is never to follow the others.
Masaru Ibuka (1908–97) Japanese co-founder and chief adviser of Sony Corporation. *Fortune* (February 1992)

27 The will to win is nothing without the will to prepare.
Juma Ikangaa (b. 1957) Tanzanian athlete. Quoted in *Running with the Legends* (Michael Sandrock; 1996)

28 I'm a bastard, but I'm a bastard who gets the mail through. And they appreciate that.
Paul Keating (b. 1944) Australian former prime minister. *Sunday Telegraph* (November 1994)

29 Sometimes it's simply about winning.
Denise Lewis (b. 1972) British athlete. Said after winning the heptathlon gold medal in the Sydney Olympics 2000. Quoted in *Time Out* (27 September 2000)

30 It is not enough to fight. It is the spirit which we bring to the fight that decides the issue. It is morale that wins the victory.
George C. Marshall (1880–1959) US military commander and politician. *Military Review* (October 1948)

31 If my enemies attack me the way they do, things must be improving.
Robert Maxwell (1923–91) British publisher, business executive, and politician. Interview during Parliamentary elections (March 1986)

32 I went back to the study hall where I met my husband at a debating competition and where, I am pleased to put it on record, I beat him.
Mary McAleese (b. 1951) Irish president. Said on a visit to her old school in Belfast. Quoted in *Irish Times* (6 December 1997)

33 I'm running to win. You don't run to lose.
Ralph Nader (b. 1934) US lawyer and consumer-rights campaigner. Said in an interview about his presidential campaign in 2000. 'On the Trail', *The Economist* (2000)

34 He who does not hope to win has already lost.
José Joaquín Olmedo (1780–1847) Ecuadorean poet and politician. Quoted in *Reader's Digest* (June 1968)

35 Winners are people who have fun—and produce results as a result of their zest.
Tom Peters (b. 1942) US management consultant and author. *A Passion for Excellence* (co-written with Nancy Austin; 1985)

36 If you think you are going to win, you'll lose. Moreover, if you think you are going to lose, you'll lose.
Toshihiko Seko (b. 1956) Japanese athlete. Quoted in *Running with the Legends* (Michael Sandrock; 1996)

37 The winner is simply someone who gets up one more time than they fall over.

Robin Sieger, British business executive and author. *Natural Born Winners* (1999)

38 Always establish a paper trail to make sure others can't take credit for what you do.
Dennis Stevenson (b. 1946) British company director. *Management Today* (April 1999)

39 Make sure it isn't possible for a lesser man or woman to seize your clothes.
Dennis Stevenson (b. 1946) British company director. *Management Today* (April 1999)

40 I am extraordinarily patient, provided I get my own way in the end.
Margaret Thatcher (b. 1925) British former prime minister. *Observer* (April 1989)

41 Control your destiny or die.
Jack Welch (b. 1935) US former chairman and CEO of General Electric. 1981. Quoted in *Observer* (October 2000)

WORK AND EMPLOYMENT

1 Work alone qualifies us for life.
Zoë Akins (1886–1958) US poet and playwright. 1924. Attrib.

2 Work was like cats were supposed to be: if you disliked and feared it…it knew at once and sought you out and jumped on your lap and climbed all over you to show how much it loved you.
Kingsley Amis (1922–95) British novelist and poet. *Take a Girl Like You* (1960), ch. 5

3 Oh, why don't you work
Like other men do?
How the hell can I work
When there's no work to do?
Anonymous. Union song. 'Hallelujah, I'm a Bum' (?1907)

4 Make the work you have to do here your means of inner spiritual rebirth.
Sri Aurobindo (1872–1950) Indian philosopher, mystic, and nationalist. Quoted in *Ethics in Management: Vedantic Perspectives* (S.K. Chakraborty; 1995)

5 There is nothing like employment, active, indispensable employment, for relieving sorrow.
Jane Austen (1775–1817) British novelist. *Mansfield Park* (1814), vol. 3, ch. 15

6 The real essence of work is concentrated energy…people who have that in a superior degree…are independent of the forms, habits and artifices by which…less active people are kept up to their labours.
Walter Bagehot (1826–77) British economist and journalist. *Literary Studies* (1879–95)

7 For workaholics, all the eggs of self-esteem are in the basket of work.
Judith M. Bardwick (b. 1933) US management consultant. *The Plateauing Trap* (1986)

8 It was the Chinese who invented the wok ethic.
Julian Barnes (b. 1946) British writer. *Observer* (4 November 1984)

9 Every man's occupation should be beneficial to his fellow-man as well as profitable to himself. All else is vanity and folly.

P.T. Barnum (1810–91) US showman and circus entrepreneur. *The Humbugs of the World* (1866)

10 Nothing is really work unless you would rather be doing something else.

James Barrie (1860–1937) British novelist and playwright. Quoted in *Woodbury Reports Archives* (June 1997)

11 Retirement is an illusion. Not a reward but a mantrap. The bankrupt underside of success. A shortcut to death. Golf courses are too much like cemeteries.

Saul Bellow (b. 1915) US novelist. *The Actuel* (1997)

12 If the condition of the industrious were not better than the condition of the idle, there would be no reason for being industrious.

Jeremy Bentham (1748–1832) British philosopher, economist, and jurist. *Principles of the Civil Code* (1836), pt 1, ch. 3

13 My formula for success is to be found in three words—work—work—work.

Silvio Berlusconi (b. 1936) Italian media entrepreneur and prime minister. Interview, *Financial Times* (1 August 1988)

14 What is work and what is not work is a question that perplexes the wisest of men.

Bhagavad Gita, Indian religious text. (?1st century BC), 4:16

15 Do thy duty, even if it be humble, rather than another's, even if it be great. To die in one's duty is life: to live in another's is death.

Bhagavad Gita, Indian religious text. (?1st century BC), 3:35

16 We spend most of our lives working. So why do so few people have a good time doing it?

Richard Branson (b. 1950) British entrepreneur, business executive, and founder of the Virgin Group. *New York Times* (28 February 1993)

17 To turn $100 into $110 is work. To turn $100 million into $110 million is inevitable.

Edgar Bronfman Jr (b. 1955) Canadian CEO of the Seagram Corporation. *Newsweek* (2 December 1985)

18 Without work, all life goes rotten, but when work is soulless, life stifles and dies.

Albert Camus (1913–60) French novelist and essayist. Quoted in *Good Work* (E.F. Schumacher; 1979)

19 The shock of unemployment becomes a pathology in its own right.

Robert Farrar Capon (b. 1925) US theologian and novelist. 'Being Let Go', *New York Times* (5 August 1984)

20 Work is the grand cure of all the maladies and miseries that ever beset mankind.

Thomas Carlyle (1795–1881) British historian and essayist. Speech, Edinburgh, Scotland (2 April 1866)

21 Having entered upon work, continue in that line of work. Fight it out on that line (except in extreme cases), for it matters little what avenue a young man finds first. Success can be attained in any branch of human labor.

There is always room at the top in every pursuit

Andrew Carnegie (1835–1919) US industrialist and philanthropist. The third of his rules of business success (the first two being don't drink and don't smoke). 'From Oakland: How to Succeed in Life', *The Pittsburgh Bulletin* (19 December 1903)

22 Work is...a means of liberation from the stifling grip of egocentric individualism to the unlimited freedom of working in tune, in *yoga* with the Universal Consciousness.

S.K. Chakraborty (b. 1957) Indian academic. *Ethics in Management: Vedantic Perspectives* (1995)

23 There's a terrific thunder-cloud advancing upon us, a mighty storm is coming to freshen us up...It's going to blow away all this idleness and indifference, and prejudice against work.

Anton Chekhov (1860–1904) Russian playwright and short-story writer. *The Three Sisters* (1901), Act 1

24 This great urge to work, heavens, how well I understand it. I've never done a hand's turn all my life.

Anton Chekhov (1860–1904) Russian playwright and short-story writer. *The Three Sisters* (1901), Act 1

25 I don't like work—no man does—but I like what is in work—the chance to find yourself. Your own reality—for yourself, not for others—what no other man can ever know.

Joseph Conrad (1857–1924) British novelist and seaman. *Heart of Darkness* (1902)

26 You really have to wonder why we ever bother to get *up* in the morning. I mean, really: *Why work?* Simply to buy more *stuff*?

Douglas Coupland (b. 1961) Canadian writer. *Generation X* (1991)

27 Work is much more fun than fun.

Noël Coward (1899–1973) British dramatist, actor, producer, and composer. Quoted in 'Sayings of the Week', *Observer* (21 June 1963)

28 Absence of occupation is not rest,
A mind quite vacant is a mind distressed.

William Cowper (1731–1800) British poet. 'Retirement', *Poems* (1782)

29 They talk about the inalienable right of a man to work; he has no such right...(he) can only work if there is a job; he can only work for a man who wants some man to work for him.

Clarence Darrow (1857–1938) US lawyer. Testimony before the US Senates Commission on Industrial Relations (1915)

30 Nothing is more humiliating than to have to beg for work, and a system in which any man has to beg for work stands condemned. No man can defend it.

Eugene V. Debs (1855–1926) US politician and trade union leader. Speech given at the founding of the Federal Council of Churches in Girard, Kansas. 'The Issue' (23 May 1908)

31 It is when you have done your work honestly, when you have contributed your share to the common fund that you begin to live.

Eugene V. Debs (1855–1926) US politician and trade union leader. Speech given at the founding of the Federal Council of Churches in Girard, Kansas. 'The Issue' (23 May 1908)

32 Industry is the soul of business and the keystone of prosperity.

Charles Dickens (1812–70) British novelist. *Barnaby Rudge* (1841)

33 Business was his aversion; pleasure was his business.

Maria Edgeworth (1767–1849) British writer. *The Contrast* (1801)

34 I have nothing against work, particularly when performed, quietly and unobtrusively, by someone else. I just don't happen to think it's an appropriate subject for an 'ethic'.

Barbara Ehrenreich (b. 1941) US writer, sociologist, and feminist. 1988. 'Goodbye to the Work Ethic', *The Worst Years of Our Lives* (1991)

35 The most important motive for work in school and in life is pleasure in work, pleasure in its result, and the knowledge of the value of the result to the community.

Albert Einstein (1879–1955) US physicist. *Ideas and Opinions* (1954)

36 Every man's work, pursued steadily, tends to become an end in itself, and so to bridge over the loveless chasms of his life.

George Eliot (1819–80) British novelist. *Silas Marner* (1861), ch. 2

37 One of the saddest things is that the only thing a man can do for eight hours a day, day after day, is work. You can't eat...nor make love for eight hours.

William Faulkner (1897–1962) US novelist. Interview, *Writers at Work* (first series) (Malcom Cowley, ed.; 1958)

38 If people really liked to work, we'd still be ploughing the ground with sticks and transporting goods on our backs.

Vic Feather (1908–76) British trade union leader. Quoted in *Woodbury Reports Archives* (December 1994)

39 The idea that to make a man work you've got to put gold in front of his eyes is a growth not an axiom. We've done it for so long we've forgotten there's any other way.

F. Scott Fitzgerald (1896–1940) US writer. *This Side of Paradise* (1920), bk 2, ch. 5

40 Business cannot eliminate unemployment, but each business can do its competitive best to expand its own sales and employment.

Henry Ford (1919–87) US car manufacturer and CEO of Ford Motor Company. Speech. Quoted in *US News & World Report* (January 1967)

41 The world is full of willing people: some willing to work, the rest willing to let them.

Robert Frost (1874–1963) US poet. Attrib.

42 The best-kept secret in America today is that people would rather work hard for something they believe in than enjoy a pampered idleness.

John W. Gardner (1912–77) US educator and social activist. Quoted in *Woodbury Reports Archives* (December 1994)

43 If you keep working, you'll last longer, and I just want to keep vertical. I'd hate to spend the rest of my life trying to outwit an 18-inch fish.

Harold S. Geneen (1910–97) US telecommunications entrepreneur and CEO of ITT. *New York Times* (23 November 1997)

44 People desperately felt the need for connection, for empathy, for open communication. In the new, stripped-down, every-job-counts business climate, these human realities will matter more than ever.

Daniel Goleman (b. 1946) US behavioural scientist, journalist, and author. *Working with Emotional Intelligence* (1998)

45 The rules for work are changing. We're being judged by a new yardstick: not just by how smart we are, or by our training and expertise, but also by how well we handle ourselves and each other.

Daniel Goleman (b. 1946) US behavioural scientist, journalist, and author. *Working with Emotional Intelligence* (1998)

46 When work is a pleasure, life is a joy! When work is a duty, life is slavery.

Maksim Gorky (1868–1936) Soviet novelist and playwright. *The Lower Depths* (1902)

47 The ethics of work should be less of a duty to produce than an invitation to excel.

Damian Grace (b. 1950) academic. *Australian Problems and Cases* (1995)

48 One less welcome byproduct of rapid economic and technological change...is the evident insecurity felt by many workers despite the tightest labor markets in decades. This anxiety stems, I suspect, from a fear of job skill obsolescence, and one very tangible measure of it is the pressure on our education and training systems to prepare and adapt workers to effectively run the new technologies.

Alan Greenspan (b. 1926) US economist and chairman of US Federal Reserve Board. Speech to the National Governors' Association 92nd Annual Meeting, State College, Pennsylvania. 'Structural Change in the New Economy' (11 July 2000)

49 There's a certain really quite unimaginable intellectual interest that one gets from working in the context where you have to put broad theoretical and fairly complex conceptual issues to a test in the marketplace.

Alan Greenspan (b. 1926) US economist and chairman of US Federal Reserve Board. Referring to why he agreed to accept a fourth term as US Federal Reserve Chairman. Speech, Washington, D.C. (4 January 2000)

50 My batting average has been good, so people ask how much luck is involved. I tell them when I work 14 hours a day, 7 days a week, I get lucky.

Armand Hammer (1898–1990) US industrialist, philanthropist, founder and CEO of Occidental Petroleum. *International Management* (June 1966)

51 The information age is one in which workers give way to professionals and managers are replaced by coaches.
Michael Hammer (b. 1948) US author and academic. 'Reversing the Industrial Revolution', *Forbes* (12 February 1996)

52 I don't think that work ever really destroyed anybody. I think that lack of work destroys them a hell of a lot more.
Katharine Hepburn (1907–2003) US actor. *Me* (1991)

53 The workplace is undergoing rapid change. So are American workers. Technology, globalization and new demographics are constantly redefining what work is.
Alexis M. Herman (b. 1947) US politician. Labor Day message (3 September 1999)

54 Work must always be about more than just a paycheck. Work is central to who we are and how we define our society.
Alexis M. Herman (b. 1947) US politician. Labor Day message (3 September 1999)

55 The race is over, but the work never is done while the power to work remains.
Oliver Wendell Holmes Jr (1841–1935) US jurist. Radio address on his ninetieth birthday (8 March 1931)

56 It is very grand to 'die in harness' but it is very pleasant to have the strap unbuckled and the heavy collar lifted from the neck and shoulders.
Oliver Wendell Holmes Jr (1841–1935) US jurist. *Over the Teacups* (1891)

57 Every thing in the world is purchased by labour; and our passions are the only causes of labour.
David Hume (1711–76) Scottish philosopher and historian. 1752. 'Of Commerce', *Essays, Moral, Political, and Literary* (1754), pt 2, essay 1

58 I like work; it fascinates me. I can sit and look at it for hours. I love to keep it by me: the idea of getting rid of it nearly breaks my heart.
Jerome K. Jerome (1859–1927) British humorist and writer. *Three Men in a Boat* (1889)

59 Who first invented work, and bound the free
And holyday-rejoicing spirit down
...To that dry drudgery at the desk's dead wood?
Charles Lamb (1775–1834) British essayist. 'Work' (1818)

60 Why should I let the toad *work*
Squat on my life?
...Six days of the week it soils
With its sickening poison—
Just for paying a few bills!
That's out of proportion.
Philip Larkin (1922–85) British poet, critic, essayist, and librarian. 'Toads', *The Less Deceived* (1955), ll. 1–2; 5–8

61 Ah, were I courageous enough
To shout *Stuff your pension!*
But I know, all too well, that's the stuff
That dreams are made on.
Philip Larkin (1922–85) British poet, critic, essayist, and librarian. 'Toads', *The Less Deceived* (1955), v.6, ll. 21–24

62 The bond between a man and his profession is similar to that which ties him to his country; it is just as complex, often ambivalent, and it is understood completely only when it is broken.
Primo Levi (1919–87) Italian novelist, essayist, and chemist. *Other People's Trades* (1989)

63 Term, holidays, term, holidays, till we leave school, and then work, work, work till we die.
C.S. Lewis (1898–1963) British scholar, critic, and novelist. *Surprised by Joy* (1955)

64 Love the little trade which you have learnt, and be content with it.
Marcus Aurelius (121–180) Roman emperor. *Meditations* (2nd century AD), bk 4, sect. 31

65 In the morning, when you are sluggish about getting up, let this thought be present: 'I am rising to a man's work'.
Marcus Aurelius (121–180) Roman emperor. *Meditations* (2nd century AD), bk 5, sect. 1

66 Labor is work that leaves no trace behind it when it is finished.
Mary McCarthy (1912–89) US author and critic. 'The Vita Activa', *New Yorker* (18 October 1958)

67 For many wage earners work is perceived as a form of punishment which is the price to be paid for various kinds of satisfactions away from the job.
Douglas McGregor (1906–64) US academic, educator, and management theorist. *The Human Side of Enterprise* (1960), ch. 3

68 I don't know any executive who ever thought about stress, although a lot of other people do. No one ever dies of hard work. But a lot of people die once they retire from an active job.
Ian McGregor (1912–98) British chairman of the National Coal Board. *Daily Mail* (19 November 1980)

69 I suspect that American workers have come to lack a work ethic. They do not live by the sweat of their brow.
Kiichi Miyazawa (b. 1919) Japanese former prime minister. Quoted in *Daily Telegraph* (5 February 1992)

70 Whether we consider the manual industry of the poor, or the intellectual exertions of the superior classes, we shall find that diligent occupation, if not criminally perverted from its purposes, is at once the instrument of virtue and the secret of happiness.
Hannah More (1745–1833) British playwright and religious writer. *Christian Morals* (1813)

71 I would live my life in nonchalance and insouciance
Were it not for making a living, which is really rather a nouciance.
Ogden Nash (1902–71) US humorist and writer. 'Introspective Reflection', *Hard Lines* (1931)

72 No torporer drowsy, no comotose slother
Will make a good banker, nor even an author.
...Torpor is harrowing, sloth it is irksome—
Everyone ready? Let's go out and worksome.

Ogden Nash (1902–71) US humorist and writer. 'Procrastination Is All of the Time', *The Face Is Familiar* (1940)

73 Flextime is the essence of respect for and trust in people.

David Packard (1912–96) US entrepreneur and co-founder of Hewlett-Packard. *The HP Way* (1995)

74 Work expands so as to fill the time available for its completion.

C. Northcote Parkinson (1909–93) British political scientist and author. This observation has become widely known as 'Parkinson's Law'. *Parkinson's Law: The Pursuit of Progress* (1958)

75 Work is accomplished by those employees who have not yet reached their level of incompetence.

Laurence J. Peter (1919–90) Canadian academic and writer. *The Peter Principle: Why Things Always Go Wrong* (co-written with Raymond Hull; 1969)

76 Work is necessary for man. Man invented the alarm clock.

Pablo Picasso (1881–1973) Spanish artist and sculptor. Attrib.

77 If you like what you do, it's not work.

Maria Fiorini Ramirez (b. 1948) US business executive. Quoted in *Women of the Street* (Sue Herera; 1997)

78 It's true hard work never killed anyone but I figure why take the chance?

Ronald Reagan (b. 1911) US former president and actor. *Speaking My Mind* (1990)

79 I think I have been talking about retiring since I was 12.

Gerry Robinson (b. 1948) Irish chairman of Granada Television and chairman of the Arts Council of England. *Management Today* (April 1999)

80 A man can be freed from the necessity of work only by the fact that he or his fathers before him have worked to good purpose.

Theodore Roosevelt (1858–1919) US president. Speech, Hamilton Club, Chicago, Illinois. 'The Doctrine of the Strenuous Life' (10 April 1899)

81 The ongoing military-industrial drive toward rationalizing, disciplining, and ultimately dehumanizing the workplace is among the foundation stones of information technology.

Theodore Roszak (1933–81) US historian, writer, and editor. *The Cult of Information* (1994)

82 The habit of labour renders idleness tiresome.

Jean-Jacques Rousseau (1712–78) French philosopher and writer. 1767. 'An Epistle from J.J. Rousseau to Mr d'Alembert', *The Portable Age of Reason Reader* (Crane Brinton, ed.; 1956)

83 I believe in hard work. It keeps the wrinkles out of the mind and spirit.

Helena Rubinstein (1870–1965) US entrepreneur, cosmetics manufacturer, and philanthropist. *My Life for Beauty* (1965)

84 Work is of two kinds: first, altering the position of matter at or near the earth's surface relative to other matter; second, telling other people to do so. The first kind is unpleasant and ill paid, the second is pleasant and highly paid.

Bertrand Russell (1872–1970) British philosopher and writer. *In Praise of Idleness* (1932)

85 One of the first things to be noted in business life is its imperialism. Business is exacting, engrossing, and inelastic.

Margaret Sangster (1838–1912) US poet and writer. *Winsome Womanhood* (1900)

86 Work, worry, toil, and trouble are indeed the lot of almost all men their whole life long. And yet if every desire were satisfied as soon as it arose how would men occupy their lives, how would they pass the time?

Arthur Schopenhauer (1788–1860) German philosopher. 'On the Suffering of the World', *The World As Will and Idea* (1819)

87 If all the year were playing holidays, To sport would be as tedious as to work.

William Shakespeare (1564–1616) English poet and playwright. *Henry IV, Part One* (1597), Act 1, Scene 2

88 A man who has no office to go to—I don't care who he is—is a trial of which you can have no conception.

George Bernard Shaw (1856–1950) Irish writer and critic. *The Irrational Knot* (1950)

89 Today, gone is craft, replaced by career. Instead of workers on our feet, we've become sedentary professionals, entering data into computers.

Clifford Stoll (b. 1950) US astrophysicist, computer security expert, and writer. *Silicon Snake Oil: Second Thoughts on the Information Highway* (1995)

90 Everyone confesses in the abstract that exertion...is the best thing for us all, but practically most people do all they can to get rid of it.

Harriet Beecher Stowe (1811–96) US writer. 'The Lady Who Does Her Own Work', *Atlantic Monthly* (1864)

91 At Amstrad the staff start early and finish late...It's all action and the atmosphere is amazing, and the *esprit de corps* is terrific. Working hard is fun.

Alan Sugar (b. 1947) British entrepreneur, founder and chairman of Amstrad electronics company. Speech, City University Business School, London (April 1987)

92 Japanese salarymen know that for pure relaxation, nothing beats a good long day in the office.

Peter Tasker, British business author. *Inside Japan* (1987)

93 Perhaps it is this specter that most haunts working men and women: the planned obsolescence of people that is of a piece with the planned obsolescence of the things they make. Or sell.

Studs Terkel (b. 1912) US writer and radio commentator. *Working* (1972), Introduction

94 If you wanted an easy job, you could be a grave digger or run a graveyard.

Ted Turner (b. 1938) US founder of Turner Broadcasting Systems. *Broadcasting* (March 1986)

95 Work consists of whatever a body is obliged to do.

Mark Twain (1835–1910) US writer. *The Adventures of Tom Sawyer* (1876), ch. 2

96 Work keeps us from three great evils: boredom, vice, and poverty.

Voltaire (1694–1778) French writer, philosopher, and reformer. *Candide* (1759)

97 Humanity cannot exist without an infinity of useful men who possess nothing at all...a man who is well off will not leave his own land to come to till yours.

Voltaire (1694–1778) French writer, philosopher, and reformer. *Dictionnaire Philosophique* (1764)

98 I yield to no one in my admiration for the office as a social centre, but it's no place actually to get any work done.

Katharine Whitehorn (b. 1926) British journalist. Attrib.

99 If I were a medical man, I should prescribe a holiday to any patient who considered his work important.

Edward O. Wilson (b. 1929) US biologist. *Autobiography* (1967)

100 The greatest testimony to the human spirit that I'm witnessing now is the fact that people still come back to work, after all that has been done to them. They are still willing to participate for a more positive future if they would be sincerely invited.

Walter Wriston (b. 1919) US banker. Interview with Scott London, US National Public Radio (November 1996)

101 The Japanese do not consider work a form of economic activity. Rather, believing that there can be no work which is not a form of religious devotion, they approach everything as a discipline akin to the practice of Zen.

Shichihei Yamamoto (b. 1921) Japanese economics commentator. Quoted in *Inside Japan* (Peter Tasker; 1987)

Keyword Index

A

advice difficult...to ask someone's a. ADVICE, 5
Get the a. of everybody ADVICE, 4
I always pass on good a. ADVICE, 7
I have yet to hear a man ask for a. CAREERS, 22
My a. to this investor INVESTMENT AND THE STOCK MARKET, 4
advise We do a. in no uncertain terms INVESTMENT AND THE STOCK MARKET, 59
affirmative action a....for the benefit of white middle-class women DISCRIMINATION, 60
afflictions If a. refine some ADVERSITY, 13
affluent The A. Society ECONOMICS, 33
African Americans tough for A. to embrace capitalism CAPITALISM, 52
agenda management a. for the next several decades KNOWLEDGE, 12
Time spent on any item of the a. BUREAUCRACY, 40
agree Do not expect everyone to a. LEADERSHIP, 103
When people a....I must be wrong DECISIONS, 31
When two men always a. EFFICIENCY, 11
agreements Men keep their a. CONTRACTS, 8
aim two things to a. at in life GOALS AND OBJECTIVES, 22
air I'm more in the a. than I am in a country GLOBALISATION, 75
airplane an a....NASA to make one INDUSTRY, 26
alarm there is always cause for a. ATTITUDE, 4
alibis The pursuit of a. BLAME, 4
alienation Large, centralized organizations foster a. ORGANISATIONS, 69
alignment a....focuses an organization ORGANISATIONS, 40
A. is...the quality of management MANAGEMENT, 43
alive I want to make people feel intensively a. PEOPLE AND RELATIONSHIPS, 23
alliances a. between workers and capitalists CAPITALISM VERSUS SOCIALISM, 18
allocation a. simply fell short of our expenditure BUDGETING, 3
all-rounder No person can hope to be an a. ACCOMPLISHMENTS, 8
alternatives something better than...two a. DECISIONS, 9
altruism emphasis on human relations...not motivated by a. EMPLOYEES, 82
always a. to do the business of the day in the day PROCRASTINATION, 30
ambition A....doing the meanest offices AMBITION, 28
A....is a great man's madness AMBITION, 34
A. should be made of sterner stuff AMBITION, 25
feeds...on the a. of others AMBITION, 27
I don't think that a. is a bad word AMBITION, 10
If a. doesn't hurt you AMBITION, 22
Nothing arouses a....as the trumpet clang of another's fame AMBITION, 15
Nothing humbler than a. AMBITION, 11
ambitious People are a. and unrealistic DETERMINATION, 13
America A. is a vast conspiracy CONSUMERS, 34
American A. brand of democratic leadership DOING BUSINESS IN EUROPE, 10
A. way...aspire to make money MONEY, 54
American Dream We've polished up the A. GOVERNMENTS, 46
Americans A. are investing in our stock markets INVESTMENT AND THE STOCK MARKET, 49
A....managers of decline GOVERNMENTS, 45
A. relate all effort...to the dollar MONEY, 68
A. want action for their money MONEY, 72
our nation's financial system works for all A. BANKING, 7
The A. are such stupid creatures WAGES, 24
analysis a. of character is the highest human entertainment CHARACTER, 58
analyst I am not a professional security a. ENTREPRENEURS, 41
analysts professional exam for these a. INVESTMENT AND THE STOCK MARKET, 77
Too many a. are being judged CORPORATE RESPONSIBILITY, 15
anarchist Tap the energy of the a. PROGRESS, 29
anchor a....in the stomach of the business MANAGEMENT, 53
have firm a. in nonsense INFORMATION, 11
anger A. can be an effective negotiating tool NEGOTIATION, 16

anonymous We live in an a. world MEDIA, 17
answer 'both' is not an admissible a. CHOICE, 8
My a. is to stay close to ordinary people CORPORATE CULTURE, 72
answers Computers...can only give us a. COMPUTERS, 14
some questions don't have a. LIMITATIONS, 3
We do not need...all the a. ACTION, 8
anticipate a. the future...by understanding the past CHANGE, 101
anticipatory Good moves are a. INVESTMENT AND THE STOCK MARKET, 32
anti-intellectualism A....the anti-Semitism INTELLIGENCE, 6
antitrust effective a. enforcement program GOVERNMENTS, 6
anything A. you can do I can do better BOASTING, 2
apartments a. are death, divorce, and transfer OPINIONS, 8
aphrodisiac Power is the ultimate a. POWER, 50
apothecary Give me...good a. IMAGINATION, 17
appearances Keep up a. IMAGE, 10
apple A. has to be more pragmatic CORPORATE CULTURE, 122
I don't think anyone can manage A. MANAGEMENT, 63
appointed You a. him...and that was that DELEGATING, 7
appointing a. a man who was not fully trained HIRING AND FIRING, 17
approach The leadership a. tends...to be elitist LEADERSHIP, 34
approval Desire for a....is a healthy motive CHARACTER, 20
approximately better to be a. right STATISTICS, 4
architect Each man the a. of his own fate RESPONSIBILITY, 4
architects Social a. LEADERSHIP, 11
argue It is...absurd to a. men CHANGE, 102
argument The stronger man's a. is always the best POWER, 52
aristocrat A., democrat, autocrat—one /Who can rule POWER, 81
armaments A., universal debt, and planned obsolescence CAPITALISM, 29
art 'I want Polaroid to stand at the intersection of a. and science', OPINIONS, 15
my a....is perhaps a wild a. CREATIVITY, 5
artist An a....produces things that people don't need BUSINESS ETHICS, 122
The a. brings something into the world INNOVATION, 90
artists Real a. ship TARGETS, 16
ashamed A man should never be a. MISTAKES, 24
ask A. what you can do for your country CHARACTER, 35
If you want anything done, a. a woman ACTION, 22
aspirations companies...in tune with the needs and a. of society CORPORATE RESPONSIBILITY, 20
My a. take a higher flight AMBITION, 7
assert a. stoutly the possession of whatever you lack CHARACTER, 40
asset companies were a. rich and cash poor ECONOMICS, 48
Intelligence becomes an a. INTELLIGENCE, 10
assets Human resources are the greatest a. EMPLOYEES, 57
asset stripping It is not a. OPINIONS, 11
association human instinct of a. TEAMS, 18
assumption a. that people cannot be trusted PRACTICE, 6
assumptions Basic a. about reality MANAGEMENT, 22
The strategist's method...challenge the prevailing a. STRATEGY, 45
atmosphere A happy a. CORPORATE CULTURE, 39
The oppressive a. in most companies CORPORATE CULTURE, 7
atom-based A. companies...competing increasingly with bit-based companies COMPETITION, 52
atrophy man will a. all his limbs TECHNOLOGY, 58
attack If my enemies a....things must be improving WINNERS AND WINNING, 31
attacking learn to hold your own by...a. PERSONAL GROWTH, 8
attempted Nothing will ever be a. BOLDNESS, 13
attention I didn't want any a. PUBLICITY, 15
I don't pay a. INVESTMENT AND THE STOCK MARKET, 22
Pay especial a. to speaking in public SPEECHES, 8
attitude Take the place and a. ATTITUDE, 8
Without the right a., a business...will fail ATTITUDE, 11
Your a. determines your altitude ATTITUDE, 6
attitudes A. are more important than facts ATTITUDE, 17

attorney when you go into an a.'s office LAWYERS, 21
audience I never failed to convince an a. SPEECHES, 41
moving from product marketing to a. marketing
  MARKETING, 35
authoritarian A. organisations tend to develop dependent
  people ORGANISATIONS, 44
authority Denying the a. of an organization
  ORGANISATIONS, 5
political a. is based upon a mystique GOVERNMENTS, 52
Where the people possess no a. POWER, 11
automated The possible use of a. equipment CHANGE, 60
automation A. does not make optimism obsolete
  TECHNOLOGY, 20
industrial order geared to a. INDUSTRY, 22
automobile fulfills a man's ego like an a. CONSUMERS, 28
autonomy a. and solidarity, serve as helpful prompters
  DECISIONS, 17
avarice A. and luxury, those evils which have been the ruin
  CIVILISATION, 25
A., the spur of industry GREED, 11
avoid A. fight or flight COMMUNICATION, 13

B

baby my b.'s the most beautiful INNOVATION, 21
back Don't look b. COMPETITION, 59
bad Nothing b.'s going to happen to us HIRING AND FIRING, 27
send...an equal amount of b. news PRACTICE, 3
The people are not b. CORPORATE CULTURE, 56
balance b. between information, knowledge, and meaning
  KNOWLEDGE, 5
balance sheets B. are meaningless BUDGETING, 4
balls they have me by the b. NEGOTIATION, 4
bananas buying b....in a virtual jungle E-COMMERCE, 16
bandwagon If you see a b., it's too late PROBLEMS, 17
bank no sane person ever enjoyed visiting a b. BANKING, 14
What is robbing a b. BUSINESS ETHICS, 17
banker A b. is a man who lends BANKING, 22
a dead skunk and a dead b. REPUTATION, 2
Every b. knows...he is worthy of credit BANKING, 3
I want to play at B.'s Trust BANKING, 18
The distinctive function of the b. BANKING, 20
What the b. sighs for...a quiet mind STRESS, 7
bankers B. are like everybody else BANKING, 17
B. need a political sense BANKING, 26
B. regard research as most dangerous CHANGE, 81
b. should become...wise counsellors BANKING, 6
banking B....more dangerous than standing armies
  BANKING, 11
bankrupt The families objected to going b. BANKING, 25
bankruptcy B. is a sacred state FAILURE, 58
B. or credit default is not an issue DEBT, 5
B. would be like...slashing your wrists FAILURE, 46
I detest b. FAILURE, 53
banks b. are...gangsters BANKING, 27
b. are not in the business of banking BANKING, 12
b. have cleaned up their act BANKING, 15
bargain Make your b. before beginning to plough
  CONTRACTS, 1
bargaining collective b....a seductive name for bilateral
  monopoly NEGOTIATION, 12
The trouble about b. NEGOTIATION, 31
bargains the rule for b. PRINCIPLES, 8
bastard I am just a hoary old b. REPUTATION, 13
I'm a b. who gets the mail through WINNERS AND WINNING, 28
battery I can charge a man's b. EMPLOYEES, 29
batting My b. average has been good WORK AND
  EMPLOYMENT, 50
battle I'm not going to claim that we fought the b.
  CHANGE, 97
In preparing for b. PLANNING, 11
The general who wins a b. PLANNING, 23
There is nothing worse than a b. LOSING, 8

battlefield In business as on the b. STRATEGY, 44
battles B. in life are never won DETERMINATION, 23
beachcomber great gift for being a b. DELEGATING, 4
beasts what distinguishes man from the other b. MONEY, 78
beat how does it feel to get b. FAILURE, 57
beauty costliness masquerading under the name of b.
  CONSUMERS, 38
Bedouin I'm merely a simple B. REPUTATION, 22
beech tree I'm the b. IMAGE, 25
beforehand He that payeth b. MONEY, 40
beggar whiles I am a b. WEALTH, 54
begin Dare to be wise; b. GETTING STARTED, 13
beginning The b. is the most important part PLANNING, 20
behaviour the existence of shared norms of ethical b.
  BUSINESS ETHICS, 49
Trying to get consumers to re-evaluate their b. is what I
  enjoy CONSUMERS, 30
beliefs American managers are influenced by b.
  MANAGEMENT, 55
believe To succeed you have to b. in something SUCCESS, 84
What the mind can b., you can achieve ACHIEVING, 24
Whether you b. you can CONFIDENCE, 15
You have to b. in the impossible DETERMINATION, 11
benchmarking b. is perfectly legal and ethical BUSINESS
  ETHICS, 9
benevolent spend the surplus each year for b. purposes
  GOALS AND OBJECTIVES, 5
best be the absolute...b. at what you do DISCRIMINATION, 74
be the b. and the smartest AMBITION, 35
get the b. out of others EXCELLENCE, 9
I want all our people to believe they are working for the b.
  agency CORPORATE CULTURE, 103
Take our 20 b. people away EMPLOYEES, 23
best-seller A b. is a book which...sold well SELLING, 2
bets place b. and not predict growth rates GROWTH, 9
better B. never means b. for everyone CHANGE, 8
b. TV shows don't cost that much more QUALITY, 3
Every day, in every way, I am getting b. PERSONAL
  GROWTH, 2
If we can't find b. (tomatoes) QUALITY, 30
I was a b. copywriter than writer-writer CAREERS, 17
When you meet someone b. than yourself GOALS AND
  OBJECTIVES, 6
big A b. man has no time...to do anything SUCCESS, 41
B. Ideas...can be shipped in blueprints GLOBALISATION, 78
There's nothing wrong with b. companies BUSINESS
  ETHICS, 70
you might as well be thinking b. BOLDNESS, 25
big business B. could do business anywhere DOING BUSINESS
  IN NORTH AMERICA, 7
The chief problem of b. CORPORATE RESPONSIBILITY, 26
billboard never see /A b. lovely as a tree ADVERTISING, 39
billion I was worth $3.2 b. WEALTH, 69
billionaire single, straight b. in Manhattan BOASTING, 3
what it's like to be a b. WEALTH, 1
biopiracy B. is the Columbian 'discovery' BUSINESS
  ETHICS, 107
black Do you know I'm b.? DISCRIMINATION, 73
blame Everyone threw the b. on me BLAME, 5
If there is no intention, there is no b. BLAME, 24
Whatever you b., that you have done yourself
  RESPONSIBILITY, 9
blameless B. people...the most exasperating BLAME, 9
blaming Our culture peculiarly honors the act of b.
  BLAME, 32
blessing There's one b. only CONFIDENCE, 38
blight This b. is management MANAGEMENT, 77
blindness B. can...affect an entire industry PROBLEMS, 20
blinkers Goals too clearly defined can become b. GOALS AND
  OBJECTIVES, 2
boa constrictor try to employ a b. as a tape-measure
  LAWYERS, 10
board best use of a b. and senior management time
  CORRUPTION AND SCANDAL, 13
The combined b....a strong signal of unity CORPORATE
  CULTURE, 4

boardroom Get me inside any b. CORRUPTION AND SCANDAL, 6
boards many b....overlook more than they oversee CORPORATE RESPONSIBILITY, 18
boast B....what thou would'st BOASTING, 8
bold Be b. BOLDNESS, 10
Be b., be b., and everywhere BOLDNESS, 23
Look with favour upon a b. beginning BOLDNESS, 26
boldly Acting b. is better than acting knowingly RISK TAKING, 41
boldness B., again b. BOLDNESS, 4
B. in business BOLDNESS, 7
B. is an ill keeper of promise BOLDNESS, 1
In civil business: what first? B. BOLDNESS, 2
bonding Male b. TEAMS, 25
bonus great big b. Really, it's almost obscene BOASTING, 7
bonuses B., as well as salaries WAGES, 47
book printed b. to create the modern school LEARNING, 20
books For tired...executives, b. are a balm EXECUTIVES, 23
B. are not sacred GLOBALISATION, 50
borders B. are not sacred GLOBALISATION, 50
borrow b. good ideas from other companies INDEPENDENCE, 3
They are the people who b. your watch RESEARCH, 23
You b. money at a certain rate PROFITS, 10
boss I'm the b. LEADERSHIP, 28
who knows 'why' will always be...b. KNOWLEDGE, 24
bosses B. tend to attract clusters of people GLOBALISATION, 3
my first two b....believed in me EMPLOYERS, 6
bottom Everything possible starts in the organization from the b. ORGANISATIONS, 73
bottom line keep the bloody b. at the bottom PROFITS, 22
The b. is in heaven PROFITS, 14
boundaries We cannot hide behind our b. PEOPLE AND RELATIONSHIPS, 39
box All we need is an old cigar b. GETTING STARTED, 27
bragging It ain't b. ACCOMPLISHMENTS, 13
brain Every human b. is...an exposed negative CREATIVITY, 51
The b. is a wonderful organ INTELLIGENCE, 1
brain-dead b., gum chewing assistant CORPORATE CULTURE, 115
brains B. are becoming the core of organisations STRATEGY, 29
We could have over 520 b. connected KNOWLEDGE, 3
brainwashed American management techniques I was b. MANAGEMENT, 81
brake a b. and an accelerator ORGANISATIONS, 71
brakes We're still trying to put the b. on STRATEGY, 16
brand a drinks b....can take over your life BRANDS, 1
B. stewardship BRANDS, 2
build a b....you want it to jump BRANDS, 27
establishing ourselves as a regional b. GLOBALISATION, 102
how can we establish a mainstream b. BRANDS, 3
How is a legend different from a b. CHARACTER, 52
If a b. screws up HONESTY, 10
I'm a b. BRANDS, 30
take on the biggest b. in the world COMPETITION, 6
the b. is what you compete on BRANDS, 20
turning yourself into a b....B. BRANDS, 24
violation of the b. BRANDS, 12
we're building a b. with depth BRANDS, 19
branding US...home of b. BRANDS, 28
brands B. are all about trust BRANDS, 23
b. were irrelevant BRANDS, 22
B. were never really dead BRANDS, 17
Disney is one of the world's most powerful b. BRANDS, 9
distinctive one-person B. BRANDS, 25
great b. are far more than just labels BRANDS, 21
bread man lives by b. alone—when there is no b. SELLING, 20
workshop of those who are winning their b. EMPLOYEES, 9
breeding-ground the b. of all procrastination PROCRASTINATION, 7
brevity B. is the soul of wit SPEECHES, 47
bribes B., backhanders and favours for 'cronies' are commonplace DOING BUSINESS IN ASIA-PACIFIC, 8
brick He is a man of b. CHARACTER, 67
bridges b. between mere mortals and...difficult technology TECHNOLOGY, 32
Never burn b. CAREERS, 27

brilliance The world has achieved b. without conscience CONSCIENCE, 5
brink scared to go to the b. RISK TAKING, 15
Britain what is good for the City is good for B. INVESTMENT AND THE STOCK MARKET, 76
British There's nothing the B. like better FAILURE, 8
broadcasting Some day we'll call it personal b. MEDIA, 26
broke If it ain't b. CHANGE, 105
broker A b....takes your fortune INVESTMENT AND THE STOCK MARKET, 86
bromides All these b. are interchangeable ADVERTISING, 53
broom I needed to teach anyone who moved a b. EMPLOYEES, 75
browser the b. no longer provides an objective search COMPUTERS, 1
brunt b. of life...a quiet conscience CONSCIENCE, 9
buck The b. stops here RESPONSIBILITY, 29
the velvet touch of a soft b. BUSINESS ETHICS, 26
Budapest it doesn't matter if you're in B. or Beijing GLOBALISATION, 99
budget It's clearly a b. MONEY, 22
The b. is God BUDGETING, 1
budget deficit you'd know why we have a b. DEBT, 10
bug It's like a b. that bites you MEDIA, 34
build When I b. something for somebody BUSINESS ETHICS, 116
Which of you, intending to b. a tower PLANNING, 2
building concentrate on b. organizations PRACTICE, 10
built I have b. my own factory ACCOMPLISHMENTS, 16
bull You've got to take the b. DECISIONS, 11
bullshit virtually limitless supply of b. CHARACTER, 65
burden Finding wealth an intolerable b. WEALTH, 53
bureaucracies B. indicate a lack of trust BUREAUCRACY, 33
b....undermined by...knowledge-based economy BUREAUCRACY, 15
The b. of the Industrial Age BUREAUCRACY, 28
bureaucracy B....function...carried by the extended family BUREAUCRACY, 21
b. has invaded...human activity BUREAUCRACY, 54
b....increasingly be replaced by adhocracy ORGANISATIONS, 14
B. is...a potentially powerful force BUREAUCRACY, 22
B. is ever desirous BUREAUCRACY, 19
b. is the greatest threat to liberty BUREAUCRACY, 30
B....modern form of despotism BUREAUCRACY, 31
B....rolls on as ineluctably BUREAUCRACY, 45
choice is only that between b. and dilettantism BUREAUCRACY, 49
Neither Stalinist b. nor Silicon Valley provide ORGANISATIONS, 29
the b. of General Motors, the Pentagon BUREAUCRACY, 17
bureaucrat a b. that does not like a poem BUREAUCRACY, 47
bureaucratic B. administration means...exercise of control BUREAUCRACY, 50
B. and risk-averse environments BUREAUCRACY, 26
b. corporation...determine 'the right sort of person' CORPORATE CULTURE, 76
B. time...slower than geologic time BUREAUCRACY, 35
The manifest picture of b. organisation BUREAUCRACY, 23
The purely b. type of administrative organization BUREAUCRACY, 53
bureaucrats young people aspire to become b. DOING BUSINESS IN ASIA-PACIFIC, 15
bush A burden in the b. RESPONSIBILITY, 27
business A b. is only as good as the sum of its parts DETAILS, 14
A b. must have a conscience CONSCIENCE, 6
America's b. problem...companies designed during the nineteenth century CHANGE, 65
a one-person global b. is...a practical reality TECHNOLOGY, 45
Being good in b. ENTHUSIASM, 17
Boxing is just show b. with blood CORPORATE CULTURE, 20
B....akin to intellectual sumo wrestling COMPETITION, 32
b. cycle has been repealed BOOM AND BUST, 7
b....depends...on paying less WAGES, 40
b. equates success or failure with profitability PROFITS, 11

C

The only irreplaceable c. an organization possesses
EMPLOYEES, 10

To create human c. TEAMS, 24

capital-intensive human c. environment EXPERIENCE, 18

capitalism acceptable face of c. REPUTATION, 16

all that will ever break c. is capitalists CAPITALISM, 51

c....a product called Windows CAPITALISM, 17

C., as practiced, is a financially profitable, non-sustainable
aberration CAPITALISM, 22

c....doesn't have an unacceptable face CAPITALISM VERSUS
SOCIALISM, 40

C....efficient for attaining economic ends CAPITALISM, 30

c. has a very bad press CAPITALISM VERSUS SOCIALISM, 26

c. has created...colossal productive forces CAPITALISM VERSUS
SOCIALISM, 22

c. has won CAPITALISM VERSUS SOCIALISM, 12

C. is a hotel CAPITALISM, 38

C. is an art form CAPITALISM, 35

C....is being tried CAPITALISM VERSUS SOCIALISM, 19

C. is truly miraculous CAPITALISM, 12

C. is using its money CAPITALISM VERSUS SOCIALISM, 4

C. re-creates itself CAPITALISM VERSUS SOCIALISM, 27

C. still possesses...exhausted resources CAPITALISM, 7

c. suffers from...incomprehension of c. CAPITALISM, 19

C....tends to foster the development of bureaucracy
BUREAUCRACY, 51

C....vested interest in social unrest CAPITALISM VERSUS
SOCIALISM, 31

C. with near-full employment CAPITALISM, 37

C. without bankruptcy...Christianity without hell
CAPITALISM, 3

c....won't survive CAPITALISM VERSUS SOCIALISM, 32

C. works better than any of us CAPITALISM, 13

free enterprise c....is brutal CAPITALISM, 10

nothing competitive about a c. that...exports
GLOBALISATION, 36

One of the dynamics of c. CAPITALISM, 14

Predatory c. created...advanced technology CAPITALISM, 8

Property and stock market crashes...history of c.
INVESTMENT AND THE STOCK MARKET, 78

Successful c....fusion of co-operation and competition
CAPITALISM, 27

The dynamics of c. CAPITALISM, 4

The flaws of c. FAILURE, 20

The ideology of c. makes us all connoisseurs CAPITALISM, 43

The spread of c. CAPITALISM, 46

The twentieth-century struggle between c. and socialism
CAPITALISM VERSUS SOCIALISM, 2

unacceptable face of c. REPUTATION, 10

War is c. with the gloves off CAPITALISM, 45

capitalist advanced c. expansion will hark back
EMPLOYEES, 70

A Texan c. couldn't care less about local government
CORPORATE RESPONSIBILITY, 1

Between the c. and communist systems of society
CAPITALISM VERSUS SOCIALISM, 21

societies in which the c. mode of production prevails
CAPITALISM, 32

struggle between c. and worker WAGES, 30

the c. roots of the racial miseries CAPITALISM VERSUS
SOCIALISM, 33

When you start making money you become a c. swine
SUCCESS, 22

You show me a c. CAPITALISM VERSUS SOCIALISM, 20

capitalists c. generally act harmoniously BUSINESS ETHICS, 77

capital markets Private c. are the fundamental building
block INVESTMENT AND THE STOCK MARKET, 34

captain I am the c. of my soul RESPONSIBILITY, 10

You can be a c. of industry MANAGEMENT, 42

captains of industry C. EXECUTIVES, 20

car five years to develop a new c. INDUSTRY, 27

Go find a c. and saw the top off PRODUCTS, 8

I have no use for a motor c. PRODUCTS, 4

motor c. for the great multitude GOALS AND OBJECTIVES, 9

cards people...want to have nice-looking visiting c.
CORPORATE CULTURE, 41

care He did not c. in which direction POWER, 13

if you don't c. ACCOMPLISHMENTS, 10

Take c. of those who work for you CORPORATE
RESPONSIBILITY, 6

career get a girl to start thinking about a c.
DISCRIMINATION, 68

getting a life instead of a c. CAREERS, 21

I've got her tits...didn't want her c. CAREERS, 19

Tomorrow's typical c....zig-zag course CAREERS, 9

total commitment to c. is possible CAREERS, 6

Your c. is literally your business CAREERS, 15

careerist competitive and c. knowledge industry
KNOWLEDGE, 25

caring C. about what you are doing QUALITY, 20

carpenter You may scold a c. CRITICISM, 9

cars I'm not going to rest until we're shipping c. DOING
BUSINESS IN ASIA-PACIFIC, 28

cartoons The British Press...fill the space between their c.
MEDIA, 13

cascades If the top 50 people are right, it just c. down
PRIORITIES, 3

cashflow I just never got involved with the c. PROFITS, 15

Prepays were the quarter-to-quarter c. lifeblood CORRUPTION
AND SCANDAL, 2

casino out of control global c. GLOBALISATION, 80

castles This is not an age of c. COMPETITION, 14

catalogue so many flukes in the c. industry CONSUMERS, 40

We use space in our c. RESEARCH, 24

catch make a fuss...c. the eye of the world CHANGE, 75

caution history counsels c. BOOM AND BUST, 5

cautious c. about going against the herd RISK TAKING, 44

cautiously do everything both c. and confidently
CONFIDENCE, 14

celebrated communications have c. what we were not
BRANDS, 13

celebrities I have no interest in c. ECONOMICS, 22

You can't shame or humiliate modern c. PUBLICITY, 17

celebrity C. gets in the way PUBLICITY, 5

c....well-known for his well-knowness PUBLICITY, 6

Celtic Tiger C. needs a human face BUSINESS ETHICS, 32

censure c....is more acute than...praise BLAME, 19

They have a right to c. BLAME, 27

central planning C. didn't work for Stalin PLANNING, 4

CEO C. of marketing. You're selling trust CORPORATE
CULTURE, 84

C.'s role...establish an atmosphere that promotes
knowledge sharing CO-OPERATION, 10

companies where the C....confuse themselves with the
company CORPORATE CULTURE, 151

I guess that's what a C.'s job is EXECUTIVES, 28

Not everyone is capable of being a C. EXECUTIVES, 61

the C. owns the brand BRANDS, 18

the C. sat on the top LISTENING, 8

certain nothing can be said to be c., except death and taxes
TAXES, 12

certainties a man will begin with c. RISK TAKING, 4

removed the c. from their life HIRING AND FIRING, 14

certainty The c. of success...destroys...its charm
SUCCESS, 11

chain entire c. of entities MEDIA, 8

chairman A c. who never wanders...becomes a hermit
LEADERSHIP, 94

Being c. of the Senate Commerce Committee POWER, 61

challenge C. the mind and capture the heart LEADERSHIP, 53

greatest c....raise the productivity of knowledge
KNOWLEDGE, 11

new systems will c. all the old executive turfs
ORGANISATIONS, 79

Usually I like more of a c. WINNERS AND WINNING, 2

challenged never be seriously c. by a new product
BRANDS, 5

Women's presence...c. the Victorian ideal DISCRIMINATION, 47

challenges c. and changes are universal GLOBALISATION, 45

the greatest c. to international business GLOBALISATION, 83

There may be no greater c. BANKING, 8

champion If you want to be a c. WINNERS AND WINNING, 9

our main c. is the automobile COMPETITION, 42
Perfect c. is a theoretical concept COMPETITION, 24
society pays for the law of c. COMPETITION, 9
the blue water between ourselves and the c. COMPETITION, 37
When the c. is moving at 200 miles an hour COMPETITION, 58
competitive business with enduring c. advantages
  INVESTMENT AND THE STOCK MARKET, 21
C. battles are Niche Inc. v. Niche Inc. COMPETITION, 62
C. strategy is about being different STRATEGY, 47
truly sustainable c. advantage ORGANISATIONS, 52
competitiveness future c. depends on treating people
  as...important EMPLOYEES, 67
competitor A prosperous c. is often less dangerous
  COMPETITION, 55
c. who wants to wipe you off the map COMPETITION, 8
understand the strengths of the c. COMPETITION, 40
unknown c. comes from nowhere COMPETITION, 16
What do you do when your c.'s drowning COMPETITION, 46
competitors Assessing the...advantages of known c.
  COMPETITION, 29
bygone days when we whipped big c. COMPETITION, 66
c....are eating your lunch COMPETITION, 61
The goal of c. is to prevail COMPETITION, 71
complain Don't criticize, condemn, or c. MANAGEMENT, 12
Men...c. about trifles OFFICE POLITICS, 4
completion A good c. takes a long time SUCCESS, 104
complex C. processes are the work of the devil CHANGE, 63
complexity manage the c. of large projects TEAMS, 16
When dealing with c. and uncertainty HONESTY, 4
compromising We are soft and c. in business CRITICISM, 5
computer A c. can tell you...what you've sold COMPUTERS, 19
A modern c. hovers COMPUTERS, 4
If the automobile had followed the same development as
  the c. TECHNOLOGY, 10
if the c. is a tool COMPUTERS, 7
most successful c. companies...buy computers STRATEGY, 48
no reason...to have a c. PRODUCTS, 18
pit crew monitors a driver by c. COMMUNICATION, 30
The Puritan work of an eyeless c. TECHNOLOGY, 5
computers C. are like bikinis COMPUTERS, 8
c....let us make bigger mistakes COMPUTERS, 3
telephones, c., and planners aren't just functional objects
  INNOVATION, 83
computing What if c. were nearly free? COMPUTERS, 9
concentrated When conscious activity is wholly c. FOCUS, 7
concentration Intense c. for hour after hour CREATIVITY, 24
The great successes of life are made by c. SUCCESS, 15
The secret of success is c. SUCCESS, 88
concepts Most individuals...built up an array of c. PEOPLE
  AND RELATIONSHIPS, 25
concessions Never make c. NEGOTIATION, 23
condemn how anyone can have the face to c. BLAME, 25
It is essential to c. PRAISE, 9
condescending Don't be c. to unskilled labor EMPLOYEES, 5
condition dynamics which...obscure the reality of a
  common c. PEOPLE AND RELATIONSHIPS, 17
condom cognitive equivalent of a c. COMPUTERS, 12
conduct Ethical c. is not a matter of conformity BUSINESS
  ETHICS, 54
ethical c. is something like a big flywheel BUSINESS ETHICS, 2
The c. of a losing party never appears right SUCCESS, 10
The c. of successful business SUCCESS, 9
conducts c. his version of Beethoven and Bach
  MANAGEMENT, 57
conference c....can decide that nothing can be done
  MEETINGS, 2
find out the shortcomings of each other...c. MEETINGS, 16
Never dump a good idea on a c. table IDEAS, 23
No grand idea was ever born in a c. MEETINGS, 4
confidence As is our c., so is our capacity CONFIDENCE, 20
Building up the c. of an organisation CONFIDENCE, 19
careful about bringing people into my c. CONFIDENCE, 6
C....embarks on great and honourable courses
  CONFIDENCE, 4
C. is a mark of respect CONFIDENCE, 32
C. is a plant of slow growth CONFIDENCE, 35

C. placed in another often compels c. CONFIDENCE, 28
C....rooted in the unpleasant, harsh aspects of life
  EXPERIENCE, 40
c. was a plant of slow growth CONFIDENCE, 9
good business for our people to have c. CORPORATE
  CULTURE, 106
I...had to battle with that c. thing GETTING STARTED, 21
I have every c. that there will be a revival BOOM AND BUST, 9
my circle of c. CONFIDENCE, 2
nurtured a lot of c. and drive AMBITION, 19
superior c....in the tall man CONFIDENCE, 17
The c....in ourselves gives birth CONFIDENCE, 24
The greatest success is c. CONFIDENCE, 13
There's nothing to build c....like real failure FAILURE, 16
You gain strength, courage and c. CONFIDENCE, 36
configuration missionary c....have its own prime
  co-ordinating mechanism CORPORATE CULTURE, 98
conflict c. between work life and personal life CORPORATE
  RESPONSIBILITY, 11
This is a c. without battlefields GOVERNMENTS, 12
conformist 'get rich' in business by being a c.
  ENTREPRENEURS, 15
conformity mystique of c. is sapping the dynamic
  individualism EXECUTIVES, 34
confrontation Constructive c. CORPORATE CULTURE, 6
confronting C. reality...is the first step HONESTY, 11
Confucius C....the basis of administrative power
  BUREAUCRACY, 48
confusion C. is a word we have invented ORDER, 19
connection People desperately felt the need for c. WORK
  AND EMPLOYMENT, 44
connectivity c....equals competitiveness
  COMMUNICATION, 14
If global c. is the...breakthrough GLOBALISATION, 25
conquer I must try to c. it ACHIEVING, 8
more than one way to c. a country ADVERTISING, 11
There are still worlds out there to c. ACHIEVING, 27
the world is not an easy place to c. AMBITION, 32
You must either c. and rule POWER, 35
conscience A man's c. begins life with him CONSCIENCE, 23
as much c. as any man in business CONSCIENCE, 39
A still and quiet c. CONSCIENCE, 35
C. and cowardice are really the same things CONSCIENCE, 42
c. does make cowards of us all CONSCIENCE, 34
C. gets a lot of credit CONSCIENCE, 2
C. is a coward CONSCIENCE, 14
C. is an imitation within ourselves CONSCIENCE, 3
C. is the guardian...preservation CONSCIENCE, 27
C. is the inner voice that warns us CONSCIENCE, 28
C. is the name...to their prejudices CONSCIENCE, 19
C.: self-esteem with a halo CONSCIENCE, 22
If there be not a c. CONSCIENCE, 36
neither safe...to do aught against c. CONSCIENCE, 26
Our c. is not the vessel of eternal verities CONSCIENCE, 24
Sufficient c. to bother him CONSCIENCE, 25
task of the c. CONSCIENCE, 8
term-time in the court of c. CONSCIENCE, 13
conscious make c. what lies unconscious LEADERSHIP, 33
consensus c. is a poor substitute for leadership LEADERSHIP, 9
consequences Only positive c. SUCCESS, 8
conservation C. is business too BUSINESS ETHICS, 121
consideration A little C. CHARACTER, 43
consolidation C....best opportunity to gain the best
  partners CHANGE, 47
consultancy The field of c. and gurus ADVICE, 2
consultant A c....takes your money and annoys your
  employees RESEARCH, 1
hire a c. on snakes CORPORATE CULTURE, 110
consultants C....excellent scapegoats for major
  management blunders EXECUTIVES, 1
I don't like to hire c. RESEARCH, 13
consumer businesses do not listen to the c. CONSUMERS, 27
c. isn't a moron CONSUMERS, 24
c....most important part of the production line
  CONSUMERS, 7
Does the c. really know who you are BRANDS, 10

crash A c....knocking at the front door by appointment INVESTMENT AND THE STOCK MARKET, 69

creation C. comes before distribution PRODUCTIVITY, 10

Our business is company c. STRATEGY, 56

creative C. people are like a wet towel ADVERTISING, 67

C. people tend to pass the responsibility CREATIVITY, 30

Every c. act...sudden cessation of stupidity CREATIVITY, 23

Firms that take a c. approach CREATIVITY, 21

I don't think I am c. CREATIVITY, 17

If it doesn't sell, it isn't c. ADVERTISING, 56

When you ask c. people CREATIVITY, 20

creativity c. in product planning and marketing INNOVATION, 62

C. is allowing oneself to make mistakes CREATIVITY, 1

C. is never enough CREATIVITY, 28

C. is thinking new things CREATIVITY, 31

C....letting go of certainties CREATIVITY, 48

C....turning up what is already there CREATIVITY, 12

Is there enough c. MEDIA, 23

My attitude was, c. will see me through BUDGETING, 5

people believe...c. leads to innovation INNOVATION, 55

people believe that c. automatically leads to innovation CREATIVITY, 29

True c. often starts where language ends CREATIVITY, 22

credit c....because I am a woman DISCRIMINATION, 16

he doesn't mind who gets the c. LIMITATIONS, 7

people who do things...people who get the c. ACCOMPLISHMENTS, 11

the c. goes to the man who convinces INNOVATION, 20

credit card A c. is a money tool MONEY, 71

c. holders being contacted, questioned, tabulated, tracked, and romanced LOYALTY, 14

creditors C. have better memories than debtors DEBT, 6

crime c. doesn't pay GOVERNMENTS, 43

every c. against one's own nature PEOPLE AND RELATIONSHIPS, 27

crises recent c....financial structure vulnerabilities ECONOMICS, 41

crisis c. really tends to help develop...an organization ORGANISATIONS, 68

C. situations are usually unanticipated PROBLEMS, 7

our business organizations...after a c. or breakdown LEARNING, 51

Things continue in government unless you feel a c. DEBT, 11

critic A c....can't drive the car MEDIA, 53

critical By failing to grasp the c. issues MISTAKES, 20

C. remarks are only made by people who love you CRITICISM, 10

we prefer c. to constructive thinking OPPORTUNITY, 4

criticism C. is one of the most important tasks CRITICISM, 7

People ask you for c. PRAISE, 14

Sandwich...c. between two layers of praise PRAISE, 1

Think before you speak is c.'s motto SPEECHES, 20

critics I don't give a damn what...c. say MEDIA, 38

what those c. don't know ACHIEVING, 39

critique My c. of the global capitalist system CAPITALISM, 44

crook the c. in modern business SINCERITY, 51

cross-cultural c. training becomes increasingly important GLOBALISATION, 10

cross selling c. ENTREPRENEURS, 30

crown He who wields the knife never wears the c. LEADERSHIP, 69

crypto-businessman The c. is the true revolutionary CAPITALISM VERSUS SOCIALISM, 13

cubby holes there are no c. SUCCESS, 9

cultural C. competence...add to an organisation's activities ORGANISATIONS, 12

responding to c. clues CORPORATE CULTURE, 32

culture A company's c. is often buried...inside rituals CORPORATE CULTURE, 49

our c. is a c. of corpses IDEAS, 8

trying to understand IBM's c. CORPORATE CULTURE, 46

what we took for granted...was...c. CAPITALISM, 20

cunning C....dark sanctuary of incapacity ACHIEVING, 7

This is an age that calls for c. CHANGE, 31

cure Work is the grand c. of all the maladies WORK AND EMPLOYMENT, 20

curiosity seek in marketing people...c. MARKETING, 30

through c. can we discover opportunities OPPORTUNITY, 2

curious C. people have an appetite CREATIVITY, 13

currency existing basis of society...c. MONEY, 58

curse c. globalization GLOBALISATION, 1

wealth most often proves a c. WEALTH, 46

customer a c. should have...different ways to shop E-COMMERCE, 13

a real c. yelling at you CUSTOMERS, 2

Better service for the c. PRINCIPLES, 15

how can you make the c. happy CORPORATE CULTURE, 68

I come with the mindset of a c. CUSTOMERS, 16

the c....determines...wages CUSTOMERS, 26

The c. is always right CUSTOMERS, 27

the c. is king CUSTOMERS, 23

The c. is never wrong CUSTOMERS, 25

the c....knows more about the goods ADVERTISING, 74

The c. will become so integrated CUSTOMERS, 28

customers a company's c....effectively control what it can and cannot do CUSTOMERS, 7

C. are in control today CONSUMERS, 3

C. are your future CUSTOMERS, 9

C. do not care about industry boundaries CONSUMERS, 18

C....most accurate barometer of what's right CUSTOMERS, 22

C. must trust an organisation BUSINESS ETHICS, 43

c. spread our message by word of mouth COMMUNICATION, 34

Don't sell c. goods SELLING, 22

give c. what they want CUSTOMERS, 18

Good c. are an asset LOYALTY, 8

if c. don't like it CUSTOMERS, 17

If you look after the c. SUCCESS, 29

In the future...lots of c. JOBS, 7

it's being friends with your c. CUSTOMERS, 21

relationship with c....question of personal identification CUSTOMERS, 24

treat the c. well...c. will return CORPORATE CULTURE, 139

cut c. its headquarters staff by 90 percent HIRING AND FIRING, 3

cycle To engage in the learning c. LEARNING, 19

cynics C. about government have much to be cynical GOVERNMENTS, 49

D

damn D. with faint praise PRAISE, 15

danger D. breeds best on too much confidence CONFIDENCE, 5

d. signals that flag problems: silence, secretiveness, or sudden outburst PROBLEMS, 31

The greatest d. is in standing still. PROCRASTINATION, 14

victory without d....triumph without glory WINNERS AND WINNING, 10

dangerous A desperate disease requires a d. remedy RISK TAKING, 17

It is d. to be sincere SINCERITY, 41

It's always d. to give interviews PUBLICITY, 13

Nothing in all the world is more d. SINCERITY, 23

Nothing is more d. than an idea IDEAS, 7

dangers Delays breed d. PROCRASTINATION, 22

Freedom of conscience entails more d. CONSCIENCE, 10

daring win respect for d. and courage RISK TAKING, 34

Darwinian capitalism is inherently D. CAPITALISM, 34

D. shakeouts in every major marketplace GLOBALISATION, 98

data hard d. may inform the intellect INFORMATION, 19

importance of collecting d. MARKETING, 6

The more the d. banks record INFORMATION, 18

datamation the new age of d. MARKETING, 33

deadlines I love d. TIME MANAGEMENT, 1

deaf When money talks, few are d. MONEY, 19

dealmaking D. beats working RISK TAKING, 14

My style of d. is quite simple CONTRACTS, 9

deals D. are my art form ACHIEVING, 40
There is always more money than d. MONEY, 96
dear Oh God, that bread should be so d. BUSINESS ETHICS, 65
death Don't study the idea to d. with experts and
  committees BOLDNESS, 11
end up being nibbled to d. COMPETITION, 48
debate art of d. lies in presenting them DECISIONS, 24
Debenhams D. is still a well-kept secret BRANDS, 8
debt D. is an evil conscience CONSCIENCE, 12
The d. is like a crazy aunt DEBT, 9
the national d. would be doubled DEBT, 3
decays A debt...never d. DEBT, 1
deceit Use no hurtful d. SINCERITY, 14
decency Have you no sense of d. CHARACTER, 72
decent how few d., honest folk there are about HONESTY, 3
decentralisation D....not the mildest form of organisation
  ORGANISATIONS, 72
Intense d....gives managers the freedom CORPORATE
  CULTURE, 40
decentralising big companies are d. ENTREPRENEURS, 29
deception Any seeming d....is costly ADVERTISING, 73
decide Advisers advise and ministers d. DECISIONS, 27
d....succumb to the preponderance of one set of influences
  DECISIONS, 4
Now who is to d. DECISIONS, 19
decided Once the *what* is d. CHOICE, 1
decidedly act d. and take the consequences
  PROCRASTINATION, 18
decision A bad d. is when you know DECISIONS, 12
A complex d. is like a great river DECISIONS, 25
a d. was made, I did not worry DECISIONS, 30
A wrong d. isn't forever PROCRASTINATION, 13
d. to do that extra bit SERVICE, 6
make a d. about a person or problem DECISIONS, 13
Modelers build intricate d. trees CORPORATE CULTURE, 88
never make mistakes...never taken a d. MISTAKES, 29
What is important is not the d. DECISIONS, 22
With every d. we make CONSUMERS, 9
you should never exclude how you feel from your
  d.-making process DECISIONS, 14
decision making D. by consensus DECISIONS, 21
decisions an environment in which others make d.
  LEADERSHIP, 110
d....made on qualitative data MARKETING, 39
Good d. come from wisdom DECISIONS, 1
make erroneous d. very quickly MISTAKES, 15
more d. are made on serendipity than people think LUCK, 10
People who are making d. about the future DECISIONS, 16
Reflective back talk increases...good d. COMMUNICATION, 6
The man who is denied the opportunity of taking d.
  OPPORTUNITY, 1
dedicated never d. to something you have complete
  confidence in CONFIDENCE, 34
deeply-entrenched d. mental models CORPORATE
  CULTURE, 126
defeat D. doesn't finish a man PERSISTENCE, 13
Never talk d. CHALLENGE, 5
defeats We all have to take d. in life LOSING, 1
defer D. no time; delays have dangerous ends
  PROCRASTINATION, 27
deficits D....when adults tell the government what they
  want DEBT, 7
define d. ourselves by reclaiming the words that d. us
  COMMUNICATION, 22
definition conventional d. of management MANAGEMENT, 1
degenerate private decisions produce a less d. capitalism
  CAPITALISM, 28
delay In d. there is advantage PROCRASTINATION, 15
delayering D. and destaffing HIRING AND FIRING, 11
delegate Do not d. an assignment LEADERSHIP, 102
people who are really, really bright...difficult to d.
  DELEGATING, 12
deliverable Buy what's d. EXPECTATIONS, 2
delivery his d. took off from the force SPEECHES, 57
delusion The d. that you're perfect PERFECTION, 3
demand We also d. our place in the sun TARGETS, 25

demands People can place d....that create uncertainty
  STRESS, 3
demarcation the grimy rules of union d. CHANGE, 46
democracy A true d....run on trust and freedom CORPORATE
  CULTURE, 123
Ordinary people may not understand...d. PEOPLE AND
  RELATIONSHIPS, 28
socialist d....more of a sham than capitalist d. CAPITALISM
  VERSUS SOCIALISM, 30
We have an underdeveloped d. CAPITALISM, 33
demographics the d. I'm looking for MARKETING, 28
department have a one-girl people d. HIRING AND FIRING, 30
departure An involuntary return to the point of d.
  PROGRESS, 35
depend D. on none but yourself INDEPENDENCE, 2
depression A d. is either a 12 percent unemployment rate
  BOOM AND BUST, 6
A d....self-fulfilling pessimism BOOM AND BUST, 12
design Good d. is good business EXCELLENCE, 13
if I need it, I d. it CUSTOMERS, 20
It is duality of d. we're concerned with PRODUCTS, 6
desire All progress is based upon a universal innate d.
  PROGRESS, 7
D. of riches, covetousness WEALTH, 30
d....to be richer than other men AMBITION, 20
It is a strange d. to seek power POWER, 8
modern corporation must manufacture...d. ADVERTISING, 23
desk know a person by the kind of d. EXECUTIVES, 32
despair D. is the prize GOALS AND OBJECTIVES, 10
despise To know all...is to d. everybody KNOWLEDGE, 8
destiny bankers' d....dangerous edge of the world
  BANKING, 24
destroyed not...the Spaniards that d....the Aztecs FAILURE, 49
detail life is frittered away by d. DETAILS, 3
details become very rich by paying attention to d. DETAILS, 11
don't get involved in the d. CORPORATE CULTURE, 101
God is in the d. DETAILS, 23
keep in touch with the d. DETAILS, 25
deteriorating response to d. business FAILURE, 36
determinant biggest d. is being in the right place LUCK, 1
development authorities makes...technological d. possible
  GOVERNMENTS, 28
d. of a successful enterprise GOALS AND OBJECTIVES, 18
The classic d. questions TECHNOLOGY, 3
the strengths of economic d. ECONOMICS, 53
devil The d. is always blaming someone BLAME, 22
dictator The customer is d. CUSTOMERS, 1
dies sell your horse before he d. LOSING, 4
difference d. between rhetoric and actuality EMPLOYEES, 28
d. between the American and the European CHARACTER, 3
What's the d. between a guy PERSISTENCE, 3
different work on something completely d....best ideas
  CREATIVITY, 14
You can't win without being...d. COMPETITION, 18
difficult nothing more d. to take in hand CHANGE, 88
There is nothing so easy but that it becomes d.
  ENTHUSIASM, 15
difficulty d. comes from lack of confidence CONFIDENCE, 37
Settle one d. PROBLEMS, 2
digital change all the processes...to be d. PRACTICE, 2
each generation will become more d. TECHNOLOGY, 40
how to make d. commerce more trustworthy
  E-COMMERCE, 17
look at the future being d. TECHNOLOGY, 43
the d. age cannot be denied TECHNOLOGY, 41
diligence D. is the mother of good fortune DETERMINATION, 7
dime Here's a d. Call up both of them EXECUTIVES, 45
diplomacy D....letting someone else have your way
  NEGOTIATION, 7
directed Action...must be d. ACTION, 20
direction Changing the d. of a large company CHANGE, 113
moving in roughly the same d. COMMUNICATION, 3
Setting the d. of the company has become one of my
  priorities PRIORITIES, 4
directors Don't try to manage from any board of d.
  MEETINGS, 10

equations What is it that breathes fire into the e. KNOWLEDGE, 17

equilibrium financial markets tend towards e. ECONOMICS, 108

equities sellers of e. in the near future INVESTMENT AND THE STOCK MARKET, 14

eraser You can't live life without an e. MISTAKES, 22

error E. is just as important a condition MISTAKES, 14

Give me fruitful e. any time MISTAKES, 21

It is the response to e. that counts MISTAKES, 11

We are...coded for e. MISTAKES, 31

errors E. using inadequate data are much less MISTAKES, 28

Honorable e. do not count as failures FAILURE, 24

essence Look to the e. of a thing DETAILS, 22

essentials e. of a fertile, creative environment RESEARCH, 18

esteem Never e. anything as of advantage SINCERITY, 30

estimate just e. of a renowned man's character CHARACTER, 66

ethic the Chinese...invented the wok e. WORK AND EMPLOYMENT, 8

ethical a decision entails e. considerations BUSINESS ETHICS, 55

America's greatest economic need is higher e. standards CORRUPTION AND SCANDAL, 11

E. traps...easy to step over moral boundaries BUSINESS ETHICS, 74

Unless managers are aware of e. issues BUSINESS ETHICS, 56

ethically create wealth legally and e. BUSINESS ETHICS, 90

etiquette It isn't e. to cut anyone BUSINESS ETHICS, 21

Europe 'going into E.'...like nine middle-aged couples GLOBALISATION, 91

E....is after all our own backyard STRATEGY, 13

E. is something happening GLOBALISATION, 81

E.'s strength is its diversity DOING BUSINESS IN EUROPE, 6

E. will become a discotheque FORECASTING, 3

One must genuinely create E. DOING BUSINESS IN EUROPE, 8

The bureaucratic method of building an integrated E. BUREAUCRACY, 43

We are part of the community of E. GLOBALISATION, 38

European The E. companies that prosper DOING BUSINESS IN EUROPE, 4

event A mistake is an e. MISTAKES, 18

events e. have controlled me POWER, 57

everlasting The Great Principles...as e. as the Pyramids PRINCIPLES, 21

everything A place for e. ORDER, 26

we've blown up e. SUCCESS, 61

evil enter into e. when necessity commands BUSINESS ETHICS, 79

the love of money is the root of all e. MONEY, 23

evils Men do not live only by fighting e. GOALS AND OBJECTIVES, 3

The e. of our big businesses GREED, 5

evolving something that is constantly e. CORPORATE CULTURE, 95

examining e....a roulette wheel RESEARCH, 22

example E. is the school of mankind LEARNING, 8

it was easy to lead by e. LEADERSHIP, 51

To take a simple e. BUSINESS ETHICS, 63

excel By different methods different men e. ACHIEVING, 9

Chinese could e. at things DOING BUSINESS IN ASIA-PACIFIC, 33

excellence e. makes people nervous EXCELLENCE, 1

excellent All things e. are as difficult EXCELLENCE, 11

The e. companies treat the rank and file PEOPLE AND RELATIONSHIPS, 32

excess Anything worth doing is worth doing to e. FOCUS, 6

excitement lower slopes of this e. E-COMMERCE, 21

excuse There is no e. FAILURE, 34

excuses Principles are only e. PRINCIPLES, 14

executed the way that concept is e. PRODUCTS, 19

executive a full-time chief e....a full-time job EXECUTIVES, 52

an e. is...as good as his health EXECUTIVES, 6

Civilization has developed e. powers CIVILISATION, 29

E.: A man who can make quick decisions EXECUTIVES, 40

e....scared of going crazy EXECUTIVES, 39

Handled creatively, getting fired allows an e. HIRING AND FIRING, 22

I am a young e. EXECUTIVES, 15

most common cause of e. failure FAILURE, 15

self-assured e....groveling shred HIRING AND FIRING, 21

The distinguishing mark of the e. responsibility CORPORATE RESPONSIBILITY, 3

the e....formulate and define purpose EXECUTIVES, 9

The successful e....the exceptional man EXECUTIVES, 35

executives Damn the great e. EXECUTIVES, 43

E. are like joggers EXECUTIVES, 12

e. continue to believe that they are 'not in the technology business' EXECUTIVES, 36

E....having a clean desk EXECUTIVES, 2

e....less well informed about the outside world KNOWLEDGE, 10

e. tend to focus downward GOALS AND OBJECTIVES, 8

If e. could learn to get things right EXECUTIVES, 24

Successful e. are great askers EXECUTIVES, 14

Today's adaptive e. EXECUTIVES, 53

Too many companies...justify e.' high salaries INVESTMENT AND THE STOCK MARKET, 27

Top e. know that they have to shift ORGANISATIONS, 22

exercise For e., I wind my watch IMAGE, 19

exertion e....is the best thing for us all WORK AND EMPLOYMENT, 90

exhilaration you'll feel a mixture of e. GETTING STARTED, 32

existence Another e. swallowed up in the fearful rush CIVILISATION, 7

expect Many people e. many things PUBLICITY, 16

expectations never listen to other people's e. INDEPENDENCE, 14

expenditure E. rises to meet income MONEY, 75

experience All e. is an arch EXPERIENCE, 1

everyone is paid in two coins: cash and e. EXPERIENCE, 19

E. has shown us that the trade of the East DOING BUSINESS IN ASIA-PACIFIC, 7

E.! Idiots do not heed it EXPERIENCE, 32

E. is a dim lamp EXPERIENCE, 6

e. is like the stern lights of a ship EXPERIENCE, 8

E. is never limited EXPERIENCE, 23

E. isn't interesting EXPERIENCE, 5

E. is the name everyone gives to their mistakes EXPERIENCE, 41

e....recognise...the folly that we have already embraced EXPERIENCE, 4

E. teaches slowly EXPERIENCE, 17

E. teaches /that it doesn't EXPERIENCE, 26

e. teaches us nothing EXPERIENCE, 30

E. teaches you that the man...is hiding something EXPERIENCE, 16

I try to avoid e. if I can EXPERIENCE, 11

We had the e. but missed the meaning INFORMATION, 8

You cannot acquire e. by making experiments EXPERIENCE, 7

experientia E. docuit EXPERIENCE, 38

E. does it—as papa used to say EXPERIENCE, 10

experimented we haven't e. ADVERTISING, 70

expert An e. is someone...to share the blame BLAME, 11

An e....knows more...about less KNOWLEDGE, 4

An e....knows...the worst errors EXPERIENCE, 21

I don't try to become an e. DELEGATING, 5

the e....wrong for more sophisticated reasons RESEARCH, 3

expertise power flows from e. POWER, 80

You build an e. around the customer CUSTOMERS, 19

explain enable me at all times satisfactorily to e. policies LEADERSHIP, 3

Never apologize and never e. NEGOTIATION, 19

explicit make your speech /not too e. SPEECHES, 25

exploitation our relationships...forms of mutual e. LOYALTY, 2

exploring end of all our e. /Will be to arrive EXPERIENCE, 13

expression I'm all in favour of free e. MEDIA, 2

extra Go the e. mile PERSISTENCE, 8

extraordinary ordinary people to create e. results MANAGEMENT, 3
eyeball We're e. to e. COMPETITION, 68
eyes looking into people's e. COMMUNICATION, 16

F

face We f. neither East nor West GLOBALISATION, 70
facilitators most effective f. in learning processes LEARNING, 40
facilities We don't have a lot of f. GETTING STARTED, 24
factories If f. are wanting ORGANISATIONS, 2
factors f. in building a self-motivated team TEAMS, 8
facts attack the f. RESEARCH, 8
Comment is free but f. are sacred OPINIONS, 34
Don't bother me with the f. GOALS AND OBJECTIVES, 28
F. are available to everyone INFORMATION, 25
F. are the most important thing in business RESEARCH, 6
F....constitute the greatest force ACCURACY, 1
f. were there to be challenged LAWYERS, 12
I am a seeker of the small f. INFORMATION, 27
The exact f....constitute a series of laws EMPLOYEES, 78
twist f. to suit theories CORRUPTION AND SCANDAL, 12
fail decide how we are going to f. FAILURE, 48
If you aren't afraid to f. FAILURE, 42
It is hard to f. FAILURE, 47
to succeed. Others must f. SUCCESS, 100
failing F. is a learning experience FAILURE, 27
F. is good FAILURE, 17
failure F. is a man who has blundered FAILURE, 32
F. is the foundation of success FAILURE, 37
f. was the only thing that worked predictably FAILURE, 28
For every f., there's an alternative FAILURE, 4
let avoiding f. become your motivator MANAGEMENT, 30
no success like f. SUCCESS, 30
respond to f. by coming back SUCCESS, 38
success can only be achieved through repeated f. FAILURE, 31
The difference between f. and success FAILURE, 52
The majority of men meet with f. FAILURE, 29
The payoff for f. FAILURE, 1
They have no fear of f. ENTREPRENEURS, 44
failures F., repeated f., are finger posts FAILURE, 35
learn from the f. and...keep going WINNERS AND WINNING, 19
fair f. and right thing to do HIRING AND FIRING, 7
Make a F. Product for a F. Price ADVERTISING, 78
faith A f. is something you die for LEADERSHIP, 10
f....makes markets INVESTMENT AND THE STOCK MARKET, 54
Have f. and pursue the unknown end ATTITUDE, 12
In America, business is going on f. DECISIONS, 23
No one can build...unless he has f. CONFIDENCE, 31
total f. in the marketplace BANKING, 21
faithfulness f. and sincerity as first principles SINCERITY, 7
fall The bigger they come the harder they f. COMPETITION, 22
Whenever you f., pick up something EXPERIENCE, 3
you can't f. off the floor CONFIDENCE, 10
falsity Recognition of the f. of material wealth WEALTH, 44
fame I must have f. PUBLICITY, 18
familiarity F. is the culmination of successful brand building BRANDS, 15
family Ambivalence about f. responsibilities...long history in the corporate world CORPORATE CULTURE, 77
average f. exists only on paper STATISTICS, 8
I know the importance of what f. means PEOPLE AND RELATIONSHIPS, 36
like breaking up a f. row as an outsider ORGANISATIONS, 66
fanaticism F. consists in redoubling your effort DETERMINATION, 21
fancies The public mind is polluted with economic f. WEALTH, 16
fancy F....mode of memory emancipated IMAGINATION, 5
Tell me where is f. bred IMAGINATION, 18
fantasy F. romps TECHNOLOGY, 4

fashion F....a gentle progression of revisited ideas INNOVATION, 70
F. is something barbarous BUSINESS ETHICS, 101
F....the lowest form of ideology CRITICISM, 13
I'm really against is the hype of f. PUBLICITY, 14
fashionable For an idea...to be f. is ominous INNOVATION, 82
fast To go f., row slowly PROGRESS, 24
faster new environment...everything happens f. CHANGE, 58
fat Through the f. years BANKING, 10
fat cats Sure, I'm one of the f. EXECUTIVES, 60
fate become the makers of our f. INNOVATION, 78
For Man is man and master of his f. RESPONSIBILITY, 26
If you can't change your f. ATTITUDE, 21
fates Men...are masters of their f. RESPONSIBILITY, 22
faults If we had no f. of our own BLAME, 23
No man can tell another his f. CRITICISM, 2
Those see nothing but f. BLAME, 14
favouritism In all industries...unashamed f. BUSINESS ETHICS, 4
fear Drive out f. LEADERSHIP, 45
The things we f. most...need not be signs ORGANISATIONS, 86
federal reserve the F. have mugged America BOOM AND BUST, 4
feel Let us say what we f. SINCERITY, 39
female I am a f. It's a mixed blessing DISCRIMINATION, 50
the emergence of a...field of f. talent DISCRIMINATION, 33
feminist f. surge...to the top of a Fortune 500 corporation DISCRIMINATION, 18
Ferrari seeing a man in a F. DOING BUSINESS IN NORTH AMERICA, 2
fetish Perfection can be a f. PERFECTION, 4
Fidel Castro Miami's single most important economic development agent...F. DOING BUSINESS IN NORTH AMERICA, 9
fidelity successful conduct...f. and zeal INDUSTRY, 19
field Whoever is first in the f. PLANNING, 24
field theory F. is a method of analyzing causal relations IDEAS, 14
fight It is not enough to f. WINNERS AND WINNING, 30
roses might f. it out with the weeds PRINCIPLES, 20
figures One can't say that f. lie BUSINESS ETHICS, 104
files Poor fellow, he suffers from f. BUREAUCRACY, 5
filing F. is concerned with the past ORDER, 35
fill f. the unforgiving minute ACHIEVING, 19
finance F. is an art MONEY, 30
International f. is always looking for new opportunities DOING BUSINESS IN AFRICA, 3
financial Derivatives are f. weapons of mass destruction INVESTMENT AND THE STOCK MARKET, 9
f. markets can affect the...fundamentals BOOM AND BUST, 14
If we want to be part of the f. mainstream SUCCESS, 93
financial markets F....resent any kind of government interference INVESTMENT AND THE STOCK MARKET, 72
finish it is how you f. that counts ACHIEVING, 13
fire the whole personnel department HIRING AND FIRING, 29
I wanted to set the world on f. ENTREPRENEURS, 36
The whole thing is f. GETTING STARTED, 23
Whenever our neighbour's house is on f. ADVERSITY, 6
firecrackers Other people set off f. EXECUTIVES, 17
fired People in the company are almost never f. HIRING AND FIRING, 15
fireflies F. throwing off sparks before the storm E-COMMERCE, 18
fireworks F. are the best fun you can have MONEY, 27
firing I have a reputation for f. editors HIRING AND FIRING, 25
first F. things f., second things never PRIORITIES, 1
there will be a f. among equals CORPORATE CULTURE, 100
fiscal responsibility mood of the country is for f. GOVERNMENTS, 24
fit If the shoe doesn't f....change the foot CHANGE, 120
fixation f. with financial measures MANAGEMENT, 58
fixed what is broken and what needs to be f. EXECUTIVES, 7
fix-it We were forced to become a f. company CORPORATE CULTURE, 65
flag trade has...tended to follow the f. INDUSTRY, 14
flamingo a very large f. DEBT, 8

G

Region-states...primary linkage is with the g. economy GLOBALISATION, 71
The new model is g. GLOBALISATION, 82
We're not going g. because we want to GLOBALISATION, 61
globalisation G....excludes nobody GLOBALISATION, 13
G. has...made the citizen disappear GLOBALISATION, 84
G....intensification of worldwide social relations GLOBALISATION, 37
G. is a long-lasting competitive advantage GLOBALISATION, 4
G. is an opportunity GLOBALISATION, 42
G. is not inevitable GLOBALISATION, 85
G. requires...a cross-cultural perspective GLOBALISATION, 11
G. will not go away CAPITALISM VERSUS SOCIALISM, 34
Our key words now are g. GLOBALISATION, 47
globally The time has...come...to think g. GLOBALISATION, 53
Think g., not locally GLOBALISATION, 34
glory The g. of good men CONSCIENCE, 21
gloves We have got to take the g. off PEOPLE AND RELATIONSHIPS, 4
gnomes little g. of Zürich BANKING, 29
goal g....as being profit-maximisation GROWTH, 3
No set. g. achieved satisfies SUCCESS, 24
The g. of a big business person GOALS AND OBJECTIVES, 13
goals g. on which hope are based TARGETS, 18
I haven't spent any time setting g. STRATEGY, 19
God Act of G....no reasonable man could have expected PLANNING, 15
G. must have loved the People in Power POWER, 68
going If you don't know where you are g. CONFIDENCE, 33
gold put g. in front of his eyes WORK AND EMPLOYMENT, 39
golden g. age of economic change SUCCESS, 57
golf Their problem is that they play a lot of g. EXECUTIVES, 11
good Being g. is g. business CORPORATE RESPONSIBILITY, 29
Start with g. people EMPLOYEES, 35
We know the g. BUSINESS ETHICS, 39
goods Arguably the only g. people need CONSUMERS, 6
g. and services can be paid for only with g. and services WAGES, 35
gossip Blood sport is...the g. columns MEDIA, 27
governance democratic and participatory g. CAPITALISM, 41
in London, the focus is on corporate g. MANAGEMENT, 31
government A g. which robs Peter to pay Paul GOVERNMENTS, 54
definitely a role for g. GOVERNMENTS, 7
extend the mastery of the G. GOVERNMENTS, 25
function of g. to invent philosophies GOVERNMENTS, 29
G....badge of lost innocence GOVERNMENTS, 38
G. could do better GOVERNMENTS, 32
G. does not solve problems GOVERNMENTS, 47
g. from a principle in nature GOVERNMENTS, 39
G. has an essential role to play in...entrepreneurial culture GOVERNMENTS, 21
g....leader in the use of technology GOVERNMENTS, 20
G. proposes, bureaucracy disposes BUREAUCRACY, 36
G. should focus on infrastructure investment GOVERNMENTS, 59
important role for g. in future economic success GOVERNMENTS, 60
most powerful force...her own g. GOVERNMENTS, 53
problem for any g. BUREAUCRACY, 13
problem in g....things are already messed up GOVERNMENTS, 11
Socialism substitutes for individual energy...g. COMMUNISM AND SOCIALISM, 1
the g. can't...run anything GOVERNMENTS, 27
the g. is big enough...to take away everything GOVERNMENTS, 16
The only good g. GOVERNMENTS, 13
There is no art which one g. sooner learns GOVERNMENTS, 55
we mean to have less of G. in business CAPITALISM, 21
governments G. can err GOVERNMENTS, 51
G. of the Industrial World...I come from Cyberspace GOVERNMENTS, 3
grab we could g. as much as we could GREED, 10
gradualness The inevitability of g. CHANGE, 132
grammar The introduction of a new g. ORGANISATIONS, 47

grand g. world plan for News Corporation STRATEGY, 43
very g. to 'die in harness' WORK AND EMPLOYMENT, 56
grasp a man's reach should exceed his g. GOALS AND OBJECTIVES, 4
gratification slaves of 'possession' and of immediate g. CIVILISATION, 21
great G. men can't be ruled POWER, 69
One sees g. things from the valley GETTING STARTED, 1
Some are born g. ORGANISATIONS, 9
To achieve g. things we must live ACHIEVING, 44
Whatever a g. man does, others imitate LEADERSHIP, 23
What's g. about this country CONSUMERS, 42
greater Four things g. than all things are POWER, 49
greatest I'm the double g. BOASTING, 1
greatness the nature of g. ACCURACY, 4
greed enough...not for everyone's g. CONSUMERS, 2
G. is all right CORRUPTION AND SCANDAL, 5
G. is right. G. works GREED, 12
G....more contagious than fear GREED, 9
people will be full of g. GREED, 3
greedy Many people have called me g. GREED, 14
you can't be too g. GREED, 15
green G....seen as the environmental colour CORPORATE CULTURE, 120
greener We can be richer by being g. BUSINESS ETHICS, 14
greenleaf profound impact on thinking about leadership...Robert G. LEADERSHIP, 112
grow businesses that fail to g....stagnate and die CHANGE, 114
Do those served g. as persons LEADERSHIP, 66
If we don't change, we don't g. CHANGE, 117
growth economic g. has the marvellous quality of stilling discontent ECONOMICS, 18
G. does not always...build on success GROWTH, 2
G. is like creativity PROGRESS, 13
level of g. that is...dangerous and deadly GROWTH, 4
Nothing seems to support...personal g. PERSONAL GROWTH, 5
Only through g....real economic deal SUCCESS, 94
The g. of a large business GROWTH, 7
grudge Advice...creates a g. ADVICE, 3
guidelines G. for bureaucrats...When in doubt, mumble BUREAUCRACY, 6
guilty Don't act too g. ADVERTISING, 10
gurus of management g. there is no...end CORPORATE CULTURE, 82
guy g. to get people to do things LEADERSHIP, 122

H

habit Excellence is not an act but a h. EXCELLENCE, 3
nothing so h. forming as money MONEY, 61
habits reconciling net income with gross h. BUDGETING, 6
hallucination It was a mass h. INVESTMENT AND THE STOCK MARKET, 11
hands when I want a pair of h. EMPLOYEES, 21
happens We know what h. DECISIONS, 3
happiness H....lies in the joy of achievement ACHIEVING, 32
It is not...prosperity that makes for h. WEALTH, 61
hard H. work is an Asian compulsion DOING BUSINESS IN ASIA-PACIFIC, 3
I'm not h. CHARACTER, 62
It is a h. world. Be harder CHARACTER, 59
hardest Sometimes the first step is the h. IDEAS, 28
hard sell A h. advertisement ADVERTISING, 66
hardships A gentleman can withstand h. PROBLEMS, 10
hardware h. is the bone of the head COMPUTERS, 16
hard work h. never killed anyone WORK AND EMPLOYMENT, 78
harmony Speaking your mind...is bad for group h. DOING BUSINESS IN ASIA-PACIFIC, 18
hatred Few top executives can even imagine the h. EMPLOYEES, 15
havoc I cause too much h. DELEGATING, 17
head Alexander at the h. of the world POWER, 87

People want to be h. of General Motors AMBITION, 13
Run with your h. the first two thirds WINNERS AND WINNING, 11
headline I'm not a h. kind of guy PUBLICITY, 10
hear the time will come when you will h. me SPEECHES, 16
heart Prepare your h. and mind SPEECHES, 15
put your h. in the business CORPORATE CULTURE, 146
put your h. in the business SUCCESS, 101
rent a brain...you can't rent a h. ENTHUSIASM, 12
heat If you can't stand the h. ADVERSITY, 25
heaven Every man is as H. made him CHARACTER, 10
help h. people see what I see VALUE, 14
helping H. someone personally...a better measure of
success CUSTOMERS, 13
Henry Ford Could H. produce the Book of Kells?
CREATIVITY, 40
heretics Modern h. are not burned at the stake HIRING AND
FIRING, 19
heterogeneous The process of developing h. resources
MANAGEMENT, 46
hiccups H. in the international business scene BRANDS, 4
hierarchical Finding the right balance of h. looseness
LEADERSHIP, 6
hierarchies We use minimal h. CORPORATE CULTURE, 125
hierarchy H. of needs SELLING, 21
high-priced a h. man has to do exactly as he is told
EMPLOYEES, 79
high-tech many companies in h. businesses will grow
much faster INVESTMENT AND THE STOCK MARKET, 12
with h....end up using scissors TECHNOLOGY, 29
hindsight H. gives everyone perfect vision JUDGEMENTS, 10
H. is always 20–20 EXPERIENCE, 42
H. is good, foresight is better PLANNING, 12
hire I worked for a menial's h. WAGES, 39
We would not knowingly h. anyone LEARNING, 48
Would you h. you HIRING AND FIRING, 31
historical Statistical figures...are h. data STATISTICS, 7
history H. cannot be reduced ECONOMICS, 44
H....includes the risks players take ORGANISATIONS, 39
I didn't come to NASA to make h. ACHIEVING, 31
I'm in h. and I like myself ACHIEVING, 43
The modern h. of economic theory ECONOMICS, 6
hit The gravy train has h. the buffers EMPLOYEES, 49
hits Swing for h. STRATEGY, 8
hoarding H. information...expressed...power
INFORMATION, 17
Men who continue h. great sums GREED, 4
hold h. office, if not resign DETERMINATION, 28
holistically Treating processes h. PRODUCTS, 3
holy there can be no h. cows CHANGE, 72
home A man who leaves h. TRAVEL, 2
homogeneous I remember how h. corporations were
DISCRIMINATION, 41
honest not impossible to conduct strictly h. business
BUSINESS ETHICS, 52
honestly If possible h....make money MONEY, 49
honesty Total commercial h. always costs something
HONESTY, 7
We often take...h. for granted CONFIDENCE, 16
honeymoon h. of small changes CHANGE, 11
honour a man of h....regrets a discreditable act
CONSCIENCE, 29
H. sinks where commerce long prevails HONESTY, 6
honours It is better to deserve h. ACCOMPLISHMENTS, 15
hope accomplished...when there seemed to be no h.
DETERMINATION, 6
H. is the power of being cheerful DETERMINATION, 8
hopeless No situation is ever absolutely h. OBSTACLES, 4
horizon the far h. will find his right road GOALS AND
OBJECTIVES, 11
horse a h. always knows when the rider is afraid CORPORATE
CULTURE, 133
horses pick h. to ride for five to ten year periods
FORECASTING, 9
hosiery queen h. masquerading as a food company
IMAGE, 23
hot air Everything he says is...h. REPUTATION, 9

hotels H. are a wonderful business ORGANISATIONS, 49
hours h. are scourges WAGES, 46
If I had eight h. to chop down a tree PROCRASTINATION, 21
It's not the h. you put in your work TIME MANAGEMENT, 7
human Microsoft's only factory asset is the h. ingredient
EMPLOYEES, 52
no h. feeling to the US securities markets INVESTMENT AND
THE STOCK MARKET, 30
human being h....forever debarred from rational
understanding EMPLOYEES, 33
human capital H. grows two ways PEOPLE AND
RELATIONSHIPS, 35
humanity H. seems bent on creating a world economy
ECONOMICS, 7
human nature general course of h. POWER, 37
human rights we cry out for h. EMPLOYEES, 7
humiliating Nothing is more h. than to have to beg WORK
AND EMPLOYMENT, 30
humiliation With publicity comes h. PUBLICITY, 12
You will find that you survive h. EXPERIENCE, 14
humility If I only had a little h. BOASTING, 14
something that transcends pride...h. ACCOMPLISHMENTS, 12
humour H....most significant activity of the human brain
CHARACTER, 15
humourless Men are quite h. CORPORATE CULTURE, 90
hunch one person's h....enough to launch a new product
INNOVATION, 80
hurdles I don't really see the h. CONFIDENCE, 30
hurts It h. to lose LOSING, 3
hygiene We sort out all the h. factors RISK TAKING, 25
hypocrite The true h....lies with sincerity SINCERITY, 15
We ought to see far enough into a h. SINCERITY, 6
hypotheses h. matter...actions matter CAREERS, 7
hypothesis discard a pet h. every day INNOVATION, 57

I

IBM I. is like the Stepford Wives CORPORATE CULTURE, 23
idea a new i. should develop out of what is already there
IDEAS, 10
An i. can turn to dust or magic TALENT, 4
An i. isn't responsible IDEAS, 16
A powerful new i. INNOVATION, 54
Every really new i. looks crazy IDEAS, 27
have your next i. waiting in the wings STRATEGY, 32
I think it would be an excellent i. CIVILISATION, 14
I want to see an i. INNOVATION, 45
perpetual i. machine INNOVATION, 4
possessed by an i....you even smell it CREATIVITY, 33
stealing an i. IDEAS, 1
ideal for an i. to become a reality CHANGE, 74
something 'i.'...lose the opportunity to improve GROWTH, 8
ideas energy, daring, and staying power to implement i.
INNOVATION, 56
guarantee a steady stream of new i. INNOVATION, 66
I. are relatively cheap to have MARKETING, 14
i. are the lifeblood IDEAS, 5
I. are useless unless used IDEAS, 13
I. do not rule the world IDEAS, 11
i. of economists and political philosophers ECONOMICS, 60
Keep on the lookout for novel i. ORIGINALITY, 3
Never invest in any i. you can't illustrate INVESTMENT AND
THE STOCK MARKET, 56
new i. are the lifeblood of any thriving organization IDEAS, 18
Our best i. come from clerks and schoolboys INNOVATION, 93
people are frightened of new i. IDEAS, 6
spontaneous exchange of fresh i. MEETINGS, 6
the best i....during the final five minutes MEETINGS, 3
The i. I stand for are not mine ORIGINALITY, 2
The mind thinks...with i. CREATIVITY, 47
The only i. that count are 'A' i. IDEAS, 26
Unless your i. are ridiculed by experts VALUE, 12
We're controlled by i. ORGANISATIONS, 83

inertia GM is so large...its i. so great CORPORATE CULTURE, 131
inevitable Change is i. in a progressive country CHANGE, 36
infected All seems i. that the i. spy ATTITUDE, 19
inferior feel i. without your consent CRITICISM, 12
inflammatory no more i. issue PEOPLE AND RELATIONSHIPS, 14
inflation i. caused by excessive money supply PLANNING, 16
i....compare it to bloodletting in the Middle Ages
  ECONOMICS, 52
I. is as violent as a mugger BOOM AND BUST, 11
i. is made...in Washington GOVERNMENTS, 18
I....taxation that can be imposed without legislation
  TAXES, 13
Steel prices cause i. BOOM AND BUST, 1
influence guard against the acquisition of unwarranted i.
  POWER, 27
I have never avoided the i. of others GETTING STARTED, 20
i. is easier when one controls tremendous sums of money
  POWER, 62
Leadership is interpersonal i. LEADERSHIP, 7
Power is the ability to i. individuals CHANGE, 92
unbelievable responsibility to i. decisions DECISIONS, 15
influential be i....and a lover of right POWER, 20
information ability to transmit accurate...i. ACCURACY, 9
all that matters...i. comes from a reputable source
  RESEARCH, 10
A wealth of i. creates a poverty of attention
  INFORMATION, 22
computerized i. services...in the public library
  TECHNOLOGY, 47
emerging i. age...filled with questions PROGRESS, 2
In an i. society BUREAUCRACY, 14
I. about money BANKING, 32
I. is a business INFORMATION, 29
I. is costly to produce INFORMATION, 23
I. is like an oyster INFORMATION, 24
I. is power INFORMATION, 28
I. is the most valuable commodity MEDIA, 37
i., knowledge applied to work to create value PROGRESS, 15
I. networks straddle the world INFORMATION, 15
i. on everything...to improve performance INFORMATION, 9
Innovation is fostered by i. INNOVATION, 97
no ideas, no i. IDEAS, 21
speed of i., things lose their sense STRESS, 1
take i. responsibly INFORMATION, 6
the better the i. INFORMATION, 7
The informated workplace...is an arena through which i.
  circulates INFORMATION, 30
The i. age...managers are replaced by coaches WORK AND
  EMPLOYMENT, 51
The i. highway will transform our culture CHANGE, 52
the I. Revolution is a fundamental revolution INDUSTRY, 43
There would be a single global i. space INNOVATION, 9
try to take i. that was hidden BUSINESS ETHICS, 37
We live in an i. economy PROBLEMS, 23
whatever i. will further our understanding of the
  company's business INVESTMENT AND THE STOCK MARKET, 15
information technology i....does not convey is perception,
  belief and motivation TECHNOLOGY, 28
ingenuity people...underestimate the i. of complete fools
  INNOVATION, 1
inimitable The true is i. ORIGINALITY, 1
initiative If offended, take the i. INITIATIVE, 1
our scheme does not ask any i. INITIATIVE, 5
innovate You can i. by not doing anything INNOVATION, 50
innovating One cannot be forever i. INNOVATION, 14
innovation Business demands i. INNOVATION, 59
Everyone likes i. INNOVATION, 98
i....a term of economics rather than of technology
  INNOVATION, 22
I....in the form of improved product quality INNOVATION, 10
I. typically occurs at the interface INNOVATION, 68
Knowledge-based i. INNOVATION, 27
measure of i....impact on the environment INNOVATION, 23
most people really don't care about i. INNOVATION, 85
Non-linear i. can be legitimized INNOVATION, 41
still room for i. in this industry INNOVATION, 48

insanity Acts of marketing i. DOING BUSINESS IN
  ASIA-PACIFIC, 19
I....logic of an accurate mind overtasked ACCURACY, 11
insecurity counterpart of a free market economy...i.
  CAPITALISM VERSUS SOCIALISM, 10
insensitivity show some i. to your past CHANGE, 55
insight A moment's i....sometimes worth a life's
  experience EXPERIENCE, 22
I am a big believer in i. EMPLOYEES, 73
insincerity great enemy of clear language is i. SINCERITY, 33
show business is...sincere i. SINCERITY, 19
insinuating i. is more useful than...persuading
  NEGOTIATION, 20
inspiration My principal i. comes from the employees
  COMMUNICATION, 7
institution business is a 'get things done' i. CREATIVITY, 32
institutional collapse seven directors or acting directors in
  six years...i. ORGANISATIONS, 50
institutions a populous backlash...against big i. BUSINESS
  ETHICS, 72
Financial i....were a powerful presence BANKING, 13
i. on the point of collapse PERFECTION, 5
i....vast mass of routine, petty malice, self interest
  ORGANISATIONS, 67
instruction Earth...no i. book came with it BUSINESS
  ETHICS, 50
instructions Written i. are seldom adequate DELEGATING, 9
insurance i. business...no statute of limitation on stupidity
  CORPORATE CULTURE, 21
integration The economic i. of the Pacific...is occuring
  GLOBALISATION, 30
virtual i....of competitive power ORGANISATIONS, 18
integrity Intellectual i....ability to see the world as it is
  LEARNING, 21
the Square of I., Education, Courtesy, and Mutuality
  HONESTY, 3
intellectual All i. improvement arises from leisure
  INTELLIGENCE, 3
I. honesty and truth are at a minimum PRACTICE, 7
Managing i. assets...most important task of business
  PRIORITIES, 5
unimaginable i. interest WORK AND EMPLOYMENT, 49
intellectual capital I....gives it a competitive edge
  INTELLIGENCE, 9
the age of i. INTELLIGENCE, 8
intelligence i. is powerless to modify character
  CHARACTER, 14
I. is quickness to apprehend CREATIVITY, 50
I....is really a kind of taste...in ideas INTELLIGENCE, 7
just enough i....to see clearly CREATIVITY, 9
intelligent rule of i. tinkering...save all the parts
  INNOVATION, 35
intent statements of i....no substitute for concrete action
  EXPERIENCE, 1
interaction personal i. is becoming more important
  COMMUNICATION, 26
interchangeable Too many companies believe people are i.
  TALENT, 3
interdependence The new electronic i. GLOBALISATION, 55
interest the energy you've wasted...to pay i. DEBT, 4
Internet All companies will be I. companies OPINIONS, 12
America has caught I. fever E-COMMERCE, 34
astonishing number of I. start-ups get established
  BOLDNESS, 16
differentiation between I. companies E-COMMERCE, 7
evidence that the I. has had any...influence MEDIA, 3
I don't think the I....change how people chew gum
  COMPUTERS, 5
I. entrepreneurs...how little cognitive behavior CRITICISM, 15
I. is an elite organization E-COMMERCE, 9
I. is like electricity KNOWLEDGE, 22
I....symbol of the new economy TECHNOLOGY, 16
I. will eventually converge with television E-COMMERCE, 26
Many view the I. merely as a sales channel COMPUTERS, 2
On the I....competitive advantage has shrunk
  COMPETITION, 53

reserve thy j. BLAME, 30
The best j. we can make ACCOMPLISHMENTS, 5
There was little real j. ORGANISATIONS, 35
We made a professional j. about...appropriate accounting
  JUDGEMENTS, 2
Where j. has wit SPEECHES, 42
judgements j. from the past may be inadequate CHALLENGE, 3
judo Masters of entrepreneurial j. ENTREPRENEURS, 9
juggler j. keeps...projects in the air EXECUTIVES, 46
justice business must build on j. BUSINESS ETHICS, 120
Injustice anywhere is a threat to j. everywhere OPINIONS, 17
Keep alive the light of j. BLAME, 10

K

KBO We must just K. PERSISTENCE, 4
kick k. in the teeth CHALLENGE, 4
KITA—K. in the ass EMPLOYEES, 31
kill If you're going to k. yourself ENTHUSIASM, 11
killing Business is often about k. CHOICE, 5
kind word to the humble PRAISE, 10
kinship I recognized my k. with all living things PEOPLE AND
  RELATIONSHIPS, 12
knew I k. my day would come AMBITION, 36
knocked Well, we k. the bastard off ACHIEVING, 17
know everything I ever needed to k. about selling
  SELLING, 33
I k. we should try harder CUSTOMERS, 5
I like to k. where things are CHARACTER, 70
know-how The possession of technological k.
  TECHNOLOGY, 54
knowing K. is different from doing DECISIONS, 7
knowledge All k. is of itself of some value DETAILS, 19
Applying k. to k. KNOWLEDGE, 7
Common-sense k. is prompt COMMON SENSE, 7
harnessing our k....to provide better solutions
  INFORMATION, 26
I have direct k. INFORMATION, 21
k. applied to the new is innovation INNOVATION, 24
K. building for an organization KNOWLEDGE, 21
k. is our most important product LEARNING, 50
K. is proportionate to being KNOWLEDGE, 18
K. may give weight KNOWLEDGE, 6
k., not buildings and machinery, is the chief resource
  KNOWLEDGE, 9
K. resides in the heads of people INVESTMENT AND THE STOCK
  MARKET, 38
make k. available BUSINESS ETHICS, 13
make k. workers out of every employee TRAINING, 3
man, in his quest for k. and progress...cannot be deterred
  KNOWLEDGE, 19
more k. about detergents anywhere in the world
  CONSUMERS, 10
The demands for new k. and skills KNOWLEDGE, 26
The use of k. is not easily restricted KNOWLEDGE, 7
To make k. productive CHANGE, 42

L

labelled If you're in jazz...you're l. commercial IMAGE, 17
labour Capital is only the fruit of l. EMPLOYEES, 45
Every thing in the world is purchased by l. WORK AND
  EMPLOYMENT, 57
l....going to be brain power COMPETITION, 41
l. is most productive where its wages are largest WAGES, 15
L. is the foundation of all CIVILISATION, 18
L. is the superior of capital EMPLOYEES, 46
L. is work that leaves no trace WORK AND EMPLOYMENT, 66
Many l. problems have spirit issues at their core
  MANAGEMENT, 9

The habit of l. renders idleness tiresome WORK AND
  EMPLOYMENT, 82
The microdivision of l. CORPORATE CULTURE, 58
The United States...manipulate cheap Mexican l. DOING
  BUSINESS IN LATIN AMERICA, 6
We are ruined by Chinese cheap l. COMPETITION, 31
We cannot survive as a cheap l. platform
  GLOBALISATION, 69
labourer l. is worthy of his hire WAGES, 3
ladder structure of an industry's rope l. CHANGE, 39
laissez-faire L., supply and demand OPINIONS, 3
land Study how a society uses its l. RESPONSIBILITY, 20
language Every company has its own l. CORPORATE
  CULTURE, 55
l. of the industrial leader LEADERSHIP, 72
male l. contained at least two vocabularies
  DISCRIMINATION, 45
our communicated thinking is done with l.
  COMMUNICATION, 15
largest only the l. companies can survive GOVERNMENTS, 17
last good guys always finish l. WINNERS AND WINNING, 5
Las Vegas L....freedom to do nutty things CONFIDENCE, 45
Latin America L....awake to the opportunity of the Internet
  DOING BUSINESS IN LATIN AMERICA, 8
US capital is...concentrated in L. DOING BUSINESS IN LATIN
  AMERICA, 7
laughing increase your brain power...by l. ATTITUDE, 9
launching L. a start-up GETTING STARTED, 2
law a contemptible l. is itself contemptible JUDGEMENTS, 9
a large business is not against the l. PRACTICE, 5
Every l. is a contract CONTRACTS, 7
every l. is an infraction of liberty GOVERNMENTS, 4
L. is a sort of hocus-pocus science LAWYERS, 13
l. seems like a sort of maze LAWYERS, 16
No brilliance is needed in the l. LAWYERS, 15
The good of the people is the chief l. BUSINESS ETHICS, 29
the l. may be...hard for the individual COMPETITION, 10
We don't break the l. CORRUPTION AND SCANDAL, 15
laws L. are like spider's webs LAWYERS, 19
L. for the regulation of trade GOVERNMENTS, 26
l. regulating the industry INDUSTRY, 8
Unnecessary l. are not good LAWYERS, 11
lawyer A l. with his briefcase LAWYERS, 18
l....One skilled in circumvention of the law LAWYERS, 4
lawyers corporate l....are often called 'hired guns'
  LAWYERS, 20
L. are like rhinoceroses LAWYERS, 14
L....ignorance of the law is not punished LAWYERS, 2
l. will be there to work out the deal LAWYERS, 7
Woe unto you, l. LAWYERS, 3
lazy you have to be efficient...to be l. EFFICIENCY, 2
lead Either l., follow, or get out of the way PRINCIPLES, 2
we l....by drawing out ideas from people LISTENING, 7
leader A fanatic is a great l. LEADERSHIP, 29
a good l....will say, 'Ready, fire, aim...' BOLDNESS, 24
a good l....without the grace of genius LEADERSHIP, 86
A l....ability to get other people to do LEADERSHIP, 121
A l. is one who...takes the risks LEADERSHIP, 65
I am a l. by default LEADERSHIP, 123
If a l....assume the role of a teacher LEADERSHIP, 39
If your role is l. LEADERSHIP, 37
l....rarely the brightest person ABILITY, 4
relationship between l. LEADERSHIP, 55
speed of the l....speed of the gang LEADERSHIP, 5
The difference between a l. and a boss LEADERSHIP, 80
the effective l....happened naturally LEADERSHIP, 83
The l. is not just a scorekeeper LEADERSHIP, 42
The l. must know LEADERSHIP, 98
The l....the articulating point between the group's genius
  LEADERSHIP, 16
The most effective l. LEADERSHIP, 93
The most successful l. TARGETS, 13
The secret of a l. lies in the tests LEADERSHIP, 113
leaders Even the best l. get submerged ORGANISATIONS, 16
From l., we need clear, consistent and honest attention
  IMAGE, 27

Good l. make people feel they're at the heart of things LEADERSHIP, 81

L....are in very short supply LEADERSHIP, 117

L. are...midwives of ideas LEADERSHIP, 20

l. are people who do the right things LEADERSHIP, 19

L. articulate and define LEADERSHIP, 17

L. configure the context while managers surrender to it LEADERSHIP, 21

L....grasp nettles BOLDNESS, 17

L. must invoke an alchemy LEADERSHIP, 78

l. must manage not just teams CO-OPERATION, 16

L. today sometimes appear to be an endangered species LEADERSHIP, 82

L. walk their talk LEADERSHIP, 14

L. who understand their organizations LEADERSHIP, 57

L. with unruly, lowly minds LEADERSHIP, 40

The best l....strong component of unorthodoxy EXECUTIVES, 47

leadership art of l....knowing how much information you're going to pass on INFORMATION, 2

Consensus is the negation of l. LEADERSHIP, 118

crisis of l. today LEADERSHIP, 32

Effective l....seems to demand continuous reflection LEADERSHIP, 38

Everyone is capable of exercising effective l. LEADERSHIP, 70

L. can be felt throughout an organization LEADERSHIP, 13

L. competence...is a matter fundamentally of competence LEADERSHIP, 71

L....inseparable from followers' needs LEADERSHIP, 31

L. is about a sense of direction LEADERSHIP, 2

L. is all hype LEADERSHIP, 47

L. is not about being nice LEADERSHIP, 74

l. is...persuasion and conciliation LEADERSHIP, 49

L. is the process of achieving a dream LEADERSHIP, 115

l. is valuing the time LEADERSHIP, 75

Legend is the missing ingredient in l. LEADERSHIP, 106

Modern business l....capacity to create large organisations LEADERSHIP, 92

Passionate l. won't succeed LEADERSHIP, 58

The art of l. LEADERSHIP, 24

The art of l....mobilize people to care LEADERSHIP, 63

the most important thing...about l. LEADERSHIP, 96

Without some element of l. LEADERSHIP, 77

learn It is the true nature of mankind to l. from mistakes LEARNING, 28

L. from the best LEARNING, 47

Never l. to do anything DELEGATING, 18

One must first l. to live BLAME, 7

You have to l. to give WEALTH, 68

learned We l. from everybody else's book EXPERIENCE, 39

learner I'm not an educator...I'm a l. LEARNING, 24

learners Lifelong l. take risks LEARNING, 26

learning every adult American must...keep on l. LEARNING, 13

Individual l. is a necessary but insufficient condition LEARNING, 5

I treat everything as a l. experience TARGETS, 19

L. and performance will become...the same thing LEARNING, 7

l. from direct experience EXPERIENCE, 43

L. how to learn LEARNING, 9

L. is a willingness LEARNING, 46

L. is not compulsory LEARNING, 52

The l. person looks forward to failure LEARNING, 6

True l. begins with unlearning LEARNING, 30

We're not in cultures which support l. CORPORATE CULTURE, 152

learns He who l. but does not think is lost LEARNING, 14

legacy Your l. should be that you made it better REPUTATION, 11

legend l. of the jungle heritage DISCRIMINATION, 56

leisure fill l. intelligently CIVILISATION, 32

Increased means and increased l. CIVILISATION, 8

lemons L. ripen faster than cherries FAILURE, 2

lending l. practices that deprive minority...neighborhoods E-COMMERCE, 32

less Always do one thing l. EXPECTATIONS, 1

L. is a bore CREATIVITY, 49

L. is more CREATIVITY, 35

the l. they have...the more noise they make CHARACTER, 47

lesson The l. I learnt was not to think small RISK TAKING, 18

lessons The l. of the past are ignored LEARNING, 2

lethargy L. bordering on sloth CORPORATE CULTURE, 22

letter reputation for keeping absolutely to the l. REPUTATION, 4

levers I shan't be pulling the l. POWER, 82

leviathans the l. have remained rich and powerful CORPORATE CULTURE, 61

liberal egg on his face...l. economist ECONOMICS, 91

liberal democracy L. is really all there is now CAPITALISM VERSUS SOCIALISM, 6

liberating Every decision is l. DECISIONS, 6

liberty L. means responsibility RESPONSIBILITY, 23

L....not too sure that it is right BUSINESS ETHICS, 60

lie striking differences between a cat and a l. BUSINESS ETHICS, 118

The camera cannot l. BUSINESS ETHICS, 40

lies A man who l. to himself CHARACTER, 17

l., damned l., and statistics DETAILS, 32

l., damned l., and statistics STATISTICS, 6

life There is l., but it's not for you ACHIEVING, 25

The shelf l. of the modern hardback writer MARKETING, 45

lifestyles L. around Europe are converging DOING BUSINESS IN EUROPE, 1

light l. at the end of the tunnel CHALLENGE, 6

lightning difference between the l. bug and the l. ACCURACY, 16

limit ecological l. to the number of paper pushers BUREAUCRACY, 9

limitations l. of the file folder ORGANISATIONS, 30

limits l. to growth under a capitalistic market economy CAPITALISM VERSUS SOCIALISM, 3

line I like to stand on l. OPINIONS, 19

lips Read my l.: no new taxes TAXES, 4

lipstick I can't do anything without first putting on l. CHARACTER, 36

liquidate L. labor, l. stocks, l. farmers BOOM AND BUST, 10

listen If you don't l. SELLING, 18

L. to everyone in your company COMMUNICATION, 36

talk and l. to a bad character COMMUNICATION, 24

The key is to get into the stores and l. CUSTOMERS, 29

You need to l. back ADVICE, 6

listeners Good l....are to be treasured LISTENING, 1

listening I...spend some time...l. in on calls CONSUMERS, 39

l. itself may not be enough LISTENING, 3

little l. things are infinitely the most important DETAILS, 8

Practise yourself in l. things DETAILS, 9

live L. within your means WAGES, 7

lives Too many l. are needed to make just one CHARACTER, 44

living A l. is made...by selling something SUCCESS, 103

living conditions everybody...to get better l. CAPITALISM VERSUS SOCIALISM, 1

loathing two sides of industry...greatest possible l. INDUSTRY, 45

locality be well acquainted with the l. DETAILS, 2

lofty No matter how l. you are MANAGEMENT, 39

logic l. is the art of demonstrating truth SPEECHES, 30

using l....where emotion played the biggest part RISK TAKING, 9

London L....the clearing house of the world GLOBALISATION, 18

long-termer Beware the manager who proclaims...he is a l. BOASTING, 11

look It depends on how we l. at things ATTITUDE, 13

loophole one man's l. is another man's livelihood TAXES, 9

lose Do not l. yourself...in your ideas FOCUS, 2

loss The l. that is unknown EXPECTATIONS, 6

love I do not l. the money MOTIVATION, 8

people can fall in l. with...business LIMITATIONS, 6

To business that we l. we rise betime ENTHUSIASM, 13

lowest the challenge of working on the l. circulations CHALLENGE, 10

loyalties Men...often bribed by their l. MONEY, 56
loyalty Forget l. LOYALTY, 13
L. programmes...turn conventional markets into lock-in markets LOYALTY, 19
L. saves the wear and tear of...decisions LOYALTY, 22
Total l. is possible LOYALTY, 1
luck guide your l. even while waiting for it LUCK, 6
l. is the inner man externalized LUCK, 4
l. may be overthrown by destiny LUCK, 5
Some folk want their l. buttered LUCK, 8
We must believe in l. LUCK, 3
lust Society drives people crazy with l. ADVERTISING, 32
luxuries l. of this life...man whose labor produces them CAPITALISM, 11
no useful distinction can be made between l. and necessities WEALTH, 25
luxury if I am travelling in l. CORPORATE CULTURE, 70
My l. is to work SUCCESS, 56

M

machine the worker has been reduced to a m. TECHNOLOGY, 36
You can be totally rational with a m. EMPLOYEES, 55
machinery M. for producing any commodity INNOVATION, 7
m....set us free to live OPINIONS, 7
machines M. have less problems INNOVATION, 94
M....impose slavery BUSINESS ETHICS, 100
used m. to lower wages or eliminate jobs TECHNOLOGY, 48
macho men are always playing their own m. games DISCRIMINATION, 7
madness M. in great ones RESPONSIBILITY, 21
magazines What I love about m. MEDIA, 20
majority The bad workmen who form the m. WAGES, 31
making find out whether something is worth m. INNOVATION, 52
Malaysian M. companies...are investing in African countries DOING BUSINESS IN AFRICA, 1
man It's still a m.'s world out there DISCRIMINATION, 64
M. belongs where he wants to go TARGETS, 24
Only m. is not content to leave things as they are CHANGE, 73
manage a creature begins to m. its environment ORDER, 25
People m. themselves CORPORATE CULTURE, 51
management 'Top' m....a tree full of owls MANAGEMENT, 80
a hot kitchen can teach you...about m. MANAGEMENT, 56
deliverer from an excess of business m. BUREAUCRACY, 46
gathering in on the part of m. MANAGEMENT, 78
Highly centralized m. can suffocate...innovative energies MANAGEMENT, 52
impossible for a top m. man...have a clean desk EXECUTIVES, 30
I only join...where I admire the m. EXECUTIVES, 22
M. and the business firm...converted into a reconciliation process LISTENING, 2
m. books for their insights LEARNING, 4
m. books should not be tossed aside lightly INFORMATION, 16
M. by trust MANAGEMENT, 34
M. by Walking About MANAGEMENT, 54
m....getting off their sometimes lazy butt MANAGEMENT, 35
M. in a global environment GLOBALISATION, 92
M. is the study of how things get done MANAGEMENT, 32
M....it's just a wastepaper basket CHANGE, 27
M....more intuitive than any textbook MANAGEMENT, 33
m. must become humanagement MANAGEMENT, 60
M. principles aim at the success of associations PRINCIPLES, 10
M. productivity...more appropriate term than labor productivity PRODUCTIVITY, 8
M....show that it loves that institution CHANGE, 129
m.'s role is simply to get the right people EMPLOYEES, 81
M.—the collective effort of intelligence MANAGEMENT, 69
m. today...role of a judge MANAGEMENT, 23
Middle level m. can be delegated DELEGATING, 8

Only m. can change the system CHANGE, 35
Professional m. is an invention MANAGEMENT, 49
Project m. is the furnace CAREERS, 23
Team m....the Chinese approach TEAMS, 27
the Civil Service is the orderly m. of decline GOVERNMENTS, 2
the core of m. is the art of mobilising DOING BUSINESS IN ASIA-PACIFIC, 23
The highest art of professional m. INFORMATION, 13
the m. wants figures QUALITY, 6
The way m. treats their associates CORPORATE CULTURE, 140
Traditional m. structures...devised when information was a scarce commodity MANAGEMENT, 73
manager A m. is an assistant to his men MANAGEMENT, 85
A tough m. may never look outside MANAGEMENT, 47
Beware the m. who proclaims...he is a long-termer EXECUTIVES, 48
first steps to becoming a really great m. MANAGEMENT, 7
good m....isn't worried about his own career MANAGEMENT, 10
tasks of a m....eliminate his people's excuses for failure FAILURE, 56
The hierarchical m. of yesterday LEADERSHIP, 36
The m. does things right LEADERSHIP, 22
managerial m. processes are enormously complex MANAGEMENT, 48
M. skill can not be painted on the outside EXECUTIVES, 26
the powers of fad surfing is...m. prozac MANAGEMENT, 65
managers American m. are too little concerned about their workers EMPLOYEES, 56
corporations m....work with one eye on their résumé CAREERS, 13
I have never compared myself to my m. DELEGATING, 1
Insecure m. create complexity MANAGEMENT, 88
M....brought up on a diet of power LEADERSHIP, 68
m. have to learn to motivate MOTIVATION, 10
M. in all too many American companies MANAGEMENT, 28
M. must manage MANAGEMENT, 29
M. should be getting everybody...doing things MANAGEMENT, 59
m....should heap on congratulations PRAISE, 4
M. should not have to choose MANAGEMENT, 40
M. should work for their people MANAGEMENT, 8
m....spend their whole careers climbing MANAGEMENT, 62
m....time for thinking MANAGEMENT, 64
M. who are skilled communicators PROBLEMS, 4
M. who extensively plan the future PLANNING, 5
Our m. are all white DISCRIMINATION, 6
managing I learned more about m. LEADERSHIP, 105
M. is getting paid for home runs someone else hits MANAGEMENT, 74
mankind Whether we like it or not m. BANKING, 30
mantra A large part of my m. STRATEGY, 17
manual work we have increased the productivity of m. PRODUCTIVITY, 6
manufactured people pounding out m. goods PRODUCTIVITY, 7
manufacturer A m. is not through CUSTOMERS, 15
manufacturers M....allured by the cheapness of provisions and labour ECONOMICS, 49
M. who don't test their products MARKETING, 26
manufacturing company No m. will ever do well PROFITS, 24
map A road m., an invariable sequence of steps QUALITY, 15
marathon The m. is my only girlfriend LOYALTY, 18
mark If you would hit the m. GOALS AND OBJECTIVES, 15
market Confronted with a fully developed world m. DOING BUSINESS IN ASIA-PACIFIC, 2
every product or service they m. COMPETITION, 2
I believe in the m. BUSINESS ETHICS, 45
I do not really understand the stock m. INVESTMENT AND THE STOCK MARKET, 60
M. competition...freedom to the individual CAPITALISM, 31
Marketing should focus on m. creation MARKETING, 22
moving towards the m. COMMUNISM AND SOCIALISM, 3
new ranges on the m. OPPORTUNITY, 3

mind Don't be afraid to...speak your m. CHARACTER, 63
It is the m. that makes the body rich WEALTH, 8
One man that has a m. and knows it CONFIDENCE, 39
the classical m....looks dingy on the surface QUALITY, 23
The m. is fearless CONSCIENCE, 15
minds M. are like parachutes CREATIVITY, 7
ministers M. and merchants love nobody BUSINESS
ETHICS, 69
mink Don't focus on the m. MARKETING, 44
minor When it comes to the m. affairs of life DETAILS, 3
minority norm demands the complete socialization of the
m. DISCRIMINATION, 20
minutes take care of the m. DETAILS, 5
miracles M. can be made DETERMINATION, 1
misdeeds m....of corporate America CORRUPTION AND
SCANDAL, 10
miserable no more m. human being
PROCRASTINATION, 19
misery half our m. from our foibles spring DETAILS, 24
mismanagement economic ills derive from m. DOING
BUSINESS IN AFRICA, 2
missed For everything you have m. FAILURE, 18
mission Our m....is to change the world STRATEGY, 12
The m. of a manufacturer BUSINESS ETHICS, 80
mission-based m. means that those in positions of
authority LEADERSHIP, 111
missteps Use m. as stepping stones MISTAKES, 30
mistake A m. is simply another way MISTAKES, 32
Every great m. has a halfway moment MISTAKES, 3
great m. to confine your imagination IMAGINATION, 9
worst m....is not to say 'Well done' PRAISE, 3
You've made a m. PROFITS, 13
mistakes A life spent making m. MISTAKES, 26
a world of m. QUALITY, 9
from the m. go on to achievement MISTAKES, 9
It is a good thing to make m. MISTAKES, 16
learning from your m. LEARNING, 16
M. are...the foundation of truth EXPERIENCE, 24
Some m. cost money MISTAKES, 6
The man who makes no m. MISTAKES, 23
The m. of the great MISTAKES, 25
worrying too much about making m. MISTAKES, 33
mistreated If someone thinks they are being m.
CUSTOMERS, 4
mobsters These m. had enjoyed power BUSINESS
ETHICS, 33
model Neoclassical economics...m. of rational
self-interested human behavior ECONOMICS, 29
The blur of business has created a new economic m.
PROFITS, 6
models seemingly 'hardest' m....frequently based on 'soft'
assumptions PLANNING, 25
moderation Exactness and neatness in m. is a virtue
ORDER, 13
M. is a fatal thing MODERATION, 5
modern M. mind has become...more calculating
LEARNING, 41
modernity M. desacralized the human body
ADVERTISING, 59
modernisation Economic m....spawns...types of
capitalism CAPITALISM VERSUS SOCIALISM, 8
molehill A m. man is a pseudo-busy executive
EXECUTIVES, 4
moment The decisive m. CREATIVITY, 4
monetarism Unfortunately m....was put into practice
ECONOMICS, 39
monetary substitution of m. values for all other values
MONEY, 87
money A bank...will lend you m. BANKING, 9
A business that makes nothing but m. BUSINESS ETHICS, 47
All m....homing instinct for the Treasury MONEY, 76
Can you make m. SUCCESS, 75
civilization produces m. CIVILISATION, 3
count your m. SUCCESS, 47
follow your passion, the m. will follow EXPECTATIONS, 4
for a woman you make a lot of m. DISCRIMINATION, 23

Getting m. is like digging with a needle MONEY, 7
Having m. is rather like being a blond WEALTH, 42
He that wants m., means, and content MONEY, 85
how I started painting m. MONEY, 94
how much m. you make INVESTMENT AND THE STOCK
MARKET, 74
How they love m. MONEY, 16
If m. is your hope for independence MONEY, 35
If m. is your motivation, forget it MONEY, 97
If there is m. in it we must move INVESTMENT AND THE STOCK
MARKET, 75
If you do anything just for the m. SUCCESS, 53
If you have enough m. WEALTH, 21
If you want to make m. IMAGE, 2
It's hard to make m. in business WEALTH, 27
love of m. is the root of all evil MONEY, 17
Making m. doesn't oblige people CONSCIENCE, 33
mistake of confounding m. and wealth WEALTH, 19
m....a bigger phallic symbol than a Porsche MONEY, 20
M. and goods are certainly the best of references
MONEY, 29
M., as a physical medium of exchange CIVILISATION, 33
M., big m. GREED, 16
m....blessing that is of no advantage MONEY, 18
M. can be translated into the beauty of living WEALTH, 41
m....can never return MONEY, 11
M. couldn't buy you friends MONEY, 67
m....degrees of desperation MONEY, 21
M. doesn't talk, it swears MONEY, 32
M. has no legs, but it runs MONEY, 8
M. is a poor man's credit card MONEY, 63
M. is better than poverty MONEY, 3
M. is like an arm or a leg MONEY, 36
M. is like a sixth sense MONEY, 62
M. is like manure MONEY, 70
M. is like muck MONEY, 13
M....is never just m. MONEY, 12
M. isn't what motivates entrepreneurs ENTREPRENEURS, 39
M....is pure inflation MONEY, 82
M....is the ruling principle MONEY, 9
M. is the seed of m. MONEY, 80
M. is...too dangerous an instrument MONEY, 48
M. itch is a bad thing MONEY, 43
M. makes a man laugh MONEY, 84
M....power sacred to most men DISCRIMINATION, 15
M....renders the motion of the wheels more smooth
MONEY, 51
M....represents the prose of life MONEY, 33
M.'s a horrid thing to follow MONEY, 57
M. should circulate like rain water MONEY, 95
M. speaks sense MONEY, 15
M. speaks...with a male voice DISCRIMINATION, 21
m....symbol of...ability as entrepreneurs WEALTH, 23
M....the poetry of our age MONEY, 50
M....translated into the beauty of living MONEY, 77
M....useful drudge of things immeasurably higher
MONEY, 24
M....was exactly like sex MONEY, 14
m. was intended to be used in exchange BANKING, 1
M. you haven't earned WEALTH, 34
m. you receive is...likely to track the recognition
WAGES, 18
never try to make all the m. GREED, 8
no m. in poetry BUSINESS ETHICS, 57
not merely satisfied in making m. DISCRIMINATION, 70
Once one has got the m. habit MONEY, 44
people like m. the way they do their...dogs MONEY, 92
rub up against m. MONEY, 81
She had a powerful regard for m. MONEY, 39
Some men turn every quality or art into...m. GREED, 2
Start with your own m. DETERMINATION, 4
sums of m. appear to vary MONEY, 53
These companies have m. thrown at them MONEY, 46
The secret point of m. WEALTH, 15
The universal regard for m. MONEY, 86
Too much m. is a dangerous thing FAILURE, 26

values which can be measured in terms of m.
ECONOMICS, 94
We haven't got the m. INNOVATION, 81
We will only do with your m. BUSINESS ETHICS, 19
When m. is at stake NEGOTIATION, 28
With m. in your pocket MONEY, 10
You've heard m. talking? MONEY, 64
monomaniac anything is being accomplished...by a m.
ACTION, 12
monopolies temporary m. are a prize for innovation
INNOVATION, 5
the real holders of power...are the great...m. ECONOMICS, 72
monopolist the m.'s sleep can never be secure SUCCESS, 44
monopoly an occasional natural m. may arise RESEARCH, 2
he...set about achieving that efficient m. GOALS AND
OBJECTIVES, 19
M. is a terrible thing OPINIONS, 26
M. is business at the end of its journey ECONOMICS, 70
monsters A continuous clash of egomaniacal m. MEDIA, 6
moon I felt like the m. RESPONSIBILITY, 30
If we hadn't put a man on the m. TECHNOLOGY, 52
moral I base all my business on m. considerations
CONSCIENCE, 4
m. problem of our age...love of money MONEY, 59
moral bankruptcy m....trickle-down economics
ECONOMICS, 55
morally It is m. as bad not to care GREED, 13
morals Food comes first, then m. CONSUMERS, 1
more if there's anything m. I can do right now
EXECUTIVES, 21
M. will mean worse QUALITY, 1
m. you get the m. you spend MONEY, 4
Morgan M., M., the Great Financial Gorgon REPUTATION, 1
Mr. M. buys his partners; I grow my own MANAGEMENT, 11
mothers m....tell their families they just lost their jobs
HIRING AND FIRING, 18
motivate how do you m. EMPLOYEES, 32
motivates Striving for excellence m. you EXCELLENCE, 2
motivation in the economic world...large part of the m.
ECONOMICS, 31
M....needs emotion MOTIVATION, 3
m. to meet Wall Street earnings CORPORATE RESPONSIBILITY, 16
True m. comes from achievement EMPLOYEES, 34
motive important m....pleasure in work WORK AND
EMPLOYMENT, 35
primary m. for setting up this company EMPLOYEES, 36
The public...will not forgive us for mistakes in m.
INVESTMENT AND THE STOCK MARKET, 37
'Tis the m. that exalts the action ACTION, 21
motives work...done without personal m. SINCERITY, 1
mouth keeping your m. shut SUCCESS, 36
move m. from one place to another GLOBALISATION, 7
movement Change means m. CHANGE, 2
movie business I wanted to work in the m. GETTING
STARTED, 17
MTV people kept saying M. wouldn't last SUCCESS, 71
muddle M. is the extra unknown personality
BUREAUCRACY, 42
multicultural If m. management is to become a reality
MANAGEMENT, 15
multimedia markets for m. applications will be
in...education INDUSTRY, 15
multinational m. companies will...play an important role
GLOBALISATION, 28
M. organisations...untainted by protectionism DOING
BUSINESS IN AFRICA, 7
the strategy involved in the m. mission GLOBALISATION, 12
multinationals M....no longer immune from violence in
Mexico DOING BUSINESS IN LATIN AMERICA, 9
multiple option free-wheeling m. society CHOICE, 6
Murdoch fish...wrapped in a M. newspaper MEDIA, 47
mushrooms Like m., they look enticing RESEARCH, 7
music M. is spiritual. The m. business is not MARKETING, 24
M. you can see MEDIA, 14
The m. industry is toast MEDIA, 22
must You m. do the thing...you cannot do CHALLENGE, 8

myself I have worked without thinking of m. SUCCESS, 48
mysterious The most beautiful thing we can experience is
the m. IDEAS, 20
myths Two of the great m. circulating MANAGEMENT, 16

N

name making a n. for yourself SUCCESS, 51
Retailers estimate...Michael Jordan's n. MARKETING, 5
This famous store needs no n. PUBLICITY, 23
names n. with X's are more memorable IMAGE, 6
Napoleon At seven I wanted to be N. AMBITION, 8
narcotic Broadband is like a n. TECHNOLOGY, 18
narrowed Our outlook is n. SUCCESS, 42
nation A n. advances in civilisation by increasing
CIVILISATION, 17
A n. is not in danger of financial disaster ECONOMICS, 77
nationalism N. is an infantile sickness GLOBALISATION, 31
natural resources N. are morally neutral CORPORATE
RESPONSIBILITY, 24
nature Accuse not N., she hath done her part
RESPONSIBILITY, 14
gross distortion of n....Newtonian machines
ORGANISATIONS, 31
Man's deeper n. is soon found out CHARACTER, 73
natures Men's n. are alike CHARACTER, 12
NCOs N. had evaluated themselves CORPORATE CULTURE, 30
necessary Make yourself n. to someone LOYALTY, 7
necessity N. never made a good bargain NEGOTIATION, 6
n. of constant change MOTIVATION, 14
the n. of work WORK AND EMPLOYMENT, 80
neck creator...purpose in equipping us with a n.
BOLDNESS, 14
need The face of evil...the face of total n. BUSINESS ETHICS, 20
needed When I saw something that n. doing ACTION, 9
needs Business is about supplying the n. CONSUMERS, 14
n. or expectations of the worker WAGES, 9
neglect A little n. may breed mischief QUALITY, 11
cannot afford to n. any gift DISCRIMINATION, 55
neglecting N. small things under the pretext of wanting to
accomplish large ones DETAILS, 7
negotiate Let us never n. out of fear NEGOTIATION, 9
strangers n. most of the arrangements HIRING AND FIRING, 24
negotiates The harder a guy n. NEGOTIATION, 13
negotiating n. for a 35 hour week NEGOTIATION, 10
N. with them reminded me of haggling over a fake Rolex
BUSINESS ETHICS, 92
negotiation n. is a game which must result in winners and
losers NEGOTIATION, 2
negotiations crunch moment when you are in n.
NEGOTIATION, 18
do not rush into n. NEGOTIATION, 24
This is about n. NEGOTIATION, 1
negotiator A n. should observe everything NEGOTIATION, 11
If you choose to be a n. NEGOTIATION, 30
neighbour Love your n....is good business OPINIONS, 21
nervous n. managers use thick, convoluted planning books
MANAGEMENT, 86
net The N. changes the balance of power E-COMMERCE, 14
network Companies gain the advantage of a n. at a price
INDEPENDENCE, 7
I didn't have the ability to n. EXECUTIVES, 8
N. of leaders ORGANISATIONS, 11
optimal form of industrial organization...n. structures
ORGANISATIONS, 23
the fundamental principle for success in the digital age is
to think n. SUCCESS, 70
networks informal n. move diagonally and eliptically
ORGANISATIONS, 27
n....the right organizational design COMMUNICATION, 35
people we get along with...strongest links in our n.
TEAMS, 11
never By and by n. comes PROCRASTINATION, 2

new n. things in n. ways INNOVATION, 11
the pain of a n. idea IDEAS, 3
new economy bells and whistles of the so-called n.
ECONOMICS, 42
how you define n....depends on where you live
ECONOMICS, 80
The n. favors...ideas, information, and relationships
CORPORATE CULTURE, 81
new media n....comes down to whether it's a good business
E-COMMERCE, 28
newness The n. of an idea matters less IDEAS, 17
news N....doesn't care much about anything MEDIA, 55
newspaper A good n....a nation talking to itself MEDIA, 36
First Duty of a n. is to be Accurate ACCURACY, 15
I see a n., I think of the poor trees MEDIA, 33
n....business is an intellectual brothel MEDIA, 52
newspapers N....remain powerful outlets MEDIA, 4
The business pages of American n. CORRUPTION AND
SCANDAL, 9
nice Be n. to people on your way up STRATEGY, 42
N. guys. Finish last WINNERS AND WINNING, 17
niche Most large markets evolve from n. markets
MARKETING, 21
nineties The nanosecond n. CHANGE, 110
nirvana n. of the Net economy OPINIONS, 25
Nobel chair from which the N. lecture is delivered
ACHIEVING, 36
Even though they had won N. prizes LEARNING, 36
nobody When n. wants something OPPORTUNITY, 16
nonchalance I would live my life in n. WORK AND
EMPLOYMENT, 71
nonperformance more difficult to measure n. EFFICIENCY, 7
normalising A n. society PEOPLE AND RELATIONSHIPS, 20
nose keeping one's n. clean at all times BLAME, 31
not-for-profit company Clearly, we're a n. PROFITS, 3
nothing man is producing n. MOTIVATION, 11
precise psychological moment when to say n.
NEGOTIATION, 26
When one does n. RESPONSIBILITY, 19
When you have n. to say, say n. COMMUNICATION, 11
notices One never n. what has been done PERSISTENCE, 6
nouveau riche Thank you for making me n. BOASTING, 4
novice the n. can often see things EXPERIENCE, 33
no win situation It's a n. OPINIONS, 31
number The n. of operations performed TIME
MANAGEMENT, 2
numbers N. written on restaurant bills...do not follow the
same mathematical laws MONEY, 1
nurture N. your mind with great thoughts CHARACTER, 16

O

obituary When people come to write my o. REPUTATION, 6
objective One's o. should be to get it right ACTION, 7
objectives You establish some o. DELEGATING, 10
objectivity eliminate...all o. MEDIA, 54
obligation The primary o. is loyalty LOYALTY, 17
obligations unsuccessful manager blames failure on his o.
OPPORTUNITY, 23
observing O....competitor's successes and failures
SUCCESS, 62
obsession great work comes from people's o. and
imagination CREATIVITY, 16
obsolescence planned o. of people WORK AND
EMPLOYMENT, 93
obsolete Every company should...o. its own product
PRODUCTS, 12
obstacle Every o. yields OBSTACLES, 5
The biggest o....changing a typewriter ribbon OBSTACLES, 1
obstacles Success is to be measured...by the o.
DETERMINATION, 25
occupation Absence of o. is not rest WORK AND
EMPLOYMENT, 28

any o....more consistently and unfairly demeaned
BANKING, 19
man's o. should be beneficial to his fellow-man WORK AND
EMPLOYMENT, 9
One must have some sort of o. now-a-days DEBT, 13
October O....one of the peculiarly dangerous months to
speculate INVESTMENT AND THE STOCK MARKET, 81
offer I'll make him an o. he can't refuse BUSINESS ETHICS, 96
office A man who has no o....is a trial WORK AND
EMPLOYMENT, 88
I wouldn't have gone to the o. at all OFFICE POLITICS, 3
movie stars run for o. MONEY, 2
No o. anywhere on earth is so puritanical CORRUPTION AND
SCANDAL, 8
O....builds up a man ACHIEVING, 3
o....no place...to get any work done WORK AND
EMPLOYMENT, 98
offices youth seek honor...as a man of o. CORPORATE
CULTURE, 89
officials O. are highly educated but one-sided
BUREAUCRACY, 25
oil O. is like a wild animal COMPETITION, 25
old I am putting o. heads on young shoulders
EXPERIENCE, 37
old-fashioned borrow money the o. way BUSINESS
ETHICS, 68
olive If you have an o. MOTIVATION, 13
omniscience My speciality is o. POWER, 38
oneself doing one's praising for o. PRAISE, 8
online It's hard to find things that won't sell o.
E-COMMERCE, 6
open It has always been Enron's policy to be o. HONESTY, 8
My door is always o. PROBLEMS, 34
opened What windows have just o. OPPORTUNITY, 17
open-mindedness What is important is our o. PRINCIPLES, 22
opinion If I want to voice my o. OPINIONS, 35
The fact that an o. has been widely held OPINIONS, 32
opinions How long halt ye between two o.
PROCRASTINATION, 6
It's not that I don't have o. OPINIONS, 27
New o. are always suspected ORIGINALITY, 6
People are responsible for their o. RESPONSIBILITY, 31
The more o. you have OPINIONS, 39
opponent Never corner an o. NEGOTIATION, 14
opponents To win against o. COMPETITION, 20
opportunities A wise man will make more o. OPPORTUNITY, 1
new o. summon new challenges CORPORATE
RESPONSIBILITY, 14
No other area offers richer o. SUCCESS, 28
One can present people with o. OPPORTUNITY, 21
O. are not offered OPPORTUNITY, 11
O. are usually disguised as hard work OPPORTUNITY, 20
o. for future growth are everywhere OPPORTUNITY, 14
Social o. of education and health care CAPITALISM, 40
opportunity Never let an o. pass by ACTION, 5
o. to break away from technological traditions PRODUCTS, 5
pay a high price for an o. RISK TAKING, 35
Seize o. by the forelock OPPORTUNITY, 15
The man who loses his o. OPPORTUNITY, 24
there is little difference between obstacle and o.
ENTREPRENEURS, 22
opposition Difficulties, o., criticism...are meant to be
overcome PROBLEMS, 27
grind the o. into the ground COMPETITION, 33
mission is only possible where there is o. COMPETITION, 19
optimistic By always being o....you will *succeed* SUCCESS, 66
Copy can be casually o. ADVERTISING, 21
Orange O....was a promise deliverer CORPORATE CULTURE, 132
orator An o. can hardly get beyond commonplaces
SPEECHES, 24
An o....feels what he says SPEECHES, 6
An o. is the worse person to tell a plain fact SPEECHES, 17
I am no o. SPEECHES, 48
The best o....can make men see with their ears SPEECHES, 1
The O. persuades and carries SPEECHES, 7
orators He is one of those o. SPEECHES, 11

What o. lack in depth SPEECHES, 37
oratory In o. the greatest art is to hide art SPEECHES, 53
Nothing is so unbelievable that o. SPEECHES, 12
O. is dying SPEECHES, 23
O. is just like prostitution SPEECHES, 40
O. is the power of beating down SPEECHES, 28
The object of o. SPEECHES, 34
orchestra I let the o. play as they like LEADERSHIP, 8
There are two golden rules for an o. SUCCESS, 5
order Bureaucracy emerged out of the organization's need for o. BUREAUCRACY, 4
I have never issued an o. LEADERSHIP, 116
Life creates o. ORDER, 23
man is a creature who needs o. ORDER, 2
O. always weighs on the individual ORDER, 33
O. is a lovely thing ORDER, 5
o. is heavenly ORDER, 31
O. is man's greatest need ORDER, 3
O. marches with weighty and measured strides ORDER, 21
o. will prevail ACTION, 17
Set thine house in o. ORDER, 4
severity is not the path to o. ORDER, 20
The desire for o. ORDER, 11
the dishonest mask of pretended o. ORDER, 17
we cannot hope for o. ORDER, 28
orders Men like to issue o. LEADERSHIP, 85
organisation a large o....thinks major change is impossible CHANGE, 83
An o. should be outstanding ORGANISATIONS, 43
basic philosophy of an o....to do with its achievements ORGANISATIONS, 84
beyond that stage of human o. CIVILISATION, 28
build a lasting competitive edge through...o. ORGANISATIONS, 6
Changing the formal o. ORGANISATIONS, 51
create a healthy o. LEADERSHIP, 129
Creative swiping provides energy to an o. CORPORATE CULTURE, 26
Developing a sound and healthy o. ORGANISATIONS, 28
development of the modern form of the o. BUREAUCRACY, 52
If an o. is to work effectively COMMUNICATION, 32
Large o. is loose o. ORDER, 9
neighborhood o....one among many methods ORGANISATIONS, 21
new theory of o. ORGANISATIONS, 48
no major change in a complex o. CHANGE, 94
no more possible to create an o. today ORGANISATIONS, 46
o....consisting of all chiefs and one human CHANGE, 134
o. exists to restrict ORGANISATIONS, 41
The O. Man ORGANISATIONS, 88
throw away the o. chart CORPORATE CULTURE, 109
Today's o....field of work needing to be done JOBS, 4
very simple, clear o. BUREAUCRACY, 24
when you become a big enough o., you...collapse ORGANISATIONS, 74
organisational O. learning style LEARNING, 18
organisational theory single assumption...conventional o. ORGANISATIONS, 45
organisations large o....block bad news ADVERSITY, 14
Many o. view people as 'things' EMPLOYEES, 59
o. have done very little to deserve...staying-power LOYALTY, 23
o. where people trust and believe in each other ORGANISATIONS, 91
Our task is to create o. ORGANISATIONS, 7
people in o. may have vision, but there's absolutely zero meaning BUREAUCRACY, 3
The o....excel in the future SUCCESS, 89
We talk about o. ORGANISATIONS, 70
Without o., there would be chaos ORGANISATIONS, 42
organise o. the unorganized MANAGEMENT, 2
There is a rage to o. ORDER, 12
organised Nobody knows how Honda is o. ORGANISATIONS, 57
organises A man is known by the company he o. CHARACTER, 5

organising o....more attention to the organization ORGANISATIONS, 89
organisms We are self-activating o. PEOPLE AND RELATIONSHIPS, 26
original Anyone who attempts anything o....must expect...ridicule ORIGINALITY, 4
businessmen are incapable of o. CREATIVITY, 41
originality O. is deliberate and forced CREATIVITY, 19
Timing; o.; forcefulness...are the hallmarks MANAGEMENT, 41
orthodoxy 'o.'...no longer means being right INNOVATION, 15
Oscar We're all dying to win an O. AMBITION, 9
out a person cannot be kept o. DISCRIMINATION, 36
outside All great change in business has come from o. CHANGE, 37
outsiders I don't want to feel responsible to o. CORPORATE CULTURE, 71
outstanding the o. man is he who thinks deeply LISTENING, 6
overbearing To be o....Is to bring calamity MODERATION, 2
overburdened o., stretched executive EXECUTIVES, 57
overcommunicated the world's first o. society COMMUNICATION, 33
overdrive when a business is in o. SUCCESS, 52
overhead O. is something that creeps in PROFITS, 20
overload perceive a situation of o. STRESS, 2
overnight success It takes years to make an o. SUCCESS, 14
overpaying We're o. him, but he's worth it WAGES, 19
overrated Holidays are often o. OPINIONS, 22
over-refinement state of o. CIVILISATION, 16
overrefines Who o. his argument DETAILS, 28
ownership The rise of o. by workers OPINIONS, 20
owning O. the intellectual property is like o. land ACHIEVING, 11
owns He who o. the most...wins WINNERS AND WINNING, 7
Whosoever o. the river bank o. the fish POWER, 6

P

pace Being in front...means that you are setting the p. RISK TAKING, 26
our p. of change is so fast CHANGE, 34
paid Ez long ez mine's p. punctooal WAGES, 28
pan-Americanism P. is a grand sentiment GLOBALISATION, 51
paper loss A p. is a very real loss MONEY, 79
paper-shuffling The modern business...ever greater p. empires BUREAUCRACY, 16
paper trail Always establish a p. WINNERS AND WINNING, 38
paradigm shift P.: A euphemism companies use when...investing in Orange County CHANGE, 3
paradox The emerging work p. CAREERS, 1
paralysed p. by the fear of major transformations CHANGE, 71
paranoia healthy p. in companies that are great at change EXCELLENCE, 6
I believe in the value of p. SUCCESS, 50
paranoid Only the p. survive EXPERIENCE, 20
pardon P. small offences EMPLOYERS, 2
pardons The offender never p. BLAME, 17
parents allow p. to balance work and family life OPPORTUNITY, 5
Paris P. is a suburb of New York and vice-versa GLOBALISATION, 56
parking The p. is easy E-COMMERCE, 2
participant challenging time to be a p. INVESTMENT AND THE STOCK MARKET, 36
participate p. for a more positive future WORK AND EMPLOYMENT, 100
participation p....is usually a sham BUSINESS ETHICS, 64
particulars P. are not to be examined DETAILS, 20
partisanship P. is our great curse LOYALTY, 15
partners If the US and Japan cannot become p. GLOBALISATION, 29
We are always willing to be trade p. GLOBALISATION, 77

party People come up to you at a p. DISCRIMINATION, 5
the office...was a p. every day CORPORATE CULTURE, 44
passably easier to write ten p. effective sonnets
ADVERTISING, 27
passion driving force in my life...p. ATTITUDE, 20
If you don't have p. ENTHUSIASM, 16
life is action and p. CHARACTER, 32
run with a p. WINNERS AND WINNING, 13
past things that are p., it is needless to blame BLAME, 6
patents P. on life...the enclosure of the intellectual BUSINESS ETHICS, 108
pathology p. of many big deals EXECUTIVES, 19
patience more you can do, the greater...your p.
DETERMINATION, 22
patient I am extraordinarily p. WINNERS AND WINNING, 40
pay Anything that promises to p. too much WAGES, 11
it's p. or perish in this world MONEY, 45
no rate of p....is low enough to compete WAGES, 50
Not a penny off the p. WAGES, 8
the larger the corporations...the smaller proportion they p.
TAXES, 5
The most un-American phrase...is 'take-home p.' WAGES, 25
we're going to p. ourselves a $1 million bonus EMPLOYEES, 66
paying cost of p. people EMPLOYERS, 10
paymaster A good p. never wants workmen EMPLOYERS, 5
payment cash p. has become the sole nexus SELLING, 3
payoffs irrational things in the pursuit of phenomenally
unlikely p. GREED, 1
PC The P. is the LSD of the 90s COMPUTERS, 11
Pearl Harbour Those Wonderful Folks Who Gave You P.
ADVERTISING, 18
pearls p. fetch a high price ECONOMICS, 119
peasants risk becoming the p. of the Western world
INDUSTRY, 6
pedantry P. is the dotage of knowledge DETAILS, 17
P. is the showy display of knowledge DETAILS, 6
peers I am compared to my p. in business SUCCESS, 65
penis few jobs...require a p. or vagina DISCRIMINATION, 43
pennies P. don't fall from heaven MONEY, 88
people get p....to where they have not been LEADERSHIP, 79
Get to know your p. EMPLOYEES, 80
P. are now becoming the most expensive optional
component PEOPLE AND RELATIONSHIPS, 16
p. are the greatest national resource GOVERNMENTS, 10
P. are the lifeblood of any airline EMPLOYEES, 17
P. can be themselves...in small comprehensible groups
TEAMS, 22
p. see that their ideas count PEOPLE AND RELATIONSHIPS, 38
P. who never get carried away ENTHUSIASM, 9
Surround yourself with the best p. DELEGATING, 13
The better p. they are CONFIDENCE, 23
The p. who get on in this world INITIATIVE, 4
what's at the heart of the business...p. MANAGEMENT, 89
You do not get good p. if HIRING AND FIRING, 16
perfect Man is born p. CAPITALISM VERSUS SOCIALISM, 29
P. numbers...are very rare PERFECTION, 2
perfection An environment which calls for p. PERFECTION, 7
The p. preached in the Gospels PERFECTION, 1
perform It's time for IBM to p. EXECUTIVES, 33
P. without fail what you resolve PRINCIPLES, 11
performance Double machine p....every year TARGETS, 17
in business...only p. is reality ACTION, 13
p. depended...on how well we worked together
CO-OPERATION, 21
P. stands out like a ton of diamonds EXCELLENCE, 5
raise individual p. by elevating...the entire system
SUCCESS, 26
perils avoid...the p....by united action CO-OPERATION, 25
perseverance Great works are performed...by p.
PERSISTENCE, 9
p. in a good cause PERSISTENCE, 16
P. is more prevailing than violence DETERMINATION, 17
P. may be just as important CHANGE, 61
persistence Nothing in the world can take the place of p.
GETTING STARTED, 16
P. and determination are omnipotent PERSISTENCE, 5

personality He had a lousy p. CHARACTER, 54
personnel Few great men could pass P. BUREAUCRACY, 18
Most people...are treated as p. LEADERSHIP, 119
The p. in India are more versatile EMPLOYEES, 44
persons I am made up of several p. CHARACTER, 42
persuade power to p. has to be demonstrated
ADVERTISING, 60
pet Whatever happens, you get your p. back ADVERTISING, 4
petitioners men who...refuse to listen to the p. POWER, 54
petrol P....a cause of international conflict GLOBALISATION, 96
petty behaving like a p. functionary CHARACTER, 13
the p. squabbles, intrigues, feuds, and airs CORPORATE
CULTURE, 60
phenomenons When new industries become p. MISTAKES, 1
phone Never pick up someone else's ringing p. CORPORATE
CULTURE, 94
picture Through the p. I see reality COMMUNICATION, 23
pig Never wrestle with a p. COMPETITION, 47
pioneers the history of p. is not that good RISK TAKING, 5
pirate It's better to be a p. INDEPENDENCE, 6
place Have a p. for everything ORDER, 32
plagiarist No p. can excuse the wrong BUSINESS ETHICS, 59
plan a five-year p....pure fantasy PLANNING, 18
I never had a business p. PLANNING, 17
p. the way a fire department plans PLANNING, 13
To p. carefully is the safest delay PROCRASTINATION, 25
planning Long-range p. does not deal with future decisions
STRATEGY, 11
P. ahead is a matter of class PLANNING, 22
P., by its very nature, defines and preserves categories
CREATIVITY, 36
p. for 100 years plant people PLANNING, 1
P. is good PLANNING, 31
P....natural to the process of success PLANNING, 21
To hell with centralized strategic p. LEADERSHIP, 120
plans I can read a lot of p. in 45 minutes PLANNING, 29
people who have got these life p. GETTING STARTED, 5
strategic p. reveal more about today's problems
PLANNING, 14
plastic A useless piece of p. LOYALTY, 6
play creative workers, give them enough time to p.
CREATIVITY, 6
players You can't play the game without all the p.
TEAMS, 29
please In him alone, 'twas Natural to p. CHARACTER, 18
pleasure An honest man can feel no p. POWER, 42
P. disappoints, possibility never OPPORTUNITY, 18
When work is a p. WORK AND EMPLOYMENT, 46
plum you have missed the p. BOLDNESS, 22
plumber try getting a p. on weekends ADVERSITY, 1
plumbing I don't do p. LEADERSHIP, 25
poet semi-talented p. CAREERS, 10
poison The strongest p. ever known POWER, 15
poker don't go to a p. table with no money RISK TAKING, 45
p. players don't hanker for jobs in casino management
CAREERS, 20
policies combining better economic p. DOING BUSINESS IN
LATIN AMERICA, 1
Outworn p. may remain in force CHANGE, 23
policy Our p. is to reduce the price TARGETS, 14
polite Be p. Write diplomatically CHARACTER, 6
political acting was good training for...p. life TRAINING, 7
P. work is the life-blood ECONOMICS, 74
political economy confused assemblage...of P.
ECONOMICS, 103
p....has a plausible idea at the root ECONOMICS, 101
P....human beings are made prosperous WEALTH, 36
P....is extremely modern ECONOMICS, 83
P. or Economics is a study of mankind ECONOMICS, 75
politician a true p....never at a loss for words SPEECHES, 38
politics I've learned one thing in p. DECISIONS, 28
p. is the art of the possible RESEARCH, 15
poll no Gallup p....no Bill Clinton INFORMATION, 3
poor He who hesitates is p. PROCRASTINATION, 8
luckily the p. provide food WEALTH, 2
poorest We are the p. rich people WEALTH, 18

private enterprise P. has no press agent PUBLICITY, 9
privatising process of p....greater room for control DOING
 BUSINESS IN AFRICA, 5
privileges p. can be no greater than our obligations
 RESPONSIBILITY, 12
prizes The world continues to offer glittering p.
 AMBITION, 26
proactive If you're p. ACTION, 11
probability A reasonable p. is the only certainty
 CONFIDENCE, 22
probity p. has eroded HONESTY, 2
problem Every solution of a p. PROBLEMS, 30
p....paying enough attention to our customers
 CUSTOMERS, 30
The p. established firms seem unable to confront BOOM
 AND BUST, 2
The p. when solved will be simple PROBLEMS, 1
they can't see the p. PROBLEMS, 8
problematically We must think p. PROBLEMS, 13
problems deep human p....not to be approached without
 some humor PROBLEMS, 11
I need p. PROBLEMS, 33
In solving our p....creating worse ones PROBLEMS, 14
P. are only opportunities in work clothes PROBLEMS, 24
P. can only be solved by the people who have them
 PROBLEMS, 22
The p. of this world PROBLEMS, 35
understand each others' p. TEAMS, 19
Work only on p....nearly impossible to solve
 INNOVATION, 53
procrastination Nothing is worse than p.
 PROCRASTINATION, 3
P. brings loss PROCRASTINATION, 11
P. is epidemic PROCRASTINATION, 20
p. is the /art of keeping /up with yesterday
 PROCRASTINATION, 23
p. is the king PROCRASTINATION, 24
P. is the thief of time PROCRASTINATION, 31
produce No man can p. great things SINCERITY, 26
producing Man is the only creature that consumes without
 p. CONSUMERS, 25
P. is more important than possessing PRODUCTIVITY, 5
real impediment to p....management MANAGEMENT, 38
product All you need is the best p. in the world
 GLOBALISATION, 59
A p. is anything that can be offered PRODUCTS, 11
A successful p. PRODUCTS, 7
companies...find planning more interesting than...p.
 PLANNING, 30
Every p. has some element of service MARKETING, 48
good p. that sits on a shelf MARKETING, 9
introduce a p. in the morning INNOVATION, 86
it's not the p. that's wrong, it's you SELLING, 15
Junk is the ideal p. PRODUCTS, 2
Make your company stock a consumer p. INVESTMENT AND
 THE STOCK MARKET, 63
plants...focused in terms of p. PRODUCTS, 1
p. is pure intellectual property PRODUCTS, 9
p. which does not exist INNOVATION, 44
When the p. is right SELLING, 12
production highest development of the techniques both
 of p. and distribution BUSINESS ETHICS, 88
P. not being the sole end of human existence
 PRODUCTIVITY, 9
routine p. is footloose ECONOMICS, 92
The mode of p. CHANGE, 91
productively The more p. one lives CONSCIENCE, 11
productiveness p. of a meeting falls with...people present
 MEETINGS, 17
productivity industrial society...confuses work and p.
 PRODUCTIVITY, 11
p....makes everything happen on time and profitably
 EFFICIENCY, 4
products All p. must be seen as experiments PRODUCTS, 14
However numerous your p. DETAILS, 15
intelligent people are offered p. CUSTOMERS, 8

new p. never get out of test markets PRODUCTS, 16
The driving force for the development of new p.
 is...imagination INNOVATION, 72
try to picture what the p. will be STRATEGY, 49
You have to love the p. SELLING, 32
profession as a p. we have taken a hit CORRUPTION AND
 SCANDAL, 3
bond between a man and his p. WORK AND
 EMPLOYMENT, 62
He has made a p. out of a business BUSINESS ETHICS, 42
No man likes...a mistake in...his p. CAREERS, 2
professional All p. men are handicapped PROBLEMS, 16
p....can do his job when he doesn't feel like it ATTITUDE, 2
professionalism Today p. is...a byword for loyalty
 LOYALTY, 5
professionals P. require little direction LEADERSHIP, 90
proficient P. is...skilled KNOWLEDGE, 14
profit excitement...figures on the p. and loss sheet
 PROFITS, 21
incentives based on p. EXECUTIVES, 37
Management's total loyalty to the maximization of p.
 CONSCIENCE, 1
P. has to be a means to other ends PROFITS, 12
P. is like health PROFITS, 1
pursuit of p....outdated and old-fashioned view GOALS AND
 OBJECTIVES, 26
The engine which drives enterprise...p. ECONOMICS, 62
The only p. center is the customer CUSTOMERS, 11
the p. system has always been...highly unprofitable
 WAGES, 49
Volatility...creates the opportunity for p. INVESTMENT AND
 THE STOCK MARKET, 68
Where p. is, loss is hidden PROFITS, 2
You don't go broke making a p. FAILURE, 50
profitability mere p. is unlikely to be sufficient CORPORATE
 RESPONSIBILITY, 22
profits 80% of business p....built around info-business
 FORECASTING, 5
Businesses which forego p. BUSINESS ETHICS, 97
keeping p. up...by keeping wages down WAGES, 37
p. and the preservation of family and community values
 BUSINESS ETHICS, 30
P. are the lifeblood PROFITS, 23
Undue p. are not made PROFITS, 4
Watch the costs...p. will take care of themselves
 BUDGETING, 2
We could have shown higher p. PROFITS, 19
when you state p. you've got to pay PROFITS, 25
profit-sharing Few ideas are as capitalist as p.
 CAPITALISM, 39
progress 'P.' involves...the technosphere PROGRESS, 18
'p.' is simply a comparative PROGRESS, 8
Change is scientific, p. is ethical CHANGE, 115
Directors desire...social p. GOALS AND OBJECTIVES, 21
economic p. means that we become anonymous cogs
 PROGRESS, 21
Problems are the price of p. PROBLEMS, 25
P....depends on retentiveness PROGRESS, 32
p. depends on the unreasonable man PROGRESS, 33
p....exchange of one nuisance for another nuisance
 PROGRESS, 10
p. has come to mean limitless movement LIMITATIONS, 5
P. is mostly the product of rogues PROGRESS, 26
P....is not an accident but a necessity PROGRESS, 37
p. is not real and cannot be permanent PROGRESS, 17
p. of human society...better apportioning of wages
 WAGES, 5
p....you can't find anyone who disagrees with you
 PROGRESS, 4
The test of our p. PROGRESS, 30
We have stopped believing in p. PROGRESS, 6
progressive a p....knows where he is going STRATEGY, 55
projects Involve people in meaningful p. PEOPLE AND
 RELATIONSHIPS, 11
prologue If past is p. INVESTMENT AND THE STOCK MARKET, 48
promise P....is the soul of an advertisement ADVERTISING, 28

promised You never reach the p. land TARGETS, 5
promises In the best institutions, p. are kept SERVICE, 7
promising Whom the gods...first call p. SUCCESS, 21
promote I never hesitated to p. someone DELEGATING, 19
promoted We want a woman schlemiel to get p. DISCRIMINATION, 1
promotion accounting system...indicators for p. MANAGEMENT, 83
P. comes from exceptional work ACHIEVING, 6
propaganda P. ends where dialogue begins COMMUNICATION, 28
propensity p. to trade...common to all men SELLING, 29
property Few rich men own their own p. WEALTH, 31
no other end but the preservation of p. GOVERNMENTS, 31
Not p. is wrong BUSINESS ETHICS, 76
Private p. is a necessary institution CAPITALISM, 47
p. is the most important guarantee of freedom CAPITALISM, 23
Thieves respect p. BUSINESS ETHICS, 27
prophecy p. is the most gratuitous MISTAKES, 7
prophets The wisest p. PLANNING, 28
proprietor I am the p. MANAGEMENT, 45
prosperity In times of great p. CONFIDENCE, 25
P. doth best discover vice ADVERSITY, 2
P. has no fixed limits WEALTH, 38
P. is a great teacher ADVERSITY, 15
P. is only an instrument WEALTH, 13
P. proves the fortunate ADVERSITY, 22
P. tries the souls WEALTH, 50
trouble with p. PROGRESS, 12
Whom p. maketh our friend ADVERSITY, 5
prosumers P. CONSUMERS, 32
protection p. is a legitimate demand INDEPENDENCE, 4
protest p., give your reasons EMPLOYEES, 11
prove Give me six months to p. myself GETTING STARTED, 12
proverbs At best we live by homely p. MANAGEMENT, 68
provision decent p. for the poor is the true test CIVILISATION, 22
provocative p. disruption CORPORATE CULTURE, 8
psychology Organisational p. CORPORATE CULTURE, 5
the market...is going to be driven by p. INVESTMENT AND THE STOCK MARKET, 29
public change the way companies go p. CORPORATE CULTURE, 92
The p. be damned CORPORATE RESPONSIBILITY, 32
The p. does not know what is possible INNOVATION, 63
public interest groups p....are using the new technology BANKING, 16
publicise We don't p. our failures FAILURE, 33
publicity The price of justice is eternal p. PUBLICITY, 4
There's no such thing as bad p. PUBLICITY, 3
public opinion P. is a weak tyrant OPINIONS, 36
public speaking P. is like the winds of the desert SPEECHES, 19
publisher As a p., we've not done acquisitions MEDIA, 18
Xerox makes everybody a p. TECHNOLOGY, 37
publishing Scale in p. is increasingly important MEDIA, 19
punctuality absolute p....a tormentor EMPLOYERS, 3
purchasers brick in his pocket...to encourage p. SELLING, 31
purpose my life's p. had been achieved ACHIEVING, 29
the best companies...have a real p. BUSINESS ETHICS, 103
The p. of getting power POWER, 14
purposes men...use you for your own p. BUSINESS ETHICS, 3
The mind is enlarged...by mere p. PERSONAL GROWTH, 6
purse the longest p. finally wins LAWYERS, 8
pursuit indefatigable p. of an unattainable perfection PERFECTION, 6
The p. of modern life is economic CAPITALISM, 6
push If you want to p. something DISCRIMINATION, 32
we must p. ourselves DISCRIMINATION, 71
Whatever I am engaged in...p. inordinately DETERMINATION, 5
pusillanimity P. disposeth men to irresolution PROCRASTINATION, 16

puzzle People weren't allowed to put the whole p. together CORPORATE CULTURE, 57
pyramid The p. inside companies is being flattened ORGANISATIONS, 54
The p....turns a business into a traffic jam EFFICIENCY, 10

Q

qualifies A man who q. himself well SUCCESS, 55
qualities We don't love q. CHARACTER, 41
quality a company presumes to judge the q. CONSUMERS, 15
Q. control was treated as a fad QUALITY, 26
Q. does not give you an advantage QUALITY, 19
Q. has to be caused QUALITY, 4
Q. is a direct experience QUALITY, 21
Q. is characteristic of a product QUALITY, 8
Q. is Free QUALITY, 5
Q. is not a thing QUALITY, 22
Q. is not...simply imposed QUALITY, 16
Q. is remembered QUALITY, 13
Q....is the protection of the investor interest INVESTMENT AND THE STOCK MARKET, 43
q. planning consists of developing the products QUALITY, 14
Q., Service, Cleanliness and Value CORPORATE CULTURE, 87
q....the best kind of advertising ADVERTISING, 26
The q. of your attention determines...other people's thinking EXCELLENCE, 7
What the hell is q. QUALITY, 24
quantitative the q. method is the victory of sterility and death STATISTICS, 3
question q. *everything* and *think big* NEGOTIATION, 15
To ask the hard q. is simple COMMUNICATION, 1
questions Go around asking a lot of damn-fool q. RISK TAKING, 28
the q....we are still asking PROGRESS, 1
quick Tell me q. ADVERTISING, 5
quit If at first you don't succeed...q. FAILURE, 19

R

race r. from the accumulation of wealth WEALTH, 9
races Winning r. gives you...satisfaction STRATEGY, 10
rack In the old days men had the r. MEDIA, 58
radical A r....feet firmly planted in the air CHARACTER, 51
raincoats not destined to be empty r. PROGRESS, 20
raise If you don't give us a r....I quit NEGOTIATION, 3
raising r. your hand for the next bid ACHIEVING, 10
rank In every r....'Tis industry supports us all INDUSTRY, 10
rashness To a few r. brings luck, to most misfortune BOLDNESS, 18
rat r. eat r., dog eat dog COMPETITION, 45
The first time a r. saved a sinking ship MEDIA, 15
rate r. we're borrowing from abroad DEBT, 12
rationalising military-industrial drive toward r. WORK AND EMPLOYMENT, 81
rat race The trouble with being in the r. STRESS, 8
rats When the r. are running for cover MANAGEMENT, 76
react r. in a business situation EXECUTIVES, 44
reactive Management today is r. behaviour MANAGEMENT, 20
readiness r. to enter a room in the dark CHANGE, 128
real Nothing ever becomes r. till it is experienced EXPERIENCE, 25
reality r. must take precedence over public relations ACCURACY, 7
the r. of inevitability is created IDEAS, 22
reasons A man always has two r. AMBITION, 21
rebuild r. our corporate world CORPORATE CULTURE, 19
recession In a r., people want to test me EMPLOYEES, 63
R. drove people to church BOOM AND BUST, 15
R. isn't the fault of the workers HIRING AND FIRING, 23

S

skills s. involved in putting together deals ENTREPRENEURS, 21
unique local s....advanced, foreign-origin production
  methods GLOBALISATION, 68
skin Most people who have been around...very vulnerable
  s. COMPETITION, 7
use my s. for lampshades CONTRACTS, 2
slack S. allows innovative projects to be pursued
  INNOVATION, 67
sleep You cannot go to s. CAPITALISM VERSUS SOCIALISM, 7
slept People assume you s. your way to the top
  DISCRIMINATION, 22
slogan The popular s. CUSTOMERS, 6
sloth an island of efficiency in a sea of s. EFFICIENCY, 6
Torpor is harrowing, s. it is irksome WORK AND
  EMPLOYMENT, 72
small I understand s. business growth ENTREPRENEURS, 8
s. is always more beautiful than big CORPORATE CULTURE, 47
S. is Beautiful ECONOMICS, 105
Think s. and act s. ATTITUDE, 14
your company so s. you...do everything for yourself
  GROWTH, 1
smart Always be s. enough to hire people brighter than
  yourself EMPLOYEES, 48
s. enough to defend ourselves from...destruction
  ORGANISATIONS, 87
smarter People also have a need to feel s. NEGOTIATION, 17
smell If you can't s. it, you can't sell it PRODUCTS, 13
smile riding on a s. and a shoestring SELLING, 25
smiling A man without a s. face SERVICE, 1
snapshot a s. of the economy today LOSING, 6
snare A s. and a delusion TAXES, 26
sneer necessary to s. at people CRITICISM, 4
soar ambition can creep as well as s. AMBITION, 5
social Brilliant minds, but no s. graces EMPLOYEES, 22
S. relations are closely bound up with productive forces
  CHANGE, 90
socialisation the s. aspect of business CORPORATE
  CULTURE, 138
socialism Marxian S....so powerful and enduring an
  influence CAPITALISM VERSUS SOCIALISM, 7
S....better wages and shorter hours COMMUNISM AND
  SOCIALISM, 8
socialist I am a revolutionary s. REPUTATION, 15
s. competition is...valour, and heroism COMMUNISM AND
  SOCIALISM, 9
society I have helped to change s. BOASTING, 6
S. acquires new arts, and loses old instincts PROGRESS, 11
S. cannot share a common communication system
  COMMUNICATION, 8
s....disposed to regard the poor as damned WEALTH, 63
S. has become unmanageable MANAGEMENT, 50
s. isn't structured on greed GREED, 6
software government...play in the growth of the s.
  industry GOVERNMENTS, 35
S. is...stupid...to invest in TECHNOLOGY, 57
The s. industry...slightly managed chaos CORPORATE
  CULTURE, 1
solidarity it is s. of labor we want EMPLOYEES, 38
solution part of the s. or part of the problem PROBLEMS, 9
solutions real s. to our problems BLAME, 3
solve S. it, s. it quickly PROBLEMS, 37
sometimes s. you just don't like somebody HIRING AND
  FIRING, 10
soul Don't subcontract your s. RISK TAKING, 3
The s. of a business OPINIONS, 10
souls Most people sell their s. CONSCIENCE, 37
sound Developing a s. and healthy organisation
  ORGANISATIONS, 82
soundbite s....is all that an interviewer allows you to say
  COMMUNICATION, 4
Soviet Union S. can be bought for dollars COMMUNISM AND
  SOCIALISM, 4
spare I always have a s. pair of pants PUBLICITY, 19
spark-gap The s. is mightier than the pen INNOVATION, 46
speak If I am to s. for ten minutes SPEECHES, 58
S. clearly, if you s. at all SPEECHES, 26

S. what you think to-day CONFIDENCE, 12
speaker The most popular s. SPEECHES, 35
speakers All the great s. were bad SPEECHES, 18
speaks The great man...simply s. SINCERITY, 31
special The voice is so s....let nothing disturb it QUALITY, 25
specialise We s. in the wholly impossible CHALLENGE, 1
specialist A s. is someone who does everything else worse
  EXCELLENCE, 10
speculate Never s....if you have savings INVESTMENT AND THE
  STOCK MARKET, 26
speculators S. may do no harm INVESTMENT AND THE STOCK
  MARKET, 41
speech A s. is poetry and cadence SPEECHES, 39
I cannot make an amusing s. SPEECHES, 51
Listening to a s. by Chamberlain SPEECHES, 2
loath to cast away my s. SPEECHES, 49
s. on economics...like pissing down your leg
  ECONOMICS, 54
the most timid man can deliver a bold s. SPEECHES, 46
the short meaning of this long s.? SPEECHES, 45
speeches His s. are like cypress trees SPEECHES, 43
S. measured by the hour SPEECHES, 27
The s. of one that is desperate SPEECHES, 3
speed our safety is in our s. RISK TAKING, 16
Unsafe at Any S. CONSUMERS, 22
speeding We are s. up our lives TIME MANAGEMENT, 8
spend To make money, you have to s. money MONEY, 74
spending every American either has a share of federal s.
  ECONOMICS, 71
executive...time for ostentatious s. EXECUTIVES, 16
spiral vicious s. of rising prices ECONOMICS, 8
sponsors s. don't know if their money is wasted
  MARKETING, 4
spontaneity shift away from mere s. LOYALTY, 11
staff If you were to hire household s. EMPLOYEES, 58
I really like my s. EMPLOYEES, 50
staffing s. decisions to minimize weaknesses HIRING AND
  FIRING, 8
stain Even doubtful accusations leave a s. BLAME, 12
stake Nobody has...built a s....without my approval WINNERS
  AND WINNING, 22
Stalin S. didn't understand the importance of business
  CAPITALISM VERSUS SOCIALISM, 11
standardised order...is a s. worker ORDER, 14
standard of living Efforts to preserve...lower the national s.
  ECONOMICS, 89
standards S. are always out of date QUALITY, 2
standing The last man s. TECHNOLOGY, 35
stars When you reach for the s. AMBITION, 6
start anything is easy to s. ENTREPRENEURS, 25
s. by giving myself a s. CAREERS, 26
starting S. companies is very hard and time-consuming
  STRATEGY, 53
start-up The challenge in a s. GETTING STARTED, 3
starve Should we really let our people s. BUSINESS ETHICS, 91
stasis Do we search for s. PROGRESS, 28
state A s. without the means of some change CHANGE, 20
That s. is a s. of slavery CORPORATE CULTURE, 48
The rulers of the s....have the privilege of lying
  GOVERNMENTS, 40
The s. is or can be master of money GOVERNMENTS, 5
static All leadership...will be useless if it becomes s.
  LEADERSHIP, 41
statistical The state of s. control STATISTICS, 5
statisticians Thou shalt not sit /With s. STATISTICS, 1
statistics s. are a form of wish fulfilment STATISTICS, 2
There are two kinds of s. STATISTICS, 9
status quo Challenging the s. BOLDNESS, 9
steer s. between the Scylla of humility RISK TAKING, 39
step In great affairs there is no little s. BOLDNESS, 20
steps I am not afraid to take s. WINNERS AND WINNING, 20
stew Don't s. about the futures STRESS, 4
stock If you aren't willing to own a s. for ten years
  INVESTMENT AND THE STOCK MARKET, 13
stockbroker A s....takes all your money INVESTMENT AND THE
  STOCK MARKET, 1

stockholders s....own companies INVESTMENT AND THE STOCK MARKET, 62

stock market s. is just like a sieve INVESTMENT AND THE STOCK MARKET, 64

The s. adopts a thesis INVESTMENT AND THE STOCK MARKET, 73

stocks 'Tis sweet to know that s. will stand INDUSTRY, 7

stores Our old s. IMAGE, 14

storms common fault of men not to reckon on s. ADVERSITY, 19

story it's enough to pull together a good s. WEALTH, 12

straightforward It's very s. IMAGE, 5

strangers do business like s. DOING BUSINESS IN ASIA-PACIFIC, 6

strategic S. market management is a system MARKETING, 2

strategic planning S. can neither provide creativity CREATIVITY, 37

strategies Creative s. seldom emerge from the annual planning STRATEGY, 28

Mould-breaking s. STRATEGY, 39

s. fail because they are overripe FAILURE, 43

S. that succeed are organic STRATEGY, 54

strategist a truly creative s....or...a true empowerer LEADERSHIP, 91

strategists consultants are the thinkers and the s. MANAGEMENT, 66

strategy break s. down to Five Forces or Seven Ss STRATEGY, 27

develop a s. against racist resistance DISCRIMINATION, 19

developing our industrial s. INDUSTRY, 2

essence of s....dynamics of its behaviour STRATEGY, 46

Marketing s. is a series of integrated actions MARKETING, 38

S. is not the consequence of planning STRATEGY, 40

S. making is an immensely complex process STRATEGY, 41

S. must attract STRATEGY, 14

S., policies and standards are set globally GLOBALISATION, 74

The essence of a company...is execution and s. PRACTICE, 4

The essence of a s. STRATEGY, 52

There is only one winning s. STRATEGY, 34

The task of business s. STRATEGY, 37

strength He knows not his own s. ADVERSITY, 17

Three failures denote uncommon s. FAILURE, 3

stress any executive who ever thought about s. WORK AND EMPLOYMENT, 68

Brain cells create ideas. S. kills brain cells STRESS, 5

stretch S. and discipline are the yin and yang of business TARGETS, 3

strike a nationwide s....'a Workman's Holiday' EMPLOYEES, 71

s. out on new paths SUCCESS, 85

The s. is the weapon of the oppressed COMMUNISM AND SOCIALISM, 2

strive Man's restlessness makes him s. AMBITION, 14

strives Man errs as long as he s. MISTAKES, 12

Man is the only creature that s. AMBITION, 17

stronger Positive feedback makes the strong grow s. SUCCESS, 90

structure S. will become a dynamic enabler CHANGE, 6

struggle The s. itself...is enough TARGETS, 6

students When s. are separated...opportunity to assess LEARNING, 33

study I went back to the s. WINNERS AND WINNING, 32

stumble You can only s. if you're moving ORGANISATIONS, 26

stupidest the very s. who cannot change CHANGE, 25

style My s. of dealmaking NEGOTIATION, 25

s., not sincerity, is the vital thing SINCERITY, 49

subject Grasp the s. SPEECHES, 9

sublime step from the s. to the ridiculous ACHIEVING, 5

subordinates s. do not talk with their boss COMMUNICATION, 20

substitute no s. for being in the right place LUCK, 7

substitutes Ours is the age of s. IDEAS, 4

subtle The s. accumulation of nuances QUALITY, 17

succeed God doesn't require us to s. SUCCESS, 98

How to S. in Business without Really Trying SUCCESS, 72

If at first you don't s. SUCCESS, 81

If we do not s. FAILURE, 45

If you can s. with a few thousand pounds GETTING STARTED, 31

If you want to s., double your failure rate SUCCESS, 12

To s....have confidence in yourself SUCCESS, 58

You only s....in survival mode SUCCESS, 91

success A minute's s. pays the failure of years FAILURE, 9

a price...for s. in a family business CORPORATE RESPONSIBILITY, 8

Doing is overrated, and s. undesirable FAILURE, 12

Eighty percent of s. is showing up SUCCESS, 3

If I'd gotten this much s. in Hollywood SUCCESS, 83

I would have been a s. in anything BUSINESS ETHICS, 82

Making a s. of the job at hand SUCCESS, 4

My formula for s. WORK AND EMPLOYMENT, 13

No one can possibly achieve...lasting s. INNOVATION, 38

No one has all the answers to s. SUCCESS, 23

no royal flower-strewn path to s. ACCOMPLISHMENTS, 17

person who wins s. PERSISTENCE, 19

S....catches the consumer's imagination ENTREPRENEURS, 33

S. goes to those with a corporate culture CORPORATE CULTURE, 105

s. in an Internet environment CO-OPERATION, 17

s. in any business CORPORATE CULTURE, 145

s. is always temporary SUCCESS, 49

S. is a science SUCCESS, 102

s. is constancy to purpose SUCCESS, 27

S. is made of 99 percent failure SUCCESS, 31

S. is more a function of consistent common sense COMMON SENSE, 9

S. is never blamed BLAME, 15

S. is relative SUCCESS, 37

S. is the final place SUCCESS, 82

S. should not be measured by earnings MARKETING, 13

S....willingness to strive for something you really want SUCCESS, 97

The best augury of a man's s. CAREERS, 5

The highest form of s. ADVERSITY, 23

The key to s. for Sony WINNERS AND WINNING, 26

The primary rule of business s. is loyalty LOYALTY, 21

The real measure of s. SUCCESS, 33

There are no secrets to s. PERSISTENCE, 14

The secret of s. PERSISTENCE, 7

The secret of s. is sincerity SINCERITY, 16

The s. of a project will depend critically upon...effort PLANNING, 3

The toughest thing about s. SUCCESS, 7

The worst tragedy...my s. PUBLICITY, 22

this has a 90 percent chance of s. INNOVATION, 42

Tis not in mortals to command s. SUCCESS, 2

to maintain this ecstasy, is s. SUCCESS, 79

Worthwhile s. is impossible in a forty hour week TIME MANAGEMENT, 4

successful A good team...stimulating, supportive, s. TEAMS, 12

Anybody who runs a s. high tech company TECHNOLOGY, 51

Brits seem to envy people who are s. SUCCESS, 67

People who are s....want it more SUCCESS, 87

s. company...solid foundations of economic success SUCCESS, 99

The secret of the truly s. SUCCESS, 35

To be s. you have to be lucky SUCCESS, 25

To be s. you...have to stand out SUCCESS, 76

successor choosing my s. EXECUTIVES, 59

sucker There's a s. born every minute SELLING, 1

suffer I s. no slings and arrows SUCCESS, 68

Life is truly known only to those who s. ADVERSITY, 18

suicide watch MGN commit s. RISK TAKING, 33

suits A few s. of clothes CIVILISATION, 36

summit they have many when they reach the s. ACHIEVING, 21

sums The s. are so large SUCCESS, 34

superficial Deep down, I'm pretty s. CHARACTER, 25

superfluous S. wealth can buy superfluities only WEALTH, 65

superior s. performance depends on s. learning LEARNING, 39

The s. man is distressed ABILITY, 5

U

useful Have nothing...you do not know to be u. CREATIVITY, 38

usefulness Do not make riches, but u., your first aim CHARACTER, 8

USP The U....lifts itself out of the ruck MARKETING, 34

People should be given the opportunity to v. BUSINESS ETHICS, 36

vulgar It is very v. to talk about one's business BOASTING, 15

vulgarisation an age of...v. CIVILISATION, 24

V

value Creating v. is an inherently cooperative process VALUE, 10

know the v. of money MONEY, 38

people...give you the v. that you believe CORPORATE CULTURE, 114

strive to add long-term v. CORPORATE RESPONSIBILITY, 12

The economic engine is always in v. E-COMMERCE, 38

There are only four ways to create v. ECONOMICS, 117

The v. of a thing VALUE, 6

V. depends entirely on utility VALUE, 8

v. in IBM...reverse in an Indian firm BUSINESS ETHICS, 24

V. is the most...impalpable of ghosts VALUE, 7

You can't measure the v. of being first COMPETITION, 50

value economy view today's economy as the V. ECONOMICS, 69

values 'Organizational v.'...derive from 'individual v.' BUSINESS ETHICS, 22

Human beings...educated for v. PRINCIPLES, 6

shifts in v....potent sources of innovation INNOVATION, 18

the idea of v....is being renewed BUSINESS ETHICS, 15

v. from the Church, the temple, the mosque CORPORATE CULTURE, 117

V. serve the process of 'becoming' BUSINESS ETHICS, 23

variety V., change, and speed...new organizational structure ORGANISATIONS, 24

vaudeville TV...Terrible V. MEDIA, 1

velocity the 2000s will be about v. CHANGE, 50

v. of decision making DECISIONS, 20

venture a joint v. imposed by foreign investing NEGOTIATION, 29

Each v. is a new beginning GETTING STARTED, 6

verbal contract A v. isn't worth the paper it's written on CONTRACTS, 4

versatility an actor's life...freedom and v. CREATIVITY, 42

viable I'm v. from ten o'clock till five JOBS, 2

vibrant It's a v. special place CORPORATE CULTURE, 33

victims We were not the v. of ancestor worship INNOVATION, 61

views My v. about economics are very simple ECONOMICS, 118

The man who v. the world at fifty ACHIEVING, 1

vigilante business...rise of v. consumers CONSUMERS, 26

violence We would never do v. BUSINESS ETHICS, 89

virtuality the voyager in v. can return home TECHNOLOGY, 55

virtue man of v....difficulty to be overcome his first business SUCCESS, 19

virtuous He preferred to be...v. SINCERITY, 37

viscera run this business on v. LEADERSHIP, 124

vision grasp and hold a v. LEADERSHIP, 99

My v. was to provide advice TARGETS, 4

Our v. controls the way we think GOALS AND OBJECTIVES, 12

V. is the art of seeing things invisible INNOVATION, 88

V.: Top management's heroic guess about the future STRATEGY, 2

Without an appropriate v....effort can easily dissolve STRATEGY, 25

visions Effective v. are lived in details DETAILS, 27

voice You could hear his v. PEOPLE AND RELATIONSHIPS, 1

volatile The more v. the market SUCCESS, 20

volatility The true investor *welcomes* v. INVESTMENT AND THE STOCK MARKET, 17

v....of deregulated financial institutions ECONOMICS, 40

Voltaire V. said that every man had two countries: his own and France GLOBALISATION, 60

vote first line of defence is to v. BUSINESS ETHICS, 106

W

wage One man's w. increase WAGES, 51

wages A fair day's w. WAGES, 4

All w. are based primarily on productive power WAGES, 23

Be content with your w. WAGES, 2

cutting down other people's w. WAGES, 34

W. are the measure of dignity WAGES, 45

W. ought...support a frugal and well-behaved wage-earner WAGES, 27

W. should be left to the fair WAGES, 38

Walkman Sony...concept of the W. INNOVATION, 69

wallet the man with a flat w. could be attracted PRODUCTS, 10

Wall Street 'W.', runs the sinister old gag INVESTMENT AND THE STOCK MARKET, 66

I'm not in W. MONEY, 69

lemmings...individuals compared with W. INVESTMENT AND THE STOCK MARKET, 24

W. is the only place people ride ADVICE, 1

W. Lays An Egg BOOM AND BUST, 13

W....Masters of the Universe INVESTMENT AND THE STOCK MARKET, 85

When W. sneezes, London catches cold INVESTMENT AND THE STOCK MARKET, 2

Wal-martise They tried to W. me and it worked CORPORATE CULTURE, 31

wanting To him that will, ways are not w. AMBITION, 16

wants Man w. but little here below CONSUMERS, 5

war comparing w. to...commerce SELLING, 4

the first live televised w. MEDIA, 41

washroom If the w. isn't good enough CORPORATE CULTURE, 130

Nobody here cares which w. you use CORPORATE CULTURE, 28

waste Never w. your attention FOCUS, 8

waste basket file your w. for 50 years INFORMATION, 1

wastes the government w. vast amounts of money GOVERNMENTS, 36

watches people looking at their w. SPEECHES, 4

water nothing beats dipping your toe in the w. STRATEGY, 5

way find a w. or make one DETERMINATION, 16

weak It is the w. and confused HONESTY, 9

weakness The chief w. in business organization ORGANISATIONS, 20

weaknesses Don't argue for other people's w. MISTAKES, 5

wealth acquisition of w....test of success SUCCESS, 86

creating w. in the third industrial revolution FAILURE, 54

men who gain from their w. WEALTH, 43

nature of w. itself...changing more fundamentally PROGRESS, 3

Nobody who has w. to distribute...omits himself MONEY, 90

servicing...the product of w. by others INDUSTRY, 46

single-minded pursuit of w. WEALTH, 52

The greater the w., the thicker...the dirt BUSINESS ETHICS, 51

the insolence of w. will creep out WEALTH, 32

The only way to create tremendous w. WEALTH, 66

The problem of our age is...w. PROBLEMS, 6

There is no fixed road to w. WEALTH, 57

three ways by which an individual can get w. WEALTH, 26

To mistake money for w. MONEY, 66

w. and knowledge...remain the primary roots CHANGE, 126

w....has not been all that evenly distributed WEALTH, 47

w. is a sacred thing WEALTH, 22

W. is like sea-water WEALTH, 51

W. is not without its advantages WEALTH, 24

W. I would have WEALTH, 60

w. should be found everywhere WEALTH, 7

W....slips like a smashed tile WEALTH, 58

w. with a person day in and day out EMPLOYEES, 4

w., w., w. till we die WORK AND EMPLOYMENT, 63

W., worry, toil, and trouble WORK AND EMPLOYMENT, 86

w....your means of inner spiritual rebirth WORK AND EMPLOYMENT, 4

You gotta think; you gotta w. SUCCESS, 59

workaholics w....are in the basket of work WORK AND EMPLOYMENT, 7

workaholism Disconnected organizations spawn w. ORGANISATIONS, 65

worked w....to discover that I didn't like it CAREERS, 24

worker The w. is the slave of the capitalist society CAPITALISM VERSUS SOCIALISM, 5

w. under capitalism...totally dependent on the machine EMPLOYEES, 16

workers My w....look at me...as a friend CORPORATE CULTURE, 69

Naturally, the w. are perfectly free EMPLOYEES, 19

The idea of making w. share in profits PROFITS, 7

They are not the w. EMPLOYEES, 85

work ethic American workers...lack a w. WORK AND EMPLOYMENT, 69

workforce By a career-resilient w. PEOPLE AND RELATIONSHIPS, 37

working hard to distinguish between w. and socialising CORPORATE CULTURE, 1

I can't stand w. and not seeing results TARGETS, 20

If you keep w., you'll last longer WORK AND EMPLOYMENT, 43

Portfolio w. CAREERS, 8

thousands of young people are w. from bedrooms ENTREPRENEURS, 24

W. hard is fun WORK AND EMPLOYMENT, 91

workplace biggest change in the w. of the future EXECUTIVES, 3

The w. is undergoing rapid change WORK AND EMPLOYMENT, 53

workstyle web w. will change the boundaries of business TECHNOLOGY, 22

world follow the property cycle around the w. GLOBALISATION, 23

The coming w. quake CHANGE, 127

The Weightless W. COMPUTERS, 6

We're gonna stay on until the end of the w. PERSISTENCE, 18

world economy The bigger the w. GLOBALISATION, 67

world records If someone breaks my w. WINNERS AND WINNING, 3

worst Some of the w. men in the world SINCERITY, 17

worth All men who have turned out w. anything LEARNING, 38

w. x amount...but you can't spend it SUCCESS, 64

worthwhile One w. task carried to a successful conclusion ACCOMPLISHMENTS, 7

wrestling Texas w. match with a new team EXECUTIVES, 62

wriggle There is so much w. room CORRUPTION AND SCANDAL, 16

writer kind of w....other people are reading IMAGE, 21

wrong If anything can go w., it will PROBLEMS, 3

It is terrible to speak well and be w. SPEECHES, 50

It was w., there's no other word for it CORRUPTION AND SCANDAL, 4

not being frightened of getting it w. ENTREPRENEURS, 11

One man saying that everything is w. COMMUNICATION, 39

something's w....it's the management PROBLEMS, 21

There is no harm in being sometimes w. MISTAKES, 17

When a business goes w. FAILURE, 14

Y

year let in the y. we're living in CHANGE, 30

yes men y. may be born...mostly they are made ACCOMPLISHMENTS, 18

yield executives expect every new idea...to y. IDEAS, 12

younger The y. you are ENTREPRENEURS, 40

young person A y. entering the work force in 2000 CAREERS, 4

Z

Zsa Zsa Gabor I feel like Z.'s fifth husband SPEECHES, 22

Zulus few people know very much about Z. INVESTMENT AND THE STOCK MARKET, 70

Author Index

A

Aaker, David A. MARKETING, 1, 2
Abdul-Jabbar, Kareem SUCCESS, 1; TEAMS, 1
Abedi, Hasan MANAGEMENT, 1
Abzug, Bella DISCRIMINATION, 1, 2
Ace, Goodman MEDIA, 1
Achebe, Chinua DEBT, 1
Acheson, Dean ADVERTISING, 1; BUREAUCRACY, 1; CAPITALISM, 1; GOVERNMENTS, 1; LEADERSHIP, 1
Ackerman, Carl William ACCURACY, 1
Acton, Lord POWER, 1
Adair, John LEADERSHIP, 2
Adams, Douglas INNOVATION, 1; MONEY, 1; TECHNOLOGY, 1, 2; TIME MANAGEMENT, 1
Adams, Henry Brooks EXPERIENCE, 1; ORDER, 1; POWER, 2
Adams, John POWER, 3
Adams, Samuel BUSINESS ETHICS, 1
Adams, Scott ADVERTISING, 2; CHANGE, 1; EXECUTIVES, 1–3; GREED, 1; MARKETING, 3; PRODUCTIVITY, 1; RESEARCH, 1; RISK TAKING, 1; TEAMS, 2
Adams, William BUSINESS ETHICS, 2; CREATIVITY, 1
Adamson, Harold RISK TAKING, 2
Addison, Joseph SUCCESS, 2
Ade, George WAGES, 1
Adenauer, Konrad J. ATTITUDE, 1
Adler, Alfred PRINCIPLES, 1
Adler, Freda ORDER, 2; PROGRESS, 1
Aeschylus AMBITION, 1
Aesop BUSINESS ETHICS, 3
Agate, James ATTITUDE, 2
Agnelli, Giovanni CORPORATE RESPONSIBILITY, 1; DELEGATING, 1; DETERMINATION, 1
Agnew, Spiro LEARNING, 1, 2; ORGANISATIONS, 1
Ahern, Bertie CORPORATE RESPONSIBILITY, 2
Aiken, Howard IDEAS, 1
Akins, Zoë BLAME, 1; WORK AND EMPLOYMENT, 1
Albright, Madeleine GLOBALISATION, 1
Aldington, Richard RESPONSIBILITY, 1
Alexander, Jason CIVILISATION, 1
Alexander, Shana EXCELLENCE, 1; MONEY, 2
Ali, Muhammad ACHIEVING, 1; BOASTING, 1; JOBS, 1; LOSING, 1; WINNERS AND WINNING, 1
Alinsky, Saul CHANGE, 2; POWER, 4
Allan, Andrew BRANDS, 1; CORPORATE CULTURE, 1
Allee, Verna KNOWLEDGE, 1
Allen, Fred ADVERTISING, 3; EXECUTIVES, 4; MEETINGS, 1
Allen, Woody ADVERSITY, 1; INVESTMENT AND THE STOCK MARKET, 1; MONEY, 3; SUCCESS, 3
Alley, Rewi CO-OPERATION, 1
Allsop, Charles MONEY, 4
Amiel, Henri-Frédéric ORDER, 3
Amis, Kingsley QUALITY, 1; WORK AND EMPLOYMENT, 2
Amoako, K.Y. DISCRIMINATION, 3; PROGRESS, 2; TECHNOLOGY, 3
Anderson, Walter LISTENING, 1
Andreotti, Giulio POWER, 5
Andrews, David NEGOTIATION, 1; PERSISTENCE, 1; WEALTH, 1
Andrews, Kenneth R. CONSCIENCE, 1
Anonymous ABILITY, 1, 2; ACCOMPLISHMENTS, 1; ACTION, 1; ADVERTISING, 4–6; BUDGETING, 1; BUSINESS ETHICS, 4, 5; CAREERS, 1; CHANGE, 3–5; CONSCIENCE, 2; CONTRACTS, 1; CORPORATE CULTURE, 2, 3; CUSTOMERS, 1; DEBT, 2; DECISIONS, 1; DETAILS, 1; DETERMINATION, 2; DISCRIMINATION, 4–7; DOING BUSINESS IN ASIA-PACIFIC, 1–6; DOING BUSINESS IN LATIN AMERICA, 1, 2; DOING BUSINESS IN NORTH AMERICA, 1, 2; E-COMMERCE, 1–3; EMPLOYEES, 1; EXECUTIVES, 5; FAILURE, 1, 2;

FOCUS, 1; FORECASTING, 1; HIRING AND FIRING, 1; INDUSTRY, 1; INNOVATION, 2–4; INVESTMENT AND THE STOCK MARKET, 2, 3; LEADERSHIP, 3, 4; LEARNING, 3, 4; MARKETING, 4, 5; MONEY, 5–10; OFFICE POLITICS, 1; PEOPLE AND RELATIONSHIPS, 1, 2; PLANNING, 1; POWER, 6; PRINCIPLES, 2; PROBLEMS, 1–3; PROCRASTINATION, 1; PROFITS, 1, 2; PUBLICITY, 1; REPUTATION, 1–3; RISK TAKING, 3; SERVICE, 1; SPEECHES, 1; STRATEGY, 1, 2; TEAMS, 3, 4; TECHNOLOGY, 4; WEALTH, 2; WORK AND EMPLOYMENT, 3
Ansoff, Igor CHANGE, 6; LISTENING, 2
Anthony, Susan B. DISCRIMINATION, 8–10
Antrim, Minna EXPERIENCE, 2; FAILURE, 3
Aouita, Said WINNERS AND WINNING, 2, 3
Archer, Jeffrey EXECUTIVES, 6; POWER, 7
Archibald, Jules INDEPENDENCE, 1
Arden, Elizabeth ENTREPRENEURS, 1; VALUE, 1; WINNERS AND WINNING, 4
Arendt, Hannah ACTION, 2; ECONOMICS, 1; LOYALTY, 1
Argyris, Chris EMPLOYEES, 2, 3; LEARNING, 5; OFFICE POLITICS, 2; PROBLEMS, 4, 5
Aristotle BANKING, 1; CONFIDENCE, 1; DETAILS, 2; GREED, 2
Armour, Philip D. MOTIVATION, 1
Armstrong, William GOVERNMENTS, 2
Arredondo, Fabiola GLOBALISATION, 2; TARGETS, 1
Arrow, Kenneth Joseph VALUE, 2
Arthur, Chester Alan DOING BUSINESS IN ASIA-PACIFIC, 7
Arthur, W. Brian COMPETITION, 1; ECONOMICS, 2–5; INNOVATION, 5
Ash, Mary Kay ACCOMPLISHMENTS, 2; DETERMINATION, 3; EMPLOYEES, 4; ENTHUSIASM, 1; FAILURE, 4; GOALS AND OBJECTIVES, 1; LEADERSHIP, 5; LISTENING, 3; PERSISTENCE, 2; PRAISE, 1, 2
Ashcroft, John PRAISE, 3
Ashe, Arthur WINNERS AND WINNING, 5
Ashkenas, Ron ABILITY, 3; LEADERSHIP, 6
Asimov, Isaac CHANGE, 7; INNOVATION, 6
Astor, John Jacob WEALTH, 3
Atkinson, Brooks EMPLOYEES, 5; IDEAS, 2
Atwood, Margaret CHANGE, 8
Auden, W.H. AMBITION, 2; COMMUNICATION, 1; JUDGEMENTS, 1; LOYALTY, 2; STATISTICS, 1
Augustine, St PROCRASTINATION, 2
Auphan, Raphael DOING BUSINESS IN AFRICA, 1
Aurobindo, Sri ATTITUDE, 3; FOCUS, 2; SINCERITY, 1; WORK AND EMPLOYMENT, 4
Austen, Jane MONEY, 11; WORK AND EMPLOYMENT, 5
Auster, Paul MONEY, 12
Avery, Oswald Theodore EXPERIENCE, 3

B

Babbage, Charles EMPLOYEES, 6; INNOVATION, 7; MARKETING, 6; ORGANISATIONS, 2, 3; PEOPLE AND RELATIONSHIPS, 3; TIME MANAGEMENT, 2
Bachelard, Gaston IMAGINATION, 1
Bacon, Francis ADVERSITY, 2, 3; BOLDNESS, 1, 2; MONEY, 13; OPPORTUNITY, 1; POWER, 8, 9; PUBLICITY, 2; RISK TAKING, 4; WEALTH, 4, 5
Bagehot, Walter BANKING, 2–4; CAPITALISM, 2; IDEAS, 3; WORK AND EMPLOYMENT, 6
Bahr, Morton MANAGEMENT, 2
Bain, Alexander CONSCIENCE, 3
Baker, Russell DOING BUSINESS IN NORTH AMERICA, 3
Baldwin, James CHANGE, 9; FAILURE, 5; MONEY, 14; POWER, 10
Baldwin, Stanley EMPLOYERS, 1

Blank, Warren LEADERSHIP, 26, 27
Block, Peter EMPLOYEES, 7; LEARNING, 7; ORGANISATIONS, 7
Bloomberg, Michael BOASTING, 3; COMPETITION, 5;
    COMPUTERS, 3; EXPECTATIONS, 2; GROWTH, 1; IMAGE, 1; LUCK, 1;
    MEDIA, 5; PLANNING, 4
Blough, Roger BOOM AND BUST, 1
Blythe, Ronald PRAISE, 6
Boesky, Ivan CORRUPTION AND SCANDAL, 5; INVESTMENT AND THE
    STOCK MARKET, 4; LEADERSHIP, 28; PROFITS, 4; WINNERS AND
    WINNING, 7
Boethius ADVERSITY, 5
Bogle, John Clifton INVESTMENT AND THE STOCK MARKET, 5–7
Bolt, Robert CONTRACTS, 2; MEDIA, 6
Bon, Michel CHANGE, 15; COMMUNICATION, 7
Bonaparte, Napoleon ACHIEVING, 5
Bond, Alan CORRUPTION AND SCANDAL, 6, 7
Bond, Bruce R. SUCCESS, 9
Bonfield, Peter CHANGE, 16; CORPORATE CULTURE, 17;
    INNOVATION, 11; ORGANISATIONS, 8
Bookchin, Murray CAPITALISM VERSUS SOCIALISM, 3
Boorstin, Daniel J. ADVERTISING, 8; ORGANISATIONS, 9;
    PUBLICITY, 6; SELLING, 2; TECHNOLOGY, 7
Boot, Jesse ENTREPRENEURS, 5
Boren, James H. BUREAUCRACY, 6
Borges, Jorge Luis EXECUTIVES, 16; PROGRESS, 6
Borman, Frank CAPITALISM, 3
Bourke, William EXECUTIVES, 17
Bouteflika, Abdul Aziz GLOBALISATION, 13
Bouvier, Jr, John V. INVESTMENT AND THE STOCK MARKET, 8
Bowen, Elizabeth ATTITUDE, 4; EXPERIENCE, 5; SINCERITY, 4
Bower, Marvin CORPORATE CULTURE, 18; EMPLOYEES, 8;
    HONESTY, 1; ORGANISATIONS, 10, 11; TARGETS, 4
Bowersock, Terri AMBITION, 3; CORPORATE CULTURE, 19;
    DETERMINATION, 4; ENTREPRENEURS, 6
Boyd, William PROCRASTINATION, 7
Brabazon of Tara, Lord SPEECHES, 5
Bradley, F.H. SINCERITY, 5
Bradley, Omar Nelson CONSCIENCE, 5
Brady, Charles GLOBALISATION, 14; WINNERS AND WINNING, 8
Bragg, Melvyn FAILURE, 8
Braiker, Harriet Beryl EXCELLENCE, 2
Branch, Anna Hempstead ORDER, 5
Brandstatter, Horst INNOVATION, 12
Branson, Richard ACCOMPLISHMENTS, 3; BUSINESS ETHICS, 16;
    CHANGE, 17; COMPETITION, 6, 7; ENTREPRENEURS, 7; GROWTH, 2;
    IDEAS, 5; MISTAKES, 2; PEOPLE AND RELATIONSHIPS, 9; WORK AND
    EMPLOYMENT, 16
Brecht, Bertolt BUSINESS ETHICS, 17; COMMUNICATION, 8;
    CONSUMERS, 1; DELEGATING, 2; LIMITATIONS, 1
Brenner, Sydney COMPUTERS, 4
Bresson, Robert ORIGINALITY, 1
Bridges, William CHANGE, 18; JOBS, 4
Bro, Margueritte CREATIVITY, 2
Brodow, Ed NEGOTIATION, 2
Bronfman, Jr, Edgar CHANGE, 19; WORK AND EMPLOYMENT, 17
Bronowski, Jacob ACTION, 6; INNOVATION, 13
Brontë, Anne TALENT, 5
Brontë, Charlotte CAREERS, 2
Brookes, Warren T. ECONOMICS, 11, 12
Brookner, Anita LUCK, 2
Brooks, Mel PROCRASTINATION, 8
Broun, Heywood LEADERSHIP, 29
Broun, Heywood Hale ACCOMPLISHMENTS, 4
Brown, Helen Gurley CORRUPTION AND SCANDAL, 8
Brown, Jan OPINIONS, 2
Brown, Norman O. CAPITALISM, 4
Brown, Shona L. LEADERSHIP, 30; PLANNING, 5

Browning, John CO-OPERATION, 4
Browning, Robert FAILURE, 9; GOALS AND OBJECTIVES, 4
Bruno, Frank CORPORATE CULTURE, 20
Bryan, Arthur BRANDS, 4; IMAGINATION, 4; TIME
    MANAGEMENT, 5
Bryan, William Jennings SPEECHES, 6
Buchwald, Art ECONOMICS, 13
Buck, Pearl S. CHOICE, 1; MISTAKES, 3; ORDER, 6
Buckman, Frank CONSUMERS, 2
Buckman, Robert KNOWLEDGE, 2, 3
Buffett, Warren ACCOMPLISHMENTS, 5; ACCURACY, 3; ACTION, 7;
    ADVICE, 1; AMBITION, 4; BUSINESS ETHICS, 18, 19; COMPUTERS, 5;
    CONFIDENCE, 2; CORPORATE CULTURE, 21, 22; EXECUTIVES, 18, 19;
    GREED, 3; HONESTY, 2; IMAGE, 2; INVESTMENT AND THE STOCK
    MARKET, 9–25; MEDIA, 7; PLANNING, 6; QUALITY, 3; RISK
    TAKING, 6–8; STATISTICS, 4; STRATEGY, 6; TAXES, 2
Bukowski, Charles PERSISTENCE, 3
Bulwer-Lytton, Edward ENTHUSIASM, 5
Bumpers, Dale DEBT, 3
Bunch, Charlotte ACTION, 8
Bungey, Michael IMAGE, 3; RISK TAKING, 9
Bureau of Labor DISCRIMINATION, 12
Burgess, Anthony MONEY, 21
Burke, Edmund ACCURACY, 4; ADVERSITY, 6; AMBITION, 5;
    CHANGE, 20; GLOBALISATION, 15; JUDGEMENTS, 3; LEARNING, 8;
    ORDER, 7; PLANNING, 7; POWER, 16, 17; PRACTICE, 1; SUCCESS, 10;
    TAXES, 3; WEALTH, 7
Burke, James DELEGATING, 3
Burke, Thomas PRAISE, 7
Burnett, Leo ADVERTISING, 9; AMBITION, 6
Burney, Fanny PERSONAL GROWTH, 1; SUCCESS, 11
Burns, H.S.M. CORPORATE RESPONSIBILITY, 6; MANAGEMENT, 10
Burns, James MacGregor LEADERSHIP, 31–35
Burroughs, Nannie CHALLENGE, 1
Burroughs, William S. BUSINESS ETHICS, 20; PRODUCTS, 2
Burson, Harold PUBLICITY, 7
Burton, Montague CONSCIENCE, 6
Bush, George CONSUMERS, 14; TAXES, 4
Bush, George W. CORRUPTION AND SCANDAL, 9–11;
    ECONOMICS, 15; ENTREPRENEURS, 8; GLOBALISATION, 16;
    GOVERNMENTS, 12; MONEY, 22; OBSTACLES, 2, 3
Bush, Jeb BLAME, 3
Busquet, Anne CONSUMERS, 3, 4
Butler, David RESEARCH, 3
Butler, Nicholas Murray KNOWLEDGE, 4
Butler, Samuel ACCURACY, 5; CONSUMERS, 5; EMPLOYEES, 9;
    FAILURE, 10; LAWYERS, 5; MONEY, 23; PRAISE, 8; PROGRESS, 7;
    RISK TAKING, 10; SUCCESS, 12
Button, John BLAME, 4; OPPORTUNITY, 3
Buzan, Tony LEARNING, 9–11; SUCCESS, 13
Byrnes, James F. POWER, 18
Byron, Lord ADVERSITY, 7

C

Cadbury, Dominic CONFIDENCE, 3
Cage, John IDEAS, 6
Cairncross, Frances GLOBALISATION, 17
Callaghan, James TARGETS, 5
Calloway, Wayne COMPETITION, 8
Calwell, Arthur PRINCIPLES, 4
Campbell, Bill CORPORATE CULTURE, 23; LEADERSHIP, 36
Campbell, Susan TEAMS, 7
Campos, Roberto DOING BUSINESS IN LATIN AMERICA, 3

E

F

L

M

T

U

V

W

X

Y

Z